GROTE'S LEGENDARY GREECE

THE PRE-HISTORY

Bust by Charles Bacon

GROTE'S

LEGENDARY GREECE

The Pre-history

Legendary Greece, Complete
Mythology & Genealogies.

– WITHOUT FOOTNOTES –

Edited by Giles Laurén

SOPHRON EDITOR
2016

ISBN 10: 0989783669
ISBN 13: 978-0989783668

Publisher's Statement

Sophron Editor endeavours to present to the Classical and Rhetorical reader the best books at the lowest prices. All of our editions are digitally typeset, *i.e.* they are not scanned reprints.

Large and complex digital editions undertaken with limited means must result in a certain number of inaccuracies in the text. For the most part these are merely irritating and do not affect the meaning of the text. The typographical oddities are to be set to the account of LibreOffice in the hope they will soon be corrected. As with all Sophron editions, I will promptly correct all errors found in the pages of these publications. Please inform me at enasophron@gmail.com.

Designed by Sophron Editor

LEGENDARY GREECE

Foreword

It has been commonly thought for some years that George Grote's *History of Greece* is obsolete because he came before Schliemann and the Golden Age of Archaeology. It is certainly true that he doubted the existence of Troy and would have been both surprised and delighted to learn of Schliemann's discoveries, the later textual discoveries and of the inscriptions still being found; but this aspect of Grote affects only a small number of his 5500 pages. Must the rest be discredited? I think not. Nobody before or after Grote has so throughly mastered the *textual* sources for Greek history or put them to paper in such a exhaustive and transparent manner. He has been called an opinionated historian, but this is what makes him so *enjoyable* to read! Moreover, the reasons for his opinions are always clearly set forth and are very hard to elude; in example, his reasons for dividing this history into Legendary and Historical periods, were first suggested by Varro and remain well founded though admittedly disputed. Many of the claims and theories made following the discovery of Troy have been found illusory; we are no closer to the date of the Trojan War, nor indeed to knowing *which* Troy fought the battle nor indeed the location of the battlefield!

A contemporary biography of Grote is included below as well as an account of the Troy discoveries and finally, A. D. Lindsay's critical introduction to the Everyman edition of 1906. They will be found useful to the critical reader.

It is in the nature of modern scholarship to betimes overstep its foundations to the point of disconnecting itself from its historical development and thereby lose to memory past scholarship that is still important. For this reason, many of Grote's interpretations may appear both fresh and penetrating to the modern reader.

The Archaeologists of today have taken over what once was the province of Classicists; however, their training and expertise depends on knowledge and methods unrelated to classical texts. Now, the history of Greece lies in the texts and and these texts tell a story without archaeology, whereas without this history archaeology has little purpose and less meaning. It is hoped that this edition of Grote will be found useful to those archaeologists and amateurs who are not also classical scholars and who enjoy a well written exposition.

This present edition contains the complete text of the that of 1872, the last published during lis lifetime; it is *intended for the general reader*, and to that end, for digital publication. The cost of realising this objective has been the loss of Grote's lovely footnotes; it is my hope that enough interest in Grote may be manifest to justify a later expanded edition to include his footnotes and perhaps with the comments of a modern editor. The specialist will know how to consult the missing footnotes.

CONTENTS

CONTENTS

LEGENDARY GREECE

CONTENTS

List of Illustrations:

The editor hopes to make the maps available from a website in the near future.

LEGENDARY GREECE

Discovery of Troy.

The ancient Greeks treated the Trojan War as a historical event that had taken place in the 13th or 12th century B.C. and believed that Troy was located near the Dardanelles in what is now Turkey. As of the mid-19th century, both the war and the city were widely believed to be non-historical. In 1868, however, the German amateur archaeologist Heinrich Schliemann (1822-90) met Frank Calvert, who convinced Schliemann that Troy was at Hissarlik and Schliemann took over Calvert's excavations on property belonging to Calvert; this claim is now accepted by most scholars. Those who believe that the stories of the Trojan War are derived from a specific historical conflict usually date it to the 12th or 11th centuries B.C., often preferring the dates given by Eratosthenes, 1194-1184 BC, which roughly corresponds with archaeological evidence of a burning of Troy VIIa.

Frank Calvert (1828-1908) was an English expatriate who was a consular official in the eastern Mediterranean region and an amateur archaeologist. He began exploratory excavations on the mound at Hissarlik (the site of the ancient city of Troy), seven years before the arrival of Heinrich Schliemann.

As early as 1822, Hissarlik was identified by Charles Maclaren as a possible site of Homeric Troy. In 1847, Calvert's brother Frederick bought a farm of over 2,000 acres (8 km²) at Akca Koy which included part of Mount Hissarlik. This was to be a momentous acquisition.

At the time Schliemann began excavating in Turkey, the site commonly believed to be Troy was at Pınarbaşı, a hilltop at the south end of the Trojan Plain. Schliemann performed soundings at Pınarbaşı, but was disappointed by his findings. Schliemann did not know where to look for Troy and was about to give up his exploration altogether. It was not until Calvert suggested excavating the mound of Hissarlik that Schliemann made any moves to dig at the site. Calvert had already searched in the mound, but he never made it down to the Bronze Age layers; still, he was determined Troy was buried somewhere within the mound.

Schliemann and Calvert found not only the possible site of Troy but thousands of artefacts such as diadems of woven gold, rings, bracelets, intricate earrings and necklaces, buttons, belts and brooches as well as anthropomorphic figures, bowls and vessels for perfumed oils. (From Wikipaedia).

LIFE OF GEORGE GROTE

From Peter Anton: *Masters in History*, Edinburgh 1880.

As the names of Greece and Rome are ever associated together in the history of antiquity, so the names of Grote and Gibbon will ever be mentioned together in the literary history of England. There is a certain propriety that a country which has surpassed Rome in the extent of her empire, and at least equals Greece in all matters of philosophical and intellectual accomplishment, should have given birth to the greatest writer on the decline and fall of the one, and the best historian of the rise and progress of the other. We cannot tell what the future may have in store for us, but it is difficult to believe the histories of Gibbon and Grote can ever be superseded. Discoveries may be made that may cast fresh light on particular points, writers may arise who may survey certain portions of the field from other and truer stand-points, isolated conclusions of the historians may be called in question or proved to be erroneous – all these things may occur, as indeed, some of them have occurred already, but that the histories of Greece and Rome, as written by Grote and Gibbon, will ever become obsolete it is very difficult to conceive. They have been written with so much genius and care, that they will survive as literary works even when they are found to be faulty as histories.

There have not been wanting those who have said that the writers of history are more worthy of our admiration than the makers of it, that it is Gibbon we admire and not Constantine, Grote and not Alcibiades. The statement is too sweeping to be accepted in its entirety, but there can be no doubt it contains in it a certain element of truth. The historian is not a mere annalist – a bare recorder of the facts of a nation's life. He differs from the latter as the painter differs from the photographer, and for the carrying out of his work the historian, like the painter, requires a severely disciplined artistic sense. To put down in then-order the dates of the births and deaths of princes, the names of the places where battles were fought, the names of the generals, and which side won, is the part of the chronicler; but it is the work of the historian to group, to paint, and to vivify, to trace the hidden stream of tendency which has brought about particular events, and to calculate the results which are likely to proceed or flow from them. It is the artistic elements which the historian embodies in his narrative that attract the attention of the reader to the genius of the former, while perusing the events of the latter. It is these elements, entering as they do in so large a measure into the substance of the "Decline and Fall of the Roman Empire" and the "History of Greece," which give these works a permanent literary value, apart altogether from the importance or accuracy of the facts they record.

While the works of Gibbon and Grote lie side by side, their lives, strikingly similar in all matters concerning literary purpose, yet present certain distinguishing contrasts. The life of Grote cannot fail to have the more salutary influence. Gibbon was a historian and nothing else: he was trained for no particular profession, he gave himself to no special business, his life-work was his history, and it formed the business and pleasure of his existence. Although an outstanding example of special devotion to a particular task, it is a life all the same which can only appeal to the few, and can never be held up as a stimulus to the great majority of men who must spend the serious hours of the day in professional or business labours, and have only a very narrow margin to devote to the intellectual pursuits of literature and science. Whilst the lives of Gibbon and Grote show what can be done by those whose good fortune it has not been to receive a university education, it is only in the life of the latter we see to what splendid purpose the leisure hours of a hard working career may be put, what rich fruits may be gathered in them, and what a fabric of learning and research may be built up by filling them with cultured activities. It is impossible to come into living contact with a mind like Grote's without finding in it the lineaments of a character singularly noble. This man of whom we speak was, no doubt, to a large extent, Grote the successful Banker, in virtue of the fact that he was his father's son, but he was altogether Grote the Great Historian, in virtue of the use to which he put his hours after he had left the counting-room for the day. He may have been speaking for many others, but certainly for himself, when he gave utterance to these words in his presidential address to the London Scientific Institution, on the 1st June 1846, in the London Tavern, "To those – whether they be many or few, I know not – who may still hold the ungenial prejudice that there is an inherent incompatibility between a day of industry in the counting-house, and an evening of study in the lecture-room, the class-room, or the library – we must continue to present the best of all refutations, in the lives and behaviour of our members. To those, on the other hand, whose sentiments are more generous and exalted, who esteem an enlightened population a greater glory than splendid edifices and unmeasurable capital, and who count it an honour to London to interweave the threads of literature and science with the staple of a commercial and professional life; to these minds we offer ourselves with confidence as auxiliaries and instruments, prepared to justify our claim upon their paternal sympathy. . . . To-morrow as well as to-day – in the times of our descendants as in our own – the life of the commercial and professional man will consist of a day of labour and an evening of leisure, which may be well or ill appropriated; to-morrow as well as to-day, the sociability of his nature may be enlisted in favour of the better employment instead of the worse – in favour of mental progress and elevating recreations, and against both seductions and lassitude. . . . Speaking as one, the best years of whose life have been passed as principal of a banking house, I contend, emphatically, that merchants and bankers will obey the call of interest as well as of duty, in seconding the voluntary efforts of our members."[Min. Wks., pp. 188, 192, 193].

In George Grote, the historian of Greece, there was a strain of foreign blood. His grandfather, Andrew Grote, came over from Bremen about the middle of the eighteenth century; and, prospering in business, he eventually entered into partnership with one George Prescott. As the result of this union of business talent, the banking house of "Grote, Prescott, and Company" was established January 1st, 1766. Andrew Grote still further added to his wealth by marrying Miss Ann Adams, a lady of position and fortune. The brother of this lady dying without issue, the estate of Badgemore and Henley-on-Thames passed into the Grote family. In 1757, Mrs Grote died, and three years later, Mr Grote took to himself another wife, in the person of Miss Mary Ann Calverden. To her husband, this lady bore three sons and six daughters; and George, the eldest son of this second marriage, was the father of the future historian of Greece. He was educated at the Charterhouse, apprenticed abroad, and most strictly trained in the arts of business by his father. In due time he came to occupy his father's position in the firm of "Grote, Prescott, & Co," and in 1793, he " married the daughter of Doctor Peckwell, a reverend divine, endowed with a handsome person, and talents of a somewhat superior quality." It may be mentioned as showing the bloods that were mixed in the historian, that the wife of Dr Peckwell was of French extraction; the revocation of the edict of Nantes had brought her family to Ireland not long after the year 1685. After his marriage with Miss Selina Peckwell, Mr George Grote settled at Clay Hill, near Beckenham, in Kent, about ten miles from London, and there, on the 17th November 1794, his son George was born unto him.

It would appear that Mrs Grote, like the minister's daughter to whom we have had occasion to refer so frequently in the previous paper, was a lady of superior intelligence and refinement. It is quite possible Dr Peckwell may have bestowed as much pains on the education of his daughter as M. Curchod did on his; but letting this be as it may, it is satisfactory to know that Mrs Grote was ambitious her son should excel in learning; and, before he was five and a-half years of age, at which period it was deemed necessary to send him to school, the mother had taught her son to read and write, and actually grounded him in the elements of Latin. With such careful maternal preparation, it is not to be wondered at, that when the youngster entered the Grammar School of Sevenoaks, he was able to rank with boys above his age, or that the master, the Rev. Mr Whitehead, immediately discovered in him "a decided aptitude for study." It is not easy to estimate a mother's influence over her son, but the pains which Mrs Grote took to fix on George's mind during his holidays what he had been learning during the session can hardly be over-valued. Habits, which masters work hard to break their pupils into, are often wholly dissipated by two months' complete idleness; and when teachers and scholars meet again, the former find they have their labours all to begin anew. In this household at Beckenham, however, it was different: what Mrs Grote's boy learned from his masters during the term, she was careful to confirm in the recess; and so, whatever intellectual ground the boy had gained, was kept, and whatever information he had gathered, was securely stored up.

LEGENDARY GREECE

When he was ten, Master Grote passed from the Grammar School to the Charterhouse. This change could hardly have taken place more opportunely. Dr Raine, an enthusiastic schoolmaster and distinguished scholar, was then at the head of the establishment; and George Waddington, afterwards Dean of Durham; Conop Thirlwall, afterwards Bishop of St David's, and historian of Greece; Henry Havelock, afterwards the fearless soldier, and others, were then boys in the classes, and the everyday companions of young Grote. Between discipline on the one hand, and clever competitors on the other, the education of the future historian of Greece could hardly have been conducted under more favourable auspices. Master George was too clever a boy ever to feel the rod for neglected lessons, or insufficienty prepared exercises, but he had also in him too much of animal spirit not to feel it often for the venial offences peculiar to boyhood, and which are more the product of an exuberant life, than of an evil spirit. It was in 1810, on the eve of his leaving school, and when, by his talents, he stood almost at the head of it, he received his last flogging. To commemorate the close of his Charterhouse days, Grote invited a number of his class-fellows and school companions to supper in the "Albion Tavern," Aldersgate Street, and for partaking somewhat amply, and inviting others to do the same, he was doomed to suffer in the flesh. What the master said to him on the occasion does not appear; but, doubtless, the good man – as teachers are wont on such occasions – predicted a depraved future from *such* a close to the career of a Charterhouse scholar!

The father and mother of George Grote formed a peculiar couple, and in many ways were singularly unsuited to each other. Even after a long life together, they could not fit in wholly to each other's habits. The elder Grote was a man who had a preference for country life, and an inborn fondness for the common rural sports of hunting and shooting, and being a man of wealth and position, and having many acquaintances, he loved from time to time to meet his friends around his board. Mrs Grote, on the other hand, was a strict Calvinist, and would associate with none but those who reflected her own religious sentiments. She disliked the society of her country neighbours, and frowned on all guests visiting her house on her husband's invitation. Such a state of matters no doubt led to a deal of domestic unpleasantness, but the elder Grote, finding her opinions were not to change, left her to pursue in all matters of household management her own course, only reserving for himself the reins in all matters connected with his children's education. It was just a pity when the husband left so much to his wife he did not leave this also, for there cannot be a doubt, if Mrs Grote had had her own way in the educational, affairs of her family, she would from the Charterhouse Academy, have sent her eldest son at once to the University. With regard, however, to the advantages to be derived from a liberal education, the elder Grote was wholly indifferent; he had no anxiety that his son should get on anywhere but in the commercial world – his only ambition being, that he might be a successful banker; and so, when his son was but sixteen years of age, he was installed, with a more imperfect education than falls to the lot of thousands of the English youth of to-day, in Threadneedle Street, to commence his banking career. This was in 1810. Let us read what this lad, when he had become a grown man, spoke six-and-thirty years after when he addressed University College, on the 1st July 1846:—"I hope, and I believe, that the administrators of University College will succeed in diffusing among the public of London larger ideas on the proper measure of a citizen's education – in correcting that mistaken impatience with which parents, often under no pressure of necessity, abridge those years requisite for their son's complete education, and hurry him into professional life a half-educated man." [Min. Wks., pp. 202, 203]. The fact was, Grote never ceased to regret his early devotion to business and consequent premature withdrawal from every system of public educational discipline.

In so far as society was concerned, the young man was placed under many disadvantages by the unfavourable condition of things existing in his own home. But as we shall more fully discover as we proceed, Grote had ever that happy pushing spirit which rose above even extraordinary difficulties. And so, while his mother was on visiting terms with but few of her neighbours, he was a general favourite, and on the best footing with all. Considering what was required of him in Threadneedle Street, he still could always find an occasional afternoon for cricket, and he had not as yet become so sufficiently studious as to love his books more than the innocent dissipations of a country ball. In going out into society his mind was poetic and impressionable; but with one exception, he was distinctly fortunate in his special friendships, and he had already that in him which made it wholly impossible for him to draw to any companion devoid of intellectual tastes. By and by this temperament got so absolutely confirmed, that intellectual worth, and that alone, was the only quality which he would allow to command his respect, or which he would acknowledge as deserving of the respect of others. The later developments of this spirit were certainly owing to the influence of James Mill. This eminent man, and historian of India, young Grote first met at the house of David Ricardo, whither he was wont to repair as often as he could, that he might listen to his conversation on a science that was already occupying much of his thought, namely, the science of Political Economy. In a letter which he wrote at this time to George W. Norman, one of Grote's most trusted and accomplished young friends, we find the following words: – " I have met Mill often at Ricardo's house, and hope to derive great pleasure and instruction from his acquaintance, as he is a very profound thinking man, and seems well disposed to communicate, as well as clear and intelligible in his manner. His mind has, indeed, all that cynicism and asperity which belong to the Benthamian School, and what I chiefly dislike in him is, the readiness and seeming preference with which he dwells on *the faults and defects* of others, even of the greatest men! But it is so very rarely that a man of any depth comes across my path, that I shall most assuredly cultivate his acquaintance a good deal farther. My friends in *Calf and*

xv

Russia still continue faithful and interesting, and if it were not for them, life would be a very waste indeed." This passage is of the greatest interest, as it shows the mind of Grote operating freely, and before it got completely entangled in Mill's intellectual coils. Above all others, James Mill was the kind of man to whose opinions Grote, by the natural constitution of his mind, was predisposed to defer, and the result brought about could have been anticipated from the beginning of their acquaintance. The philosopher was an eager propagandist, and in the course of a remarkably short space of time he had his young disciple at his feet. It would no doubt have been better for Grote, it would most certainly have left him with a sweeter tone of mind, if he had been more discriminating in his admiration of his master. While he received many good lessons, he also imbibed many unreasonable prejudices. No mind ever kept so faithfully the direction it received from the impulse of another than did the mind of Grote the direction given it by the mind of Mill. The metaphysician gave him a love for philosophy, and that love was never quenched; he made him a student, and a student he remained. His Radicalism and democratic sympathies Grote also took from the teaching of his early master. It would have been well could the future Historian of Greece have stopped short at this part of his master's educating process; but Mill's fanaticism against the governing classes simply because they were the governing classes, his rancorous hatred of the aristocracy, his "profound prejudice" against the Established Church and her ministers, all had their reflection more or less in the sentiments of the pupil.

To the credit of Grote this must be said, however, that while the good influences of Mill remained, the antipathies died out, and eventually the sweeter mind prevailed. Along with Ricardo and Mill, Grote was also at this time associating with Bentham, but what permanent impression this able man left on the mind of his young friend does not appear. Bentham was peculiar in his conversation: he would bear with no interruption; so, although he talked fluently, it is just possible one so enquiring as Grote would feel his meetings with him, pleasant though they were in their way, yet somewhat unsatisfactory in their results.

The unfortunate acquaintanceship [*Per. Life*, p. 15, *et seq.*] already alluded to was with a clergyman of the Church. Mrs Grote in her "Personal Life" of her husband, a work written with admirable delicacy, condensation, and grace, but here and there disfigured by touches of asperity, has not told us either who he was, or to what congregation it was his privilege to minister, and it is well she has kept her own counsel, giving the world no further clue to the man than it can have in the sufficiently hazy symbolism of E — .

To this man, the Rev. Mr E—, Grote had been attracted by the suavity of his manners, the extent and variety of his reading, and the fact that he was acknowledged as a scholar and a masterly critic. In the company of this reverend individual Grote was wont to talk freely and openly, and while he still believed him to be a gentleman, he submitted to him in confidence the secrets of his heart. It is every way to be regretted this confidence was so completely misplaced, as it would have been of incalculable advantage to the young man to have discussed over again with a clergyman of cultured intelligence the philosophical positions of Mill; and there can be no doubt in the society of such an one this further advantage would have accrued – the unreasoning antipathies of the teacher would have been immediately corrected, and possibly wholly neutralized before they had fixed themselves in the temperament of the future Historian.

Grate's break with the Rev. Mr E— flowed from his dishonourable conduct in a love affair of the young man. In the winter of 1814-15, Grate became acquainted with Miss Harriet Lewin, on the introduction of his friend G. M. Norman, and towards this young lady he soon cherished the tenderest of sentiments. Now, as it would happen, the young man, in the first place, confided his passion to his friend E—, and by this individual he was told the pursuit was hopeless, as it consisted with his knowledge her hand was already promised to another. In his innocence, George Grote suspected no duplicity; he gave up the hopes of happiness he had been cherishing, and tried to forget his pain by increased devotion to business and study. His father observed his son's changed deportment, and interrogating him on the matter, he was told all that had occurred. The parent was in no way sorry at the result, and, to guard against all future difficulties, he extorted from his son the promise that he would never marry until he had obtained his father's sanction in the matter. Soon after this promise had been given, the treachery of E—'s conduct was disclosed. The fact was, he himself had been an importunate suitor for Miss Lewin's hand. "E— is a villain; and Harriet completely exculpated" was the glad news sent by G. W. Norman to his friend Grote in the autumn of 1813. So far all was well, but wakening to a knowledge of E—'s trickery, he woke also to the consciousness of his rash and hasty promise to his father. Grote appealed to his father to release him, considering the circumstances in which the promise had been made; but the heart of the old banker was in no way touched by the passion of the youth. The young man's last difficulty was like to be worse than his first, for, as he was entirely dependent on his father, there remained no alternative for him but to bow to his stern decree, and relinquish all intercourse with the Lewin family.

In his second perplexity Grote again returned, and with increased eagerness, for consolation to his books. He made a special study of Sismondi's "Italian History." Like Gibbon, he took copious notes as he went on, and never considered himself master of any subject until he had put down on paper the thoughts that had occurred to him about it. He confessed to his friend Norman, "I have always found that, in order to make myself master of a subject, the best mode was to sit down and give an account of it myself." So "literature continued to form the greatest attraction to his mind," and was, he acknowledged, "the only pleasure he could enjoy which left no repentance behind it," until the March of 1818, when all his former passion was awakened by finding himself unexpectedly in the presence of its object. The effect produced was unmistakeable, as his own words sufficiently testify. "I had the happiness or misfortune (I know not which to call it, the feelings are so mixed) to see my dear and favourite, Harriet Lewin, the other day in Bromley. She was sitting with Charlotte and another lady in the carriage, which was waiting at the door of the 'Bell.' I stood there and conversed with her for about ten minutes, but something – I know not what it is – kept me, during the whole of the time, in such a state of indescribable tremor and uneasiness, that I could hardly utter a rational sentence. She looked lovely beyond expression. Her features still retained the same life and soul which once did so magnetize me; I never have seen it, and I never shall see it, on any other face. My dear Harriet! It is terrible work. It is most cruelly painful to think that I can only appear to her in the light of one who has occasioned nothing but pain and uneasiness to her. Yet so it must be. I am sometimes tempted to wish myself an isolated being, without any family or relations, and nothing but those friends whom my own merit (little as it is) may attach to me, and to whom my affections flow spontaneously and ardently. Relations are a chain which drags a man on by means of his sense of duty. "Happy is he who has fewest" After this first meeting, and, no doubt, also after many others, for Miss Lewin was now staying with Lord Harewood, at his residence in Hanover Square, the son petitioned the father with increased emphasis, and eventually the old banker agreed to his son's proposals, on condition that the nuptials should not take place for two years. The new arrangement was judged of in the worst spirit by the Lewin family; it was distasteful, in the highest degree, that they were obliged to accept the young man's suit with so distant a prospect of union. Miss Lewin also said, "it was not without mortification and embarrassing reflections she made up her mind to forget the painful circumstances of 1815, and to submit to enter into this harsh compact." All things considered, it was natural the lady should have had some feeling in the matter; on the whole, however, the young man seems to have been contented with the final turn of events. He opened up his mind to his old Charterhouse friend, Waddington, on the subject of his future marriage, and, in return, he had a characteristic letter with certain caustic touches: "I saw a monster yesterday – an English monster – [the letter is written from Paris] – that weighs about 20 stone, and yet, perhaps is still as much like a man as any other animal; I mean in appearance. It calls itself E—. Going to dine at the *table d'hote* with my cousin, I observed this phenomenon waiting to be fed."

The two years preceding Grate's marriage were divided between bank work and study. He kept a regular diary, and by it Miss Lewin was kept perfectly posted up in the events of his daily life. His diary would have its special interest for Miss Lewin, but it has also now its general interest for the educated world. Here are two entries – one of a Sunday, and another of a week day – taken at random. *January*, 1819. *Tuesday* – "Rose at 1/4 past 8. Breakfasted and unlocked. Read some more of 'Say's preface.' Thought much this day on the subject of Foreign Trade. Dined at 1/2 past 5; played on the bass for an hour, and then read some of Lessing's theological writings. Drank tea, and spent the evening in writing down my thoughts on Foreign Trade. Bed at 12." *Sunday, March* 28 – "Rose at 1/2 past 5. Studied Kant until 1/2 past 8, when I set off to breakfast with Mr Ricardo. Met Mr Mill there, and enjoyed some most interesting and instructive discourse with them, indoors and out walking in Kensington Gardens, until 1/2 past three, when I mounted my horse, and set off to Beckenham. Was extremely exhausted with fatigue and hunger when I arrived there, and ate and drank plentifully, which quenched my intellectual vigour for the night. Bed at 1/2 past 10."

Early in the month of March 1820, at Bexley Church, Kent, George Grote and Miss Harriet Lewin were married by the Rev. Edward Barnard, the vicar. Before this consummation was brought about they had endured much for each other's sake, but that endurance was fully rewarded by the lifetime of happiness they had with each other. Mrs Grote was a woman of rich native talents, and by her contributions to the *Westminster Review*, she helped to increase the household income during her first married years. Such exertions on her part should not have been at all necessary if her husband had been paid according to the duties he performed, and his position as working partner in the Bank. The narrow establishment they were obliged to keep – merely a dingy unhealthy house at the Bank, and furnished lodgings in the suburbs – was owing to the parsimony of the elder Grote. When they began life with each other the pair had a heart for any fate, and, considering the affluent circumstances in which they afterwards moved, it was possibly for the advantage of both that they were called on for two or three years to practise a rigid frugality. Miss Harriet Lewin was in every way fitted to be the wife of such a man as George Grote. She knew what such a man needed was sympathy and companionship in his higher work; and before her marriage she had so disciplined her mind by study in view of the life before her, that when she became Mrs Grote there was no need for her husband to decline to the narrower heart and the range of lower feelings. What Grote might have done with a less accomplished wife we cannot tell, but this we know, it was Mrs Grote kept his literary impulse ever active, and his intellectual passions ever warm; she entered into the spirit of his every endeavour, and she suggested his greatest work. It was from the well-springs of his domestic life he drew strength for his every achievement, and to them he ever went for solace and refreshment.

The married pair had not gone far together in the path of life when they were met by severe domestic affliction. The unhealthy nature of their house in Threadneedle Street acted very injuriously on Mrs Grote's health. Her reduced constitution brought about premature labour, and a boy was born, who only survived a week. Puerperal fever followed on the birth, and after three days the doctors said there could only be one termination to the illness. They were very happily, however, disappointed; their patient rallied, and, after a slow convalescence, recovered.

While Grote's days were spent in his office, his evenings were now almost exclusively devoted to study, and more than ever did he court the acquaintanceship of intellectual men. Mr David Ricardo, Mr John Smith, M. P., Mr John Black of the *Morning Chronicle*, Thomas Campbell the poet, John and Charles Austin, John Romilly, Charles Buller, Lord William Bentinck, Eyton Tooke, John Stuart Mill, John R. Macculloch, and M. de Santa Rosa, were all frequent visitors at Threadneedle Street between the years 1822 and 1830. Mrs Grote had many connections amongst the aristocracy, whom it would have been her pleasure to visit and entertain, but such a decided aversion had her husband to "everything tinctured with aristocratic tastes and forms of opinion," that she was obliged, for the sake of domestic quietness, and that she might not directly displease "her somewhat intolerant" husband, to relinquish to a very large extent her aristocratic friendships. He would not suffer that Mrs Grote should be dictated to by the very highest officers in the State. Witness the following to his wife, then staying at the noble residence of Gilston Park, Herts: – "I trust you will not be kept longer than Thursday or Friday: and I really think that neither you nor Mrs Lewin ought to suffer your time and your expectations to be tampered with any longer, *even* by the Governor-General of India. If he does not come on Monday or Tuesday, I would not wait for him at all."

Getting up early, for the most part about six, reading all manner of learned works in the morning and in the evening, Grote accumulated vast quantities of notes on the volumes perused. One day Mrs Grote said to her husband, "You are always studying the ancient authors whenever you have a moment's leisure; now here would be a fine subject for you to treat. Suppose you try your hand!" Mrs Grote's reference was to a subject frequently under discussion, namely, the history of Greece. Grote accepted the suggestion of his wife. The idea of a great new History of Greece fixed itself in his mind, and from that time – the autumn of 1823 – his studies became directed towards the accomplishment of his vast self-imposed task. The historian himself gives no clue to the first idea of his work, he merely says in one place, [*Hist.* i., *Pref.*, p. 5]. "The first idea of this history was conceived many years ago, at a time when ancient Hellas was known to the English public chiefly through the pages of Mitford."

It is not to be thought for a moment that while Grote was thus earnestly devoting himself to study, he was even in the smallest way neglecting his business. The fact was he did not find private study and public duty in any way incompatible, and whilst he was enlarging his reputation amongst men of letters, he was at the same time establishing himself amongst mercantile men as a wise and considerate banker. So far from the interests of the house "Prescott, Grote, & Co." suffering in his hands, after the concern had been for some time under almost his sole management, it was found, on his father's death in 1830, that he had very materially enlarged the business.

By the decease of the elder Grote, his son inherited the family estate in Lincolnshire and, £40,000 of personal property. This event put him on a perfectly different social footing. So far – his views on many things differing so substantially from his father's – his life had been subject to considerable restraint;

now he was in a position to do what seemed to him good in his own eyes. As yet he had taken no personal part in the politics of his time; and the only matter in which he had interested himself, acting along with Macaulay, Mill, Waymouth, Hume, and Hallam, had been the founding of the London University. Now, however, his democratic sympathies were keenly affected by the aspect of affairs in the country. The people were agitated, and the Reform Bill was being debated in Parliament. At the request of Mill he gave some weeks to the thinking out of the whole question then before the country, and in a very short space he issued from the press a fibrous and closely reasoned essay on the *Essentials of Parliamentary Reform*. The subject suited the temper of the author's mind, and finding his ground firm beneath him he struck out fiercely. He even allowed his antipathies play – but this is not the strong point of his paper – and declaimed against the aristocracy in language not the most measured. In these sentences there is something both of the thought and sarcasm of the complete paper: – "Superior income affords no ground for guessing at the capacities of men, even as a general rule. In comparing men of middling incomes, from £100 per annum upwards, there is no presumption of superior capacity on either side; but when we reach the very high figure in the scale, it will be found that not only is there no presumption in favour of mental eminence, but there is a probability not easy to be rebutted against it. The position and circumstances of a very rich man cut off all motive to mental labour: he is caressed and deified by his circle without any of those toils whereby others purchase an attentive hearing; and the purple, the fine linen, and the sumptuous fare every day of Dives are impediments to solid improvement hardly less fatal than the sores and wretchedness of Lazarus." [*Minor Works*, pp. 18, 19.]

It was evident to all that a man who could write such a paper as the *Essentials of Parliamentary Reform*, was a man to be looked up to by his party. After its publication great endeavours were made to get him to contest the City of London, but at first he positively refused. Apart from the little work above referred to, he had not as yet won fame as an author, and beyond his business connections and a small circle, there were comparatively few acquainted in any way with the sterling worth of the man. Mrs Grote was right when she held that for her husband to enter on a successful parliamentary contest, and to be heard with respect and attention in the House, it was necessary he should first have made himself a name. It was only after the publication of the history, and "when it had reflected a literary renown upon its author, he could hope to derive an importance in the public eye adequate to sustain him in a political course."

The views of Mrs Grote were just and sensible; but the stream of influence steadily increasing in volume, eventually its force was not to be resisted, and in 1832, after the Reform Bill had been passed in its final shape, he issued his address to the electors of the City of London. This carefully drawn up document went on to say that he regarded the Reform Bill as but the first step "towards a series of great and essential ameliorations," and he would not consider it had even got a fair trial until two improvements indispensable to the efficacy of the Representative System had been completed. These improvements were Vote by Ballot and Triennial Elections. To the constituency of the City, Grote simply and plainly declared himself a Radical, and that the electors were neither afraid of the man nor the name they showed by their votes, for the name of "George Grote" was at the head of the poll with a majority of 924 votes, the total number given in his favour being 8788. Mrs Grote confessed "it was a proud day to her when she looked down on 4000 citizens in Guildhall, cheering and echoing the sentiments which for years we had privately cherished, but which were now first fearlessly avowed."

During these exciting times the history had been progressing favourably; but for a period it was now laid on the shelf, – currency, the Bank Charter, and cognate subjects engaging the new M.P.'s attention. At a dinner party in Threadneedle Street, at which-were present Henry Warburton, John Romilly, Joseph Hume, and James Mill, it was agreed that Grote should be the person who should undertake to bring the Ballot before the House in the ensuing parliamentary session. The entrusting of Grote with this duty virtually constituted him leader of the Radical party. Although his brother Charles had been now settled in his old house at the bank, thus easing him considerably in affairs of business, still, from the position he occupied, it was difficult to get spare time for extraordinary labours. However, as best he could, he surmounted all difficulties, and on the 25th April 1833, he made his first motion in favour of the Ballot, concluding it with these words: "That this House might be so constituted, that it should enjoy and command and deserve the confidence of the people." Grote occupied the time of the House for an hour, and although he had not yet studied the graces of elocution and the arts of distinct speaking, still he was perfectly heard by the whole assembly. He had a difficult question to deal with, and he succeeded in putting the issues before the House with absolute clearness. The speech contains many forcible passages, and in such pieces as these we find unmistakeable traces of his severe classical culture, and the pith and directness of the Socratic dialogue: – "How much influence over votes ought a rich man to have? As much as he can purchase? No, certainly; for even the present law forbids all idea of his purchasing any influence. Not as much as he can purchase, but as much as he deserves, and as much as unconstrained freemen are willing to pay him. Amongst unconstrained freemen, the man of recognised superiority will be sure to acquire spontaneous esteem and deference: these are his just deserts, and they come to him unbidden and unbespoken. But they will come to him multiplied tenfold, if along with such intrinsic excellencies, he possesses the extrinsic recommendation of birth and fortune; if he be recommended to the attention of his neighbours by the conspicuous blazon of established opulence and station, and if he be thus furnished with the means of giving ample range and effect to an enlightened beneficence. This is the meed which awaits men of birth and station, if they do but employ their faculties industriously and to the proper ends. Poorer men may, doubtless, attain it also; but with them the ascent is toilsome, the obstructions numerous, and the success at best uncertain: to the rich man the path is certain and easy – the willing public meet him half way, and joyfully hail the gradual opening of his virtues. He is the man to whom they delight to pay homage, and their idolatrous fancy forestalls and exaggerates his real merits. This, sir, is, in my opinion, the legitimate influence of wealth and station: to serve as the passport, the ally, and the handmaid of superior worth and talent. This influence is as gentle and kindly as it is lasting and infallible; it is self-created and self-preserving; and it is, moreover, twice blest, for it blesses as well the few who exercise it, as the many over whom it is exercised." The M.P. for the City closed with the following appeal: – "If ever there was a case in which the address to your reason was vehemently and powerfully seconded by the appeal to your feelings, that case is the emancipation of honest voters – the making peace between a man's duty and his worldly cares – the rescue of political morality from the snares which now beset it, and from the storms which now lay it prostrate. You are called upon to protect the rights and to defend the integrity of the electoral conscience; to shield the innocent from persecution at the hands of the guilty; to guard the commonwealth against innumerable breaches of trust committed by the reluctant hands of well-meaning citizens. . . . Above all, you are called on to make this House what it professes and purports to be, a real emanation from the pure and free-spoken choice of the electors; an assembly of men commanding the general esteem and confidence of the people, and consisting of persons – the fittest which the nation affords – for executing the true end and aim of government. When all these vast interests, collective and individual, are at stake in one measure, am I not justified in demanding from you, not merely a cold and passive attention, but an earnest sympathy and solicitude?" [Hansard's Parliamentary Speeches.] The motion of Grote was supported by Dr Lushington, Cobbett, and O'Connell; but the result of the voting was—ayes, 106; noes, 211; pairs, 26. Again and again Grote returned to the attack, but each time only to sustain defeat. During his parliamentary career, six times in all did he bring forward his motion. On the 3rd June 1835, he only secured 146 in his favour, whilst 319 votes were recorded against him. In the following year the tone of parliamentary feeling was unchanged, 88 was the number of the ayes, and 139 the number of the noes. On the 8th March 1837, the division stood – for, 155 ; against, 267; pairs, 5. The last time Grote made the motion was on the 18th June 1839. He said he had no novel arguments to bring forward, and hoped even although "they intended the Reform Act to be final, they did not mean also to embalm its deformities." The mover was ably supported by the brilliancy of Macaulay, but when the count came, only 216 members declared "aye," while 333 declared "no."

During Grote's Parliamentary career from 1833 to 1841, there had been two dissolutions; and when he sought, on the last of these occasions, re-election for the city, he stood at the bottom of the four returned, and only escaped defeat by six votes. For Grote, this very narrow majority was in reality a defeat; but it was not so much the man as the decay of the party, which brought about a result at the election, which the historian could not but feel. In the Parliament of 1836, there were only half-a-dozen members "to sustain the Radical opinions of the House of Commons." One evening in Grote's house, when all the other guests had departed, and Sir William Molesworth and Charles Buller remained late to talk about the state of affairs, the latter said to his host, "I see what we are coming to, Grote; in no very long time from this, you and I shall be left to 'tell' Molesworth!"

The ballot was, no doubt, the measure with which Grote's name as a Member of Parliament was chiefly identified, but it was certainly very far from engaging his whole attention; he made important speeches on other matters and did a great amount of parliamentary work. Between the preparation of speeches, attendance at the House, and the engrossing nature of private and the excitement of public business, his years of parliamentary life were wholly barren of literary products strictly so called. His friend, Molesworth, at the suggestion of Mrs Grote, published an edition of the works of Hobbes; and his old schoolmate, Waddington – now Dean of Durham – also gave to the world a "History of the Reformation," both of which works, at great trouble to himself, Grote revised. But this was all. It may be said he found both tasks uncongenial – the latter especially so.

Although Grote was a man of an exceedingly powerful constitution, he found House-of-Commons life extremely fagging. No evil results, however, accrued to his health, for so soon as his tone was perceptibly lowered, Mrs Grote had him immediately away from the foetid atmosphere of London and its assemblies. In this way the historian had most agreeable trips to Paris, Belgium, Switzerland, the Rhine, and the South of England; and thus his public life was pleasantly diversified by private recreation.

That the life of a Member of Parliament, ever full of wrangle and noise, but ever barren of practical result, could long have continued satisfactory to such a man as George Grote, it is wholly impossible to believe. It was certainly good for him he had entered Parliament, for in discussing the constitution of the Grecian States it furnished him with personal experiences of a popular assembly, but all the same, he soon grew weary of it, or, perhaps, more properly speaking, he bethought himself of the long evenings he had had to himself before he entered Parliament, his long spells of improving study, and the chapters of his "History of Greece" that were lying on the shelf. At anyrate, in the February of 1838, we find him writing thus to his friend, Mr John Austin, then Senior Commissioner of Inquiry at Malta: – "The degeneracy of the Liberal party, and their passive acquiescence in everything, good or bad, which emanates from the present Ministry, puts the accomplishment of any political good out of the question, and it is not at all worth while to undergo the fatigue of a nightly attendance in Parliament for the simple purpose of sustaining *Whig* Conservatism against *Tory*

Conservatism. I now look wistfully back to my unfinished Greek History. I hope the time will soon arrive when I can resume it."

After the dissolution in 1841, Grote and his wife carried out a long-thought-of idea of visiting Rome. The first time the historian of Greece caught sight of the Eternal City, he could hardly restrain his emotion; but plain fact often treads rudely on the skirts of sentiment, and the future historian was called away from musing amid the ruins of antiquity to pay the April Bank dividends in Threadneedle Street!

Immediately he was back in England, his old pre-parliamentary habits came back upon him. His leisure was again filled with profitable study. At his house at Burnham Beeches, he laid out in detail the scheme of his first two volumes of his "History of Greece," and in the *Westminster Review* for May 1843, he gave the learned world a foretaste of their contents in an elaborate article on Early Grecian Legends.

In the autumn of 1843, after having been thirty years connected with the banking-house, Grote retired from the firm of Prescott, Grote, & Co. The clerks in the establishment paid him a valued compliment on the occasion; but apart from the death of Mrs Grote's father, his meeting with the reverend wit, Sydney Smith, at his residence Combe Florey, in Somersetshire, with the French philosopher M. Comte in Paris, and with that great musical genius, Felix Mendelssohn in London, this year and the one following passed quietly and uneventfully.

Before going on to speak of the publication of the History, it will be well to pause for a little and consider the preparation the historian had made for his work.

It is to be noted, in the first place, that the languages of which he was master were Greek, Latin, French, Italian, German, and, of course, English. By means of these instruments he had made himself acquainted with the manners and customs, the habits and institutions of a great number of countries, making himself specially conversant with the facts and circumstances attending the rise of their national life. Every fact connected with the growth of a people's power was interesting to him, and having secured, in his young days, an extensive vocabulary by the perusal of all kinds of imaginative literature, it was ever a pleasure to him to write down his opinions of books, men, and historical events. When he sat down in earnest to his work, he had thus beside him commonplace books, filled with learned references, and a great accumulation of short sketches and essays on matters particularly bearing on Grecian history.

The turn of mind which he received from James Mill is not to be lost sight of. If the chief defects of Mitford's history flowed from the monarchical tendencies of the writer, it was the democratic habit of thought planted in his pupil by the philosopher which brought Grote into sympathetic connection with the Hellenic race, and gave him that principle of living interpretation which even more than his scholarship and assiduity was to unlock the hidden secrets of Grecian life. The knowledge and research Grote brought to bear on the whole range of his work, no doubt surpassed that of any other Grecian historian, but, in reality, it was the *spirit* he brought to bear on the cold facts which gave his pages fresh interest, and his conclusions their inestimable value. Mr Murray's confidential adviser, after perusing the MSS. of Grote's first two volumes, and without knowing who the author was, said to the publisher, "Sir, you have got hold of a *good thing* here, and one likely to produce a great effect upon the scholar world. If I am not mistaken, this will prove to be a work of profound interest to us all." Mill pronounced on the general effect in these words: – "Though the statement has the air of an exaggeration, yet, after much study of Mr Grote's book, we do not hesitate to assert, that there is hardly a fact of importance in Grecian history which was perfectly understood before his re-examination of it."

Furthermore, when account is taken of the large place in Grecian history filled by necessary accounts of works of philosophy and art, it is at once evident that something more must be possessed by the historian of Hellas than merely "a historical or narrative interest." The phenomena of Grecian culture required its historian to be at the same time a psychologist and philosopher. Excepting in Hume and Mill, these qualities have seldom been found in the same individual. Grote, however, is another exception, and in him the analytic habit of the philosopher was happily blended with the discriminating power of the historian; and it was in virtue of possessing these faculties he was as able to follow the footsteps of Alexander as to thread the mazes of the Platonic philosophy. Thus, in most comfortable worldly circumstances, freed from business entanglements, with languages learned, with studious habits confirmed, with stores of past industry to draw from, with a large knowledge of the world, and with a mind ready to mark and sympathise with every popular effort after freedom, Grote, in the seclusion of Burnham Beeches, sat down to his great self-imposed task.

The scope of the historian's work was "to exhaust the free life of collective Hellas," to put down in their order all the events that marked, and the activities that quickened, the Grecian race from the time of the Homeric poems to the death of Alexander. The work was to be divided into two great parts – Legendary and Historical Greece. The latter part again, the historian proposed to subdivide into six great divisions. From 776 B.C. to the accession of Peisistratus at Athens was to constitute the first period of Historical Greece; from Peisistratus to the repulse of Xerxes, the second; from the repulse of Xerxes to the overthrow of Athens, the third; from the close of the Peloponnesian war to the battle of Leuktra, the fourth; from the battle of Leuktra to that of Chaeroneia, the fifth; and from the battle of Chaeroneia to the end of the generation of Alexander, the sixth.

By the beginning of 1846 the first two volumes were ready for the press. After some difficulty, Mr Murray, of Albemarle Street, was secured by Mr Grote, as publisher. Strange to say, Grote would take nothing to do with the publishing arrangements. He only ventured to hope "that the poor man might not be a loser by him, and then he would be content, come what might." The truth was, Grote was in doubt, considering the legendary and generally uninteresting nature of their contents, about the success of these two first volumes. He was conscious he had spent a deal of labour on them, but he had misgivings with regard to their reception by the public. He wrote to J. S. Mill, "It is repugnant to me, rather, to publish the legendary matter, together with so small a portion of the real history as I shall be able to comprise in this first batch; but a beginning *must* be made."

In the March of the year 1846, the first instalment of the "History of Greece" was given to the world. This was twenty-two years after the idea of such a work had been suggested to Grote by his wife. The fears of the author were quickly dissipated by the success of the work. Lewis was the first to congratulate him, and thought he "had completely succeeded in placing the whole question of the mythology and legendary narrations of the Greeks upon what he believed to be their true footing." Not long after the publication, Henry Hallam, at a dinner at Sir T. Frankland Lewis's, drew aside the historian's wife, and said to her, "I have been familiar with the literary world for a very long period, and I can safely affirm that I never knew a book take so *rapid* a flight to the highest summits of fame as George's new 'History of Greece.' It has produced a striking sensation among scholars."

The chief charge which Grote anticipated would be made against him with regard to the subject-matter of Vols. I. and II., that he had not inquired sufficiently into that kernel of fact in which the legends had their beginning, he most ably repelled even before it had been preferred. "I describe," says the historian, "the earlier times by themselves, as conceived by the faith and feeling of the first Greeks, and known only through then-legends – without presuming to measure how much or how little of historical matter these legends may contain. If the reader blame me for not assisting him in determining this – if he ask me why I do not withdraw the curtain and disclose the picture – I reply in the words of the painter Zeuxis, when the same question was addressed to him on exhibiting his masterpiece of imitative art – 'The curtain *is* the picture.' What we now read as poetry and legend was once accredited history, and the only genuine history which the first Greeks could conceive or relish of their past time: the curtain conceals nothing behind, and cannot, by any ingenuity, be withdrawn." [*Hist.* i., *Pref.* pp. 12-13]

During the next two years Grote and his wife had a great deal of intercourse with the stars of the musical world. Felix Mendelssohn had come to town to bring out his oratorio of "Elijah." Jenny Lind stayed with them at Burnham Beeches, and they became her warm friends and active partisans. They also came a great deal into contact with Moscheles, Ernst, Thalberg, and others. With such lively and interesting company about him, the historian still proceeded steadily with his work, and in the April of 1847 two other volumes made their appearance. The latter of these concludes with the battle of Marathon, "the narrative of which," said one, "cannot be read for the hundredth time without deep emotion."

In the description of this battle the characteristic features of Grote's style are apparent It was as different from Gibbon's as could be well conceived. In Grote the balance of Gibbon's polished paragraphs, and the roll of his long sentences are wanting. Grote's sentences ever flow simply and sweetly. You realize while you read the author is not declaiming but speaking to you. The more massive figures of speech – hyperbole, interrogation, climax – are all wanting, but the simpler figures – metaphor and simile – he uses frequently and to good purpose. He is sometimes blamed for lack of warmth, but if his narrative is anywhere cold it was not that he wanted the poetic spirit, but because he knew that in historical work poetry could never pass for proof, nor emotion for matter of fact. Not the least remarkable of the many good qualities of his style is that it is never clouded, but always simple and perspicuous, and the sense to be conveyed always apparent to the very lowest capacity. We have said the description of the battle of Marathon may be taken as a specimen of Grote's simple and lucid style: – "Of the two opposing armies at Marathon, we are told that the Athenians were 10,000 hoplites, either including, or besides, the 1000 who came from Platæa. Nor is this statement in itself improbable, though it does not come from Herodotus, who is our only really valuable authority on the case, and who mentions no numerical total. Indeed, the number named seems smaller than we should have expected, considering that no less than 4000 Kleruchs or out-settled citizens had just come over from Eubœa. A sufficient force of citizens must, of course, have been left behind to defend the city. The numbers of the Persians we cannot be said to know at all; nor is there anything certain except that they were greatly superior to the Greeks. We hear from Herodotus that their armament originally consisted of 600 ships of war, but we are not told how many transports there were; and moreover, re-inforcements had been procured as they came across the Ægean from the islands successfully conquered. The aggregate crews on board of all their ships must have been between 150,000 and 200,000 men; but what proportion of these were fighting men, or how many actually did fight at Marathon we have no means of determining. There was a certain proportion of cavalry, and some transports expressly prepared for the conveyance of horses. Moreover, Herodotus tells us that Hippias selected the plain of Marathon for a landing-place, because it was the most convenient spot in Attica for cavalry movements – though it is singular that in the battle the cavalry are not mentioned.

"Marathon, situated near to a bay on the eastern coast of Attica, and in a direction E.N.E. from Athens, is divided by the high ridge of Mount Pentelikus from the city, with which it communicated by two roads – one to the north, another to the south of that mountain. Of these two roads, the northern, at once the shortest and most difficult, is twenty-two miles in length; the southern – longer, but more easy, and the only one practicable for chariots – is twenty-six miles in length, or about six and a half hours of computed march. It passed between Mount Pentelikus and Hymettus, through the ancient demes of Gargettus and Pallenè, and was the road by which Peisistratus and Hippias, when they landed at Marathon forty-seven years before, had marched to Athens. The bay of Marathon, sheltered by a projecting cape from the northward, affords both deep water and a shore convenient for landing, while its plain (says a careful modern observer [Findlay on the Battle of Marathon]) extends in a perfect level along this fine bay, and is in length about six miles, in breadth never less than about one mile and a half. Two marshes bound the extremity of the plain; the southern is not very large, and is always dry at the conclusion of the great heats; but the northern, which generally covers considerably more than a square mile, offers several parts which are at all seasons impassable. Both, however, leave a broad, firm, sandy beach between them and the sea. The uninterrupted flatness of the plain is hardly relieved by a single tree, and an amphitheatre of rocky hills and rugged mountains separate it from the rest of Attica, over the lower ridges of which some steep and difficult paths communicate with the districts of the interior.

"The position occupied by Miltiades before the battle, identified as it was to all subsequent Athenians by the sacred grove of Herakles, near Marathon, was probably on some portion of the high ground above this plain, and Cornelius Nepos tells us that he protected it from the attacks of the Persian cavalry by felled trees obstructing the approach. The Persians occupied a position on the plain; while their fleet was arranged along the beach, and Hippias himself marshalled them for the battle. The native Persians and Sakae, the best troops in the whole army, were placed in the centre, which they considered as the post of honour, and which was occupied by the Persian king himself when present at battle. The right wing was so regarded by the Greeks, and the polemarch Kallmiachus had the command of it; the hoplites being arranged in the order of their respective tribes from right to left. At the extreme left stood the Platæans. It was necessary for Miltiades to present a front equal, or nearly equal, to that of the more numerous Persian host, in order to guard himself from being taken in flank: and with this view he drew up the central tribes, including the Leontis and Antiochis, in shallow files, occupying large breadth of ground: while each of the wings was in stronger and deeper order, so as to make his attack efficient on both sides. His whole army consisted of hoplites, with some slaves as unarmed or light-armed attendants, but without either bowmen or cavalry. Nor could the Persians have been very strong in this latter force, seeing that their horses had to be transported across the Ægean. But the elevated position of Miltiades enabled them to take some measure of the numbers under his command; and the entire absence of cavalry among their enemies could not but confirm the confidence with which a long career of uninterrupted victory had impressed their generals.

"At length the sacrifices in the Greek camp were favourable for battle, and Miltiades, who had everything to gain by coming immediately to close quarters, ordered his army to advance at a running step over the interval of one mile which separated the two armies. This rapid forward movement, accompanied by the war-cry or paean which always animated the charge of the Greek soldier, astounded the Persian army; who construed it as an act of desperate courage little short of insanity, in a body not only small, but destitute of cavalry or archers – but who, at the same time, felt their conscious superiority sink within them. It seems to have been long remembered among the Greeks as the peculiar characteristic of the battle of Marathon, and Herodotus tells us that the Athenians were the first Greeks who ever charged at a run. It doubtless operated beneficially in rendering the Persian cavalry and archers comparatively innocuous, but we may reasonably suppose it also disordered the Athenian ranks, so that when they reached the Persian front, they were both out of breath and unsteady in that line of presented spears and shields which constituted their force. On the two wings, where the files were deep, this disorder produced no mischievous effect; the Persians, after a certain resistance, were overborne and driven back. But in the centre, where the files were shallow, and where, moreover, the native Persians and other choice troops of the army were posted, the breathless and disordered Athenian hoplites found themselves in far greater difficulties. The tribes Leontis and Antioches, with Thomastikles and Aristides among them, were actually defeated, broken, driven back, and pursued by the Persians and Sakae. Miltiades seems to have foreseen the possibility of such a check when he found himself compelled to diminish so materially the depth of his centre; for his wings having routed the enemies opposed to them, were stayed from pursuit until the centre was extricated, and the Persians and Sakae put to flight along with the rest. The pursuit then became general, and the Persians were chased to their ships, ranged in line along the shore; some of them became involved in the impassable marsh and there perished. The Athenians tried to set the ships on fire, but the defence here was both vigorous and successful – several of the forward warriors of Athens were slain, and only seven ships out of the numerous fleet destroyed. This part of the battle terminated to the advantage of the Persians. They repulsed the Athenians from the sea-shore, and secured a safe re-embarkation; leaving few or no prisoners, but a rich spoil of tents and equipments which had been disembarked and could not be carried away.

"Herodotus estimates the number of those who fell on the Persian side in this memorable action at 6400 men; the number of Athenian dead is accurately known since all were collected for the last solemn obsequies – they were 192. How many were wounded we do not hear. The brave Kallimachus, the polemarch, and Stezilaus one of the ten generals, were among the slain; together with Kynegeirus, son of Euphorion, who, in laying hold of the poop-staff of one of the vessels, had his hand cut off by an axe, and died of the wound. He was brother to the poet Æschylus, himself present at the fight; to whose imagination this battle at the ships must have emphatically recalled the fifteenth book of the

Iliad. Both these Athenian generals are said to have perished in the assault of the ships, apparently the hottest part of the conflict. The statement of the Persian loss as given by Herodotus appears moderate and reasonable, but he does not specify any distinguished individuals as having fallen." [*Hist.* iv., pp. 467-476, *et sup.*]

The battle of Marathon being one of the outstanding events in Grecian History, and its proudest scene of heroism and victorious valour, it has been again and again objected to Grote's account that it does not sufficiently excite the imagination. But it is worthy of remark, that those who have had the deepest knowledge of military affairs have never had for the historian's description anything but unqualified praise. One-and-twenty years after the publication of the fourth volume, one of the few survivors of Waterloo, Sir William Gomm, confessed that he burned with a desire to view the site of Marathon with Grote's book in his hand. On Mrs Grote saying, "It has been objected by the critics that the story of Marathon was too coldly narrated in Grote;" the veteran replied, "Not at all I It is excellently told, and I have read it over, often, with delight."

To resume. After the publication of the third and fourth volumes, Grote became eagerly interested in the condition of affairs in Switzerland. The politics of the country were strangely agitated, and Grote believing that the condition of the Cantons formed a good practical illustration of the autonomy – a word, by the way, first brought into repute by the historian – of the ancient Grecian States, at once took ship for the Continent, that he might make a personal inspection of this peculiar form of government. He made his inspection with that thoroughness and masterliness which characterised his every work, and eventually he published a little book on the subject. In the beginning of the volume he states how the purpose of his visit had been entirely that he might be enabled to carry those enlightened views to the elucidation of the politics of Greece.

"The inhabitants of the twenty-two Cantons of Switzerland are interesting on every ground to the general intelligent public of Europe. But to one whose studies lie in the contemplation and interpretation of historical phenomena, they are especially instructive – partly from the many specialities and differences of race, language, religion, civilization, wealth, habits, &c., which distinguish one part of the population from another, comprising between the Rhine and the Alps, a miniature of all Europe, and exhibiting the fifteenth century in juxtaposition with the nineteenth – partly from the free and unrepressed action of the people, which brings out such distinctive attributes in full relief and contrast. To myself in particular, they present an additional ground of interest from a certain political analogy (nowhere else to be found in Europe) with those who prominently occupy my thoughts, and on whose history I am still engaged – the ancient Greeks." [Pref. to *Ltrs. on Switzerland*]

In Switzerland, Grote spent a day with Mendelssohn at his home at

Interlachen. This was only some weeks before the death of the great musician. Next winter, when Grote and his wife were entertaining during the opera season, Jenny Lind, Chopin, Thalberg, and Dorus Gras at the "Beeches," it seemed, without Felix Mendelssohn's vivacious company, most unlike the happy party they had formed there in past days. The sudden death of the composer was a great blow to the musical world, but by few in the country excepting that solitary couple at Burnham Beeches, was it felt as a personal bereavement

Diversified though they were by occasional company, still those quiet years that the historian passed at his suburban residence were filled to the full by studious labours, and they saw his scholarly passion ever deepening and intensifying. The historian was full of his subject; he felt he was able for it – that he was master of it; and thenceforward to nearly the close of his life, he frequently complained, not in any spirit of exasperation, but mildly and blandly, that "the days were too short." Gibbon's regret was when he looked back on his Oxford years, that he had not done more in the past; Grote's, on the other hand, was, that he could not make enough of the present – that the golden hours passed too swiftly by, and all too quickly after the dawn came the close of the working day. How frugal he was of his time, the extent of his works bears sufficient testimony. In the autumn of 1848, appeared the fifth and sixth volumes, only to be followed in the March of 1850 by the seventh and eighth.

It has always been common with the writers of books to show their manuscripts to trusted friends before putting them into the hands of the printer; but while Grote often performed the part of reader for others, he never required for himself any other adviser than his wife. Excepting part of the sixth volume, the whole of the manuscript and proof came under her eye, and many were the corrections, emendations and excisions which at her instance were made on the work. There cannot be the least doubt that such extraordinary capacity on the part of his wife, if it was not at the root, must at least have very distinctly stimulated those active efforts he put forth, while member of the Council of University College, for the higher education of women.

During the winter of the last mentioned year, Grote, with his wife, attended, on the invitation of the Queen, the theatrical "Soirées" of Her Majesty at Windsor. This was not the first time, for ever since the publication of the "Swiss Letters," which greatly pleased Prince Albert, the ex-M.P. for the city had not been lost sight of at Court. Mrs Grote confessed she did not know whether to feel "flattered or insulted" at the frequent inquiries which these invitations called forth from certain quarters. She felt the honour in her heart, but still she was a woman after all – a woman and a wife; and what honour could be too much for George. It would appear, notwithstanding the Windsor theatricals, Grote was still as much a Radical as ever, and not yet had any change passed over his political sentiments. One night in Drury Lane, when Grote and his wife were in a pit box, Monckton Milnes came and talked with Mrs Grote. "You see," said Mr Milnes, "that man in the stalls opposite, that is the envoy from the French Republic." The wife passed the information along with an opera glass to her husband. "Bless me," said the historian, using the binocular, "I must go and call on that gentleman immediately." Next morning Grote was at the door of the "Ambassador of the Republic," and two days after the Ambassador was dining with him in his town establishment, now in Saville Row. In 1849, when the historian paid a short visit to his friends in Paris, he was "unwontedly excited" at the idea that he was then actually *living under a Republic.*

On the 15th of March 1850, the name of Grote, along with the names of Lords Monteagle and Overstone, Sir James Graham, Thomas B. Macaulay, Sir George Cornewall Lewis, and Henry Hallam, were added by the Crown to the Senate of University College, and in this institution he took the very warmest interest to the end. During the twenty-one years Grote was a member of the Senate, many critical questions came to be discussed and voted on, and the historian was invariably found on the side of progress and liberality. It said much for Grote's inherent breadth of spirit that, while all his years had been taken up with erudite and classical studies, still he was willing to believe that other studies than those in which he had found a special charm might be equally useful and salutary. To the claims of science he was never indifferent. In two measures he took a particular interest; the one was the claim of the graduates to be admitted into the corporate body, and the other was the admission of women to the examinations of the university. The agitation concerning the first measure was successful, and that concerning the second was only defeated by the narrowest of majorities; indeed, just by the casting vote of the Chancellor. The speech made by Grote, when this vote was taken in the Senate, was one of the most temperate, exhaustive, and genuinely liberal he ever uttered. In one part of it he said: "The conviction has spread much, and is spreading more, among both sexes, that women must be taught much more than they have been, to earn for themselves and by their own efforts, an honourable and independent living. There is a larger proportion of women now than formerly who are dissatisfied with a life of mere dependence, without any active purposes or prospects. To throw open to them the field of professional competition more largely than is now done, appears to me most desirable as well as most equitable; but it is an essential preliminary to success in any line that habits of steady, accurate application should be formed at an early period of life. Wherever a female has that genuine aspiration to attain an independent and self-maintaining position, which in my judgment is a virtue alike in both sexes, the prospect of access to our examinations and certificates will tend to stimulate the diligent and serious application in early life which is now wanting, because it goes untested and unrewarded. Complaints of the general inaccuracy of women's minds are sufficiently frequent to have reached everyone. Let those women who are superior to this very frequent infirmity, and who are prepared to prove themselves superior, have the opportunity of doing so by admission to our examinations."

The ninth and tenth volumes of the "History of Greece" were brought out in the month of February 1852, and the eleventh about the end of April of the following year, but what substantial reward, besides fame and honour, the work was bringing to the historian we are, for the most part, left to guess. Grote did not write for money; no historian can. To George C. Lewis our author once remarked in a letter, "No man can write a long work on history or philosophy who has not means of support independent of what the work is to produce." Grote's hope at first had been, "that the poor man, the publisher, might lose nothing by him." But as the work was extensively read, as it appeared, and as the first volumes were already in their third edition, there is no doubt the history must have been by this time a source of very considerable profit. What the extent of the profit was we are not told, but Mrs Grote informs us that the residence they built for themselves at East Burnham was named "History Hut," from the fact that it was wholly built and furnished from the proceeds of the sale of the history.

Although Grote certainly had not "cultivated literature on a little oatmeal," still, from the force of circumstances above set forth, he had never been able to call himself a university man. That he thus had to educate himself in the higher branches of literature, and that this work in no way could be considered as the product of college training, may have been the reasons why he was so long in being recognised by the authorities of the national universities. But, at any rate, from whatever cause, it was not until the historian was verging on sixty years of age he received academical distinction. In the middle of 1853, Henry Milman, then Dean of St Paul's, communicated with Grote on the matter of the honorary degree of D.C.L. Milman acted on behalf of his university, and his offer of the degree was in terms the most flattering. "My own feeling of reverence," said the Dean, "and love for the university induces me to wish most earnestly, that by proposing some higher names, more worthy of the honour, more worthy of being joined with Macaulay, Oxford may redeem herself from the somewhat inglorious list, which, in fact, according to old usage, she receives from the Chancellor at his installation." In due course, Grote was invested with the degree of doctor of civil law. He received his distinction at the hands of the late Earl of Derby, and he confessed to being somewhat nervous in finding himself for the first time surrounded by the scholarship of Oxford. At a banquet given in honour of the new Chancellor, Grote replied for the "British Historians," and Sir Roderick Murchison said, that "he made by far the best speech of the evening."

The pursuits of literature are very far removed from those of banking, and those of agriculture stand far apart from both. Now, it might be thought that any man who had it in him to excel in the higher walks of scholarship and trade could hardly fail in the lower walk of farming. Experience, however, has shown again and again that the very greatest men may make the most unsuccessful agriculturists. Amongst the very considerable number of names great in literature, but beaten and disappointed in farming, must be placed the name of Grote. About this time he got entangled with a 600 acre farm of his own in

Lincolnshire, but after entering into it with the utmost spirit, and spending a deal of money on implements, cattle, and draining, and after also, it must be said, reading the best works on the subject, he was obliged eventually to let it to another, as finding in it a source of continued irritation, vexation, and loss. When we know the historian had got his ideas of farming from Virgil's "Bucolics," we can hardly wonder he suffered defeat and disappointment when himself put his hand to the plough.

On the 23d December the last sheets of the "History of Greece" were sent from History Hut to the publishers. Thus, thirty-two years after the first idea of the work had been suggested to him by his wife, and twelve years after he had left the firm of "Prescott, Grote, & Co.," from which time he had given himself almost exclusively to its preparation, George Grote had the satisfaction, amid the applause of educated England and Germany, to bring, what was acknowledged by all as one of the greatest literary and historical efforts of his time, to a triumphant conclusion. Gibbon, as we have seen, after finishing his great work on the "Decline and Fall of the Roman Empire," left his writing-table to muse for a little, in the soft stillness of the evening, and while the silver orb of the moon was showing its shimmering reflection in the Genevese lake, on the uncertainty of all human life, and the possible brevity of his own. The conclusion of the "History of Greece" calls us to view a homelier scene altogether, and the historian in a less romantic situation. Mrs Grote tells us it was Christmas Eve, and, along with one or two of her husband's brother's children – for they had none of their own – they were all very happy together. While the children played by themselves, Mrs Grote brewed a bowl of punch, in celebration of the completion of the "*opus magnum;*" and she further discloses, that as the Doctor continued to sip "the delicious mixture," for the most part in silence, but "giving unmistakeable signs of inward complacency," she grew garrulous in her wifely happiness, bringing to mind the scenes of thirty years ago, and sooner, when they had met in their golden prime, when she had first spoken of *the history;* and descanting upon "the happiness of their living to see this day," and the termination of the work. As we have said, this is a homelier scene than a similar one we depicted in our previous sketch, but on that account it hath not the less a broader human appeal.

As the historian had advanced, he had warmed to his work, and his zeal and thoroughness had so increased with his progress, that the twelfth volume may be taken as containing the best part of the whole history. In this volume the outstanding feature is the startling and marvellous career of Alexander the Great. On the whole life of this great warrior the historian had bestowed the utmost pains; but he had so mastered the subject that we never see in any part of this narrative, what we frequently behold in other departments of the history, the writer bent down with such a weight of authorities that his step wants elasticity and his advance seems painful and slow. In the story of Alexander we find the greatest possible amount of research united to the greatest suppleness of style and rapidity of narrative. The last hours of the son of Philip of Macedon are thus described: – " On the morrow, though desperately ill, he still made the effort requisite for performing the sacrifice: he was then carried across from the garden-house to the palace, giving orders that the generals and officers should remain in permanent attendance in and near the hall. He caused some of them to be called to his bedside; but though he knew them perfectly, he had by this time become incapable of utterance. One of his last words spoken is said to have been, on being asked to whom he bequeathed his kingdom, '*To the strongest:*' one of his last acts was to take his signet ring and hand it to Perdikkas. For two nights and a day he continued in this state, without either amendment or repose. Meanwhile, the news of his malady had spread through the army, filling them with grief and consternation. Many of the soldiers, eager to see him once more, forced their way into the palace, and were admitted unarmed. They passed along by the bedside, with all the demonstrations of affliction and sympathy, Alexander knew them, and made show of friendly recognition as well as he could, but was unable to say a word. Several of the generals slept in the Temple of Serapis, hoping to be informed by the god in a dream whether they ought to bring Alexander into it, as a suppliant, to experience the divine healing power. The god informed them in their dream that Alexander ought not to be brought into the temple – that it would be better for him to be left where he was. In the afternoon he expired – June 323 B.C. – after a life of thirty-two years and eight months, and a reign of twelve years and eight months. . . . Alexander had mastered, in defiance of fatigue, hardship, and combat, not merely all the eastern half of the Persian empire, but unknown Indian regions beyond its easternmost limits. Besides Macedonia, Greece, and Thrace, he possessed all that immense treasure and military force which had once rendered the great king so formidable. By no such contemporary man had any such power ever been known or conceived. With the turn of imagination then prevalent, many were doubtless disposed to take him for a god on earth, as Grecian spectators had once supposed with regard to Xerxes, when they beheld the innumerable Persian host crossing the Hellespont. Exalted to this prodigious grandeur, Alexander was at the time of his death little more than thirty-two years old – the age at which a citizen of Athens was growing into important commands; ten years less than the age for a consul at Rome; two years younger than the age at which Timour first acquired the crown, and began his foreign conquests. His extraordinary bodily powers were unabated; he had acquired a large stock of military experience; and, what was still more important, his appetite for further conquest was as voracious, and his readiness to purchase it at the largest cost of toil or danger as complete, as it had been when he had first crossed the Hellespont. Great as his past career had been, his future achievements, with such increased means and experience, were likely to be yet greater. His ambition would have been satisfied with nothing less than the conquest of the whole habitable world as then known; and if his life had been prolonged he would probably have accomplished it. Nowhere (so far as our knowledge reaches) did there reside any military power capable of making head against him; nor were his soldiers, when he commanded them, daunted or baffled by any extremity of cold, heat, or fatigue." [*Hist.* xii., pp. 344, 345, 348, 349]

Carlyle somewhere says that the writing of his books has invariably made him ill: and when we consider the number of years Grote had spent on his history – the steady devotion and intellectual energy with which he prosecuted his task – we cannot wonder after it was done he seemed so thoroughly jaded that Mrs Grote was glad to get him away to the Italian lakes to recruit. Before, however, the History had been well out of his hands, and before setting out for his well-earned tour, he had put his papers together in prospect of attacking the Philosophy of Plato. Ever as he grew older the idea of the short days and the long work made him ever more eager to seize the opportunity of the passing hour.

The next two or three years after his return from Italy were passed at History Hut in study and comparative retirement. Left to himself, Grote would never have become member of any club, but by the exertions of Lord Overstone, and the connivance of his wife, his resistance was overcome, and he was enrolled a member of "The Club," as it is called, *par excellence.* It was the club of which Johnson, Reynolds, Goldsmith, and Gibbon had all been members in their day. Grote never regretted the step, but used to recount the conversation of the rooms, and was often highly delighted with the superior literary talk of the members. Amongst the visitors who enlivened the historian's leisure were Mrs Stanley, Lady Trelawny, Lady Lewis, Dr William Smith, John Mill, Mr Lowe, and Professor Bain. Grote also met by accident while on a visit to the country the Hon. Lothrop Motley, the famous historian of the Low Countries. There is no account of what passed between the two men, but from the nature of their sentiments, we may well suppose they would find in each other the most congenial companionship. Motley was travelling with his wife and daughter in England, and after this casual meeting they all paid a short visit to Grote at Barrow Green, whither he had removed after disposing of History Hut.

On the 9th of January his old friend Henry Hallam died, and was interred in Westminster Abbey. Hallam had been a trustee of the British Museum, and it had been one of his last wishes that Grote might be appointed in his place after he was gone. This wish was realised in the appointment of Grote to the vacant seat; but although he had already sufficient "Board" work, the duties of a Museum Trustee were at once interesting and peculiar, and after the brain was fatigued by philosophical writing, he always found it a pleasing diversity to participate in labours requiring practical discernment

In the beginning of January 1862, John Stuart Mill was anxious Grote should accompany him in a tour to Greece. Finding himself, however, now too old for the foot and horse exercise inevitable in such a journey, Grote was obliged to decline visiting in person those scenes of which he had written so much, and which since his earliest years had ever shone before his imagination. A consciousness of growing years and failing strength made Grote now more cautious in his exercises and methodical in his studies than he had ever been. He now rose regularly at 8 A.M., and after a short walk and light breakfast, he repaired to his study, where he remained till dinner, with only a short cessation from work at luncheon time. From breakfast till luncheon he was invariably accompanied by "Dora," a little favourite pet-dog. "Dora" took up her position on the historian's knees, and Mrs Grote "will vouch for it that the greater portion of the volumes of his Plato were written over the back of this little favourite." After luncheon, having spent the morning with "the Master," "Dora" devoted the remainder of the day to attending on the "Mistress."

In 1863 Grote paid a visit to Canon Stanley, Professor of Ecclesiastical History at Oxford, and met with a most flattering reception from young England. In the year following he had the high honour to be elected "Foreign Member" of the Institute of France, "The muster roll of which," said the Count Adolphe de Circourt, in giving him notice of his election, "is probably the highest and fullest representation of the genius and learning of the age."

Vast as was the conception of the "History of Greece," it was in reality but part of a grander design in the mind of the historian. His object was to write a great Greek Trilogy: the first part being the History of Greece, the second was to be an elucidation of the Philosophy of Plato and his contemporaries, and the third a discussion of the life, influences, and ethics of Aristotle. In May 1865, nine years after the completion of the History, appeared the second part of this great work, under the title of "Plato and the other Companions of Sokrates." The subject was one which commended itself specially to the historian's intelligence, as he regarded the writings of Plato as the pure and unadulterated products of the Hellenic mind. They had a rich value of their own, because they were unmixed by foreign speculations, and "preceded the development of Alexandria and the amalgamation of Oriental views of thought with the inspirations of the Academy or the Lyceum." "The Orontes and the Jordan had not yet begun to flow westward, and to impart their own colour to the waters of Attica and Latium."[*Plato et al.* i. Pref., p. 12]

The year following the publication of the "Plato" was embittered by a severe sectarian struggle. The Professorship of Logic in University College had become vacant, and as the Dissenters had ever looked with interest to the rise of this institution, they were most anxious to have their party represented amongst its Professors. For this purpose they brought forward the Rev. James Martineau as a candidate for the vacant chair. Grote was dismayed for the moment. But not losing courage, his wife says, like "Christian" when he found Apollyon be-straddling the pathway, Grote "immediately felt for his sword." The fight was acrimonious and envenomed; but Grote succeeded in swaying the vote against the Unitarian. This matter we need scarcely have alluded to; it is only worthy of mention from the fact that defeat would have severed Grote's forty years connection with an institution whose prosperity was in great measure owing to his own disinterested endeavours.

Grote began his work on Aristotle in his seventy-first year, so anxious was he to complete his account, if he were able, not only of the active, but also of the speculative history of Hellas. Apart from writing some contributions to Professor Bain's "Manual," including the *De Anima*, which occupied eight months in composition, the Aristotle engaged the whole of his studious hours. This work, however, was never to see the light in Grote's lifetime; indeed, although the author had advanced it far, still he did not live to complete it. It is but a fragment – a sad memorial of the defeat which awaits the most courageous human endeavours. While Grote thus strove to exhaust the life of collective Hellas, it is strange we have nowhere any hint that the artistic powers of the Greek intelligence were as worthy of examination, and just as great as either their active or speculative capabilities. With his books on the works of Plato and Aristotle before us, we cannot help thinking of possible books as full and elaborate on the works of Phidias and Praxiteles.

In a letter to Professor Bain, dated 4th December 1868, we find Grote saying – "I am sure my intellect is as good as ever it was. I shall be 74, Nov. 17." While the historian was writing in this manner to his friend, Mrs Grote was writing to the following effect in her diary: – " Mr Grote's health, I fully expect, will ere long give way under the unwholesome habits in which he permits himself to indulge; spending about twenty-two hours out of the twenty-four – indeed sometimes twenty-three – within four walls. . . . Mr Grote's personal aspect is sensibly changed within the last eight months, whilst I discern a lessening capacity for bodily exertion, not fairly referable to his being one year older. His hand shakes worse than it did, his gait has altered to that of an old man, from being remarkably steady and elastic up to a recent date." During the hot June of 1869 he stuck to his "Board" work in town, and his studious labours at his desk, but his wife getting him to consult a physician, he was ordered off at once to Hombourg-les-Bains, to drink the waters for three weeks, and thereafter to travel in Switzerland.

Honours, as we have seen, had been falling thick on him lately, but shortly after his return from the Continent he had the greatest of all placed before him for his acceptance. With the authority of Her Majesty, Mr Gladstone proposed to him that he should become a peer of the United Kingdom. In a long letter to the Prime Minister, Grote set forth his reasons for refusing the generous offer, and one paragraph of it was characteristic: – " Last, though not least, I am engaged in a work on Aristotle, forming a sequel to my work on Plato: and, as I am thoroughly resolved to complete this, if health and energy be preserved to me, I feel that (being now nearly seventy-five) I have no surplus force for other purposes." This reflects the man: he could never think of position apart from corresponding duties to be discharged, and from no duty, however onerous, would he ever turn to grasp at any position, however honourable.

LEGENDARY GREECE

Since the time Grote had first given utterance to his views on the ballot, now nearly forty years ago, his opinions had been slowly ripening in the country; but when, in the month of February 1870, a member of Parliament moved for "leave to bring in a bill for ballot at elections," and Lord Harrington gave no sign of any intention on the part of the Government of the day to oppose the bill, the near prospect of the passing of this measure which the historian had struggled so earnestly for in his younger years, created in him no concern whatever. The fact was he had already anticipated the results that were to accrue from its action, clearly perceiving it was not likely to bring more radical members to the House than the open voting system. When the ballot act was about to be carried into effect, Mrs Grote said to the historian one day, "You will soon have lived to see your own favourite measure triumph over all obstacles, and you will, of course, feel great satisfaction thereat?" The husband made answer, "I should have done so had it not been for the recent alteration of the suffrage. Since the wide expansion of the voting element, I confess that the value of the ballot has sunk in my estimation; I do not, in fact, think that the elections will be affected by it, one way or another, as far as party interests are concerned." The wife made the further inquiry, "Still you will, at all events, get at the genuine preference of the constituency in choosing their candidate?" "No doubt," answered Grote, "but then, again, I have come to perceive that the choice between one man and another, among the English people, signifies less than I formerly used to think it did. Take a section of society, cut it from top to bottom, and examine the composition of the successive layers. They are much alike throughout the scale. The opinions all based upon the same social instincts: never upon a clear or enlightened perception of *general interests*. Every particular class pursuing its own, the result is a universal struggle for the advantages accruing from *party* supremacy. The English mind is much of one pattern take whatever class you will. The same favourite prejudices, amiable and otherwise; the same antipathies, coupled with ill-regulated, though benevolent efforts to eradicate human evils, are well nigh universal: modified, naturally, by instruction among the highly educated few; but *they* hardly affect the course of out-of-doors sentiment. I believe, therefore, that the actual composition of Parliament represents, with tolerable fidelity, the British people. And it will never be better than it is, for a House of Commons cannot afford to be above its own constituencies, in intelligence, knowledge, or patriotism." Again, such a remark as the historian made to Mrs Grote, when talking to her about the affairs of the United States, gives too great insight into his later opinions to be passed without notice. "I have outlived," said Grote, "my faith in the efficacy of republican government regarded as a check upon the vulgar passions of the majority in a nation, and I recognise the fact that supreme power lodged in their hands *may* be exercised quite as mischievously as by a despotic ruler like the first Napoleon. The conduct of the Northern States, in the late conflict with the Southern States, has led me to the conclusion, though it costs me much to avow it, even to myself." It is not to be thought, from these remarks, that Grote's early democratic opinions had suffered eclipse; in reality, it was not so; his spirit never ceased to the last to cherish a lofty ideal of popular freedom; but, in mature years, he had had too much experience, meditated too profoundly on the drawbacks and impulses to civilisation, and had become, in short, too much of a philosopher to believe that a perfect government could be organised out of the defective and broken materials of human life. To the end, if he had had to choose between monarchy and republicanism, he would have preferred the latter, but out of no spirit of enmity to the former.

in the spring of 1870, the Members of Convocation of the University of London, asked Grote, their now respected Vice-Chancellor, to sit for his portrait – the picture, when finished, to be placed in the senate-room of their new buildings in Burlington Gardens. The historian complied, but it was while "sitting" in Mr Millais's studio he received a chill, from which he never perfectly recovered. He had taken off his great-coat on coming into the painter's workshop, and although he felt uncomfortable, being ever more zealous about the comfort of others than himself, he thought it might have been an injustice to the artist if he had asked to be allowed to put it on again. The illness which supervened would certainly have been triumphed over but for the historian's continued disobedience to medical orders. Dividend warrants had to be signed at the Bank of England, and he had to be there to sign them; the British Museum Standing Committee had important work before it, and he had to be there to give his vote and see to everything being satisfactorily done. On the 16th May, the University Senate held a committee meeting in his house in Savile Row. The Vice-Chancellor presided. The matters on hand "taxed his cerebral faculties severely." This was the last effort Grote ever made for the public good, – the last meeting he ever attended. On the morning of the 18th June, the great historian passed away tranquilly and without pain; and thus was brought to a close, a career singularly devoted, conscientious, and laborious, a life rich in virtue and honour and the esteem of the wise and the good. The remains were buried in Westminster Abbey. "I selected," says Dean Stanley, "the spot in the south transept, in what Fuller calls the learned side of Poet's Corner. Camden and Causaubon look down upon the grave, and Macaulay lies a few feet distant."

The eulogy which Grote pronounced over the life of Solon, [*Hist.* iii., p. 212] is a eulogy which with equal justice can be pronounced over his own: "He represents the best tendencies of his age, combined with much that is personally excellent; the improved ethical sensibility; the thirst for enlarged knowledge and observation, not less potent in old age than in youth; the conception of regularised popular institutions, departing sensibly from the type and spirit of the governments around him, and calculated to found a new character in the Athenian [in Grote's case English] people; a genuine and reflecting sympathy with the mass of the poor, anxious not merely to rescue them from the oppression of the rich, but to create in them habits of self-relying industry: lastly, during his temporary possession of a power altogether arbitrary, not merely an absence of all selfish ambition, but a rare discretion in seizing the mean between conflicting exigencies." Like the endeavours of him who was "neither Lancelot nor another," all the aim of this knight of literature was:

"To keep down the base in man,
To teach high thought, and amiable words,
And courtliness and the desire of fame,
And love of truth, and all that makes a man."

The following is a list of Grote's published works:

Statement of the Question of Parliamentary Reform, 1821 (summarised in Chapter I of "Minor Works"); Analysis of the Influence of Natural Religion on the Temporal Happiness of Mankind (published under the pseudonym of Philip Beauchamp), 1822; Essentials of Parliamentary Reform, 1831 (reprinted in "Minor Works"); Two Speeches on Vote by Ballot, 1833, 1836; Seven Letters on the Recent Politics of Switzerland (from the "Spectator"), 1847-1856 (with additional Letter); History of Greece, 12 vols., 1846-1856 (several volumes were re-published before the completion of the whole work); Later Editions, 1862, 1869, 1872, 1888; Plato's Doctrine Concerning the Rotation of the Earth, and Aristotle's Comment upon that Doctrine, 1860 ("Minor Works"); Plato and the other Companions of Sokrates, 3 vols., 1865, 1867, 1874, 4 vols. 1885; ed. by A. Bain, 4 vols. 1888; Review of John Stuart Mill on the Philosophy of Sir William Hamilton (from "Westminster Review," 1866), 1868 ("Minor Works").

Posthumous Publications: Aristotle, ed. by A. Bain and G. C. Robertson, 2 vols., 1872, 1880 (the "Psychology of Aristotle" had already appeared in 1868 as an appendix to the third edition of Bain's "Senses and Intellect"; and the section on Universals in the same year as appendix to the same author's "Mental and Moral Science").

Poems, 1815-1822 (printed for private circulation 1872).

The Minor Works of George Grote, with Critical Remarks on his Intellectual Character, Writings, and Speeches, by A. Bain, 1873 (including, besides the articles already mentioned, a "Notice of Sir William Molesworth's edition of the Works of Hobbes," from the "Spectator," 1839; Grecian Legends and Early History, from the "Westminster Review," 1843; On Ancient Weights, Coins, and Measures, from the "Classical Museum," 1844; Presidential Address, In Commemoration of the Twenty-first Anniversary of the London Scientific Institution, 1846; Address on Delivering the Prizes at University College, 1846; Review of Sir G. C. Lewis on the Credibility of Early Roman History, from the "Edinburgh Review," 1856).

Posthumous Papers, printed for private circulation, 1874; Fragments on Ethical Subjects, a selection from Grote's Posthumous Papers, by A. Bain, 1876.

Personal Life of George Grote, by his widow, 1873.

LIFE OF GEORGE GROTE

Introduction to the Everyman Edition of 1906.

Grote's "History of Greece" was first published just sixty years ago. Since then many histories of Greece have been written, but of those written in England, Grote's still remains in some respects the greatest. It was the first great history of Greece written in the spirit of scientific criticism which marked the renaissance of classical studies in the nineteenth century. Grote had an unrivalled knowledge of and command over the literary sources, and so far as Greek history depends on such sources, his history is still, and will remain, up to date. He has been condemned as a partisan, and we can hardly claim him as an impartial historian. He is throughout the fervent defender of Athenian democracy. For him Athens, and especially Athenian democrats, are always in the right, and he outdoes even Herodotus in his contempt for tyrants, oligarchs and Spartans. He commits too often the fault of reading the prejudices and passions of modern politics into ancient history. But for this attitude there are excuses, and it has its compensations. His impassioned defence of Athenian democracy was a natural reaction against the foolish carpings of anti-democratic historians like Mitford. His enthusiasm for Athens is not always to be regretted. His wholehearted appreciation of her ideals may not always result in "scientific" history, but it gave him a sympathy and insight into Greek democracy at its best, a realisation of the debt which civilisation owes to Greece in politics as well as in art and speculation, which we should be sorry to be without. If he sometimes becomes a party advocate rather than an historian, his advocacy is always based on knowledge and critical insight. If Greek history still relied solely on literary sources, Grote's history would remain a great and adequate account.

Since the publication of his history a great change has come over our knowledge of Greek civilisation. We no longer rely solely on literary sources, on Herodotus, Thucydides and Xenophon, and other historians. We have also the important evidence of archaeology. All over Greece archaeologists have brought to light countless memorials of Greek civilisation. In Grote's time the sources for Greek history were scanty, and we had no means of checking the statements of one historian, except comparison with those of another. Contradictions between Herodotus and Thucydides, or between Thucydides and later writers, could be resolved only by conjecture, by a discussion of the inherent probabilities of each case. Since that time inscriptions have been discovered in great number which throw new light on such subjects as, for example, the working of the Athenian constitution, and by which we can often check, corroborate or correct the statements of historians. Further, our literary sources have been increased by the important discovery in Egypt of a copy of Aristotle's lost Ἀθηναίων πολιτεία. The result is that since Grote's time Greek history has been to a large extent amplified, and in some respects reconstructed.

In the light of such fresh discoveries can we say that any history of Greece published sixty years ago is still of value? The answer to this question depends upon our conception of the respective contributions to history of archaeology and the contemporary records. We learn far more of the history of any period from its literature, and particularly from its historical literature than from its monuments. The consequence is that where our knowledge of any period of history depends upon contemporary written sources, archaeology cannot usually do much to change our conception of the period. It may and does make it much more vivid and fresh, but its part, supposing that our written sources are at all trustworthy, is much more to corroborate than to correct. Now from the end of the sixth century B.C., we have fairly ample literary sources for Greek history; and archaeology, with all its fresh discoveries, has on the whole only corroborated Herodotus and Thucydides and Xenophon in so far as they dealt with the history of their own time. It has to some extent amplified our knowledge, filled up certain lacunæ, and corrected certain details. But the general conception of the history of the period remains the same. Thanks to recent discoveries, we know, for example, that the conspiracy of Kylon preceded the legislation of Dracon instead of following it, as was previously thought. We know that the Athenians in 425 very greatly increased the tribute paid by the allies. Grote had argued that the silence of Thucydides disproved this. We have found the actual inscription recording the assessment and know that he was wrong, and this new fact is of considerable importance for our estimate of the policy of Cleon and his successors. Thanks to the discovery of many of the tribute lists and of inscriptions recording treaties between Athens and her allies, we know far more of the organisation of the Athenian empire and of its history in the years between 476 and 432. But archaeological evidence for this period is of great importance only because our literary records of it are so scanty. The most recent discoveries affect a later period. Only last year Messrs. Grenfell and Hunt discovered at Oxyrhynchus a portion of the fourth century historian Cratippus. It will enable us to correct certain details in Xenophon's account of the history of the years 396-395. It also fills up a conspicuous gap in our knowledge by its description of the Federal Constitution of Bœotia. A fragment of papyrus found recently at Strasburg and known as Anonymus Argentensis enables us to conclude that Grote was wrong in thinking that the Nomophylakes were an institution of Athens under Pericles. These are specimens of our new knowledge. But all this new information, interesting as it is, is concerned with points of detail. Our knowledge of Greece from the beginning of the fifth century still rests mainly on literary sources and must always do so. Because Grote, with all his faults, was a great imaginative historian, his history of this later period has a permanent and real value which archaeological discoveries cannot materially effect.

It is otherwise with the history of Greece before the end of the sixth century. For here our literary records are scantier and more untrustworthy. Thanks to Herodotus and certain passages in Thucydides we know a good deal about the history of Athens in the sixth century; we can form some notion of the early constitution of Sparta and of the stages by which it rose to the hegemony of the Peloponnese. The poems of Solon, the fragments of such early poets as Archilochus, Tyrtæus, and Theognis give us contemporary literary sources of a kind. We know something of the relations of the cities of Asia Minor to the kingdom of Lydia, more of the age of the tyrants. As we go further back our sources become still more imperfect. We have to rely on vague legends and untrustworthy genealogies. Grote began his account of historical Greece with the Dorians already settled in the Peloponnese. He accepted 776, the first Olympiad, as the earliest historical date; but for at least a hundred and fifty years after that he had almost no historical information. Before 776 he had only legends of Dorian and Æolian migrations, genealogies going hack to the gods, curious tales of early non-Hellenic races in Greece, Pelasgians, Leleges and Karians, and stories of heroes and gods. Somewhere in this dim region came the great Homeric poems, with their elaborate accounts of a civilisation that was strangely different from that of historical Greece. Accurate historical data there were none.

Under these circumstances Grote resolved with much reason to make an absolute distinction between history and legend. It was of no use, he declared, to try to extract historical information from legend, for we have no criterion as to what in it is historical and what is not. He therefore condemned all discussions, *e.g.* about the exact site of Troy and all conjectures about the historical truth underlying the stories of Minos or Agamemnon. Legend, he insisted, is the creation of the poetic mind, and as such it must be treated. The Homeric poems might be used as evidences for the early civilisation in which the writer or writers of these poems lived, but for nothing more. The importance of the legends was poetical and religious, not historical. Grote therefore began his history with a systematic account of the Greek legends and myths, which was for him an account of Greek religion. We could know, he argued, what the Greeks of the fifth century thought about the beginnings of their history, but we could also know, thanks to our superior critical insight, that what they thought was historically untrue.

At the time at which Grote wrote, this attitude was not only defensible but praiseworthy. It was a great service to insist that rationalised legend and history are very different things. But even taken on his own lines the first part has its disadvantages. It is a most misleading account of Greek religion. It represents that as far more systematic, uniform and intellectual than it actually was, and to begin a history of Greece with a systematic account of Greek religion in which the Homeric stories of the gods and the Orphic myths are treated as parts of one uniform system is misleading and anachronistic.

No one could now begin a history of Greece in the same way. Our whole conception of the beginnings of Greek civilisation has been entirely changed since Grote's time, and this change is due to archaeological discoveries. Of the period between the Dorian migration and the sixth century, indeed, archaeology has even less to tell us than our literary records. The tradition of the Dorian migration is confirmed by archaeological evidences. These seem to show that about 900 B.C. the civilisation represented by Mycenae was overthrown by a race who used iron and whose rude pottery was incised with geometrical designs. The older civilisation lingered on in such places as Rhodes and Cyprus, and remains of that period have been discovered by archaeologists. There are a few inscriptions of the seventh and sixth centuries, but only a very few. The two or three centuries succeeding the Dorian invasion remain, and probably will always remain, the least known period in Greek history.

It is otherwise with the earlier period, that on which the Homeric poems and the early legends have always shed a glorious, if tantalising light. This has become peculiarly the domain of archaeological discovery. Where the cautious and well-warranted scepticism of Grote proved fruitless, Schliemann's almost foolish credulity and lack of historical sense produced astonishing results. In 1870 Schliemann began to excavate the mound of Hissarlik in the Troad, in the hope of finding the ruins of the city of Troy. Grote, in his fifteenth chapter, reviews the discussion as to whether Hissarlik or Bounarbashi was the real site of Troy, and dismisses any attempt to locate the city of which Homer sang as necessarily futile. Schliemann began to dig at Hissarlik and made most startling discoveries. The mound was found to have been the site of a very early settlement, going back to Neolithic times, where one city had been built upon another. One of these was a city with strong ramparts which showed traces of having been burned. Greatest discovery of all, a coffer was found containing a store of worked gold, a collection of ornaments which were like nothing previously known to us as Greek, but which did answer to certain descriptions in Homer. Encouraged by this success, Schliemann in 1878 began to excavate the traditional site of Mycenae. Here his discoveries were almost more astonishing. He found five tombs, hewn in the rock, filled with a profusion of gold, ivory, silver, bronzes and alabaster. The gold was beaten into face-masks, bracelets, breast-pieces and all manner of ornaments. On the site were excavated the remains of a palace, which corresponded in many ways to the description of the Homeric house. Schliemann in his enthusiasm went too far, and held that we might now consider the poems of Homer as authenticated history. Had he not found the actual death-masks of Agamemnon and Clytemnestra? But this was entirely to mistake the relations of archaeology, legend and history. These discoveries no more prove that the details of the Homeric story are true, than the discovery of the Round Table would prove the historical reality of the vision of Sir Galahad. They prove the general truth of the picture of Greece given in Homer, where Mycenae Mycenae is the capital of a great kingdom.

But the question of the relation of these discoveries to the Homeric poems was soon lost in the questions raised concerning the discoveries themselves. For all over the Ægean similar finds were made. On the Acropolis rock at Athens, at Tiryns, at Vaphio near Sparta, at Orchomenos, at Thebes and Delphi, and in many of the islands, Naxos, Paros, Thera, and especially in Melos, remains of a similar civilisation have been discovered. These remains were at first given the general title of Mycenaean. Some of the distinctive pottery of this period was found as far afield as Egypt, and pictures of foreigners bringing Mycenaean vases as tribute "from the islands of the very green," were found upon a tomb of the eighteenth dynasty, dating from about 1200 B.C. But in the last few years fresh and even more surprising discoveries have been made. Mr. Arthur Evans has excavated Knossos, the traditional site of the palace of Minos, and we now know that the civilisation of which Mycenae was the chief town, was itself the successor of an earlier civilisation now known as Minoan, whose centre was Crete. The artistic remains of Mycenaean civilisation were wonderful, but they are nothing to the splendour of the discoveries at Knossos. Knossos was the site of a vast and elaborate palace, whose buildings rose to two or three storeys. It was ornamented with frescoes and statues of great naturalistic beauty. Its inhabitants had brought the ceramic arts to great perfection. Besides producing vases painted with great skill and beauty, they could make delicate articles of faience. Further, this civilisation was acquainted with the art of writing, and we possess many inscriptions in a hitherto unknown script used by the inhabitants of Knossos somewhere in the third milenium B.C. Remains of this same earlier civilisation have been found at other places in Crete, notably at Phaistos, and also at Phylakopi in the island of Melos. The legends of Minos, equally with the story of Troy, are shown to have had a real foundation. Mr. Evans has discovered what was certainly the origin of the story of the labyrinth. Frescoes of bull-fights, even of a minotaur, were discovered upon the walls of the palace. Discoveries in Sicily have shown that there was a connection between the Minoan kingdom and that island, of which the story told by Herodotus, how Minos met his death there, seems to be an echo. In any case we can be certain that before the rise of Mycenae the Ægean was ruled from Knossos.

Any general description of those remains would be beyond the scope of this introduction. The reader must be referred to the volume which will shortly be published by Mr. Evans. It will be sufficient if a brief account is given of their importance for the beginnings of Greek history.

The traces of civilisation at Knossos are as early as anything in Egypt. The Neolithic strata seem to go back to as far as the twelfth millennium before Christ. There are traces of connection with Egypt from the fourth millennium onwards. The Ægean was then, as it was so often in later history, the meeting ground of the civilisations of North and South. Mr. Evans distinguishes nine periods of Minoan civilisation. Of these, the fifth, sixth, seventh and eighth are the period of the great palace and represent the Minoan thalassocracy of the Ægean. At the end of the eighth, presumably about 1600 B.C., the palace was destroyed, and Mycenae took the place of Knossos as the centre of Ægean civilisation. Somewhere about the ninth century this civilisation was destroyed by iron-using conquerors from the North, who are presumably the Dorians of history.

Greek art therefore was not a new discovery. It was a renascence, and Greek civilisation and Greek religion had their roots in an immemorial past. The Greeks, as we know them in history, were not a homogeneous people who had come from the North into a previously uninhabited country. That a conquering race did come from the North on at least two different occasions is more than likely. They brought with them their language and imposed it and much else upon the earlier inhabitants. The Greeks of history are a composite race, and they retained in their legends, in their religion, and in their art traces of their relation to the earlier civilisations of the Ægean. Those legends are no doubt largely mythical and unhistorical; but they have a historical foundation, and for the first part of Grote's history, which treats these legends as mere inventions of the poetic faculty of the Greeks, we must substitute the account which archaeology gives us of the civilisation of Crete and Mycenae.

For the history of Greece from the sixth century onward, Grote is still almost as valuable as ever. In the words of Canon Hicks, who has done as much as any one else to emphasise the importance of archaeology for the historical period of Greece, "For most English students Grote's History is of paramount value. True that only in his later volumes does Grote awake to the importance of epigraphical evidence, and then he only cites it cautiously and at second hand. But from first to last the reader is brought face to face with the existing literary evidence. Herodotus, Thucydides, Xenophon, Demosthenes, acquire life and voice, seed are made to tell us their own tale of what they themselves Have seen and heard."

A.(lexander) D.(unlop) Lindsay (1879-1952). *Oxford,* 1906.

LIFE OF GEORGE GROTE

PREFACE

The first idea of this History was conceived many years ago, at a time when ancient Hellas was known to the English public chiefly through the pages of Mitford [William Mitford, 1744-1827]: and my purpose in writing it was to rectify the erroneous statements as to matter of fact which that History contained, as well as to present the general phenomena of the Grecian world under what I thought a juster and more comprehensive point of view. My leisure, however, was not at that time equal to the execution of any large literary undertaking: nor is it until within the last three or four years that I have been able to devote to the work that continuous and exclusive labour, without which, though much may be done to illustrate detached points, no entire or complicated subject can ever be set forth in a manner worthy to meet the public eye.

Meanwhile the state of the English literary world, in reference to ancient Hellas, has been materially changed in more ways than one. If my early friend Dr. Thirlwall's [Connop Thirwall, 1797-1875] *History of Greece* had appeared a few years sooner, I should probably never have conceived the design of the present work at all: I should certainly not have been prompted to the task by any deficiencies, such as those which I felt and regretted in Mitford. The comparison of the two authors affords, indeed, a striking proof of the progress of sound and enlarged views respecting the ancient world during the present generation. Having studied of course the same evidences as Dr Thirlwall, I am better enabled than others to bear testimony to the learning, the sagacity, and the candour which pervade his excellent work: and it is the more incumbent on me to give expression to this sentiment, since the particular points on which I shall have occasion to advert to it will, unavoidably, be points of dissent oftener than of coincidence.

The liberal spirit of criticism, in which Dr. Thirlwall stands so much distinguished from Mitford, is his own: there are other features of superiority which belong to him conjointly with his age. For during the generation since Mitford's work, philological studies have been prosecuted in Germany with remarkable success: the stock of facts and documents, comparatively scanty, handed down from the ancient world, has been combined and illustrated in a thousand different ways: and if our witnesses cannot be multiplied, we at least have numerous interpreters to catch, repeat, amplify, and explain their broken and half-inaudible depositions. Some of the best writers in this department – Boeckh, Niebuhr, O. Müller – have been translated into our language: so that the English public has been enabled to form some idea of the new lights thrown upon many subjects of antiquity by the inestimable aid of German erudition. The poets, historians, orators, and philosophers of Greece, have thus been all rendered both more intelligible and more instructive than they were to a student in the last century: and the general picture of the Grecian world may now be conceived with a degree of fidelity, which, considering our imperfect materials, it is curious to contemplate.

It is that general picture which an historian of Greece is required first to embody in his own mind, and next to lay out before his readers: a picture not merely such as to delight the imagination by brilliancy of colouring and depth or sentiment, but also suggestive and improving to the reason. Not omitting the points of resemblance as well as of contrast with the better-known forms of modern society, he will especially study to exhibit the spontaneous movement of Grecian intellect, sometimes aided but never borrowed from without, and lighting up a small portion of a world otherwise clouded and stationary. He will develop the action of that social system, which, while insuring to the mass of freemen a degree of protection elsewhere unknown, acted as a stimulus to the creative impulses of genius, and left the superior minds sufficiently unshackled to soar above religious and political routine, to overshoot their own age, and to become the teachers of posterity.

To set forth the history of a people by whom the first spark was set to the dormant intellectual capacities of our nature, Hellenic phenomena, as illustrative of the Hellenic mind and character, is the task which I propose to myself in the present work: not without a painful consciousness how much the deed falls short of the will, and a yet more painful conviction, that full success is rendered impossible by an obstacle which no human ability can now remedy, the insufficiency of original evidence. For, in spite of the valuable expositions of so many able commentators, our stock of information respecting the ancient world still remains lamentably inadequate to the demands of an enlightened curiosity. We possess only what has drifted ashore from the wreck of a stranded vessel: and though this includes some of the most precious articles amongst its once abundant cargo, yet if any man will cast his eyes over the citations in Diogenes Laërtius, Athenæus, or Plutarch, or the list of names in Vossius de *Historicis Græcis*, he will see with grief and surprise how much larger is the proportion which, through the enslavement of the Greeks themselves, the decline of the Roman Empire, the change of religion, and the irruption of barbarian conquerors, has been irrecoverably submerged. We are thus reduced to judge of he whole Hellenic world, eminently multiform as it was, from a few compositions: excellent, indeed, in themselves, but bearing too exclusively the stamp of Athens. Of Thucydidês and Aristotle, indeed, both as inquirers into matter of fact, and as free from narrow local feeling, it is impossible to speak too highly: but, unfortunately, that work of the latter which would have given us the most copious information regarding Grecian political life – his collection and comparison of one hundred and fifty distinct town constitutions – has not been preserved: and the brevity of Thucydidês often gives us but a single word where a sentence would not have been too much, and sentences which we should be glad to see expanded into paragraphs.

Such insufficiency of original and trustworthy materials, as compared with those resources which are thought hardly sufficient for the historian of any modern kingdom, is neither to be concealed nor extenuated, however much we may lament it. I advert to the point here on more grounds than one. For it not only limits the

PREFACE

amount of information which an historian of Greece can give to his readers, compelling him to leave much of his picture an absolute blank, but it also greatly spoils the execution of the remainder. The question of credibility is perpetually obtruding itself, and requiring a decision, which, whether favourable or unfavourable, always introduces more or less of controversy: and gives to those out lines, which the interest of the picture requires to be straight and vigorous, a faint and faltering character. Expressions of qualified and hesitating affirmation are repeated until the reader is sickened: while the writer himself, to whom this restraint is more painful still, is frequently tempted to break loose from the unseen spell by which a conscientious criticism binds him down, – to screw up the possible and probable into certainty, to suppress counterbalancing considerations, and to substitute a pleasing romance in place of half-known and perplexing realities. Desiring, in the present work, to set forth all which can be ascertained, together with such conjectures and inferences as can be reasonably deduced from it, but nothing more – I notice at the outset that faulty state of the original evidence which renders discussions of credibility, and hesitation in the language of the judge, unavoidable Such discussions, though the reader may be assured that they will become less frequent as we advance into times better known, are tiresome enough even with the comparatively late period which I adopt as the historical beginning; much more intolerable would they have proved had I thought it my duty to start from the primitive terminus of Deukaliôn or Inachus, or from the unburied Pelasgi and Leleges, and to subject the heroic ages to a similar scrutiny. I really know nothing so disheartening or unrequited as the elaborate balancing of what is called evidence – the comparison of infinitesimal probabilities and conjectures, all uncertified – in regard to these shadowy times and persons.

The law respecting sufficiency of evidence ought to be the same for ancient times as for modern; and the reader will find in this history an application to the former, of criteria analogous to those which have been long recognised in the latter. Approaching, though with a certain measure of indulgence, to this standard, I begin the real history of Greece with the first recorded Olympiad, or 776 B.C. To such as are accustomed to the habits once universal, and still not uncommon, in investigating the ancient world, I may appear to be striking off one thousand years from the scroll of history; but to those whose canon of evidence is derived from Mr. Hallam, M. Sismondi, or any other eminent historian of modern events, I am well assured that I shall appear lax and credulous rather than exigent or sceptical. For the truth is, that historical records, properly so called, do not begin until long after this date; nor will any man, who candidly considers the extreme paucity of attested facts for two centuries after 776 B.C., be astonished to learn that the state of Greece in 900, 1000, 1100, 1200, 1300, 1400 B.C., &c. – or any earlier century which it may please chronologists to include in their computed genealogies – cannot be described to him upon anything like decent evidence. I shall hope, when I come to the lives of Sokratês and Plato, to illustrate one of the most valuable of their principles – that conscious and confessed ignorance is a better state of mind, than the fancy, without the reality, of knowledge. Meanwhile I begin by making that confession, in reference to the real world of Greece anterior to the Olympiads; meaning the disclaimer to apply to anything like a general history, – not to exclude rigorously every individual event.

The times which I thus set apart from the region of history are discernible only through a different atmosphere – that of epic poetry and legend. To confound together these disparate matters is, in my judgement, essentially unphilosophical. I describe the earlier times by themselves, as conceived by the faith and feeling of the first Greeks, and known only through their legends – without presuming to measure how much or how little of historical matter these legends may contain. If the reader blame me for not assisting him to determine this – if he ask me why I do not undraw the curtain and disclose the picture – I reply in the words of the painter Zeuxis, when the same question was addressed to him on exhibiting his masterpiece of imitative art – "The curtain *is* the picture." What we now read as poetry and legend was once accredited history, and the only genuine history which the first Greeks could conceive or relish of their past-time: the curtain conceals nothing behind, and cannot by any ingenuity be withdrawn. I undertake only to show it as it stands – not to efface, still less to repaint it.

Legendary Greece, as now presented to the public is destined to elucidate this age of historical faith, as distinguished from the later age of historical reason: to exhibit its basis in the human mind – an omnipresent religious and personal interpretation of nature; to illustrate it by comparison with the like mental habit in early modern Europe; to show its immense abundance and variety of narrative matter, with little care for consistency between one story and another: lastly, to set forth the causes which overgrew and partially supplanted the old epical sentiment, and introduced, in the room of literal faith, a variety of compromises ind interpretations.

The legendary age of the Greeks receives its principal charm and dignity from the Homeric poems: to these, therefore, and to the other poems included in the ancient epic, an entire chapter is devoted, the length of which must be justified by the names of the Iliad and Odyssey. I have thought it my duty to take some notice of the Wolfian controversy as it now stands in Germany, and have even hazarded some speculations respecting the structure of the Iliad. The society and manners of the heroic age, considered as known in a general way from Homer's descriptions and allusions, are also described and criticised.

I next pass to the historical age, beginning at 776 B.C.: prefixing some remarks upon the geographical features of Greece. I try to make out, amidst obscure and scanty indications, what the state of Greece was at this period: and I indulge some cautious conjectures, founded upon the earliest verifiable facts, respecting the steps immediately antecedent by which that condition was brought about. In the present volumes, I have only been able to include the history of Sparta and the Peloponnesian

PREFACE

Dôrians, down to the age of Peisistratus and Croesus. I had hoped to have comprised in them the entire history of Greece down to this last-mentioned period, but I find the space insufficient.

The history of Greece falls most naturally into six compartments, of which the first may be looked at as a period of preparation for the five following, which exhaust the free life of collective Hellas.

I. Period from 776 B.C. to 560 B.C., the accession of Peisistratus at Athens and of Croesus in Lydia.

II. From the accession of Peisistratus and Croesus to the repulse of Xerxês from Greece.

III. From the repulse of Xerxês to the close of the Peloponnesian war and overthrow of Athens.

IV. From the close of the Peloponnesian war to the battle of Leuktra.

V. From the battle of Leuktra to that of Chæroneia.

VI. From the battle of Chæroneia to the end of the generation of Alexander.

The five periods, from Peisistratus down to the death of Alexander and of his generation, present the acts of an historical drama capable of being recounted in perspicuous succession, and connected by a sensible thread of unity. I shall interweave in their proper places the important but outlying adventures of the Sicilian and Italian Greeks, introducing such occasional notices of Grecian political constitutions, philosophy, poetry, and oratory, as are requisite to exhibit the many-sided activity of this people during their short but brilliant career.

After the generation of Alexander, the political action of Greece becomes cramped and degraded, no longer interesting to the reader, or operative on the destinies of the future world. We may, indeed, name one or two incidents, especially the revolutions of Agis and Kleomenês at Sparta, which are both instructive and affecting: but as a whole, the period, between 300 B.C. and the absorption of Greece by the Romans, is of no interest in itself, and is only so far of value as it helps us to understand the preceding centuries. The dignity and value of the Greeks from that time forward belong to them only as individual philosophers, preceptors, astronomers, and mathematicians, literary men and critics, medical practitioners, &c. In all these respective capacities, especially in the great schools of philosophical speculation they still constitute the light of the Roman world: though, as communities, they have lost their own orbit, and have become satellites of more powerful neighbours.

I propose to bring down the history of the Grecian communities to the year 300 B.C., or the close of the generation which takes its name from Alexander the Great.

There are great disadvantages in the publication of one portion of a history apart from the remainder: for neither the earlier nor the later phenomena can be fully comprehended without the light which each mutually casts upon the other. But the practice has become habitual, and is indeed more than justified by the well-known inadmissibility of "long hopes" into the short span of human life. I venture, however, to forewarn the reader, that there will occur numerous circumstances in the after political life of the Greeks, which he will not comprehend unless he be initiated into the course of their legendary associations. He will not understand the frantic terror of the Athenian public during the Peloponnesian war, on the occasion of the mutilation of the statues called Hermæ, unless he enters into the way in which they connected their stability and security with the domiciliation of the gods in the soil: nor will he adequately appreciate the habit of the Spartan king on military expeditions, when he offered his daily public sacrifices on behalf of his army and his country, "always to perform this morning service immediately before sunrise, in order that he might be beforehand in obtaining the favour of the gods," if he be not familiar with the Homeric conception of Zeus going to rest at night and awaking to rise at early dawn from the side of the "white-armed Hêrê." The occasion will, indeed, often occur for remarking how these legends illustrate and vivify the political phenomena of the succeeding times, and I have only now to urge the necessity of considering them as the beginning of a series, not as an entire work.

G.G., *London, March* 5, 1846.

PREFACE

Names of Gods, Goddesses, and Heroes.

Following the example of Dr. Thirlwall and other excellent scholars, I call the Greek deities by their real Greek names, and not by the Latin equivalents used among the Romans. For the assistance of those readers to whom the Greek names may be less familiar, I here annex a table of the one and the other.

GREEK.	LATIN.
Zeus,	Jupiter.
Poseidôn,	Neptune.
Arês,	Mars.
Dionysus,	Bacchus.
Hermês,	Mercury.
Hêlios,	Sol.
Hêphæstus,	Vulcan.
Hadês,	Pluto.
Hêrê,	Juno.
Athênê,	Minerva.
Artemis,	Diana.
Aphroditê,	Venus.
Eôs,	Aurora.
Hestia,	Vesta.
Lêtô,	Latona.
Dêmêtêr,	Ceres.
Hêraklês,	Hercules.
Asklêpius,	Æsculapius.

A few words are here necessary respecting the orthography of Greek names adopted in the above table and generally throughout this history. I have approximated as nearly as I dared to the Greek letters in preference to the Latin: and on this point I venture upon an innovation which I should have little doubt of vindicating before the reason of any candid English student. For the ordinary practice of substituting, in a Greek name, the English C in place of the Greek K, is, indeed, so obviously incorrect, that it admits of no rational justification. Our own K, precisely and in every point, coincides with the Greek K: we have thus the means of reproducing the Greek name to the eye as well as to the ear, yet we gratuitously take the wrong letter in preference to the right. And the precedent of the Latins is here against us rather than in our favour, for their C really coincided in sound with the Greek K, whereas our C entirely departs from it, and becomes an S, before e, i, æ, œ, and y. Though our C has so far deviated in sound from the Latin C, yet there is some warrant for our continuing to use it in writing Latin names, because we thus reproduce the name to the eye, though not to the ear. But this is not the case when we employ our C to designate the Greek K, for we depart here not less from the visible than from the audible original: while we mar the unrivalled euphony of the Greek language by that multiplied sibilation which constitutes the least inviting feature in our own. Among German philologists, the K is now universally employed in writing Greek names, and I have adopted it pretty largely in this work, making exception for such names as the English reader has been so accustomed to hear with the C, that they may be considered as being almost Anglicised. I have, farther, marked the long *e* and the long *o* (η, ω) by a circumflex (Hêrê) when they occur in the last syllable in the penultimate of a name.

I. LEGENDS RESPECTING THE GODS.

The mythical world of the Greeks opens with the gods, anterior as well as superior to man: it gradually descends, first to heroes, and next to the human race. Along with the gods are found various monstrous natures, ultra-human and extra-human, who cannot with propriety be called gods, but who partake with gods and men in the attributes of freewill, conscious agency, and susceptibility of pleasure and pain, such as the Harpies, the Gorgons, the Græææ, the Sirens, Scylla and Charybdis, Echidna, Sphinx, Chimæra, Chrysaor, Pegasus, the Cyclôpes, the Centaurs, &c. The first acts of what may be termed the great mythical cycle describe the proceedings of these gigantic agents – the crash and collision of certain terrific and over-boiling forces, which are ultimately reduced to obedience, or chained up, or extinguished, under the more orderly government of Zeus, who supplants his less capable predecessors, and acquires precedence and supremacy over gods and men – subject however to certain social restraints from the chief gods and goddesses around him, as well as to the custom of occasionally convoking and consulting the divine agora.

I recount these events briefly, but literally, treating them simply as mythes springing from the same creative imagination, addressing themselves to analogous tastes and feelings, and depending upon the same authority, as the legends of Thêbes and Troy. It is the inspired voice of the Muse which reveals and authenticates both, and from which Homer and Hesiod alike derive their knowledge – the one, of the heroic, the other, of the divine, fore-time. I maintain, moreover, fully, the character of these great divine agents as Persons, which is the light in which they presented themselves to the Homeric or Hesiodic audience. Uranos, Nyx, Hypnos and Oneiros (Heaven, Night, Sleep and Dream), are Persons, just as much as Zeus and Apollo. To resolve them into mere allegories, is unsafe and unprofitable: we then depart from the point of view of the original hearers, without acquiring any consistent or philosophical point of view of our own. For although some of the attributes and actions ascribed to these persons are often explicable by allegory the whole series and system of them never are so. The theorist who adopts this course of explanation finds that, after one or two simple and obvious steps, the path is no longer open, and he is forced to clear a way for himself by gratuitous refinements and conjectures. The allegorical persons and attributes are always found mingled with other persons and attributes not allegorical: but the two classes cannot be severed without breaking up the whole march of the mythical events, nor can any explanation which drives us to such a necessity be considered as admissible. To suppose indeed that these legends could be all traced by means of allegory into a coherent body of physical doctrine, would be inconsistent with all reasonable presumptions respecting the age or society in which they arose. Where the allegorical mark is clearly set upon any particular character, or attribute, or event, to that extent we may recognise it; but we can rarely venture to divine further, still less to alter the legends themselves on the faith of any such surmises. The theogony of the Greeks contains some cosmogonic ideas: but it cannot be considered as a system of cosmogony, or translated into a string of elementary, planetary, or physical changes.

In the order of legendary chronology, Zeus comes after Kronos and Uranos: but in the order of Grecian conception, Zeus is the prominent person, and Kronos and Uranos are inferior and introductory precursors, set up in order to be overthrown and to serve as mementos of the prowess of their conqueror. To Homer and Hesiod, as well as to the Greeks universally, Zeus is the great and predominant god, "the father of gods and men," whose power none of the other gods can hope to resist, or even deliberately think of questioning. All the other gods have their specific potency and peculiar sphere of action and duty, with which Zeus does not usually interfere; but it is he who maintains the lineaments of a providential superintendence, as well over the phenomena of Olympus as over those of earth. Zeus and his brothers Poseidôn and Hadês have made a division of power: he has reserved the ether and the atmosphere to himself – Poseidôn has obtained the sea – and Hadês the under-world or infernal regions: while earth, and the events which pass upon earth, are common to all of them, together with free access to Olympus.

Zeus, then, with his brethren and colleagues, constitute the present gods, whom Homer and Hesiod recognise as in full dignity and efficiency. The inmates of this divine world are conceived upon the model, but not upon the scale, of the human. They are actuated by the full play and variety of those appetites, sympathies, passions and affections, which divide the soul of man: invested with a far larger and indeterminate measure of power, and an exemption as well from death as (with some rare exceptions) from suffering and infirmity. The rich and diverse types thus conceived, full of energetic movement and contrast, each in his own province, and soaring confessedly above the limits of experience, were of all themes the most suitable for adventure and narrative, and operated with irresistible force upon the Grecian fancy. All

2

I. LEGENDS RESPECTING THE GODS.

nature was then conceived as moving and working through a number of personal agents, amongst whom the gods of Olympus were the most conspicuous: the reverential belief in Zeus and Apollo being only one branch of this omnipresent personifying faith. The attributes of all these agents had a tendency to expand themselves into illustrative legends – especially those of the gods, who were constantly invoked in the public worship. Out of this same mental source sprang both the divine and heroic mythes – the former being often the more extravagant and abnormal in their incidents, in proportion as the general type of the gods was more vast and awful than that of the heroes.

As the gods have houses and wives like men, so the present dynasty of gods must have a past to repose upon; and the curious and imaginative Greek, whenever he does not find a recorded past ready to his hand, is uneasy until he has created one. Thus the Hesiodic theogony explains, with a certain degree of system and coherence, first the antecedent circumstances under which Zeus acquired the divine empire, next the number of his colleagues and descendants.

First in order of time (we are told by Hesiod) came Chaos: next Gæa, the broad, firm, and flat Earth, with deep and dark Tartarus at her base. Erôs (Love), the subduer of gods as well as men, came immediately afterwards.

From Chaos sprung Erebos and Nyx: from these latter Æthêr and Hêmera, Gæa also gave birth to Uranos, equal in breadth to herself, in order to serve both as an overarching vault to her, and as a residence for the immortal gods: she further produced the mountains, habitations of the divine nymphs, and Pontus, the barren and billowy sea.

Then Gæa intermarried with Uranos, and from this union came a numerous offspring – twelve Titans and Titanides, three Cyclôpes, and three Hekatoncheires or beings with a hundred hands each. The Titans were Oceanus, Kœos, Krios, Hyperiôn, Iapetos, and Kronos: the Titanides, Theia, Rhea, Themis, Mnêmosynê, Phoebê, and Têhys. The Cyclôpes were Brontês, Steropês, and Argês, formidable persons, equally distinguished for strength and for manual craft, so that they made the thunder which afterwards formed the irresistible artillery of Zeus. The Hekatoncheires were Kottos, Briareus, and Gygês, of prodigious bodily force.

Uranos contemplated this powerful brood with fear and horror: as fast as any of them were born, he concealed them in cavities of the earth, and would not permit them to come out. Gæa could find no room for them, and groaned under

3

the pressure; she produced iron, made a sickle, and implored her sons to avenge both her and themselves against the oppressive treatment of their father. But none of them, except Kronos, had courage to undertake the deed. He, the youngest and the most daring, was armed with the sickle and placed in suitable ambush by the contrivance of Gæa. Presently night arrived, and Uranos descended to the embraces of Gæa: Kronos then emerged from his concealment, cut off the genitals of his father, and cast the bleeding member behind him far away into the sea. Much of the blood was spilt upon the earth, and Gæa in consequence gave birth to the irresistible Erinnys, the vast and muscular Gigantes, and the Melian nymphs. Out of the genitals themselves, as they swam and foamed upon the sea, emerged the goddess Aphroditê, deriving her name from the foam out of which she had sprung. She first landed at Kythêra, and then went to Cyprus: the island felt her benign influence, and the green herb started up under her soft and delicate tread. Eros immediately joined her, and partook with her the function of suggesting and directing the amorous impulses both of gods and men.

Uranos being thus dethroned and disabled, Kronos and the Titans acquired their liberty and became predominant; the Cyclôpes and the Hekatoncheires had been cast by Uranos into Tartarus, and were still allowed to remain there.

Each of the Titans had a numerous offspring: Oceanus, especially, marrying his sister Têthys, begat three thousand daughters, the Oceanic nymphs, and as many sons: the rivers and springs passed for his offspring. Hyperiôn and his sister Theia had for their children Hêlios, Selênê, and Eôs; Kœos with Phosbê begat Lêtô and Asteria; the children of Krios were Astræos, Pallas, and Persês, from Astræos and Eôs sprang the winds Zephyrus, Boreas, and Notus. Iapetos, marrying the Oceanic nymph Klymenê, counted as his progeny the celebrated Promêtheus, Epimêtheus, Menœtius, and Atlas. But the offspring of Kronos were the most powerful and transcendent of all. He married his sister Rhea, and had by her three daughters – Hestia, Dêmêtêr, and Hêrê – and three sons, Hadês, Poseidôn, and Zeus, the latter at once the youngest and the greatest.

Kronos foreboded to himself destruction from one of his own children, and accordingly, as soon as any of them were born, he immediately swallowed them and retained them in his own belly. In this manner had the first five been treated, and Rhea was on the point of being delivered of Zeus. Grieved and indignant at the loss of her children, she applied for counsel to her father and mother, Uranos and Gæa, who aided her to conceal the birth of Zeus. They conveyed her by night to Lyktus in Crête, hid the new-born child in a woody

I. LEGENDS RESPECTING THE GODS.

cavern on Mount Ida, and gave to Kronos, in place of it, a stone wrapped in swaddling clothes, which he greedily swallowed, believing it to be his child. Thus was the safety of Zeus ensured. As he grew up his vast powers fully developed themselves; at the suggestion of Gæa, he induced Kronos by stratagem to vomit up, first the stone which had been given to him, next, the five children whom he had previously devoured. Hestia, Dêmêtêr, Hêrê, Poseidôn and Hadês, were thus allowed to grow up along with Zeus; and the stone to which the latter owed his preservation was placed near the temple of Delphi, where it ever afterwards stood, as a conspicuous and venerable memorial to the religious Greek.

We have not yet exhausted the catalogue of beings generated during this early period, anterior to the birth of Zeus. Nyx alone and without any partner, gave birth to a numerous progeny: Thanatos, Hypnos and Oneiros: Mômus and Oïzys (Grief): Klôthô, Lachesis and Atropos, the three Fates: the retributive and equalising Nemesis: Apatê and Philotês (Deceit and amorous Propensity), Geras (Old Age) and Eris (Contention). From Eris proceeded an abundant offspring, all mischievous and maleficent: Ponos (Suffering), Lêthê, Limos (Famine), Phonos and Machê (Slaughter and Battle), Dysnomia and Atê (Lawlessness and reckless Impulse), and Horkos, the ever-watchful sanctioner of oaths, as well as the inexorable punisher of voluntary perjury.

Gæa, too, intermarrying with Pontus, gave birth to Nereus, the just and righteous old man of the sea: to Thaumas, Phorkys and Kêtô. From Nereus, and Doris daughter of Oceanus, proceeded the fifty Nêreids or Sea-nymphs. Thaumus also married Elektra daughter of Oceanus, and had by her Iris and the two Harpies, Aellô and Okypetê, winged and swift as the winds. From Phorkys and Kêtô sprung the Dragon of the Hesperides. and the monstrous Grææ: and Gorgons: the blood of Medusa, one of the Gorgons, when killed by Perseus, produced Curysaôr and the horse Pegasus. Chrysaôr and Kallirhoê gave birth to Geryôn as well as to Echidna, a creature half-nymph and half-serpent, unlike both to gods and to men. Other monsters arose from the union of Echidna with Typhaôn, Orthros, the two-headed dog of Geryôn: Cerberus, the dog of Hadês, with fifty heads, and the Lernæan Hydra. From the latter proceded the Chimaera, the Sphinx of Thêbes, and the Nemean lion.

A powerful and important progeny, also, was that of Styx, daughter of Oceanus, by Pallas: she had Zêlos and Nikê (Imperiousness and Victory), and

Kratos and Bia (Strength and Force) The hearty and early coöperation of Styx and her four sons with Zeus was one of the main causes which enabled him to achieve his victory over the Titans.

Zeus had grown up not less distinguished for mental capacity than for bodily force. He and his brothers now determined to wrest the power from the hands of Kronos and the Titans, and a long and desperate struggle commenced, in which all the gods and all the goddesses took part. Zeus convoked them to Olympus, and promised to all who would aid him against Kronos, that their functions and privileges should remain undisturbed. The first who responded to the call, came with her four sons, and embraced his cause, was Styx. Zeus took them all four as his constant attendants, and conferred upon Styx the majestic distinction of being the Horkos, or oath-sanctioner of the Gods, what Horkos was to men, Styx was to the Gods.

Still further to strengthen himself, Zeus released the other Uranids who had been imprisoned in Tartarus by their father, the Cyclôpes and the Centimanes, and prevailed upon them to take part with him against the Titans. The former supplied him with thunder and lightning, and the latter brought into the fight their boundless muscular strength. Ten full years did the combat continue: Zeus and the Kronids occupying Olympus, and the Titans being established on the more southerly mountain-chain of Othrys. All nature was convulsed, and the distant Oceanus, though he took no part in the struggle, felt the boiling, the noise, and the shock, not less than Gæa and Pontus. The thunder of Zeus, combined with the crags and mountains torn up and hurled by the Centimanes, at length prevailed, and the Titans were defeated and thrust down into Tartarus. Iapetos, Kronos, and the remaining Titans (Oceanus excepted) were imprisoned, perpetually and irrevocably, in that subterranean dungeon, a wall of brass being built around them by Poseidôn, and the three Centimanes being planted as guards.

Of the two sons of Iapetos, Menœtius was made to share this prison, while Atlas was condemned to stand forever at the extreme west, and to bear upon his shoulders the solid vault of heaven.

Thus were the Titans subdued, and the Kronids with Zeus at their head placed in possession of power. They were not, however, yet quite secure; for Gæa, intermarrying with Tartarus, gave birth to a new and still more formidable monster called Typhôsus, of such tremendous properties and promise, that, had he been allowed to grow into full development, nothing could have prevented him from vanquishing all rivals and becoming supreme. But Zeus foresaw the danger, smote him at once with a thunderbolt

I. LEGENDS RESPECTING THE GODS.

from Olympus, and burnt him up: he was cast along with the rest into Tartarus, and no further enemy remained to question the sovereignty of the Kronids.

With Zeus begins a new dynasty and a different order of beings. Zeus, Poseidôn, and Hadês agree upon the distribution before noticed, of functions and localities: Zeus retaining the Æthêr and the atmosphere, together with the general presiding function: Poseidôn obtaining the sea, and administering subterranean forces generally: and Hadês ruling the under-world or region in which the half-animated shadows of departed men reside

It has been already stated, that in Zeus, his brothers and his sisters, and his and their divine progeny, we find the *present* Gods: that is, those, for the most part, whom the Homeric and Hesiodic Greeks recognised and worshipped. The wives of Zeus were numerous as well as his offspring. First he married Mêtis, the wisest and most sagacious of the goddesses: but Gæa and Uranos forewarned him that if he permitted himself to have children by her, they would be stronger than himself and dethrone him. Accordingly when Mêtis was on the point of being delivered of Athênê, he swallowed her up, and her wisdom and sagacity thus became permanently identified with his own being. His head was subsequently cut open, in order to make way for the exit and birth of the goddess Athênê. By Themis, Zeus begat the Hôræ, by Eurynomê, the three Charities or Graces: by Mnêmosynê, the Muses: by Lêtô (Latona), Apollo and Artemis; and by Dêmêtêr, Persephonê. Last of all he took for his wife Hêrê, who maintained permanently the dignity of queen of the Gods: by her he had Hêbê. Arês, and Eileithyia. Hermês also was born to him by Maia, the daughter of Atlas. Hêphæstos was born to Hêrê, according to some accounts, by Zeus; according to others, by her own unaided generative force. He was born lame, and Hêrê was ashamed of him: she wished to secrete him away, but he made his escape into the sea, and found shelter under the maternal care of the Nêreids Thetis and Eurynomê. Our enumeration of the divine race, under the presidency of Zeus, will thus give us:

1. The twelve great gods and goddesses of Olympus, Zeus, Poseidôn, Apollo, Arês, Hêphæstos, Hermês, Hêrê, Athênê, Artemis, Aphroditê, Hestia, Dêmêtêr.

2. An indefinite number of other deities, not included among the Olympic, seemingly because the number *twelve* was complete without them, but some of them not inferior in power and dignity to many of the twelve: Hadês,

Hêlios. Hekatê, Dionysos, Lêtô, Diônê, Persephonê, Selênê, Themis, Eôs, Harmonia, the Charities, the Muses, the Eilaithyiæ, the Mœræ, the Oceanids and the Nêreids, Proteus, Eidothea, the Nymphs, Leukothea, Phorkys, Æolus, Nemesis, &c.

3. Deities who perform special services to the greater gods: Iris, Hêbê, the Horæ, &c.

4. Deities whose personality is more faintly and unsteadily conceived: Atê, the Litæ, Eris, Thanatos, Hypnos, Kratos, Bia, Ossa, &c. The same name is Hêrê employed sometimes to designate the person, sometimes the attribute or event not personified, an unconscious transition of ideas, which, when consciously performed, is called Allegory.

5. Monsters, offspring of the Gods: the Harpies, the Gorgons, the Græræ, Pegasus, Chrysaôr, Echidna, Chimæra, the Dragon of the Hesperides, Cerberus, Orthros, Geryôn, the Lernæan Hydra, the Nemean lion, Scylla and Charybdis, the Centaurs, the Sphinx, Xanthos and Balios the immortal horses, &c.

From the gods we slide down insensibly, first to heroes, and then to men; but before we proceed to this new mixture, it is necessary to say a few words on the theogony generally. I have given it briefly as it stands in the Hesiodic Theogonia, because that poem – in spite of great incoherence and confusion, arising seemingly from diversity of authorship as well as diversity of age – presents an ancient and genuine attempt to cast the divine fore-time into a systematic sequence. Homer and Hesiod were the grand authorities in the pagan world respecting theogony. But in the Iliad and Odyssey nothing is found except passing allusions and implications, and even in the Hymns (which were commonly believed in antiquity to be the productions of the same author as the Iliad and the Odyssey) there are only isolated, unconnected narratives. Accordingly men habitually took their information respecting their theogonic antiquities from the Hesiodic poem, where it was ready laid out before them; and the legends consecrated in that work acquired both an extent of circulation and a firm hold on the national faith, such as independent legends could seldom or never rival. Moreover the scrupulous and sceptical Pagans, as well as the open assailants of Paganism in later times, derived their subjects of attack from the same source; so that it has been absolutely necessary to recount in their naked simplicity the Hesiodic stories, in order to know what it was that Plato deprecated and Xenophanês denounced. The strange proceedings ascribed to Uranos, Kronos and Zeus, have been more frequently alluded to, in the way of ridicule or condemnation, than any other portion of the mythical world.

I. LEGENDS RESPECTING THE GODS.

Differences between Homer and Hesiod.

But though the Hesiodic theogony passed as orthodox among the later Pagans, because it stood before them as the only system anciently set forth and easily accessible, it was evidently not the only system received at the date of the poem itself. Homer knows nothing of Uranos, in the sense of an arch-God anterior to Kronos. Uranos and Gæa, like Oceanus, Têthys and Nyx, are with him great and venerable Gods, but neither the one nor the other present the character of predecessors of Kronos and Zeus. The Cyclôpes, whom Hesiod ranks as sons of Uranos and fabricators of thunder, are in Homer neither one nor the other: they are not noticed in the Iliad at all, and in the Odyssey they are gross gigantic shepherds and cannibals, having nothing in common with the Hesiodic Cyclôpes except the one round central eye. Of the three Centimanes enumerated by Hesiod, Briareus only is mentioned in Homer, and to all appearance, not as the son of Uranos, but as the son of Poseidôn; not as aiding Zeus in his combat against the Titans, but as rescuing him at a critical moment from a conspiracy formed against him by Hêrê, Poseidôn and Athênê. Not only is the Hesiodic Uranos (with the Uranids) omitted in Homer, but the relations between Zeus and Kronos are also presented in a very different light. No mention is made of Kronos swallowing his young children: on the contrary, Zeus is the eldest of the three brothers instead of the youngest, and the children of Kronos live with him and Rhea: there the stolen intercourse between Zeus and Hêrê first takes place without the knowledge of their parents. When Zeus puts Kronos down into Tartarus, Rhea consigns her daughter Hêrê to the care of Oceanus: no notice do we find of any terrific battle with the Titans as accompanying that event. Kronos, Iapetos, and the remaining Titans are down in Tartarus, in the lowest depths under the earth, far removed from the genial rays of Hêlios; but they are still powerful and venerable, and Hypnos makes Hêrê swear an oath in their name, as the most inviolable that he can think of.

In Homer, then, we find nothing beyond the simple fact that Zeus thrust his father Kronos together with the remaining Titans into Tartarus; an event to which he affords us a tolerable parallel in certain occurrences even under the presidency of Zeus himself. For the other gods make more than one rebellious attempt against Zeus, and are only put down, partly by his unparalleled strength, partly by the presence of his ally the Centimane Briareus. Kronos, like Laërtes or Pêleus, has become old, and has been supplanted by a force vastly superior to his own. The Homeric epic treats Zeus as present, and, like all the interesting heroic characters, a father must be assigned to him: that father has once been the chief of the Titans, but has been superseded and put down into Tartarus along with the latter, so soon as Zeus and the superior breed of the Olympic gods acquired their full development.

That antithesis between Zeus and Kronos – between the Olympic gods and the Titans – which Homer has thus briefly brought to view, Hesiod has amplified into a theogony, with many things new, and some things contradictory to his predecessor; while Eumêlus or Arktinus in the poem called Titanomachia (now lost) also adopted it as their special subject. As Stasinus, Arktinus, Leschês, and others, enlarged the Legend of Troy by composing poems relating to a supposed time anterior to the commencement, or subsequent to the termination of the Iliad, as other poets recounted adventures of Odysseus subsequent to his landing in Ithaka, so Hesiod enlarged and systematized, at the same time that he corrupted, the skeleton theogony which we find briefly indicated in Homer. There is violence and rudeness in the Homeric gods, but the great genius of Grecian epic is no way accountable for the stories of Uranos and Kronos, the standing reproach against Pagan legendary narrative.

How far these stories are the invention of Hesiod himself is impossible to determine. They bring us down to a cast of fancy more coarse and indelicate than the Homeric, and more nearly resembling some of the Holy Chapters (ἱεποῖ λόγοι) of the more recent mysteries, such (for example) as the tale of Dionysos Zagreus. There is evidence in the Theogony itself that the author was acquainted with local legends current both at Krête and at Delphi; for he mentions both the mountain-cave in Krête wherein the new-born Zeus was hidden, and the stone near the Delphian temple – the identical stone (ὀμφαλός) which Kronos had swallowed – "placed by Zeus himself as a sign and wonder to mortal men." Both these two monuments, which the poet expressly refers to, and had probably seen, imply a whole train of accessory and explanatory local legends – current probably among the priests of Krête and Delphi, between which places, in ancient times, there was an intimate religious connection. And we may trace further in the poem, that which would be the natural feeling of Krêtan worshippers of Zeus, an effort to make out that Zeus was justified in his aggression on Kronos, by the conduct of Kronos himself both towards his father and towards his children: the treatment of Kronos by Zeus appears in Hesiod as the retribution foretold and threatened by the mutilated Uranos against the son who had outraged him. In fact the relations of Uranos and Gæa are in almost all their particulars a mere copy and duplication of those between Kronos and Rhea, differing

I. LEGENDS RESPECTING THE GODS.

only in the mode whereby the final catastrophe is brought about. Now castration was a practice thoroughly abhorrent both to the feelings and to the customs of Greece; but it was seen with melancholy frequency in the domestic life as well as in the religious worship of Phrygia and other parts of Asia, and it even became the special qualification of a priest of the Great Mother Cybelê, as well as of the Ephesian Artemis. The employment of the sickle ascribed to Kronos seems to be the product of an imagination familiar with the Asiatic worship and legends, which were connected with and partially resembled the Krêtan. And this deduction becomes the more probable when we connect it with the first genesis of iron, which Hesiod mentions to have been produced for the express purpose of fabricating the fatal sickle; for metallurgy finds a place in the early legends both of the Trojan and of the Krêtan Ida and the three Idæan Dactyls, the legendary inventors of it, are assigned sometimes to one and sometimes to the other.

As Hesiod had extended the Homeric series of gods by prefixing the dynasty of Uranos to that of Kronos, so the Orphic theogony lengthened it still further. First came Chronos, or Time, as a person, after him Æthêr and Chaos, out of whom Chronos produced the vast mundane egg. Hence emerged in process of time the first-born god Phanês, or Mêtis, or Hêrikapæos, a person of double sex, who first generated the Kôsmos, or mundane system, and who carried within him the seed of the gods. He gave birth to Nyx, by whom he begat Uranos and Gæa: as well as to Hêlios and Selênê.

From Uranos and Gæa sprang the three Mœræ, or Fates, the three Centimanes and the three Cyclôpes: these latter were cast by Uranos into Tartarus, under the foreboding that they would rob him of his dominion. In revenge for this maltreatment of her sons, Gæa produced of herself the fourteen Titans, seven male and seven female: the former were Kœos, Krios, Phorkys, Kronos, Oceanus, Hyperiôn and Iapetos; the latter were Themis, Têthys, Mnêmosynê, Theia, Diônê, Phoebê and Rhea. They received the name of Titans because they avenged upon Uranos the expulsion of their elder brothers. Six of the Titans, headed by Kronos the most powerful of them all, conspiring against Uranos, castrated and dethroned him: Oceanus alone stood aloof and took no part in the aggression. Kronos assumed the government and fixed his seat on Olympos; while Oceanus remained apart, master of his own divine stream. The reign of Kronos was a period of tranquillity and happiness, as well as of extraordinary longevity and vigour.

Kronos and Rhea gave birth to Zeus and his brothers and sisters. The

11

concealment and escape of the infant Zeus, and the swallowing of the stone by Kronos, are given in the Orphic Theogony substantially in the same manner as by Hesiod, only in a style less simple and more mysticised. Zeus is concealed in the cave of Nyx, the seat of Phanês himself, along with Eidê and Adraeteia, who nurse and preserve him, while the armed dance and sonorous instruments of the Kurêtês prevent his infant cries from reaching the ears of Kronos. When grown up, he lays a snare for his father, intoxicates him with honey, and having surprised him in the depth of sleep, enchains and castrates him. Thus exalted to the supreme mastery, be swallowed and absorbed into himself Mêtis, or Phanês, with all the pre-existing elements of things, and then generated all things anew out of his own being and conformably to his own divine ideas. So scanty are the remains of this system, that we end it difficult to trace individually the gods and goddesses sprung from Zeus beyond Apollo, Dionysos, and Persephonê, the latter being confounded with Artemis and Hekatê.

There is one new personage, begotten by Zeus, who stands pre-eminently marked in the Orphic Theogony, and whose adventures constitute one of its peculiar features. Zagreus, "the horned child," is the son of Zeus by his own daughter Persephonê: he is the favourite of his father, a child of magnificent promise, and predestined, if he grow up, to succeed to supreme dominion as well as to the handling of the thunderbolt. He is seated, whilst an infant, on the throne beside Zeus, guarded by Apollo and the Kurêtês. But the jealous Hêrê intercepts his career and incites the Titans against him, who, having first smeared their faces with plaster, approach him on the throne, tempt his childish fancy with playthings, and kill him with a sword while he is contemplating his face in a mirror. They then cut up his body and boil it in a caldron, leaving only the heart, which is picked up by Athênê and carried to Zeus, who in his wrath strikes down the Titans with thunder into Tartarus: whilst Apollo is directed to collect the remains of Zagreus and bury them at the foot of Mount Parnassus. The heart is given to Semelê, and Zagreus is born again from her under the form of Dionysos.

Such is the tissue of violent fancies comprehended under the title of the Orphic Theogony, and read as such, it appears, by Plato, Isokratês and Aristotle. It will be seen that it is based upon the Hesiodic Theogony, but according to the general expansive tendency of Grecian legend, much new matter is added: Zeus has in Homer one predecessor, in Hesiod two, and in Orpheus four.

I. LEGENDS RESPECTING THE GODS.

Hesiod and Orpheus

The Hesiodic Theogony, though later in date than the Iliad and Odyssey, was coeval with the earliest period of what may be called Grecian history, and certainly of an age earlier than 700 B.C. It appears to have been widely circulated in Greece, and being at once ancient and short, the general public consulted it as their principal source of information respecting divine antiquity. The Orphic Theogony belongs to a later date, and contains the Hesiodic ideas and persons, enlarged and mystically disguised. Its vein of invention was less popular, adapted more to the contemplation of a sect specially prepared than to the taste of a casual audience, and it appears accordingly to have obtained currency chiefly among purely speculative men. Among the majority of these latter, however, it acquired greater veneration, and above all was supposed to be of greater antiquity, than the Hesiodic. The belief in its superior antiquity (disallowed by Herodotus, and seemingly also by Aristotle), as well as the respect for its contents, increased during the Alexandrine age and through the declining centuries of Paganism, reaching its maximum among the New-Platonists of the third and fourth century after Christ. Both the Christian assailants, as well as the defenders, of paganism, treated it as the most ancient and venerable summary of the Grecian faith. Orpheus is celebrated by Pindar as the harper and companion of the Argônautic maritime heroes: Orpheus and Musæus, as well as Pamphos and Olên, the great supposed authors of theogonic, mystical, oracular, and prophetic verses and hymns, were generally considered by literary Greeks as older than either Hesiod or Homer; and such was also the common opinion of modern scholars until a period comparatively recent. It has now been shown, on sufficient ground, that the compositions which passed under these names emanate for the most part from poets of the Alexandrine age, and subsequent to the Christian æra; and that even the earliest among them, which served as the stock on which the later additions were engrafted, belong to a period far more recent than Hesiod: probably to the century preceding Onomakritus (B.C. 610-510). It seems, however, certain, that both Orpheus and Musæus were names of established reputation at the time when Onomakritus flourished; and it is distinctly stated by Pausanias that the latter was himself the author of the most remarkable and characteristic mythe of the Orphic Theogony – the discerption of Zagreus by the Titans, and his resurrection as Dionysos.

The names of Orpheus and Musæus (as well as that of Pythagoras, looking at one side of his character) represent facts of importance in the history of the Grecian mind – the gradual influx of Thracian, Phrygian, and Egyptian, religious ceremonies and feelings, and the increasing diffusion of special mysteries, schemes for religious purification, and orgies (I venture to anglicise the Greek word, which contains in its original meaning no implication of the ideas of excess to which it was afterwards diverted) in honour of some particular god – distinct both from the public solemnities and from the gentile solemnities of primitive Greece, celebrated apart from the citizens generally, and approachable only through a certain course of preparation and initiation – sometimes even forbidden to be talked of in the presence of the uninitiated, under the severest threats of divine judgment. Occasionally such voluntary combinations assumed the form of permanent brotherhoods, bound together by periodical solemnities as well as by vows of an ascetic character: thus the Orphic life (as it was called) or regulation of the Orphic brotherhood, among other injunctions partly arbitrary and partly abstinent, forbade animal food universally, and on certain occasions, the use of woollen clothing. The great religious and political fraternity of the Pythagoreans, which acted so powerfully on the condition of the Italian cities, was one of the many manifestations of this general tendency, which stands in striking contrast with the simple, open-hearted, and demonstrative worship of the Homeric Greeks.

Festivals at seed-time and harvest – at the vintage and at the opening of the new wine – were doubtless coeval with the earliest habits of the Greeks: the latter being a period of unusual joviality. Yet in the Homeric poems, Dionysos and Dêmêtêr, the patrons of the vineyard and the cornfield, are seldom mentioned, and decidedly occupy little place in the imagination of the poet as compared with the other gods; nor are they of any conspicuous importance even in the Hesiodic Theogony. But during the interval between Hesiod and Onomakritus, the revolution in the religious mind of Greece was such as to place both these deities in the front rank. According to the Orphic doctrine, Zagreus, son of Persephonê, is destined to be the successor of Zeus, and although the violence of the Titans intercepts this lot, yet even when he rises again from his discerption under the name of Dionysos, he is the colleague and coequal of his divine father.

This remarkable change, occurring as it did during the sixth and a part of the seventh century before the Christian sera, may be traced to the influence of communication with Egypt (which only became fully open to the Greeks about B.C. 660), as well as with Thrace, Phrygia, and Lydia. From hence new

14

I. LEGENDS RESPECTING THE GODS.

religious ideas and feelings were introduced, which chiefly attached themselves to the characters of Dionysos and Dêmêtêr. The Greeks identified these two deities with the great Egyptian Osiris and Isis, so that what was borrowed from the Egyptian worship of the two latter naturally fell to their equivalents in the Grecian system. Moreover the worship of Dionysos (under what name cannot be certainly made out) was indigenous in Thrace, as that of the Great Mother was in Phyrgia, and in Lydia – together with those violent ecstasies and manifestations of temporary frenzy, and that clashing of noisy instruments, which we find afterwards characterising it in Greece. The great masters of the pipe – as well as the dithyramb, and indeed the whole musical system appropriated to the worship of Dionysos, which contrasted so pointedly with the quiet solemnity of the Pæan addressed to Apollo – were all originally Phrygian.

From all these various countries, novelties, unknown to the Homeric men, found their way into the Grecian worship; and there is one amongst them which deserves to be specially noticed, because it marks the generation of the new class of ideas in their theology. Homer mentions many persons guilty of private or involuntary homicide, and compelled either to go into exile or to make pecuniary satisfaction; but he never once describes any of them to have either received or required purification for the crime. Now in the time subsequent to Homer, purification for homicide comes to be considered as indispensable: the guilty person is regarded as unfit for the society of man or the worship of the gods until he has received it, and special ceremonies are prescribed whereby it is to be administered. Herodotus tells us that the ceremony of purification was the same among the Lydians and among the Greeks; we know that it formed no part of the early religion of the latter, and we may perhaps reasonably suspect that they borrowed it from the former. The oldest instance known to us of expiation for homicide was contained in the epic poem of the Milesian Arktinus, wherein Achilles is purified by Odysseus for the murder of Thersitês: several others occurred in the later or Hesiodic epic – Hêraklês, Pêleus, Bellerophôn, Alkmæôn, Amphiktyôn, Pœmander, Triopas, from whence they probably passed through the hands of the logographers to Apollôdorus, Diodôrus, and others. The purification of the murderer was originally operated, not by the hands of any priest or specially sanctified man, but by those of a chief or king, who goes through the appropriate ceremonies in the manner recounted by Herodotus in his pathetic narrative respecting Crœsus and Adrastus.

The idea of a special taint of crime, and of the necessity as well as the sufficiency of prescribed religious ceremonies as a means of removing it, appears thus to have got footing in Grecian practice subsequent to the time of Homer. The peculiar rites or orgies, composed or put together by Onomakritus, Methapus, and other men of more than the ordinary piety, were founded upon a similar mode of thinking,and adapted to the same mental exigencies. They were voluntary religious manifestations, superinduced upon the old public sacrifices of the king or chiefs on behalf of the whole society, and of the father on his own family hearth – they marked out the details of divine service proper to appease or gratify the god to whom they were addressed, and to procure for the believers who went through them his blessings and protection here or hereafter – the exact performance of the divine service in all its specialty was held necessary, and thus the priests or Hierophants, who alone were familiar with the ritual, acquired a commanding position. Generally speaking, these peculiar orgies obtained their admission and their influence at periods of distress, disease, public calamity and danger, or religious terror and despondency, which appear to have been but too frequent in their occurrence.

The minds of men were prone to the belief that what they were suffering arose from the displeasure of some of the gods, and as they found that the ordinary sacrifices and worship were insufficient for their protection, so they grasped at new suggestions proposed to them with the view of regaining the divine favour. Such suggestions were more usually copied, either in whole or in part, from the religious rites of some foreign locality, or from some other portion of the Hellenic world; and in this manner many new sects or voluntary religious fraternities, promising to relieve the troubled conscience and to reconcile the sick or suffering with the offended gods, acquired permanent establishment as well as considerable influence. They were generally under the superintendence of hereditary families of priests, who imparted the rites of confirmation and purification to communicants generally; no one who went through the prescribed ceremonies being excluded. In many cases, such ceremonies fell into the hands of jugglers, who volunteered their services to wealthy men, and degraded their profession as well by obtrusive venality as by extravagant promises. Sometimes the price was lowered to bring them within reach of the poor and even of slaves. But the wide diffusion, and the number of voluntary communicants of these solemnities, proves how much they fell in with the feeling of the time and how much respect they enjoyed – a

I. LEGENDS RESPECTING THE GODS.

respect, which the more conspicuous establishments, such as Eleusis and Samothrace, maintained for several centuries. And the visit of the Krêtan Epimenidês to Athens – in the time of Solôn, and at a season of the most serious disquietude and dread of having offended the gods – illustrates the tranquillizing effect of new orgies and rites of absolution, when enjoined by a man standing high in the favour of the gods and reputed to be the son of a nymph. The supposed Erythræan Sibyl, and the earliest collection of Sibylline prophecies, afterwards so much multiplied and interpolated, and referred (according to Grecian custom) to an age even earlier than Homer, appear to belong to a date not long posterior to Epimenidês. Other oracular verses, such as those of Bakis, were treasured up in Athens and other cities: the sixth century before the Christian æra was fertile in these kinds of religious manifestations.

Principal mysteries.

Amongst the special rites and orgies of the character just described, those which enjoyed the greatest Pan-Hellenic reputation were attached to the Idæan Zeus in Krête, to Dêmêtêr at Eleusis, to the Kabeiri in Samothrace, and to Dionysos at Delphi and Thêbes. That they were all to a great degree analogous, is shown by the way in which they unconsciously run together and become confused in the minds of various authors. The ancient inquirers themselves were unable to distinguish one from the other, and we must be content to submit to the like ignorance. But we see enough to satisfy us of the general fact, that during the century and a half which elapsed between the opening of Egypt to the Greeks and the commencement of their struggle with the Persian kings, the old religion was largely adulterated by importations from Egypt, Asia Minor, and Thrace. The rites grew to be more furious and ecstatic, exhibiting the utmost excitement, bodily as well as mental: the legends became at once more coarse, more tragical, and less pathetic. The manifestations of this frenzy were strongest among the women, whose religious susceptibilities were often found extremely unmanageable, and who had everywhere congregative occasional ceremonies of their own, part from the men – indeed, in the case of the colonists, especially of the Asiatic colonists, the women had been originally women of the country, and as such retained to a great degree their non-Hellenic manners and feelings. The god Dionysos, whom the legends described as clothed in feminine attire, and leading a troop of frenzied women, inspired a temporary ecstasy, and those who resisted the inspiration, being supposed to disobey his will, were punished either by particular judgments or

17

by mental terrors; while those who gave full loose to the feeling, in the appropriate season and with the received solemnities, satisfied his exigencies, and believed themselves to have procured immunity from such disquietudes for the future. Crowds of women, clothed with fawn-skins and bearing the sanctified thyrsus, flocked to the solitudes of Parnassus, or Kithærôn, or Taygetus, during the consecrated triennial period, passed the night there with torches, and abandoned themselves to demonstrations of frantic excitement, with dancing and clamorous invocation of the god. They were said to tear animals limb from limb, to devour the raw flesh, and to cut themselves without feeling the wound. The men yielded to a similar impulse by noisy revels in the streets, sounding the cymbals and tambourine, and carrying the image of the god in procession. It deserves to be remarked, that the Athenian women never practised these periodical mountain excursions, so common among the rest of the Greeks: they had their feminine solemnities of the Thesmophoria, mournful in their character and accompanied with fasting, and their separate congregations at the temples of Aphroditê, but without any extreme or unseemly demonstrations. The state festival of the Dionysia, in the city of Athens, was celebrated with dramatic entertainments, and the once rich harvest of Athenian tragedy and comedy was thrown up under its auspices. The ceremonies of the Kurêtes in Krête, originally armed dances in honour of the Idæan Zeus, seem also to have borrowed from Asia so much of fury, of self-infliction, and of mysticism, that they became at last inextricably confounded with the Phrygian Korybantes or worshippers of the Great Mother; though it appears that Grecian reserve always stopped short of the irreparable self-mutilation of Atys.

The influence of the Thracian religion upon that of the Greeks cannot be traced in detail, but the ceremonies contained in it were of a violent and fierce character, like the Phrygian, and acted upon Hellas in the same general direction as the latter. And the like may be said of the Egyptian religion, which was in this case the more operative, inasmuch as all the intellectual Greeks were naturally attracted to go and visit the wonders on the banks of the Nile; the powerful effect produced upon them is attested by many evidences, but especially by the interesting narrative of Herodotus. Now the Egyptian ceremonies were at once more licentious, and more profuse in the outpouring both of joy and sorrow, than the Greek; but a still greater difference sprang from the extraordinary power, separate mode of life, minute observances, and elaborate organisation, of the priesthood. The

I. LEGENDS RESPECTING THE GODS.

ceremonies of Egypt were multitudinous, but the legends concerning them were framed by the priests, and as a general rule, seemingly, known to the priests alone; at least they were not intended to be publicly talked of, even by pious men. They were "holy stories," which it was sacrilege publicly to mention, and which from this very prohibition only took firmer hold of the minds of the Greek visitors who heard them. And thus the element of secrecy and mystic silence – foreign to Homer, and only faintly glanced at in Hesiod – if it was not originally derived from Egypt, at least received from thence its greatest stimulus and diffusion. The character of the legends themselves was naturally affected by this change from publicity to secrecy; the secrets when revealed would be such as to justify by their own tenor the interdict on public divulgation. Instead of being adapted, like the Homeric mythe, to the universal sympathies and hearty interest of a crowd of hearers, they would derive their impressiveness from the tragical, mournful, extravagant, or terror-striking character of the incidents. Such a tendency, which appears explicable and probable even on general grounds, was in this particular case rendered still more certain by the coarse taste of the Egyptian priests. That any recondite doctrine, religious or philosophical, was attached to the mysteries or contained in the holy stories, has never been shown, and is to the last degree improbable though the affirmative has been asserted by many learned men

Herodotus seems to have believed that the worship and ceremonies of Dionysos generally were derived by the Greeks from Egypt, brought over by Kadmus and taught by him to Melampus. and the latter appears in the Hesiodic Catalogue as having cured the daughters of Prœtus of the mental distemper with which they had been smitten by Dionysos for rejecting his ritual. He cured them by introducing the Bacchic dance and fanatical excitement: this mythical incident is the most ancient mention of the Dionysiac solemnities presented in the same character as they hear in Euripidês. It is the general tendency of Herodotus to apply the theory of derivation from Egypt far too extensively to Grecian institutions: the orgies of Dionysos were not originally borrowed from thence, though they may have been much modified by connection with Egypt as well as with Asia. The remarkable mythe composed by Onomakritus respecting the dismemberment of Zagreus was founded upon an Egyptian tale very similar respecting the body of Osiris, who was supposed to be identical with Dionysos nor was it unsuitable to the reckless fury of the Bacchanals during their state of temporary excitement, which found a still more awful expression in the mythe of Pentheus, torn in pieces by his own mother Agavê at the head of her companions in the ceremony, as an intruder upon the feminine rites as well as a scoffer at the god. A passage in the Iliad (the authenticity of which has been contested, but even as an interpolation it must be old) also recounts how Lykurgus was struck blind by Zeus for having chased away with a whip "the nurses of the mad Dionysos," and frightened the god himself into the sea to take refuge in the arms of Thetis; and the fact, that Dionysos is so frequently represented in his mythes as encountering opposition and punishing the refractory, seems to indicate that his worship under its ecstatic form was a late phenomenon and introduced not without difficulty. The mythical Thracian Orpheus was attached as eponymous to a new sect, who seem to have celebrated the ceremonies of Dionysos with peculiar care, minuteness and fervour, besides observing various rules in respect to food and clothing.It was the opinion of Herodotus, that these rules, as well as the Pythagorean, were borrowed from Egypt. But whether this be the fact or not, the Orphic brotherhood is itself both an evidence, and a cause, of the increased importance of the worship of Dionysos, which indeed is attested by the great dramatic poets of Athens.

The Homeric Hymns present to us, however, the religious ideas and legends of the Greeks at an earlier period, when the enthusiastic and mystic tendencies had not yet acquired their full development. Though not referable to the same age or to the same author as either the Iliad or the Odyssey, they do to a certain extent continue the same stream of feeling, and the same mythical tone and colouring, as these poems – manifesting but little evidence of Egyptian, Asiatic, or Thracian adulterations. The difference is striking between the god Dionysos as he appears in the Homeric hymn and in the Bacchæ of Euripidês. The hymnographer describes him as standing on the sea-shore, in the guise of a beautiful and richly-clothed youth, when Tyrrhenian pirates suddenly approach: they seize and bind him and drag him on board their vessel. But the bonds which they employ burst spontaneously, and leave the god free. The steersman, perceiving this with affright, points out to his companions that they have unwittingly laid bands on a god, perhaps Zeus himself, or Apollo, or Poseidôn. He conjures them to desist, and to replace Dionysos respectfully on the shore, lest in his wrath he should visit the ship with wind and hurricane: but the crew deride his scruples, and Dionysos is carried prisoner out to sea with the ship under full sail. Miraculous circumstances soon attest both his presence and his power. Sweet-scented wine is seen to flow spontaneously about the ship, the sail and mast appear adorned with vine and ivy-leaves, and the oar-pegs with garlands. The terrified crew now too late entreat the helmsman to steer his course for the shore, and crowd round him for protection on the poop. But their destruction is at hand; Dionysos assumes the form of a lion – a bear is seen standing near him – this bear rushes with a loud roar upon the captain, while the crew leap overboard in their agony of fright, and are changed into dolphins. There remains none but the discreet and pious steersman, to whom Dionysos addresses words of affectionate encouragement, revealing his name, parentage and dignity.

This hymn, perhaps produced at the Naxian festival of Dionysos, and earlier than the time when the dithyrambic chorus became the established mode of singing the praise and glory of that god, is conceived in a spirit totally different from that of the Bacchic Teletæ, or special rites which the Bacchic of Euripidês so abundantly extol, rites introduced from Asia by Dionysos himself at the head of a thiasus or troop of enthusiastic women, inflaming with temporary frenzy the minds of the women of Thêbes, not communicable except to those who approach as pious communicants, and followed by the most tragical results to all those who fight against the god. The Bacchic Teletæ, and the Bacchic feminine frenzy, were importations from abroad, as Euripidês represents them, engrafted upon the joviality of the primitive Greek Dionysia; they were borrowed, in all probability, from more than one source and channel, the Orphic life or brotherhood being one of the varieties. Strabo ascribes to this latter a Thracian original, considering Orpheus, Musæus, and Eumolpus as having been all Thracians. It is curious to observe how, in the Bacchæ of Euripidês, the two distinct and even conflicting ideas of Dionysos come alternately forward; sometimes the old Grecian idea of the jolly and exhilarating god of wine – but more frequently the recent and imported idea of the terrific and irresistible god who unseats the reason, and whose *æstrus* can only be appeased by a willing, though temporary obedience. In the fanatical impulse which inspired the votaries of the Asiatic Rhea or Cybelê, or of the Thracian Kotys, there was nothing of spontaneous joy; it was a sacred madness, during which the soul appeared to be surrendered to a stimulus from without, and accompanied by preternatural strength and temporary sense of power, altogether distinct from the unrestrained hilarity of the original Dionysia, as we see them in the rural dêmes of Attica, or in the gay city of Tarentum. There was indeed a side on which the two bore some analogy, inasmuch as, according to the religions point of view of the Greeks, even the spontaneous joy of the vintage feast was conferred by the favour and enlivened by the companionship of Dionysos. It was upon this analogy that the framers of the Bacchic orgies proceeded; but they did not the less disfigure the genuine character of the old Grecian Dionysia.

Dionysos is in the conception of Pindar the Paredros or companion in worship of Dêmêtêr; the worship and religious estimate of the latter has by that time undergone as great a change as that of the former, if we take our comparison with the brief description of Homer and Hesiod; she has acquired much of the awful and soul-disturbing attributes of the Phrygian Cybelê. In Homer, Dêmêtêr is the goddess of the corn-field, who becomes attached to the mortal man Jasiôn: an unhappy passion, since Zeus, jealous of the connection between goddesses and men, puts him to death. In the Hesiodic Theogony, Dêmêtêr is the mother of Persephonê by Zeus, who permits Hadês to carry off the latter as his wife: moreover Dêmêtêr has, besides, by Jasiôn a son called Plutos, born in Krête. Even from Homer to Hesiod, the legend of Dêmêtêr, has been expanded and her dignity exalted: according to the usual tendency of Greek legend, the expansion goes on still further. Through Jasiôn, Dêmêtêr becomes connected with the mysteries of Samothrace; through Persephonê, with those of Eleusis. The former connection it is difficult to follow out in detail, but the latter is explained and traced to its origin in the Homeric Hymn to Dêmêtêr.

Though we find different statements respecting the date as well as the origin of the Eleusinian mysteries, yet the popular belief of the Athenians, and the story which found favour at Eleusis, ascribed them to the presence and dictation of the goddess Dêmêtêr herself: just as the Bacchic rites are, according to the Bacchæ of Euripidês, first communicated and enforced on the Greeks by the personal visit of Dionysos to Thêbes, the metropolis of the Baccic ceremonies In the Eleusinian legend, preserved by the author of the Homeric Hymn, she comes voluntarily and identifies herself with Eleusis: her past abode in Krête being briefly indicated. Her visit to Eleusis is connected with the deep sorrow caused by the loss of her daughter Persephonê, who had been seized by Hadês, while gathering flowers in a meadow along with the Oceanic Nymphs, and carried off to become his wife in the under-world. In vain did the reluctant Persephonê shriek and invoke the aid of her father Zeus: he had consented to give her to Hadês, and her cries were heard only by Hekatê and Hêlios. Dêmêtêr was inconsolable at the disappearance of her daughter, but knew not where to look for her: she wandered for nine days and nights with torches in search of the lost maiden without success. At length Hêlios, the "spy of gods and men," revealed to her, in reply to her urgent prayer, the rape of Persephonê, and the permission given to Hadês by Zeus. Dêmêtêr was smitten with anger and despair; she renounced Zeus and the society of Olympus, abstained from nectar and ambrosia, and wandered on earth in grief and fasting until her form could no longer be known. In this condition she came to Eleusis, then governed by the prince Keleos. Sitting down by a well at the wayside in the guise of an old woman, she was found by the daughters of Keleos, who came hither with their pails of brass for water. In reply to their questions, she told them that she had been brought by pirates from Krête to Thorikos, and had made her escape; she then solicited from them succour and employment as a servant or as a nurse. The damsels prevailed upon their mother Metaneira to receive her, and to entrust her with the nursing of the young Dêmophoôn, their late-born brother, the only son of Keleos. Dêmêtêr was received into the house of Metaneira, her dignified form still borne down by grief; she sat long silent and could not be induced either to smile or to taste food, until the maid-servant Iambê, by jests and playfulness, succeeded in amusing and rendering her cheerful. She would not taste wine, but requested a peculiar mixture of barley-meal with water and the herb mint.

The child Dêmophoôn, nursed by Dêmêtêr, throve and grew up like a god, to the delight and astonishment of his parents: she gave him no food, but anointed him daily with ambrosia, and plunged him at night in the fire like a torch, where he remained unburnt. She would have rendered him immortal, had she not been prevented by the indiscreet curiosity and alarm of Metaneira, who secretly looked in at night, and shrieked with horror at the sight of her child in the fire. The indignant goddess, setting the infant on the ground, now revealed her true character to Metaneira; her wan and aged look disappeared, and she stood confest in the genuine majesty of her divine shape, diffusing a dazzling brightness which illuminated the whole house. "Foolish mother," she said, "thy want of faith has robbed thy son of immortal life. I am the exalted Dêmêtêr, the charm and comfort both of gods and men: I was preparing for thy son exemption from death and old age; now it cannot be but he must taste of both. Yet shall he be ever honoured, since he has sat upon my knee and slept in my arms. Let the people of Eleusis erect for me a temple and altar on yonder hill above the fountain. I will myself prescribe to them the orgies which they must religiously perform in order to propitiate my favour."

The terrified Metaneira was incapable even of lifting up her child from the ground; her daughters entered at her cries, and began to embrace and tend their infant brother, but he sorrowed and could not be pacified for the loss of his divine nurse. All night they strove to appease the goddess.

Strictly executing the injunctions of Dêmêtêr, Keleos convoked the people of Eleusis and erected the temple on the spot which she had pointed out. It was speedily completed, and Dêmêtêr took up her abode in it, apart from the remaining gods, still pining with grief for the loss of her daughter, and withholding her beneficent aid from mortals. And thus she remained a whole year, a desperate and terrible year; in vain did the oxen draw the plough, and in vain was the barley-seed cast into the furrow, Dêmêtêr suffered it not to emerge from the earth. The human race would have been starved, and the gods would have been deprived of their honours and sacrifice, had not Zeus found means to conciliate her. But this was a hard task: for Dêmêtêr resisted the entreaties of Iris and of all the other goddesses and gods whom Zeus successively sent to her. She would be satisfied with nothing less than the recovery of her daughter. At length Zeus sent Hermês to Hadês, to bring Persephonê away: Persephonê joyfully obeyed, but Hadês prevailed upon her before she departed to swallow a grain of pomegranate, which rendered it impossible for her to remain the whole year away from him.

With transport did Dêmêtêr receive back her lost daughter, and the faithful Hekatê sympathised in the delight felt by both at the reunion. It was now an easier undertaking to reconcile her with the gods. Her mother Rhea, sent down expressly by Zeus, descended from Olympus on the fertile Rharian plain, then smitten with barrenness like the rest of the earth. She succeeded in appeasing the indignation of Dêmêtêr, who consented again to put forth her relieving hand. The buried seed came up in abundance, and the earth was covered with fruit and flowers. She would have wished to retain Persephonê constantly with her, but this was impossible, and she was obliged to consent that her daughter should go down for one-third of each year to the house of Hadês, departing from her every spring at the time when the seed is sown. She then revisited Olympus, again to dwell with the gods, but before her departure, she communicated to the daughters of Keleos, and to Keleos himself, together with Triptolemus, Dioklês and Eumolpus, the divine service and the solemnities which she required to be observed in her honour. And thus began the venerable mysteries of Eleusis, at her special command: the lesser mysteries, celebrated in February, in honour of Persephonê; the greater, in August, to the honour of

I. LEGENDS RESPECTING THE GODS.

Dêmêtêr herself. Both are jointly patronesses of the holy city and temple.

Such is a brief sketch of the temple legend of Eleusis, set forth at length in the Homeric Hymn to Dêmêtêr. It is interesting not less as a picture of the Mater Dolorosa (in the mouth of an Athenian, Dêmêtêr and Persephonê were always the Mother and Daughter, by excellence), first an agonised sufferer, and then finally glorified, the weal and woe of man being dependent upon her kindly feeling, than as an illustration of the nature and the growth of Grecian legend generally. Though we now read this Hymn as pleasing poetry, to the Eleusinians, for whom it was composed, it was genuine and sacred history. They believed in the visit of Dêmêtêr to Eleusis, and in the mysteries as a revelation from her, as implicitly as they believed in her existence and power as a goddess. The Eleusinian psalmist shares this belief in common with his countrymen, and embodies it in a continuous narrative, in which the great goddesses of the place, as well as the great heroic families, figure in inseparable conjunction. Keleos is the son of the Eponymous hero Eleusis, and his daughters, with the old epic simplicity, carry their basons to the well for water. Eumolpus, Triptolemus, Dioklês, heroic ancestors of the privileged families who continued throughout the historical times of Athens to fulfil their special hereditary functions in the Eleusinian solemnities, are among the immediate recipients of inspiration from the goddess; but chiefly does she favour Metaneira and her infant son Dêmophoôn, for the latter of whom her greatest boon is destined, and intercepted only by the weak faith of the mother. Moreover, every incident in the Hymn has a local colouring and a special reference. The well, overshadowed by an olive-tree near which Dêmêtêr had rested, the stream Kallichorus and the temple-hill, were familiar and interesting places in the eyes of every Eleusinian. The peculiar posset prepared from barley-meal with mint was always tasted by the Mysts (or communicants) after a prescribed fast, as an article in the ceremony, while it was also the custom, at a particular spot in the processional march, to permit the free interchange of personal jokes and taunts upon individuals for the general amusement. These two customs are connected in the Hymn with the incidents, that Dêmêtêr herself had chosen the posset as the first interruption of her long and melancholy fast, and that her sorrowful thoughts had been partially diverted by the coarse playfulness of the servant-maid Iambê. In the enlarged representation of the Eleusinian ceremonies, which became established after the incorporation of Eleusis with Athens, the part of Iambê herself was enacted by a woman, or man in woman's attire, of suitable wit and

25

imagination, who was posted on the bridge over the Kephissos, and addressed to the passers-by in the procession, especially the great men of Athens, saucy jeers, probably not less piercing than those of Aristophanês on the stage. The torch-bearing Hekatê received a portion of the worship in the nocturnal ceremonies of the Eleusinia; this too is traced, in the Hymn, to her kind and affectionate sympathy with the great goddesses.

Though all these, incidents were sincerely believed by the Eleusinians as a true history of the past, and as having been the real initiatory cause of their own solemnities, it is not the less certain that they are simply mythes or legends, and not to be treated as history, either actual or exaggerated. They do not take their start from realities of the past, but from realities of the present, combined with retrospective feeling and fancy, which fills up the blank of the afore-time in a manner at once plausible and impressive. What proportion of fact there may be in the legend, or whether there be any at all, it is impossible to ascertain and useless to inquire, for the story did not acquire belief from its approximation to real fact, but from its perfect harmony with Eleusinian faith and feeling, and from the absence of any standard of historical credibility. The little town of Eleusis derived all its importance from the solemnity of the Dêmêtria, and the Hymn which we have been considering (probably at least as old as 600 B.C.) represents the town as it stood before its absorption into the larger unity of Athens, which seems to have produced an alteration of its legends and an increase of dignity in its great festival. In the faith of an Eleusinian, the religious as well as the patriotic antiquities of his native town were connected with this capital solemnity. The divine legend of the sufferings of Dêmêtêr and her visit to Eleusis was to him that which the heroic legend of Adrastus and the Siege of Thêbes was to a Sikyônian, or that of Erechtheus and Athênê to an Athenian – grouping together in the same scene and story the goddess and the heroic fathers of the town. If our information were fuller, we should probably find abundance of other legends respecting the Dêmêtria; the Gephyræi of Athens, to whom belonged the celebrated Harmodios and Aristogeitôn, and who possessed special Orgies of Dêmêtêr the Sorrowful, to which no man foreign to their Gens was ever admitted, would doubtless have told stories not only different but contradictory; and even in other Eleusinian mythes we discover Eumolpus as king of Eleusis, son of Poseidôn, and a Thracian, completely different from the character which he bears in the Hymn before us. Neither discrepancies nor want of evidence, in reference to alleged antiquities, shocked the faith of a non-historical public What they wanted

I. LEGENDS RESPECTING THE GODS.

was a picture of the past, impressive to their feelings and plausible to their imagination; and it is important to the reader to remember, while he reads either the divine legends which we are now illustrating or the heroic legends to which we shall soon approach, that he is dealing with a past which never was present, a region essentially mythical, neither approachable by the critic nor mensurable by the chronologer.

The tale respecting the visit of Dêmêtêr, which was told by the ancient Gens, called the Phytalids, in reference to another temple of Dêmêtêr between Athens and Eleusis, and also by the Megarians in reference to a Dêmêtrion near their city, acquired under the auspices of Athens still further extension. The goddess was reported to have first communicated to Triptolemus at Eleusis the art of sowing corn, which by his intervention was disseminated all over the earth. Thus the Athenians took credit to themselves for having been the medium of communication from the gods to man of all the inestimable blessings of agriculture, which they affirmed to have been first exhibited on the fertile Rharian plain near Eleusis. Such pretensions are not to be found in the old Homeric hymn. The festival of the Thesmophoria, celebrated in honour of Dêmêtêr Thesmophoros at Athens, was altogether different from the Eleusinia, in this material respect, as well as others, that all males were excluded, and women only were allowed to partake in it: the surname Thesmophorus gave occasion to new legends in which the goddess was glorified as the first authoress of laws and legal sanctions to mankind. This festival, for women apart and alone, was also celebrated at Thêbes, at Paros, at Ephesus, and in many other parts of Greece.

Altogether, Dêmêtêr and Dionysos, as the Grecian counterparts of the Egyptian Isis and Osiris, seem to have been the great recipients of the new sacred rites borrowed from Egypt, before the worship of Isis in her own name was introduced into Greece: their solemnities became more frequently recluse and mysterious than those of the other deities. The importance of Dêmêtêr to the collective nationality of Greece may be gathered from the fact that her temple was erected at Dôrus, the spot where the Amphiktyonic assemblies were held, close by the temple of the Eponymous hero Amphiktyôn himself, and under the surname of the Amphiktyonic Dêmêtêr.

We now pass to another and not less important celestial personage – Apollo.

Legends of Apollo.

The legends of Dêlos and Delphi, embodied in the Homeric Hymn to Apollo,

27

indicate, if not a greater dignity, at least a more widely diffused worship of that god than even of Dêmêtêr. The Hymn is, in point of fact, an aggregate of two separate compositions, one emanating from an Iônic bard at Dêlos, the other from Delphi. The first details the birth, the second the mature divine efficiency of Apollo; but both alike present the unaffected charm as well as the characteristic peculiarities of Grecian mythical narrative. The hymnographer sings, and his hearers accept in perfect good faith, a history of the past; but it is a past, imagined partly as an introductory explanation to the present, partly as a means of glorifying the god. The island of Dêlos was the accredited birth-place of Apollo, and is also the place in which he chiefly delights, where the great and brilliant Iônic festival is periodically convened in his honour. Yet it is a rock narrow, barren, and uninviting; how came so glorious a privilege to be awarded to it? This the poet takes upon himself to explain. Lêtô, pregnant with Apollo, and persecuted by the jealous Hêrê, could find no spot wherein to give birth to her offspring. In vain did she address herself to numerous places in Greece, the Asiatic coast and the intermediate islands; all were terrified at the wrath of Hêrê, and refused to harbour her. As a last resort, she approached the rejected and repulsive island of Dêlos, and promised that, if shelter were granted to her in her forlorn condition, the island should become the chosen resort of Apollo as well as the site of his temple with its rich accompanying solemnities. Dêlos joyfully consented, but not without many apprehensions that the potent Apollo would despise her unworthiness, and not without exacting a formal oath from Lêtô, who was then admitted to the desired protection, and duly accomplished her long and painful labour. Though Diônê, Rhea, Themis and Amphitritê came to soothe and succour her, yet Hêrâ kept away the goddess presiding over childbirth, Eileithyia, and thus cruelly prolonged her pangs. At length Eileithyia came, and Apollo was born. Hardly had Apollo tasted, from the hands of Themis, the immortal food, nectar and ambrosia, when he burst at once his infant bands, and displayed himself in full divine form and strength, claiming his characteristic attributes of the bow and the harp, and his privileged function of announcing beforehand to mankind the designs of Zeus. The promise made by Lêtô to Dêlos was faithfully performed: amidst the numberless other temples and groves which men provided for him, he ever preferred that island as his permanent residence, and there the Iônians with their wives and children, and all their "bravery," congregated periodically from their different cities to glorify him. Dance and song and athletic contests adorned the solemnity, and the countless ships, wealth, and grace of the multitudinous Iônians had the air of an assembly of gods. The Delian maidens, servants of

28

I. LEGENDS RESPECTING THE GODS.

Apollo, sang hymns to the glory of the god, as well as of Artemis and Lêtô, intermingled with adventures of foregone men and women, to the delight of the listening crowd. The blind itinerant bard of Chios (composer of this the Homeric hymn, and confounded in antiquity with the author of the Iliad) had found honour and acceptance at this festival, and commends himself, in a touching farewell strain, to the remembrance and sympathy of the Delian maidens.

Yet Dêlos was not an oracular spot; Apollo did not manifest himself there as revealer of the futurities of Zeus. A place must be found where this beneficent function, without which mankind would perish under the innumerable doubts and perplexities of life, may be exercised and rendered available. Apollo himself descends from Olympus to make choice of a suitable site: the hymnographer knows a thousand other adventures of the god which he might sing, but he prefers this memorable incident, the charter and patent of consecration for the Delphian temple. Many different places did Apollo inspect: he surveyed the country of the Magnêtes and the Perræbians, came to Iôlkos, and passed over from thence to Eubœa and the plain of Lelanton. But even this fertile spot did not please him: he crossed the Euripus to Bœotia, passed by Teumêssus and Mykalêssus, and the then inaccessible and unoccupied forest on which the city of Thêbes afterwards stood. He next proceeded to Onchêstos, but the grove of Poseidôn was already established there: next across the Kêphissus to Okalea, Haliartus, and the agreeable plain and much-frequented fountain of Delphusa, or Tilphusa. Pleased with the place, Apollo prepared to establish his oracle there, but Tilphusa was proud of the beauty of her own site, and did not choose that her glory should be eclipsed by that of the god. She alarmed him with the apprehension that the chariots which contended in her plain, and the horses and mules which watered at her fountain would disturb the solemnity of his oracle: and she thus induced him to proceed onward to the southern side of Parnassus, overhanging the harbour of Krissa. Here he established his oracle, in the mountainous site not frequented by chariots and horses, and near to a fountain, which however was guarded by a vast and terrific serpent, once the nurse of the monster Typhaôh. This serpent Apollo slew with an arrow, and suffered its body to rot in the sun: hence the name of the place, Pythô, and the surname of the Pythian Apollo. The plan of his temple being marked out, it was built by Trophônios and Agamêdês, aided by a crowd of forward auxiliaries from the neighbourhood. He now discovered with indignation, however, that Tilphusa had cheated him, and went back with swift step to resent it. "Thou shalt not thus," he said, "succeed in thy fraud and retain thy beautiful water: the glory of the place shall be mine, and not thine alone." Thus saying, he tumbled down a crag upon the fountain, and obstructed her limpid current: establishing an altar for himself in a grove hard by near another spring, where men still worship him as Apollo Tilphusios, because of his severe vengeance upon the once beautiful Tilphusa.

Apollo next stood in need of chosen ministers to take care of his temple and sacrifice, and to pronounce his responses at Pythô. Descrying a ship, "containing many and good men," bound on traffic from the Minoian Knossus in Krête, to Pylus in Peloponnêsus, he resolved to make use of the ship and her crew for his purpose. Assuming the shape of a vast dolphin, he splashed about and shook the vessel so as to strike the mariners with terror, while he sent a strong wind, which impelled her along the coast of Peloponnêsus into the Corinthian Gulf, and finally to the harbour of Krissa, where she ran aground. The affrighted crew did not dare to disembark: but Apollo was seen standing on the shore in the guise of a vigourous youth, and inquired who they were, and what was their business. The leader of the Krêtans recounted in reply their miraculous and compulsory voyage, when Apollo revealed himself as the author and contriver of it, announcing to them the honourable function and the dignified post to which he destined them. They followed him by his orders to the rocky Pythô on Parnassus, singing the solemn Io-Paian such as it is sung in Krête, while the god himself marched at their head, with his fine form and lofty step, playing on the harp. He showed them the temple and site of the oracle, and directed them to worship him as Apollo Delphinios, because they had first seen him in the shape of a dolphin. "But how," they inquired, "are we to live in a spot where there is neither corn, nor vine, nor pasturage?" "Ye silly mortals," answered the god, "who look only for toil and privation, know that an easier lot is yours. Ye shall live by the cattle whom crowds of pious visitors will bring to the temple: ye shall need only the knife to be constantly ready for sacrifice. Your duty will be to guard my temple, and to officiate as ministers at my feasts, but if ye be guilty of wrong or insolence, either by word or deed, ye shall become the slaves of other men, and shall remain so forever. Take heed of the word and the warning."

Such are the legends of Dêlos and Delphi, according to the Homeric Hymn to Apollo. The specific functions of the god, and the chief localities of his worship, together with the surnames attached to them, are thus historically explained, being connected with his past acts and adventures. Though these

30

I. LEGENDS RESPECTING THE GODS.

are to us only interesting poetry, yet to those who heard them sung they possessed all the requisites of history, and were fully believed as such, not because they were partially founded in reality, but because they ran in complete harmony with the feelings; and, so long as that condition was fulfilled, it was not the fashion of the time to canvass truth or falsehood. The narrative is purely personal, without any discernible symbolised doctrine or allegory, to serve as a supposed ulterior purpose. The particular deeds ascribed to Apollo grow out of the general preconceptions as to his attributes, combined with the present realities of his worship. It is neither history nor allegory, but simple mythe or legend.

The worship of Apollo is among the most ancient, capital, and strongly marked facts of the Grecian world, and widely diffused over every branch of the race. It is older than the Iliad or Odyssey, in the latter of which both Pythô and Dêlos are noted, though Dêlos is not named in the former. But the ancient Apollo is different in more respects than one from the Apollo of later times. He is in an especial manner the god of the Trojans, unfriendly to the Greeks, and especially to Achillês: he has, moreover, only two primary attributes, his bow and his prophetic powers, without any distinct connection either with the harp, or with medicine, or with the sun, all which in later times he came to comprehend. He is not only, as Apollo Karneius, the chief god of the Doric race, but also (under the surname of Patrôus) the great protecting divinity of the gentile tie among the Iônians; he is moreover the guide and stimulus to Grecian colonisation, scarcely any colony being ever sent out without encouragement and direction from the oracle at Delphi: Apollo Archêgetês is one of his great surnames. His temple lends sanctity to the meetings of the Amphiktyonic assembly, and he is always in filial subordination and harmony with his father Zeus: Delphi and Olympia are never found in conflict. In the Iliad, the warm and earnest patrons of the Greeks are Hêrê, Athênê, and Poseidôn: here too Zeus and Apollo are seen in harmony, for Zeus is decidedly well-inclined to the Trojans, and reluctantly sacrifices them to the importunity of the two great goddesses. The worship of the Sminthian Apollo, in various parts of the Troad and the neighbouring territory, dates before the earliest periods of Æolic colonisation; hence the zealous patronage of Troy ascribed to him in the Iliad. Altogether, however, the distribution and partialities of the gods in that poem are different from what they become in later times, a difference which our means of information do not enable us satisfactorily to explain. Besides the Delphian temple, Apollo had numerous temples throughout Greece, and oracles at Abæ in Phôkis, on the Mount Ptôon, and at Tegyra in Bœotia, where he was said to have been born, at Branchidæ near Milêtus, at Klarus in Asia Minor, and at Patara in Lykia. He was not the only oracular god; Zeus at Dôdôna and at Olympia gave responses also; the gods or heroes Trophônius, Amphiaraus, Amphilochus, Mopsus, &c., each at his own sanctuary and in his own prescribed manner, rendered the same service.

The two legends of Delphi and Dêlos, above noticed, form of course a very insignificant fraction of the narratives which once existed respecting the great and venerated Apollo. They serve only as specimens, and as very early specimens, to illustrate what these divine mythes were, and what was the turn of Grecian faith and imagination. The constantly recurring festivals of the gods caused an incessant demand for new mythes respecting them, or at least for varieties and reproductions of the old mythes. Even during the third century of the Christian era, in the time of the rhetor Menander, when the old forms of Paganism were waning and when the stock of mythes in existence was extremely abundant, we see this demand in great force: but it was incomparably more operative in those earlier times when the creative vein of the Grecian mind yet retained its pristine and unfaded richness. Each god had many different surnames, temples, groves, and solemnities: with each of which was connected more or less of mythical narrative, originally hatched in the prolific and spontaneous fancy of a believing neighbourhood, to be afterwards expanded, adorned and diffused by the song of the poet. The earliest subject of competition at the great Pythian festival was the singing of a hymn in honour of Apollo; other *agones* were subsequently added, but the ode or hymn constituted the fundamental attribute of the solemnity: the Pythia at Sikyôn and elsewhere were probably framed on a similar footing. So too at the ancient and celebrated Charitêsia, or festival of the Charites, at Orchomenos, the rivalry of the poets in their various modes of composition both began and continued as the predominant feature; and the inestimable treasures yet remaining to us of Attic tragedy and comedy, are gleanings from the once numerous dramas exhibited at the solemnity of the Dionysia. The Ephesians gave considerable rewards for the best hymns in honour of Artemis, to be sung at her temple. The early lyric poets of Greece, though their works have not descended to us, devoted their genius largely to similar productions, as may be seen by the titles and fragments yet remaining.

Both the Christian and the Mahomedan religions have begun during the

I. LEGENDS RESPECTING THE GODS.

historical age, have been propagated from one common centre, and have been erected upon the ruins of a different pre-existing faith. With none of these particulars did Grecian Paganism correspond. It took rise in an age of imagination and feeling simply, without the restraints, as well as without the aid, of writing or records, of history or philosophy. It was, as a general rule, the spontaneous product of many separate tribes and localities, imitation and propagation operating as subordinate causes; it was moreover a primordial faith, as far as our means of information enable us to discover.

These considerations explain to us two facts in the history of the early Pagan mind: first, the divine mythes, the matter of their religion, constituted also the matter of their earliest history: next, these mythes harmonised with each other only in their general types, but differed incurably in respect of particular incidents. The poet who sung a new adventure of Apollo, the trace of which he might have heard in some remote locality, would take care that it should be agreeable to the general conceptions which his hearers entertained respecting the god. He would not ascribe the cestus or amorous influences to Athênê, nor armed interference and the ægis to Aphroditê; but, provided he maintained this general keeping, he might indulge his fancy without restraint in the particular events of the story. The feelings and faith of his hearers went along with him, and there were no critical scruples to hold them back; to scrutinise the alleged proceedings of the gods was repulsive, and to disbelieve them impious. And thus these divine mythes, though they had their root simply in religious feelings, and though they presented great discrepancies of fact, served nevertheless as primitive matter of history to an early Greek: they were the only narratives, at once publicly accredited and interesting, which he possessed. To them were aggregated the heroic mythes (to which we shall proceed presently), indeed the two are inseparably blended, gods, heroes and men almost always appearing in the same picture, analogous both in their structure and their genesis, and differing chiefly in the circumstance that they sprang from the type of a hero instead of from that of a god.

We are not to be astonished if we find Aphroditê, in the Iliad, born from Zeus and Dionê, and in the Theogony of Hesiod, generated from the foam on the sea after the mutilation of Uranos; nor if in the Odyssey she appears as the wife of Hêphæstos, while in the Theogony the latter is married to Aglaia, and Aphroditê is described as mother of three children by Arês. The Homeric hymn to Aphroditê details the legend of Aphroditê and Anchisês, which is presupposed in the Iliad as the parentage of Æneas: but the author of the hymn, probably sung at one of the festivals of Aphroditê in Cyprus, represents the goddess as ashamed of her passion for a mortal, and as enjoining Anchisês under severe menaces not to reveal who the mother of Æneas was; while in the Iliad she has no scruple in publicly owning him, and he passes everywhere as her acknowledged son. Aphroditê is described in the hymn as herself cold and un-impressible, but ever active and irresistible in inspiring amorous feelings, to gods, to men, and to animals. Three goddesses are recorded as memorable exceptions to her universal empire, Athênê, Artemis, and Hestia or Vesta. Aphroditê was one of the most important of all the goddesses in the mythical world; for the number of interesting, pathetic and tragical adventures deducible from misplaced or unhappy passion was of course very great; and in most of these cases the intervention of Aphroditê was usually prefixed, with some legend to explain why she manifested herself. Her range of action grows wider in the later epic and lyric and tragic poets than in Homer.

Athênê, the man-goddess, born from the head of Zeus, without a mother and without feminine sympathies, is the antithesis partly of Aphroditê, partly of the effeminate or womanised god Dionysos – the latter is an importation from Asia, but Athênê is a Greek conception – the type of composed, majestic and unrelenting force. It appears however as if this goddess had been conceived in a different manner in different parts of Greece. For we find ascribed to her, in some of the legends, attributes of industry and home-keeping; she is represented as the companion of Hêphæstos, patronising handicraft, and expert at the loom and the spindle; the Athenian potters worshipped her along with Promêtheus. Such traits of character do not square with the formidable ægis and the massive and crushing spear which Homer and most of the mythes assign to her. There probably were at first at least two different types of Athênê, and their coalescence has partially obliterated the less marked of the two. Athênê is the constant and watchful protectress of Hêraklês; she is also locally identified with the soil and people of Athens, even in the Iliad. Erechtheus, the Athenian, is born of the earth, but Athênê brings him up, nourishes him, and lodges him in her own temple, where the Athenians annually worship him with sacrifice and solemnities. It was altogether impossible to make Erechtheus son of Athênê, the type of the goddess forbade it; but the Athenian mythe-creators, though they found this barrier impassable, strove to approach to it as near as they could, and the description which they give of the birth of Erichthonios, at once un-Homeric and unseemly, presents something like the phantom of maternity.

The huntress Artemis, in Arcadia and in Greece proper generally, exhibits a

I. LEGENDS RESPECTING THE GODS.

well-defined type with which the legends respecting her are tolerably consistent. But the Ephesian as well as the Tauric Artemis partakes more of the Asiatic character, and has borrowed the attributes of the Lydian Great Mother as well as of an indigenous Tauric Virgin; this Ephesian Artemis passed to the colonies of Phokæa and Milêtus. The Homeric Artemis shares with her brother Apollo in the dexterous use of the far-striking bow, and sudden death is described by the poet as inflicted by her gentle arrow. The jealousy of the gods at the withholding of honours and sacrifices, or at the presumption of mortals in contending with them, a point of character so frequently recurring in the types of the Grecian gods, manifests itself in the legends of Artemis. The memorable Kalydônian boar is sent by her as a visitation upon Œneus, because he had omitted to sacrifice to her, while he did honour to other gods. The Arcadian heroine Atalanta is however a reproduction of Artemis, with little or no difference, and the goddess is sometimes confounded even with her attendant nymphs.

The mighty Poseidôn, the earth-shaker and the ruler of the sea, is second only to Zeus in power, but has no share in those imperial and superintending capacities which the Father of gods and men exhibits. He numbers a numerous heroic progeny, usually men of great corporeal strength, and many of them belonging to the Æolic race; the great Nêleid family of Pylus trace their origin up to him; and he is also the father of Polyphêmus the Cyclôps, whose well-earned suffering he cruelly revenges upon Odysseus. His Dêlos is the island of Kalaureia, wherein there was held in it an old local Amphiktyony, for the purpose of rendering to him joint honour and sacrifice. The isthmus of Corinth, Helikê in Achaia, and Onchêstos in Bœotia, are also residences which he much affects, and where he is solemnly worshipped. But the abode which he originally and specially selected for himself was the Acropolis of Athens, where by a blow of his trident he produced a well of water in the rock: Athênê came afterwards and claimed the spot for herself, planting in token of possession the olive-tree which stood in the sacred grove of Pandrosos: and the decision either of the indigenous Cecrops, or of Erechthous, awarded to her the preference, much to the displeasure of Poseidôn. Either on this account, or on account of the death of his son Eumolpus, slain in assisting the Eleusinians against Erechtheus, the Attic mythes ascribed to Poseidôn great enmity against the Erechtheid family, which he is asserted to have ultimately overthrown: Thesêus, whose glorious reign and deeds succeeded to that family, is said to have been really his son.

In several other places, in Ægina, Argôs and Naxos, Poseidôn had disputed the privileges of patron-god with Zeus, Hêrê and Dionysos: he was worsted in all, but bore his defeat patiently. Poseidôn endured a long slavery, in common with Apollo, gods as they were, under Laomedôn, king of Troy, at the command and condemnation of Zeus: the two gods rebuilt the walls of the city, which had been destroyed by Hêraklês. When their time was expired, the insolent Laomedôn withheld from them the stipulated reward, and even accompanied its refusal with appalling threats: and the subsequent animosity of the god against Troy was greatly determined by the sentiment of this injustice. Such periods of servitude, inflicted upon individual gods, are among the most remarkable of all the incidents in the divine legends. We find Apollo on another occasion condemned to serve Admêtus, king of Pheræ, as a punishment for having killed the Cyclôpes, and Hêraklês also is sold as a slave to Omphalê. Even the fierce Arês, overpowered and imprisoned for a long time by the two Alôids, is ultimately liberated only by extraneous aid. Such narratives attest the discursive range of Grecian fancy in reference to the gods, as well as the perfect commingling of things and persons, divine and human, in their conceptions of the past. The god who serves is for the time degraded; but the supreme god who commands the servitude is in the like proportion exalted, whilst the idea of some sort of order and government among these superhuman beings was never lost sight of. Nevertheless the mythes respecting the servitude of the gods became obnoxious afterwards, along with many others, to severe criticism on the part of philosophers.

The proud, jealous, and bitter Hêrê, the goddess of the once-wealthy Mykênæ, the *fax et focus* of the Trojan war, and the ever-present protectress of Jasôn in the Argônautic expedition, occupies an indispensable station in the mythical world. As the daughter of Kronos and wife of Zeus, she fills a throne from whence he cannot dislodge her, and which gives her a right perpetually to grumble and to thwart him. Her unmeasured jealousy of the female favourites of Zeus, and her antipathy against his sons, especially against Hêraklês, has been the suggesting cause of innumerable mythes. The general type of her character stands here clearly marked, as furnishing both stimulus and guide to the mythopœic fancy. The "Sacred Wedding," or marriage of Zeus and Hêrê, was familiar to epithalamic poets long before it became a theme for the spiritualising ingenuity of critics.

Hêphæstos is the son of Hêrê without a father, and stands to her in the same relation as Athênê to Zeus: her pride and want of sympathy are manifested by her casting him out at once in consequence of his deformity. He is the god of fire, and especially of fire in its practical applications to handicraft, and is indispensable as the right-hand and instrument of the gods. His skill and his deformity appear alternately as the source of mythical stories: wherever exquisite and effective fabrication is intended to be designated, Hêphæstos is announced as the maker, although in this function the type of his character is reproduced in Dædalos. In the Attic legends he appears intimately united both with Promêtheus and with Athênê, in conjunction with whom he was worshipped at Kolônus near Athens. Lêmnos was the favourite residence of Hêphæstos; and if we possessed more knowledge of this island and its town Hêphæstias, we should doubtless find abundant legends detailing his adventures and interventions.

The chaste, still, and home-keeping Hestia, goddess of the family hearth, is far less fruitful in mythical narratives, it spite of her very superior dignity, than the knavish, smooth-tongued, keen, and acquisitive Hermês. His function of messenger of the gods brings him perpetually on the stage, and affords ample scope for portraying the features of his character. The Homeric hymn to Hermês describes the scene and circumstances of his birth, and the almost instantaneous manifestation, even in infancy, of his peculiar attributes; it explains the friendly footing on which he stood with Apollo, the interchange of gifts and functions between them, and lastly, the inviolate security of all the wealth and offerings in the Delphian temple, exposed as they were to thieves without any visible protection. Such was the innate cleverness and talent of Hermês, that on the day he was born he invented the lyre, stringing the seven chords on the shell of a tortoise; and he also stole the cattle of Apollo in Pieria, dragging them backwards to his cave in Arcadia, so that their track could not be detected. To the remonstrances of his mother Maia, who points out to him the danger of offending Apollo, Hermês replies, that he aspires to rival the dignity and functions of Apollo among the immortals, and that if his father Zeus refuses to grant them to him, he will employ his powers of thieving in breaking open the sanctuary at Delphi, and in carrying away the gold and the vestments, the precious tripods and vessels. Presently Apollo discovers the loss of his cattle, and after some trouble finds his way to the Kyllênian cavern, where he sees Hermês asleep in his cradle. The child denies the theft with effrontery, and even treats the surmise as a ridiculous impossibility; he persists in such denial even before Zeus, who however detects him at once, and compels him to reveal the place where the cattle are concealed. The lyre was as yet unknown to Apollo, who has heard nothing except the voice of the Muses and the sound of the pipe. So powerfully is he fascinated by hearing the tones of the lyre from Hermês, and so eager to become possessed of it, that he is willing at once to pardon the past theft, and even to conciliate besides the friendship of Hermês. Accordingly a bargain is struck between the two gods and sanctioned by Zeus. Hermês surrenders to Apollo the lyre, inventing for his own use the syrinx or panspipe, and receiving from Apollo in exchange the golden rod of wealth, with empire over flocks and herds as well as over horses and oxen and the wild animals of the woods. He presses to obtain the gift of prophecy, but Apollo is under a special vow not to impart that privilege to any god whatever: He instructs Hermês however how to draw information, to a certain extent, from the Mœræ or Fates themselves; and assigns to him, over and above, the function of messenger of the gods to Hadês.

Although Apollo has acquired the lyre, the particular object of his wishes, he is still under apprehension that Hermês will steal it away from him again, together with his bow, and he exacts a formal oath by Styx as security. Hermês promises solemnly that he will steal none of the acquisitions, nor ever invade the sanctuary of Apollo; while the latter on his part pledges himself to recognise Hermês as his chosen friend and companion, amongst all the other sons of Zeus, human or divine.

So came to pass, under the sanction of Zeus, the marked favour shown by Apollo to Hermês. But Hermês (concludes the hymnographer, with frankness unusual in speaking of a god) "does very little good; he avails himself of the darkness of night to cheat without measure the tribes of mortal men."

Here the general types of Hermês and Apollo, coupled with the present fact that no thief ever approached the rich and seemingly accessible treasures of Delphi, engender a string of expository incidents cast into a quasi-historical form and detailing how it happened that Hermês had bound himself by especial convention to respect the Delphian temple. The types of Apollo seem to have been different in different times and parts of Greece; in some places he was worshipped as Apollo Nomios, or the patron of pasture and cattle, and this attribute, which elsewhere passed over to his son Aristæus, is by our hymnographer voluntarily surrendered to Hermês, combined with the golden rod of fruitfulness. On the other hand, the lyre did not originally belong to the Far-striking King, nor is he at all an inventor: the hymn explains both its first invention and how it came into his possession. And the value of the incidents

I. LEGENDS RESPECTING THE GODS.

is thus partly expository, partly illustrative, as expanding in detail the general preconceived character of the Kyllênian god.

To Zeus more amours are ascribed than to any of the other gods, probably because the Grecian kings and chieftains were especially anxious to trace their lineage to the highest and most glorious of all, each of these amours having its representative progeny on earth. Such subjects were among the most promising and agreeable for the interest of mythical narrative, and Zeus as a lover thus became the father of a great many legends, branching out into innumerable interferences, for which his sons, all of them distinguished individuals, and many of them persecuted by Hêrê, furnished the occasion. But besides this, the commanding functions of the supreme god, judicial and administrative, extending both over gods and men, was a potent stimulus to the mythopoeic activity. Zeus has to watch over his own dignity, the first of all considerations with a god: moreover as Horkios, Xenios. Ktêsios, Meilichios, (a small proportion of his thousand surnames), he guaranteed oaths and punished perjurers, he enforced the observance of hospitality, he guarded the family hoard and the crop realised for the year, and he granted expiation to the repentant criminal. All these different functions created a demand for mythes, as the means of translating a dim, but serious, presentiment into distinct form, both self-explaining and communicable to others. In enforcing the sanctity of the oath or of the tie of hospitality, the most powerful of all arguments would be a collection of legends respecting the judgments of Zeus, Horkios or Xenios; the more impressive and terrific such legends were, the greater would be their interest, and the less would any one dare to disbelieve them. They constituted the natural outpourings of a strong and common sentiment, probably without any deliberate ethical intention. The preconceptions of the divine agency, expanded into legend, form a product analogous to the idea of the divine features and symmetry embodied in the bronze or the marble statue.

But it was not alone the general type and attributes of the gods which contributed to put in action the mythopœic propensities. The rites and solemnities forming the worship of each god, as well as the details of his temple and its locality, were a fertile source of mythes, respecting his exploits and sufferings, which to the people who heard them served the purpose of past history. The exegetes, or local guide and interpreter, belonging to each temple, preserved and recounted to curious strangers these traditional narratives, which lent a certain dignity even to the minutiæ of divine service. Out of a stock of materials thus ample, the poets extracted individual collections, such as the

"Causes" (Αἴτια) of Kallimachus, now lost, and such as the Fasti of Ovid are for the Roman religious antiquities.

It was the practice to offer to the gods in sacrifice the bones of the victim only, enclosed in fat; how did this practice arise? The author of the Hesiodic Theogony has a story which explains it. Promêtheus tricked Zeus into an imprudent choice, at the period when the gods and mortal men first came to an arrangement about privileges and duties (in Mekônê). Promêtheus, the tutelary representative of man, divided a large steer into two portions: on the one side he placed the flesh and guts, folded up in the omentura and covered over with the skin; on the other, he put the bones enveloped in fat. He then invited Zeus to determine which of the two portions the gods would prefer to receive from mankind. Zeus "with both hands" decided for and took the white fat, but was highly incensed on finding that he had got nothing at the bottom except the bones. Nevertheless the choice of the gods was now irrevocably made; they were not entitled to any portion of the sacrificed animal beyond the bones and the white fat, and the standing practice is thus plausibly explained. I select this as one amongst a thousand instances to illustrate the genesis of legend out of religious practices. In the belief of the people, the event narrated in the legend was the real producing cause of the practice; but when we come to apply a sound criticism, we are compelled to treat the event as existing only in its narrative legend, and the legend itself as having been, in the greater number of cases, engendered by the practice, thus reversing the supposed order of production.

In dealing with Grecian mythes generally, it is convenient to distribute them into such as belong to the Gods and such at belong to the Heroes, according as the one or the other are the prominent personages. The former class manifests, more palpably than the latter, their real origin, as growing out of the faith and the feelings, without any necessary basis, either of matter of fact or allegory; moreover, they elucidate more directly the religion of the Greeks, so important an item in their character as a people. In point of fact, most of the mythes present to us Gods, Heroes and Men, in juxtaposition one with the other and the richness of Grecian mythical literature arises from the infinite diversity of combinations thus opened out: first by the three class-types, God, Hero, and Man; next by the strict keeping with which each separate class and character is handled. We shall now follow downward the stream of mythical time, which begins with the Gods, to the Heroic legends, or those which principally concern the Heroes and Heroines; for the latter were to the full as important in legend as the former.

II. LEGENDS RELATING TO HEROES AND MAN.

II. LEGENDS RELATING TO HEROES AND MAN.

The Hesiodic theogony gives no account of anything like a creation of man, nor does it seem that such an idea was much entertained in the legendary vein of Grecian imagination, which commonly carried back the present men by successive generations to some primitive ancestor, himself sprung from the soil, or from a neighbouring river or mountain, or from a god, a nymph, &c. But the poet of the Hesiodic "Works and Days" has given us a narrative conceived in a very different spirit respecting the origin of the human race, more in harmony with the sober and melancholy ethical tone which reigns through that poem.

First (he tells us) the Olympic gods made the golden race, good, perfect, and happy men, who lived from the spontaneous abundance of the earth, in ease and tranquillity like the gods themselves; they suffered neither disease nor old age, and their death was like a gentle sleep. After death they became, by the award of Zeus, guardian terrestrial dæmons, who watch unseen over the proceedings of mankind – with the regal privilege of dispensing to them wealth, and taking account of good and bad deeds.

Next, the gods made the silver race, unlike and greatly inferior, both in mind and body, to the golden. The men of this race were reckless and mischievous towards each other, and disdainful of the immortal gods, to whom they refused to offer either worship or sacrifice. Zeus in his wrath buried them in the earth; but there they still enjoy a secondary honour, as the Blest of the under-world.

Thirdly, Zeus made the brazen race, quite different from the silver. They were made of hard ash-wood, pugnacious and terrible; they were of immense strength and adamantine soul, nor did they raise or touch bread. Their arms, their houses, and their implements were all of brass; there was then no iron. This race, eternally fighting, perished by each other's hands, died out, and descended without name or privilege to Hadês.

Next, Zeus made a fourth race, far juster and better than the last preceding. These were the Heroes or demigods, who fought at the sieges of Troy and Thêbes. But this splendid stock also became extinct; some perished in war, others were removed by Zeus to a happier state in the islands of the Blest. There they dwell in peace and comfort, under the government of Kronos, reaping thrice in the year the spontaneous produce of the earth.

The fifth race, which succeeds to the Heroes, is of iron; it is the race to which the poet himself belongs, and bitterly does he regret it. He finds his contemporaries mischievous, dishonest, unjust, ungrateful, given to perjury, careless both of the ties of consanguinity and of the behests of the gods: Nemesis and Ædôs (Ethical Self-reproach) have left earth and gone back to Olympus. How keenly does he wish that his lot had been cast either earlier or later! This iron race is doomed to continual guilt, care, and suffering, with a small infusion of good; but the time will come when Zeus will put an end to it. The poet does not venture to predict what sort of race will succeed.

Such is the series of distinct races of men, which Hesiod, or the author of the "Works and Days," enumerates as having existed down to his own time. I give it as it stands, without placing much confidence in the various explanations which critics have offered. It stands out in more than one respect from the general tone and sentiment of Grecian legend; moreover the sequence of races is neither natural nor homogeneous, the heroic race not having any metallic denomination, and not occupying any legitimate place in immediate succession to the brazen. Nor is the conception of the dæmons in harmony either with Homer or with the Hesiodic theogony. In Homer, there is scarcely any distinction between gods and dæmons, while the gods are stated to go about and visit the cities of men in various disguises for the purpose of inspecting good and evil proceedings. But in the poem now before us, the distinction between gods and dæmons is generic. The latter are invisible tenants of earth, remnants of the once happy golden race whom the Olympic gods first made: the remnants of the second or silver race are not dæmons, nor are they tenants of earth, but they still enjoy an honourable posthumous existence as the Blest of the under-world. Nevertheless the Hesiodic dæmons are in no way authors or abettors of evil; on the contrary, they form the unseen police of the gods, for the purpose of repressing wicked behaviour in the world.

We may trace, I think, in this quintuple succession of earthly races, set forth by the author of the "Works and Days," the confluence of two veins of sentiment, not consistent one with the other, yet both coexisting in the author's mind. The drift of his poem is thoroughly didactic and ethical; though deeply penetrated with the injustice and suffering which darken the face of human life, he nevertheless strives to maintain, both in himself and in others, a conviction that on the whole the just and laborious man will come off well, and he enforces in considerable detail the lessons of practical prudence and virtue. This ethical sentiment, which dictates his appreciation of the present, also guides his imagination as to the past. It is pleasing to him to bridge over the chasm

II. LEGENDS RELATING TO HEROES AND MAN.

between the gods and degenerate man, by the supposition of previous races, the first altogether pure, the second worse than the first, and the third still worse than the second; and to show further how the first race passed by gentle death-sleep into glorious immortality; how the second race was sufficiently wicked to drive Zeus to bury them in the under-world, yet still leaving them a certain measure of honour; while the third was so desperately violent as to perish by its own animosities, without either name or honour of any kind. The conception of the golden race passing after death into good guardian dæmons, which some suppose to have been derived from a comparison with oriental angels, presents itself to the poet partly as approximating this race to the gods, partly as a means of constituting a triple gradation of post-obituary existence, proportioned to the character of each race whilst alive. The denominations of gold and silver, given to the first two races, justify themselves, like those given by Simonidês of Amorgos and by Phokylidês to the different characters of women, derived from the dog, the bee, the mare, the ass, and other animals; and the epithet of brazen is specially explained by reference to the material which the pugnacious third race so plentifully employed for their arms and other implements.

So far we trace intelligibly enough the moralising vein; we find the revolutions of the past so arranged as to serve partly as an ethical lesson, partly as a suitable preface to the present. But fourth in the list comes "the divine race of Heroes." Here a new vein of thought is opened by the poet. The symmetry of his ethical past is broken up, in order to make way for these cherished beings of the national faith. For though the author of the "Works and Days" was himself of a didactic cast of thought, like Phokylidês, or Solôn, or Theognis, yet he had present to his feelings, in common with his countrymen, the picture of Grecian fore-time, as it was set forth in the current mythes, and still more in Homer and those other epical productions which were then the only existing literature and history. It was impossible for him to exclude from his sketch of the past, either the great persons or the glorious exploits which these poems ennobled; and even if he himself could have consented to such an exclusion, the sketch would have become repulsive to his hearers. The chiefs who figured before Thêbes and Troy could not be well identified either with the golden, the silver, or the brazen race; moreover it was essential that they should be placed in immediate contiguity with the present race, because their descendants, real or supposed, were the most prominent and conspicuous of existing men. Hence the poet is

43

obliged to assign to them the fourth place in the series, and to interrupt the descending ethical movement in order to interpolate them between the brazen and the iron race, with neither of which they present any analogy. The iron race, to which the poet himself unhappily belongs, is the legitimate successor, not of the heroic, but of the brazen. Instead of the fierce and self-annihilating pugnacity which characterizes the bitter, the iron race manifests an aggregate of smaller and meaner vices and mischiefs. It will not perish by suicidal extinction – but it is growing worse and worse, and is gradually losing its vigour, so that Zeus will not vouchsafe to preserve much longer such a race upon the earth.

I conceive that the series of races imagined by the poet of the "Works and Days" is the product of two distinct and incongruous veins of imagination, the didactic or ethical blending with the primitive mythical or epical. His poem is remarkable as the most ancient didactic production of the Greeks, and as one of the first symptoms of a new tone of sentiment finding its way into their literature, never afterwards to become extinct. The tendency of the "Works and Days" is antiheroic; far from seeking to inspire admiration for adventurous enterprise, the author inculcates the strictest justice, the most unremitting labour and frugality, and a sober, not to say anxious, estimate of all the minute specialties of the future. Prudence and probity are his means, practical comfort and happiness his end. But he deeply feels, and keenly exposes, the manifold wickedness and short-comings of his contemporaries, in reference to this capital standard. He turns with displeasure from the present men, not because they are too feeble to hurl either the spear of Achilles or some vast boundary-stone, but because they are rapacious, knavish, and unprincipled.

Dæmons.

The dæmons first introduced into the religious atmosphere of the Grecian world by the author of the "Works and Days," as generically different from the gods, but as essentially good, and as forming the intermediate agents and police between gods and men, are deserving of attention as the seed of a doctrine which afterwards underwent many changes, and became of great importance, first as one of the constituent elements of pagan faith, then as one of the helps to its subversion. It will be recollected that the buried remnants of the half-wicked silver race, though they are not recognised as dæmons, are still considered as having a substantive existence, a name, and

II. LEGENDS RELATING TO HEROES AND MAN.

dignity, in the under-world. The step was easy, to treat them as dæmons also, but as dæmons of a defective and malignant character; this step was made by Empedoclês and Xenocratês, and to a certain extent countenanced by Plato. There came thus to be admitted among the pagan philosophers dæmons both good and bad, in every degree: and these dæmons were found available as a means of explaining many phænomena for which it was not convenient to admit the agency of the gods. They served to relieve the gods from the odium of physical and moral evils, as well as from the necessity of constantly meddling in small affairs: and the objectionable ceremonies of the pagan world were defended upon the ground that in no other way could the exigencies of such malignant beings be appeased. They were most frequently noticed as causes of evil, and thus the name (*dæmon*) came insensibly to convey with it a bad sense, the idea of an evil being as contrasted with the goodness of a god. So it was found by the Christian writers when they commenced their controversy with paganism. One branch of their argument led them to identify the pagan gods with dæmons in the evil sense, and the insensible change in the received meaning of the word lent them a specious assistance. For they could easily show that not only in Homer, but in the general language of early pagans, all the gods generally were spoken of as dæmons – and therefore, verbally speaking, Clemens and Tatian seemed to affirm nothing more against Zeus or Apollo than was employed in the language of Paganism itself Yet the audience of Homer or Sophoklês would have strenuously repudiated the proposition, if it had been put to them in the sense which the word *dæmon* bore in the age and among the circle of these Christian writers. In the imagination of the author of the "Works and Days," the dæmons occupy an important place, and are regarded as being of serious practical efficiency. When he is remonstrating with the rulers around him upon their gross injustice and corruption, he reminds them of the vast number of these immortal servants of Zeus who are perpetually on guard amidst mankind, and through whom the visitations of the gods will descend even upon the most potent evil doers. His supposition that the dæmons were not gods, but departed men of the golden race, allowed him to multiply their number indefinitely, without too much cheapening the divine dignity.

As this poet has been so much enslaved by the current legends as to introduce the Heroic race into a series to which it does not legitimately belong, so he has under the same influence inserted in another part of his poem the mythe of Pandôra and Promêtheus, as a means of explaining the primary diffusion, and

45

actual abundance, of evil among mankind. Yet this mythe can in no way consist with his quintuple scale of distinct races, and is in fact a totally distinct theory to explain the same problem, the transition of mankind from a supposed state of antecedent happiness to one of present toil and suffering. Such an inconsistency is not a sufficient reason for questioning the genuineness of either passage, for the two stories, though one contradicts the other, both harmonise with that central purpose which governs the author's mind, a querulous and didactic appreciation of the present. That such was his purpose appears not only from the whole tenor of his poem, but also from the remarkable fact that his own personality, his own adventures and kindred, and his own sufferings, figure in it conspicuously. And this introduction of self imparts to it a peculiar interest. The father of Hesiod came over from the Æolic Kymê, with the view of bettering his condition, and settled at Askra in Bœotia, at the foot of Mount Helicon. After his death his two sons divided the family inheritance; but Hesiod bitterly complains that his brother Persês cheated and went to law with him, and obtained through corrupt judges an unjust decision. He farther reproaches his brother with a preference for the suits and unprofitable bustle of the agora, at a time when he ought to be labouring for his subsistence in the field. Askra indeed was a miserable place, repulsive both in summer and winter. Hesiod had never crossed the sea, except once from Aulis to Eubœa, whither he went to attend the funeral games of Amphidamas, the chief of Chalkis: he sung a hymn, and gained as prize a tripod, which he consecrated to the muses in Helicon.

These particulars, scanty as they are, possess a peculiar value, as the earliest authentic memorandum respecting the doing or suffering of any actual Greek person. There is no external testimony at all worthy of trust respecting the age of the "Works and Days." Herodotus treats Hesiod and Homer as belonging to the same age, four hundred years before his own time, and there are other statements besides, some placing Hesiod at an earlier date than Homer, some at a later. Looking at the internal evidences, we may observe that the pervading sentiment, tone and purpose of the poem is widely different from that of the Iliad and Odyssey, and analogous to what we read respecting the compositions of Archilochus and the Amorgian Simonidês. The author of the "Works and Days" is indeed a preacher and not a satirist; but with this distinction, we find in him the same predominance of the present and the positive, the same disposition to turn the muse into an exponent of his own personal wrongs, the same employment of Æsopic fable by way of illustration, and the same

II. LEGENDS RELATING TO HEROES AND MAN.

unfavourable estimate of the female sex, all of which may be traced in the two poets above mentioned, placing both of them in contrast with the Homeric epic. Such an internal analogy, in the absence of good testimony, is the best guide which we can follow in determining the date of the "Works and Days," which we should accordingly place shortly after the year 700 B.C. The style of the poem might indeed afford a proof that the ancient and uniform hexameter, though well adapted to continuous legendary narrative or to solemn hymns, was somewhat monotonous when called upon either to serve a polemical purpose or to impress a striking moral lesson. When poets, then the only existing composers, first began to apply their thoughts to the cut and thrust of actual life, aggressive or didactic, the verse would be seen to require a new, livelier and smarter metre: and out of this want grew the elegiac and the iambic verse, both seemingly contemporaneous, and both intended to supplant the primitive hexameter for the short effusions then coming into vogue.

III. LEGEND OF THE IAPEITDS.

The sons of the Titan god Iapetus, as described in the Hesiodic theogony, are Atlas, Menœtius, Promêtheus and Epimêtheus. Of these, Atlas alone is mentioned by Homer in the Odyssey, and even he not as the son of Iapetus; the latter himself is named in the Iliad as existing in Tartarus along with Kronos. The Homeric Atlas "knows the depths of the whole sea, and keeps by himself those tall pillars which hold the heaven apart from the earth."

As the Homeric theogony generally appears much expanded in Hesiod, so also does the family of Iapetus, with their varied adventures. Atlas is here described, not as the keeper of the intermediate pillars between heaven and earth, but as himself condemned by Zeus to support the heaven on his head and hands: while the fierce Menœtius is thrust down to Erebus as a punishment for his ungovernable insolence. The remaining two brothers, Promêtheus and Epimêtheus, are among the most interesting creations of Grecian legend, and distinguished in more than one respect from all the remainder.

First, the main battle between Zeus and the Titan gods is a contest of force purely and simply – mountains are hurled and thunder is launched, and the victory remains to the strongest. But the competition between Zeus and Promêtheus is one of craft and stratagem; the victory does indeed remain to the former, but the honours of the fight belong to the latter. Secondly, Promêtheus and Epimêtheus (the fore-thinker and the after-thinker) are characters stamped at the same mint and by the same effort, the express contrast and antithesis of each other. Thirdly, mankind are here expressly brought forward, not indeed as active partners in the struggle, but as the grand and capital subjects interested, as gainers or sufferers by the result Promêtheus appears in the exalted character of champion of the human race, even against the formidable superiority of Zeus.

In the primitive or Hesiodic legend, Promêtheus is not the creator or moulder of man; it is only the later additions which invest him with this character. The race are supposed as existing, and Promêtheus, a member of the dispossessed body of Titan gods, comes forward as their representative and defender. The advantageous bargain which he made with Zeus on their behalf, in respect to the partition of the sacrificial animals, has been recounted in the preceding chapter. Zeus felt that he had been outwitted, and was exceeding wroth. In his displeasure he withheld from mankind the inestimable comfort of

48

fire, so that the race would have perished, had not Promêtheus stolen fire, in defiance of the command of the Supreme Ruler, and brought it to men in the hollow of a ferule.

Zeus was now doubly indignant, and determined to play off a still more ruinous stratagem. Hêphæstos, by his direction, moulded the form of a beautiful virgin; Athênê dressed her, Aphroditê and the Charities bestowed upon her both ornament and fascination, while Hermês infused into her the mind of a dog, a deceitful spirit, and treacherous words. The messenger of the gods conducted this "fascinating mischief" to mankind, at a time when Promêtheus was not present. Now Epimêtheus had received from his brother peremptory injunctions not to accept from the hands of Zeus any present whatever; but the beauty of Pandôra (so the newly-formed female was called) was not to be resisted. She was received and admitted among men, and from that moment their comfort and tranquillity was exchanged for suffering of every kind. The evils to which mankind are liable had been before enclosed in a cask in their own keeping; Pandôra in her malice removed the lid of the cask, and out flew these thousand evils and calamities, to exercise forever their destroying force. Hope alone remained imprisoned, and therefore without efficacy, as before – the inviolable lid being replaced before she could escape. Before this incident (says the legend) men had lived without disease or suffering; but now both earth and sea are full of mischiefs, while maladies of every description stalk abroad by day as well as by night, without any hope for man of relief to come.

The Theogony gives the legend here recounted, with some variations – leaving out the part of Epimêtheus altogether, as well as the cask of evils. Pandôra is the ruin of man, simply as the mother and representative of the female sex. And the variations are thus useful, as they enable us to distinguish the essential from the accessory circumstances of the story.

"Thus (says the poet, at the conclusion of his narrative) it is not possible to escape from the purposes of Zeus." His mythe, connecting the calamitous condition of man with the malevolence of the supreme god, shows, first, by what cause such an unfriendly feeling was raised; next, by what instrumentality its deadly results were brought about. The human race are not indeed the creation, but the protected flock of Promêtheus, one of the elder or dispossessed Titan gods. When Zeus acquires supremacy, mankind along with the rest become subject to him, and are to make the best bargain they can respecting worship and service to be yielded. By the stratagem of their advocate Promêtheus, Zeus is cheated into such a partition of the victims as is eminently unprofitable to him; whereby his wrath is so provoked, that he tries to subtract from man the use of fire. Here however his scheme is frustrated by the theft of Promêtheus; but his second attempt is more successful, and he in his turn cheats the unthinking Epimêtheus into the acceptance of a present (in spite of the peremptory interdict of Promêtheus) by which the whole of man's happiness is wrecked. This legend grows out of two feelings: partly as to the relations of the gods with man, partly as to the relation of the female sex with the male. The present gods are unkind towards man, but the old gods, with whom man's lot was originally cast, were much kinder – and the ablest among them stands forward as the indefatigable protector of the race. Nevertheless, the mere excess of his craft proves the ultimate ruin of the cause which he espouses. He cheats Zeus out of a fair share of the sacrificial victim, so as both to provoke and justify a retaliation which he cannot be always at hand to ward off. The retaliation is, in his absence, consummated by a snare laid for Epimêtheus and voluntarily accepted. And thus, though Hesiod ascribes the calamitous condition of man to the malevolence of Zeus, his piety suggests two exculpatory pleas for the latter: mankind have been the first to defraud Zeus of his legitimate share of the sacrifice – and they have moreover been consenting parties to their own ruin. Such are the feelings, as to the relation between the gods and man, which have been one of the generating elements of this legend. The other element, a conviction of the vast mischief arising to man from women, whom yet they cannot dispense with, is frequently and strongly set forth in several of the Greek poets – by Simonidês of Amorgos and Phokylidês, not less than by Euripidês.

But the miseries arising from woman, however great they might be, did not reach Promêtheus himself. For him, the rash champion who had ventured "to compete in sagacity" with Zeus, a different punishment was in store. Bound by heavy chains to a pillar, he remained fast imprisoned for several generations; every day did an eagle prey upon his liver, and every night did the liver grow afresh for the next day's suffering. At length Zeus, eager to enhance the glory of his favourite son Hêraklês, permitted the latter to kill the eagle and rescue the captive.

Such is the Promethean mythe as it stands in the Hesiodic poems; its earliest form, as far as we can trace. Upon it was founded the sublime tragedy of Æschylus, "The Enchained Promêtheus," together with at least one more tragedy, now lost, by the same author. Æschylus has made several important alterations: describing the human race, not as having once enjoyed and subsequently lost a state of tranquillity and enjoyment, but as originally feeble and wretched. He suppresses both the first trick played off by Promêtheus upon Zeus respecting the partition of the victim – and the final formation and sending of Pandôra – which are the two most marked portions of the Hesiodic story; while on the other hand be brings out prominently and enlarges upon the theft of fire, which in Hesiod is but slightly touched. If he has thus relinquished the antique simplicity of the story, he has rendered more than ample compensation by imparting to it a grandeur of *idéal,* a large reach of thought combined with appeals to our earnest and admiring sympathy, and a pregnancy of suggestion in regard to the relations between the gods and man, which soar far above the Hesiodic level – and which render his tragedy the most impressive, though not the most artistically composed, of all Grecian dramatic productions. Promêtheus there appears not only as the heroic champion and sufferer in the cause and for the protection of the human race, but also as the gifted teacher of all the arts, helps, and ornaments of life, amongst which fire is only one; all this against the will and in defiance of the purpose of Zeus, who, on acquiring his empire, wished to destroy the human race and to beget some new breed. Moreover, new relations between Promêtheus and Zeus are superadded by Æschylus. At the commencement of the struggle between Zeus and the Titan gods, Promêtheus had vainly attempted to prevail upon the latter to conduct it with prudence; but when he found that they obstinately declined all wise counsel, and that their ruin was inevitable, he abandoned their cause and joined Zeus. To him and to his advice Zeus owed the victory: yet the monstrous ingratitude and tyranny of the latter is now manifested by nailing him to a rock, for no other crime than because he frustrated the purpose of extinguishing the human race, and furnished to them the means of living with tolerable comfort. The new ruler Zeus, insolent with his victory over the old gods, tramples down all right, and sets at naught sympathy and obligation, as well towards gods as towards man. Yet the prophetic Promêtheus, in the midst of intense suffering, is consoled by the foreknowledge that the time will come when Zeus must again send for him, release him, and invoke his aid, as the sole means of averting from himself dangers otherwise insurmountable. The security and means of continuance for mankind have now been placed beyond the reach of Zeus – whom Promêtheus proudly defies, glorying in his generous and successful championship, despite the terrible price which he is doomed to pay for it.

As the Æschylean Promêtheus, though retaining the old lineaments, has acquired a new colouring, soul and character, so he has also become identified with a special locality. In Hesiod, there is no indication of the place in which he is imprisoned, but Æschylus places it in Scythia, and the general belief of the Greeks supposed it to be on Mount Caucasus. So long and so firmly did this belief continue, that the Roman general Pompey, when in command of an army in Kolchis, made with his companion, the literary Greek Theophanês, a special march to view the spot in Caucasus where Promêtheus had been transfixed.

IV. HEROIC LEGENDS.- GENEALOGY OF ARGOS.

Having briefly enumerated the gods of Greece, with their chief attributes as described in legend, we come to those genealogies which connected them with historical men.

In the retrospective faith of a Greek, the ideas of worship and ancestry coalesced. Every association of men, large or small, in whom there existed a feeling of present union, traced back that union to some common initial progenitor; that progenitor being either the common god whom they worshipped, or some semi-divine person closely allied to him. What the feelings of the community require is a continuous pedigree to connect them with this respected source of existence, beyond which they do not think of looking back. A series of names, placed in filiation or fraternity, together with a certain number of family or personal adventures ascribed to some of the individuals among them, constitute the ante-historical past through which the Greek looks back to his gods. The names of this genealogy are, to a great degree, gentile or local names familiar to the people, rivers, mountains, springs, lakes, villages, dêmes, etc, embodied as persons, and introduced as acting or suffering. They are moreover called kings or chiefs, but the existence of a body of subjects surrounding them is tacitly implied rather than distinctly set forth; for their own personal exploits or family proceedings constitute for the most part the whole matter of narrative. Thus the genealogy was made to satisfy at once the appetite of the Greeks for romantic adventure, and their demand for an unbroken line of filiation between themselves and the gods. The eponymous personage, from whom the community derive their name, is sometimes the begotten son of the local god, sometimes an indigenous man sprung from the earth, which is indeed itself divinised.

It will be seen from the mere description of these genealogies that they included elements human and historical, as well as elements divine and extra-historical. If we could determine the time at which any genealogy was first framed, we should be able to assure ourselves that the men then represented as present, together with their fathers and grandfathers, were real persons of flesh and blood. But this is a point which can seldom be ascertained; moreover, even if it could be ascertained, we must at once set it aside, if we wish to look at the genealogy in the point of view of the Greeks. For to them, not only all the members were alike real, but the gods and heroes at the commencement were in a certain sense the most real; at least, they were the most esteemed and indispensable of all. The value of the genealogy consisted, not in its length, but in its continuity; not (according to the feeling of modern aristocracy) in the power of setting out a prolonged series of human fathers and grandfathers, but in the sense of ancestral union with the primitive god. And the length of the series is traceable rather to humility, inasmuch as the same person who was gratified with the belief that he was descended from a god in the fifteenth generation, would have accounted it criminal insolence to affirm that a god was his father or grandfather. In presenting to the reader those genealogies which constitute the supposed primitive history of Hellas, I make no pretence to distinguish names real and historical from fictitious creations; partly because I have no evidence upon which to draw the line, and partly because by attempting it I should altogether depart from the genuine Grecian point of view.

Nor is it possible to do more than exhibit a certain selection of such as were most current and interesting, for the total number of them which found place in Grecian faith exceeds computation. As a general rule, every dême, every gens, every aggregate of men accustomed to combined action, religious or political, had its own. The small and unimportant dêmes into which Attica was divided had each its ancestral god and heroes, just as much as the great Athens herself. Even among the villages of Phôkis, which Pausanias will hardly permit himself to call towns, deductions of legendary antiquity were not wanting. And it is important to bear in mind, when we are reading the legendary genealogies of Argôs, or Sparta, or Thêbes, that these are merely samples amidst an extensive class, all perfectly analogous, and all exhibiting the religious and patriotic retrospect of some fraction of the Hellenic world. They are no more matter of historical tradition than any of the thousand other legendary genealogies which men delighted to recall to memory at the periodical festivals of their gens, their dême, or their village.

With these few prefatory remarks, I proceed to notice the most conspicuous of the Grecian heroic pedigrees, and first, that of Argôs.

The earliest name in Argeian antiquity is that of Inachus, the son of Oceanus and Têthys, who gave his name to the river flowing under the walls of the town. According to the chronological computations of those who regarded the mythical genealogies as substantive history, and who allotted a given number of years to each generation, the reign of Inachus was placed 1986 B.C., or about 1100 years prior to the commencement of the recorded Olympiads.

The sons of Inachus were Phorôneus and Ægialeus; both of whom however

IV. HEROIC LEGENDS.- GENEALOGY OF ARGOS.

were sometimes represented as indigenous or indigenous men, the one in the territory of Argôs, the other in that of Sikyôn. Ægialeus gave his name to the north-western region of the Peloponnêsus, on the southern coast of the Corinthian Gulf. The name of Phorôneus was of great celebrity in the Argeian mythical genealogies, and furnished both the title and the subject of the ancient poem called Phorônis, in which he is styled "the father of mortal men." He is said to have imparted to mankind, who had before him lived altogether isolated, the first notion and habits of social existence, and even the first knowledge of fire: his dominion extended over the whole Peloponnêsus. His tomb at Argôs, and seemingly also the place called the Phorônic city, in which he formed the first settlement of mankind, were still shown in the days of Pausanias. The offspring of Phorôneus, by the nymph Teledikê, were Apis and Niobê. Apis, a harsh ruler, was put to death by Thelxiôn and Telchin, having given to Peloponnêsus the name of Apia; he was succeeded by Argôs, the son of his sister Niobê by the god Zeus. From this sovereign Peloponnêsus was denominated Argôs. By his wife Evadnê, daughter of Strymôn, he had four sons, Ekbasus, Peiras, Epidaurus, and Kriasus. Ekbasus was succeeded by his son Agênôr, and he again by his son Argôs Panoptês, a very powerful prince who is said to have had eyes distributed over all his body, and to have liberated Peloponnêsus from several monsters and wild animals which infested it; Akusilaus and Æschylus make this Argôs an earth-born person, while Pherekydês reports him as son of Arestôr. Iasus was the son of Argôs Panoptês by Ismênê, daughter of Asôpus. According to the authors whom Apollodôrus and Pausanias prefer, the celebrated Iô was his daughter; but the Hesiodic epic (as well as Akusilaus) represented her as daughter of Peiras, while Æschylus and Kastôr the chronologist affirmed the primitive king Inachus to have been her father. A favourite theme, as well for the ancient genealogical poets as for the Attic tragedians, were the adventures of Iô, of whom, while priestess of Hêrê, at the ancient and renowned Hêræon between Mykênæ and Tiryns, Zeus became amorous. When Hêrê discovered the intrigue and taxed him with it, he denied the charge, and metamorphosed Iô into a white cow. Hêrê, requiring that the cow should be surrendered to her, placed her under the keeping of Argôs Panoptês; but this guardian was slain by Hermês, at the command of Zeus: and Hêrê then drove the cow Iô away from her native land by means of the incessant stinging of a gad-fly, which compelled her to wander without repose or sustenance over an immeasurable extent of foreign regions. The wandering Iô gave her name to the Iônian Gulf, traversed Epirus and Ilyria, passed the chain of Mount Hæmus and the lofty summits of Caucasus, and swam across the

55

Thracian or Cimmerian Bosporus (which also from her derived its appellation) into Asia. She then went through Scythia, Cimmeria, and many Asiatic regions, until she arrived in Egypt, where Zeus at length bestowed upon her rest, restored her to her original form, and enabled her to give birth to his black son Epaphos.

Such is a general sketch of the adventures which the ancient poets, epic, lyric, and tragic, and the logographers after them, connect with the name of the Argeian Iô, one of the numerous tales which the fancy of the Greeks deduced from the amorous dispositions of Zeus and the jealousy of Hêrê. That the scene should be laid in the Argeian territory appears natural, when we recollect that both Argôs and Mykênæ were under the special guardianship of Hêrê, and that the Hêræon Mykênæ was one of the oldest and most celebrated temples in which she was worshipped. It is useful to compare this amusing fiction with the representation reported to us by Herodotus, and derived by him as well from Phœnician as from Persian antiquarians, of the circumstances which occasioned the transit of Iô from Argôs to Egypt, an event recognised by all of them as historical matter of fact. According to the Persians, a Phœnician vessel had arrived at the port near Argôs, freighted with goods intended for sale to the inhabitants of the country. After the vessel had remained a few days, and disposed of most of her cargo, several Argeian women, and among them Iô the king's daughter, coming on board to purchase, were seized and carried off by the crew, who sold Iô in Egypt. The Phœnician antiquarians, however, while they admitted the circumstance that Iô had left her own country in one of their vessels, gave a different colour to the whole by affirming that she emigrated voluntarily, having been engaged in an amour with the captain of the vessel and fearing that her parents might come to the knowledge of her pregnancy. Both Persians and Phœnicians described the abduction of Iô as the first of a series of similar acts between Greeks and Asiatics, committed each in revenge for the preceding. First came the rape of Europe from Phoenicia by Grecian adventurers, perhaps, as Herodotus supposed, by Krêtans: next, the abduction of Mêdeia from Kolchis by Jasôn, which occasioned the retaliatory act of Paris, when he stole away Helena from Menelaos. Up to this point the seizures of women by Greeks from Asiatics, and by Asiatics from Greeks, had been equivalent both in number and in wrong. But the Greeks now thought fit to equip a vast conjoint expedition to recover Helen, in the course of which they took and sacked Troy. The invasions of Greece by Darius and Xerxês were intended, according to the

IV. HEROIC LEGENDS.- GENEALOGY OF ARGOS.

Persian antiquarians, as a long-delayed retribution for the injury inflicted on the Asiatics by Agamemnôn and his followers.

The account thus given of the adventures of Iô, when contrasted with the genuine legend, is interesting, as it tends to illustrate the phænomenon which early Grecian history is constantly presenting to us, the way in which the epical furniture of an unknown past is recast and newly coloured so as to meet those changes which take place in the retrospective feelings of the present. The religious and poetical character of the old legend disappears; nothing remains except the names of persons and places, and the voyage from Argôs to Egypt. We have in exchange a sober, quasi-historical narrative, the value of which consists in its bearing on the grand contemporary conflicts between Persia and Greece, which filled the imagination of Herodotus and his readers.

To proceed with the genealogy of the kings of Argôs, Iasus was succeeded by Krotôpus, son of his brother Agênôr; Krotôpus by Sthenelas, and he again by Gelanôr. In the reign of the latter, Danaos came with his fifty daughters from Egypt to Argôs; and here we find another of those romantic adventures which so agreeably decorate the barrenness of the mythical genealogies. Danaos and Ægyptos were two brothers descending from Epaphos, son of Iô: Ægyptos had fifty sons, who were eager to marry the fifty daughters of Danaos, in spite of the strongest repugnance of the latter. To escape such a necessity, Danaos placed his fifty daughters on board of a pentecoter (or vessel with fifty oars) and sought refuge at Argôs; touching in his voyage at the island of Rhodes, where he erected a statue of Athênê at Lindos, which was long exhibited as a memorial of his passage. Ægyptos and his sons followed them to Argôs and still pressed their suit, to which Danaos found himself compelled to assent; but on the wedding night he furnished each of his daughters with a dagger, and enjoined them to murder their husbands during the hour of sleep. His orders were obeyed by all, with the single exception of Hypermnêstra, who preserved her husband Lynkeus, incurring displeasure and punishment from her father. He afterwards, however, pardoned her, and when, by the voluntary abdication of Gelanôr, he became king of Argôs, Lynkeus was recognised as his son-in-law and ultimately succeeded him. The remaining daughters, having been purified by Athênê and Hermês, were given in marriage to the victors in a gymnic contest publicly proclaimed. From Danaos was derived the name of Danai, applied to the inhabitants of the Argeian territory, and to the Homeric Greeks

57

generally.

From the legend of the Danaïdes we pass to two barren names of kings, Lynkeus and his son Abas. The two sons of Abas were Akrisios and Prœtos, who, after much dissension, divided between them the Argeian territory: Akrisios ruling at Argôs, and Prœtos at Tiryns. The families of both formed the theme of romantic stories. To pass over for the present the legend of Bellerophôn, and the unrequited passion which the wife of Prestos conceived for him, we are told that the daughters of Prœtos, beautiful, and solicited in marriage by suitors from all Greece-were smitten with leprosy and driven mad, wandering in unseemly guise throughout Peloponnêsus. The visitation had overtaken them, according to Hesiod, because they refused to take part in the Bacchic rites; according to Pherekydês and the Argeian Akusilaus, because they had treated scornfully the wooden statue and simple equipments of Hêrê. The religious character of the old legend here displays itself in a remarkable manner. Unable to cure his daughters, Prœtos invoked the aid of the renowned Pylian prophet and leech, Melampus son of Amythaôn, who undertook to remove the malady on condition of being rewarded with the third part of the kingdom. Prœtos indignantly refused these conditions, but the state of his daughters becoming aggravated and intolerable, he was compelled again to apply to Melampus, who, on the second request, raised his demands still higher, and required another third of the kingdom for his brother Bias. These terms being acceded to, he performed his part of the covenant. He appeased the wrath of Hêrê by prayer and sacrifice; or, according to another account, he approached the deranged women at the head of a troop of young men, with shouting and ecstatic dance, the ceremonies appropriate to the Bacchic worship of Dionysos, and in this manner effected their cure. Melampus, a name celebrated in many different Grecian mythes, is the legendary founder and progenitor of a great and long-continued family of prophets. He and his brother Bias became kings of separate portions of the Argeian territory; he is recognised as ruler there even in the Odyssey, and the prophet Theoklymenos, his grandson, is protected and carried to Ithaca by Têlemachus. Herodotus also alludes to the cure of the women, and to the double kingdom of Melampus and Bias in the Argeian land. He recognises Melampus as the first person who introduced to the knowledge of the Greeks the name and worship of Dionysos, with its appropriate sacrifices and phallic processions. Here again he historicises various features of the old legend in a manner not unworthy of notice.

But Danaê, the daughter of Akrisios, with her son Perseus acquired still greater celebrity than her cousins the Prœtides. An oracle had apprised Akrisios that his daughter would give birth to a son by whose hand he would himself be slain. To guard against this danger, he imprisoned Danaê in a chamber of brass under ground. But the god Zeus had become amorous of her, and found means to descend through the roof in the form of a shower of gold; the consequence of his visits was the birth of Perseus. When Akrisios discovered that his daughter had given existence to a son, he enclosed both the mother and the child in a coffer, which he cast into the sea. The coffer was carried to the isle of Seriphos, where Diktys, brother of the king Polydektês, fished it up, and rescued both Danaê and Perseus. The exploits of Perseus, when he grew up, against the three Phorkydes or daughters of Phorkys, and the three Gorgons, are among the most marvellous and imaginative in all Grecian legend: they bear a stamp almost Oriental. I shall not here repeat the details of those unparalleled hazards which the special favour of Athênê enabled him to overcome, and which ended in his bringing back from Libya the terrific head of the Gorgon Medusa, endued with the property of turning every one who looked upon it into stone. In his return, he rescued Andromeda, daughter of Kêpheus, who had been exposed to be devoured by a sea-monster, and brought her back as his wife. Akrisios trembled to see him after this victorious expedition, and retired into Thessaly to avoid him; but Perseus followed him thither, and having succeeded in calming his apprehensions, became competitor in a gymnic contest where his grandfather was among the spectators. By an incautious swing of his quoit, he unintentionally struck Akrisios, and caused his death: the predictions of the oracle were thus at last fulfilled. Stung with remorse at the catastrophe, and unwilling to return to Argôs, which had been the principality of Akrisios, Perseus made an exchange with Megapenthês, son of Prœtos king of Tiryns. Megapenthês became king of Argôs, and Perseus of Tiryns; moreover, the latter founded, within ten miles of Argôs, the far-famed city of Mykênæ. The massive walls of this city, like those of Tiryns, of which remains are yet to be seen, were built for him by the Lykian Cyclôpes.

We here reach the commencement of the Perseid dynasty of Mykênæ. It should be noticed, however, that there were among the ancient legends contradictory accounts of the foundation of this city. Both the Odyssey and the Great Eoiai enumerated, among the heroines, Mykênê, the Eponyma of the city; the former poem classifying her with Tyrô and Alkmênê, the latter describing her as the daughter of Inachus and wife of Arestôr. And Akusilaus mentioned an eponymous Mykêheus, the son of Spartôn and grandson of

LEGENDARY GREECE

Phorôneus.

The prophetic family of Melampus maintained itself in one of the three parts of the divided Argeian kingdom for five generations, down to Amphiaraos and his sons Alkmæon and Amphilochos. The dynasty of his brother Bias, and that of Megapenthês, son of Prœtos, continued each for four generations: a list of barren names fills up the interval. The Perseids of Mykênæ boasted a descent long and glorious, heroic as well as historical, continuing down to the last sovereigns of Sparta. The issue of Perseus was numerous; his son Alkæos was father of Amphitryon; another of his sons, Elektryon, was father of Alkmênê; a third, Sthenelos, father of Eurystheus.

After the death of Perseus, Alkæos and Amphitryôn dwelt at Tiryns. The latter became engaged in a quarrel with Elektryôn respecting cattle, and in a fit of passion killed him; moreover the piratical Taphians from the west coast of Akarnania invaded the country, and slew the sons of Elektryôn, so that Alkmênê alone was left of that family. She was engaged to wed Amphitryôn: but she bound him by oath not to consummate the marriage until he had avenged upon the Têleboæ the death of her brothers. Amphitryôn, compelled to flee the country as the murderer of his uncle, took refuge in Thêbes, whither Alkmênê accompanied him; Sthenelos was left in possession of Tiryns. The Kadmeians of Thêbes, together with the Lokrians and Phokians, supplied Amphitryôn with troops, which he conducted against the Têleboæ and the Taphians, yet he could not have subdued them without the aid of Komætho, daughter of the Taphian king Pterelaus, who conceived a passion for him, and cut off from her father's head the golden lock to which Poseidôn had attached the gift of immortality. Having conquered and expelled his enemies, Amphitryôn returned to Thêbes, impatient to consummate his marriage; but Zeus on the wedding-night assumed his form and visited Alkmênê before him: he had determined to produce from her a son superior to all his prior offspring, "a specimen of invincible force both to gods and men." At the proper time, Alkmênê was delivered of twin sons: Hêraklês the offspring of Zeus, and the inferior and unhonoured Iphiklês, offspring of Amphitryôn.

Birth of Hêraklês.

When Alkmênê was on the point of being delivered at Thêbes, Zeus publicly boasted among the assembled gods, at the instigation of the mischief-making Atê, that there was on that day about to be born on earth, from his breed, a son who should rule over all his neighbours. Hêrê treated this as an empty boast, calling upon him to bind himself by an irremissible oath that the prediction should be realised. Zeus incautiously pledged his solemn word, upon which Hêrê darted swiftly down from Olympus to the Achaic Argus, where the wife of Sthenelos (son of Perseus, and therefore grandson of Zeus) was already seven months gone with child. By the aid of the Eileithyiæ, the special goddesses of parturition, she caused Eurystheus, the son of Sthenelos, to be born before his time on that very day, while she retarded the delivery of Alkmênê. Then returning to Olympus, she announced the fact to Zeus. "The good man Eurystheus, son of the Perseid Sthenelos, is this day born of thy loins, the sceptre of the Argeians worthily belongs to him." Zeus was thunderstruck at the consummation which he had improvidently bound himself to accomplish. He seized Atê his evil counsellor by the hair, and hurled her forever away from Olympus, but he had no power to avert the ascendency of Eurystheus and the servitude of Hêraklês. "Many a pang did he suffer, when he saw his favourite son going through his degrading toil in the tasks imposed upon him by Eurystheus."

The legend, of unquestionable antiquity, here transcribed from the Iliad, is one of the most pregnant and characteristic in the Grecian mythology. It explains, according to the religious ideas familiar to the old epic poets, both the distinguishing attributes and the endless toil and endurances of Hêraklês, the most renowned and most ubiquitous of all the semi-divine personages worshipped by the Hellenes, a being of irresistible force, and especially beloved by Zeus, yet condemned constantly to labour for others and to obey the commands of a worthless and cowardly persecutor. His recompense is reserved to the close of his career, when his afflicting trials are brought to a close; he is then admitted to the godhead and receives in marriage Hêbê. The twelve labours, as they are called, too notorious to be here detailed, form a very small fraction of the exploits of this mighty being, which ruled the Hêrakleian epics of the ancient poets. He is found not only in most parts of Hellas, but throughout all the other regions then known to the Greeks, from Gadês to the river Thermôdon in the Euxine and to Scythia, overcoming all difficulties and vanquishing all opponents. Distinguished families are everywhere to be traced who bear his patronymic, and glory in the belief that they are his descendants. Among Achæans, Kadmeians, and Dôrians, Hêraklês, is venerated; the latter especially treat him as their principal hero, the Patron Hero-God of the race; the Hêrakleids form among all Dôrians a privileged gens, in which at Sparta the special lineage of the two kings was included.

His character lends itself to mythes countless in number as well as disparate in their character. The irresistible force remains constant, but it is sometimes applied with reckless violence against friends as well us enemies, sometimes devoted to the relief of the oppressed. The comic writers often brought him out as a coarse and stupid glutton, while the Keian philosopher Prodikos, without at all distorting the type, extracted from it the simple, impressive, and imperishable apologue still known as the Choice of Hercules.

After the death and apotheosis of Hêraklês, his son Hyllos and his other children were expelled and persecuted by Eurystheus; the fear of his vengeance deterred both the Trachinian king Kêyx and the Thêbans from harbouring them, and the Athenians alone were generous enough to brave the risk of offering them shelter. Eurystheus invaded Attica, but perished in the attempt by the hand of Hyllos, or by that of Iolaos, the old companion and nephew of Hêraklês. The chivalrous courage which the Athenians had on this occasion displayed in behalf of oppressed innocence, was a favourite theme for subsequent eulogy by Attic poets and orators.

All the sons of Eurystheus lost their lives in the battle along with him, so that the Perseid family was now represented only by the Hêrakleids, who collected an army and endeavoured to recover the possessions from which they had been expelled. The united forces of Iônians, Achæans, and Arcadians, then inhabiting Peloponnêsus, met the invaders at the isthmus, when Hyllos, the eldest of the sons of Hêraklês, proposed that the contest should be determined by a single combat between himself and any champion of the opposing army. It was agreed, that if Hyllos were victorious, the Hêrakleids should be restored to their possessions – if he were vanquished, that they should forego all claim for the space of a hundred years, or fifty years, or three generations, for in the specification of the time, accounts differ. Echemos, the hero of Tegea in Arcadia, accepted the challenge, and Hyllos was slain in the encounter; in consequence of which the Hêrakleids retired, and resided along with the Dôrians under the protection of Ægimios, son of Dôrus. As soon as the stipulated period of truce had expired, they renewed their attempt upon Peloponnêsus conjointly with the Dôrians, and with complete success; the great Dôrian establishments of Argôs, Sparta, and Messênia were the result. The details of this victorious invasion will be hereafter recounted.

Sikyôn, Phlios, Epidauros, and Trœzen all boasted of respected eponyms and a genealogy of dignified length, not exempt from the usual discrepancies – but all just as much entitled to a place on the tablet of history as the more renowned Æolids or Hêrakleids. I omit them here because I wish to impress upon the reader's mind the salient features and character of the legendary world, not to load his memory with a full list of legendary names.

LEGENDARY GREECE

V. DEUKALIÔN, HELLÊN, SONS OF HELLÊN.

In the Hesiodic Theogony, as well as in the "Works and Days," the legend of Promêtheus and Epimêtheus presents an import religious, ethical, and social, and in this sense it is carried forward by Æschylus; but to neither of the characters is any genealogical function assigned. The Hesiodic Catalogue of Women brought both of them into the stream of Grecian legendary lineage, representing Deukaliôn as the son of Promêtheus and Pandôra, and seemingly his wife Pyrrha as daughter of Epimêtheus.

Deukaliôn is important in Grecian mythical narrative under two points of view. First, he is the person specially saved at the time of the general deluge; next, he is the father of Hellen, the great eponym of the Hellenic race; at least this was the more current story, though there were other statements which made Hellên the son of Zeus.

The name of Deukaliôn is originally connected with the Lokrian towns of Kynos and Opus, and with the race of the Leleges, but he appears finally as settled in Thessaly, and ruling in the portion of that country called Phthiôtis. According to what seems to have been the old legendary account, it is the deluge which transferred him from the one to the other; but according to another statement, framed in more historicising times, he conducted a body of Kurêtês and Leleges into Thessaly. and expelled the prior Pelasgian occupants.

The enormous iniquity with which earth was contaminated – as Apollodôrus says, by the then existing brazen race, or at others say, by the fifty monstrous sons of Lykaôn – provoked Zeus to send a general deluge. An unremitting and terrible rain laid the whole of Greece under water, except the highest mountain-tops, whereon a few stragglers found refuge. Deukaliôn was saved in a chest or ark, which he had been forewarned by his father Promêtheus to construct. After floating for nine days on the water, he at length landed on the summit of Mount Parnassus. Zeus having sent Hermês to him, promising to grant whatever he asked, he prayed that men and companions might be sent to him in his solitude: accordingly Zeus directed both him and Pyrrha to cast stones over their heads; those cast by Pyrrha became women, those by Deukaliôn men. And thus the "stony race of men" (if we may be allowed to translate an etymology which the Greek language presents exactly, and which has not been disdained by Hesiod, by Pindar, by Epicharmus, and by Virgil) came to tenant the soil of Greece. Deukaliôn on greater celebrity than her cousins the Prœtides. An oracle had apprised Akrisios that his daughter would give birth to a son by whose hand he would himself be slain. To guard against this danger, he imprisoned Danaê in a chamber of brass under ground. But the god Zeus had become amorous of her, and found means to descend through the roof in the form of a shower of gold; the consequence of his visits was the birth of Perseus. When Akrisios discovered that his daughter had given existence to a son, he enclosed both the mother and the child in a coffer, which he cast into the sea. The coffer was carried to the isle of Seriphos, where Diktys, brother of the king Polydektês, fished it up, and rescued both Danaê and Perseus. The exploits of Perseus, when he grew up, against the three Phorkydes or daughters of Phorkys, and the three Gorgons, are among the most marvellous and imaginative in all Grecian legend: they bear a stamp almost Oriental. I shall not here repeat the details of those unparalleled hazards which the special favour of Athênê enabled him to overcome, and which ended in his bringing back from Libya the terrific head of the Gorgon Medusa, endued with the property of turning every one who looked upon it into stone. In his return, he rescued Andromeda, daughter of Kêpheus, who had been exposed to be devoured by a sea-monster, and brought her back as his wife. Akrisios trembled to see him after this victorious expedition, and retired into Thessaly to avoid him; but Perseus followed him thither, and having succeeded in calming his apprehensions, became competitor in a gymnic contest where his grandfather was among the spectators. By an incautious swing of his quoit, he unintentionally struck Akrisios, and caused his death: the predictions of the oracle were thus at last fulfilled. Stung with remorse at the catastrophe, and unwilling to return to Argôs, which had been the principality of Akrisios, Perseus made an exchange with Megapenthês, son of Prœtos king of Tiryns. Megapenthês became king of Argôs, and Perseus of Tiryns; moreover, the latter founded, within ten miles of Argôs, the far-famed city of Mykênæ. The massive walls of this city, like those of Tiryns, of which remains are yet to be seen, were built for him by the Lykian Cyclôpes.

We here reach the commencement of the Perseid dynasty of Mykênæ. It should be noticed, however, that there were among the ancient legends contradictory accounts of the foundation of this city. Both the Odyssey and the Great Eoiai enumerated, among the heroines, Mykênê, the Eponyma of the city; the former poem classifying her with Tyrô and Alkmênê, the latter describing her as the daughter of Inachus and wife of Arestôr. And Akusilaus mentioned an eponymous Mykêheus, the son of Spartôn and grandson of

Phorôneus.

The prophetic family of Melampus maintained itself in one of the three parts of the divided Argeian kingdom for five generations, down to Amphiaraos and his sons Alkmæon and Amphilochos. The dynasty of his brother Bias, and that of Megapenthês, son of Prœtos, continued each for four generations: a list of barren names fills up the interval. The Perseids of Mykênæ boasted a descent long and glorious, heroic as well as historical, continuing down to the last sovereigns of Sparta. The issue of Perseus was numerous; his son Alkæos was father of Amphitryon; another of his sons, Elektryon, was father of Alkmênê; a third, Sthenelos, father of Eurystheus.

After the death of Perseus, Alkæos and Amphitryôn dwelt at Tiryns. The latter became engaged in a quarrel with Elektryôn respecting cattle, and in a fit of passion killed him; moreover the piratical Taphians from the west coast of Akarnania invaded the country, and slew the sons of Elektryôn, so that Alkmênê alone was left of that family. She was engaged to wed Amphitryôn: but she bound him by oath not to consummate the marriage until he had avenged upon the Têleboæ the death of her brothers. Amphitryôn, compelled to flee the country as the murderer of his uncle, took refuge in Thêbes, whither Alkmênê accompanied him; Sthenelos was left in possession of Tiryns. The Kadmeians of Thêbes, together with the Lokrians and Phokians, supplied Amphitryôn with troops, which he conducted against the Têleboæ and the Taphians, yet he could not have subdued them without the aid of Komæthô, daughter of the Taphian king Pterelaus, who conceived a passion for him, and cut off from her father's head the golden lock to which Poseidôn had attached the gift of immortality. Having conquered and expelled his enemies, Amphitryôn returned to Thêbes, impatient to consummate his marriage; but Zeus on the wedding-night assumed his form and visited Alkmênê before him: he had determined to produce from her a son superior to all his prior offspring, "a specimen of invincible force both to gods and men." At the proper time, Alkmênê was delivered of twin sons: Hêraklês the offspring of Zeus, and the inferior and unhonoured Iphiklês, offspring of Amphitryôn.

Birth of Hêraklês.

When Alkmênê was on the point of being delivered at Thêbes, Zeus publicly boasted among the assembled gods, at the instigation of the mischief-making Atê, that there was on that day about to be born on earth, from his breed, a son who should rule over all his neighbours. Hêrê treated

V. DEUKALIÔN, HELLÊN, SONS OF HELLÊN.

landing from the ark sacrificed a grateful offering to Zeus Phyxios, or the God of escape; he also erected altars in Thessaly to the twelve great gods of Olympus.

The reality of this deluge was firmly believed throughout the historical ages of Greece; the chronologers, reckoning up by genealogies, assigned the exact date of it, and placed it at the same time as the conflagration of the world by the rashness of Phaëthôn, during the reign of Krotôpas king of Argus, the seventh from Inachus. The meteorological work of Aristotle admits and reasons upon this deluge as an unquestionable fact, though he alters the locality by placing it west of Mount Pindus, near Dôdôna and the river Achelôus. He at the same time treats it as a physical phænomenon, the result of periodic cycles in the atmosphere, thus departing from the religious character of the old legend, which described it as a judgment inflicted by Zeus upon a wicked race. Statements founded upon this event were in circulation throughout Greece even to a very late date. The Megarians affirmed that Megaros, their hero, son of Zeus by a local nymph, had found safety from the waters on the lofty summit of their mountain Geraneia, which had not been completely submerged. In the magnificent temple of the Olympian Zeus at Athens, a cavity in the earth was shown, through which it was affirmed that the waters of the deluge had retired. Even in the time of Pausanias, the priests poured into this cavity holy offerings of meal and honey. In this, as in other parts of Greece, the idea of the Deukalionian deluge was blended with the religious impressions of the people and commemorated by their sacred ceremonies.

The offspring of Deukaliôn and Pyrrha were two sons, Hellên and Amphiktyôn, and a daughter, Prôtogeneia, whose son by Zeus was Aëthlius: it was however maintained by many, that Hellên was the son of Zeus and not of Deukaliôn. Hellên had by a nymph three sons, Dôrus, Xuthus, and Æolus. He gave to those who had been before called Greeks, the name of Hellenes, and partitioned his territory among his three children. Æolus reigned in Thessaly; Xnthus received Peloponnêsus, and had by Kreüsa as his sons, Achæus and Iôn; while Dôrus occupied the country lying opposite to the Peloponnêsus, on the northern side of the Corinthian Gulf. These three gave to the inhabitants of their respective countries the names of Æolians, Achæans and Iônians, and Dôrians.

Such is the genealogy as we find it in Apollodôrus. In so far as the names and filiation are concerned, many points in it are given differently, or

65

implicitly contradicted, by Euripidês and other writers. Though as literal and personal history it deserves no notice, its import is both intelligible and comprehensive. It expounds and symbolises the first fraternal aggregation of Hellenic men, together with their territorial distribution and the institutions which they collectively venerated.

There were two great holding-points in common for every section of Greeks. One was the Amphiktyonic assembly, which met half-yearly, alternately at Delphi and at Thermopylæ; originally and chiefly for common religious purposes, but indirectly and occasionally embracing political and social objects along with them. The other was, the public festivals or games, of which the Olympic came first in importance; next, the Pythian, Nemean and Isthmian, institutions which combined religious solemnities with recreative effusion and hearty sympathies, in a manner so imposing and so unparalleled. Amphiktyôn represents the first of these institutions, and Aëthlius the second. As the Amphiktyonic assembly was always especially connected with Thermopylæ and Thessally; Amphiktyôn is made the son of the Thessalian Deukaliôn, but as the Olympic festival was nowise locally connected with Deukaliôn, Aëthlius is represented as having Zeus for his father, and as touching Deukaliôn only through the maternal line. It will be seen presently, that the only matter predicated respecting Aëthlius is, that he settled in the territory of Elis, and begat Endymiôn: this brings him into local contact with the Olympic games, and his function is then ended.

Division of Hellas: Æolians, Dôrians, Iônians.

Having thus got Hellas as an aggregate with its main cementing forces, we march on to its subdivision into parts, through Æolus, Dôrus and Xuthus, the three sons of Hellen; a distribution which is far from being exhaustive, nevertheless, the genealogists whom Apollodôrus follows recognise no more than three sons.

The genealogy is essentially post-Homeric, for Homer knows Hellas and the Hellenes only in connection with a portion of Achaia Phthiôtis. But as it is recognised in the Hesiodic Catalogue – composed probably within the first century after the commencement of recorded Olympiads, or before 676 B.C. – the peculiarities of it, dating from so early a period, deserve much attention. We may remark, first, that it seems to exhibit to us Dôrus and Æolus as the only pure and genuine offspring of Hellen. For their brother Xuthus is not enrolled as an eponymous, he neither founds nor names any people; it is only his sons

V. DEUKALIÔN, HELLÊN, SONS OF HELLÊN.

Achæus and Iôn, after his blood has been mingled with that of the Erechtheid Kreüsa, who become eponyms and founders, each of his own separate people. Next, as to the territorial distribution, Xuthus receives Peloponnêsus from his father, and unites himself with Attica (which the author of this genealogy seems to have conceived as originally unconnected with Hellen) by his marriage with the daughter of the indigenous hero, Erechtheus. The issue of this marriage, Achæus and Iôn, present to us the population of Peloponnêsus and Attica conjointly as related among themselves by the the the of brotherhood, but as one degree more distant both from Dôrians and Æolians. Æolus reigns over the regions about Thessaly, and called the people in those parts Æolians; while Dôrus occupies "the country over against Peloponnêsus on the opposite side of the Corinthian Gulf," and calls the inhabitants after himself, Dôrians. It is at once evident that this designation is in no way applicable to the confined district between Parnassus and Œta, which alone is known by the name of Dôris, and its inhabitants by that of Dôrians, in the historical ages. In the view of the author of this genealogy, the Dôrians are the original occupants of the large range of territory north of the Corinthian Gulf, comprising Ætôlia, Phôkis, and the territory of the Ozolian Lokrians. And this farther harmonises with the other legend noticed by Apollodôrus, when he states that Ætôlus, son of Endymiôn, having been forced to expatriate from Peloponnêsus, crossed into the Küretid territory, and was there hospitably received by Dôrus, Laodokus and Polypœtês, sons of Apollo and Phthia. He slew his hosts, acquired the territory, and gave to it the name of Ætôlia; his son Pleurôn married Xanthippê, daughter of Dôrus, while his other son, Kalydôn, marries Æolia, daughter of Amythaôn. Here again we have the name of Dôrus, or the Dôrians, connected with the tract subsequently termed Ætôlia. That Dôrus should in one place be called the son of Apollo and Phthia, and in another place the son of Hellên by a nymph, will surprise no one accustomed to the fluctuating personal nomenclature of these old legends; moreover the name of Phthia is easy to reconcile with that of Hellen, as both are identified with the same portion of Thessaly, even from the days of the Iliad.

This story, that the Dôrians were at one time the occupants, or the chief occupants, of the range of territory between the river Achelôus and the northern shore of the Corinthian Gulf, is at least more suitable to the facts attested by historical evidence than the legends given in Herodotus, who represents the Dôrians as originally in the Phthiôtid, then as passing under Dôrus, the son of Hellen, into the Histiæôtid, under the mountains of Ossa and Olympus; next, as driven by the Kadmeians into the regions of Pindus; from thence passing into the Dryopid territory, on Mount Œta; lastly, from thence into Peloponnêsus. The received story was, that the great Dôrian establishments in Peloponnêsus were formed by invasion from the north, and that the invaders crossed the gulf from Naupaktus, a statement which, however disputable with respect to Argôs, seems highly probable in regard both to Sparta and Messênia. That the name of Dôrians comprehended far more than the inhabitants of the insignificant tetrapolis of Dôris Proper, must be assumed, if we believe that they conquered Sparta and Messênia; both the magnitude of the conquest itself, and the passage of a large portion of them from Naupaktus. harmonise with the legend as given by Apollodorus, in which the Dôrians are represented as the principal inhabitants of the northern shore of the gulf. The statements which we find in Herodotus, respecting the early migrations of the Dôrians, have been considered as possessing greater historical value than those of the fabulist Apollodôrus. Both are equally matter of legend, while the brief indications of the latter seem to be most in harmony with the facts which we afterwards find attested by history.

It has already been mentioned that the genealogy which makes Æolus, Xuthus and Dôrus sons of Hellen, is as old as the Hesiodic Catalogue: probably also that which makes Hellên son of Deukaliôn. Aëthlius also is an Hesiodic personage; whether Amphiktyôn be so or not, we have no proof. They could not have been introduced into the legendary genealogy until after the Olympic games and the Amphiktyonic council had acquired an established an established and extensive reverence throughout Greece.

Respecting Dôrus the son of Hellên, we find neither legends nor legendary genealogy; respecting Xuthus, very little beyond the tale of Kreüsa and Iôn, which has its place more naturally among the Attic fables. Achæus however, who is here represented as the son of Xuthus, appears in other stories with very different parentage and accompaniments. According to the statement which we find in Dionysius of Halicarnassus, Achæus, Phthius and Pelasgus are sons of Poseidôn and Larissa. They migrate from Peloponnêsus into Thessaly, and distribute the Thessalian territory between them, giving their names to its principal divisions; their descendants in the sixth generation were driven out of that country by the invasion of Deukaliôn at the head of the Kurêtês and the Leleges. This was the story of those who wanted to provide an eponymous for the Achæans in the southern districts of Thessaly; Pausanias accomplishes the same object by different means, representing Achæus, the son of Xuthus as having gone back to Thessaly and occupied the portion of it to which his father was entitled. Then, by way of explaining how it was that there were Achæans at Sparta and at Argôs, he tells us that Archander and Architelês, the sons of Archaeus, came back from Thessaly to Peloponnêsus, and married two daughters of Danaus; they acquired great influence at Argôs and Sparta, and gave to the people the name of Achæans after their father Achæus.

Euripidês also deviates very materially from the Hesiodic genealogy in respect to these eponymous persons. In the drama called Iôn, he describes Iôn as son of Kreüsa by Apollo, but adopted by Xuthus; according to him, the real sons of Xuthus and Kreüsa are Dôrus and Achæus, eponyms of the Dôrians and Achæans in the interior of Peloponnêsus. It is a still more capital point of difference, that he omits Hellên altogether – making Xuthus an Achæan by race, the son of Æolus, who is the son of Zeus. This is the more remarkable, as in the fragments of two other dramas of Euripidês, the Melanippê and the Æolus, we find Hellên mentioned both as father of Æolus and son of Zeus. To the general public even of the most instructed city of Greece, fluctuations and discrepancies in these mythical genealogies seem to have been neither surprising nor offensive.

VI. ÆOLIDS - SONS & DAUGHTERS OF ÆOLUS.

If two of the sons of Hellên, Dôrus and Xuthus, present to us families comparatively unnoticed in mythical narrative, the third son, Æolus, richly makes up for the deficiency. From him we pass to his seven sons and five daughters, amidst a great abundance of heroic and poetical incident.

In dealing however with these extensive mythical families, it is necessary to observe, that the legendary world of Greece, in the manner in which it is presented to us, appears invested with a degree of symmetry and coherence which did not originally belong to it. For the old ballads and stories which were sung or recounted at the multiplied festivals of Greece, each on its special theme, have been lost: the religious narratives, which the Exegêtês of every temple had present to his memory, explanatory of the peculiar religious ceremonies and local customs in his own town or Dême, have passed away. All these primitive elements, originally distinct and unconnected, are removed out of our sight, and we possess only an aggregate result, formed by many confluent streams of fable, and connected together by the agency of subsequent poets and logographers. Even the earliest agents in this work of connecting and systematising – the Hesiodic poets – have been hardly at all preserved. Our information respecting Grecian mythology is derived chiefly from the prose logographers who followed them, and in whose works, since a continuous narrative was above all things essential to them, the fabulous personages are woven into still more comprehensive pedigrees, and the original isolation of the legends still better disguised. Hekatæus, Pherekydês, Hellanikus, and Akusilaus lived at a time when the idea of Hellas as one great whole, composed of fraternal sections, was deeply rooted in the mind of every Greek: and when the hypothesis of a few great families, branching out widely from one common stem, was more popular and acceptable than that of a distinct indigenous origin in each of the separate districts. These logographers, indeed, have themselves been lost; but Apollodôrus and the various scholiasts, our great immediate sources of information respecting Grecian mythology, chiefly borrowed from them. So that the legendary world of Greece is in fact known to us through them, combined with the dramatic and Alexandrine poets, their Latin imitators, and the still later class of scholiasts – except indeed such occasional glimpses as we obtain from the Iliad and the Odyssey, and the remaining Hesiodic fragments, which exhibit but too frequently a hopeless diversity when confronted with the narratives of the logographers.

VI. ÆOLIDS - SONS & DAUGHTERS OF ÆOLUS.

Though Æolus (as has been already stated) is himself called the son of Hellên along with Dôrus and Xuthus, yet the legends concerning the Æolids, far from being dependent upon this genealogy, are not all even coherent with it; moreover the name cf Æolus in the legend is older than that of Hellên, inasmuch as it occurs both in the Iliad and Odyssey. Odysseus sees in the under-world the beautiful Tyrô, daughter of Salmôneus, and wife of Krêtheus, son of Æolus.

Æolus is represented as having reigned in Thessaly; his seven sons were Krêtheus, Sisyphus, Athamas, Salmôneus, Deiôn, Magnês and Periêrês; his fire daughters, Canacê, Alcyonê, Peisidikê, Calycê and Perimêdê. The fables of this race seem to be distinguished by a constant introduction of the god Poseidôn, as well as by an unusual prevalence of haughty and presumptuous attributes among the Æolid heroes, leading them to affront the gods by pretences of equality, and sometimes even by defiance The worship of Poseidôn must probably have been diffused and pre-eminent among a people with whom these legends originated.

I. Sons of Æolus.

Salmôneus is not described in the Odyssey as son of Æolus, but he is so denominated both in the Hesiodic Catalogue, and by the subsequent logographers. His daughter Tyrô became enamoured of the river Enipeus, the most beautiful of all streams that traverse the earth; she frequented the banks assiduously, and there the god Poseidôn found means to indulge his passion for her, assuming the character of the river god himself. The fruit of this alliance were the twin brothers, Pelias and Nêleus. Tyrô afterwards was given in marriage to her uncle Krêtheus, another son of Æolus, by whom she had Æsôn, Pherês and Amythaôn – all names of celebrity in the heroic legends. The adventures of Tyrô formed the subject of an affecting drama of Sophokles, now lost. Her father had married a second wife, named Sidêrô, whose cruel counsels induced him to punish and torture his daughter on account of her intercourse with Poseidôn. She was shorn of her magnificent hair, beaten and ill-used in various ways, and confined in a loathsome dungeon. Unable to take care of her two children, she had been compelled to expose them immediately on their birth in a little boat on the river Enipeus; they were preserved by the kindness of a herdsman, and when grown up to manhood, rescued their mother, and revenged her wrongs by putting to death the iron-hearted Sidêrô. This pathetic tale respecting the long imprisonment of Tyrô is substituted by

Sophokles in place of the Homeric legend, which represented her to have become the wife of Krêtheus and mother of a numerous offspring.

Her father, the unjust Salmôneus, exhibited in his conduct the most insolent impiety towards the gods. He assumed the name and title even of Zeus, and caused to be offered to himself the sacrifices destined for that god; he also imitated the thunder and lightning, by driving about with brazen caldrons attached to his chariot and casting lighted torches towards heaven. Such wickedness finally drew upon him the wrath of Zeus, who smote him with a thunderbolt, and effaced from the earth the city which he had founded, with all its inhabitants.

Pelias and Nêleus, "both stout vassals of the great Zeus," became engaged in dissension respecting the kingdom of Iôlkos in Thessaly. Pelias got possession of it, and dwelt there in plenty and prosperity, but he had offended the goddess Hêrê by killing Sidêrô upon her altar, and the effects of her wrath were manifested in his relations with his nephew Jasôn.

Nêleus quitted Thessaly, went into Peloponnêsus, and there founded the kingdom of Pylos. He purchased by immense marriage presents, the privilege of wedding the beautiful Chlôris, daughter of Amphiôn, king of Orchomenos, by whom he had twelve sons and but one daughter – the fair and captivating Pêrô, whom suitors from all the neighbourhood courted in marriage. But Nêleus, "the haughtiest of living men," refused to entertain the pretensions of any of them; he would grant his daughter only to that man who should bring to him the oxen of Iphiklos, from Phylakê in Thessaly. These precious animals were carefully guarded, as well by herdsmen as by a dog whom neither man nor animal could approach. Nevertheless, Bias, the son of Amythaôn, nephew of Nêleus, being desperately enamoured of Pêrô, prevailed upon his brother Melampus to undertake for his sake the perilous adventure, in spite of the prophetic knowledge of the latter, which forewarned him that though he would ultimately succeed, the prize must be purchased by severe captivity and suffering. Melampus, in attempting to steal the oxen, was seized and put in prison, from whence nothing but his prophetic powers rescued him. Being acquainted with the language of worms, he heard these animals communicating to each other, in the roof over his head, that the beams were nearly eaten through and about to fall in. He communicated this intelligence to his guards, and demanded to be conveyed to another place of confinement, announcing that the roof would presently fall in and bury them. The prediction was fulfilled, and Phylakos, father of Iphiklos, full of wonder at this specimen of prophetic power,

VI. ÆOLIDS - SONS & DAUGHTERS OF ÆOLUS.

immediately caused him to be released. He further consulted him respecting the condition of his son Iphiklos, who was childless, and promised him the possession of the oxen on condition of his suggesting the means whereby offspring might be ensured. A vulture having communicated to Melampus the requisite information, Podarkês, the son of Iphiklos, was born shortly afterwards. In this manner Melampus obtained possession of the oxen, and conveyed them to Pylos, obtaining for his brother Bias the hand of Pêrô. How this great legendary character, by miraculously healing the deranged daughters of Prœtos, procured both for himself and for Bias dominion in Argôs, has been recounted in a preceding chapter.

Of the twelve sons of Nêleus, one at least, Periklymenos, besides the ever-memorable Nestôr, was distinguished for his exploits as well as for his miraculous gifts. Poseidôn, the divine father of the race, had bestowed upon him the privilege of changing his form at pleasure into that of any bird, beast, reptile, or insect. He had occasion for all these resources, and he employed them for a time with success in defending his family against the terrible indignation of Hêraklês, who, provoked by the refusal of Nêleus to perform for him the ceremony of purification after his murder of Iphitus, attacked the Nêleids at Pylos. Periklymenos by his extraordinary powers prolonged the resistance, but the hour of his fate was at length brought upon him by the intervention of Athênê, who pointed him out to Hêraklês while he was perched as a bee upon the hero's chariot. He was killed, and Hêraklês became completely victorious, overpowering Poseidôn, Hêrê, Arês, and Hadês, and even wounding the three latter, who assisted in thedefence. Eleven of the sons of Nêleus perished by his hand, while Nestôr, then a youth, was preserved only by his accidental absence at Gerêna. away from his father's residence.

The proud house of the Nêleids was now reduced to Nestôr, but Nestôr singly sufficed to sustain its eminence. He appears not only as the defender and avenger of Pylos against the insolence and rapacity of his Epeian neighbours in Elis, but also as aiding the Lapithæ in their terrible combat against the Centaurs, and as companion of Thesêus, Peirithöus, and the other great legendary heroes who preceded the Trojan war. In extreme old age his once marvellous power of handling his weapons has indeed passed away, but his activity remains unimpaired, and his sagacity as well as his influence in counsel is greater than ever. He not only assembles the various Grecian chiefs for the armament, against Troy, perambulating the districts of Hellas along with Odysseus, but takes a vigorous part in the siege itself, and is of pre-eminent service to Agamemnôn. After the conclusion of the siege, he is one of the few Grecian princes who returns to his original dominions, and is found, in a strenuous and honoured old age, in the midst of his children and subjects, sitting with the sceptre of authority on the stone bench before his house at Pylos, offering sacrifice to Poseidôn, as his father Nêleus had done before him, and mourning only over the death of his favourite son Antilochus, who had fallen, along with so many brave companions in arms, in the Trojan war.

After Nestôr the line of the Nêleids numbers undistinguished names, Börus, Penthilus, and Andropompus, three successive generations down to Melanthus, who on the invasion of Peloponnêsus by the Herakleids, quitted Pylos and retired to Athens, where he became king, in a manner which I shall hereafter recount. His son Kodrus was the last Athenian king, and Nêleus, one of the sons of Kodrus, is mentioned as the principal conductor of what is called the Iônic emigration from Athens to Asia Minor. It is certain that during the historical age, not merely the princely family of the Kodrids in Milêtus, Ephesus, and other Iônic cities, but some of the greatest families even in Athens itself, traced their heroic lineage through the Nêleids up to Poseidôn; and the legends respecting Nestôr and Periklymenos would find especial favour amidst Greeks with such feelings and belief. The Kodrids at Ephesus, and probably some other Iônic towns, long retained the title and honorary precedence of kings, even after they had lost the substantial power belonging to the office. They stood in the same relation, embodying both religious worship and supposed ancestry, to the Nêleids and Poseidôn, as the chiefs of the Æolic colonies to Agamemnôn and Orestês. The Athenian despot Peisistratus was named after the son of Nestôr in the Odyssey, and we may safely presume that the heroic worship of the Nêleids was as carefully cherished at the Iônic Milêtus as at the Italian Metapontum.

Having pursued the line of Salmôneus and Nêleus to the end of its legendary career, we may now turn back to that of another son of Æolus, Krêtheus, a line hardly less celebrated in respect of the heroic names which it presents. Alkêstis, the most beautiful of the daughters of Pelias, was promised by her father in marriage to the man that could bring him a lion and a boar tamed to the yoke and drawing together. Admêtus, son of Pherês, the eponymous of Pheræ in Thessaly, and thus grandson of Krêtheus, was enabled by the aid of Apollo to fulfil this condition, and to win her; for Apollo happened at that time to be in his service as a slave (condemned to this penalty by Zeus for having put to death the Cyclôpes), in which capacity he tended the herds and horses with such success, as to equip Eumêlus (the son of Admêtus) to the Trojan war with the finest horses in the Grecian army. Though menial duties were imposed upon him, even to the drudgery of grinding in the mill, he yet carried away with him a grateful and friendly sentiment towards his mortal master, whom he interfered to rescue from the wrath of the goddess Artemis, when she was indignant at the omission of her name in his wedding sacrifices. Admêtus was about to perish by a premature death, when Apollo, by earnest solicitation to the Fates, obtained for him the privilege that his life should be prolonged, if he could find any person to die a voluntary death in his place. His father and his mother both refused to make this sacrifice for him, but the devoted attachment of his wife Alkêstis disposed her to embrace with cheerfulness the condition of dying to preserve her husband. She had already perished when Hêraklês, the ancient guest and friend of Admêtus, arrived during the first, hour of lamentation; his strength and daring enabled him to rescue the deceased Alkêstis even from the grasp of Thanatos (Death), and to restore her alive to her disconsolate husband.

The son of Pelias, Akastus, had received and sheltered Pêleus when obliged to fly his country in consequence of the involuntary murder of Eurytiôn. Krêthêis, the wife of Akastus, becoming enamoured of Pêleus, made to him advances which he repudiated. Exasperated at his refusal, and determined to procure his destruction, she persuaded her husband that Pêleus had attempted her chastity, upon which Akastus conducted Pêleus out upon a hunting excursion among the woody regions of Mount Pêlion, contrived to steal from him the sword fabricated and given by Hêphæstos, and then left him, alone and unarmed, to perish by the hands of the Centaurs or by the wild beasts. By the friendly aid of the Centaur Cheirôn, however, Pêleus was preserved, and his sword restored to him; returning to the city, he avenged himself by putting to death both Akastus and his perfidious wife.

But amongst all the legends with which the name of Pelias is connected, by far the most memorable is that of Jasôn and the Argônautic expedition. Jasôn was son of Æsôn, grandson of Krêtheus, and thus great-grandson of Æolus. Pelias, having consulted the oracle respecting the security of his dominion at Iôlkos, had received in answer a warning to beware of the man who should appear before him with only one sandal. He was celebrating a festival in honour of Poseidôn, when it so happened that Jasôn appeared before him with one of his feet un-sandalled; he had lost one sandal in wading through the swollen current of the river Anauros. Pelias immediately understood that this was the enemy against whom the oracle had forewarned him. As a means of averting the danger, he imposed upon Jasôn the desperate task of bringing back to Iôlkos the Golden Fleece, the fleece of that ram which had carried Phryxos from Achaia to Kolchis, and which Phryxos had dedicated in the latter country as an offering to the god Arês. The result of this injunction was the memorable expedition – of the ship Argô and her crew called the Argônauts, composed of the bravest and noblest youths of Greece – which cannot be conveniently included among the legends of the Æolids, and is reserved for a separate chapter.

The voyage of the Argô was long protracted, and Pelias, persuaded that neither the ship nor her crew would ever return, put to death both the father and mother of Jasôn together with their infant son. Æsôn, the father, being permitted to choose the manner of his own death, drank bull's blood while performing a sacrifice to the gods. At length, however, Jasôn did return, bringing with him not only the golden fleece, but also Mêdea, daughter of Æêtês, king of Kolchis, as his wife; a woman distinguished for magical skill and cunning, by whose assistance alone the Argônauts had succeeded in their project. Though determined to avenge himself upon Pelias, Jasôn knew he could only succeed by stratagem; he remained with his companions at a short distance from Iôlkos, while Mêdea, feigning herself a fugitive from his ill-usage, entered the town alone, and procured access to the daughters of Pelias. By exhibitions of her magical powers she soon obtained unqualified ascendency over their minds. For example, she selected from the flocks of Pelias a ram in the extremity of old age, cut him up and boiled him in a caldron with herbs, and brought him out in the shape of a young and vigorous lamb; the daughters of Pelias were made to believe that their old father could in like manner be restored to youth. In this persuasion they cut him up with their own hands and cast his limbs into the caldron, trusting that Mêdea would produce upon him the same magical effect. Mêdea pretended that an invocation to the moon was a necessary part of the ceremony; she went up to the top of the house as if to pronounce it, and there lighting the fire-signal concerted with the Argônauts. Jasôn and his companions burst in and possessed themselves of the town. Satisfied with having thus revenged himself, Jasôn yielded the principality of Iôlkos to Akastus, son of Pelias, and retired with Mêdea to Corinth. Thus did the goddess Hêrê gratify her ancient wrath against Pelias; she had constantly watched over Jasôn, and had carried the "all-notorious" Argô through its innumerable perils, in order that

Jasôn might bring home Mêdea to accomplish the ruin of his uncle. The misguided daughters of Pelias departed as voluntary exiles to Arcadia; Akastus his son celebrated splendid funeral games in honour of his deceased father.

Jasôn and Mêdea retired from Iôlkos to Corinth, where they resided ten years: their children were – Medeius, whom the Centaur Cheirôn educated in the regions of Mount Pêlion, and Mermerus and Pherês, born at Corinth. After they had resided there ten years in prosperity, Jasôn set his affections on Glaukê, daughter of Kreôn king of Corinth; and as her father was willing to give her to him in marriage, he determined to repudiate Mêdea, who received orders forthwith to leave Corinth. Stung with this insult and bent upon revenge, Mêdea prepared a poisoned robe, and sent it as a marriage present to Glaukê; it was unthinkingly accepted and put on, and the body of the unfortunate bride was burnt up and consumed. Kreôn, her father, who tried to tear from her the burning garment, shared her fate and perished. The exulting Mêdea escaped by means of a chariot with winged serpents furnished to her by her grandfather Hêlios; she placed herself under the protection of Ægeus at Athens, by whom she had a son named Mêdus. She left her young children in the sacred enclosure of the Arkræan Hêrê, relying on the protection of the altar to ensure their safety, but the Corinthians were so exasperated against her for the murder of Kreôn and Glaukê, that they dragged the children away from the altar and put them to death. The miserable Jasôn perished by a fragment of his own ship Argô, which fell upon him while he was asleep under it, being hauled on shore, according to the habitual practice of the ancients.

The first establishment at Ephyrê, or Corinth, had been founded by Sisyphus, another of the sons of Æolas, brother of Salmôneus and Krêtheus. The Æolid Sisyphus was distinguished as an unexampled master of cunning and deceit. He blocked up the road along the isthmus, and killed the strangers who came along it by rolling down upon them great stones from the mountains above. He was more than a match even for the arch thief Autolycus, the son of Hermês, who derived from his father the gift of changing the colour and shape of stolen goods, so that they could no longer be recognised. Sisyphus, by marking his sheep under the foot, detected Autolycus when he stole them, and obliged him to restore the plunder. His penetration discovered the amour of Zeus with the nymph Ægina, daughter of the river-god Asôpus. Zeus had carried her off to the island of Œnônê (which subsequently bore the name of Ægina), upon which Asôpus, eager to recover her, inquired of Sisyphus whither she was gone; the latter told him what had happened, on condition that he should provide a spring of water on the summit of the Acro-Corinthus. Zeus, indignant with Sisyphus for this revelation, inflicted upon him in Hadês the punishment of perpetually heaving up a hill a great and heavy stone, which, so soon as it attained the summit, rolled back again in spite of all his efforts, with irresistible force into the plain.

In the application of the Æolid genealogy to Corinth, Sisyphus, the son of Æolus, appears as the first name, but the old Corinthian poet Eumêlus either found or framed an heroic genealogy for his native city independent both of Æolus and Sisyphus. According to this genealogy, Ephyrê, daughter of Oceanus and Têthys, was the primitive tenant of the Corinthian territory, Asôpus of the Sikyônian: both were assigned to the god Hêlios, in adjusting a dispute between him and Poseidôn, by Briareus. Hêlios divided the territory between his two sons Æêtês and Alôeus: to the former he assigned Corinth, to the latter Sikyôn. Æêtês, obeying the admonition of an oracle, emigrated to Kolchis, leaving his territory under the rule of Bunos, the son of Hermês, with the stipulation that it should be restored whenever either he or any of his descendants returned. After the death of Bunos, both Corinth and Sikyôn were possessed by Epôpeus, son of Alôeus, a wicked man. His son Marathôn left him in disgust and retired into Attica, but returned after his death and succeeded to his territory, which he in turn divided between his two sons Corinthos and Sikyôn, from whom the names of the two districts were first derived. Corinthos died without issue, and the Corinthians then invited Mêdea from Iôlkos as the representative of Æêtês: she with her husband Jasôn thus obtained the sovereignty of Corinth. This legend of Eumêlus, one of the earliest of the genealogical poets, so different from the story adopted by Neophrôn or Euripidês, was followed certainly by Simonidês and seemingly by Theopompus. The incidents in it are imagined and arranged with a view to the supremacy of Mêdea: the emigration of Æêtês and the conditions under which he transferred his sceptre, being so laid out as to confer upon Mêdea an hereditary title to the throne. The Corinthians paid to Mêdea and to her children solemn worship, either divine or heroic, in conjunction with Hêrê Akræa, and this was sufficient to give to Mêdea a prominent place in the genealogy composed by a Corinthian poet, accustomed to blend together gods, heroes and men in the antiquities of his native city. According to the legend of Eumêlus, Jasôn became (through Mêdea) king of Corinth, but she concealed the children of their marriage in

78

the temple of Hêrê, trusting that the goddess would render them immortal. Jasôn, discovering her proceedings, left her and retired in disgust to Iôlkos; Mêdea also, being disappointed in her scheme, quitted the place, leaving the throne in the hands of Sisyphus, to whom, according to the story of Theopompus, she had become attached. Other legends recounted, that Zeus had contracted a passion for Mêdea, but that she had rejected his suit from fear of the displeasure of Hêrê; who, as a recompense for such fidelity, rendered her children immortal; moreover Mêdea had erected, by special command of Hêrê, the celebrated temple of Aphroditê at Corinth. The tenor of these fables manifests their connection with the temple of Hêrê, and we may consider the legend of Mêdea as having been originally quite independent of that of Sisyphus, but fitted on to it, in seeming chronological sequence, so as to satisfy the feelings of those Æolids of Corinth who passed for his descendants.

Sisyphus had for his sons Glaukos and Ornytiôn. From Glaukos sprang Bellerophôn, whose romantic adventures commence with the Iliad, and are further expanded by subsequent poets: according to some accounts he was really the son of Poseidôn, the prominent deity of the Æolid family. The youth and beauty of Bellerophôn rendered him the object of a strong passion on the part of the Anteia, wife of Prœtos king of Argôs. Finding her advances rejected, she contracted a violent hatred towards him, and endeavoured by false accusations to prevail upon her husband to kill him. Prœtos refused to commit the deed under his own roof, but despatched him to his son-in-law the king of Lykia in Asia Minor, putting into his hands a folded tablet full of destructive symbols. Conformably to these suggestions, the most perilous undertakings were imposed upon Bellerophôn. He was directed to attack the monster Chimæra and to conquer the warlike Solymi as well as the Amazons; as he returned victorious from these enterprises, an ambuscade was laid for him by the bravest Lykian warriors, all of whom he slew. At length the Lykian king recognised him "as the genuine son of a god," and gave him his daughter in marriage together with half of his kingdom. The grand-children of Bellerophôn, Glaukos and Sarpêdôn, the latter a son of his daughter Laodameia by Zeus, combat as allies of Troy against the host of Agamemnôn.

We now pass from Sisyphus and the Corinthian fables to another son of Æolus, Athamas, whose family history is not less replete with mournful and tragical incidents, abundantly diversified by the poets. Athamas, we are told, was king of Orchomenos; his wife Nephelê was a goddess, and he had by her two children, Phryxus and Hellê. After a certain time he neglected Nephelê, and took to himself as a new wife Inô, the daughter of Kadmus, by whom he had two sons, Learchus and Melikerttês. Inô, looking upon Phryxus with the hatred of a step-mother, laid a snare for his life. She persuaded the women to roast the seed-wheat, which, when sown in this condition, yielded no crop, so that famine overspread the land. Athamas sent to Delphi to implore counsel and a remedy: he received for answer, through the machinations of Inô with the oracle, that the barrenness of the fields could not be alleviated except by offering Phryxus as a sacrifice to Zeus. The distress of the people compelled him to execute this injunction, and Phryxus was led as a victim to the altar. But the power of his mother Nephelê snatched him from destruction, and procured for him from Hermês a ram with a fleece of gold, upon which he and his sister Hellê mounted and were carried across the sea. The ram took the direction of the Euxine sea and Kolchis: when they were crossing the Hellespont, Hellê fell off into the narrow strait, which took its name from that incident. Upon this, the ram, who was endued with speech, consoled the terrified Phryxus, and ultimately carried him safe to Kolchis. Æêtês, king of Kolchis son of the god Hêlios and brother of Circê, received Phryxus kindly, and gave him his daughter Chalciope in marriage. Phryxus sacrificed the ram to Zeus Phyxios, and suspended the golden fleece in the sacred grove of Arês.

Athamas – according to some both Athamas and Inô – were afterwards driven mad by the anger of the goddess Hêrê; insomuch that the father shot his own son Learchus, and would also have put to death his other son Melikertê if Inô had not snatched him away. She fled with the boy, across the Megarian territory and Mount Geraneia, to the rock Moluris, overhanging the Sarônic Gulf: Athamas pursued her, and in order to escape him she leaped into the sea. She became a sea-goddess under the title of Leukothea; while the body of Melikertês was cast ashore on the neighbouring territory of Schœnus, and buried by his uncle Sisyphus, who was directed by the Nereïds to pay to him heroic honours under the name of Pahæmôn. The Isthmian games, one of the great periodical festivals of Greece, were celebrated in honour of the god Poseidôn in conjunction with Palæmôn as a hero. Athamas abandoned his territory, and became the first settler of a neighbouring region called from him Athmantia, or the Athamantian plain.

The legend of Athamas connects itself with some sanguinary religious rites and very peculiar family customs, which prevailed at Alos, in Achaia Phthiôtis, down to a time later than the historian Herodotus, and of which some remnant existed at Orchomenos even in the days of Plutarch. Athamas was worshipped at Aloe as a hero, having both a chapel and a consecrated grove, attached to the temple of Zeus Laphystios. On the family of which he was the heroic progenitor, a special curse and disability stood affixed. The eldest of the race was forbidden to enter the prytaneion or government-house: if he was found within the doors of the building, the other citizens laid hold of him on his going out, surrounded him with garlands, and led him in solemn procession to be sacrificed as a victim at the altar of Zeus Laphystios. The prohibition carried with it an exclusion from all the public meetings and ceremonies, political as well at religious, and from the sacred fire of the state: many of the individuals marked out had therefore been bold enough to transgress it. Some had been seized on quitting the building and actually sacrificed; others had fled the country for a long time to avoid a similar fate.

The guides who conducted Xerxês and his army through southern Thessaly detailed to him this existing practice, coupled with the local legend, that Athamas, together with Inô, had sought to compass the death of Phryxus, who however had escaped to Kolchis: that the Achæans had been enjoined by an oracle to offer up Athamas himself as an expiatory sacrifice to release the country from the anger of the gods, but that Kytissoros, son of Phryxus, coming back from Kolchis, had intercepted the sacrifice of Athamas, whereby the anger of the gods remained still unappeased, and an undying curse rested upon the family.

That such human sacrifices continued to a greater or less extent, even down to a period later than Herodotus, among the family who worshipped Athamas as their heroic ancestor, appears certain: mention is also made of similar customs in parts of Arcadia, and of Thessaly, in honour of Pêleus and Cheirôn. But we may reasonably presume, that in the period of greater humanity which Herodotus witnessed, actual sacrifice had become very rare. The curse and the legend still remained, but were not called into practical working, except during periods of intense national suffering or apprehension, during which the religious sensibilities were always greatly aggravated. We cannot at all doubt, that during the alarm created by the presence of the Persian king with his immense and ill-disciplined host, the minds of the Thessalians must have been keenly alive to all that was terrific in their national stories, and all that was expiatory in their religious solemnities.

Moreover, the mind of Xerxês himself was so awe-struck by the tale, that he reverenced the dwelling-place consecrated to Athamas. The guides who recounted to him the romantic legend, gave it as the historical and generating cause of the existing rule and practice: a critical inquirer is forced (as has been remarked before) to reverse the order of precedence, and to treat the practice as having been the suggesting cause of its own explanatory legend.

The family history of Athamas, and the worship of Zeus Laphystios, are expressly connected by Herodotus with Alos in Achæa Phthiôtis – one of the towns enumerated in the Iliad as under the command of Achillês. But there was also a mountain called Laphystion, and a temple and worship of Zeus Laphystios between Orchomenos and Korôneia, in the northern portion of the territory known in the historical ages as Bœotia. Here also the family story of Athamas is localised, and Athamas is presented to us as king of the districts of Korôneia, Haliartus and Mount Laphystion: he is thus interwoven with the Orchomenian genealogy. Andreas (we are told), son of the river Pêneios, was the first person who settled in the region: from him it received the name Andrêis. Athamas, coming subsequently to Andreus, received from him the territory of Korôneia and Haliartus with Mount Laphystion: he gave in marriage to Andreus, Euippê, daughter of his son Leucôn, and the issue of this marriage was Eteoklies, said to be the son of the river Kêphisos. Korônos and Haliartus, grandsons of the Corinthian Sisyphus, were adopted by Athamas, as he had lost all his children; but when his grandson Presbôn, son of Phryxus, returned to him from Kolchis, he divided his territory in such manner that Korônos and Haliartus became the founders of the towns which bore their names. Almôn, the son of Sisyphus, also received from Eteoklês a portion of territory, where he established the village Almônes.

With Eteoklês began, according to a statement in one of the Hesiodic poems, the worship of the Charites or Graces, so long and so solemnly continued at Orchomenos in the periodical festival of the Charitêsia, to which many neighbouring towns and districts seem to have contributed. He also distributed the inhabitants into two tribes – Eteokleia and Kêphisias. He died childless, and was succeeded by Almos, who had only two daughters, Chrysê and Chrysogeneia. The son of Chrysê by the god Arês was Phlegyas, the father and founder of the warlike and predatory Phlegyæ, who despoiled every one within their reach, and assaulted not only the pilgrims on their road to Delphi, but even the treasures of the temple itself. The offended god punished them by continued thunder, by earthquakes, and by pestilence, which extinguished all this impious race, except a scanty remnant who fled into Phôkis.

Chrysogeneia, the other daughter of Almos, had for issue, by the god Poseidôn, Minyas: the son of Minyas was Orchomenos. From these two was derived the name both of Minyæ for the people, and of Orchomenos for the town. During the reign of Orchomenos, Hyêttus came to him from Argôs, having become an exile in consequence of the death of Molyros: Orchomenos assigned to him a portion of land, where he founded the village called Hyêttus. Orchomenos, having no issue, was succeeded by Klymenos, son of Presbôn, of the house of Athamas: Klymenos was slain by some Thêbans during the festival of Poseidôn at Onchêstos, and his eldest son, Erginus, to avenge his death, attacked the Thêbans with his utmost force – an attack, in which he was so successful, that the latter were forced to submit, and to pay him an annual tribute.

The Orchomenian power was now at its height: both Minyas and Orchomenos had been princes of surpassing wealth, and the former had built a spacious and durable edifice which he had filled with gold and silver. But the success of Erginus against Thêbes was soon terminated and reversed by the hand of the irresistible Hêraklês, who rejected with disdain the claim of tribute, and even mutilated the envoys sent to demand it: he not only emancipated Thêbes, but broke down and impoverished Orchomenos. Erginus in his old age married a young wife, from which match sprang the illustrious heroes, or gods, Trophônius and Agamêdês: though many (amongst whom is Pausanius himself) believed Trophônius to be the son of Apollo. Trophônius, one of the most memorable persons in Grecian mythology, was worshipped as a god in various places, but with especial sanctity as Zeus Trophônius at Lebadeia: in his temple at this town, the prophetic manifestations outlasted those of Delphi itself. Trophônius and Agamêdês, enjoying matchless renown as architects, built the temple of Delphi, the thalamus of Amphitryôn at Thêbes, as well as the inaccessible vault of Hyrieus at Hyria, in which they are said to have left one stone removable at pleasure, so as to reserve for themselves a secret entrance. They entered so frequently, and stole so much gold and silver, that Hyrieus, astonished at his losses, at length spread a fine net, in which Agamêdês was inextricably caught: Trophônius cut off his brother's head and carried it away, so that the body, which alone remained, was insufficient to identify the thief. Like Amphiaraos, whom he resembles in more than one respect, Trophônius was swallowed up by the earth near Lebadeia.

From Trophônius and Agamêdês the Orchomenian genealogy passes to Ascalaphos and Ialmenos, the sons of Arês by Astyochê, who are named in the Catalogue of the Iliad as leaders of the thirty ships from Orchomenos against Troy. Azeus, the grandfather of Astyochê in the Iliad, is introduced as the brother of Erginus by Pausanias, who does not carry the pedigree lower.

The genealogy here given out of Pausanias is deserving of the more attention, because it seems to have been copied from the special history of Orchomenos by the Corinthian Kallippus, who again borrowed from the native Orchomenian poet, Chersias: the works of the latter had never come into the hands of Pausanias. It illustrates forcibly the principle upon which these mythical genealogies were framed, for almost every personage in the series is an Eponymous. Andreus gave his name to the country, Athamas to the Athamantian plain: Minyas, Orchomenos, Korônus, Haliartus, Almos and Hyêttos, are each in like manner connected with some name of people, tribe, town or village: while Chrysê and Chrysogeneia have their origin in the reputed ancient wealth of Orchomenos. Abundant discrepancies are found, however, in respect to this old genealogy, if we look to other accounts. According to one statement, Orchomenos was the son of Zeus by Isionê, daughter of Danaus: Minyas was the son of Orchomenos (or rather of Poseidôn) by Hermippê, daughter of Bœôtos: the sons of Minyas were Presbôn, Orchomenos, Athamas and Diochthôndas. Others represented Minyas as son of Poseidôn by Kallirrhoê, an Oceanic nymph, while Dionysius called him son of Arês, and Aristodêmus, son of Aleas: lastly, there were not wanting authors who termed both Minyas and Orchomenos sons of Eteoklês. Nor do we find in any one of these genealogies the name of Amphiôn, the son of Iasus, who figures so prominently in the Odyssey as king of Orchomenos, and whose beautiful daughter Chlôris is married to Nêleus. Pausanias mentions him, but not as king, which is the denomination given to him in Homer.

The discrepancies here cited are hardly necessary in order to prove that these Orchomenian genealogies possess no historical value. Yet some probable inferences appear deducible from the general tenor of the legends, whether the facts and persons of which they are composed be real or fictitious.

Throughout all the historical age, Orchomenos is a member of the Bœotian confederation. But the Bœotians are said to have been immigrants into the territory which bore their name from Thessaly; and prior to the time of their

84

VI. ÆOLIDS - SONS & DAUGHTERS OF ÆOLUS.

immigration, Orchomenos and the surrounding territory appear as possessed by the Minyae, who are recognised in that locality both in the Iliad and in the Odyssey, and from whom the constantly recurring Eponymous, King Minyas, is borrowed by the genealogists. Poetical legend connects the Orchomenian Minyas on the one side, with Pylos and Tryphylia in Peloponnêsus: on the other side, with Phthiôtis and the town of Iôlkos in Thessaly; also with Corinth, through Sisyphus and his sons. Pherekydês represented Nêleus, king of Pylos, as having also been king of Orchomenos. In the region of Triphylia, near to or coincident with Pylos, a Minyeian river is mentioned by Homer; and we find traces of residents called Minyæ: even in the historical times, though the account given by Herodotus of the way in which they came thither is strange and unsatisfactory.

Before the great changes which took place in the inhabitants of Greece from the immigration of the Thesprôtians into Thessaly, of the Bœotians into Bœotia, and of the Dôrians and Ætôlians into Peloponnêsus, at a date which we have no means of determining, the Minyæ and tribes fraternally connected with them seem to have occupied a large portion of the surface of Greece, from Iôlkos in Thessaly to Pylos in the Peloponnêsus. The wealth of Orchomenos is renowned even in the Iliad; and when we study its topography in detail, we are furnished with a probable explanation both of its prosperity and its decay. Orchomenos was situated on the northern bank of the lake Kôpaïs, which receives not only the river Kêphisos from the valleys of Phôkis, but also other rivers from Parnassus and Helicôn. The waters of the lake find more than one subterranean egress – partly through natural rifts and cavities in the limestone mountains, partly through a tunnel pierced artificially more than a mile in length – into the plain on the north-eastern side, from whence they flow into the Eubœan sea near Larymna and it appears that, so long as these channels were diligently watched and kept clear, a large portion of the lake was in the condition of alluvial land, pre-eminently rich and fertile. But when the channels came to be either neglected, or designedly choked up by an enemy, the water accumulated to such a degree, as to occupy the soil of more than one ancient town, to endanger the position of Kôpæ, and to occasion the change of the site of Orchomenos itself from the plain to the declivity of Mount Hyphanteion. An engineer, Kratês, began the clearance of the obstructed water-courses in the reign of Alexander the Great, and by his commission – the destroyer of Thêbes being anxious to re-establish the extinct prosperity of Orchomenos. He succeeded so far as partially to drain and diminish the lake, whereby the site of more than one ancient city was rendered visible: but the revival of Thêbes by Kassander, after the decease of Alexander, arrested the progress of the undertaking, and the lake soon regained its former dimensions, to contract which no farther attempt was made.

According to the Thêban legend, Hêraklês, after his defeat of Erginus had blocked up the exit of the waters, and converted the Orchomenian plain into a lake. The spreading of these waters is thus connected with the humiliation of the Minyæ; and there can be little hesitation in ascribing to these ancient tenants of Orchomenos, before it became bœotised, the enlargement and preservation of these protective channels. Nor could such an object have been accomplished, without combined action and acknowledged ascendency on the part of that city over its neighbours, extending even to the sea at Larymna, where the river Kêphisos discharges itself. Of its extended influence, as well as of its maritime activity, we find a remarkable evidence in the ancient and venerated Amphiktyony at Kalauria. The little island so named, near the harbour of Trœzên, in Peloponnêsus, was sacred to Poseidôn, and an asylum of inviolable sanctity. At the temple of Poseidôn, in Kalauria, there had existed, from unknown date, a periodical sacrifice, celebrated by seven cities in common – Hermionê, Epidaurus, Ægina, Athens, Prasiæ, Nauplia, and the Minyeian Orchomenos. This ancient religious combination dates from the time when Nauplia was independent of Argôs, and Prasiæ of Sparta: Argôs and Sparta, according to the usual practice in Greece, continued to fulfil the obligation each on the part of its respective dependent. Six out of the seven states are at once sea-towns, and near enough to Kalauria to account for their participation in this Amphiktyony. The junction of Orchomenos, from its comparative remoteness, becomes inexplicable, except on the supposition that its territory reached the sea, and that it enjoyed a considerable maritime traffic – a fact which helps to elucidate both its legendary connection with Iôlkos, and its partnership in what is called the Iônic emigration.

The great power of Orchomenos was broken down, and the city reduced to a secondary and half-dependent position by the Bœotians of Thêbes; at what time, and under what circumstances, history has not preserved. The story, that the Thêban hero, Hêraklês, rescued his native city from servitude and tribute to Orchomenos, since it comes from a Kadmeian and not from an Orchomenian legend, and since the details of it were favourite subjects of commemoration in the Thêbian temples, affords a presumption that Thêbes was really once dependent on Orchomenos. Moreover the savage mutilations

VI. ÆOLIDS - SONS & DAUGHTERS OF ÆOLUS.

inflicted by the hero on the tribute seeking envoys, so faithfully portrayed in his surname Rhinokoloustês, infuse into the mythe a portion of that bitter feeling which so long prevailed between Thêbes and Orchomenos, and which led the Thêbans, as soon as the battle of Leuktra had placed supremacy in their hands, to destroy and depopulate their rival. The ensuing generation saw the same fate retorted upon Thêbes, combined with the restoration of Orchomenos. The legendary grandeur of this city continued, long after it had ceased to be distinguished for wealth and power, imperishably recorded both in the minds of the nobler citizens and in the compositions of the poets: the emphatic language of Pausanius shows how much he found concerning it in the old epic.

II. Daughters of Æolus.

With several of the daughters of Æolus memorable mythical pedigrees and narratives are connected. Alcyonê married Kêyx, the son of Eôsphoros, but both she and her husband displayed in a high degree the overweening insolence common in the Æolic race. The wife called her husband Zeus, while he addressed her as Hêrê, for which presumptuous act Zeus punished them by changing both into birds.

Canacê had by the god Poseidôn several children, amongst whom were Epôpeus and Alôeus. Aldôus married Iphimêdea, who became enamoured of the god Poseidôn, and boasted of her intimacy with him. She had by him two sons, Otos and Ephialtês, the huge and formidable Alôids, Titanic beings, nine fathoms in height and nine cubits in breadth, even in their boy-hood, before they had attained their full strength. These Alôids defied and insulted the gods in Olympus: they paid their court to Hêrê and Artemis, and they even seized and bound Arês, confining him in a brazen chamber for thirteen months. No one knew where he was, and the intolerable chain would have worn him to death, had not Eribœa, the jealous stepmother of the Alôids, revealed the place of his detention to Hermês, who carried him surreptitiously away when at the last extremity; nor could Arês obtain any atonement for such an indignity. Otos and Ephialtês even prepared to assault the gods in heaven, piling up Ossa on Olympus and Pelion on Ossa, in order to reach them. And this they would have accomplished had they been allowed to grow to their full maturity; but the arrows of Apollo put a timely end to their short-lived career.

The genealogy assigned to Kalykê, another daughter of Æolus, conducts us from Thessaly to Elis and Ætôlia. She married Aëthlius (the son of Zeus by

Prôtogeneia, daughter of Deukaliôn and sister of Hellên), who conducted a colony out of Thessaly and settled in the territory of Elis. He had for his son Endymiôn, respecting whom the Hesiodic Catalogue and the Eoiai related several wonderful things. Zeus granted him the privilege of determining the hour of his own death, and even translated him into heaven, which he forfeited by daring to pay court to Hêrê: his vision in this criminal attempt was cheated by a cloud, and he was cast out into the under-world. According to other stories, his great beauty caused the goddess Selênê to become enamoured of him, and to visit him by night during his sleep: – the sleep of Endymiôn became a proverbial expression for enviable, undisturbed, and deathless repose. Endymiôn had for issue (Pausanias gives us three different accounts, and Apollodôrus a fourth, of the name of his wife) Epeios, Ætôlus, Pæôn, and a daughter Eurykydê. He caused his three sons to run a race on the stadium at Olympia, and Epeios, being victorious, was rewarded by becoming his successor in the kingdom: it was after him that the people, were denominated Epeians.

Epeios had no male issue, and was succeeded by his nephew Eleios, son of Euykydê by the god Poseidôn: the name of the people was then changed from Epeians to Eleians. Ætôlus, the brother of Epeios, having slain Apis, son of Phorôneus, was compelled to flee from the country: he crossed the Corinthian gulf and settled in the territory then called Kurêtis, but to which he gave the name of Ætôlia.

The son of Elios, or, according to other accounts, of the god Hêlios, of Poseidôn, or of Phorbas, is Augeas, whom is mentioned in the Iliad as king of the Epeians or Eleians. Augeas was rich in all sorts of rural wealth, and possessed herds of cattle so numerous, that the dung of the animals accumulated in the stable or cattle-enclosures beyond all power of endurance. Eurystheus, as an insult to Hêraklês, imposed upon him the obligation of cleansing this stable: the hero, disdaining to carry off the dung upon his shoulders, turned the course of the river Alpheios through the building, and thus swept the encumbrance away. But Augeas, in spite of so signal a service, refused to Hêraklês the promised reward, though his son Phyleus protested against such treachery, and when he found that he could not induce his father to keep faith, retired in sorrow and wrath to the island of Dulichion. To avenge the deceit practised upon him, Hêraklês invaded Elis; but Augeas had powerful auxiliaries, especially his nephews, the two Molionids (sons of Poseidôn by Molionê, the wife of Aktôr), Eurytos and

VI. ÆOLIDS - SONS & DAUGHTERS OF ÆOLUS.

Kteatos. These two miraculous brothers, of transcendent force, grew together, having one body, but two heads and four arms. Such was their irresistible might, that Hêraklês was defeated and repelled from Elis: but presently the Eleians sent the two Molionid brothers as *Theôri* (sacred envoys) to the Isthmian games, and Hêraklês, placing himself in ambush at Kleônæ, surprised and killed them as they passed through. For this murderous act the Eleians in vain endeavoured to obtain redress both at Corinth and at Argôs: which is assigned as the reason for the self-ordained exclusion, prevalent throughout all the historical age, that no Eleian athlete would ever present himself as a competitor at the Isthmian games. The Molionids being thus removed, Hêraklês again invaded Elis, and killed Augeas along with his children, all except Phyleus, whom he brought over from Dulichion, and put in possession of his father's kingdom. According to the more gentle narrative which Pausanias adopts, Augeas was not killed, but pardoned at the request of Phyleus. He was worshipped as a hero even down to the time of that author.

It was on occasion of this conquest of Elis, according to the old mythe which Pindar has ennobled in a magnificent ode, that Hêraklês first consecrated the ground of Olympia, and established the Olympic games. Such at least was one of the many fables respecting the origin of that memorable institution.

It has already been mentioned that Ætôlus, son of Endymiôn, quitted Peloponnêsus in consequence of having slain Apis. The country on the north of the Corinthian gulf, between the rivers Euênus and Achelôus. received from him the name of Ætôlia instead of that of Kurêtis. He acquired possession of it after having slain Dôrus, Laodokus and Polypœstes, sons of Apollo and Phthia, by whom he had been well received. He had by his wife Pronoê (the daughter of Phorbas) two sons, Pleurôn and Kalydôn, and from them the two chief towns in Ætolia were named. Pleurôn married Xanthippê, daughter of Dôrus, and had for his son Agênôr, from whom sprang Portheus, or Porthaôn, and Demonikê: Euênos and Thestius were children of the latter by the god Arês.

Portheus had three sons, Agrius, Melas and Œneus: among the offspring of Thestius were Althæa and Lêda, names which bring us to a period of interest in the legendary history. Lêda marries Tyndareus and becomes mother of Helena and the Dioscuri: Althæa marries Œneus, and has, among other children, Meleager and Deianeira; the latter being begotten by the god Dionysus, and the former by Arês. Tydeus also is his son, the father of Diomêdês: warlike eminence goes hand in hand with tragic calamity among the members of this memorable family.

We are fortunate enough to find the legend of Althæa and Meleager set forth at considerable length in the Iliad, in the speech addressed by Phœnix to appease the wrath of Achillês. Œneus, king of Kalydôn, in the vintage sacrifices which he offered to the gods, omitted to include Artemis: the misguided man either forgot her or cared not for her; and the goddess, provoked by such an insult, sent against the vineyards of Œneus a wild boar, of vast size and strength, who tore up the trees by the root and laid prostrate all their fruit. So terrible was this boar, that nothing less than a numerous body of men could venture to attack him: Meleager, the son of Œneus, however, having got together a considerable number of companions, partly from the Kurêtês of Pleurôn, at length slew him. But the anger of Artemis was not yet appeased, and she raised a dispute among the combatants respecting the possession of the boar's head and hide, the trophies of victory. In this dispute, Meleager slew the brother of his mother Althæa, prince af the Kurêtês of Pleurôn: these Kurêtês attacked the Ætôlians of Kalydôn in order to avenge their chief. So long as Meleager contended in the field the Ætôlians had the superiority. But he presently refused to come forth, indignant at the curses imprecated upon him by his mother. For Althæa, wrung with sorrow for the death of her brother, flung herself upon the ground in tears, beat the earth violently with her hands, and implored Hadês and Persephonê to inflict death upon Meleager, a prayer which the unrelenting Erinnys in Erebus heard but too well. So keenly did the hero resent this behaviour of his mother, that he kept aloof from the war; and the Kurêtês not only drove the Ætôlians from the field, but assailed the walls and gates of Kalydôn, and were on the point of overwhelming its dismayed inhabitants. There was no hope of safety except in the arm of Meleager; but Meleager lay in his chamber by the side of his beautiful wife Klœpatra, the daughter of Idas, and heeded not the necessity. While the shouts of expected victory were heard from the assailants at the gates, the ancient men of Ætôlia and the priests of the gods earnestly besought Meleager to come forth, offering him his choice of the fattest land in the plain of Kalydôn. His dearest friends, his father Œneus, his sisters, and even his mother herself added their supplications, but he remained inflexible. At length the Kurêtês penetrated into the town and began to burn it: at this last moment, Kleopatra his wife addressed to him her pathetic appeal, to avert from her and from his family the desperate horrors impending over them all. Meleager could no longer resist, he put on his armour, went forth from his chamber, and repelled the enemy. But when the danger was over, his countrymen withheld from him the splendid presents which they had promised, because he had rejected their prayers, and had come forth only when his own haughty caprice dictated.

Such is the legend of Meleager in the Iliad: a verse in the second book mentions simply the death of Meleager, without farther details, as a reason why Thoas appeared in command of the Ætôlians before Troy.

Later poets both enlarged and altered the fable. The Hesiodic Eoiai, as well as the old poem called the Minyas, represented Meleager as having been slain by Apollo, who aided the Kurêtês in the war; and the incident of the burning brand, though quite at variance with Homer, is at least as old as the tragic poet Phrynichus, earlier than Æschylus. The Mœræ, or Fates, presenting themselves to Althæa shortly after the birth of Meleager, predicted that the child would die so soon as the brand then burning on the fire near at hand should be consumed. Althæa snatched it from the flames and extinguished it, preserving it with the almost care, until she became incensed against Meleager for the death of her brother. She then cast it into the fire, and as soon as it was consumed the life of Meleager was brought to a close.

We know, from the sharp censure of Pliny, that Sophoklês heightened the pathos of this subject by his account of the mournful death of Meleager's sisters, who perished from excess of grief. They were changed into the birds called Meleagrides, and their never-ceasing tears ran together into amber. In the hands of Euripidês – whether originally through him or not, we cannot tell – Atalanta became the prominent figure and motive of the piece, while the party convened to hunt the Kalydônian boar was made to comprise all the distinguished heroes from every quarter of Greece. In fact, as Heyne justly remarks, this event is one of the four aggregate dramas of Grecian heroic life, along with the Argônautic expedition, the siege of Thêbes, and the Trojan war.

To accomplish the destruction of the terrific animal which Artemis in her wrath had sent forth, Meleager assembled not merely the choice youth among the Kurêtes and Ætôlians (as we find in the Iliad), but an illustrious troop, including Kastôr and Pollux, Idas and Lynkeus, Pêleus and Telamôn, Thêseus and Peirithous, Ankæus and Kêpheus, Jasôn, Amphiaraus, Admêtus, Eurytiôn and others. Nestôr and Phœnix, who appear as old men before the walls of Troy, exhibited their early prowess as auxiliaries to the suffering Kalydônians. Conspicuous amidst them all stood the virgin Atalanta, daughter of the Arcadian Schœneus: beautiful and matchless for swiftness of foot, but living in the forest as a huntress and unacceptable to Aphrodîtê. Several of the heroes were slain by the boar, others escaped by various stratagems: at length Atalanta first shot him in the back, next Amphiaraus in the eye, and, lastly, Meleager killed him. Enamoured of the beauty of Atalanta, Meleager made over to her the chief spoils of the animal, on the plea that she had inflicted the first wound. But his uncles, the brothers of Thestius, took them away from her, asserting their rights as next of kin, if Meleager declined to keep the prize for himself, the latter, exasperated at this behaviour, slew them. Althæa, in deep sorrow for her brothers and wrath against her son, is impelled to produce the fatal brand which she had so long treasured up, and consign it to the flames. The tragedy concludes with the voluntary death both of Althæa and Kleopatra.

Interesting as the Arcadian huntress, Atalanta, is in herself, she is an intrusion, and not a very convenient intrusion, into the Homeric story of the Kalydônian boar-hunt, wherein another female Kleopatra, already occupied the foreground. But the more recent version became accredited throughout Greece, and was sustained by evidence which few persons in those days felt any inclination to controvert. For Atalanta carried away with her the spoils and head of the boar into Arcadia; and there for successive centuries hung the identical hide and the gigantic tusks of three feet in length, in the temple of Athênê Alea at Tegea. Kallimachus mentions them as being there preserved, in the third century before the Christian æra; but the extraordinary value set upon them is best proved by the fact that the emperor Augustus took away the tusks from Tegea, along with the great statue of Athênê Alea, and conveyed them to Rome, to be there preserved among the public curiosities. Even a century and a half afterwards, when Pausanias visited Greece, the skin worn out with age was shown to him, while the robbery of the tusks had not been forgotten. Nor were these relics of the boar the only memento preserved at Tegea of the heroic enterprise. On the pediment of the temple of Athênê Alea, unparalleled in Peloponnêsus for beauty and grandeur, the illustrious statuary Skopas had executed one of his most finished reliefs, representing the Kalydônian hunt. Atalanta and Meleager were placed in the front rank of the assailants, and Ankæus, one of the Tegean heroes, to whom the tusks of the boar had proved fatal, was represented as sinking under his death-wound into the arms of his brother Epochos. Pausanias observes, that the Tegeans, while they had manifested the same honourable forwardness as other Arcadian communities in the conquest of Troy, the repulse of Xerxês, and the battle of Dipæa against Sparta – might fairly claim to themselves, through Ankæus and Atalanta, that they alone amongst all Arcadians had participated in the glory of the Kalydônian boar-hunt. So entire and unsuspecting is the faith both of the Tegeans and of Pausanias in the past historical reality of this romantic adventure. Strabo indeed tries to transform the romance into something which has the outward semblance of history, by remarking that the quarrel respecting the boar's head and hide cannot have been the real cause of war between the Kurêtes and the Ætôlians: the true ground of dispute (he contends) was probably the possession of a portion of territory. His remarks on this head are analogous to those of Thucydidês and other critics, when they ascribe the Trojan war, not to the rape of Helen, but to views of conquest or political apprehensions. He treats the general fact of the battle between the Kurêtes and the Ætôlians, mentioned in the Iliad, as something unquestionably real and historical – recapitulating at the same time a variety of discrepancies on the part of different authors, but not giving any decision of his own respecting their truth or falsehood.

In the same manner as Atalanta was intruded into the Kalydônian hunt, so also she seems to have been introduced into the memorable funeral games celebrated after the decease of Pelias at Iôlkos, in which she had no place at the time when the works on the chest of Kypselus were executed. Her native and genuine locality is Arcadia: where her race-course, near to the town of Methydrion, was shown even in the days of Pausanias. This race-course had been the scene of destruction for more than one unsuccessful suitor. For Atalanta, averse to marriage, had proclaimed that her hand should only be won by the competitor who could surpass her in running: all who tried and failed were condemned to die, and many were the persons to whom her beauty and swiftness, alike unparalleled, had proved fatal. At length Meilaniôn, who had vainly tried to win her affections by assiduous services in her hunting excursions, ventured to enter the perilous lists. Aware that he could not hope to outrun her except by stratagem, he had obtained by the kindness of Aphroditê, three golden apples from the garden of the Hesperides, which he successively let fall near to her while engaged in the race. The maiden could not resist the temptation of picking them up, and was thus overcome: she became the wife of Meilaniôn and the mother of the Arcadian Parthenopæus, one of the seven chiefs who perished in the siege of Thêbes.

We have yet another female in the family of Œneus, whose name the legend has immortalised. His daughter Deianeira was sought in marriage by the river Achelôus, who presented himself in various shapes, first as a serpent and afterwards as a bull. From the importunity of this hateful suitor she was rescued be the arrival of Hêraklês, who encountered Achelôus, vanquished him and broke off one of his horns, which Achelôus ransomed by surrendering to him the horn of Amaltheia, endued with the miraculous property of supplying the possessor with abundance of any food or drink which he desired. Hêraklês was rewarded for his prowess by the possession of Deianeira, made over the horn of Amaltheia as his marriage-present to Œneus. Compelled to leave the residence of Œneus in consequence of having in a fit of anger struck the youthful attendant Eunomus, and involuntarily killed him, Hêraklês retired to Trachin, crossing the river Euênus at the place where the Centaur Nessus was accustomed to carry over passengers for hire. Nessus carried over Deianeira, but when he had arrived on the other side, began to treat her with rudeness, upon which Hêraklês slew him with an arrow tinged by the poison of the Lernæan hydra. The dying Centaur advised Deianeira to preserve the poisoned blood which flowed from his wound, telling her that it would operate as a philtre to regain for her the affections of Hêraklês, in case she should ever be threatened by a rival. Some time afterwards the hero saw and loved the beautiful Iolê, daughter of Eurytos, king of Œchalia: he stormed the town, killed Eurytos, and made Iolê his captive. The misguided Deianeira now had recourse to her supposed philtre: she sent as a present to Hêraklês a splendid tunic, imbued secretly with the poisoned blood of the Centaur. Hêraklês adorned himself with the tunic on the occasion of offering a solemn sacrifice to Zeus on the promontory of Kênæon in Eubœa; but the fatal garment, when once put on, clung to him indissolubly, burnt his skin and flesh, and occasioned an agony of pain from which he was only relieved by death. Deianeira slew herself in despair at this disastrous catastrophe.

We have not yet exhausted the eventful career of Œneus and his family – ennobled among the Ætôlians especially, both by religious worship and by poetical eulogy – and favourite themes not merely in some of the Hesiodic poems, but also in other ancient epic productions, the Alkmæônis and the Cyclic Thêbais. By another marriage, Œbeus had for his son Tydeus, whose poetical celebrity is attested by the many different accounts given both of the name and condition of his mother. Tydeus, having slain his cousins, the sons of Melas, who were conspiring against Œneus, was forced to become an exile, and took refuge at Argôs with Adrastus, whose daughter Deipylê he married. The issue of this marriage was Diomêdês, whose brilliant exploits in the siege of Troy were not less celebrated than those of his father at the siege of Thêbes. After the departure of Tydeus, Œneus was deposed by the sons of Agrios, and fell

VI. ÆOLIDS - SONS & DAUGHTERS OF ÆOLUS.

into extreme poverty and wretchedness, from which he was only rescued by his grandson Diomêdês, after the conquest of Troy. The sufferings of this ancient warrior, and the final restoration and revenge by Diomêdês, were the subject of a lost tragedy of Euripidês, which even the ridicule of Aristophanes demonstrates to have been eminently pathetic.

Though the genealogy just given of Œneus is in part Homeric, and seems to have been followed generally by the mythographers, yet we find another totally at variance with it in Hekatæus, which he doubtless borrowed from some of the old poets: the simplicity of the story annexed to it seems to attest its antiquity. Orestheus, son of Deukaliôn, first passed into Ætôlia, and acquired the kingdom: he was father of Phytios, who was father of Œneus. Ætôlus was son of Œneus.

The original migration of Ætôlus from Elis to Ætôlia – and the subsequent establishment in Elis of Oxylus, his descendant in the tenth generation, along with the Dôrian invaders of Peloponnêsus – were commemorated by two inscriptions, one in the agora of Elis, the other in that of the Ætôlian chief town, Thermum, engraved upon the statues of Ætôlus and Oxylus, respectively.

LEGENDARY GREECE

VII. THE PELOPIDS.

Among the ancient legendary genealogies, there was none which figured with greater splendour, or which attracted to itself a higher degree of poetical interest and pathos, than that of the Pelopids – Tantalus, Pelops, Atreus and Thyestês, Agamemnôn and Menelaus and Ægisthus, Helen and Klytæmnêstra, Orestês and Elektra and Hermionê. Each of these characters is a star of the first magnitude in the Grecian hemisphere: each name suggests the idea of some interesting romance or some harrowing tragedy: the curse which taints the family from the beginning inflicts multiplied wounds at every successive generation. So, at least, the story of the Pelopids presents itself, after it had been successively expanded and decorated by epic, lyric and tragic poets. It will be sufficient to touch briefly upon events with which every reader of Grecian poetry is more or less familiar, and to offer some remarks upon the way in which they were coloured and modified by different Grecian authors.

Pelops is the eponym or name-giver of the Peloponnêsus: to find an eponym for every conspicuous local name was the invariable turn of Grecian retrospective fancy. The name Peloponnêsus is not to be found either in the Iliad or the Odyssey, nor any other denomination which can be attached distinctly and specially to the entire peninsula. But we meet with the name in one of the most ancient post-Homeric poems of which any fragments have been preserved – the Cyprian Verses – a poem which many (seemingly most persons) even of the contemporaries of Herodotus ascribed to the author of the Iliad, though Herodotus contradicts the opinion. The attributes by which the Pelopid Agamemnôn and his house are marked out and distinguished from the other heroes of the Iliad, are precisely those which Grecian imagination would naturally seek in an eponymous – superior wealth, power, splendour and regality. Not only Agamemnôn himself, but his brother Menelaus, is "more of a kin" even than Nestôr or Diomêdês. The gods have not given to the king of the "much-golden" Mykênæ greater courage, or strength, or ability, than to various other chiefs; but they have conferred upon him a marked superiority in riches, power and dignity, and have thus singled him out as the appropriate leader of the forces. He enjoys this pre-eminence as belonging to a privileged family and as inheriting the heaven-descended sceptre of Pelops, the transmission of which is described by Homer in a very remarkable way. The sceptre was made "by Hêphæstos, who presented it to Zeus; Zeus gave it to Hermês, Hermês to the charioteer Pelops; Pelops gave it to Atreus, the ruler of men;

VII. THE PELOPIDS.

Atreus at his death left it to Thyestês, the rich cattle-owner; Thyestês in his turn left it to his nephew Agamemnôn to carry, that he might hold dominion over many islands and over all Argôs."

We have here the unrivalled wealth and power of the "king of men, Agamemnôn," traced up to his descent from Pelops, and accounted for, in harmony with the recognised epical agencies, by the present of the special sceptre of Zeus through the hands of Hermês: the latter being the wealth-giving god, whose blessing is most efficacious in furthering the process of inquisition, whether by theft or by accelerated multiplication of flocks and herds. The wealth and princely character of the Atreids were proverbial among the ancient epic poets. Paris not only carries away Helen, but much property along with her; the house of Menelaus, when Têlemachus visits it in the Odyssey, is so resplendent with gold and silver and rare ornament, as to strike the beholder with astonishment and admiration. The attributes assigned to Tantalus, the father of Pelops, are in conformity with the general idea of the family – superhuman abundance and enjoyments, and intimate converse with the gods, to such a degree that his head is turned, and he commits inexpiable sin. Though Tantalus himself is mentioned, in one of the most suspicious passages of the Odyssey (as suffering punishment in the under-world), he is not announced, nor is any one else announced, as father of Pelops, unless we are to construe the lines in the Iliad as implying that the latter was son of Hermês. In the conception of the author of the Iliad, the Pelopids are, if not of divine origin, at least a mortal breed specially favoured and ennobled by the gods – beginning with Pelops, and localised at Mykênæ. No allusion is made to any connection of Pelops either with Pisa or with Lydia.

The legend which connected Tantalus and Pelops with Mount Sipylus may probably have grown out of the Æolic settlements at Magnêsia and Kymê. Both the Lydian origin and the Pisatic sovereignty of Pelops are adapted to times later than the Iliad, when the Olympic games had acquired to themselves the general reverence of Greece, and had come to serve as the religious and recreative centre of the Peloponnêsus – and when the Lydian and Phrygian heroic names, Midas and Gygês, were the types of wealth and luxury, as well as of chariot driving, in the imagination of a Greek. The inconsiderable villages of the Pisatid derived their whole importance from the vicinity of Olympia: they are not deemed worthy of notice in the Catalogue of Homer. Nor could the genealogy which connected the eponym of the entire peninsula with Pisa have obtained currency in Greece unless it had been sustained by pre-established veneration for the locality of Olympia. But if the sovereign of the humble Pisa was to be recognised as forerunner of the thrice-wealthy princes of Mykênæ, it became necessary to assign some explanatory cause of his riches. Hence the supposition of his being an immigrant, son of a wealthy Lydian named Tantalus, who was the offspring of Zeus and Ploutô. Lydian wealth and Lydian chariot-driving rendered Pelops a fit person to occupy his place in the legend, both as ruler of Pisa and progenitor of the Mykênæan Atreids. Even with the admission of these two circumstances there is considerable difficulty, for those who wish to read the legends as consecutive history, in making the Pelopids pass smoothly and plausibly from Pisa to Mykênæ.

I shall briefly recount the legends of this great heroic family as they came to stand in their full and ultimate growth, after the localisation of Pelops at Pisa had been tacked on as a preface to Homer's version of the Pelopid genealogy.

Tantalus, residing near Mount Sipylus in Lydia, had two children, Pelops and Niobê. He was a man of immense possessions and pre-eminent happiness, above the lot of humanity: the gods communicated with him freely, received him at their banquets, and accepted of his hospitality in return. Intoxicated with such prosperity, Tantalus became guilty of gross wickedness. He stole nectar and ambrosia from the table of the gods, and revealed their secrets to mankind: he killed and served up to them at a feast his own son Pelops. The gods were horror-struck when they discovered the meal prepared for them: Zeus restored the mangled youth to life, and as Dêmêtêr, then absorbed in grief for the loss of her daughter Persephonê, had eaten a portion of the shoulder, he supplied an ivory shoulder in place of it Tantalus expiated his guilt by exemplary punishment. He was placed in the under-world, with fruit and water seemingly close to him, yet eluding his touch as often as he tried to grasp them and leaving his hunger and thirst incessant and unappeased. Pindar, in a very remarkable passage, finds this old legend revolting to his feelings: he rejects the tale of the flesh of Pelops having been served up and eaten, as altogether unworthy of the gods.

Niobê, the daughter of Tantalus, was married to Amphiôn, and had a numerous and flourishing offspring of seven sons and seven daughters. Though accepted as the intimate friend and companion of Lêtô, the mother of Apollo and Artemis, she was presumptuous enough to triumph over that goddess, and to place herself on a footing of higher dignity, on account of the superior number of her children, Apollo and Artemis avenged this insult by killing all the sons and all the daughters: Niobê, thus left a childless and disconsolate mother, wept herself to death, and was turned into a rock, which the later Greeks continued always to identify on Mount Sipylus.

Some authors represented Pelops as not being a Lydian, but a king of Paphlagônia: by others it was said that Tantalus, having become detested from his impieties, had been expelled from Asia by Ilus the king of Troy, an incident which served the double purpose of explaining the transit of Pelops to Greece, and of imparting to the siege of Troy by Agamemnôn the character of retribution for wrongs done to his ancestor. When Pelops came over to Greece, he found Œnomaus, son of the god Arês and Harpinna, in possession of the principality of Pisa, immediately bordering on the district of Olympia. Œnomaus, having been apprised by an oracle that death would overtake him if he permitted his daughter Hippodameia to marry, refused to give her in marriage except to some suitor who should beat him in a chariot-race from Olympia to the isthmus of Corinth; the ground here selected for the legendary victory of Pelops deserves attention, inasmuch as it is a line drawn from the assumed centre of Peloponnêsus to its extremity, and thus comprises the whole territory with which Pelops is connected as eponym. Any suitor overmatched in the race was doomed to forfeit his life; and the fleetness of the Pisan horses, combined with the skill of the charioteer Myrtilus, had already caused thirteen unsuccessful competitors to perish by the lance of Œnomaus. Pelops entered the lists as a suitor: his prayers moved the god Poseidôn to supply him with a golden chariot and winged horses: or according to another story, he captivated the affections of Hippodameia herself, who persuaded the charioteer Myrtilus to loosen the wheels of Œnomaus before he started, so that the latter was overturned and perished in the race. Having thus won the hand of Hippodameia, Pelops became Prince of Pisa, He put to death the charioteer Myrtilus, either from indignation at his treachery to Œnomaus, or from jealousy on the score of Hippodameia; but Myrtilus was the son of Hermês, and though Pelops erected a temple in the vain attempt to propitiate that god, he left a curse upon his race which future calamities were destined painfully to work out.

Pelops had a numerous issue by Hippodameia: Pittheus, Trœzen and Epidaurus, the eponyms of the two Argôlic cities so called, are said to have been among them: Atreus and Thyestês were also his sons, and his daughter Nikippê married Sthenelus of Mykênaæ and became the mother of Eurystheus.

LEGENDARY GREECE

We hear nothing of the principality of Pisa afterwards: the Pisatid villages became absorbed into the larger aggregate of Elis, after a vain struggle to maintain their separate right of presidency over the Olympic festival. The legend ran that Pelops left his name to the whole peninsula: according to Thucydidês, he was enabled to do this because of the great wealth which he had brought with him from Lydia into a poor territory. The historian leaves out all the romantic interest of the genuine legends – preserving only this one circumstance, which, without being better attested than the rest, carries with it, from its common-place and prosaic character, a pretended historical plausibility.

Besides his numerous issue by Hippodameia, Pelops had an illegitimate son named Chrysippus, of singular grace and beauty, towards whom he displayed so much affection as to rouse the jealousy of Hippodameia and her sons. Atreus and Thyestês conspired together to put Chrysippus to death, for which they were banished by Pelops and retired to Mykênæ, an event which brings us into the track of the Homeric legend. For Thucydidês. having found in the death of Chrysippus a suitable ground for the secession of Atreus from Pelops, conducts him at once to Mykênæ, and shows a train of plausible circumstances to account for his having mounted the throne. Eurystheus, king of Mykênæ, was the maternal nephew of Atreus: when he engaged in any foreign expedition, he naturally entrusted the regency to his uncle; the people of Mykênæ thus became accustomed to be governed by him, and he on his part made efforts to conciliate them, so that when Eurystheus was defeated and slain in Attica, the Mykênæan people, apprehensive of an invasion from the Hêrakleids, chose Atreus as at once the most powerful and most acceptable person for his successor. Such was the tale which Thucydidês derived "from those who had learnt ancient Peloponnesian matters most clearly from their forefathers." The introduction of so much sober and quasi-political history, unfortunately unauthenticated, contrasts strikingly with the highly poetical legends of Pelops and Atreus, which precede and follow it.

Atreus and Thyestês are known in the Iliad only as successive possessors of the sceptre of Zeus, which Thyestês at his death bequeathes to Agamemnôn. The family dissensions among this fated race commence, in the Odyssey, with Agamemnôn the son of Atreus, and Ægisthus the son of Thyestês. But subsequent poets dwelt upon an implacable quarrel between the two fathers. The cause of the bitterness was differently represented: some alleged that Thyestês had intrigued with the Krêtan Aeropê, the wife of his brother: other narratives mentioned that Thyestês procured for himself surreptitiously the possession of

VII. THE PELOPIDS.

a lamb with a golden fleece, which had been designedly introduced among the flocks of Atreus by the anger of Hermês, as a cause of enmity and ruin to the whole family. Atreus, after a violent burst of indignation, pretended to be reconciled, and invited Thyestês to a banquet, in which he served up to him the limbs of his own son, and the father ignorantly partook of the fatal meal. Even the all-seeing Hêlios is said to have turned back his chariot to the east in order that he might escape the shocking spectacle of this Thyestêan banquet: yet the tale of Thyestêan revenge – the murder of Atreus perpetrated by Ægisthus, the incestuous offspring of Thyestês by his daughter Pelopia – is no less replete with horrors.

Homeric legend is never thus revolting. Agamemnôn and Menelaus are known to us chiefly with their Homeric attributes, which have not been so darkly overlaid by subsequent poets as those of Atreus and Thyestês. Agamemnôn and Menelaus are affectionate brothers: they marry two sisters, the daughters of Tyndareus king of Sparta, Klytæmnêstra and Helen: for Helen, the real offspring of Zeus, passes as the daughter of Tyndarius. The "king of men" reigns at Mykênæ: Menelaus succeeds Tyndareus at Sparta. Of the rape of Helen, and the siege of Troy consequent upon it, I shall speak elsewhere; I now touch only upon the family legends of the Atreids. Menelaus, on his return from Troy with the recovered Helen, is driven by storms far away to the distant regions of Phœnicia and Egypt, and is exposed to a thousand dangers and hardships before he again sets foot in Peloponnêsus. But at length he reaches Sparta, resumes his kingdom, and passes the rest of his days in uninterrupted happiness and splendour: being moreover husband of the godlike Helen and son-in-law of Zeus, he is even spared the pangs of death. When the fulness of his days is past he is transported to the Elysian fields, there to dwell along with "the golden-haired Rhadamanthus" in a delicious climate and in undisturbed repose.

Far different is the fate of the king of men, Agamemnôn. During his absence, the unwarlike Ægisthus, son of Thyestês, had seduced his wife Klytæmnêstra, in spite of the special warning of the gods, who, watchful over this privileged family, had sent their messenger Hermês expressly to deter him from the attempt. A venerable bard had been left by Agamemnôn as the companion and monitor of his wife, and so long as that guardian was at hand, Ægisthus pressed his suit in vain. But he got rid of the bard by sending him to perish in a desert island, and then won without difficulty the undefended Klyæmnêstra. Ignorant of what had passed, Agamemnôn returned from Troy victorious and full of hope to his native country: but he had scarcely landed when Ægisthus invited him to a banquet, and there with the aid of the treacherous Klytæmnêstra, in the very hall of festivity and congratulation, slaughtered him and his companions "like oxen tied to the manger." His concubine Kassandra, the prophetic daughter of Priam, perished along with him by the hand of Klytæmnêstra herself. The boy Orestês, the only male offspring of Agamemnôn, was stolen away by his nurse, and placed in safety at the residence of the Phôkian Strophius.

For seven years Ægisthus and Klytæmnêstra reigned in tranquillity at Mykênæ on the throne of the murdered Agamemnôn. But in the eighth year the retribution announced by the gods overtook them: Orestês, grown to manhood, returned and avenged his father by killing Ægisthus, according to Homer: subsequent poets add, his mother also. He recovered the kingdom of Mykênæ, and succeeded Menelaus in that of Sparta. Hermionê, the only daughter of Menelaus and Helen, was sent into the realm of the Myrmidons in Thessaly, as the bride of Neoptolemus, son of Achillês, according to the promise made by her father during the siege of Troy.

Here ends the Homeric legend of the Pelopids, the final act of Orestês being cited as one of unexampled glory. Later poets made many additions: they dwelt upon his remorse and hardly earned pardon for the murder of his mother, and upon his devoted friendship for Pylades: they wove many interesting tales, too, respecting his sisters Iphigeneia and Elektra and his cousin Hermionê, names which have become naturalised in every climate and incorporated with every form of poetry.

These poets did not at all scruple to depart from Homer, and to give other genealogies of their own, with respect to the chief persons of the Pelopid family. In the Iliad and Odyssey, Agamemnôn is son of Atreus: in the Hesiodic Eoiai and in Stesichorus, he is son of Pleisthenês the son of Atreus. In Homer, he is specially marked as reigning at Mykênæ: but Stesichorus, Simonidês and Pindar represented him as having both resided and perished at Sparta or at Amyklæ. According to the ancient Cyprian Verses, Helen was represented as the daughter of Zeus and Nemesis: in one of the Hesiodic poems she was introduced as an Oceanic nymph, daughter of Oceanus and Têthys. The genealogical discrepancies, even as to the persons of the principal heroes and heroines, are far too numerous to be cited, nor is it necessary to advert to them, except as they bear upon the unavailing attempt to convert such legendary parentage into a basis of historical record or chronological calculation.

The Homeric poems probably represent that form of the legend, respecting Agamemnôn and Orestês which was current and popular among the Æolic colonists. Orestês was the great heroic chief of the Æolic emigration: he, or his sons, or his descendants, are supposed to have conducted the Achæans to seek a new home, when they were no longer able to make head against the invading Dôrians: the great families at Tenedos and other Æolic cities even during the historical æra, gloried in tracing back their pedigrees to this illustrious source. The legends connect it with the heroic worship of these mythical ancestors form the basis of the character and attributes of Agamemnôn and his family, as depicted in Homer, in which Mykênæ appears as the first place in Peloponnêsus, and Sparta only as the second: the former the special residence of "the king of men;" the latter that of his younger and inferior brother, yet still the seat of a member of the princely Pelopids, and moreover the birth-place of the divine Helen. Sparta, Argôs and Mykênæ are all three designated in the Iliad by the goddess Hêrê as her favourite cities; yet the connection of Mykênæ with Argôs, though the two towns were only ten miles distant, is far less intimate than the connection of Mykênæ with Sparta. When we reflect upon the very peculiar manner in which Homer identifies Hêrê with the Grecian host and its leader, for she watches over the Greeks with the active solicitude of a mother, and her antipathy against the Trojans is implacable to a degree which Zeus cannot comprehend, and when we combine this with the ancient and venerated Hêræon, or temple of Hêrê, near Mykênæ, we may partly explain to ourselves the pre-eminence conferred upon Mykênæ in the Iliad and Odyssey. The Hêræon was situated between Argôs and Mykenæ; in later times its priestesses were named and its affairs administered by the Argeians; but as it was much nearer to Mykênæ than to Argos, we may with probability conclude that it originally belonged to the former, and that the increasing power of the latter enabled them to usurp to themselves a religious privilege which was always an object of envy and contention among the Grecian communities. The Æolic colonists doubtless took out with them in their emigration the divine and heroic legends, as well as the worship and ceremonial rites, of the Hêræon: and in those legends the most exalted rank would be assigned to the close-adjoining and administering city.

Mykênæ maintained its independence even down to the Persian invasion. Eighty of its heavy-armed citizens, in the ranks of Leonidas at Thermopylæ, and a number not inferior at Platæa, upheld the splendid heroic celebrity of their city during a season of peril, when the more powerful Argos disgraced itself by a treacherous neutrality. Very shortly afterwards Mykênæ was enslaved and its inhabitants expelled by the Argeians. Though this city so long maintained a separate existence, its importance had latterly sunk to nothing, while that of the Dôrian Argos was augmented very much, and that of the Dôrian Sparta still more.

The name of Mykênæ is imperishably enthroned in the Iliad and Odyssey, but all the subsequent fluctuations of the legend tend to exalt the glory of other cities at its expense. The recognition of the Olympic games as the grand religions festival of Peloponnêsus gave vogue to that genealogy which connected Pelops with Pisa or Elis and withdrew him from Mykênæ. Moreover, in the poems of the great Athenian tragedians, Mykênæ is constantly confounded and treated as one with Argos. If any one of the citizens of the former, expelled at the time of its final subjugation by the Argeians, had witnessed at Athens a drama of Æschylus, Sophoklês, or Euripidês, or the recital of an ode of Pindar, he would have heard with grief and indignation the city of his oppressors made a partner in the heroic glories of his own. The great political ascendency acquired by Sparta contributed still farther to degrade Mykênæ, by disposing subsequent poets to treat the chief of the Grecian armament against Troy as having been a Spartan. It has been already mentioned that Stêsichorus, Simonidês and Pindar adopted this version of the legend: we know that Zeus Agamemnôn, as well as the hero Menelaus, was worshipped at the Dôrian Sparta, and the feeling of intimate identity, as well as of patriotic pride, which had grown up in the minds of the Spartans connected with the name of Agamemnôn, is forcibly evinced by the reply the Spartan Syagrus to Gelôn of Syracuse at the time of the Persian invasion of Greece. Gelôn was solicited to lend his aid in the imminent danger of Greece before the battle of Salamis: he offered to furnish an immense auxiliary force, on condition that the supreme command should be allotted to him. "Loudly indeed would the Pelopid Agamemnôn cry out (exclaimed Syagrus in rejecting this application), if he were to learn that the Spartans had been deprived of the headship by Gelôn and the Syracusans." Nearly a century before this event, in obedience to the injunctions of the Delphian oracle, the Spartans had brought back from Tegea to Sparta the bones of "the Lacônian Orestês," as Pindar denominates him: the recovery of these bones was announced to them as the means of reversing a course of ill-fortune, and of procuring victory in their war against Tegea. The value which they set upon this acquisition, and the decisive results ascribed to it, exhibit a precise analogy with the recovery of the bones of Thêseus from Skyros by the Athenian Kimôn shortly after the Persian invasion. The remains sought were those of a hero properly belonging to their own soil, but who had died in a foreign land, and of whose protection and assistance they were for that reason deprived. The superhuman magnitude of the bones, which were contained in a coffin seven cubits long, is well suited to the legendary grandeur of the son of Agamemnôn.

VIII. LACONIAN & MESSÊNIAN GENEALOGIES.

The earliest names in Lacônian genealogy are, an indigenous Lelex and a Naiad nymph Kleochareia. From this pair sprung a son Eurôtas, and from him a daughter Sparta, who became the wife of Lacedæmôn, son of Zeus and Taygetê, daughter of Atlas. Amyklas, son of Lacedæmôn, had two sons, Kynortas and Hyakinthus – the latter a beautiful youth, the favourite of Apollo, by whose hand he was accidentally killed while playing at quoits: the festival of the Hyakinthia, which the Lacedæmônians generally, and the Amyklæans with special solemnity, celebrated throughout the historical ages, was traced back to this legend. Kynortas was succeeded by his son Periêrês, who married Gorgophonê, daughter of Perseus, and had a numerous issue – Tyndareus, Ikarius, Aphareus, Leukippus, and Hippokoôn. Some authors gave the genealogy differently, making Periêrês, son of Æolus, to be the father of Kynortas, and Œbalus son of Kynortas, from whom sprung Tyndareus, Ikarius and Hippokoôn.

Both Tyndareus and Ikarius, expelled by their brother Hippokoôn, were forced to seek shelter at the residence of Thestius, king of Kalydôn, whose daughter, Lêda, Tyndareus espoused. It is numbered among the exploits of the omnipresent Hêraklês, that he slew Hippokoôn and his sons, and restored Tyndareus to his kingdom, thus creating for the subsequent Hêrakleidan kings a mythical title to the throne. Tyndareus, as well as his brothers, are persons of interest in legendary narrative: he is the father of Kastôr, of Timandra, married to Echemus, the hero of Tegea, and of Klyæmnêstra. married to Agamemnôn. Pollux and the ever-memorable Helen are the offspring of Lêda by Zeus. Ikarius is the father of Penelopê, wife of Odysseus: the contrast between her behaviour and that of Klytæmnêstra and Helen became the more striking in consequence of their being so nearly related. Aphareus is the father of Idas and Lynkeus, while Leukippus has for his daughters, Phœbê and Ilaëira. According to one of the Hesiodic poems, Kastôr and Pollux were both sons of Zeus by Lêda, while Helen was neither daughter of Zeus nor of Tyndareus, but of Oceanus and Têthys.

The brothers Kastôr and (Polydeukês, or) Pollux are no less celebrated for their fraternal affection than for their great bodily accomplishments: Kastôr, the great charioteer and horse-master: Pollux, the first of pugilists. They are enrolled both among the hunters of the Kalydônian boar and among the heroes of the Argônautic expedition, in which Pollux represses the insolence of

106

Amykus, king of the Bebrykes, on the coast of Asiatic Thrace – the latter, a gigantic pugilist, from whom no rival has ever escaped, challenges Pollux, but is vanquished and killed in the fight.

The two brothers also undertook an expedition into Attica, for the purpose of recovering their sister Helen, who had been carried off by Thêseus in her early youth, and deposited by him at Aphidna, while he accompanied Peirithous to the under-world, in order to assist his friend in carrying off Persephonê. The force of Kastôr and Pollux was irresistible, and when they re-demanded their sister, the people of Attica were anxious to restore her, but no one knew where Thêseus had deposited his prize. The invaders, not believing in the sincerity of this denial, proceeded to ravage the country, which would have been utterly ruined, had not Dekelus, the eponymous of Dekeleia, been able to indicate Aphidna as the place of concealment. The indigenous Titakus betrayed Aphidna to Kastôr and Pollux, and Helen was recovered: the brothers in evacuating Attica, carried away into captivity Æthra, the mother of Thêseus. In after-days, when Kastôr and Pollux, under the title of the Dioskuri, had come to be worshipped as powerful gods, and when the Athenians were greatly ashamed of this act of Thesêus – the revelation made by Dekelus was considered as entitling him to the lasting gratitude of his country, as well as to the favourable remembrance of the Lacedæmônians, who maintained the Dekeleians in the constant enjoyment of certain honorary privileges at Sparta, and even spared that dême in all their invasions of Attica. Nor is it improbable that the existence of this legend had some weight in determining the Lacedæmônians to select Dekelia as the place of their occupation during the Peleponnesian war.

The fatal combat between Kastôr and Polydeukês on the one side, and Idas and Lynkeus on the other, for the possession of the daughters of Leukippus, was celebrated by more than one ancient poet, and forms the subject of one of the yet remaining Idylls of Theokritus. Leukippus had formally betrothed his daughters to Idas and Lynkeus: but the Tyndarids, becoming enamoured of them, outbid their rivals in the value of the customary nuptial gifts, persuaded the father to violate his promise, and carried off Phœbê and Ilaëira as their brides. Idas and Lynkeus pursued them and remonstrated against the injustice: according to Theokritus, this was the cause of the combat. But there was another tale, which seems the older, and which assigns a different cause to the quarrel. The four had jointly made a predatory incursion into Arcadia, and had driven off some cattle, but did not agree about the partition of the booty – Idas carried off into Messênia a portion of it which the Tyndarids claimed as their own. To revenge and reimburse themselves, the Tyndarids invaded Messênia, placing themselves in ambush in the hollow of an ancient oak. But Lynkeus, endued with preternatural powers of vision, mounted to the top of Taygetos, from whence, as he could see over the whole Peleponnêsus and detected them in their chosen place of concealment. Such was the narrative of the ancient Cyprian Verses. Kastôr perished by the band of Idas, Lynkeus by that of Pollux. Idas, seizing a stone pillar from the tomb of his father Aphareus, hurled it at Pollux, knocked him down and stunned him, but Zeus, interposing at the critical moment for the protection of his son, killed Idas with a thunderbolt. Zeus would have conferred upon Pollux the gift of immortality, but the latter could not endure existence without his brother: he entreated permission to share the gift with Kastôr, and both were accordingly permitted to live, but only on every other day.

The Dioskuri, or sons of Zeus, as the two Spartan heroes, Kastôr and Pollux, were denominated, were recognised in the historical days of Greece as gods, and received divine honours. This is even noticed in a passage of the Odyssey, which is at any rate a very old interpolation, as well as in one of the Homeric hymns. What is yet more remarkable is that they were invoked during storms at sea, as the special and all-powerful protectors of the endangered mariner, although their attributes and their celebrity seem to be of a character so dissimilar. They were worshipped throughout most parts of Greece, but with pre-eminent sanctity at Sparta.

Kastôr and Pollux being removed, the Spartan genealogy passes from Tyndareus to Menelaus, and from him to Orestês.

Originally it appears that Messênê was a name for the western portion of Lacônia, bordering on what was called Pylos: it is so represented in the Odyssey, and Ephorus seems to have included it amongst the possessions of Orestês and his descendants. Throughout the whole duration of the Messênico-Dôrian kingdom, there never was any town called Messênê: the town was first founded by Epameinôndas, after the battle of Leuktra. The heroic genealogy of Messênia, starts from the same name as that of Lacônia – from the indigenous Lelex: his younger son, Polykaôn, marries Messênê, daughter of the Argeian Triopas, and settles the country. Pausanias tells us that the posterity of this pair occupied the country for five generations; but he in vain searched the ancient genealogical poems to find the names of their descendants. To them succeeded Periêrês, son of Æolus; and Aphareus and Leukippus, according to Pausanias, were sons of Periêrês.

VIII. LACONIAN & MESSÊNIAN GENEALOGIES.

Aphareus, after the death of his sons, founded the town of Arênê, and made over most part of his dominions to his kinsman Nêleus, with whom we pass into the Pylian genealogy.

IX. ARCADIAN GENEALOGY.

The Arcadian divine or heroic pedigree begins with Pelasgus, whom both Hesiod and Asius considered as an indigenous man, though Akusilaus the Argeian represented him as brother of Argôs and son of Zeus by Niobê, daughter of Phorôneus. Akusilaus wished to establish a community of origin between the Argeians and the Arcadians.

Lykaôn, son of Pelasgus and king of Arcadia, had by different wives, fifty sons, the most savage, impious and wicked of mankind: Mænalus was the eldest of them. Zeus, in order that he might himself become a witness of their misdeeds, presented himself to them in disguise. They killed a child and served it up to him for a meal, but the god overturned the table and struck dead with thunder Lykaôn and all his fifty sons, with the single exception of Nyktimus, the youngest, whom he spared at the earnest intercession of the goddess Gæa (the Earth). The town near which the table was overturned received the name of Trapezus (Tabletown).

This singular legend (framed on the same etymological type as that of the ants in Ægina, recounted elsewhere) seems ancient, and may probably belong to the Hesiodic Catalogue. Pausanias tells us a story in many respects different, which was represented to him in Arcadia as the primitive local account, and which becomes the more interesting, as he tells us that he himself fully believes it. Both tales indeed go to illustrate the same point – the ferocity of Lykaôn's character, as well as the cruel rites which he practised. The latter was the first who established the worship and solemn games of Zeus Lykæos: he offered up a child to Zeus, and made libations with the blood upon the altar. Immediately after having perpetrated this act, he was changed into a wolf.

"Of the truth of this narrative (observes Pausanias) I feel persuaded: it has been repeated by the Arcadians from old times, and it carries probability along with it. For the men of that day, from their justice and piety, were guests and companions at table with the gods, who manifested towards them approbation when they were good, and anger if they behaved ill, in a palpable manner: indeed at that time there were some, who having once been men, became gods, and who yet retain their privileges as such – Aristæus, the Krêtan Britomartis, Hêraklês son of Alkmêna, Amphiaraus the son of Oiklês, and Pollux and Kastôr besides. We may therefore believe that Lykaôn became a wild beast, and that Niobê, the daughter of Tantalus, became a stone. But in my time, wickedness having enormously increased, so as to overrun the whole earth and all the

110

IX. ARCADIAN GENEALOGY.

cities in it, there are no farther examples of men exalted into gods, except by mere title and from adulation towards the powerful; moreover the anger of the gods falls tardily upon the wicked, and is reserved for them after their departure from hence."

Pausanias then proceeds to censure those who, by multiplying false miracles in more recent times, tended to rob the old and genuine miracles of their legitimate credit and esteem. The passage illustrates forcibly the views which a religious and instructed pagan took of his past time – how inseparably be blended together in it gods and men, and how little he either recognised or expected to find in it the naked phenomena and historical laws of connection which belonged to the world before him. He treats the past as the province of legend, the present as that of history: and in doing this he is more sceptical than the persons with whom he conversed, who believed not only in the ancient, but even in the recent and falsely reported miracles. It is true that Pausanias does not always proceed consistently with this position: he often rationalises the stories of the past, as if he expected to find historical threads of connection; and sometimes, though more rarely, accepts the miracles of the present. In the present instance he draws a broad line of distinction between present and past, or rather between what is recent and what is ancient: his criticism is, in the main, analogous to that of Arrian in regard to the Amazons – denying their existence during times of recorded history, but admitting it during the early and unrecorded ages.

In the narrative of Pausanias, the sons of Lykaôn, instead of perishing by thunder from Zeus, become the founders of the various towns in Arcadia. And as that region was subdivided into a great number of small and independent townships, each having its own eponym, so the Arcadian heroic genealogy appears broken up and subdivided. Pallas, Orestheus, Phigalus, Trapezeus, Mænalus, Mantineus, and Tegeatês, are all numbered among the sons of Lykaôn, and are all eponyms of various Arcadian towns.

The legend respecting Kallistô and Arkas, the eponym of Arcadia generally, seems to have been originally quite independent of and distinct from that of Lykaôn. Eumêlus, indeed, and some other poets made Kallistô daughter of Lykaôn, but neither Hesiod, nor Asius, nor Pherekydês, acknowledged any relationship between them. The beautiful Kallistô, companion of Artemis in the chase, had bound herself by a vow of chastity: Zeus, either by persuasion or by force, obtained a violation of the vow, to the grievous displeasure both of Hêrê and Artemis. The former changed Kallistô into a bear, the latter when she

111

was in that shape killed her with an arrow. Zeus gave to the unfortunate Kallistô a place among the stars, as the constellation of the Bear: he also preserved the child Arkas, of which she was pregnant by him, and gave it to the Atlantid nymph Maia to bring up.

Arkas, when he became king, obtained from Triptolemus and communicated to his people the first rudiments of agriculture: he also taught them to make bread, to spin, and to weave. He had three sons – Azan, Apheidas, and Elatus: the first was the eponym of Azania, the northern region of Arcadia: the second was one of the heroes of Tegea: the third was father of Ischys (rival of Apollo for the affections of Korônis), as well as of Æpytus and Kyllên: the name of Æpytus among the heroes of Arcadia is as old as the Catalogue in the Iliad.

Aleus, son of Apheidas and king of Tegea, was the founder of the celebrated temple and worship of Athênê Alea in that town. Lykurgus and Kêpheus were his sons, Augê his daughter, who was seduced by Hêraklês, and secretly bore to him a child: the father, discovering what had happened, sent Augê to Nauplius to be sold into slavery: Teuthras, king of Mysia in Asia Minor, purchased her and made her his wife: her tomb was shown at Pergamus on the river Kaikus even in the time of Pausanias.

From Lykurgus, the son of Aleus and brother of Augê, we pass to his son Ankæus, numbered among the Argônauts, finally killed in the chase of the Kalydônian boar, and father of Agapenôr, who leads the Arcadian contingent against Troy, (the adventurers of his niece, the Tegeatic huntress Atalanta, have already been touched upon), then to Echemus, son of Aëropus and grandson of the brother of Lykurgus, Kepheus. Echemus is the chief heroic ornament of Tegea. When Hyllus, the son of Hêraklês, conducted the Hêrakleids on their first expedition against Peloponnêsus, Echemus commanded the Tegean troops who assembled along with the other Peloponnêsians at the isthmus of Corinth to repel the invasion: it was agreed that the dispute should be determined by single combat, and Echemus, as the champion of Peloponnêsus, encountered and killed Hyllus. Pursuant to the stipulation by which they had bound themselves, the Hêrakleids retired, and abstained for three generations from pressing their claim upon Peloponnêsus. This valorous exploit of their great martial hero was cited and appealed to by the Tegeates before the battle of Platæa, as the principal evidence of their claim to the second post in the combined army, next in point of honour to that of the Lacedæmônians, and superior to that of the Athenians: the latter replied to them by producing as counter-evidence the splendid heroic deeds of Athens, the protection of the

IX. ARCADIAN GENEALOGY.

Hêrakleids against Eurystheus, the victory over the Kadmeians of Thêbes, and the complete defeat of the Amazons in Attica. Nor can there be any doubt that these legendary glories were both recited by the speakers, and heard by the listeners, with profound and undoubting faith, as well as with heart-stirring admiration.

One other person there is – Ischys, son of Elatus and grandson of Arkas – in the fabulous genealogy of Arcadia whom it would be improper to pass over, inasmuch as his name and adventures are connected with the genesis of the memorable god or hero Æsculapius, or Asklêpius. Korônis, daughter of Phlegyas, and resident near the lake Bœbêis in Thessaly, was beloved by Apollo and became pregnant by him: unfaithful to the god, she listened to the propositions of Ischys son of Elatus, and consented to wed him: a raven brought to Apollo the fatal news, which so incensed him that he changed the colour of the bird from white, as it previously had been, into black. Artemis, to avenge the wounded dignity of her brother, put Korônis to death, but Apollo preserved the male child of which she was about to be delivered, and consigned it to the Centaur Cheirôn to be brought up. The child was named Asklêpius or Æsculapius, and acquired, partly from the teaching of the beneficent leech Cheirôn, partly from inborn and superhuman aptitude, a knowledge of the virtues of herbs and a mastery of medicine and surgery, such as had never before been witnessed. He not only cured the sick, the wounded, and the dying, but even restored the dead to life. Kapaneus, Eriphylê, Hippolytus, Tyndareus and Glaukus were all affirmed by different poets and logographers to have been endued by him with a new life. But Zeus nowfound himself under the necessity of taking precautions lest mankind, thus unexpectedly protected against sickness and death, should no longer stand in need of the immortal gods: he smote Asklêpius with thunder and killed him. Apollo was so exasperated by this slaughter of his highly-gifted son, that he killed the Cyclôpes who had fabricated the thunder, and Zeus was about to condemn him to Tartarus for doing so, but on the intercession of Latôna he relented, and was satisfied with imposing upon him a temporary servitude in the house of Admêtus at Pheræ.

Asklêpius was worshipped with very great solemnity at Trikka, at Kôs, at Knidus, and in many different parts of Greece, but especially at Epidaurus, so that more than one legend had grown up respecting the details of his birth and adventures: in particular, his mother was by some called Arsinoê. A formal application had been made on this subject (so the Epidaurians told Pausanias) to

113

the oracle of Delphi, and the god in reply acknowledged that Asklêpius was his son by Korônis. The tale above recounted seems to have been both the oldest and the most current. It is adorned by Pindar in a noble ode, wherein however he omits all mention of the raven as messenger – not specifying who or what the spy was from whom Apollo learnt the infidelity of Korônis. By many this was considered as an improvement in respect of poetical effect, but it illustrates the mode in which the characteristic details and simplicity of the old fables came to be exchanged for dignified generalities, adapted to the altered taste of society.

Machaôn and Podaleirius, the two sons of Asklêpius, commaud the contingent from Trikka, in the north-west region of Thessaly, at the siege of Troy by Agamemnôn. They are the leeches of the Grecian army, highly prized and consulted by all the wounded chiefs. Their medical renown was further prolonged in the subsequent poem of Arktinus, the Iliu-Persis, wherein the one was represented as unrivalled in surgical operations, the other as sagacious in detecting and appreciating morbid symptoms. It was Podaleirius who first noticed the glaring eyes and disturbed deportment which preceded the suicide of Ajax.

Galen appears uncertain whether Asklêpius (as well as Dionysus) was originally a god, or whether he was first a man and then became afterwards a god; but Apollodôrus professed to fix the exact date of his apotheosis. Throughout all the historical ages the descendants of Asklêpius were numerous and widely diffused. The many families or gentes called Asklêpiads, who devoted themselves to the study and practice of medicine, and who principally dwelt near the temples of Asklêpius, whither sick and suffering men came to obtain relief – all recognised the god not merely as the object of their common worship, but also as their actual progenitor. Like Solôn, who reckoned Nêleus and Poseidôn as his ancestors, or the Milêsian Hekatæus, who traced his origin through fifteen successive links to a god – like the privileged gens at Pêlion in Thessaly, who considered the wise Centaur Cheirôn as their progenitor, and who inherited from him their precious secrets respecting the medicinal herbs of which their neighbourhood was full; Asklêpiads even of the later times, numbered and specified all the intermediate links which separated them from their primitive divine parent. One of these genealogies has been preserved to us, and we may be sure that there were many such, as the Asklêpiads were found in many different places. Among them were enrolled highly instructed and accomplished men, such as the great Hippocratês and the historian Ktêsias, who prided themselves on the divine origin of themselves and

IX. ARCADIAN GENEALOGY.

their gens – so much did the legendary element pervade even the most philosophical and positive minds of historical Greece. Nor can there be any doubt that their means of medical observation must have been largely extended by their vicinity to a temple so much frequented by the sick, who came in confident hopes of divine relief, and who, whilst they offered up sacrifice and prayer to Æsculapius, and slept in his temple in order to be favoured with healing suggestions in their dreams, might, in case the god withheld his supernatural aid, consult his living descendants. The sick visitors at Kôs, or Trikka, or Epidaurus, were numerous and constant, and the tablets usually hung up to record the particulars of their maladies, the remedies resorted to, and the cures operated by the god, formed both an interesting decoration of the sacred ground and an instructive memorial to the Asklêpiads.

The genealogical descent of Hippocratês and the other Asklêpiads from the god Asklêpius is not only analogous to that of Hekatæus and Solôn from their respective ancestoral gods, but also to that of the Lacedæmônian kings from Hêraklês, upon the basis of which the whole supposed chronology of the ante-historical times has been built, from Eratosthenês and Apollodôrus down to the chronologers of the present century. I shall revert to this hereafter.

X. ÆAKUS & HIS DESCENDANTS - ÆGINA, SALAMIS, PHTHIA.

The memorable heroic genealogy of the Æakids establishes a fabulous connection between Ægina, Salamis, and Phthia, which we can only recognise as a fact without being able to trace its origin.

Æakus was the son of Zeus, born of Ægina, daughter of Asôpus, whom the god had carried off and brought into the island to which he gave her name: she was afterwards married to Aktôr, and had by him Menœtius, father of Patroclus. As there were two rivers named Asôpus, one between Phlius and Sikyôn, and another between Thêbes and Platæa – so the Æginêtan heroic genealogy was connected both with that of Thêbes and with that of Phlius, and this belief led to practical consequences in the minds of those who accepted the legends as genuine history. For when the Thêbans, in the 68th Olympiad, were hard-pressed in war by Athens, they were directed by the Delphian oracle to ask assistance of their next of kin: recollecting that Thêbê and Ægina had been sisters, common daughters of Asôpus, they were induced to apply to the Æginêtans as their next of kin, and the Æginêtans gave them aid, first by sending to them their common heroes, the Æakids, next by actual armed force. Pindar dwells emphatically on the heroic brotherhood between Thêbes, his native city, and Ægina.

Æakus was alone in Ægina: to relieve him from this solitude, Zeus changed all the ants in the island into men, and thus provided him with a numerous population, who, from their origin, were called Myrmidons. By his wife Endêis, daughter of Cheirôn, Æakus had for his sons Pêleus and Telamôn: by the Nêreid Psamathê, he had Phôkus. A monstrous crime had then recently been committed by Pelops, in killing the Arcadian prince, Stymphalus, under a simulation of friendship and hospitality: for this the gods had smitten all Greece with famine and barrenness. The oracles affirmed that nothing could relieve Greece from this intolerable misery except the prayers of Æakus, the most pious of mankind. Accordingly, envoys from all quarters flocked to Ægina, to prevail upon Æakus to put up prayers for them: on his supplications the gods relented, and the suffering immediately ceased. The grateful Greeks established in Ægina the temple and worship of Zeus Panhellênius, one of the lasting monuments and institutions of the island, on the spot where Æakus had offered up his prayer. The statues of the envoys who had come to solicit him were yet to be seen in the Æakeion, or sacred edifice of Æakus, in the time of Pausanias; and the Athenian Isokratês, in his eulogy of Evagoras, the despot of Salamis in Cyprus (who traced his descent through Teukrus to Æakus), enlarges upon this signal miracle, recounted and believed by other Greeks as well as by the Æginêtans, as a proof both of the great qualities and of the divine favour and patronage displayed in the career of the Æakids. Æakus was also employed to aid Poseidôn and Apollo in building the walls of Troy.

Pêleus and Telamôn, the sons of Æakus, contracting a jealousy of their bastard brother, Phôkus, in consequence of his eminent skill in gymnastic contests, conspired to put him to death. Telamôn flung his quoit at him while they were playing together, and Pêleus despatched him by a blow with his hatchet in the back. They then concealed the dead body in a wood, but Æakus, having discovered both the act and the agents, banished the brothers from the island. For both of them eminent destinies were in store.

While we notice the indifference to the moral quality of actions implied in the old Hesiodic legend, when it imputes distinctly and nakedly this proceeding to two of the most admired persons of the heroic world – it is not less instructive to witness the change of feeling which had taken place in the age of Pindar. That warm eulogist of the great Æakid race hangs down his head with shame, and declines to recount, though he is obliged darkly to glance at the cause which forced the pious Æakus to banish his sons from Ægina. It appears that Kallimachus, if we may judge by a short fragment, manifested the same repugnance to mention it.

Telamôn retired to Salamis, then ruled by Kychreus, the son of Poseidôn and Salamis, who had recently rescued the island from the plague of a terrible serpent. This animal, expelled from Salamis, retired to Eleusis in Attica, where it was received and harboured by the goddess Dêmêtêr in her sacred domicile. Kychreus dying childless left his dominion to Telamôn, who, marrying Periboea, daughter of Alkathoos, and granddaughter of Pelops, had for his son the celebrated Ajax. Telamôn took part both in the chase of the Kalidônian boar and in the Argônautic expedition: he was also the intimate friend and companion of Hêraklês, whom he accompanied in his enterprise against the Amazons, and in the attack made with only six ships upon Laomedôn, king of Troy. This last enterprise having proved completely successful, Telamôn was rewarded by Hêraklês with the possession of the daughter of Laomedôn, Hêsionê – who bore to him Teukros, the most distinguished archer amidst the host of Agamemnôn, and the founder of Salamis in Cyprus.

Pêleus went to Phthia, where he married the daughter of Eurytiôn, son of

Aktôr, and received from him the third part of his dominions. Taking part in the Kalydônian boar-hunt, he unintentionally killed his father-in-law Eurytiôn, and was obliged to flee to Iôlkos, where he received purification from Akastus, son of Pelias: the danger to which he became exposed by the calumnious accusations of the enamoured wife of Akastus has already been touched upon in a previous section. Pêleus also was among the Argônauts: the most memorable event in his life however was his marriage with the sea-goddess Thetis. Zeus and Poseidôn had both conceived a violent passion for Thetis. But the former, having been forewarned by Promêtheus that Thetis was destined to give birth to a son more powerful than his father, compelled her, much against her own will, to marry Pêleus: who, instructed by the intimations of the wise Cheirôn, was enabled to seize her on the coast called Sêpias in the southern region of Thessaly. She changed her form several times, but Pêleus held her fast until she resumed her original appearance, and she was then no longer able to resist. All the gods were present, and brought splendid gifts to these memorable nuptials: Apollo sang with his harp, Poseidôn gave to Pêleus the immortal horses Xanthus and Balius, and Cheirôn presented a formidable spear, cut from an ash-tree on Mount Pêlion. We shall have reason hereafter to recognise the value of both these gifts in the exploits of Achillês.

The prominent part assigned to Thetis in the Iliad is well known, and the post-Homeric poets of the Legend of Troy introduced her as actively concurring first to promote the glory, finally to bewail the death of her distinguished son. Pêleus, having survived both his son Achilles and his grandson Neoptolemus, is ultimately directed to place himself on the very spot where he had originally seized Thetis, and thither the goddess comes herself to fetch him away, in order that he may exchange the desertion and decrepitude of age for a life of immortality along with the Nêreids. The spot was indicated to Xerxês when he marched into Greece by the Iônises who accompanied him, and his magi offered solemn sacrifices to her as well as to the other Nêreids, as the presiding goddesses and mistresses of the coast.

Neoptolemus or Pyrrhus, the son of Achillês, too young to engage in the commencement of the siege of Troy, comes on the stage after the death of his father as the indispensable and prominent agent in the final capture of the city. He returns victor from Troy, not to Phthia, but to Epirus, bringing with him the captive Andromachê, widow of Hectôr, by whom Molossus is born to him. He himself perishes in the full vigour of life at Delphi by the machinations of Orestês, son of Agamemnôn. But his son Molossus – like Fleance, the son of Banquo, in Macbeth – becomes the father of the powerful race of Molossian kings, who played so conspicuous a part during the declining vigour of the Grecian cities, and to whom the title and parentage of Æakids was a source of peculiar pride, identifying them by community of heroic origin with genuine and undisputed Hellênes.

The glories of Ajax, the second grandson of Æakus, before Troy, are surpassed only by those of Achillês. He perishes by his own hand, the victim of an insupportable feeling of humiliation, because a less worthy claimant is allowed to carry off from him the arms of the departed Achillês. His son Philæus receives the citizenship of Athens, and the gens or dême called Philaidæ traced up to him its name and its origin: moreover the distinguished Athenians, Militiadês and Thucydidês, were regarded as members of this heroic progeny.

Teukrus escaped from the perils of the siege of Troy as well as from those of the voyage homeward, and reached Salamis in safety. But his father Telamôn, indignant at his having returned without Ajax, refused to receive him, and compelled him to expatriate. He conducted his followers to Cyprus, where he founded the city of Salamis: his descendant Evagoras was recognised as a Teukrid and as an Æakid even in the time of Isokratês.

Such was the splendid heroic genealogy of the Æakids, – a family renowned for military excellence. The Æakeion at Ægina, in which prayer and sacrifice were offered to Æakus, remained in undiminished dignity down to the time of Pausanias. This genealogy connects together various eminent gentes in Achaia Phthiôtis, in Ægina, in Salamis, in Cyprus, and amongst the Epirotic Molossians. Whether we are entitled to infer from it that the island of Ægina was originally peopled by Myrmidones from Achaia Phthiotia, as O. Müller imagines, I will not pretend to affirm. These mythical pedigrees seem to unite together special clans or gentes, rather than the bulk of any community – just as we know that the Athenians generally had no part in the Æakid genealogy, though certain particular Athenian families laid claim to it. The intimate friendship between Achilles and the Opuntian hero Patroclus – and the community of name and frequent conjunction between the Locrian Ajax, son of Oïlous, and Ajax, son of Telamôn – connect the Æakids with Opus and the Opuntian Locrians, in a manner which we have no farther means of explaining. Pindar too represents Menœtius, father of Patroclus, as son of Aktôr and Ægina, and therefore maternal brother of Æakus.

XI. ATTIC LEGENDS AND GENEALOGIES.

The most ancient name in Attic archaeology, as far as our means of information reach, is that of Erechtheus, who is mentioned both in the Catalogue of the Iliad and in a brief allusion of the Odyssey. Born of the Earth, he is brought up by the goddess Athênê, adopted by her as her ward, and installed in her temple at Athens, where the Athenians offer to him annual sacrifices. The Athenians are styled in the Iliad, "the people of Erechtheus." This is the most ancient testimony concerning Erechtheus, exhibiting him as a divine or heroic, certainly a superhuman person, and identifying him with the primitive germination (if I may use a term, the Grecian equivalent of which would have pleased an Athenian ear) of Attic man. He was recognised in this same character, even at the close of the fourth century before the Christian æra, by the Butadæ, one of the most ancient and important Gentes at Athens, who boasted of him as their original ancestor: the genealogy of the great Athenian orator Lykurgus, a member of this family, drawn up by his son Abrôn, and painted on a public tablet in the Erechtheion, contained as its first and highest name, Erechtheus, son of Hêphæstos and the Earth. In the Erechtheion, Erechtheus was worshipped conjointly with Athênê: he was identified with the god Poseidôn, and bore the denomination of Poseidôn Erechtheus: one of the family of the Butadæ, chosen among themselves by lot, enjoyed the privilege and performed the functions of hereditary priest. Herodotus also assigns the same earth-born origin to Erechtheus; but Pindar, the old poem called the Danais, Euripidês and Apollodôrus – all name Erichthonius, son of Hêphæstos and the Earth, as the being who was thus adopted and made the temple-companion of Athênê, while Apollodôrus in another place identifies Erichthonius with Poseidôn. The Homeric scholiast treated Erechtheus and Erichthonius as the same person under two names; and since, in regard to such mythical persons, there exists no other test of identity of the subject except perfect similarity of the attributes, this seems the reasonable conclusion.

We may presume, from the testimony of Homer, that the first and oldest conception of Athens and its sacred acropolis places it under the special protection, and represents it as the settlement and favourite abode of Athênê, jointly with Poseidôn: the latter being the inferior, though the chosen companion of the former, and therefore exchanging his divine appellation for the cognomen of Erechtheus. The country called Attica, which, during the

XI. ATTIC LEGENDS AND GENEALOGIES.

historical ages, forms one social and political aggregate with Athens, was originally distributed into many independent dêmes or cantons, and included, besides, various religious clans or hereditary sects (if the expression may be permitted): that is, a multitude of persons not necessarily living together in the same locality, but bound together by an hereditary communion of sacred rites, and claiming privileges, as well as performing obligations, founded upon the traditional authority of divine persons for whom they had a common veneration. Even down to the beginning of the Peloponnêsian war, the demots of the various Attic dêmes, though long since embodied in the larger political union of Attica, and having no wish for separation, still retained the recollection of their original political autonomy. They lived in their own separate localities, resorted habitually to their own temples, and visited Athens only occasionally for private or political business, or for the great public festivals. Each of these aggregates, political as well as religious, had its own eponymous god or hero, with a genealogy more or less extended, and a train of mythical incidents more or less copious, attached to his name, according to the fancy of the local exegetes and poets. The eponymous heroes Marathôn, Dekelus, Kolônus, or Phlyus, had each their own title to worship, and their own position as themes of legendary narrative, independent of Erechtheus, or Poseidôn, or Athênê, the patrons of the acropolis common to all of them.

But neither the archæology of Attica, nor that of its various component fractions, was much dwelt upon by the ancient epic poets of Greece. Thesêus is noticed both in the Iliad and Odyssey as having carried off from Krête Ariadnê, the daughter of Minôs – thus commencing that connection between the Krêtan and Athenian legends which we afterwards find so largely amplified – and the sons of Thesêus take part in the Trojan war. The chief collectors and narrators of the Attic mythes were, the prose logographers, authors of the many compositions called Atthides, or works on Attic archæology. These writers – Hellanikus, the contemporary of Herodotus, is the earliest composer of an Atthis expressly named, though Pherekydês also touched upon the Attic fables – these writers, I say, interwove into one chronological series the legends which either greatly occupied their own fancy, or commanded the most general reverence among their countrymen. In this way the religions and political legends of Eleusis, a town originally independent of Athens, but incorporated with it before the historical age, were worked into one continuous sequence along with those of the Erechtheids. In this way, Kekrops, the eponymous hero of the portion of Attica called Kekropia, came to be placed in the mythical chronology at a higher point even than the primitive god or hero Erechtheus.

Ogygês is said to have reigned in Attica 1020 years before the first Olympiad, or 1796 years B.C. In his time happened the deluge of Deukaliôn, which destroyed most of the inhabitants of the country: after a long interval, Kekrops, an indigenous person, half man and half serpent, is given to us by Apollodôrus as the first king of the country: he bestowed upon the land, which had before been called Actê, the name of Kekropia. In his day there ensued a dispute between Athênê and Poseidôn respecting the possession of the acropolis at Athens, which each of them coveted. First, Poseidôn struck the rock with his trident, and produced the well of salt water which existed in it, called the Erechthêis: next came Athênê, who planted the sacred olive-tree ever afterwards seen and venerated in the portion of Erechtheion called the cell of Pandrosus. The twelve gods decided the dispute; and Kekrops having testified before them that Athênê had rendered this inestimable service, they adjudged the spot to her in preference to Poseidôn. Both the ancient olive-tree and the well produced by Poseidôn were seen on the acropolis, in the temple consecrated jointly to Athênê and Erechtheus, throughout the historical ages. Poseidôn, as a mark of his wrath for the preference given to Athênê, inundated the Thriasian plain with water.

During the reign of Kekrops, Attica was laid waste by Karian pirates on ths coast, and by invasions of the Aônian inhabitants from Bœotia. Kekrops distributed the inhabitants of Attica into twelve local sections – Kekropia, Tetrapolis, Epakria, Dekeleia, Eleusis, Aphidna, Thorikus, Braurôn, Kythêrus, Sphêttus, Kêphisius, Phalêrus. Wishing to ascertain the number of inhabitants, he commanded each man to cast a single stone into a general heap: the number of stones was counted, and it was found that there were twenty thousand.

Kekrops married the daughter of Aktæus, who (according to Pausanias's version) had been king of the country before him, and had called it by the name of Aktæa. By her he had three daughters, Aglaurus, Ersê and Pandrosus, and a son, Erysichthôn.

Erysichthôn died without issue, and Kranaus succeeded him, another indigenous person and another eponymous, for the name Kranai was an old denomination of the inhabitants of Attica. Kranaus was dethroned by Amphiktyôn, by some called an indigenous man: by others, a son of Deukaliôn: Amphiktyôn in his turn was expelled by Erichthonius, son of Hêphæstos and the Earth, the same person apparently as Erechtheus, but inserted by Apollodôrus at this point of the series. Erichthonius, the pupil and favoured companion of Athênê, placed in the acropolis the original Palladium or wooden statue of that goddess, said to have dropped from heaven: he was moreover the first to celebrate the festival of the Panathenæa. He married the nymph Pasithea, and had for his son and successor Pandiôn. Erichthonius was the first person who taught the art of breaking in horses to the yoke, and who drove a chariot and four.

In the time of Pandiôn, who succeeded to Erichthonius, Dionysus and Dêmêtêr both came into Attica: the latter was received by Keleos at Eleusis. Pandiôn married the nymph Zeuxippê, and had twin sons, Erechtheus and Butês, and two daughters, Proknê and Philomêla. The two latter are the subjects of a memorable and well-known legend. Pandiôn having received aid in repelling the Thêbans from Têreus, king of Thrace, gave him his daughter Proknê in marriage, by whom he had a son, Itys. The beautiful Philomêla, going to visit her sister, inspired the barbarous Thracian with an irresistible passion: he violated her person, confined her in a distant pastoral hut, and pretended that she was dead, cutting out her tongue to prevent her from revealing the truth. After a long interval, Philomêla found means to acquaint her sister of the cruel deed which had been perpetrated: she wove into a garment words describing her melancholy condition, and despatched it by a trusty messenger. Proknê, overwhelmed with sorrow and anger, took advantage of the free egress enjoyed by women during the Bacchanalian festival to go and release her sister: the two sisters then revenged themselves upon Têreus by killing the boy Itys, and serving him up for his father to eat: after the meal had been finished, the horrid truth was revealed to him. Têreus snatched a hatchet to put Proknê to death: she fled, along with Philomêla, and all the three were changed into birds – Proknê became a swallow, Philomêla a nightingale, and Têreus an hoopoe. This tale, so popular with the poets, and so illustrative of the general character of Grecian legend, is not less remarkable in another point of view – that the great historian Thucydidês seems to allude to it as an historical fact, not however directly mentioning the final metamorphosis.

After the death of Pandiôn, Erechtheus succeeded to the kingdom, and his brother, Butês, became priest of Poseidôn Erichthonius, a function which his descendants ever afterwards exercised, the Butadæ or Eteobutadæ. Erechtheus seems to appear in three characters in the fabulous history of Athens – as a god, Poseidôn Erechtheus – as a hero, Erechtheus, son of the Earth – and now, as a king, son of Pandiôn: so much did the ideas of divine and human rule become confounded and blended together in the imagination of the Greeks in reviewing their early times.

The daughters of Erechtheus were not less celebrated in Athenian legend than those of Pandiôn. Prokris, one of them, is among the heroines seen by Odysseus in Hadês: she became the wife of Kephalus, son of Deionês, and lived in the Attic dême of Thorikus.

Kreüsa, another daughter of Erechtheus, seduced by Apollo, becomes the mother of Iôn, whom she exposes immediately after his birth in the cave north of the acropolis, concealing the fact from every one. Apollo prevails upon Hermês to convey the new-born child to Delphi, where he is brought up as a servant of the temple, without knowing his parents. Kreüsa marries Xuthus, son of Æolus, but continuing childless, she goes with Xuthus to the Delphian oracle to inquire for a remedy. The god presents to them Iôn, and desires them to adopt him as their son: their son Achæus is afterwards born to them, and Iôn and Achæus become the eponyms of the Iônians and Achæans.

Oreithyia, the third daughter of Erechtheus, was stolen away by the god Boreas while amusing herself on the banks of the Ilissus, and carried to his residence in Thrace. The two sons of this marriage, Zêtês and Kalais, were born with wings: they took part in the Argônautic expedition, and engaged in the pursuit of the harpies: they were slain at Tênos by Hêraklês, Kleopatra, the daughter of Boreas and Oreithyia, was married to Phineus, and had two sons, Plexippus and Pandiôn: but Phineus afterwards espoused a second wife, Idæa, the daughter of Dardanus, who, detesting the two sons of the former bed, accused them falsely of attempting her chastity, and persuaded Phineus in his wrath to put out the eyes of both. For this cruel proceeding he was punished by the Argônauts in the course of their voyage.

On more than one occasion the Athenians derived, or at least believed themselves to have derived, important benefits from this marriage of Boreas with the daughter of their primaeval hero: one inestimable service, rendered at a juncture highly critical for Grecian independence deserves to be specified. At the time of the invasion of Greece by Xerxês, the Grecian fleet was assembled at Chalkis and Artemision in Eubœa, awaiting the approach of the Persian force, so overwhelming in its numbers as well by sea as on land. The Persian fleet had reached the coast of Magnêsia and the south-eastern corner of Thessaly without any material damage, when the Athenians were instructed by an oracle "to invoke the aid of their son-in-law." Understanding the advice to point to Boreas, they supplicated his aid and that of Oreithyia, most earnestly, as well by prayer as by sacrifice, and the event corresponded to their wishes. A furious north-easterly wind immediately arose, and continued for three days to afflict the Persian fleet as it lay on an unprotected coast: the number of ships driven ashore, both vessels of war and of provision, was immense, and the injury done to the armament was never thoroughly repaired. Such was the powerful succour which the Athenians derived, at a time of their utmost need, from their son-in-law Boreas; and their gratitude was shown by consecrating to him a new temple on the banks of the Ilissus.

The three remaining daughters of Erechtheus – he had six in all – were in Athenian legend yet more venerated than their sisters, on account of having voluntarily devoted themselves to death for the safety of their country. Eumolpus of Eleusis was the son of Poseidôn and the eponymous hero of the sacred gens called the Eumolpids, in whom the principal functions, appertaining to the mysterious rites of Dêmêtêr at Eleusis, were vested by hereditary privilege: he made war upon Erechtheus and the Athenians, with the aid of a body of Thracian allies: indeed it appears that the legends of Athens, originally foreign and unfriendly to those of Eleusis, represented him as having been himself a Thracian born and an immigrant into Attica. Respecting Eumolpus however and his parentage, the discrepancies much exceed even the measure of license usual in the legendary genealogies, and some critics, both ancient and modern, have sought to reconcile these contradictions by the usual stratagem of supposing two or three different persons of the same name. Even Pausanias, so familiar with this class of unsworn witnesses, complains of the want of native Eleusinian genealogists, and of the extreme license of fiction in which other authors had indulged.

In the Homeric Hymn to Dêmêtêr, the most ancient testimony before us, composed, to all appearance, earlier than the complete incorporation of Eleusis with Athens, Eumolpus appears (to repeat briefly what has been stated in a previous chapter) as one of the native chiefs or princes of Eleusis, along with Triptolemus, Dioklês, Polyxeinus and Dolichus: Keleos is the king, or principal among these chiefs, the son or lineal descendant of the eponymous Eleusis himself. To these chiefs, and to the three daughters of Keleos, the goddess Dêmêtêr comes in her sorrow for the loss of her daughter Persephonê: being hospitably entertained by Keleos she reveals her true character, commands that a temple shall be built to her at Eleusis, and prescribes to them the rites according to which they are to worship her. Such seems to have been the ancient story of the Eleusinians respecting their own religious antiquities: Keleos, with Metaneira his wife, and the other chiefs here mentioned, were

125

LEGENDARY GREECE

worshipped at Eleusis, and from thence transferred to Athens as local gods or heroes. Eleusis became incorporated with Athens, apparently not very long before the time of Solôn: and the Eleusinian worship of Dêmêtêr was then received into the great religious solemnities of the Athenian state, to which it owes its remarkable subsequent extension and commanding influence. In the Atticised worship of the Eleusinian Dêmêtêr, the Eumolpids and the Kêrykes were the principal hereditary functionaries: Eumolpus, the eponym of this great family, came thus to play the principal part in the Athenian legendary version of the war between Athens and Eleusis. An oracle had pronounced that Athens could only be rescued from his attack by the death of the three daughters of Erechtheus: their generous patriotism consented to the sacrifice, and their father put them to death. He then went forth confidently to the battle, totally vanquished the enemy, and killed Eumolpus with his own hand. Erechtheus was worshipped as a god, and his daughters as goddesses, at Athens. Their names and their exalted devotion were cited along with those of the warriors of Marathôn, in the public assembly of Athens, by orators who sought to arouse the languid patriot, or to denounce the cowardly deserter; and the people listened both to one and the other with analogous feelings of grateful veneration, as well as with equally unsuspecting faith in the matter of fact.

Though Erechtheus gained the victory over Eumolpus, yet the story represents Poseidôn as having put an end to the life and reign of Erechtheus, who was (it seems) slain in the battle. He was succeeded by his son Kekrops II., and the latter again by his son Pandiôn II., two names unmarked by any incidents, and which appear to be mere duplication of the former Kekrops and Pandiôn, placed there by the genealogisers for the purpose of filling up what seemed to them a chronological chasm.

Apollodôrus passes at once from Erechtheus to his son Kekrops II., then to Pandiôn II., next to the four sons of the latter, Ægeus, Pallas, Nisus and Lykus. The tragedians here insert the story of Xuthus, Krüsa and Iôn: the latter being the son of Kreüsa by Apollo, but given by the god to Xuthus, and adopted by the latter as his own. Iôn becomes the successor of Erechtheus, and his sons Teleon, Hoplês, Argadês and Aigikorês) become the eponyms of the four ancient tribes of Athens, which subsisted until the revolution of Kleisthenês. Iôn himself is the eponym of the Iônic race both in Asia, in Europe, and in the Ægean islands: Dôrus and Achæus are the sons of Kreüsa by Xuthus, so that Iôn is distinguished from both of them by being of divine parentage. According to the story given by Philochorus. Iôn rendered such

126

essential service in rescuing the Athenians from the attack of the Thracians under Eumolpus, that he was afterwards made king of the country, and distributed all the inhabitants into four tribes or castes, corresponding to different modes of life, – soldiers, husbandmen, goatherds, and artisans. It seems that the legend explanatory of the origin of the festival Boëdromia, originally important enough to furnish a name for one of the Athenian months, was attached to the aid thus rendered by Iôn.

We pass from Iôn to persons of far greater mythical dignity and interest, Ægeus and his son Thêseus.

Pandiôn had four sons, Ægeus, Nisus, Lykus, and Pallas, between whom he divided his dominions. Nisus received the territory of Megaris, which had been under the sway of Pandiôn, and there founded the seaport of Nisæa. Lykus was made king of the eastern coast, but a dispute afterwards ensued, and he quitted the country altogether, to establish himself on the southern coast of Asia Minor among the Termilæ, to whom he gave the name of Lykians. Ægeus, as the eldest of the four, became king of Athens: but Pallas received a portion both of the southwestern coast and the interior, and he as well as his children appear as frequent enemies both to Ægeus and to Thesêus. Pallas is the eponym of the dême Pallênê, and the stories respecting him and his sons seem to be connected with old and standing feuds among the different dêmes of Attica, originally independent communities. These feuds penetrated into the legend, and explain the story which we find that Ægeus and Thesêus were not genuine Erechtheids, the former being denominated a supposititious child to Pandiôn.

Thêseus.

Ægeus has little importance in the mythical history except as the father of Thesêus: it may even be doubted whether his name is anything more than a mere cognomen of the god Poseidôn, who was (as we are told) the real father of this great Attic Hêraklês. As I pretend only to give a very brief outline of the general territory of Grecian legend, I cannot permit myself to recount in detail the chivalrous career of Thesêus, who is found both in the Kalydônian boar-hunt and in the Argônautic expedition – his personal and victorious encounters with the robbers Sinnis, Procrustês, Periphêtês, Skiron and others – his valuable service in ridding his country of the Krommyonian sow and the Marathônian bull – his conquest of the Minôtaur in Krête, and his escape from the dangers of the labyrinth by the aid of Ariadnê, whom he subsequently carries off and abandons – his many amorous adventures, and his expeditions both against the Amazons and into the under-world along with Peirithous.

Thucydidês delineates the character of Thesêus as a man who combined sagacity with political power, and who conferred upon his country the inestimable benefit of uniting all the separate and self-governing dêmes of Attica into one common political society. From the well-earned reverence attached to the assertion of Thucydidês, it has been customary to reason upon this assertion as if it were historically authentic, and to treat the romantic attributes which we find in Plutarch and Diodôrus as if they were fiction superinduced upon this basis of fact. Such a view of the case is in my judgment erroneous. The athletic and amorous knight-errant is the old version of the character – the profound and long-sighted politician is a subsequent correction, introduced indeed by men of superior mind, but destitute of historical warranty, and arising out of their desire to find reasons of their own for concurring in the veneration which the general public paid more easily and heartily to their national hero. Thesêus, in the Iliad and Odyssey, fights with the Lapithæ against the Centaurs: Thesêus, in the Hesiodic poems, is misguided by his passion for the beautiful Æglê, daughter of Panopeus; and the Thesêus described in Plutarch's biography is in great part a continuation and expansion of these same or similar attributes, mingled with many local legends, explaining, like the Fasti of Ovid, or the lost Aitia of Kallimachus, the original genesis of prevalent religious and social customs. Plutarch has doubtless greatly softened down and modified the adventures which he found in the Attic logographers as well as in the poetical epics called Thêsêis. For in his preface to the life of Thesêus, after having emphatically declared that he is about to transcend the boundary both of the known and the knowable, but that the temptation of comparing the founder of Athens with the founder of Rome is irresistible, he concludes with the following remarkable words: "I pray that this fabulous matter may be so far obedient to my endeavours as to receive, when purified by reason, the aspect of history: in those cases where it haughtily scorns plausibility and will admit no alliance with what is probable, I shall beg for indulgent hearers, willing to receive antique narrative in a mild spirit." We see here that Plutarch sat down, not to recount the old fables as he found them, but to purify them by reason and to impart to them the aspect of history. We have to thank him for having retained, after this purification, so much of what is romantic and marvellous: but we may be sure that the sources from which be borrowed were more romantic and marvellous still. It was the tendency of the enlightened men of Athens, from the days of Solôn downwards, to refine and politicise the character of Thesêus; even Peisistratus expunged from one of the Hesiodic poems the line which described the violent passion of the hero for the fair Æglê; and the tragic poets found it more congenial to the feelings of their audience to exhibit him as a dignified and liberal sovereign, rather than as an adventurous single-handed fighter. The logographers and the Alexandrine poets remained more faithful to the old fables. The story of Hekalê, the hospitable old woman who received and blessed Thesêus when he went against the Marathônian bull, and whom he found dead when he came back to recount the news of his success, was treated by Kallimachus; and Virgil must have had his mind full of the unrefined legends when he numbered this Attic Hêraklês among the unhappy sufferers condemned to endless penance in the under-world.

Two however among the Thêseian fables cannot be dismissed without some special notice, – the war against the Amazons, and the expedition against Krête. The former strikingly illustrates the facility as well as the tenacity of Grecian legendary faith: the latter embraces the story of Dædalus and Minôs, two of the most eminent among Grecian ante-historical personages.

Legend of the Amazons.

The Amazons, daughters of Arês and Harmonia, are both early creations and frequent reproductions of the ancient epic – which was indeed, we may generally remark, largely occupied both with the exploits and sufferings of women, or heroines, the wives and daughters of the Grecian heroes – and which recognised in Pallas Athênê the finished type of an irresistible female warrior. A nation of courageous, hardy and indefatigable women, dwelling apart from men, permitting only a short temporary intercourse for the purpose of renovating their numbers, and burning out their right breast with a view of enabling themselves to draw the bow freely, this was at once a general type stimulating to the fancy of the poet and a theme eminently popular with his hearers. Nor was it at all repugnant to the faith of the latter – who had no recorded facts to guide them, and no other standard of credibility as to the past except such poetical narratives themselves – to conceive communities of Amazons as having actually existed in anterior time. Accordingly we find these warlike females constantly reappearing in the ancient poems, and universally accepted as past realities. In the Iliad, when Priam wishes to illustrate emphatically the most numerous host in which he ever found himself included, he tells us that it was assembled in Phyrgia, on the banks of the Sangarius, for the purpose of resisting the formidable Amazons. When Bellerophôn is to be employed on a deadly and perilous undertaking, by those who indirectly wish to procure his death, he is despatched against the Amazons. In the Æthiopis of Arktinus, describing the post-Homeric war of Troy, Penthesileia, queen of the Amazons, appears as the most effective ally of the besieged city, and as the most formidable enemy of the Greeks, succumbing only to the invincible might of Achillês. The Argônautic heroes find the Amazons on the river Thermôdôn, in their expedition along the southern coast of the Euxine. To the same spot Hêraklês goes to attack them, in the performance of the ninth labour imposed upon him by Eurystheus, for the purpose of procuring the girdle of the Amazonian queen, Hippolytê; and we are told that they had not yet recovered from the losses sustained in this severe aggression when Thesêus also assaulted and defeated them, carrying off their queen, Antiopê. This injury they avenged by invading Attica, an undertaking as Plutarch justly observes) "neither trifling nor feminine," especially if according to the statement of Hellanikus, they crossed the Cimmerian Bosporus on the winter ice, beginning their march from the Asiatic side of the Paulus Mæotis. They overcame all the resistances and difficulties of this prodigious march, and penetrated even into Athens itself, where the final battle, hard-fought and at one time doubtful, by which Thesêus crushed them, was fought – in the very heart of the city. Attic antiquaries confidently pointed out the exact position of the two contending armies: the left wing of the Amazons rested upon the spot occupied by the commemorative monument called the Amazoneion: the right wing touched the Pnyx, the place in which the public assemblies of the Athenian democracy were afterwards held. The details and fluctuations of the combat, as well as the final triumph and consequent truce, were recounted by these authors with as complete faith and as much circumstantiality as those of the battle of Platæa by Herodotus. The sepulchral edifice called the Amazoneion, the tomb or pillar of Antiopê near the western gate of the city – the spot called the Horkomosion near the temple of Thesêus – even the hill of Areiopagus itself, and the sacrifices which it was customary to offer to the Amazons at the periodical festival of the Thêseia – were all so many religious mementos of this victory; which was moreover a favourite subject of art both with the sculptor and the painter, at Athens as well as in other parts of Greece.

No portion of the ante-historical epic appears to have been more deeply worked

XI. ATTIC LEGENDS AND GENEALOGIES.

into the national mind of Greece than this invasion and defeat of the Amazons. It was not only a constant theme of the logographers, but was also familiarly appealed to by the popular orators along with Marathôn and Salamis, among those antique exploits of which their fellow-citizens might justly be proud. It formed a part of the retrospective faith of Herodotus, Lysias, Plato and Isokratês, and the exact date of the event was settled by the chronologists. Nor did the Athenians stand alone in such a belief. Throughout many other regions of Greece, both European and Asiatic, traditions and memorials of the Amazons were found. At Megara, at Trœzen, in Lacônia near Cape Tænarus, at Chæroneia in Bœôtia, and in more than one part of Thessaly, sepulchres or monuments of the Amazons were preserved. The warlike women (it was said), on their way to Attica, had not traversed those countries, without leaving some evidences of their passage.

Amongst the Asiatic Greeks the supposed traces of the Amazons were yet more numerous. Their proper territory was asserted to be the town and plain of Themiskyra, near the Grecian colony of Amisus, on the river Thermôdôn, a region called after their name by Roman historians and geographers. But they were believed to have conquered and occupied in early times a much wider range of territory, extending even to the coast of Iônia and Æolis. Ephesus, Smyrna, Kymê, Myrina, Paphos and Sinopê were affirmed to have been founded and denominated by them. Some authors placed them in Libya or Ethiopia: and when the Pontic Greeks on the north-western shore of the Euxine had become acquainted with the hardy and daring character of the Sarmatian maidens, who were obliged to have slain each an enemy in battle as the condition of obtaining a husband, and who artificially prevented the growth of the right breast during childhood, they could imagine no more satisfactory mode of accounting for such attributes than by deducing the Sarmatians from a colony of vagrant Amazons, expelled by the Grecian heroes from their territory on the Thermôdôn. Pindar ascribed the first establishment of the memorable temple of Artemis at Ephesus to the Amazons. And Pausanias explains in part the pre-eminence which this temple enjoyed over every other in Greece by the widely diffused renown of its female founders, respecting whom he observes (with perfect truth, if we admit the historical character of the old epic), that women possess an unparalleled force of resolution in resisting adverse events, since the Amazons, after having been first roughly handled by Hêraklês and then completely defeated by Thesêus, could yet find courage to play so conspicuous a part in the defence of Troy against the Grecian besiegers.

It is thus that in what is called early Grecian history, as the Greeks themselves looked back upon it, the Amazons were among the most prominent and undisputed personages. Nor will the circumstance appear wonderful if we reflect, that the belief in them was first established at a time when the Grecian mind was fed with nothing else but religious legend and epic poetry, and that the incidents of the supposed past, as received from these sources, were addressed to their faith and feelings, without being required to adapt themselves to any canons of credibility drawn from present experience. But the time came when the historians of Alexander the Great audaciously abused this ancient credence. Amongst other tales calculated to exalt the dignity of that monarch, they affirmed that after his conquest and subjugation of the Persian empire, he had been visited in Hyrcania by Thalêstris, queen of the Amazons, who admiring his warlike prowess, was anxious to be enabled to return into her own country in a condition to produce offspring of a breed so invincible. But the Greeks had now been accustomed for a century and a half to historical and philosophical criticism – and that un-inquiring faith, which was readily accorded to the wonders of the past, could no longer be invoked for them when tendered as present reality. For the fable of the Amazons was here reproduced in its naked simplicity, without being rationalized or painted over with historical colours.

Some literary men indeed, among whom were Dêmêtrius of Skêpsis, and the Mitylenæan Theophanês, the companion of Pompey in his expeditions, still continued their belief both in Amazons present and Amazons past; and when it became notorious that at least there were none such on the banks of the Thermôdôn, these authors supposed them to have migrated from their original locality, and to have settled in the unvisited regions north of Mount Caucasus. Strabo, on the contrary, feeling that the grounds of disbelief applied with equal force to the ancient stories and to the modern, rejected both the one and the other. He remarks at the same time, not without some surprise, that it was usual with most persons to adopt a middle course, to retain the Amazons as historical phenomena of the remote past, but to disallow them as realities of the present, and to maintain that the breed had died out. The accomplished intellect of Julius Cæsar did not scruple to acknowledge them as having once conquered and held in dominion a large portion of Asia; and the compromise between early, traditional, and religious faith on the one hand, and established habits of critical research on the other, adopted by the historian Arrian, deserves to be transcribed in his own words, as illustrating strikingly the powerful sway of the old legends even over the most positive-minded Greeks: "Neither

XI. ATTIC LEGENDS AND GENEALOGIES.

Aristobulus nor Ptolemy (he observes), nor any other competent witness, has recounted this (visit of the Amazons and their queen to Alexander): nor does it seem to me that the race of the Amazons was preserved down to that time, nor have they been noticed either by any one before Alexander, or by Xenophôn, though he mentions both the Phasians and the Kolchians, and the other barbarous nations which the Greeks saw both before and after their arrival at Trapezus, in which marches they must have met with the Amazons, if the latter had been still in existence. Yet *it is incredible to me* that this race of women, celebrated as they have been by authors so many and so commanding, s*hould never have existed at all.* The story tells of Hêraklês, that he set out from Greece and brought back with him the girdle of their queen Hippolytê: also of Theseûs and the Athenians, that they were the first who defeated in battle and repelled these women in their invasion of Europe: and the combat of the Athenians with the Amazons has been painted by Mikôn, not less than that between the Athenians and the Persians. Moreover Herodotus has spoken in many places of these women, and those Athenian orators who have pronounced panegyrics on the citizens slain in battle, have dwelt upon the victory over the Amazons as among the most memorable of Athenian exploits. If the satrap of Media sent any equestrian women at all to Alexander, I think that they must have come from some of the neighbouring tribes, practised in riding and equipped in the costume generally called Amazonian."

There cannot be a more striking evidence of the indelible force with which these ancient legends were worked into the national faith and feelings of the Greeks, than these remarks of a judicious historian upon the fable of the Amazons. Probably if any plausible mode of rationalising it, and of transforming it into a quasi-political event, had been offered to Arrian, he would have been better pleased to adopt such a middle term, and would have rested comfortably in the supposition that he believed the legend in its true meaning, while his less inquiring countrymen were imposed upon by the exaggerations of poets. But as the story was presented to him plain and unvarnished, either for acceptance or rejection, his feelings as a patriot and a religious man prevented him from applying to the past such tests of credibility as his untrammelled reason acknowledged to be paramount in regard to the present. When we see moreover how much his belief was strengthened, and all tendency to scepticism shut out by the familiarity of his eye and memory with sculptured or painted Amazons – we may calculate the irresistible force of this sensible demonstration on the convictions of the unlettered public, at once more deeply retentive of passive impressions, and unaccustomed to the countervailing habit of rational investigation into evidence. Had the march of an army of warlike women, from the Thermôdôn or the Tanais into the heart of Attica, been recounted to Arrian as an incident belonging to the time of Alexander the Great, he would have rejected it no less emphatically than Strabo; but cast back as it was into an undefined past, it took rank among the hallowed traditions of divine or heroic antiquity, gratifying to extol by rhetoric, but repulsive to scrutinise in argument.

XII. KRÊTAN LEGENDS - MINÔS AND HIS FAMILY.

To understand the adventures of Thesêus in Krête, it will be necessary to touch briefly upon Minôs and the Krêtan heroic genealogy.

Minôs and Rhadamanthus, according to Homer, are sons of Zeus, by Europe, daughter of the widely-celebrated Phœnix, born in Krête. Minôs is the father of Deukaliôn, whose son Idomeneus, in conjunction with Mêrionês, conducts the Krêtan troops to the host of Agamemnôn before Troy. Minôs is ruler of Knôssus, and familiar companion of the great Zeus. He is spoken of as holding guardianship in Krête – not necessarily meaning the whole of the island: he is farther decorated with a golden sceptre, and constituted judge over the dead in the underworld to settle their disputes, in which function Odysseus finds him – this however by a passage of comparatively late interpolation into the Odyssey. He also had a daughter named Ariadnê, for whom the artist Dædalus fabricated in the town of Knôssus the representation of a complicated dance, and who was ultimately carried off by Thesêus: she died in the island of Dia, deserted by Thesêus and betrayed by Dionysos to the fatal wrath of Artemis. Rhadamanthus seems to approach to Minôs both in judicial functions and posthumous dignity. He is conveyed expressly to Eubœa, by the semi-divine sea-carriers the Phæacians, to inspect the gigantic corpse of the earth-born Tityus – the longest voyage they ever undertook. He is moreover after death promoted to an abode of undisturbed bliss in the Elysian plain at the extremity of the earth.

According to poets later than Homer, Europê is brought over by Zeus from Phœnicia to Krête, where she bears to him three sons, Minôs, Rhadamanthus and Sarpêdôn. The latter leaves Krête and settles in Lykia, the population of which, as well as that of many other portions of Asia Minor, is connected by various mythical genealogies with Krête, though the Sarpêdôn of the Iliad has no connection with Krête, and is not the son of Europê. Sarpêdôn having become king of Lykia, was favoured by his father, Zeus, with permission to live for three generations. At the same time the youthful Milêtus, a favourite of Sarpêdôn, quitted Krête, and established the city which bore his name on the coast of Asia Minor. Rhadamanthus became sovereign of and lawgiver among the islands in the Ægean: he subsequently went to Bœôtia, where he married the widowed Alkmênê, mother of Hêraklês.

Europê finds in Krête a king Astêrius, who marries her and adopts her children by Zeus: this Astêrius is the son of Krês, the eponym of the island, or (according to another genealogy by which it was attempted to be made out that Minôs was of Dôrian race) he was a son of the daughter of Krês by Tektamus, the son of Dôrus, who had migrated into the island from Greece.

Minôs married Pasiphaê, daughter of the god Hêlios and Perseïs, by whom he had Katreus, Deukaliôn, Glaukus, Androgeos, names marked in the legendary narrative, together with several daughters, among whom were Ariadnê and Phædra. He offended Poseidôn by neglecting to fulfil a solemnly-made vow, and the displeased god afflicted his wife Pasiphaê with a monstrous passion for a bull. The great artist Dædalus, son of Eupalamus, a fugitive from Athens, became the confidant of this amour, from which sprang the Minôtaur, a creature half man and half bull. This Minôtaur was imprisoned by Minôs in the labyrinth, an inextricable inclosure constructed by Dædalus for that express purpose, by order of Minôs.

Minôs acquired great nautical power, and expelled the Karian inhabitants from many of the islands of the Ægean, which he placed under the government of his sons on the footing of tributaries. He undertook several expeditions against various places on the coast – one against Nisus, the son of Pandiôn, king of Megara, who had amongst the hair of his head one peculiar lock of a purple colour: an oracle had pronounced that his life and reign would never be in danger so long as he preserved this precious lock. The city would have remained inexpugnable, if Skylla, the daughter of Nisus, had not conceived a violent passion for Minôs. While her father was asleep, she cut off the lock on which his safety hung, so that the Krêtan king soon became victorious. Instead of performing his promise to carry Skylla away with him to Krête, he cast her from the stern of his vessel into the sea: both Skylla and Nisus were changed into birds.

Androgeos, son of Minôs having displayed such rare qualities as to vanquish all his competitors at the Panathenaic festival in Athens, was sent by Ægeus the Athenian king to contend against the bull of Marathôn, an enterprise in which he perished, and Minôs made war upon Athens to avenge his death. He was for a long time unable to take the city: at length he prayed to his father Zeus to aid him in obtaining redress from the Athenians, and Zeus sent upon them pestilence and famine. In vain did they endeavour to avert these calamities by offering up as propitiatory sacrifices the four daughters of Hyakinthus. Their sufferings still continued, and the oracle directed them to submit to any terms which Minôs might exact. He required that they should send to Krête a tribute of seven youths and seven maidens, periodically, to be devoured by the

Minôtaur, offered to him in a labyrinth constructed by Dædalus, including countless different passages, out of which no person could escape.

Every ninth year this offering was to be despatched. The more common story was, that the youths and maidens thus destined to destruction were selected by lot – but the logographer Hellanikus said that Minôs came to Athens and chose them himself. The third period for despatching the victims had arrived, and Athens was plunged in the. deepest affliction, when Thêseus determined to devote himself as one of them, and either to terminate the sanguinary tribute or to perish. He prayed to Poseidôn for help, and the Delphian god assured him that Aphroditê would sustain and extricate him. On arriving at Knôssus he was fortunate enough to captivate the affections of Ariadnê, the daughter of Minôs, who supplied him with a sword and a clue of thread. With the former he contrived to kill the Minôtaur, the latter served to guide his footsteps in escaping from the labyrinth. Having accomplished this triumph, he left Krête with his ship and companions unhurt, carrying off Ariadnê, whom however he soon abandoned on the island of Naxos. On his way home to Athens, he stopped at Delos, where he offered a grateful sacrifice to Apollo for his escape, and danced along with the young men and maidens whom he had rescued from the Minôtaur, a dance called the Geranus, imitated from the twists and convolutions of the Krêtan labyrinth. It had been concerted with his father Ægeus, that if he succeeded in his enterprise against the Minôtaur, he should on his return hoist white sails in his ship in place of the black canvas which she habitually carried when employed on this mournful embassy. But Thesêus forgot to make the change of sails: so that Ægeus, seeing the ship return with her equipment of mourning unaltered, was impressed with the sorrowful conviction that his son had perished, and cast himself into the sea. The ship which made this voyage was preserved by the Athenians with careful solicitude, being constantly repaired with new timbers, down to the time of the Phalerian Dêmêtrius: every year she was sent from Athens to Dêlos with a solemn sacrifice and specially-nominated envoys. The priest of Apollo decked her stern with garlands before she quitted the port, and during the time which elapsed until her return, the city was understood to abstain from all acts carrying with them public impurity, so that it was unlawful to put to death any person even under formal sentence by the dikastery. This accidental circumstance becomes especially memorable, from its having postponed for thirty days the death of the lamented Sokratês.

The legend respecting Thesêus, and his heroic rescue of the seven noble youths and maidens from the jaws of the Minôtaur, was thus both commemorated and certified to the Athenian public, by the annual holy ceremony and by the unquestioned identity of the vessel employed in it. There were indeed many varieties in the mode of narrating the incident; and some of the Attic logographers tried to rationalise the fable by transforming the Minôtaur into a general or a powerful athlete, named Taurus, whom Thesêus vanquished in Krête. But this altered version never overbore the old fanciful character of the tale as maintained by the poets. A great number of other religious ceremonies and customs, as well as several chapels or sacred enclosures in honour of different heroes, were connected with different acts and special ordinances of Thesêus. To every Athenian who took part in the festivals of the Oschophoria, the Pyanepsia, or the Kybernêsia, the name of this great hero was familiar, and the motives for offering to him solemn worship at his own special festival of the Thêseia, became evident and impressive.

The same Athenian legends which ennobled and decorated the character of Thesêus, painted in repulsive colours the attributes of Minôs: and the traits of the old Homeric comrade of Zeus were buried under those of the conqueror and oppressor of Athens. His history like that of the other legendary personages of Greece, consists almost entirely of a string of family romances and tragedies. His son Katreus, father of Aëropê, wife of Atreus, was apprised by an oracle that he would perish by the hand of one of his own children: he accordingly sent them out of the island, and Althæmenês, his son, established himself in Rhodes. Katreus having become old, and fancying that he had outlived the warning of the oracle, went over to Rhodes to see Althæmenês. In an accidental dispute which arose between his attendants and the islanders, Althæmenês inadvertently took part and slew his father without knowing him. Glaukus, the youngest son of Minôs, pursuing a mouse, fell into a reservoir of honey and was drowned. No one knew what had become of him and his father was inconsolable: at length the Argeian Polyeidus, a prophet wonderfully endowed by the gods, both discovered the boy and restored him to life, to the exceeding joy of Minôs.

The latter at last found his death in an eager attempt to overtake and punish Dædalus. This great artist, the eponymous hero of the Attic gens or dême called the Dædalidæ, and the descendant of Erechtheus through Mêtion, had been tried at the tribunal of Areiopagus and banished for killing his nephew Talos, whose rapidly improving skill excited his envy. He took refuge in Krête, where he acquired the confidence of Minôs, and was employed (as has been already mentioned) in constructing the labyrinth: subsequently however he fell under the displeasure of Minôs, and was confined as a close prisoner in the inextricable windings of his own edifice. His unrivalled skill and resource however did not forsake him. He manufactured wings both for himself and for his son Ikarus, with which they flew over the sea: the father arrived safely in Sicily at Kamikus, the residence of the Sikanian king Kokalus, but the son, disdaining paternal example and admonition, flew so high that his wings were melted by the sun and he fell into the sea, which from him was called the Ikarian sea.

Dædalus remained for some time in Sicily, leaving in various parts of the island many prodigious evidences of mechanical and architectural skill. At length Minôs bent upon regaining possession of his person, undertook an expedition against Kokalus with a numerous fleet and army. Kokalus affecting readiness to deliver up the fugitive, and receiving Minôs with apparent friendship, ordered a bath to be prepared for him by his three daughters, who, eager to protect Dædalus at any price, drowned the Krêtan king in the bath with hot water. Many of the Krêtans who had accompanied him remained in Sicily and founded the town of Minoa, which they denominated after him. But not long afterwards Zeus instigated all the inhabitants of Krête (except the towns of Polichna and Præsus) to undertake with one accord an expedition against Kamikus for the purpose of avenging the death of Minôs. They besieged Kamikus in vain for five years, until at last famine compelled them to return. On their way along the coast of Italy, in the Gulf of Tarentum, a terrible storm destroyed their fleet and obliged them to settle permanently in the country: they founded Hyria with other cities, and became Messapian Iapygians. Other settlers, for the most part Greeks, immigrated into Krête to the spots which this movement had left vacant. In the second generation after Minôs, occurred the Trojan war. The departed Minôs was exceedingly offended with the Krêtans for co-operating in avenging the injury to Menelaus, since the Greeks generally had lent no aid to the Krêtans in their expedition against the town of Kamikus. He sent upon Krête, after the return of Idomeneus from Troy, such terrible visitations of famine and pestilence, that the population again died out or expatriated, and was again renovated by fresh immigrations. The intolerable suffering thus brought upon the Krêtans by the anger of Minôs, for having co-operated in the general Grecian aid to Menelaus, was urged by them to the Greeks as the reason why they could take no part in resisting the invasion of Xerxês: and it is even pretended that they were advised and encouraged to adopt this ground of excuse by the Delphian oracle.

Such is the Minôs of the poets and logographers, with his legendary and romantic attributes: the familiar comrade of the great Zeus, the judge among the dead in Hadês, the husband of Pasiphaê, daughter of the god Hêlios, the father of the goddess Ariadnê, as well as of Androgeos, who perishes and is worshipped at Athens, and of the boy Glaukus, who is miraculously restored to life by a prophet, the person beloved by Skylla, and the amorous pursuer of the nymph or goddess Britomartis, the proprietor of the Labyrinth and of the Minôtaur, and the exactor of a periodical tribute of youths and maidens from Athens as food for this monster, lastly, the follower of the fugitive artist Dædalus to Kamikus, and the victim of the three ill-disposed daughters of Kokalus in a bath. With this strongly-marked portrait, the Minôs of Thucydidês and Aristotle has scarcely anything in common except the name. He is the first to acquire *Thalassokraty,* or command of the Ægean sea: he expels the Karian inhabitants from the Cyclades islands, and sends thither fresh colonists under his own sons: he puts down piracy, in order that he may receive his tribute regularly: lastly, he attempts to conquer Sicily, but fails in the enterprise and perishes. Here we have conjectures, derived from the analogy of the Athenian maritime empire in the historical times, substituted in place of the fabulous incidents, and attached to the name of Minôs.

In the fable, a tribute of seven youths and seven maidens in paid to him periodically by the Athenians: in the historicised narrative this character of a tribute-collector is preserved, but the tribute is money collected from dependent islands; and Aristotle points out to us how conveniently Krête is situated to exercise empire over the Ægean. The expedition against Kamikus, instead of being directed to the recovery of the fugitive Dædalus, is an attempt on the part of the great thalassokrat to conquer Sicily. Herodotus gives us generally the same view of the character of Minôs as a great maritime king, but his notice of the expedition against Kamicus includes the mention of Dædalus as the intended object of it. Ephorus, while he described Minôs as a commanding and comprehensive lawgiver imposing his commands under the sanction of Zeus, represented him as the imitator of an earlier lawgiver named Rhadamanthus, and also as an immigrant into Krête from the Æolic Mount Ida, along with the priests or sacred companions of Zeus called the Idæi Dactyli. Aristotle too points him out as the author of the Syssitia, or public meals common in Krête as well as at Sparta, other divergences in a new direction from the spirit of the old fables.

The contradictory attributes ascribed to Minôs, together with the perplexities

XII. KRÊTAN LEGENDS - MINÔS AND HIS FAMILY.

experienced by those who wished to introduce a regular chronological arrangement into these legendary events, has led both in ancient and in modern times to the supposition of two kings named Minôs, one the grandson of the other, Minôs I., the son of Zeus, lawgiver and judge, Minôs II., the thalassokrat, a gratuitous conjecture, which, without solving the problem required, only adds one to the numerous artifices employed for imparting the semblance of history to the disparate matter of legend. The Krêtans were at all times, from Homer downward, expert and practised seamen. But that they were ever united under one government, or ever exercised maritime dominion in the Ægean is a fact which we are neither able to affirm nor to deny. The Odyssey, in so far as it justifies any inference at all, points against such a supposition, since it recognises a great diversity both of inhabitants and of languages in the island, and designates Minôs as king specially of Knossus: it refutes still more positively the idea that Minôs put down piracy, which the Homeric Krêtans as well as others continue to practise without scruple.

Herodotus, though he in some places speaks of Minôs as a person historically cognisable, yet in one passage severs him pointedly from the generation of man. The Samian despot "Polykratês (he tells us) was the first person who aspired to nautical dominion, excepting Minôs of Knôssus, and others before him (if any such there ever were) who may have ruled the sea: but Polykrates is the first of that which is called *the generation of man* who aspired with much chance of success to govern Iônia and the islands of the Ægean." Here we find it manifestly intimated that Minôs did not belong to the generation of man, and the tale given by the historian respecting the tremendous calamities which the wrath of the departed Minôs inflicted on Krête confirms the impression. The king of Knôssus is a god or a hero, but not a man: he belongs to legend, not to history. He is the son as well as the familiar companion of Zeus: he marries the daughter of Hêlios, and Ariadnê is numbered among his offspring. To this superhuman person are ascribed the oldest and most revered institutions of the island, religious and political, together with a period of supposed ante-historical dominion. That there is much of Krêtan religious ideas and practice embodied in the fables concerning Minôs can hardly be doubted: nor is it improbable that the tale of the youths and maidens sent from Athens may be based in some expiatory offerings rendered to a Krêtan divinity. The orgiastic worship of Zeus, solemnised by the armed priests with impassioned motions and violent excitement, was of ancient date in that island, as well as the connection with the worship of Apollo both at Delphi and at Dêlos. To analyse the fables and to elicit from them any trustworthy particular facts, appears to me a fruitless attempt. The religious recollections, the romantic invention, and the items of matter of fact, if any such there be, must forever remain indissolubly amalgamated as the poet originally blended them, for the amusement or edification of his auditors. Hoeckh, in his instructive and learned collection of facts respecting ancient Krête, construes the mythical genealogy of Minôs to denote a combination of the orgiastic worship of Zeus, indigenous among the Eteokrêtes, with the worship of the moon imported from Phœnicia, and signified by the names Europê, Pasiphaê, and Ariadnê. This is specious as a conjecture, but I do not venture to speak of it in terms of greater confidence.

From the connection of religious worship and legendary tales between Krête and various parts of Asia Minor, the Troad, the coast of Milêtus and Lykia, especially between Mount Ida in Krête and Mount Ida in Æolis, it seems reasonable to infer an ethnographical kindred or relationship between the inhabitants anterior to the period of Hellenic occupation. The tales of Krêtan settlement at Minoa and Engyôn on the south-western coast of Sicily, and in Iapygia on the Gulf of Tarentum, conduct us to a similar presumption, though the want of evidence forbids our tracing it farther. In the time of Herodotus, the Eteokrêtes, or aboriginal inhabitants of the island, were confined to Polichna and Præsus; but in earlier times, prior to the encroachments of the Hellenes, they had occupied the larger portion, if not the whole of the island. Minôs was originally their hero, subsequently adopted by the immigrant Hellenes, at least Herodotus considers him as barbarian, not Hellenic.

XIII. ARGONAUTIC EXPEDITION.

The ship Argô was the theme of many songs during the oldest periods of the Grecian epic, even earlier than the Odyssey. The king Æêtês, from whom she is departing, the hero Jasôn, who commands her, and the goddess Hêrê, who watches over him, enabling the Argô to traverse distances and to escape dangers which no ship had ever before encountered, are all circumstances briefly glanced at by Odysseus in his narrative to Alkinous. Moreover, Eunêus, the son of Jasôn and Hypsipylê. governs Lêmnos during the siege of Troy by Agamemnôn, and carries on a friendly traffic with the Grecian camp, purchasing from them their Trojan prisoners.

The legend of Halus in Achaia Phthiôtis, respecting the religious solemnities connected with the family of Athamas and Phryxus (related in a previous chapter), is also interwoven with the voyage of the Argônauts: and both the legend and the solemnities seem evidently of great antiquity. We know further, that the adventures of the Argô were narrated not only by Hesiod and in the Hesiodic poems, but also by Eumêlus and the author of the Naupaktian verses – by the latter seemingly at considerable length. These poems are unfortunately lost, nor have we any means of determining what the original story was: for the narrative, as we have it, borrowed from later sources, is enlarged by local tales from the subsequent Greek colonies – Kyzikus, Hêrakleia, Sinopê, and others.

Jasôn, commanded by Pelias to depart in quest of the golden fleece belonging to the speaking ram which had carried away Phryxus and Hellê, was encouraged by the oracle to invite the noblest youth of Greece to his aid, and fifty of the most distinguished amongst them obeyed the call. Hêraklês, Thesêus, Telamôn and Pêleus, Kastôr and Pollux, Idas and Lynkeus – Zêtês and Kalaïs, the winged sons of Boreas – Meleager, Amphiaraus, Kêpheus, Laertês, Autolykus, Menœtius, Aktôr, Erginus, Euphêmus, Ankæus, Pœas, Periklymenus, Augeas, Eurytus, Admêtus, Akastus, Kæneus, Euryalus, Pênêleôs and Lêitus, Askalaphus and Ialmenus, were among them. Argus the son of Phryxus, directed by the promptings of Athênê, built the ship, inserting in the prow a piece of timber from the celebrated oak of Dôdôna, which was endued with the faculty of speech: Tiphys was the steersman, Idmôn the son of Apollo and Mopsus accompanied them as prophets, while Orpheus came to amuse their weariness and reconcile their quarrels with his harp.

First they touched at the island of Lêmnos, in which at that time there were no men: for the women, infuriated by jealousy and ill-treatment, had put to death their fathers, husbands and brothers. The Argônauts, after some difficulty, were received with friendship, and even admitted into the greatest intimacy. They staid some months, and the subsequent population of the island was the fruit of their visit. Hypsipylê, the queen of the island, bore to Jasôn two sons.

They then proceeded onward along the coast of Thrace, up the Hellespont, to the southern coast of the Propontis, inhabited by the Doliones and their king Kyzikus. Here they were kindly entertained, but after their departure were driven back to the same spot by a storm; and as they landed in the dark, the inhabitants did not know them. A battle took place, in which the chief, Kyzikus, was killed by Jasôn, whereby much grief was occasioned as soon as the real facts became known. After Kyzikus had been interred with every demonstration of mourning and solemnity, the Argônauts proceeded along the coast of Mysia. In this part of the voyage they left Hêraklês behind. For Hylas, his favourite youthful companion, had been stolen away by the nymphs of a fountain, and Hêraklês, wandering about in search of him, neglected to return. At last he sorrowfully retired, exacting hostages from the inhabitants of the neighbouring town of Kius that they would persist in the search.

They next stopped in the country of the Bebrykians, where the boxing contest took place between the king Amykus and the Argônaut Pollux: they then proceeded onward to Bithynia, the residence of the blind prophet Phineus. His blindness had been inflicted by Poseidôn as a punishment for having communicated to Phryxus the way to Kolchis. The choice had been allowed to him between death and blindness, and he had preferred the latter. He was also tormented by the harpies, winged monsters who came down from the clouds whenever his table was set, snatched the food from his lips and imparted to it a foul and unapproachable odour. In the midst of this misery, he hailed the Argônauts as his deliverers – his prophetic powers having enabled him to foresee their coming. The meal being prepared for him, the harpies approached as usual, but Zêtês and Kalais, the winged sons of Boreas, drove them away and pursued them. They put forth all their speed, and prayed to Zeus to be enabled to overtake the monsters; when Hermês appeared and directed them to desist, the harpies being forbidden further to molest Phineus, and retiring again to their native cavern in Krête.

Phineus, grateful for the relief afforded to him by the Argônauts, forewarned them of the dangers of their voyage and of the precautions necessary for their safety; and through his suggestions they were enabled to pass through the terrific rocks called Symplêgades. These were two rocks which alternately opened and shut, with a swift and violent collision, so that it was difficult even for a bird to fly through during the short interval. When the Argô arrived at the dangerous spot, Euphêmus let loose a dove, which flew through and just escaped with the loss of a few feathers of her tail. This was a signal to the Argônauts, according to the prediction of Phineus, that they might attempt the passage with confidence. Accordingly they rowed with all then might, and passed safely through: the closing rocks, held for a moment asunder by the powerful arms of Athênê, just crushed the ornaments at the stern of their vessel. It had been decreed by the gods, that so soon as any ship once got through, the passage should forever afterwards be safe and easy to all. The rocks became fixed in their separate places, and never again closed.

After again halting on the coast of the Maryandinians, where their steersman Tiphys died, as well as in the country of the Amazons, and after picking up the sons of Phryxus, who had been cast away by Poseidôn in their attempt to return from Kolchis to Greece, they arrived in safety at the river Phasis and the residence of Æêtês. In passing by Mount Caucasus, they saw the eagle which gnawed the liver of Promêtheus nailed to the rock, and heard the groans of the sufferer himself. The sons of Phryxus were cordially welcomed by their mother Chalkioê. Application was made to Æêtês, that he would grant to the Argônauts, heroes of divine parentage and sent forth by the mandate of the gods, possession of the golden fleece: their aid in return was proffered to him against any or all of his enemies. But the king was wroth, and peremptorily refused, except upon conditions which seemed impracticable. Hêphæstos had given him two ferocious and untameable bulls, with brazen feet, which breathed fire from their nostrils: Jasôn was invited, as a proof both of his illustrious descent and of the sanction of the gods to his voyage, to harness these animals to the yoke, so as to plough a large field and sow it with dragon's teeth. Perilous as the condition was, each one of the heroes volunteered to make the attempt. Idmôn especially encouraged Jasôn to undertake it and the goddesses Hêrê and Aphroditê made straight the way for him. Mêdea, the daughter of Æêtês and Eidyia, having seen the youthful hero in his interview with her father, had conceived towards him a passion which disposed her to employ every means for his salvation and success. She had received from Hekatê pre-eminent magical powers, and she prepared for Jasôn the powerful Prometheian unguent, extracted from an herb which had grown where the blood of Promêtheus dropped. The body of Jasôn having been thus pre-medicated, became invulnerable either by fire or by warlike weapons. He undertook the enterprise, yoked the bulls without suffering injury, and ploughed the field: when he had sown the dragon's teeth, armed men sprung out of the furrows. But he had been forewarned by Mêdea to cast a vast rock into the midst of them, upon which they began to fight with each other, so that he was easily enabled to subdue them all.

The task prescribed had thus been triumphantly performed. Yet Æêtês not only refused to hand over the golden fleece, but even took measures for secretly destroying the Argônauts and burning their vessel. He designed to murder them during the night after a festal banquet; but Aphroditê, watchful for the safety of Jasôn, inspired the Kolchian king at the critical moment with an irresistible inclination for his nuptial bed. While he slept, the wise Idmôn counselled the Argônauts to make their escape, and Mêdea agreed to accompany them. She lulled to sleep by a magic potion the dragon who guarded the golden fleece, placed that much-desired prize on board the vessel, and accompanied Jasôn with his companions in their flight, carrying along with her the young Apsyrtus, her brother.

Æêtês, profoundly exasperated at the flight of the Argônauts with his daughter, assembled his forces forthwith, and put to sea in pursuit of them. So energetic were his efforts that he shortly overtook the retreating vessel, when the Argônauts again owed their safety to the stratagem of Mêdea, She killed her brother Apsyrtus, cut his body in pieces and strewed the limbs round about in the sea. Æêtês on reaching the spot found these sorrowful traces of his murdered son, but while he tarried to collect the scattered fragments, and bestow upon the body an honourable interment, the Argônauts escaped. The spot on which the unfortunate Apsyrtus was cut up received the name of Tomi. This fratricide of Mêdea, however, so deeply provoked the indignation of Zeus, that he condemned the Argô and her crew to a trying voyage, full of hardship and privation, before she was permitted to reach home. The returning heroes traversed an immeasurable length both of sea and of river: first of the river Phasis into the ocean which flows round the earth – then following the course of that circumfluous stream until its junction with the Nile, they came down the Nile into Egypt, from whence they carried the Argô on their shoulders by a fatiguing land-journey to the lake Tritônis in Libya. Here they were rescued from the extremity of want and exhaustion by the kindness of the local god Tritôn, who treated them hospitably, and even presented to

XIII. ARGONAUTIC EXPEDITION.

Euphêmus a clod of earth, as a symbolical promise that his descendants should one day found a city on the Libyan shore. The promise was amply redeemed by the flourishing and powerful city of Kyrênê, whose princes the Battiads boasted themselves as lineal descendants of Euphêmus.

Refreshed by the hospitality of Tritôn, the Argônauts found themselves again on the waters of the Mediterranean in their way homeward. Before they arrived at Iôlkos they visited Circê, at the island of Æaea, where Mêdea was purified for the murder of Apsyrtus: they also stopped at Korkyra, then called Drepanê, where Alkinous received and protected them. The cave in that island where the marriage of Mêdea with Jasôn was consummated, was still shown in the time of the historian Timæus, as well as the altars to Apollo which she had erected, and the rites and sacrifices which she had first instituted. After leaving Korkyra, the Argô was overtaken by a perilous storm near the island of Thêra. The heroes were saved from imminent peril by the supernatural aid of Apollo, who, shooting from his golden bow an arrow which pierced the waves like a track of light, caused a new island suddenly to spring up in their track and present to them a port of refuge. The island was called Anaphê: and the grateful Argônauts established upon it an altar and sacrifices in honour of Apollo Æglêtês, which were ever afterwards continued, and traced back by the inhabitants to this originating adventure.

On approaching the coast of Krête, the Argônauts were prevented from landing by Talôs, a man of brass, fabricated by Hêphæstos, and presented by him to Minôs for the protection of the island. This vigilant sentinel hurled against the approaching vessel fragments of rock, and menaced the heroes with destruction. But Mêdea deceived him by a stratagem and killed him: detecting and assailing the one vulnerable point in his body. The Argônauts were thus enabled to land and refresh themselves. They next proceeded onward to Ægina, where however they again experienced resistance before they could obtain water — then along the coast of Euboea and Locris back to Iôlkos in the gulf of Pagesæ, the place from whence they had started. The proceedings of Pelias during their absence, and the signal revenge taken upon him by Mêdea after their return, have already been narrated in a preceding section. The ship Argô herself, in which the chosen heroes of Greece had performed so long a voyage and braved so many dangers, was consecrated by Jasôn to Poseidôn at the isthmus of Corinth. According to another account, she was translated to the stars by Athênê, and became a constellation.

147

LEGENDARY GREECE

Numerous monuments to the Argô.

Traces of the presence of the Argônauts were found not only in the regions which lay between Iôlkos and Kolchis, but also in the western portion of the Grecian world – distributed more or less over all the spots visited by Grecian mariners or settled by Grecian colonists, and scarcely less numerous than the wanderings of the dispersed Greeks and Trojans after the capture of Troy. The number of Jasônia, or temples for the heroic worship of Jasôn, was very great, from Abdêra in Thrace, eastward along the coast of the Euxine, to Armenia and Media. The Argônauts had left their anchoring-stone on the coast of Bebrykia, near Kyzikus, and there it was preserved during the historical ages in the temple of the Jasônian Athênê. They had founded the great temple of the Idæan mother on the mountain Dindymon, near Kyzikus, and the Hieron of Zeus Urios on the Asiatic point at the mouth of the Euxine, near which was also the harbour of Phryzus. Idmôn, the prophet of the expedition, who was believed to have died of a wound by a wild hoar on the Mariandynian coast, was worshipped by the inhabitants of the Pontic Hêrakleia with great solemnity, as their Heros Poliuchus, and that too by the special direction of the Delphian god. Autolykus, another companion of Jasôn, was worshipped as Œkist by the inhabitants of Sinopê. Moreover, the historians of Hêrakleia pointed out a temple of Hekatê in the neighbouring country of Paphlagonia, first erected by Mêdea; and the important town of Pantikapæon, on the European side of the Cimmerian Bosporus, ascribed its first settlement to a son of Æêtês. When the returning ten thousand Greeks sailed along the coast, called the Jasônian shore, from Sinopê to Hêrakleia, they were told that the grandson of Æêtês was reigning king of the territory at the mouth of the Phasis, and the anchoring-places where the Argô had stopped were specially pointed out to them. In the lofty regions of the Moschi, near Kolchis, stood the temple of Leukothea, founded by Phryxus, which remained both rich and respected down to the times of the kings of Pontus, and where it was an inviolable rule not to offer up a ram. The town of Dioskurias, north of the river Phasis, was believed to have been hallowed by the presence of Kastôr and Pollux in the Argô, and to have received from them its appellation. Even the interior of Media and Armenia was full of memorials of Jasôn and Mêdea and their son Mêdus, or of Armenus the son of Jasôn, from whom the Greeks deduced not only the name and foundation of the Medes and Armenians, but also the great operation of cutting a channel through the mountains for the efflux of the river Araxes, which they compared to that of the Peneius in Thessaly. The Roman general Pompey, after having completed the conquest and

148

XIII. ARGONAUTIC EXPEDITION.

expulsion of Mithridatês, made long marches through Kolchis into the regions of Caucasus, for the express purpose of contemplating the spots which had been ennobled by the exploits of the Argônauts, the Dioskuri and Hêraklês.

In the west, memorials either of the Argônauts or of the pursuing Kolchians were pointed out in Korkyra, in Krête, in Epirus near the Akrokeraunian mountains, in the islands called Apsyrtides near the Illyrian coast, at the bay of Caieta as well as at Poseidônia on the southern coast of Italy, in the island of Æthalia or Elba, and in Libya.

Such is a brief outline of the Argônautic expedition, one of the most celebrated and widely-diffused among the ancient tales of Greece. Since so many able men have treated it as an undisputed reality, and even made it the pivot of systematic chronological calculations, I may here repeat the opinion long ago expressed by Heyne, and even indicated by Burmann, that the process of dissecting the story, in search of a basis of fact, is one altogether fruitless. Not only are we unable to assign the date, or identify the crew, or decipher the log-book, of the Argô, but we have no means of settling even the preliminary question, whether the voyage be matter of fact badly reported, or legend from the beginning. The widely-distant spots in which the monuments of the voyage were shown, no less than the incidents of the voyage itself, suggest no other parentage than epical fancy. The supernatural and the romantic not only constitute an inseparable portion of the narrative, but even embrace all the prominent and characteristic features: if they do not comprise the whole, and if there be intermingled along with them any sprinkling of historical or geographical fact, a question to us indeterminable, there is at least no solvent by which it can be disengaged, and no test by which it can be recognised. Wherever the Grecian mariner sailed, he carried his religious and patriotic mythes along with him. His fancy and his faith were alike full of the long wanderings of Jasôn, Odysseus, Perseus, Hêraklês, Dionysus, Triptolemus or Iô: it was pleasing to him in success, and consoling to him in difficulty, to believe that their journeys had brought them over the ground which he was himself traversing. There was no tale amidst the wide range of the Grecian epic more calculated to be popular with the seaman, than the history of the primaeval ship Argô and her distinguished crew, comprising heroes from all parts of Greece, and especially the Tyndarids Kastôr and Pollux, the heavenly protectors invoked during storm and peril. He localised the legend anew wherever he went, often with some fresh circumstances suggested either by his own adventures or by the scene before him. He took a sort of religious possession of the spot, connecting it by a bond of faith with his native land, and erecting in it a temple or an altar with appropriate commemorative solemnities. The Jasônium thus established, and indeed every visible object called after the name of the hero, not only served to keep alive the legend of the Argô in the minds of future comers or inhabitants, but was accepted as an obvious and satisfactory proof that this marvellous vessel had actually touched there in her voyage.

The epic poets, building both on the general love of fabulous incident and on the easy faith of the people, dealt with distant and unknown space in the same manner as with past and unrecorded time. They created a mythical geography for the former, and a mythical history for the latter. There was this material difference between the two: that while the unrecorded time was beyond the reach of verification, the unknown space gradually became trodden and examined. In proportion as authentic local knowledge was enlarged, it became necessary to modify the geography, or shift the scene of action, of the old mythes; and this perplexing problem was undertaken by some of the ablest historians and geographers of antiquity, for it was painful to them to abandon any portion of the old epic, as if it were destitute of an ascertainable basis of truth.

Many of these fabulous localities are to be found in Homer and Hesiod, and the other Greek poets and logographers, Erytheia, the garden of the Hesperides, the garden of Phœbus, to which Boreas transported the Attic maiden Oreithyia, the delicious country of the Hyperboreans, the Elysian plain, the floating island of Æolus, Thrinakia, the country of the Æthiopians, the Læstrygones, the Kyklôpes, the Lotophagi , the Sirens, the Cimmerians and the Gorgons, &c. These are places which (to use the expression of Pindar respecting the Hyperboreans) you cannot approach either by sea or by land: the wings of the poet alone can carry you thither. They were not introduced into the Greek mind by incorrect geographical reports, but, on the contrary, had their origin in the legend, and passed from thence into the realities of geography, which they contributed much to pervert and confuse. For the navigator or emigrant, starting with an unsuspicious faith in their real existence, looked out for them in his distant voyages, and constantly fancied that he had seen or heard of them, so as to be able to identify their exact situation The most contradictory accounts indeed, as might be expected, were often given respecting the latitude and longitude of each fanciful spots, but this did not put an end to the general belief in their real existence

In the present advanced state of geographical knowledge, the story of that man who after reading Gulliver's Travels went to look in his map for Lilliput, appears an absurdity. But those who fixed the exact locality of the floating island of Æolus or the rocks of the Sirens did much the same; and, with their ignorance of geography and imperfect appreciation of historical evidence, the error was hardly to be avoided. The ancient belief which fixed the Sirens on the islands of Sirenusæ off the coast of Naples – the Kyklôpes, Erytheia, and the Læstrygones in Sicily – the Lotophagi on the island of Mêninx near the Lesser Syrtis – the Phæakians at Korkyra – and the goddess Circê at the promontory of Circeium – took its rise at a time when these regions were first Hellenised and comparatively little visited. Once embodied in the local legends, and attested by visible monuments and ceremonies, it continued for a long time un-assailed; and Thucydidês seems to adopt it, in reference to Korkyra and Sicily before the Hellenic colonisation, as matter of fact generally unquestionable, though little avouched as to details. But when geographical knowledge became extended, and the criticism upon the ancient epic was more or less systematized by the literary men of Alexandria and Pergamus, it appeared to many of them impossible that Odysseus could have seen so many wonders, or undergone such monstrous dangers within limits so narrow, and in the familiar track between the Nile and the Tiber. The scene of his weather-driven course was then shifted further westward. Many convincing evidences were discovered, especially by Asklepiadês of Myrlea, of his having visited various places in Iberia: several critics imagined that he had wandered about in the Atlantic Ocean outside of the Strait of Gibraltar, and they recognised a section of Lotophagi on the coast of Mauritania, over and above those who dwelt on the island of Mêninx. On the other hand, Eratosthenês and Apollodôrus treated the places visited by Odysseus as altogether unreal, for which scepticism they incurred much reproach.

The fabulous island of Erytheia, – the residence of the three headed Geryôn with his magnificent herd of oxen, under the custody of the two-headed dog Orthrus, and described by Hesiod, like the garden of the Hesperides, as extra-terrestrial, on the farther side of the circumfluous ocean, this island was supposed by the interpreters of Stesichorus the poet to be named by him off the south-western region of Spain called Tartêssus, and in the immediate vicinity of Gadês. But the historian Hekatæus, in his anxiety to historicise the old fable, took upon himself to remove Erytheia from Spain nearer home to Epirus. He thought it incredible that Hêraklês should have traversed Europe from East to West, for the purpose of bringing the cattle of

Geryôn to Eurystheus at Mykênæ, and he pronounced Geryôn to have been a king of Epirus, near the Gulf of Ambrakia. The oxen reared in that neighbourhood were proverbially magnificent, and to get them even from thence and bring them to Mykênæ (he contended) was no inconsiderable task. Arrian, who cites this passage from Hekatæus, concurs in the same view, an illustration of the license with which ancient authors fitted on their fabulous geographical names to the real earth, and brought down the ethereal matter of legend to the lower atmosphere of history.

Both the, track and the terminus of the Argônantic voyage appear in the most ancient epic as little within the conditions of reality, as the speaking timbers or the semi-divine crew of the vessel. In the Odyssey, Æêtês and Circê (Hesiod names Mêdea also) are brother and sister, offspring of Hêlios. The Æææan island, adjoining the circumfluous ocean, "where the house and dancing-ground of Eôs are situated, and where Hêlios rises," is both the residence of Circê and of Æêtês, inasmuch as Odysseus, in returning from the former, follows the same course as the Argô had previously taken in returning from the latter. Even in the conception of Mimnermus, about 600 B.C., Æa still retained its fabulous attributes in conjunction with the ocean and Hêlios, without having been yet identified with any known portion of the solid earth; and it was justly remarked by Dêmetrius of Skêpsis in antiquity (though Strabo vainly tries to refute him), that neither Homer nor Mimnermus designates Kolchis either as the residence of Æêtês, or as the terminus of the Argônautic voyage. Hesiod carried the returning Argônauts through the river Phasis into the ocean. Some of the poems ascribed to Eumêlus were the first which mentioned Æêtês and Kolchis, and interwove both of them into the Corinthian mythical genealogy. These poems seem to have been composed subsequent to the foundation of Sinopê, and to the commencement of Grecian settlement on the Borysthenês, between the years 600 and 500 B.C. The Greek mariners who explored and colonised the southern coast of the Euxine, found at the extremity of their voyage the river Phasis and its barbarous inhabitants: it was the easternmost point which Grecian navigation (previous to the time of Alexander the Great) ever attained, and it was within sight of the impassable barrier of Caucasus. They believed, not unnaturally, that they had here found "the house of Eôs (the morning) and the rising place of the sun," and that the river Phasis, if they could follow it to its unknown beginning, would conduct them to the circumfluous ocean. They gave to the spot the name of Æa, and the fabulous and real title gradually became associated together into one compound appellation, the Kolchian Æa, or Æa of

XIII. ARGONAUTIC EXPEDITION.

Kolchis. While Kolchis was thus entered on the map as a fit representative for the Homeric "house of the morning," the narrow strait of the Thracian Bosporus attracted to itself the poetical fancy of the Symplêgades, or colliding rocks, through which the heaven-protected Argô had been the first to pass. The powerful Greek cities of Kyzikus, Hêrakleia and Sinopê, each fertile in local legends, still farther contributed to give this direction to the voyage: so that in the time of Hekatæus it had become the established belief that the Argô had started from Iôlkos and gone to Kolchis.

Æêtês thus received his home from the legendary faith and fancy of the eastern Greek navigators: his sister Circê, originally his fellow-resident, was localised by the western. The Hesiodic and other poems, giving expression to the imaginative impulses of the inhabitants of Cumæ and other early Grecian settlers in Italy and Sicily, had referred the wanderings of Odysseus to the western or Tyrrhenian sea, and had planted the Cyclôpes, the Læstrigones, the floating island of Æolus, the Lotophagi, the Phæacians, &c., about the coast of Sicily, Italy, Libya, and Korkyra. In this way the Ææan island, – the residence of Circê, and the extreme point of the wanderings of Odysseus, from whence he passes only to the ocean and into Hadês – came to be placed in the far west, while the Æa of Æêtês was in the far east, not unlike our East and West Indies. The Homeric brother and sister were separated and sent to opposite extremities of the Grecian terrestrial horizon.

The track from Iôlkos to Kolchis, however, though plausible as far as it went, did not realise all the conditions of the genuine fabulous voyage: it did not explain the evidences of the visit of these maritime heroes which were to be found in Libya, in Krête at Anaphê, in Korkyra, in the Adriatic Gulf, in Italy and in Æthalia. It became necessary to devise another route for them in their return, and the Hesiodic narrative was (as I have before observed), that they came back by the circumfluous ocean: first going up the river Phasis into the cicumfluous ocean: then following that deep and gentle stream until they entered the Nile, and came down its course to the coast of Libya. This seems also to have been the belief of Hekatæus. But presently several Greeks (and Herodotus among them) began to discard the idea of a circumfluous ocean-stream, which had pervaded their old geographical and astronomical fables, and which explained the supposed easy communication between one extremity of the earth and another. Another idea was then started for the returning voyage of the Argônauts. It was supposed that the river Ister, or Danube, flowing from the Rhipæan mountains in the north-west of Europe, divided itself into two branches, one of which fell into the Euxine Sea, and the other into the Adriatic

The Argônauts, fleeing from the pursuit of Æêtês, had been obliged to abandon their regular course homeward, and had gone from the Euxine Sea up the Ister: then passing down the other branch of that river, they had entered into the Adriatic, the Kolchian pursuers following them. Such is the story given by Apollônius Rhodius from Timagêtus, and accepted even by so able a geographer as Eratosthenês – who preceded him by one generation, and who, though sceptical in regard to the localities visited by Odysseus, seems to have been a firm believer in the reality of the Argônautic voyage. Other historians again, among whom was Timæus, though they considered the ocean as an outer sea, and no longer admitted the existence of the old Homeric ocean-stream, yet imagined a story for the return-voyage of the Argônauts somewhat resembling the old tale of Hesiod and Hekatæus. They alleged that the Argô, after entering into the Palus Mæotis, had followed the upward course of the river Tanais: that she had then been carried overland and launched in a river which had its mouth in the ocean or great outer sea. When in the ocean, she had coasted along the north and west of Europe until she reached Gadês and the Strait of Gibraltar, where she entered into the Mediterranean, and there visited the many places specified in the fable. Of this long voyage, in the outer sea to the north and west of Europe, many traces were affirmed to exist along the coast of the ocean. There was again a third version, according to which the Argônauts came back as they went, through the Thracian Bosporus and the Hellespont. In this way geographical plausibility was indeed maintained, but a large portion of the fabulous matter was discarded.

Such were the various attempts made to reconcile the Argônautic legend with enlarged geographical knowledge and improved historical criticism. The problem remained unsolved, but the faith in the legend did not the less continue. It was a faith originally generated at a time when the unassisted narrative of the inspired poet sufficed for the conviction of his hearers: it consecrated one among the capital exploits of that heroic and superhuman race, whom the Greek was accustomed at once to look back upon as his ancestors and to worship conjointly with has gods: it lay too deep in his mind either to require historical evidence for its support, or to be overthrown by geographical difficulties as they were then appreciated. Supposed traces of the past event, either preserved in the names of places, or embodied in standing religious customs with their explanatory comments, served as sufficient authentication in the eyes of the curious inquirer. And even men trained in a more severe school of criticism contented themselves with eliminating the palpable contradictions and softening down the supernatural and romantic events, so as to produce an Argônautic expedition of their own invention as the true and accredited history. Strabo, though he can neither overlook nor explain the geographical impossibilities of the narrative, supposes himself to have discovered the basis of actual fact, which the original poets had embellished or exaggerated. The golden fleece was typical of the great wealth of Kolchis, arising from gold-dust washed down by the rivers: and the voyage of Jasôn was in reality an expedition at the head of a considerable army, with which he plundered this wealthy country and made extensive conquests in the interior. Strabo has nowhere laid down what he supposes to have been the exact measure and direction of Jasôn's march, but he must have regarded it as very long, since he classes Jasôn with Dionysus and Hêraklês, and emphatically characterises all the three as having traversed wider spaces of ground than any moderns could equal. Such was the compromise which a mind like that of Strabo made with the ancient legends. He shaped or cut them down to the level of his own credence, and in this waste of historical criticism, without any positive evidence, he took to himself the credit of greater penetration than the literal believers, while he escaped the necessity of breaking formally with the bygone heroic world.

LEGENDARY GREECE

XIV. LEGENDS OF THÊBES.

The Bœôtians generally, throughout the historical age, though well endowed with bodily strength and courage, are represented as proverbially deficient in intelligence, taste and fancy. The legendary population of Thêbes, the Kadmeians, are rich in mythical antiquities, divine as well as heroic. Both Dionysus and Hêraklês recognise Thêbes as their natal city. Moreover, the two sieges of Thêbes by Adrastus, even taken apart from Kadmus, Antiopê, Amphiôn and Zêthus, &c., are the most prominent and most characteristic exploits, next to the siege of Troy, of that pre-existing race of heroes who lived in the imagination of the historical Hellenes.

It is not Kadmus, but the brothers Amphiôn and Zêthus, who are given to us in the Odyssey as the first founders of Thêbes and the first builders of its celebrated walls. They are the sons of Zeus by Antiopê, daughter of Asôpus. The scholiasts who desire to reconcile this tale with the more current account of the foundation of Thêbes by Kadmus, tell us that after the death of Amphiôn and Zêthus, Eurymachus, the warlike king of the Phlegyæ, invaded and ruined the newly-settled town, so that Kadmus on arriving was obliged to re-found it. But Apollodôrus, and seemingly the older logographers before him, placed Kadmus at the top, and inserted the two brothers at a lower point in the series. According to them, Bêlus and Agênor were the sons of Epaphus, (sons of the Argeian Iô) by Libya. Agênor went to Phœnicia and there he became their king: he had for his offspring Kadmus, Phœnix, Kilix, and a daughter Eurôpa; though in the Iliad Eurôpa is called daughter of Phœnix. Zeus fell in love with Eurôpa, and assuming the shape of a bull, carried her across the sea upon his back from Egyyt to Krête, where she bore to him Minôs, Rhadamanthus and Sarpêdôn. Two out of the three sons sent out by Agenôr in search of their lost sister, wearied out by a long-protracted as well as fruitless voyage, abandoned the idea of returning home: Kilix settled in Kilikia, and Kadmus in Thrace. Thasus, the brother or nephew of Kadmus, who had accompanied them in the voyage, settled and gave name to the island of Thasus.

Both Herodotus and Euripidês represent Kadmus as an emigrant from Phœnicia, conducting a body of followers in quest of Eurôpa. The account of Apollôdorus describes him as having come originally from Libya or Egypt to Phœnicia: we may presume that this was also the statement of the earlier logographers Pherekydês and Hellanikus. Conôn, who historicises and politicises the whole legend, seems to have found two different accounts: one connecting Kadmus with Egypt, another bringing him from Phœnicia. He tries to melt down the two into one, by representing that the Phœnicians, who sent out Kadmus, had acquired great power in Egypt – that the seat of their kingdom was the Egyptian Thêbes – that Kadmus was despatched, under pretence indeed of finding his lost sister, but really on a project of conquest – and that the name Thêbes, which be gave to his new establishment in Bœotia, was borrowed from Thêbes in Egypt, his ancestoral seat.

Kadmus went from Thrace to Delphi to procure information respecting his sister Eurôpa, but the god directed him to take no further trouble about her: he was to follow the guidance of a cow, and to found a city on the spot where the animal should lie down. The condition was realised on the site of Thêbes. The neighbouring fountain Areia was guarded by a fierce dragon, the offspring of Arês, who destroyed all the persons sent to fetch water. Kadmus killed the dragon, and at the suggestion of Athênê sowed the dragon's teeth in the earth: there sprang up at once the armed men called the Sparti, among whom he flung stones, and they immediately began to assault each other until all were slain except five. Arês, indignant at this slaughter, was about to kill Kadmus; but Zeus appeased him, condemning Kadmus to an expiatory servitude of eight years, after which he married Harmonia, the daughter of Arês and Aphroditê – presenting to her the splendid necklace fabricated by the hand of Hêphæstos, which had been given by Zeus to Eurôpa. All the gods came to the Kadmeia, the citadel of Thêbes, to present congratulations and gifts at these nuptials, which seem to have been hardly less celebrated in the mythical world than those of Pêleus and Thetis. The issue of the marriage was one son, Polydôrus, and four daughters, Autonoê, Inô, Semelê and Agavê.

From the five who alone survived of the warriors sprung from the dragon's teeth, arose five great families or gentes in Thêbes: the oldest and noblest of its inhabitants, coeval with the foundation of the town. They were called Sparti, and their name seems to have given rise, not only to the fable of the sowing of the teeth, but also to other etymological narratives.

All the four daughters of Kadmus are illustrious in fabulous history. Inô, wife of Athamas, the son of Æolus, has already been included among the legends of the Æolids. Semelê became the mistress of Zeus, and inspired Hêrê with jealousy. Misguided by the malicious suggestions of that goddess, she solicited Zeus to visit her with all the solemnity and terrors which surrounded him when he approached Hêrê herself. The god unwillingly consented, and came in his chariot in the midst of thunder and lightning, under which awful accompaniments the mortal frame of Semelê perished. Zeus, taking from her the child of which she was pregnant, sewed it into his own thigh: after the proper interval the child was brought out and born, and became the great god Dionysus or Bacchus. Hermês took him to Inô and Athamas to receive their protection. Afterwards, however, Zeus having transformed him into a kid to conceal him from the persecution of Hêrê, the nymphs of the mountain Nysa became his nurses.

Autonoê, the third daughter of Kadmus, married the pastoral hero or god Aristæus, and was mother of Aktæôn, a devoted hunter and a favourite companion of the goddess Artemis. She however became displeased with him – either because he looked into a fountain while she was bathing and saw her naked – or according to the legend set forth by the poet Stesichorus, because he loved and courted Semelê – or according to Euripidês, because he presumptuously vaunted himself as her superior in the chase. She transformed him into a stag, so that his own dogs set upon and devoured him. The rock upon which Aktæôn used to sleep when fatigued with the chase, and the spring whose transparent waters had too clearly revealed the form of the goddess, were shown to Pausanias near Platæa, on the road to Megara.

Agavê, the remaining daughter of Kadmus, married Echiôn, one of the Sparti. The issue of these nuptials was Pentheus, who, when Kadmus became old succeeded him as king of Thêbes. In his reign Dionysus appeared as a god, the author or discoverer of the vine with all its blessings. He had wandered over Asia, India and Thrace, at the head of an excited troop of female enthusiasts – communicating and inculcating everywhere the Bacchic ceremonies, and rousing in the minds of women that impassioned religious emotion which led them to ramble in solitary mountains at particular seasons, there to give vent to violent fanatical excitement, apart from the men, clothed in fawn-skins and armed with the thyrsus. The obtrusion of a male spectator upon these solemnities was esteemed sacrilegious. Though the rites had been rapidly disseminated and fervently welcomed in many parts of Thrace, yet there were some places in which they had been obstinately resisted and their votaries treated with rudeness: especially by Lykurgus, king of the Edonian Thracians, upon whom a sharp and exemplary punishment was inflicted by Dionysus.

Thêbes was the first city of Greece to which Dionysus came, at the head of his Asiatic troop of females, to obtain divine honours and to establish his peculiar rites in his native city. The venerable Kadmus, together with his daughters and the prophet Teiresias, at once acknowledged the divinity of the new god, and began to offer their worship and praise to him along with the solemnities which he enjoined. But Pentheus vehemently opposed the new ceremonies, reproving and maltreating the god who introduced them: nor was his unbelief at all softened by the miracles which Dionysus wrought for his own protection and for that of his followers. His mother Agavê: with her sisters and a large body of other women from Thêbes, had gone out from Thêbes to Mount Kithærôn to celebrate their solemnities under the influence of the Bacchic frenzy. Thither Pentheus followed to watch them, and there the punishment due to his impiety overtook him. The avenging touch of the god having robbed him of his senses, he climbed a tall pine for the purpose of overlooking the feminine multitude, who detected him in this position, pulled down the tree, and tore him in pieces. Agavê, mad and bereft of consciousness, made herself the foremost in this assault, and carried back in triumph to Thêbes the head of her slaughtered son. The aged Kadmus, with his wife Harmonia, retired among the Illyrians, and at the end of their lives were changed into serpents, Zeus permitting them to be transferred to the Elysian fields.

Polydôrus and Labdakus successively became kings of Thêbes: the latter at his death left an infant son, Laius, who was deprived of his throne by Lykus. And here we approach the legend of Antiopê, Zêthus and Amphiôn, whom the fabulists insert at this point of the Thêban series. Antiopê is here the daughter of Nykteus, the brother of Lykus. She is deflowered by Zeus, and then, while pregnant, flies to Epôpeus king of Sikyôn: Nykteus dying entreats his brother to avenge the injury, and Lykus accordingly invades Sikyôn, defeats and kills Epôpeus, and brings back Antiopê prisoner to Thêbes. In her way thither, in a cave near Eleutheræ, which was shown to Pausanias, she is delivered of the twin sons of Zeus – Amphiôn and Zêthus – who, exposed to perish, are taken up and nourished by a shepherd, and pass their youth amidst herdsmen, ignorant of their lofty descent.

Antiopê is conveyed to Thêbes, where, after undergoing a long persecution from Lykus and his cruel wife Dirkê, she at length escapes, and takes refuge in the pastoral dwelling of her sons, now grown to manhood. Dirkê pursues and requires her to be delivered up: but the sons recognise and protect their mother, taking an ample revenge upon her persecutors. Lykus is slain, and Dirkê is dragged to death, tied to the horns of a bull. Amphiôn and Zêthus, having banished Laius, become kings at Thêbes. The former, taught by Hêrmes, and possessing exquisite skill on the lyre, employs it in fortifying the city, the stones of the walls arranging themselves spontaneously in obedience to the rhythm of his song.

Zêthus marries Aêdôn, who, in the dark and under a fatal mistake, kills her son Itylus: she is transformed into a nightingale, while Zêthus dies of grief. Amphiôn becomes the husband of Niobê, daughter of Tantalus, and the father of a numerous offspring, the complete extinction of which by the hands of Apollo and Artemis has already been recounted in these pages.

Here ends the legend of the beautiful Antiopê and her twin sons – the rude and unpolished, but energetic, Zêthus – and the refined and amiable, but dreamy, Amphiôn. For so Euripidês, in the drama of Antiopê unfortunately lost, presented the two brothers, in affectionate union as well as in striking contrast. It as evident that the whole story stood originally quite apart from the Kadmeian family, and so the rudiments of it yet stand in the Odyssey: but the logographers, by their ordinary connecting artifices, have opened a vacant place for it in the descending series of Thêban mythes. And they have here proceeded in a manner not usual with them. For whereas they are generally fond of multiplying entities, and supposing different historical personages of the same name, in order to introduce an apparent smoothness in the chronology – they have here blended into one person Amphiôn the son of Antiopê and Amphiôn the father of Chlôris, who seem clearly distinguished from each other in the Odyssey. They have further assigned to the same person all the circumstances of the legend of Niobê, which seems to have been originally framed quite apart from the sons of Antiopê.

Amphiôn and Zêthus being removed, Laius became king of Thêbes. With him commences the ever-celebrated series of adventures of Œdipus and his family. Laius forewarned by the oracle that any son whom he might beget would kill him, caused Œdipus as soon as he was born to be exposed on Mount Kithærôn. Here the herdsmen of Polybus king of Corinth accidentally found him and conveyed him to their master, who brought him up as his own child. In spite of the kindest treatment, however, Œdipus when he grew up found himself exposed to taunts on the score of his unknown parentage, and went to Delphi to inquire of the god the name of his real father. He received for answer an admonition not to go back to his country: if he did so, it was his destiny to kill his father and become the husband of his mother. Knowing no other country but

XIV. LEGENDS OF THÊBES.

Corinth, he accordingly determined to keep away from that city, and quitted Delphi by the road towards Bœôtia and Phôkis. At the exact spot where the roads leading to these two countries forked, he met Laius in a chariot drawn by mules, when the insolence of one of the attendants brought on an angry quarrel, in which Œdipus killed Laius, not knowing him to be his father.

On the death of Laius, Kreôn, the brother of Jokasta, succeeded to the kingdom of Thêbes. At this time the country was under the displeasure of the gods, and was vexed by a terrible monster, with the face of a woman, the wings of a bird, and the tail of a lion, called the Sphinx – sent by the wrath of Hêrê, and occupying the neighbouring mountain of Phikium. The Sphinx had learned from the Muses a riddle, which she proposed to the Thêbans to resolve: on every occasion of failure she took away one of the citizens and ate him up. Still no person could solve the riddle, and so great was the suffering occasioned, that Kreôn was obliged to offer both the crown and the nuptials of his sister Jokasta to any one who could achieve the salvation of the city. At this juncture Œdipus arrived and solved the riddle; upon which the Sphinx immediately threw herself from the acropolis and disappeared. As a recompense for this service, Œdipus was made king of Thêbes, and married Jokasta, not aware that she was his mother.

These main tragical circumstances – that Œdipus had ignorantly killed his father and married his mother – belong to the oldest form of the legend as it stands in the Odyssey. The gods (it is added in that poem) quickly made the facts known to mankind. Epikasta (so Jokasta is here called) in an agony of sorrow hanged herself: Œdipus remained king of the Kadmeians, but underwent many and great miseries, such as the Erinnyes, who avenge an injured mother, inflict. A passage in the Iliad implies that he died at Thêbes, since it mentions the funeral games which were celebrated there in honour of him. His misfortunes were recounted by Nestôr, in the old Cyprian verses, among the stories of afore-time. A fatal curse hung both upon himself and upon his children, Eteoklês, Polynikês, Antigonê and Ismênê. According to that narrative which the Attic tragedians have rendered universally current, they were his children by Jokasta, the disclosure of her true relationship to him having been very long deferred. The ancient epic called Œdipodia, treading more closely in the footsteps of Homer, represented him as having after her death married a second wife, Euryganeia, by whom the four children were born to him: and the painter Onatas adopted this story in preference to that of Sophoklês.

The disputes of Eteoklês and Polynikês for the throne of their father gave occasion not only to a series of tragical family incidents, but also to one of the great quasi-historical events of legendary Greece – the two sieges of Thêbes by Adrastus, king of Argôs. The two ancient epic poems called the Thêbaïs and the Epigoni (if indeed both were not parts of one very comprehensive poem) detailed these events at great length, and as it appears, with distinguished poetical merit: for Pausanias pronounces the Cyclic Thêbaïs (so it was called by the subsequent critics to distinguish it from the more modern Thêbaïs of Antimachus) inferior only to the Iliad and Odyssey: and the ancient elegiac poet Kallinus treated it as an Homeric composition. Of this once-valued poem we unfortunately possess nothing but a few scanty fragments. The leading points of the legend are briefly glanced at in the Iliad: but our knowledge of the details is chiefly derived from the Attic tragedians, who transformed the narratives of their predecessors at pleasure, and where popularity constantly eclipsed and obliterated the ancient version. Antimachus of Kolophôn, contemporary with Euripidês, in his long epic, probably took no less liberties with the old narrative. His Thêbaïd never became generally popular, but it exhibited marks of study and elaboration which recommended it to the esteem of the Alexandrine critics, and probably contributed to discredit in their eyes the old cyclic poem.

The logographers, who gave a continuous history of this siege of Thêbes, had at least three pre-existing epic poems – the Thêbaïs, the Œdipodia, and the Alkmæônis, from which they could borrow. The subject was also handled in some of the Hesiodic poems, but we do not know to what extent. The Thêbaïs was composed more in honour of Argôs than of Thêbes, as the first line of it, one of the few fragments still preserved, betokens.

Sieges of Thêbes.

The legend, about to recount fraternal dissension ol the most implacable kind, comprehending in its results not only the immediate relations of the infuriated brothers, but many chosen companions of the heroic race along with them, takes its start from the paternal curse of Œdipus, which overhangs and determines all the gloomy sequel.

Œdipus, though king of Thêbes and father of four children by Euryganeia (according to the Œdipodia). has become the devoted victim of the Erinnyes, in consequence of the self-inflicted death of his mother, which he has unconsciously caused, as well as of his unintentional parricide. Though he had long forsworn the use of all the ornaments and luxuries which his father had inherited from his kingly progenitors, yet when through age he had come to be dependent upon his two sons, Polynikês one day broke through this interdict, and set before him the silver table and the splendid wine-cup of Kadmus, which Laius had always been accustomed to employ. The old king had no sooner seen these precious appendages of the regal life of his father, than his mind was overrun by a calamitous phrenzy, and he imprecated terrible curses on his sons, predicting that there would be bitter and endless warfare between them. The goddess Erinnys heard and heeded him; and he repeated the curse again on another occasion, when his sons, who had always been accustomed to send to him the shoulder of the victims sacrificed on the altar, caused the buttock to be served to him in place of it. He resented this as an insult, and prayed the gods that they might perish each by the hand of the other. Throughout the tragedians as well as in the old epic, the paternal curse, springing immediately from the misguided Œdipus himself, but remotely from the parricide and incest with which he has tainted his breed, is seen to domineer over the course of events – the Erinnys who executes that curse being the irresistible, though concealed, agent. Æschylus not only preserves the fatal efficiency of the paternal curse, but even briefly glances at the causes assigned for it in the Thêbaïs, without superadding any new motives. In the judgment of Sophoklês, or of his audience, the conception of a father cursing his sons upon such apparently trifling grounds was odious: and that great poet introduced many aggravating circumstances, describing the old blind father as having been barbarously turned out of doors by his sons to wander abroad in exile and poverty. Though by this change he rendered his poem more coherent and self-justifying, yet he departed, from the spirit of the old legend, according to which Œdipus has contracted by his unconscious misdeeds an incurable taint destined to pass onward to his progeny. His mind is alienated, and he curses them, not because he has suffered seriously by their guilt, but because he is made the blind instrument of an avenging Erinnys for the ruin of the house of Laius.

After the death of Œdipus and the celebration of his funeral games, at which amongst others, Argeia, daughter of Adrastus (afterwards the wife of Polynikês), was present, his two sons soon quarrelled respecting the succession. The circumstances are differently related: but it appears that, according to the original narrative, the wrong and injustice was on the part of Polynikês, who, however, was obliged to leave Thêbes and to seek shelter with Adrastus, king of Argôs. Here he met Tydeus, a fugitive, at the same time, from Ætôlia: it was dark when they arrived, and a broil ensued between the two exiles, but Adrastus came out and parted them. He had been enjoined by an oracle to give his two daughters in marriage to a lion and a boar, and he thought this occasion had now arrived, inasmuch as one of the combatants carried on his shield a lion, the other a boar. He accordingly gave Deipylê in marriage to Tydeus, and Argeia to Polynikês: moreover, he resolved to restore by armed resistance both his sons-in-law to their respective countries.

On proposing the expedition to the Argeian chiefs around him he found most of them willing auxiliaries: but Amphiaraüs – formerly his bitter opponent, though now reconciled to him, and husband of his sister Eriphylê – strongly opposed him. He denounced the enterprise as unjust and contrary to the will of the gods. Again, being of a prophetic stock, descended from Melampus, he foretold the certain death both of himself and of the principal leaders, should they involve themselves as accomplices in the mad violence of Tydeus or the criminal ambition of Polynikês. Amphiaraüs, already distinguished both in the Kalydônian boar-hunt and in the funeral games of Pelias, was in the Thêban war the most conspicuous of all the heroes, and absolutely indispensable to its success. Yet his reluctance to engage in it was invincible, nor was it possible to prevail upon him except through the influence of his wife Eriphylê. Polynikês, having brought with him from Thêbes the splendid robe and necklace given by the gods to Harmonia on her marriage with Kadmus, offered it as a bribe to Eriphylê, on condition that she would influence the determination of Amphiaraüs. The sordid wife, seduced by so matchless a present, betrayed the lurking-place of her husband, and involved him in the fatal expedition. Amphiaraüs, reluctantly dragged forth, and foreknowing the disastrous issue of the expedition both to himself and to his associates, addressed his last injunctions, at the moment of mounting his chariot, to his sons Alkmæôn and Amphilochus, commanding Alkmæôn to avenge his approaching death by killing the venal Eriphylê, and by undertaking a second expedition against Thêbes.

The Attic dramatists describe this expedition as having been conducted by seven chiefs, one to each of the seven celebrated gates of Thêbes. But the Cyclic Thêbaïs gave to it a much more comprehensive character, mentioning auxiliaries from Arcadia, Messênê, and various parts of Peloponnêsus; and the application of Tydeus and Polynikês at Mykênæ in the course of their circuit made to collect allies, is mentioned in the Iliad. They were well received at Mykênæ: but the warning signals given by the gods were so

XIV. LEGENDS OF THÊBES.

terrible that no Mykênæan could venture to accompany them. The seven principal chiefs however were Adrastus, Amphiaraüs, Kapaneus, Hippomedôn, Parthenopæus Tydeus and Polynikês.

The Kadmeians, assisted by their allies the Phôkians and the Phlegyæ, marched out to resist the invaders, and fought a battle near the Ismênian hill, in which they were defeated and forced to retire within the walls. The prophet Teiresias acquainted them that if Menœkeus, son of Kreôn would offer himself as a victim to Arês, victory would be assured to Thêbes. The generous youth, as soon as he learnt that his life was to be the price of safely to his country, went and slew himself before the gates. The heroes along with Adrastus now commenced a vigorous attack upon the town, each of the seven selecting one of the gates to assault. The contest was long and strenuously maintained, but the devotion of Menœkeus had procured for the Thêbans the protection of the gods. Parthenopæus was killed with a stone by Periklymenus: and when the furious Kapaneus, having planted a scaling-ladder, had mounted the walls, he was smitten by a thunderbolt from Zeus and cast down dead upon the earth. This event struck terror into the Argeians, and Adrastus called back his troops from the attack. The Thêbans now sallied forth to pursue them, when Eteoklês, arresting the battle, proposed to decide the controversy by single combat with his brother. The challenge, eagerly accepted by Polynikês, was agreed to by Adrastus: a single combat ensued between the two brothers, in which both were exasperated to fury and both ultimately slain by each other's hand. This equal termination left the result of the general contest still undetermined, and the bulk of the two armies renewed the fight. In the sanguinary struggle which ensued the sons of Astakus on the Thêban side displayed the most conspicuous and successful valour. One of them, Melanippus, mortally wounded Tydeus – while two others, Leades and Amphidikus, killed Eteoklus and Hippomedôn. Amphiaraüs avenged Tydeus by killing Melanippus; but unable to arrest the rout of the army, he fled with the rest, closely pursued by Periklymenus. The latter was about to pierce him with his spear, when the beneficence of Zeus rescued him from this disgrace – miraculously opening the earth under him, so that Amphiaraüs with his chariot and horses was received unscathed into her bosom. The exact spot where this memorable incident happened was indicated by a sepulchral building, and shown by the Thêbans down to the days of Pausanias – its sanctity being attested by the fact, that no animal would consent to touch the herbage which grew within the sacred inclosure. Amphiaraüs, rendered immortal by Zeus, was worshipped as a god at Argôs, at Thêbes and at Orôpus – and for many centuries gave answers at his oracle to the questions of the pious applicant.

Adrastus, thus deprived of the prophet and warrior whom he regarded as "the eye of his army," and having seen the other chiefs killed in the disastrous fight, was forced to take flight singly, and was preserved by the matchless swiftness of his horse Areiôn, the offspring of Poseidôn. He reached Argôs on his return, bringing with him nothing except "his garments of woe and his black-maned steed."

Kreôn, father of the heroic youth Menœkeus, succeeding to the administration of Thêbes after the death of the two hostile brothers and the repulse of Adrastus, caused Eteoklês to be buried with distinguished honour, but cast out ignominiously the body of Polynikês as a traitor to his country, forbidding every one on pain of death to consign it to the tomb. He likewise refused permission to Adrastus to inter the bodies of his fallen comrades. This proceeding, so offensive to Grecian feeling, gave rise to two further tales: one of them at least of the highest pathos and interest. Antigonê, the sister of Polynikês, heard with indignation the revolting edict consigning her brother's body to the dogs and vultures, and depriving it of those rites which were considered essential to the repose of the dead. Unmoved by the dissuading counsel of an affectionate but timid sister, and unable to procure assistance, she determined to brave the hazard and to bury the body with her own hands. She was detected in the act, and Kreôn, though forewarned by Teiresias of the consequences, gave orders that she should be buried alive, as having deliberately set at naught the solemn edict of the city. His son Hæmôn, to whom she was engaged to be married, in vain interceded for her life. In an agony of despair he slew himself in the sepulchre to which the living Antigonê had been consigned; and his mother Eurydikê, the wife of Kreôn, inconsolable for his death, perished by her own hand. Thus the new light which seemed to be springing up over the last remaining scion of the devoted family of Œdipus, is extinguished amidst gloom and horrors – which overshadowed also the house and dynasty of Kreôn.

The other tale stands more apart from the original legend, and seems to have had its origin in the patriotic pride of the Athenians. Adrastus, unable to obtain permission from the Thêbans to inter the fallen chieftains, presented himself in suppliant guise, accompanied by their disconsolate mothers, to Thesêus at Eleusis. He implored the Athenian warrior to extort from the perverse Thêbans that last melancholy privilege which no decent or pious Greeks ever thought of withholding, and thus to stand forth as the champion of Grecian public morality in one of its most essential points, not less than of the rights of the subterranean gods. The Thêbans obstinately persisting in their refusal, Thesêus undertook an expedition against their city, vanquished them in the field, and compelled them by force of arms to permit the sepulture of their fallen enemies. This chivalrous interposition, celebrated in one of the preserved dramas of Euripidês, formed a subject of glorious recollection to the Athenians throughout the historical age: their orators dwelt upon it in terms of animated panegyric: and it seems to have been accepted as a real fact of the past time, with not less implicit conviction than the battle of Marathôn. But the Thêbans, though equally persuaded of the truth of the main story, dissented from the Athenian version of it, maintaining that they had given up the bodies for sepulture voluntarily and of their own accord. The tomb of the chieftains was shown near Eleusis even in the days of Pausanias.

The defeat of the seven chiefs before Thêbes was amply avenged by their sons, again under the guidance of Adrastus: Ægialeus son of Adrastus, Thersander son of Polynikês, Alkmæôn and Amphilochus, sons of Amphiaraüs, Diomêdês son of Tydeus, Sthenelus son of Kapaneus, Promachus son of Parthenopæus, and Euryalus son of Mekistheus, joined in this expedition. Though all these youthful warriors, called the Epigoni, took part in the expedition, the grand and prominent place appears to have been occupied by Alkmæôn, son of Amphiaraüs. Assistance was given to them from Corinth and Megara, as well as from Messênê and Arcadia; while Zeus manifested his favourable dispositions by signals not to be mistaken. At the river Glisas the Epigoni were met by the Thêbans in arms, and a battle took place in which the latter were completely defeated. Laodamas, son of Eteoklês, killed Ægialeus, son of Adrastus; but he and his army were routed and driven within the walls by the valour and energy of Alkmæôn. The defeated Kadmeians consulted the prophet Teiresias, who informed them that the gods had declared for their enemies, and that there was no longer any hope of successful resistance. By his advice they sent a herald to the assailants offering to surrender the town, while they themselves conveyed away their wives and children, and fled under the command of Laodamas to the Illyrians, upon which the Epigoni entered Thêbes, and established Thersander, son of Polynikês. on the throne.

Adrastus, who in the former expedition had been the single survivor amongst so many fallen companions, now found himself the only exception to the general triumph and joy of the conquerors: he had lost his son Ægialeus, and the violent sorrow arising from the event prematurely cut short his life. His soft voice and persuasive eloquence were proverbial in the ancient epic. He was worshipped as a hero both at Argôs and at Sikyôn, but with especial solemnity in the last-mentioned place, where his Herôum stood in the public agora, and where his exploits as well as his sufferings were celebrated periodically in lyric tragedies. Melanippus, son of Astakus, the brave defender of Thêbes, who had slain both Tydeus and Mekistheus, was worshipped with no less solemnity by the Thêbans. The enmity of these two heroes rendered it impossible for both of them to be worshipped close upon the same spot. Accordingly it came to pass during the historical period, about the time of the Solônian legislation at Athens, that Kleisthenês, despot of Sikyôn, wishing to banish the hero Adrastus and abolish the religious solemnities celebrated in honour of the latter by the Sikyônians, first applied to the Delphian oracle for permission to carry this banishment into effect directly and forcibly. That permission being refused, he next sent to Thêbes an intimation that he was anxious to introduce their hero Melanippus into Sikyôn. The Thêbans willingly consented, and he assigned to the new hero a consecrated spot in the strongest and most commanding portion of the Sikyônian prytaneium. He did this (says the historian) "knowing that Adrastus would forthwith go away of his own accord: since Melanippus was of all persons the most odious to him, as having slain both his son-in-law and his brother." Kleisthenês moreover diverted the festivals and sacrifices which had been offered to Adrastus, to the newly established hero Melanippus; and the lyric tragedies from the worship of Adrastus to that of Dionysus. But his dynasty did not long continue after his decease, and the Sikyônians then re-established their ancient solemnities.

Near the Prœtid gate of Thêbes were seen the tombs of two combatants who had hated each other during life even more than Adrastus and Melanippus – the two brothers Eteoklês and Polynikês. Even as heroes and objects of worship, they still continued to manifest their inextinguishable hostility: those who offered sacrifices to them observed that the flame and the smoke from the two adjoining altars abhorred all communion, and flew off in directions exactly opposite. The Thêban exegetes assured Pausanias of this fact. And though he did not himself witness it, yet having seen with his own eyes a miracle not very dissimilar at Pioniæ in Mysia, he had no difficulty in crediting their assertion.

XIV. LEGENDS OF THÊBES.

Amphiaraüs when forced into the first attack of Thêbes – against his own foreknowledge and against the warnings of the gods – had enjoined his sons Alkmsæôn and Amphilochus not only to avenge his death upon the Thêbans, but also to punish the treachery of their mother, "Eriphylê, the destroyer of her husband." In obedience to this command, and having obtained the sanction of the Delphian oracle, Alkmæôn slew his mother; but the awful Erinnys, the avenger of matricide, inflicted on him a long and terrible punishment, depriving him of his reason, and chasing him about from place to place without the possibility of repose or peace of mind. He craved protection and cure from the god at Delphi, who required him to dedicate at the temple, as an offering, the precious necklace of Kadmus, that irresistible bribe which had originally corrupted Eriphylê. He further intimated to the unhappy sufferer, that though the whole earth was tainted with his crime, and had become uninhabitable for him, yet there was a spot of ground which was not under the eye of the sun at the time when the matricide was committed, and where therefore Alkmæôn yet might find a tranquil shelter. The promise was realised at the mouth of the river Achelôus, whose turbid stream was perpetually depositing new earth and forming additional islands. Upon one of these, near Œniadæ, Alkmæôn settled, permanently and in peace: he became the primitive hero of Akarnania, to which his son Akarnan gave name. The necklace was found among the treasures of Delphi, together with that which had been given by Aphroditê to Helen, by the Phôkian plunderers who stripped the temple in the time of Philip of Macedôn. The Phôkian women quarrelled about these valuable ornaments, and we are told that the necklace of Eriphylê was allotted to a woman of gloomy and malignant disposition, who ended by putting her husband to death: that of Helen to a beautiful but volatile wife, who abandoned her husband from a preference for a young Epirot.

There were several other legends respecting the distracted Alkmæôn, either appropriated or invented by the Attic tragedians. He went to Phêgeus, king of Psôphis in Arcadia, whose daughter Arsinoê he married, giving as a nuptial present the necklace of Eriphylê. Being however unable to remain there, in consequence of the unremitting persecutions of the maternal Erinnys, he sought shelter at the residence of king Achelôus, whose daughter Kallirhoê he made his wife, and on whose soil he obtained repose. But Kallirhoê would not be satisfied without the possession of the necklace of Eriphylê, and Alkmæôn went back to Psôphis to fetch it, where Phêgeus and his sons slew him. He had left twin sons, infants, with Kallirhoê, who prayed fervently to Zeus that they might be preternaturally invested with immediate manhood, in order to revenge the murder of their father. Her prayer was granted, and her sons Amphoterus and Akarnan, having instantaneously sprung up to manhood, proceeded into Arcadia, slew the murderers of their father, and brought away the necklace of Eriphylê, which they carried to Delphi.

Euripidês deviated still more widely from the ancient epic, by making Alkmæôn the husband of Mantô, daughter of Teiresias, and the father of Amphilochus. According to the Cyclic Thêbaïs, Mantô was consigned by the victorious Epigoni as a special offering to the Delphian god, and Amphilochus was son of Amphiaraüs, not son of Alkmæôn. He was the eponymous hero of the town called the Amphilochian Argôs, in Akarnania, on the shore of the Gulf of Ambrakia. Thucydidês tells us that he went thither on his return from the Trojan war, being dissatisfied with the state of affairs which he found at the Peloponnêsian Argôs. The Akarnanians were remarkable for the numerous prophets which they supplied to the rest of Greece: their heroes were naturally drawn from the great prophetic race of the the Melampodids.

Thus ends the legend of the two sieges of Thêbes: the greatest event, except the siege of Troy, in the ancient epic: the greatest enterprise of war, between Greeks and Greeks, during the time of those who are called the Heroes.

XV. LEGEND OF TROY.

XV. LEGEND OF TROY.

We now arrive at the capital and culminating point of the Grecian epic, – the two sieges and capture of Troy, with the destinies of the dispersed heroes, Trojan as well as Grecian, after the second and most celebrated capture and destruction of the city.

It would require a large volume to convey any tolerable idea of the vast extent and expansion of this interesting fable, first handled by so many poets, epic, lyric and tragic, with their endless additions, transformations and contradictions, then purged and recast by historical inquirers, who under colour of setting aside the exaggerations of the poets, introduced a new vein of prosaic invention, lastly, moralised and allegorised by philosophers. In the present brief outline of the general field of Grecian legend, or of that which the Greeks believed to be their antiquities, the Trojan war can be regarded as only one among a large number of incidents upon which Hekatæus and Herodotus looked back as constituting their fore-time. Taken as a special legendary event, it is indeed of wider and larger interest than any other, but it is a mistake to single it out from the rest as if it rested upon a different and more trustworthy basis. I must therefore confine myself to an abridged narrative of the current and leading facts; and amidst the numerous contradictory statements which are to be found respecting every one of them, I know no better ground of preference than comparative antiquity, though even the oldest tales which we possess – those contained in the Iliad – evidently presuppose others of prior date.

The primitive ancestor of the Trojan line of kings is Dardanus, son of Zeus, founder and eponymous of Dardania: in the account of later authors, Dardanus was called the son of Zeus by Elektra, daughter of Atlas, and was further said to have come from Samothrace, or from Arcadia, or from Italy; but of this Homer mentions nothing. The first Dardanian town founded by him was in a lofty position on the descent of Mount Ida; for he was not yet strong enough to establish himself on the plain. His son Erichthonius, by the favour of Zeus, became the wealthiest of mankind. His flocks and herds having multiplied, he had in his pastures three thousand mares, the offspring of some of whom, by Boreas, produced horses of preternatural swiftness. Trôs, the son of Erichthonius, and the eponym of the Trojans, had three sons – Ilus, Assaracus, and the beautiful Ganymêdês, whom Zeus stole away to become his cup-bearer in Olympus, giving to his father Trôs, as the price of the youth, a team of immortal horses.

From Ilus and Assaracus the Trojan and Dardanian lines diverge: the former passing from Ilus to Laomedôn, Priam and Hectôr: the latter from Assaracus to Capys, Anchisês and Æneas. Ilus founded in the plain of Troy the holy city of Ilium: Assaracus and his descendants remained sovereigns of Dardania.

It was under the proud Laomedôn, son of Ilus, that Poseidôn and Apollo underwent, by command of Zeus, a temporary servitude: the former building the walls of the town, the latter tending the flocks and herds. When their task was completed and the penal period had expired, they claimed the stipulated reward; but Laomedôn angrily repudiated their demand, and even threatened to cut off their ears, to tie them hand and foot, and to sell them in some distant island as slaves. He was punished for this treachery by a sea-monster, whom Poseidôn sent to ravage his fields and to destroy his subjects. Laomedôn publicly offered the immortal horses given by Zeus to his father Trôs, as a reward to any one who would destroy the monster. An oracle declared that a virgin of noble blood must be surrendered to him, and the lot fell upon Hesionê, daughter of Laomedôn himself. Hêraklês arriving at this critical moment, killed the monster by the aid of a fort built for him by Athênê and the Trojans, so as to rescue both the exposed maiden and the people; but Laomedôn, by a second act of perfidy, gave him mortal horses in place of the matchless animals which had been promised. Thus defrauded of his due, Hêraklês equipped six ships, attacked and captured Troy and killed Laomedôn, giving Hesionê to his friend and auxiliary Telamôn, to whom she bore the celebrated archer Teukros. A painful sense of this expedition was preserved among the inhabitants of the historical town of Ilium, who offered no worship to Hêraklês.

Among all the sons of Laomedôn, Priam was the only one who had remonstrated against the refusal of the well-earned guerdon of Hêraklês; for which the hero recompensed him by placing him on the throne. Many and distinguished were his sons and daughters, as well by his wife Hekabê, daughter of Kisseus, as by other women. Among the sons were Hectôr, Paris, Dêiphobus, Helenus, Trôilus, Politês, Polydôrus: among the daughters Laodikê, Kreüsa, Polyxena, and Kassandra.

The birth of Paris was preceded by formidable presage; for Hekabê dreamt that she was delivered of a firebrand, and Priam, on consulting the soothsayers, was informed that the son about to be born would prove fatal to him. Accordingly he directed the child to be exposed on Mount Ida: but the inauspicious kindness of the gods preserved him, and he grew up amidst the

172

flocks and herds, active and beautiful, fair of hair and symmetrical in person, and the special favourite of Aphroditê.

It was to this youth, in his solitary shepherd's walk on Mount Ida, that the three goddesses Hêrê, Athênê, and Aphroditê were conducted, in order that he might determine the dispute respecting their comparative beauty, which had arisen at the nuptials of Pêleus and Thetis, a dispute brought about in pursuance of the arrangement, and in accomplishment of the deep-laid designs, of Zeus. For Zeus, remarking with pain the immoderate numbers of the then existing heroic race, pitied the earth for the overwhelming burden which she was compelled to bear, and determined to lighten it by exciting a destructive and long-continued war. Paris awarded the palm of beauty to Aphroditê, who promised him in recompense the possession of Helena, wife of the Spartan Menelaus, the daughter of Zeus and the fairest of living women. At the instance of Aphroditê, ships were built for him, and he embarked on the enterprise so fraught with eventual disaster to his native city, in spite of the menacing prophecies of his brother Helenus, and the always neglected warnings of Kassandra.

Paris, on arriving at Sparta, was hospitably entertained by Menelaus as well as by Kastôr and Pollux, and was enabled to present the rich gifts which he had brought to Helen. Menelaus then departed to Krête, leaving Helen to entertain his Trojan guest – a favourable moment which was employed by Aphroditê to bring about the intrigue and the elopement. Paris carried away with him both Helen and a large sum of money belonging to Menelaus – made a prosperous voyage to Troy – and arrived there safely with his prize on the third day.

Menelaus, informed by Iris in Krête of the perfidious return made by Paris for his hospitality, hastened home in grief and indignation to consult with his brother Agamemnôn, as well as with the venerable Nestôr, on the means of avenging the outrage. They made known the event to the Greek chiefs around them, among whom they found universal sympathy: Nestôr, Palamêdês and others went round to solicit aid in a contemplated attack of Troy, under the command of Agamemnôn, to whom each chief promised both obedience and unwearied exertion until Helen should be recovered. Ten years were spent in equipping the expedition. The goddesses Hêrê and Athênê, incensed at the preference given by Paris to Aphroditê, and animated by steady attachment to Argôs, Sparta and Mykênæ, took an active part in the cause: and the horses of Hêrê were fatigued with her repeated visits to the different parts of Greece.

By such efforts a force was at length assembled at Aulis in Bœôtia, consisting of 1186 ships and more than 100,000 men, a force outnumbering by more than ten to one anything that the Trojans themselves could oppose, and superior to the defenders of Troy even with all her allies included. It comprised heroes with their followers from the extreme points of Greece – from the north-western portions of Thessaly under Mount Olympus, as well as the western islands of Dulichium and Ithaca, and the eastern islands of Krête and Rhodes. Agamemnôn himself contributed 100 ships manned with the subjects of his kingdom of Mykênæ, besides furnishing 60 ships to the Arcadians, who possessed none of their own. Menelaus brought with him 60 ships, Nestôr from Pylus 90, Idomeneus from Krête and Diomêdês from Argôs 80 each. Forty ships were manned by the Eleians, under four different chiefs: the like number under Meges from Dulichium and the Echinades, and under Thoas from Kalydôn and the other Ætôlian towns. Odysseus from Ithaca, and Ajax from Salamis, brought 12 ships each. The Abantes from Eubœa, under Elephênôr, filled 40 vessels: the Bœotians, under Peneleôs and Lêitus, 50: the inhabitants of Orchomenus and Aspledôn, 30: the light-armed Locrians, under Ajax son of Oïleus, 40: the Phôkians as many. The Athenians, under Menestheus, a chief distinguished for his skill in marshalling an army, mustered 50 ships: the Myrmidons from Phthia and Hellas, under Achillês, assembled in 50 ships: Protesilaus from Phylakê and Pyrasus, and Eurypylus from Ormenium, each came with 40 ships: Machaôn and Podaleirius, from Trikka, with 30: Eumêlus, from Pheræ and the lake Bœbêis, with 11: and Philoktêtês from Melibœa with 7: the Lapithæ, under Polypœtes, son of Peirithous, filled 40 vessels: the Ænianes and Perrhæbians, under Guneus, 22: and the Magnêtês under Prothous, 40: these last two were from the northernmost parts of Thessaly, near the mountains Pêlion and Olympus. From Rhodes, under Tlêpolemus, son of Hêraklês, appeared 9 ship: from Symê, under the comely but effeminate Nireus, 3: from Kôs, Krapathus and the neighbouring islands, 30, under the orders of Pheidippus and Antiphus, sons of Thessalus and grandsons of Hêraklês.

Among this band of heroes were included the distinguished warriors Ajax and Diomêdês, and the sagacious Nestôr; while Agamemnôn himself, scarcely inferior to either of them in prowess, brought with him a high reputation for prudence in command. The most marked and conspicuous of all were Achilles and Odysseus: the former a beautiful youth born of a divine mother, swift in the race, of fierce temper and irresistible might: the latter not less efficient as an ally from his eloquence, his untiring endurance, his inexhaustible resources under difficulty, and the mixture of daring courage with deep-laid cunning which never deserted him; the blood of the arch-deceiver Sisyphus, through an illicit connection with his mother Antikleia, was said to flow in his veins, and he was especially patronised and protected by the goddess Athênê. Odysseus, unwilling at first to take part in the expedition, had even simulated insanity; but Palamêdês, sent to Ithaca to invite him, tested the reality of his madness by placing in the furrow where Odysseus was ploughing, his infant son Têlemachus. Thus detected, Odysseus could not refuse to join the Achæan host, but the prophet Halithersês predicted to him that twenty years would elapse before he revisited his native land. To Achilles the gods had promised the full effulgence of heroic glory before the walls of Troy: nor could the place be taken without both his co-operation and that of his son after him. But they had forewarned him that this brilliant career would be rapidly brought to a close, and that if he desired a long life, he must remain tranquil and inglorious in his native land. In spite of the reluctance of his mother Thetis, he preferred few years with bright renown, and joined the Achæan host. When Nestôr and Odysseus came to Phthia to invite him, both he and his intimate friend Patroklus eagerly obeyed the call.

Agamemnôn and his powerful host set sail from Aulis; but being ignorant of the locality and the direction, they landed by mistake in Teuthrania, a part of Mysia near the river Kaïkus, and began to ravage the country under the persuasion that it was the neighbourhood of Troy. Têlephus, the king of the country, opposed and repelled them, but was ultimately defeated and severely wounded by Achillês. The Greeks now, discovering their mistake, retired, but their fleet was dispersed by a storm and driven back to Greece. Achilles attacked and took Skyrus, and there married Deidamia, the daughter of Lycomêdês. Têlephus, suffering from his wounds, was directed by the oracle to come to Greece and present himself to Achilles to be healed, by applying the scrapings of the spear with which the wound had been given: thus restored, he became the guide of the Greeks when they were prepared to renew their expedition.

The armament was again assembled at Aulis, but the goddess Artemis, displeased with the boastful language of Agamemnôn, prolonged the duration of adverse winds, and the offending chief was compelled to appease her by the well-known sacrifice of his daughter Iphigeneia. They then proceeded to Tenedos, from whence Odysseus and Menelaus were despatched as envoys to Troy, to re-demand Helen and the stolen property. In spite of the prudent counsels of Antenôr, who received the two Grecian chiefs with friendly hospitality, the Trojans rejected the demand, and the attack was resolved upon. It was foredoomed by the gods that the Greek who first landed should perish: Protesilaus was generous enough to put himself upon this forlorn hope, and accordingly fell by the hand of Hectôr.

Meanwhile the Trojans had assembled a large body of allies from various parts of Asia Minor and Thrace: Dardanians under Æneas, Lykians under Sarpêdôn, Mysians, Karians, Mæonians, Alizonians, Phrygians, Thracians, and Pæonians. But vain was the attempt to oppose the landing of the Greeks: the Trojans were routed, and even the invulnerable Kyknus, son of Poseidôn, one of the great bulwarks of the defence, was slain by Achillês. Having driven the Trojans within their walls, Achilles attacked and stormed Lyrnêssus, Pêdasus, Lesbos and other places in the neighbourhood, twelve towns on the sea-coast and eleven in the interior: he drove off the oxen of Æneas and pursued the hero himself, who narrowly escaped with his life: he surprised and killed the youthful Trôilus, son of Priam, and captured several of the other sons, whom he sold as prisoners into the islands of the Ægean. He acquired as his captive the fair Brisêis, while Chrysêis was awarded to Agamemnôn: he was moreover eager to see the divine Helen, the prize and stimulus of this memorable struggle, and Aphroditê and Thetis contrived to bring about an interview between them.

At this period of the war the Grecian army was deprived of Palamêdês, one of its ablest chiefs. Odysseus had not forgiven the artifice by which Palamêdês had detected his simulated insanity, nor was he without jealousy of a rival clever and cunning in a degree equal, if not superior, to himself: one who had enriched the Greeks with the invention of letters, of dice for amusement, of night-watches, as well as with other useful suggestions. According to the old Cyprian epic, Palamêdês was drowned while fishing, by the hands of Odysseus and Diomêdês. Neither in the Iliad nor the Odyssey does the name of Palamêdês occur: the lofty position which Odysseus occupies in both those poems – noticed with some degree of displeasure even by Pindar, who described Palamêdês as the wiser man of the two – is sufficient to explain the omission. In the more advanced period of the Greek mind, when intellectual superiority came to acquire a higher place in the public esteem as compared with military prowess, the character of Palamêdês, combined with his unhappy fate, rendered him one of the most interesting personages in the Trojan legend. Æschylus, Sophoklês and

XV. LEGEND OF TROY.

Euripidês each consecrated to him a special tragedy; but the mode of his death as described in the old epic was not suitable to Athenian ideas, and accordingly he was represented as having been falsely accused of treason by Odysseus, who caused gold to be buried in his tent, and persuaded Agamemnôn and the Grecian chiefs that Palamêdês had received it from the Trojans. He thus forfeited his life, a victim to the calumny of Odysseus and to the delusion of the leading Greeks. In the last speech made by the philosopher Sokratês to his Athenian judges, he alludes with solemnity and fellow-feeling to the unjust condemnation of Palamêdês, as analogous to that which he himself was about to suffer, and his companions seem to have dwelt with satisfaction on the comparison. Palamêdês passed for an instance of the slanderous enmity and misfortune which so often wait upon superior genius.

Epic chronology historicised.

In these expeditions the Grecian army consumed nine years, during which the subdued Trojans dared not give battle without their walls for fear of Achillês. Ten years was the fixed epical duration of the siege of Troy, just as five years was the duration of the siege of Kamikus by the Krêtan armament which came to avenge the death of Minôs; ten years of preparation, ten years of siege, and ten years of wandering for Odysseus, were periods suited to the rough chronological dashes of the ancient epic, and suggesting no doubts nor difficulties with the original hearers. But it was otherwise when the same events came to be contemplated by the historicising Greeks, who could not be satisfied without either finding or inventing satisfactory bonds of coherence between the separate events. Thucydidês tells us that the Greeks were less numerous than the poets have represented, and that being moreover very poor, they were unable to procure adequate and constant provisions: hence they were compelled to disperse their army, and to employ a part of it in cultivating the Chersonese, a part in marauding expeditions over the neighbourhood. Could the whole army have been employed against Troy at once (he says), the siege would have been much more speedily and easily concluded. If the great historian could permit himself thus to amend the legend in so many points, we might have imagined that the simpler course would have been to include the duration of the siege among the list of poetical exaggerations, and to affirm that the real siege had lasted only one year instead of ten. But it seems that the ten years' duration was so capital a feature in the ancient tale, that no critic ventured to meddle with it.

A period of comparative intermission however was now at hand for the

Trojans. The gods brought about the memorable fit of anger of Achillês, under the influence of which he refused to put on his armour, and kept his Myrmidons in camp. According to the Cypria, this was the behest of Zeus, who had compassion on the Trojans: according to the Iliad, Apollo was the originating cause, from anxiety to avenge the injury which his priest Chrysês had endured from Agamemnôn. For a considerable time, the combats of the Greeks against Troy were conducted without their best warrior, and severe indeed was the humiliation which they underwent in consequence. How the remaining Grecian chiefs vainly strove to make amends for his absence – how Hectôr and the Trojans defeated and drove them to their ships – how the actual blaze of the destroying flame, applied by Hectôr to the ship of Protesilaus, roused up the anxious and sympathising Patroclus, and extorted a reluctant consent from Achillês, to allow his friend and his followers to go forth and avert the last extremity of ruin – how Achillês, when Patroclus had been killed by Hectôr, forgetting his anger in grief for the death of his friend, re-entered the fight, drove the Trojans within their walls with immense slaughter, and satiated his revenge both upon the living and the dead Hectôr – all these events have been chronicled, together with those divine dispensations on which most of them are made to depend, in the immortal verse of the Iliad.

Homer breaks off with the burial of Hectôr, whose body has just been ransomed by the disconsolate Priam: while the lost poem of Arktinus, entitled the Æthiopis, so far as we can judge from the argument still remaining of it, handled only the subsequent events of the siege. The poem of Quintus Smyrnæus, composed about the fourth century of the Christian aera, seems in its first books to coincide with the Æthiopis, in the subsequent books partly with the Ilias Minor of Leschês.

The Trojans, dismayed by the death of Hectôr, were again animated with hope by the appearance of the warlike and beautiful queen of the Amazons, Penthesileia, daughter of Arês, hitherto invincible in the field, who came to their assistance from Thrace at the head of a band of her countrywomen. She again led the besieged without the walls to encounter the Greeks in the open field: and under her auspices the latter were at first driven back, until she too was slain by the invincible arm of Achillês. The victor, on taking off the helmet of his fair enemy as she lay on the ground, was. profoundly affected and captivated by her charms, for which he was scornfully taunted by Thersitês: exasperated by this rash insult, he killed Thersitês on the spot with a blow of his fist. A violent dispute among the Grecian chiefs was the result, for Diomêdês, the kinsman of Thersitês, warmly resented the proceeding; and Achilles was obliged to go to Lesbos, where he was purified from the act of homicide by Odysseus.

Next arrived Memnôn, son of Tithônus and Eôs, the most stately of living men, with a powerful band of black Æthiopians, to the assistance of Troy. Sallying forth against the Greeks, he made great havoc among them: the brave and popular Antilochus perished by his hand, a victim to filial devotion in defence of Nestôr. Achilles at length attacked him, and for a long time the combat was doubtful between them: the prowess of Achilles and the supplication of Thetis with Zeus finally prevailed; whilst Eôs obtained for her vanquished son the consoling gift of immortality. His tomb, however, was shown near the Propontis, within a few miles of the mouth of the river Æsêpus, and was visited annually by the birds called Memnonides, who swept it and bedewed it with water from the stream. So the traveller Pausanias was told, even in the second century after the Christian æra, by the Hellespontine Greeks.

The fate of Achilles himself was now at hand. After routing the Trojans and chasing them into the town, he was slain near the Skæan gate by an arrow from the quiver of Paris, directed under the unerring auspices of Apollo. The greatest efforts were made by the Trojans to possess themselves of the body, which was however rescued and borne off to the Grecian camp by the valour of Ajax and Odysseus. Bitter was the grief of Thetis for the loss of her son: she came into the camp with the Muses and the Nêreids to mourn over him; and when a magnificent funeral-pile had been prepared by the Greeks to burn him with every mark of honour, she stole away the body and conveyed it to a renewed and immortal life in the island of Leukê in the Euxine Sea. According to some accounts he was there blest with the nuptials and company of Helen.

Thetis celebrated splendid funeral games in honour of her son, and offered the unrivalled panoply, which Hêphæstos had forged and wrought for him, as a prize to the most distinguished warrior in the Grecian army. Odysseus and Ajax became rivals for the distinction, when Athênê, together with some Trojan prisoners, who were asked from which of the two their country had sustained greatest injury, decided in favour of the former. The gallant Ajax lost his senses with grief and humiliation: in a fit of phrenzy he slew some sheep, mistaking them for the men who had wronged him, and then fell upon his own sword.

Odysseus now learnt from Helenus son of Priam, whom he had captured in an ambuscade, that Troy could not be taken unless both Philoktêtês and

Neoptolemus, son of Achillês, could be prevailed upon to join the besiegers. The former, having been stung in the foot by a serpent, and becoming insupportable to the Greeks from the stench of his wound, had been left at Lemnus in the commencement of the expedition, and had spent ten years in misery on that desolate island; but he still possessed the peerless bow and arrows of Hêraklês, which were said to be essential to the capture of Troy. Diomêdês fetched Philoktetes from Lemnus to the Grecian camp, where he was healed by the skill of Machaôn, and took an active part against the Trojans – engaging in single combat with Paris, and killing him with one of the Hêrakleian arrows. The Trojans were allowed to carry away for burial the body of this prince, the fatal cause of all their sufferings; but not until it had been mangled by the hand of Menelaus. Odysseus went to the island of Skyrus to invite Neoptolemus to the army. The untried but impetuous youth gladly obeyed the call, and received from Odysseus his father's armour, while on the other hand, Eurypylus, son of Têlephus, came from Mysia as auxiliary to the Trojans and rendered to them valuable service – turning the tide of fortune for a time against the Greeks, and killing some of their bravest chiefs, amongst whom was numbered Peneleôs, and the unrivalled leech Machaôn. The exploits of Neoptolemus were numerous, worthy of the glory of his race and the renown of his father. He encountered and slew Eurypylus, together with numbers of the Mysian warriors: he routed the Trojans and drove them within their walls, from whence they never again emerged to give battle: nor was he less distinguished for his good sense and persuasive diction, than for forward energy in the field.

Troy however was still impregnable so long as the Palladium, a statue given by Zeus himself to Dardanus, remained in the citadel: and great care had been taken by the Trojans not only to conceal this valuable present, but to construct other statues so like it as to mislead any intruding robber. Nevertheless the enterprising Odysseus, having disguised his person with miserable clothing and self-inflicted injuries, found means to penetrate into the city and to convey the Palladium by stealth away. Helen alone recognised him, but she was now anxious to return to Greece, and even assisted Odysseus in concerting means for the capture of the town.

To accomplish this object, one final stratagem was resorted to. By the hands of Epeius of Panopeus, and at the suggestion of Athênê, a capacious hollow wooden horse was constructed, capable of containing one hundred men: the *élite* of the Grecian heroes, Neoptolemus, Odysseus, Menelaus and others, concealed themselves in the inside of it, and the entire Grecian army sailed away to Tenedos, burning their tents and pretending to have abandoned the siege. The Trojans, overjoyed to find themselves free, issued from the city and contemplated with astonishment the fabric which their enemies had left behind: they long doubted what should be done with it; and the anxious heroes from within heard the surrounding consultations, as well as the voice of Helen when she pronounced their names and counterfeited the accents of their wives. Many of the Trojans were anxious to dedicate it to the gods in the city as a token of gratitude for their deliverance; but the more cautious spirits inculcated distrust of an enemy's legacy, and Laocoôn, the priest of Poseidôn, manifested his aversion by striking the side of the horse with his spear. The sound revealed that the horse was hollow, but the Trojans heeded not this warning of possible fraud, and the unfortunate Laocoôn, a victim to his own sagacity and patriotism, miserably perished before the eyes of his countrymen, together with one of his sons, two serpents being sent expressly by the gods out of the sea to destroy him. By this terrific spectacle, together with the perfidious counsels of Sinon, a traitor whom the Greeks had left behind for the special purpose of giving false information, the Trojans were induced to make a breach in their own walls, and to drag the fatal fabric with triumph and exultation into their city.

The destruction of Troy, according to the decree of the gods, was now irrevocably sealed. While the Trojans indulged in a night of riotous festivity, Sinon kindled the fire-signal to the Greeks at Tenedos, loosening the bolts of the wooden horse, from out of which the enclosed heroes descended. The city, assailed both from within and from without, was thoroughly sacked and destroyed, with the slaughter or captivity of the larger portion of its heroes as well as its people. The venerable Priam perished by the hand of Neoptolemus, having in vain sought shelter at the domestic altar of Zeus Herkeios; but his son Deiphobus, who since the death of Paris had become the husband of Helen, defended his house desperately against Odysseus and Menalaus, and sold his life dearly. After he was slain, his body was fearfully mutilated by the latter.

Thus was Troy utterly destroyed – the city, the altars and temples, and the population. Æneas and Antenôr were permitted to escape, with their families, having been always more favourably regarded by the Greeks than the remaining Trojans. According to one version of the story, they had betrayed the city to the Greeks: a panther's skin had been hung over the door of Antenôr's house as a signal for the victorious besiegers to spare it in the general plunder. In the distribution of the principal captives, Asryanax, the infant son of Hectôr, was cast from the top of the wall and killed by Odysseus or Neoptolemus: Polyxena, the daughter of Priam, was immolated on the tomb of Achillês, in compliance with a requisition made by the shade of the deceased hero to his countrymen; while her sister Kassandra was presented as a prize to Agamemnôn. She had sought sanctuary at the altar of Athênê, where Ajax, the son of Oïleus, making a guilty attempt to seize her, had drawn both upon himself and upon the army the serious wrath of the goddess, insomuch that the Greeks could hardly be restrained from stoning him to death. Andromachê and Helenus were both given to Neoptolemus, who, according to the Ilias Minor, carried away also Æneas as his captive.

Helen gladly resumed her union with Menelaus: she accompanied him back to Sparta, and lived with him there many years in comfort and dignity, passing afterwards to a happy immortality in the Elysian fields. She was worshipped as a goddess with her brothers the Dioskari and her husband, having her temple, statue and altar at Therapnæ and elsewhere. Various examples of her miraculous interventions were cited among the Greeks. The lyric poet Stêsichorus had ventured to denounce her, conjointly with her sister Klytæmnêstra, in a tone of rude and plain-spoken severity, resembling that of Euripidês and Lycophrôn afterwards, but strikingly opposite to the delicacy and respect with which she is always handled by Homer, who never admits reproaches against her except from her own lips. He was smitten with blindness, and made sensible of his impiety: but having repented and composed a special poem formally retracting the calumny, was permitted to recover his sight. In his poem of recantation (the famous palinode now unfortunately lost) he pointedly contradicted the Homeric narrative, affirming that Helen had never been to Troy at all, and that the Trojans had carried thither nothing but her image or *eidôlon*. It is, probably, to the excited religious feelings of Stêsichorus that we owe the first idea of this glaring deviation from the old legend, which could never have been recommended by any considerations of poetical interest.

Other versions were afterwards started, forming a sort of compromise between Homer and Stêsichorus, admitting that Helen had never really been at Troy, without altogether denying her elopement. Such is the story of her having been detained in Egypt during the whole term of the siege. Paris, on his departure from Sparta, had been driven thither by storms, and the Egyptian king Prôteus, hearing of the grievous wrong which he had committed towards Menelaus, had sent him away from the country with severe menaces, detaining Helen until her lawful husband should come to seek her. When the Greeks reclaimed Helen from Troy, the Trojans assured them solemnly, that she neither was, nor ever had been, in the town; but the Greeks, treating this allegation as fraudulent, prosecuted the siege until their ultimate success confirmed the correctness of the statement. Menelaus did not recover Helen until, on his return from Troy, he visited Egypt. Such was the story told by the Egyptian priests to Herodotus, and it appeared satisfactory to his historicising mind. "For if Helen had really been at Troy (he argues) she would certainly have been given up, even had she been mistress of Priam himself instead of Paris: the Trojan king, with all his family and all his subjects, would never knowingly have incurred utter and irretrievable destruction for the purpose of retaining her: their misfortune was, that while they did not possess, and therefore could not restore her, they yet found it impossible to convince the Greeks that such was the fact." Assuming the historical character of the war of Troy, the remark of Herodotus admits of no reply: nor can we greatly wonder that he acquiesced in the tale of Helen's Egyptian detention, as a substitute for the "incredible insanity" which the genuine legend imputes to Priam and the Trojans. Pansanias, upon the same ground and by the same mode of reasoning, pronounces that the Trojan horse must have been in point of fact a battering-engine, because to admit the literal narrative would be to impute utter childishness to the defenders of the city. Mr. Payne Knight rejects Helen altogether as the real cause of the Trojan war, though she may have been the pretext of it: for he thinks that neither the Greeks nor the Trojans could have been so mad and silly as to endure calamities of such magnitude "for one little woman." Mr. Knight suggests various political causes as substitutes; these might deserve consideration, either if any evidence could be produced to countenance them, or if the subject on which they are brought to bear could be shown to belong to the domain of history.

The return of the Grecian chiefs from Troy furnished matter to the ancient epic hardly less copious than the siege itself, and the more susceptible of indefinite diversity, inasmuch as those who had before acted in concert were now dispersed and isolated. Moreover the stormy voyages and compulsory wanderings of the heroes exactly fell in with the common aspirations after an heroic founder, and enabled even the most remote Hellenic settlers to connect the origin of their town with this prominent event of their ante-historical and semi-divine world. An absence of ten years afforded room for the supposition of many domestic changes in their native abode, and many family misfortunes and misdeeds during the interval. One of these heroic "Returns," that of Odysseus, has been immortalised by the verse if Homer. The hero, after a series of long-protracted suffering and expatriation, inflicted on him by the anger of Poseidôn, at last reaches his native island, but finds his wife beset, his youthful son insulted, and his substance plundered, by a troop of insolent suitors; he is forced to appear as a wretched beggar, and to endure in his own person their scornful treatment; but finally, by the interference of Athênê coming in aid of his own courage and stratagem, he is enabled to overwhelm his enemies, to resume his family position, and to recover his property. The return of several other Grecian chiefs was the subject of an epic poem by Hagias, which is now lost, but of which a brief abstract or argument still remains: there were in antiquity various other poems of similar title and analogous matter.

As usual with the ancient epic, the multiplied sufferings of this back-voyage are traced to divine wrath, justly provoked by the sins of the Greeks; who, in the fierce exultation of a victory purchased by so many hardships, had neither respected nor even spared the altars of the gods in Troy. Athênê, who had been their most zealous ally during the siege, was so incensed by their final recklessness, more especially by the outrage of Ajax, son of Oïleus, that she actively harassed and embittered their return, in spite of every effort to appease her. The chiefs began to quarrel among themselves: their formal assembly became a scene of drunkenness; even Agamemnôn and Menelaus lost their fraternal harmony, and each man acted on his own separate resolution. Nevertheless, according to the Odyssey, Nestôr, Diomêdês, Neoptolemus, Idomeneus and Philoktêtês reached home speedily and safely; Agamemnôn also arrived in Peloponnêsus, to perish by the hand of a treacherous wife; but Menelaus was condemned to long wanderings and to the severest privations in Egypt, Cyprus and elsewhere, before he could set foot in his native land. The Lokrian Ajax perished on the Gyræan rock. Though exposed to a terrible storm, he had already reached this place of safety, when he indulged in the rash boast of having escaped in defiance of the gods. No sooner did Poseidôn hear this language, than he struck with his trident the rock which Ajax was grasping and precipitated both into the sea. Kalchas the soothsayer, together with Leonteus and Polypœtes, proceeded by land from. Troy to Kolophon.

XV. LEGEND OF TROY.

Wanderings of the heroes.

In respect however to these and other Grecian heroes, tales were told different from those in the Odyssey, assigning to them a long expatriation and a distant home. Nestôr went to Italy, where he founded Metapontum, Pisa and Hêrakleia; Philoktêtês also went to Italy, founded Petilia and Krimisa, and sent settlers to Egesta in Sicily. Neoptolemus, under the advice of Thetis, marched by land across Thrace, met with Odysseus, who had come by sea, at Maroneia, and then pursued his journey to Epirus, where he became king of the Molossians. Idomeneus came to Italy, and founded Uria in the Salentine peninsula. Diomêdês, after wandering far and wide, went along the Italian coast into the innermost Adriatic Gulf, and finally settled in Daunia, founding the cities of Argyrippa, Beneventum, Atria and Diomêdeia: by the favour of Athênê he became immortal, and was worshipped as a god in many different places. The Lokrian followers of Ajax founded the Epizephyrian Lokri on the southernmost corner of Italy, besides another settlement in Libya. I have spoken in another place of the compulsory exile of Teukros, who, besides founding the city of Salamis in Cyprus, is said to have established some settlements in the Iberian peninsula. Menestheus the Athenian did the like, and also founded both Elæa in Mysia and Skylletium in Italy. The Arcadian chief Agapenôr founded Paphus in Cyprus. Epeius, of Panopeus in Phôkis, the constructor of the Trojan horse with the aid of the goddess Athênê, settled at Lagaria near Sybaris on the coast of Italy; and the very tools which he had employed in that remarkable fabric were shown down to a late date in the temple of Athênê at Metapontum. Temples, altars and towns were also pointed out in Asia Minor, in Samos and in Krête, the foundation of Agamemnôn or of his followers. The inhabitants of the Grecian town of Skionê, in the Thracian peninsula called Pallênê or Pellênê, accounted themselves the offspring of the Pellênians from Achæa in Peloponnêsus, who had served under Agamemnôn before Troy, and who on their return from the siege had been driven on the spot by a storm and there settled. The Pamphylians, on the southern coast of Asia Minor, deduced their origin from the wanderings of Amphilochus and Kalchas after the siege of Troy: the inhabitants of the Amphilochian Argôs on the Gulf of Ambrakia revered the same Amphilochus as their rounder. The Orchomenians under Ialmenus, on quitting the conquered city, wandered or were driven to the eastern extremity of the Euxine Sea; and the barbarous Achæans under Mount Caucasus were supposed to have derived their first establishment from this source. Merionês with his Krêtan followers settled at Engyion in Sicily, along with the preceding Krêtans who had remained there after the invasion of Minôs. The Elymians in Sicily also were composed of Trojans and Greeks separately driven to the spot, who, forgetting their previous differences, united in the joint settlements of Eryx and Egesta. We hear of Podaleirius both in Italy and on the coast of Karia; of Akamas, son of Thesêus, at Amphipolis in Thrace, at Soli in Cyprus, and at Synnada in Phrygia; of Guneus, Prothous and Eurypylus, in Krête as well as in Libya. The obscure poem of Lycophrôn enumerates many of these dispersed and expatriated heroes, whose conquest of Troy was indeed a Kadmeian victory (according to the proverbial phrase of the Greeks), wherein the sufferings of the victor were little inferior to those of the vanquished. It was particularly among the Italian Greeks, where they were worshipped with very special solemnity, that their presence as wanderers from Troy was reported and believed.

I pass over the numerous other tales which circulated among the ancients, illustrating the ubiquity of the Grecian and Trojan heroes as well as that of the Argônauts, one of the most striking features in the Hellenic legendary world. Amongst them all, the most interesting, individually, is Odysseus, whose romantic adventures in fabulous places and among fabulous persons have been made familiarly known by Homer. The goddesses Kalypso and Circê; the semi-divine mariners of Phæacia, whose ships are endowed with consciousness and obey without a steersman; the one-eyed Cyclôpes, the gigantic Læstrygones, and the wind-ruler Æolus: the Sirens who ensnare by their song, as the Lotophagi fascinate by their food – all these pictures formed integral and interesting portions of the old epic. Homer leaves Odysseus re-established in his house and family; but so marked a personage could never be permitted to remain in the tameness of domestic life: the epic poem called the Telegonia ascribed to him a subsequent series of adventures. Telegonus, his son by Circê, coming to Ithaka in search of his father, ravaged the island and killed Odysseus without knowing who he was. Bitter repentance overtook the son for his undesigned parricide: at his prayer and by the intervention of his mother Circê, both Penelopê and Têlemachus were made immortal: Telegonus married Penelopê, and Têlemachus married Circê.

We see by this poem that Odysseus was represented as the mythical ancestor of the Thesprotian kings, just as Neoptolemus was of the Molossian.

It has already been mentioned that Antenôr and Æneas stand distinguished from the other Trojans by a dissatisfaction with Priam and a sympathy with the

Greeks, which is by Sophoklês and others construed as treacherous collusion, a suspicion indirectly glanced, at though emphatically repelled, by the Æneas of Virgil. In the old epic of Arktinus, next in age to the Iliad and Odyssey, Æneas abandons Troy and retires to Mount Ida, in terror at the miraculous death of Laocoôn, before the entry of the Greeks into the town and the last night-battle: yet Leschês, in another of the ancient epic poems, represented him as having been carried away captive by Neoptolemus. In a remarkable passage of the Iliad, Poseidôn describes the family of Priam as having incurred the hatred of Zeus, and predicts that Æneas and his descendants shall reign over the Trojans; the race of Dardanus, beloved by Zeus more than all his other sons, would thus be preserved, since Æneas belonged to it. Accordingly, when Æneas is in imminent peril from the hands of Achillês, Poseidôn specially interferes to rescue him, and even the implacable miso-Trojan goddess Hêrê assents to the proceeding. These passages have been construed by various able critics to refer to a family of philo-Hellenic or semi-Hellenic Æeadæ, known even in the time of the early singers of the Iliad as-masters of some territory in or near the Troad, and professing to be descended from, as well as worshipping, Æneas. In the town of Skêpsis, situated in the mountainous range of Ida, about thirty miles eastward of Ilium, there existed two noble and priestly families who professed to be descended, the one from Hectôr, the other from Æneas. The Skêpsian critic Dêmêtrius (in whose time both these families were still to be found) informs us that Skamandrius son of Hectôr, and Ascanius son of Æneas, were the archegets or heroic founders of his native city, which had been originally situated on one of the highest ranges of Ida, and was subsequently transferred by them to the less lofty spot on which it stood in his time. In Arisbê and Gentinus there seem to have been families professing the same descent, since the same archegets were acknowledged. In Ophrynium, Hectôr had his consecrated edifice, and in Ilium both he and Æneas were worshipped as gods: and it was the remarkable statement of the Lesbian Menekratês, that Æneas, "having been wronged by Paris and stripped of the sacred privileges which belonged to him, avenged himself by betraying the city, and then became one of the Greeks."

One tale thus among many respecting Æneas, and that too the most ancient of all, preserved among the natives of the Troad, who worshipped him as their heroic ancestor, was, that after the capture of Troy he continued in the country as king of the remaining Trojans, on friendly terms with the Greeks. But there were other tales respecting him, alike numerous and irreconcilable: the hand of destiny marked him as a wanderer (*fato profugus*), and his ubiquity is not exceeded even by that of Odysseus. We hear of him at Ænus in Thrace, in Pallenê, at Æneia in the Thermaic Gulf, in Delus, at Orchomenus and Mantineia in Arcadia, in the islands of Kythêra and Zakynthus, in Leukas and Ambrakia, at Buthrotum in Epirus, on the Salentine peninsula and various other places in the southern region of Italy; at Drepana and Segesta in Sicily, at Carthage, at Cape Palinurus, Cumæ, Misenum, Caieta, and finally in Latium, where he lays the first humble foundation of the mighty Rome and her empire. The reason why his wanderings were not continued still further was, that the oracles and the pronounced will of the gods directed him to settle in Latium. In each of these numerous places his visit was commemorated and certified by local monuments or special legends, particularly by temples and permanent ceremonies in honour of his mother Aphroditê, whose worship accompanied him everywhere: there were also many temples and many different tombs of Æneas himself. The vast ascendency acquired by Rome, the ardour with which all the literary Romans espoused the idea of a Trojan origin, and the fact that the Julian family recognised Æneas as their gentile primary ancestor, all contributed to give to the Roman version of his legend the preponderance over every other. The various other places in which monuments of Æneas were found came thus to be represented as places where he had halted for a time on his way from Troy to Latium. Though the legendary pretensions of these places were thus eclipsed in the eyes of those who constituted the literary public, the local belief was not extinguished; they claimed the hero as their permanent property, and his tomb was to them a proof that he had lived and died among them.

Antenôr, who shares with Æneas the favourable sympathy of the Greeks, is said by Pindar to have gone from Troy along with Menelaus and Helen into the region of Kyrênê in Libya. But according to the more current narrative, he placed himself at the head of a body of Eneti or Veneti from Paphlagonia, who had come as allies of Troy, and went by sea into the inner part of the Adriatic Gulf, where he conquered the neighbouring barbarians and founded the town of Patavium (the modern Padua): the Veneti in this region were said to owe their origin to his immigration. We learn further from Strabo, that Opsikellas, one of the companions of Antenôr, had continued his wanderings even into Ibêria, and that he had there established a settlement bearing his name.

Thus ended the Trojan war: together with its sequel, the dispersion of the heroes, victors as well as vanquished. The account here given of it has been unavoidably brief and imperfect; for in a work intended to follow consecutively the real history of the Greeks, no greater space can be allotted even to the most splendid gem of their legendary period. Indeed, although it would be easy to fill a large volume with the separate incidents which have been introduced into the "Trojan cycle," the misfortune is that they are for the most part so contradictory as to exclude all possibility of weaving them into one connected narrative. We are compelled to select one out of the number, generally without any solid ground of preference, and then to note the variations of the rest. No one who has not studied the original documents can imagine the extent to which this discrepancy proceeds: it covers almost every portion and fragment of the tale.

Though much may have been thus omitted of what the reader might expect to find in an account of the Trojan war, its genuine character has been studiously preserved, without either exaggeration or abatement. The real Trojan war is that which was recounted by Homer and the old epic poets, and continued by all the lyric and tragic composers. For the latter, though they took great liberties with the particular incidents, and introduced to some extent a new moral tone, yet worked more or less faithfully on the Homeric scale; and even Euripidês, who departed the most widely from the feeling of the old legend, never lowered down his matter to the analogy of contemporary life. They preserved its well-defined object, at once righteous and romantic, the recovery of the daughter of Zeus and sister of the Dioskuri – its mixed agencies, divine, heroic and human – the colossal force and deeds of its chief actors – its vast magnitude and long duration, as well as the toils which the conquerors underwent, and the Nemesis which followed upon their success. These were the circumstances which, set forth in the full blaze of epic and tragic poetry, bestowed upon the legend its powerful and imperishable influence over the Hellenic mind. The enterprise was one comprehending all the members of the Hellenic body, of which each individually might be proud, and in which, nevertheless, those feelings of jealous and narrow patriotism, so lamentably prevalent in many of the towns, were as much as possible excluded. It supplied them with a grand and inexhaustible object of common sympathy, common faith, and common admiration; and when occasions arose for bringing together a Pan-Hellenic force against the barbarians, the precedent of the Homeric expedition was one upon which the elevated minds of Greece could dwell with the certainty of rousing an unanimous impulse, if not always of counter-working sinister by-motives, among their audience. The incidents comprised in the Trojan cycle were familiarised, not only to the public mind but also to the public eye, by innumerable representations both of the sculptor and the painter, those which were romantic and chivalrous being better adapted for this purpose, and therefore more constantly employed, than any other.

Of such events the genuine Trojan war of the old epic was for the most part composed. Though literally believed, reverentially cherished, and numbered among the gigantic phænomena of the past, by the Grecian public, it is in the eyes of modern inquiry essentially a legend and nothing more. If we are asked whether it be not a legend embodying portions of historical matter, and raised upon a basis of truth, whether there may not really have occurred at the foot of the hill of Ilium a war purely human and political, without gods, without heroes, without Helen, without Amazons, without Ethiopians under the beautiful son of Eôs, without the wooden horse, without the characteristic and expressive features of the old epical war, like the mutilated trunk of Deïphobus in the under-world: if we are asked whether there was not really some such historical Trojan war as this, our answer must be, that as the possibility of it cannot be denied, so neither can the reality of it be affirmed. We possess nothing but the ancient epic itself without any independent evidence: had it been an age of records indeed, the Homeric epic in its exquisite and unsuspecting simplicity would probably never have come into existence. Whoever therefore ventures to dissect Homer, Arktinus and Leschês, and to pick out certain portions as matters of fact, while he sets aside the rest as fiction, must do so in full reliance on his own powers of historical divination, without any means either of proving or verifying his conclusions. Among many attempts, ancient as well as modern, to identify real objects in this historical darkness, that of Dio Chrysostom deserves attention for its extraordinary boldness. In his oration addressed to the inhabitants of Ilium, and intended to demonstrate that the Trojans were not only blameless as to the origin of the war, but victorious in its issue – he overthrows all the leading points of the Homeric narrative, and re-writes nearly the whole from beginning to end: Paris is the lawful husband of Helen, Achilles if slain by Hectôr, and the Greeks retire without taking Troy, disgraced as well as baffled. Having shown without difficulty that the Iliad, if it be looked at as a history, is full of gaps, incongruities and absurdities, he proceeds to compose a more plausible narrative of his own, which he tenders as so much authentic matter of fact. The most important point, however, which his Oration brings to view is, the literal and confiding belief with which the Homeric narrative was regarded, as if it were actual history, not only by the inhabitants of Ilium, but also by the general Grecian public.

Site of Troy.

The small town of Ilium, inhabited by Æolic Greeks, and raised into importance only by the legendary reverence attached to it, stood upon an elevated ridge forming a spur from Mount Ida, rather more than three miles from the town and promontory of Sigeium, and about twelve stadia, or less than two miles, from the sea at its nearest point. From Sigeium and the neighbouring town of Achilleium (with its monument and temple of Achillês), to the town of Rhœteium on a hill higher up the Hellespont (with its monument and chapel of Ajax called the Aianteium), was a distance of sixty stadia, or seven miles and a half in the straight course by sea: in the intermediate space was a bay and an adjoining plain, comprehending the embouchure of the Scamander, and extending to the base of the ridge on which Ilium stood. This plain was the celebrated plain of Troy, in which the great Homeric battles were believed to have taken place: the portion of the bay near to Sigeium went by the name of the Naustathmon of the Achæans (*i.e.* the spot where they dragged their ships ashore), and was accounted to have been the camp of Agamemnôn and his vast army.

Historical Ilium was founded. according to the questionable statement of Strabo, during the last dynasty of the Lydian kings, that is, at some period later than 720 B.C. Until after the days of Alexander the Great – indeed until the period of Roman preponderance – it always remained a place of inconsiderable power and importance, as we learn not only from the assertion of the geographer, but also from the fact that Achilleium, Sigeium and Rhœteium were all independent of it. Inconsiderable as it might be, it was the only place which ever bore the venerable name immortalised by Homer. Like the Homeric Ilium, it had its temple of Athênê, wherein she was worshipped as the presiding goddess of the town: the inhabitants affirmed that Agamemnôn had not altogether destroyed the town, but that it had been re-occupied after his departure, and had never ceased to exist. Their acropolis was called Pergamum, and in it was shown the house of Priam and the altar of Zeus Herkeius where that unhappy old man had been slain; moreover there were exhibited, in the temples, panoplies which had been worn by the Homeric heroes, and doubtless many other relics appreciated by admirers of the Iliad.

These were testimonies which few persons in those ages were inclined to question, when combined with the identity of name and general locality; nor

191

does it seem that any one did question them until the time of Dêmêtrius of Skêpsis. Hellanikus expressly described this Ilium as being the Ilium of Homer, for which assertion Strabo (or probably Dêmêtrius, from whom the narrative seems to be copied) imputes to him very gratuitously an undue partiality towards the inhabitants of the town. Herodotus relates, that Xerxês in his march into Greece visited the place, went up to the Pergamum of Priam, inquired with much interest into the details of the Homeric siege, made libations to the fallen heroes, and offered to the Athênê of Ilium his magnificent sacrifice of a thousand oxen: he probably represented and believed himself to be attacking Greece as the avenger of the Priamid family. The Lacedæmonian admiral Mindarus, while his fleet lay at Abydus, went personally to Ilium to offer sacrifice to Athênê, and saw from that elevated spot the battle fought between the squadron of Dorieus and the Athenians, on the shore near Rhœteium. During the interval between the Peloponnesian war and the Macedonian invasion of Persia. Ilium was always garrisoned as a strong position; but its domain was still narrow, and did not extend even to the sea which was so near to it. Alexander, on crossing the Hellespont, sent his army from Sestos to Abydos, under Parmenio, and sailed personally from Elæeus in the Chersonese, after having solemnly sacrificed at the Ekæntian shrine of Prôtesilaus, to the harbour of the Achæans between Sigeium and Rhœteium. He then ascended to Ilium, sacrificed to the Iliean Athênê, and consecrated in her temple his own panoply, in exchange for which he took some of the sacred arms there suspended, which were said to have been preserved from the time of the Trojan war. These arms were carried before him when he went to battle by his armour-bearers. It is a fact still more curious, and illustrative of the strong working of the old legend on an impressible and eminently religious mind, that he also sacrificed to Priam himself, on the very altar of Zeus Herkeius from which the old king was believed to have been torn by Neoptolemus. As that fierce warrior was his heroic ancestor by the maternal side, he desired to avert from himself the anger of Priam against the Achilleid race.

Alexander made to the inhabitants of Ilium many munificent promises, which he probably would have executed, had he not been prevented by untimely death. One of his successors, Antigonus, founded the city of Alexandreia in the Trôad, between Sigeium and the more southerly promontory Lektum; compressing into it the inhabitants of many of the neighbouring Æolic towns in the region of Ida, Skêpsis, Kebrên, Hamaxitus, Kolônæ, and Neandria, though the inhabitants of Skêpsis were subsequently permitted by Lysimachus to resume their own city and autonomous government. Ilium however remained without any special mark of favour until the arrival of the Romans in Asia and their triumph over Antiochus (about 190 B.C.). Though it retained its walls and its defensible position, Dêmêtrius of Skêpsis, who visited it shortly before that event, described it as being then in a state of neglect and poverty, many of the houses not even having tiled roofs. In this dilapidated condition, however, it was still mythically recognised both by Antiochus and by the Roman consul Livius, who went up thither to sacrifice to the Iliean Athênê. The Romans, proud of their origin from Troy and Æneas, treated Ilium with signal munificence: not only granting to it immunity from tribute, but also adding to its domain the neighbouring territories of Gergis, Rhœteium and Sigeium – and making the Ilieans masters of the whole coast from the Peræa (or continental possessions) of Tenedos (southward of Sigeium) to the boundaries of Dardanus, which had its own title to legendary reverence as the special sovereignty of Æneas. The inhabitants of Sigeium could not peaceably acquiesce in this loss of their autonomy, and their city was destroyed by the Ilieans.

The dignity and power of Ilium being thus prodigiously enhanced, we cannot doubt that the inhabitants assumed to themselves exaggerated importance as the recognised parents of all-conquering Rome. Partly, we may naturally suppose, from the jealousies thus aroused on the part of their neighbours at Skêpsis and Alexandreia Trôas – partly from the pronounced tendency of the age (in which Kratês at Pergamus and Aristarchus at Alexandria divided between them the palm of literary celebrity) towards criticism and illustration of the old poets – a blow was now aimed at the mythical legitimacy of Ilium. Dêmêtrius of Skêpsis, one of the most laborious of the Homeric critics, had composed thirty books of comment upon the Catalogue in the Iliad: Hestiæa, an authoress of Alexandreia Trôas, had written on the same subject: both of them, well-acquainted with the locality, remarked that the vast battles described in the Iliad could not be packed into the narrow space between Ilium and the Naustathmon of the Greeks: the more so, as that space, too small even as it then stood, had been considerably enlarged since the date of the Iliad by deposits at the mouth of the Skamander. They found no difficulty in pointing out topographical incongruities and impossibilities as to the incidents in the Iliad, which they professed to remove by the startling theory that the Homeric Ilium had not occupied the site of the city so called. There was a village, called the village of the Ilieans, situated rather less than four miles from the city in the direction of Mount Ida, and further removed from the sea: here, they affirmed the "holy Troy" had stood.

No positive proof was produced to sustain the conclusion, for Strabo expressly states that not a vestige of the ancient city remained at the Village of the Ilieans; but the fundamental supposition was backed by a second accessory supposition, to explain how it happened that all such vestiges had disappeared. Nevertheless Strabo adopts the unsupported hypothesis of Dêmêtrius as if it were an authenticated fact – distinguishing pointedly between Old and New Ilium, and even censuring Hellanikus for having maintained the received local faith. But I cannot find that Dêmêtrius and Hestiæa have been followed in this respect by any other writer of ancient times excepting Strabo. Ilium still continued to be talked of and treated by every one as the genuine Homeric Troy: the cruel jests of the Roman rebel Fimbria, when he sacked the town and massacred the inhabitants – the compensation made by Sylla, and the pronounced favour of Julius Cæsar and Augustus, all prove this continued recognition of identity. Arrian, though a native of Nicomedia, holding a high appointment in Asia Minor, and remarkable for the exactness of his topographical notices, describes the visit of Alexander to Ilium without any suspicion that the place with all its relics was a mere counterfeit: Aristidês, Dio Chrysostom, Pausanias, Appian, and Plutarch hold the same language. But modern writers seem for the most part to have taken up the supposition from Strabo as implicitly as he took it from Dêmêtrius. They call Ilium by the disrespectful appellation of *New* Ilium – while the traveller in the Trôad looks for old *Old* Ilium as if it were the unquestionable spot where Priam had lived and moved: the name is even formally enrolled on the best maps recently prepared of the ancient Trôad.

Strabo has here converted into geographical matter of fact an hypothesis purely gratuitous, with a view of saving the accuracy of the Homeric topography; though in all probability the locality of the pretended old Ilium would have been found open to difficulties not less serious than those which it was introduced to obviate. It may be true that Dêmêtrius and he were justified in their negative argument, so as to show that the battles described in the Iliad could not possibly have taken place if the city of Priam had stood on the hill inhabited by the Ilieans. But the legendary faith subsisted before, and continued without abatement afterwards, notwithstanding such topographical impossibilities. Hellanikus, Herodotus, Mindarus, the guides of Xerxês, and Alexander, had not been shocked by them: the case of the latter is the

194

strongest of all, because he had received the best education of his time under Aristotle – he was a passionate admirer and constant reader of the Iliad – he was moreover personally familiar with the movements of armies, and lived at a time when maps, which began with Anaximander, the disciple of Thalês, were at least known to all who sought instruction. Now if, notwithstanding such advantages, Alexander fully believed in the identity of Ilium, unconscious of these many and glaring topographical difficulties, much less would Homer himself, or the Homeric auditors, be likely to pay attention to them, at a period, five centuries earlier, of comparative rudeness and ignorance, when prose records as well as geographical maps were totally unknown. The inspired poet might describe, and his hearers would listen with delight to the tale, how Hectôr, pursued by Achillês, ran thrice round the city of Troy, while the trembling Trojans were all huddled into the city, not one daring to come out even at this last extremity of their beloved prince – and while the Grecian army looked on, restraining unwillingly their uplifted spears at the nod of Achillês, in order that Hectôr might perish by no other hand than his: nor were they, while absorbed by this impressive recital disposed to measure distances or calculate topographical possibilities with reference to the site of the real Ilium. The mistake consists in applying to Homer and to the Homeric siege of Troy, criticisms which would be perfectly just if brought to bear on the Athenian siege of Syracuse, as described by Thucydidês; in the Peloponnesian war – but which are not more applicable to the epic narrative than they would be to the exploits of Amadis or Orlando.

There is every reason for presuming that the Ilium visited by Xerxês and Alexander was really the "holy Ilium" present to the mind of Homer; and if so, it must have been inhabited, either by Greeks or by some anterior population, at a period earlier than that which Strabo assigns. History recognises neither Troy the city, nor Trojans, as actually existing; but the extensive region called Trôas, or the Trôad (more properly Trôias), is known both to Herodotus and to Thucydidês: it seems to include the territory westward of an imaginary line drawn from the northeast comer of the Adramyttian gulf to the Propontis at Parium, since both Antandrus, Kolônæ, and the district immediately round Ilium, are regarded as belonging to the Trôad. Herodotus further notices the Teukrians of Gergis (a township conterminous with Ilium, and lying to the eastward of the road from Ilium to Abydus), considering them as the remnant of a larger Teukrian population which once resided in the country, and which had in very early times undertaken a vast migration from Asia into Europe. To that Teukrian population he thinks that the Homeric Trojans belonged; and by later writers, especially by Virgil and the other Romans, the names Teukrians and Trojans are employed as equivalents. As the name *Trojans* is not mentioned in any contemporary historical monument, so the name *Teukrians* never once occurs in the old Epic. It appears to have been first noticed by the elegiac poet Kallinius, about 660 B.C, who connected it by an alleged immigration of Teukrians from Krête into the region round about Ida. Others again denied this, asserting that the primitive ancestor, Teukrus, had come into the country from Attica, or that he was of indigenous origin, born from Skamander and the nymph Idæa – all various manifestations of that eager thirst after an eponymous hero which never deserted the Greeks. Gergithians occur in more than one spot in Æolis, even so far southward as the neighbourhood of Kymê: the name has no place in Homer, but he mentions Gorgythion and Kebriones as illegitimate sons of Priam, thus giving a sort of epical recognition both to Gergis and Kebrên. As Herodotus calls the old epical Trojans by the name Teukrians, so the Attic tragedians call them Phrygians; though the Homeric hymn to Aphroditê represents Phrygians and Trojans as completely distinct, specially noting the diversity of language; and in the Iliad the Phrygians are simply numbered among the allies of Troy from the far Ascania, without indication of any more intimate relationship. Nor do the tales which connect Dardanus with Samothrace and Arcadia find countenance in the Homeric poems, wherein Dardanus is the son of Zeus, having no root anywhere except in Dardania. The mysterious solemnities of Samothrace, afterwards so highly venerated throughout the Grecian world, date from a period much later than Homer; and the religious affinities of that island as well as of Krête with the territories of Phrygia and Æolis, were certain, according to the established tendency of the Grecian mind, to beget stories of a common genealogy.

To pass from this legendary world, an aggregate of streams distinct and heterogeneous, which do not willingly come into confluence, and cannot be forced to intermix, into the clearer vision afforded by Herodotus, we learn from him that in the year 500 B.C. the whole coast-region from Dardanus southward to the promontory of Lektum (including the town of Ilium), and from Lektum eastward to Adramyttium, had been Æolised, or was occupied by Æolic Greeks – likewise the inland towns of Skêpsis and Kebrên. So that if we draw a line northward from Adramyttium to Kyzikus on the Propontis, throughout the whole territory westward from that line, to the Hellespont and the Ægean Sea, all the considerable towns would be Hellenic, with the exception of Gergis and the

Teukrian population around it, all the towns worthy of note were either Iônic or Æolic. A century earlier, the Teukrian population would have embraced a wider range – perhaps Skêpsis and Krebên, the latter of which places was colonised by Greeks from Kymê: a century afterwards, during the satrapy of Pharnabazus, it appears that Gergis had become Hellenised as well as the test. The four towns, Ilium, Gergis, Kebrên and Skêpsis, all in lofty and strong positions, were distinguished each by a solemn worship and temple of Athênê, and by the recognition of that goddess as their special patroness.

The author of the Iliad conceived the whole of this region as occupied by people not Greek; Trojans, Dardanians, Lykians, Lelegians, Pelasgians, and Kilikians. He recognises a temple and worship of Athênê in Ilium, though the goddess is bitterly hostile to the Trojans; and Arktinus described the Palladium as the capital protection of the city. Perhaps the most remarkable feature of identity between the Homeric and the historical Æolis, is the solemn and diffused worship of the Sminthian Apollo. Chrysê, Killa and Tenedos, and more than one place called Sminthium. maintain the surname and invoke the protection of that god during later times, just as they are emphatically described to do by Homer.

When it is said that the Post-Homeric Greeks gradually Hellenised this entire region, we are not to understand that the whole previous population either retired or was destroyed. The Greeks settled in the leading and considerable towns, which enabled them both to protect one another and to gratify their predominant tastes. Partly by force – but greatly also by that superior activity, and power of assimilating foreign ways of thought to their own, which distinguished them from the beginning – they invested all the public features and management of the town with an Hellenic air, distributed all about it their gods, their heroes and their legends, and rendered their language the medium of public administration, religions songs and addresses to the gods, and generally for communications wherein any number of persons were concerned. Two remarks are here to be made: first, in doing this they could not avoid taking to themselves more or less of that which belonged to the parties with whom they fraternised, so that the result was not pure Hellenism: next, that even this was done only in the towns, without being fully extended to the territorial domain around, or to those smaller townships which stood to the town in a dependent relation. The Æolic and Iônic Greeks borrowed from the Asiatics whom they had Hellenised, musical instruments and new laws of rhythm and melody, which they knew how to turn to account: they further adopted more or less of those violent and maddening religious rites, manifested occasionally in self-inflicted suffering and mutilation, which were indigenous in Asia Minor in the worship of the Great Mother. The religion of the Greeks in the region of Ida as well as at Kyzikus was more orgiastic than the native worship of Greece Proper, just as that of Lampsacus, Priapus and Parium was more licentious. From the Teukrian region of Gergis, and from the Gergithes near Kymê, sprang the original Sibylline prophecies, and the legendary Sibyll who plays so important a part in the tale of Æneas: the mythe of the Sibyll, whose prophecies are supposed to be heard in the hollow blast bursting out from obscure caverns and apertures in the rocks, was indigenous among the Gergithian Teukrians, and passed from the Kymæans in Æolis, along with the other circumstances of the tale of Æneas, to their brethren the inhabitants of Cumæ in Italy. The date of the Gergithian Sibyll, or rather of the circulation of her supposed prophecies, is placed during the reign of Crœsus, a period when Gergis was thoroughly Teukrian. Her prophecies, though embodied in Greek verses, had their root in a Teukrian soil and feelings: and the promises of future empire which they so liberally make to the fugitive hero escaping from the flames of Troy into Italy, become interesting from the remarkable way in which they were realised by Rome.

At what time Ilium and Dardanus became Æolised we have no information. We find the Mitylenæans in possession of Sigeium in the time of the poet Alkæus, abont 600 B.C: and the Athenians during the reign of Peisistratus, having wrested it from them and trying to maintain their possession, vindicate the proceeding by saying that they had as much right to it as the Mitylenæans, "for the latter had no more claim to it than any of the other Greeks who had aided Menelaus in avenging the abduction of Helen." This is a very remarkable incident, as attesting the celebrity of the legend of Troy, and the value of a mythical title in international disputes – yet seemingly implying that the establishment of the Mitylenæans on that spot must have been sufficiently recent. The country near the junction of the Hellespont and the Propontis is represented as originally held by Bebrykian Thracians, while Abydus was first occupied by Milesian colonists in the reign and by the permission of the Lydian king Gyges – to whom the whole Trôad and the neighbouring territory belonged, and upon whom therefore the Teukrians of Ida must have been dependent. This must have been about 700 B.C., a period considerably earlier than the Mitylenæan occupation of Sigeium Lampsacus and Pæsus, on the neighbouring shores of the Propontis, were also Milesian colonies, though we do not know their date Parium was jointly settled from Milêtus, Erythræ and Parus.

XVI. GRECIAN MYTHES, AS SEEN BY THE GREEKS.

The preceding sections have been intended to exhibit a sketch of that narrative matter, so abundant, so characteristic and so interesting, out of which early Grecian history and chronology have been extracted. Raised originally by hands unseen and from data un-assignable, it existed first in the shape of floating talk among the people, from whence a large portion of it passed into the song of the poets, who multiplied, transformed and adorned it in a thousand various ways.

These mythes or current stories, the spontaneous and earliest growth of the Grecian mind, constituted at the same time the entire intellectual stock of the age to which they belonged. They are the common root of all those different ramifications into which the mental activity of the Greeks subsequently diverged; containing, as it were, the preface and germ of the positive history and philosophy, the dogmatic theology and the professed romance, which we shall hereafter trace each in its separate development. They furnished aliment to the curiosity, and solution to the vague doubts and aspirations of the age: they explained the origin of those customs and standing peculiarities with which men were familiar: they impressed moral lessons, awakened patriotic sympathies, and exhibited in detail the shadowy, but anxious presentiments of the vulgar as to the agency of the gods; moreover they satisfied that craving for adventure and appetite for the marvellous, which has in modern times become the province of fiction proper.

It is difficult, we may say impossible, for a man of mature age to carry back his mind to his conceptions such as they stood when he was a child, growing naturally out of his imagination and feelings, working upon a scanty stock of materials, and borrowing from authorities whom he blindly followed but imperfectly apprehended. A similar difficulty occurs when we attempt to place ourselves in the historical and quasi-philosophical point of view which the ancient mythes present to us. We can follow perfectly the imagination and feeling which dictated these tales, and we can admire and sympathise with them as animated, sublime, and affecting poetry; but we are too much accustomed to matter of fact and philosophy of a positive kind to be able to conceive a time when these beautiful fancies were construed literally and accepted as serious reality.

Nevertheless it is obvious that Grecian mythes cannot be either understood or appreciated except with reference to the system of conceptions and belief of the ages in which they arose. We must suppose a public not reading and writing, but seeing, hearing and telling – destitute of all records, and careless as well as ignorant of positive history with its indispensable tests, yet at the same time curious and full of eagerness for new or impressive incidents – strangers even to the rudiments of positive philosophy and to the idea of invariable sequences of nature either in the physical or moral world, yet requiring some connecting theory to interpret and regularize the phenomena before them. Such a theory was supplied by the spontaneous inspirations of an early fancy, which supposed the habitual agency of beings intelligent and voluntary like themselves, but superior in extent of power, and different in peculiarity of attributes. In the geographical ideas of the Homeric period, the earth was flat and round, with the deep and gentle ocean-stream flowing around and returning into itself: chronology, or means of measuring past time, there existed none; but both unobserved regions might be described, the forgotten past unfolded, and the unknown future predicted – through particular men specially inspired by the gods, or endowed by them with that peculiar vision which detected and interpreted passing signs and omens.

If even the rudiments of scientific geography and physics, now so universally diffused and so invaluable as a security against error and delusion, were wanting in this early stage of society, their place was abundantly supplied by vivacity of imagination and by personifying sympathy. The unbounded tendency of the Homeric Greeks to multiply fictitious persons, and to construe interesting or formidable phænomena into manifestations of design, is above all things here to be noticed, because the form of personal narrative, universal in their mythes, is one of its many manifestations. Their polytheism (comprising some elements of an original fetichism, in which particular objects had themselves been supposed to be endued with life, volition, and design) recognised agencies of unseen beings identified and confounded with the different localities and departments of the physical world. Of such beings there were numerous varieties, and many gradations both in power and attributes: there were differences of age, sex and local residence, relations both conjugal and filial between them, and tendencies sympathetic as well as repugnant. The gods formed a sort of political community of their own, which had its hierarchy, its distribution of ranks and duties, its contentions for power and occasional revolutions, its public meetings in the agora of Olympus, and its multitudinous banquets or festivals. The great Olympic gods were in fact only the most exalted amongst an aggregate of quasi-human or ultra-human personages, dæmons, heroes, nymphs, eponymous (or name-giving) genii, identified with each river, mountain, cape, town, village, or known circumscription of territory, besides horses, bulls, and dogs, of immortal breed and peculiar attributes, and monsters of strange lineaments and combinations, "Gorgons and Harpies and Chimæras dire." As there were in every *gens* or family special gentile deities and foregone ancestors who watched over its members, forming in each the characteristic symbol and recognised guarantee of their union, so there seem to have been in each guild or trade peculiar beings whose vocation it was to co-operate or to impede in various stages of the business.

The extensive and multiform personifications, here faintly sketched, pervaded in every direction the mental system of the Greeks, and were identified intimately both with their conception and with their description of phenomena, present as well as past. That which to us is interesting as the mere creation of an exuberant fancy, was to the Greek genuine and venerated reality. Both the earth and the solid heaven (Gæa and Uranos) were both conceived and spoken of by him as endowed with appetite, feeling, sex, and most of the various attributes of humanity. Instead of a sun such as we now see, subject to astronomical laws, and forming the centre of a system the changes of which we can ascertain and foreknow, he saw the great god Hêlios, mounting his chariot in the morning in the east, reaching at mid-day the height of the solid heaven, and arriving in the evening at the western horizon, with horses fatigued and desirous of repose. Hêlios, having favourite spots wherein his beautiful cattle grazed, took pleasure in contemplating them during the course of his journey, and was sorely displeased if any man slew or injured them: he had moreover sons and daughters on earth, and as his all-seeing eye penetrated everywhere, he was sometimes in a situation to reveal secrets even to the gods themselves – while on other occasions he was constrained to turn aside in order to avoid contemplating scenes of abomination. To us these now appear puerile though pleasing fancies, but to an Homeric Greek they seemed perfectly natural and plausible. In his view, the description of the sun, as given in a modern astronomical treatise, would have appeared not merely absurd, but repulsive and impious. Even in later times, when the positive spirit of inquiry had made considerable progress, Anaxagoras and other astronomers incurred the charge of blasphemy for dis-personifying Hêlios, and trying to assign invariable laws to the solar phænomena. Personifying fiction was in this way blended by the Homeric Greeks with their conception of the physical phænomena before them, not simply in the way of poetical ornament, but as a genuine portion of their every-day belief.

LEGENDARY GREECE

The gods and heroes of the land and the tribe belonged, in the conception of a Greek, alike to the present and to the past: he worshipped in their groves and at their festivals: he invoked their protection, and believed in their superintending guardianship, even in his own day; but their more special, intimate, and sympathising agency was cast back into the unrecorded past. To give suitable utterance to this general sentiment, to furnish body and movement and detail to these divine and heroic pre-existences, which were conceived only in shadowy outline, to lighten up the dreams of what the past must have been, in the minds of those who knew not what it really had been – such was the spontaneous aim and inspiration of productive genius in the community, and such were the purposes which the Grecian mythes pre-eminently accomplished.

The love of antiquities, which Tacitus notices as so prevalent among the Greeks of his day, was one of the earliest, the most durable, and the most widely diffused of the national propensities. The antiquities of every state were divine and heroic, reproducing the lineaments, but disregarding the measure and limits, of ordinary humanity. The gods formed the starting-point, beyond which no man thought of looking, though some gods were more ancient than others: their progeny, the heroes, many of them sprung from human mothers, constitute an intermediate link between god and man. The ancient epic usually recognises the presence of a multitude of nameless men, but they are introduced chiefly for the purpose of filling the scene, and of executing the orders, celebrating the valour, and bringing out the personality, of a few divine or heroic characters. It was the glory of bards and storytellers to be able to satisfy those religious and patriotic predispositions of the public, which caused the primary demand for their tales, and which were of a nature eminently inviting and expansive. For Grecian religion was many-sided and many coloured: it comprised a great multiplicity of persons, together with much diversity in the types of character: it divinised every vein and attribute of humanity, the lofty as well as the mean – the tender as well as the warlike – the serf-devoting and adventurous as well as the laughter-loving and sensual. We shall hereafter reach a time when philosophers protested against such identification of the gods with the more vulgar appetites and enjoyments, believing that nothing except the spiritual attributes of man could properly be transferred to superhuman beings, and drawing their predicates respecting the gods exclusively from what was awful, majestic and terror-striking in human affairs. Such restrictions on the religious fancy were continually on the increase, and the mystic and didactic stamp which marked the last century of paganism in the days of Julian and Libanius, contrasts forcibly with the concrete and vivacious forms, full of vigorous impulse and alive to all the capricious gusts of the human temperament, which people the Homeric Olympus. At present, however, we have only to consider the early, or Homeric and Hesiodic paganism, and its operation in the genesis of the mythical narratives. We cannot doubt that it supplied the most powerful stimulus, and the only one which the times admitted, to the creative faculty of the people; as well from the sociability, the gradations, and the mutual action and reaction of its gods and heroes, as from the amplitude, the variety, and the purely human cast, of its fundamental types.

Though we may thus explain the mythopœic fertility of the Greeks, I am far from pretending that we can render any sufficient account of the supreme beauty of their chief epic and artistical productions. There is something in the first-rate productions of individual genius which lies beyond the compass of philosophical theory: the special breath of the Muse (to speak the language of ancient Greece) must be present in order to give them being. Even among her votaries, many are called, but few are chosen; and the peculiarities of those few remain as yet her own secret.

We shall not however forget that Grecian language was also an indispensable requisite to the growth and beauty of Grecian mythes – its richness, its flexibility and capacity of new combinations, its vocalic abundance and metrical pronunciation: and many even among its proper names, by their analogy to words really significant, gave direct occasion to explanatory or illustrative stories. Etymological mythes are found in sensible proportion among the whole number.

To understand properly then the Grecian mythes, we must try to identify ourselves with the state of mind of the original mythopœic age; a process not very easy, since it requires as to adopt a string of poetical fancies not simply as realities, but as the governing realities of the mental system; yet a process which would only reproduce something analogous to our childhood. The age was one destitute both of recorded history and of positive science, but full of imagination and sentiment and religious impressibility. From these sources sprung that multitude of supposed persons around whom all combinations of sensible phænomena were grouped, and towards whom curiosity, sympathies, and reverence were earnestly directed. The adventures of such persons were the only aliment suited at once both to the appetites and to the comprehension of an early Greek; and the mythes which detailed them, while powerfully interesting his emotions, furnished to him at the same time a quasi-history and quasi-philosophy: they filled up the vacuum of the unrecorded past, and explained many of the puzzling incognita of the present. Nor need we wonder that the same plausibility which captivated his imagination and his feelings was sufficient to engender spontaneous belief; or rather, that no question as to truth or falsehood of the narrative suggested itself to his mind. His faith is ready, literal and un-inquiring, apart from all thought of discriminating fact from fiction, or of detecting hidden and symbolised meaning: it is enough that what he hears be intrinsically plausible and seductive, and that there be no special cause to provoke doubt. If indeed there were, the poet overrules such doubts by the holy and all-sufficient authority of the Muse, whose omniscience is the warrant for his recital, as her inspiration is the cause of his success.

The state of mind, and the relation of speaker to hearers, thus depicted, stand clearly marked in the terms and tenor of the ancient epic, if we only put a plain meaning upon what we read. The poet – like the prophet, whom he so much resembles – sings under heavenly guidance, inspired by the goddess to whom he has prayed for her assisting impulse: she puts the word into his mouth and the incidents into his mind: he is a privileged man, chosen as her organ and speaking from her revelations. As the Muse grants the gift of song to whom she will, so she sometimes in her anger snatches it away, and the most consummate human genius is then left silent and helpless. It is true that these expressions, of the Muse inspiring and the poet singing a tale of past times, have passed from the ancient epic to compositions produced under very different circumstances, and have now degenerated into unmeaning forms of speech; but they gained currency originally in their genuine and literal acceptation. If poets had from the beginning written or recited, the predicate of singing would never have been ascribed to them; nor would it have ever become customary to employ the name of the Muse as a die to be stamped on licensed fiction, unless the practice had begun when her agency was invoked and hailed in perfect good faith. Belief, the fruit of deliberate inquiry and a rational scrutiny of evidence, is in such an age unknown. The simple faith of the time slides in unconsciously when the imagination and feeling are exalted; and inspired authority is at once understood, easily admitted, and implicitly confided in.

The word mythe (μῦθος, *fabula*, story) in its original meaning , signified simply a statement or current narrative, without any connotative implication either of truth or falsehood. Subsequently the meaning of the word (in Latin and English as well as in Greek) changed and came to carry with it the idea of an old personal narrative, always uncertified, sometimes untrue or avowedly fictitious. This change was the result of a silent alteration in the mental state of the society, of a transition on the part of the superior minds (and more or less on the part of all) to a stricter and more elevated canon of credibility, in consequence of familiarity with recorded history, and its essential tests, affirmative as well as negative. Among the original hearers of the mythes, all such tests were unknown: they had not yet learned the lesson of critical disbelief: the mythe passed unquestioned from the mere fact of its currency, and from its harmony with existing sentiments and preconceptions. The very circumstances which contributed to rob it of literal belief in after-time, strengthened its hold upon the mind of the Homeric man. He looked for wonders and unusual combinations in the past: he expected to hear of gods, heroes and men, moving and operating together upon earth: he pictured to himself the fore-time as a theatre in which the gods interfered directly, obviously and frequently, for the protection of their favourites and the punishment of their foes. The rational conception, then only dawning in his mind, of a systematic course of nature was absorbed by this fervent and lively faith. If he could have been supplied with as perfect and philosophical a history of his own real past time, as we are now enabled to furnish with regard to the last century of England or France, faithfully recording all the successive events, and accounting for them by known, positive laws, but introducing no special interventions of Zeus and Apollo – such a history would have appeared to him not merely unholy and unimpressive, but destitute of all plausibility or title to credence. It would have provoked in him the same feeling of incredulous aversion as a description of the sun (to repeat the previous illustration) in a-modern book on scientific astronomy.

To us these mythes are interesting fictions: to the Homeric and Hesiodic audience they were "rerum divinarum et humanarum scientia," an aggregate of religious, physical and historical revelations, rendered more captivating, but not less true and real, by the bright colouring and fantastic shapes in which they were presented. Throughout the whole of "mythe-bearing Hellas" they formed the staple of the uninstructed Greek mind, upon which history and philosophy were by so slow decrees superinduced; and they continued to be the aliment of ordinary thought and conversation, even after history and philosophy had partially supplanted the mythical faith among the leading men, and disturbed it more or less in the ideas of all. The men, the women, and the children of the remote dêmes and villages of Greece, to whom Thucydidês, Hippocratês, Aristotle, or

Hipparchus were unknown, still continued to dwell upon the local fables which formed their religious and patriotic antiquity. Pausanias, even in his time, heard everywhere divine or heroic legends yet alive, precisely of the type of the old epic: he found the conceptions of religious and mythical faith, co-existent with those of positive science, and contending against them at more or less of odds, according to the temper of the individual. Now it is the remarkable characteristic of the Homeric age, that no such co-existence or contention had yet begun. The religious and mythical point of view covers, for the most part, all the phenomena of nature; while the conception of invariable sequence exists only in the background, itself personified under the name of the Mœræ, or Fates, and produced generally as an exception to the omnipotence of Zeus for all ordinary purposes. Voluntary agents, visible and invisible, impel and govern everything. Moreover this point of view is universal throughout the community, – adopted with equal fervour, and carried out with equal consistency, by the loftiest minds and by the lowest. The great man of that day is he who, penetrated like others with the general faith, and never once imagining any other system of nature than the agency of these voluntary Beings, can clothe them in suitable circumstances and details, and exhibit in living body and action those types which his hearers dimly prefigure.

History, philosophy, &c., properly so called and conforming to our ideas (of which the subsequent Greeks were the first creators), never belonged to more than a comparatively small number of thinking men, though their influence indirectly affected more or less the whole national mind. When positive science and criticism, and the idea of an invariable sequence of events, came to supplant in the more vigorous intellects the old mythical creed of omnipresent personification, an inevitable scission was produced between the instructed few and the remaining community. The opposition between the scientific and the religious point of view was not slow in manifesting itself: in general language, indeed, both might seem to stand together, but in every particular case the admission of one involved the rejection of the other. According to the theory which then became predominant, the course of nature was held to move invariably on, by powers and attributes of its own, unless the gods chose to interfere and reverse it; but they had the power of interfering as often and to as great an extent as they thought fit. Here the question was at once opened, respecting a great variety of particular phænomena, whether they were to be regarded as natural or miraculous. No constant or discernible test could be suggested to discriminate the two: every man was called upon to settle the doubt for himself, and each settled it according to the extent of his knowledge, the force of his logic, the state of his health, his hopes, his fears, and many other considerations affecting his separate conclusion. In a question thus perpetually arising, and full of practical consequences, instructed minds, like Periklês, Thucydidês, and Euripidês, tended more and more to the scientific point of view, in cases where the general public were constantly gravitating towards the religious.

The age immediately prior to this unsettled condition of thought in the really mythopœic age: in which the creative faculties of the society know no other employment, and the mass of the society no other mental demand. The perfect expression of such a period, in its full peculiarity and grandeur, is to be found in the Iliad and Odyssey, poems of which we cannot determine the exact date, but which seem both to have existed prior to the first Olympiad, 776 B.C., our earliest trustworthy mark of Grecian time. For some time after that event, the mythopœic tendencies continued in rigour (Arktinus, Leschês, Eumêlus, and seemingly most of the Hesiodic poems, fall within or shortly after the first century of recorded Olympiads); but from and after this first century, we may trace the operation of causes which gradually enfeebled and narrowed them, altering the point of view from which the mythes were looked at. What these causes were, it will be necessary briefly to intimate.

The foremost and most general of all is, the expansive force of Grecian intellect itself, a quality in which this remarkable people stand distinguished from all their neighbours and contemporaries. Most, if not all nations have had mythes, but no nation except the Greeks have imparted to them immortal charm and universal interest; and the same mental capacities, which raised the great men of the poetic age to this exalted level, also pushed forward their successors to outgrow the early faith in which the mythes had been generated and accredited.

One great mark, as well as means, of such intellectual expansion, was the habit of attending to, recording, and combining, positive and present facts, both domestic and foreign. In the genuine Grecian epic, the theme was an unknown and aoristic past; but even as early as the Works and Days of Hesiod, the present begins to figure: the man who tills the earth appears in his own solitary nakedness, apart from gods and heroes – bound indeed by serious obligations to the gods, but contending against many difficulties which are not to be removed by simple reliance on their help. The poet denounces his age in the strongest terms as miserable, degraded and profligate, and looks back with reverential envy to the extinct heroic races who fought at Troy and Thêbes. Yet bad as the present time is, the Muse condescends to look at it along with him, and to prescribe rules for human life – with the assurance that if a man be industrious, frugal, provident, just and friendly in his dealings, the gods will recompense him with affluence and security. Nor does the Muse disdain, while holding out such promise, to cast herself into the most homely details of present existence and to give advice thoroughly practical and calculating. Men whose minds were full of the heroes of Homer, called Hesiod in contempt the poet of the Helots; and the contrast between the two is certainly a remarkable proof of the tendency of Greek poetry towards the present and the positive.

Other manifestations of the same tendency become visible in the age of Archilochus (B.C. 680-660). In an age when metrical composition and the living voice are the only means whereby the productive minds of a community make themselves felt, the invention of a new metre, new forms of song and recitation, or diversified accompaniments, constitute an epoch. The iambic, elegiac, choric, and lyric poetry, from Archilochus downwards, all indicate purposes in the poet, and impressibilities of the hearers, very different from those of the ancient epic. In all of them the personal feeling of the poet and the specialties of present time and place, are brought prominently forward, while in the Homeric hexameter the poet is a mere nameless organ of the historical Muse – the hearers are content to learn, believe, and feel, the incidents of a foregone world, and the tale is hardly leas suitable to one time and place than to another. The iambic metre (we are told) was first suggested to Archilochus by the bitterness of his own private antipathies; and the mortal wounds inflicted by his lampoons, upon the individuals against whom they were directed, still remain attested, though the verses themselves have perished. It was the metre (according to the well-known judgment of Aristotle) most nearly approaching to common speech, and well suited both to the coarse vein of sentiment, and to the smart and emphatic diction of its inventor. Simonidês of Amorgus, the younger contemporary of Archilochus, employed the same metre, with less bitterness, but with an anti-heroic tendency not less decided. His remaining fragments present a mixture of teaching and sarcasm, having a distinct bearing upon actual life, and carrying out the spirit which partially appears in the Hesiodic Works and Days. Of Alkæus and Sappho, though unfortunately we are compelled to speak of them upon hearsay only, we know enough to satisfy us that their own personal sentiments and sufferings, their relations private or public with the contemporary world, constituted the soul of those short effusions which gave them so much celebrity; and in the few remains of the elegiac poets preserved to us – Kallinus, Mimnermus, Tyrtæus – the impulse of some present motive or circumstance is no less conspicuous. The same may also be said of Solôn, Theognis and Phokylidês, who preach, encourage, censure, at complain, but do not recount – and in whom a profound ethical sensibility, unknown to the Homeric poems, manifests itself: the form of poetry (to use the words of Solôn himself) is made the substitute for the public speaking of the agora.

Doubtless all these poets made abundant use of the ancient mythes, but it was by turning them to present account, in the way of illustration, or flattery, or contrast, a tendency which we may usually detect even in the compositions of Pindar, in spite of the lofty and heroic strain which they breathe throughout. That narrative or legendary poetry still continued to be composed during the seventh and sixth centuries before the Christian æra is not to be questioned; but it exhibited the old epical character without the old epical genius; both the inspiration of the composer and the sympathies of the audience had become more deeply enlisted in the world before them, and disposed to fasten on incidents of their own actual experience. From Solôn and Theognis we pass to the abandonment of all metrical restrictions and to the introduction of prose writing, a fact, the importance of which it is needless to dwell upon, marking as well the increased familiarity with written records, as the commencement of a separate branch of literature for the intellect, apart from the imagination and emotions wherein the old legends had their exclusive root.

Egypt was first unreservedly opened to the Greeks during the reign of Psammetichus, about B.C. 660: gradually it became much frequented by them for military or commercial purposes, or for simple curiosity, and enlarged the range of their thoughts and observations, while it also imparted to them that vein of mysticism, which overgrew the primitive simplicity of the Homeric religion, and of which I have spoken in a former chapter They found in it a long-established civilisation, colossal wonders of architecture, and a certain knowledge of astronomy and geometry, elementary indeed, but in advance of their own. Moreover it was a portion of their present world, and it contributed to form in them an interest for noting and describing the actual realities before them. A sensible progress is made in the Greek mind during the two centuries from B.C. 700 to B.C. 500, in the record and arrangement of historical facts: an *historical sense* arises in the superior intellects, and some idea of evidence as a discriminating test between fact and fiction. This progressive tendency was further stimulated by increased communication and by more settled and peaceful social relations between the various members of the Hellenic world, to which may be added material improvements, purchased at the expense of a period of turbulence and revolution, in the internal administration of each separate state. The Olympic, Pythian, Nemean, and Isthmian games became frequented by visitors from the most distant parts of Greece: the great periodical festival in the island of Dêlos brought together the citizens of every Iônic community, with their wives and children, and an ample display of wealth and ornaments. Numerous and flourishing colonies were founded In Sicily, the south of Italy, the coasts of Epirus and of the Euxine Sea: the Phokæans explored the whole of the Adriatic, established Massalia, and penetrated even as far as the south of Ibêria, with which they carried on a lucrative commerce. The geographical ideas of the Greeks were thus both expanded and rectified: the first preparation of a map, by Anaximander the disciple of Thalês, is an epoch in the history of science. We may note the ridicule bestowed by Herodotus both upon the supposed people called Hyperboreans and upon the idea of a circumfluous ocean-stream, as demonstrating the progress of the age in this department of inquiry. Even earlier than Herodotus, Xanthus had noticed the occurrence of fossil marine productions in the interior of Asia Minor, which led him to reflections on the changes of the earth's surface with respect to land and water.

If then we look down the three centuries and a half which elapsed between the commencement of the Olympic æra and the age of Herodotus and Thucydidês, we shall discern a striking advance in the Greeks, ethical, social and intellectual. Positive history and chronology has not only been created, but in the ease of Thucydidês, the qualities necessary to the historiographer, in their application to recent events, have been developed with a degree of perfection never since surpassed. Men's minds have assumed a gentler as well as a juster cast; and acts come to he criticised with reference to their bearing on the internal happiness of a well-regulated community, as well as upon the standing harmony of fraternal states. While Thucydidês treats the habitual and licensed piracy, so coolly alluded to in the Homeric poems, as an obsolete enormity, many of the acts described in the old heroic and Theogonic legends were found not less repugnant to this improved tone of feeling. The battles of the gods with the Giants and Titans, the castration of Uranus by his son Kronus, the cruelty, deceit and licentiousness, often supposed both in the gods and heroes, provoked strong disapprobation. The language of the philosopher Xenophanês, who composed both elegiac and iambic poems for the express purpose of denouncing such tales, is as vehement and unsparing as that of the Christian writers, who, eight centuries afterwards, attacked the whole scheme of paganism.

It was not merely as an ethical and social critic that Xenophanês stood distinguished. He was one of a great and eminent triad – Thalês and Pythagoras being the others – who, in the sixth century before the Christian æra, first opened up those veins of speculative philosophy which occupied afterwards so large a portion of Grecian intellectual energy. Of the material differences between the three I do not here speak: I regard them only in reference to the Homeric and Hesiodic philosophy which preceded them, and from which all three deviated by a step, perhaps the most remarkable in all the history of philosophy.

They were the first who attempted to dis-enthral the philosophic intellect from this all-personifying religions faith, and to constitute a method of interpreting nature distinct from the spontaneous inspirations of untaught mind. It is in them that we first find the idea of Person tacitly set aside or limited, and an impersonal Nature conceived as the object of study. The divine husband and wife, Oceanus and Têthys, parents of many gods and of the Oceanic nymphs, together with the avenging goddess Styx, are translated into the material substance *water*, or, as we ought rather to say, the Fluid; and Thalês set himself to prove that water was the primitive element, out of which all the different natural substances had been formed. He, as well as Xenophanês and Pythagoras, started the problem of physical philosophy, with its objective character and invariable laws, to be discoverable by a proper and methodical application of the human intellect. The Greek word Φύσις, denoting *nature*, and its derivatives *physics* and *physiology*, unknown in that large sense to Homer or Hesiod, as well as the word *Kôsmos*, to denote the mundane system, first appears with these philosophers. The elemental analysis of Thalês – the one unchangeable cosmic substance, varying only in appearance, but not in reality, as suggested by Xenophanês, and the geometrical and arithmetical combinations of Pythagoras, all these were different ways of approaching the explanation of physical phenomena, and each gave rise to a distinct school or succession of philosophers. But they all agreed in departing from the primitive method, and in recognising determinate properties, invariable sequences, and objective truth, in nature – either independent of willing or designing agents, or serving to these latter at once as an indispensable subject-matter and as a limiting condition. Xenophanês disclaimed openly all knowledge respecting the gods, and pronounced that no man could have any means of ascertaining when he was right and when he was wrong, in affirmations respecting them; while Pythagoras represents in part the scientific tendencies of his age, in part also the spirit of mysticism and of special fraternities for religious and ascetic observance, which became diffused throughout Greece in the sixth century before the Christian æra. This was another point which placed him in antipathy with the simple, unconscious and demonstrative faith of the old poets, as well as with the current legends.

If these distinguished men, when they ceased to follow the primitive instinct of tracing the phenomena of nature to personal and designing agents, passed over, not at once to induction and observation, but to a misemployment of abstract words, substituting metaphysical *eidôla* in the place of polytheism, and to an exaggerated application of certain narrow physical theories – we must remember that nothing else could be expected from the scanty stock of facts then accessible, and that the most profound study of the human mind points out such transition as an inevitable law of intellectual progress. At present, we have to compare them only with that state of the Greek mind which they partially superseded, and with which they were in decided opposition. The rudiments of physical science were conceived and developed among superior men; but the religious feeling of the mass was averse to them; and the aversion, though gradually mitigated, never wholly died away. Some of the philosophers were not backward in charging others with irreligion, while the multitude seems to have felt the same sentiment more or less towards all – or towards that postulate of constant sequences, with determinate conditions of occurrence, which scientific study implies, and which they could not reconcile with their belief in the agency of the gods, to whom they were constantly praying for special succour and blessings.

The discrepancy between the scientific and the religious point of view was dealt with differently by different philosophers. Thus Sokratês openly admitted it, and assigned to each a distinct and independent province. He distributed phenomena into two classes: one, wherein the connection of antecedent and consequent was invariable and ascertainable by human study, and therefore future results accessible to a well-instructed foresight: the other and those, too, the most comprehensive and important, which the gods had reserved for themselves and their own unconditional agency, wherein there was no invariable or ascertainable sequence, and where the result could only be foreknown by some omen, prophecy, or other special inspired communication from themselves. Each of these classes was essentially distinct, and required to be looked at and dealt with in a manner radically incompatible with the other. Sokratês held it wrong to apply the scientific interpretation to the latter, or the theological interpretation to the former. Physics and astronomy, in his opinion, belonged to the divine class of phenomena, in which human research was insane, fruitless, and impious.

On the other hand, Hippocratês, the contemporary of Sokratês, denied the discrepancy, and merged into one those two classes of phenomena – the divine and the scientifically determinable, which the latter had put asunder. Hippocratês treated all phenomena as at once both divine and scientifically determinable. In discussing certain peculiar bodily disorders found among the Scythians, he observes, "The Scythians themselves ascribe the cause of this to god, and reverence and bow down to such sufferers, each man fearing that he may suffer the like; and I myself think too that these affections, as well as all others, are divine: no one among them is either more divine or more human than another, but all are on the same footing, and all divine; nevertheless each of them has its own physical conditions, and not one occurs without such physical conditions."

A third distinguished philosopher of the same day, Anaxagoras, allegorising Zeus and the other personal gods, proclaimed the doctrine of one common pervading Mind, as having first established order and system in the mundane aggregate, which had once been in a state of chaos – and as still manifesting its uninterrupted agency for wise and good purposes. This general doctrine obtained much admiration from Plato and Aristotle; but they at the same time remarked with surprise, that Anaxagoras never made any use at all of his own general doctrine for the explanation of the phenomena of nature, that he looked for nothing but physical causes and connecting laws, so that in fact the spirit of his particular researches was not materially different from those of Demokritus or Leukippus, whatever might be the difference in their general theories. His investigations in meteorology and astronomy, treating the heavenly bodies as subjects for calculation, have been already noticed as offensive, not only to the general public of Greece, but even to Sokratês himself among them: he was tried at Athens, and seems to have escaped condemnation only by voluntary exile.

The three eminent men just named, all essentially different from each other, may be taken as illustrations of the philosophical mind of Greece during the last half of the fifth century B.C. Scientific pursuits had acquired a powerful hold, and adjusted themselves in various ways with the prevalent religions feelings of the age. Both Hippocratês and Anaxagoras modified their ideas of the divine agency so as to suit their thirst for scientific research. According to the former, the gods were the really effluent agents in the production of all phenomena, the mean and indifferent not less than the terrific or tutelary. Being thus alike connected with all phænomena, they were specially associated with none – and the proper task of the inquirer was, to find out those rules and conditions by which (he assumed) their agency was always determined, and according to which it might be foretold. Now such a view of the divine agency could never be reconciled with the religious feelings of the ordinary Grecian believer, even as they stood in the time of Anaxagoras; still less could it have been reconciled with those of the Homeric man, more than three centuries earlier. By him Zeus and Athênê were conceived as definite Persons, objects of special reverence, hopes, and fears, and animated with peculiar feelings, sometimes of favour, sometimes of wrath, towards himself or his family or country. They were propitiated by his prayers, and prevailed upon to lend him succour in danger – but offended and disposed to bring evil upon him if he omitted to render thanks or sacrifice. This sense of individual communion with, and dependence upon them was the essence of his faith. While he prayed with sincerity for special blessings or protection from the gods, he could not acquiesce in the doctrine of Hippocratês, that their agency was governed by constant laws and physical conditions.

That radical discord between the mental impulses of science and religion, which manifests itself so decisively during the most cultivated ages of Greece, and which harassed more or less so many of the philosophers, produced its most afflicting result in the condemnation of Sokratês by the Athenians. According to the remarkable passage recently cited from Xenophôn, it will appear that Sokratês agreed with his countrymen in denouncing physical speculations as impious, that he recognised the religious process of discovery as a peculiar branch, co-ordinate with the scientific, and that he laid down a theory, of which the basis was, the confessed divergence of these two processes from the beginning – thereby seemingly satisfying the exigencies of religious hopes and fears on the one hand, and those of reason, in her ardour for ascertaining the invariable laws of phænomena, on the other. We may remark that the theory of this religious and extra-scientific process of discovery was at that time sufficiently complete: for Sokratês could point out, that those anomalous phænomena which the gods had reserved for themselves, and into which science was forbidden to pry, were yet accessible to the seekings of the pious man, through oracles, omens, and other exceptional means of communication which divine benevolence vouchsafed to keep open.

Now the scission thus produced between the superior minds and the multitude, in consequence of the development of science and the scientific point of view, is a fact of great moment in the history of Greek progress, and forms an important contrast between the age of Homer and Hesiod and that of Thucydidês: though in point of fact even the multitude, during this later age, were partially modified by those very scientific views which they regarded with disfavour. We must keep in view the primitive religious faith, once universal and unobstructed, but subsequently disturbed by the intrusions of science: we must follow the great change, as well in respect to enlarged intelligence as to refinement of social and ethical feeling, among the Greeks, from the Hesiodic times downward, in order to render some account of the altered manner in which the ancient mythes came to be dealt with. These mythes, the spontaneous growth of a creative and personifying interpretation of nature, had struck root in Grecian associations at a time when the national faith required no support from what we call evidence. They were *now* submitted, not simply to a feeling, imagining, and believing public, but also to special classes of instructed men, philosophers, historians, ethical teachers, and critics, and to a public partially modified by their ideas as well as improved by a wider practical experience. They were not intended for such an audience: they had ceased to be in complete harmony even with the lower strata of intellect and sentiment, much more so with the higher. They were the cherished inheritance of a past time: they were interwoven in a thousand ways with the religious faith, the patriotic retrospect, and the national worship, of every Grecian community: the general type of the mythe was the ancient, familiar, and universal form of Grecian thought, which even the most cultivated men had imbibed in their childhood from the poets, and by which they were to a certain degree unconsciously enslaved. Taken as a whole the mythes had acquired prescriptive and ineffaceable possession: to attack, call in question, or repudiate them, was a task painful even to undertake, and far beyond the power of any one to accomplish.

For these reasons the anti-mythic vein of criticism was of no effect as a destroying force, but nevertheless its dissolving decomposing and transforming influence was very considerable. To accommodate the ancient mythes to an improved tone of sentiment and a newly created canon of credibility, was a function which even the wisest Greeks did not disdain, and which occupied no small proportion of the whole intellectual activity of the nation. The mythes were looked at from a point of view completely foreign to the reverential curiosity and literal imaginative faith of the Homeric man: they were broken up and recast in order to force them into new moulds such as their authors had never conceived. We may distinguish four distinct classes of minds, in the literary age now under examination, as having taken them in hand – the poets, the logographers, the philosophers, and the historians.

With the poets and logographers, the mythical persons are real predecessors, and the mythical world an antecedent fact; but it is divine and heroic reality, not human: the present is only half-brother of the past (to borrow an illustration from Pindar in his allusion to gods and men), remotely and generically, but not closely and specifically, analogous to it As a general habit, the old feelings and the old unconscious faith, apart from all proof or evidence, still remain in their minds; but recent feelings have grown up which compel them to omit, to alter, sometimes even to reject and condemn, particular narratives.

Pindar repudiates some stories and transforms others, because they are inconsistent with his conceptions of the gods. Thus he formally protests against the tale that Pelops had been killed and served up at table by his father, for the immortal gods to eat: he shrinks from the idea of imputing to them so horrid an appetite: he pronounces the tale to have been originally fabricated by a slanderous neighbour. Nor can he bring himself to recount the quarrels between different gods. The amours of Zeus and Apollo are no way displeasing to him; but he occasionally suppresses some of the simple details of the old mythe, as deficient in dignity: thus, according to the Hesiodic narrative, Apollo was informed by a raven of the infidelity of the nymph Korônis: but the mention of the raven did not appear to Pindar consistent with the majesty of the god, and he therefore wraps up the mode of detection in vague and mysterious language. He feels considerable repugnance to the character of Odysseus, and intimates more than once that Homer has unduly exalted him by force of poetical artifice. With the character of the Æakid Ajax, on the other hand, he has the deepest sympathy, as well as with his untimely and inglorious death, occasioned by the undeserved preference of a less worthy rival. He appeals for his authority usually to the Muse, but sometimes to "ancient sayings of men," accompanied with a general allusion to story-tellers and bards, admitting, however, that these stories present great discrepancy, and sometimes that they are false. Yet the marvellous and the supernatural afford no ground whatever for rejecting a story: Pindar makes an express declaration to this effect in reference to the romantic adventures of Perseus and the Gorgon's head. He treats even those mythical characters, which conflict the most palpably with positive experience, as connected by a real genealogical thread with the world before him. Not merely the heroes of Troy and Thêbes, and the demigod seamen of Jasôn and the ship Argô, but also the Centaur Cheirôn, the hundred-headed Typhôs, the giant Alkyoneus, Antæus, Bellerophôn and Pegasus, the Chimæra, the Amazons and the Hyperboreans – all appear painted on the same canvas, and touched with the same colours, as the men of the recent and recorded past, Phalaris and Krœsus: only they are thrown back to a greater distance in the perspective. The heroic ancestors of those great Æginetan, Thessalian, Thêban, Argeian, &c. families, whose present members the poet celebrates for their agonistic victories, sympathise with the exploits and second the efforts of their descendants: the inestimable value of a privileged breed and of the stamp of nature is powerfully contrasted with the impotence of unassisted teaching and practice. The power and skill of the Argeian Thesêus and his relatives as wrestlers, are ascribed partly to the fact that their ancestors Pamphaês in afore-time had hospitably entertained the Tyndarids Kastôr and Pollux. Perhaps however the strongest proof of the sincerity of Pindar's mythical faith is afforded when he notices a guilty incident with shame and repugnance, but with an unwilling confession of its truth, as in the case of the fratricide committed on Phôkus by his brothers Pêleus and Telamôn.

Æschylus and Sophoklês exhibit the same spontaneous and un-inquiring faith as Pindar in the legendary antiquities of Greece, taken as a whole; but they allow themselves greater license as to the details. It was indispensable to the success of their compositions that they should recast and group anew the legendary events, preserving the names and general understood relation of those characters whom they introduced. The demand for novelty of combination increased with the multiplication of tragic spectacles at Athens; moreover the feelings of the Athenians, ethical as well as political, had become too critical to tolerate the literal reproduction of many among the ancient stories.

Both of them exalted rather than lowered the dignity of the mythical world, as something divine and heroic rather than human. The Promêtheus of Æschylus is a far more exalted conception than his keen-witted namesake in Hesiod, and the more homely details of the ancient Thêbaïs and Œdipodia were in like manner modified by Sophoklês. The religious agencies of the old epic are constantly kept prominent ny Both. The paternal curse, the wrath of deceased persons against those from whom they here sustained wrong, the judgments of the Erinnys against guilty or foredoomed persons, sometimes inflicted directly, sometimes brought about through dementation of the sufferer himself (like the Homeric Atê), are frequent in their tragedies.

Æschylus in two of his remaining pieces brings forward the gods as the chief personages. Far from sharing the objection of Pindar to dwell upon dissensions of the gods, he introduces Promêtheus and Zeus in the one, Apollo and the Eumenides in the other, in marked opposition. The dialogue, first superinduced by him upon the primitive Chorus, gradually became the most important portion of the drama, and is more elaborated in Sophoklês than in Æschylus. Even in Sophoklês, however, it still generally retains its ideal majesty as contrasted with the rhetorical and forensic tone which afterwards crept in: it grows out of the piece, and addresses itself to the emotions more than to the reason of the audience. Nevertheless, the effect of Athenian political discussion and democratical feeling is visible in both these dramatists. The idea of rights and legitimate privileges as opposed to usurping force, is applied by Æschylus even to the society of the gods: the Eumenides accuse Apollo of having, with the insolence of youthful ambition, "ridden down" their old prerogatives – while the Titan Promêtheus, the champion of suffering humanity against the unfriendly dispositions of Zeus, ventures to depict the latter as a recent usurper reigning only by his superior strength, exalted by one successful revolution, and destined at some future time to be overthrown by another, a fate which cannot be averted except through warnings communicable only by Promêtheus himself.

Though Æschylus incurred reproaches of impiety from Plato, and seemingly also from the Athenian public, for particular speeches and incidents in his tragedies, and though he does not adhere to the received vein of religious tradition with the same strictness as Sophoklês – yet the ascendency and interference of the gods is never out of sight, and the solemnity with which they are represented, set off by a bold, figurative, and elliptical style of expression (often but imperfectly intelligible to modern readers) reaches its maximum in his tragedies. As he throws round the gods a kind of airy grandeur, so neither do his men or heroes appear like tenants of the common earth, The mythical world from which he borrows his characters is peopled only with "the immediate seed of the gods, in close contact with Zeus, in whom the divine blood has not yet had time to degenerate:" his individuals are taken, not from the iron race whom Hesiod acknowledges with shame as his contemporaries, but from the extinct heroic race which had fought at Troy and Thêbes. It is to them that his conceptions aspire, and he is even chargeable with frequent straining, beyond the limits of poetical taste, to realise his picture. If he does not consistently succeed in it, the reason is because consistency in such a matter is unattainable, since, after all, the analogies of common humanity, the only materials which the most creative imagination has to work upon, obtrude themselves involuntarily, and the lineaments of the man are thus seen even under a dress which promises superhuman proportions.

Sophoklês, the most illustrious ornament of Grecian tragedy, dwells upon the same heroic characters, and maintains their grandeur, on the whole, with little abatement, combining with it a far better dramatic structure, and a wider appeal to human sympathies. Even in Sophoklês, however, we find indications that an altered ethical feeling and a more predominant sense of artistic perfection are allowed to modify the harsher religious agencies of the old epic. Occasional misplaced effusions of rhetoric, as well as of didactic prolixity, may also be detected. It is Æschylus, not Sophoklês, who forms the marked antithesis to Euripidês: it is Æschylus, not Sophoklês, to whom Aristophanes awards the prize of tragedy, as the poet who assigns most perfectly to the heroes of the past those weighty words, imposing equipments, simplicity of great deeds with little talk, and masculine energy superior to the corruptions of Aphroditê, which beseem the comrades of Agamemnôn and Adrastus.

How deeply this feeling, of the heroic character of the mythical world, possessed the Athenian mind, may be judged by the bitter criticisms made on Euripidês, whose compositions were pervaded, partly by ideas of physical philosophy learnt under Anaxagoras, partly by the altered tone of education and the wide diffusion of practical eloquence, forensic as well as political, at Athens. While Aristophanês assails Euripidês as the representative of this "young Athens," with the utmost keenness of sarcasm, other critics also concur in designating him as having vulgarised the mythical heroes, and transformed them into mere characters of common life, loquacious, subtle, and savouring of the market-place. In some of his plays, sceptical expressions and sentiments were introduced, derived from his philosophical studies, sometimes confounding two or three distinct gods into one, sometimes translating the personal Zeus into a substantial Æther with determinate attributes. He put into the months of some of his unprincipled dramatic characters, apologetic speeches which were denounced as ostentatious sophistry, and as setting out a triumphant case for the criminal. His thoughts, his words, and the rhythm of his choric songs, were all accused of being deficient in dignity and elevation. The mean attire and miserable attitude in which he exhibited Œneus, Têlephus, Thyestês, Inô, and other heroic characters, were unmercifully derided, though it seems that their position and circumstances had always been painfully melancholy; but the effeminate pathos which Euripidês brought so nakedly into the foreground, was accounted unworthy of the majesty of a legendary hero. He incurred still greater obloquy on another point, on which he is allowed even by his enemies to have only reproduced in substance the pre-existing tales, the illicit and fatal passion depicted in several of his female characters, each as Phædra and Sthenobœa. His opponents admitted that these stories were true, but contended that they ought to be kept back and not produced upon the stage, a proof both of the continued mythical faith and of the more sensitive ethical criticism of his age. The marriage of the six daughters to the six sons of Æolas is of Homeric origin, and stands now, though briefly stated, in the Odyssey; but the incestuous passion of Makareus and Kanakê, embodied by Euripidês in the lost tragedy called *Æolus,* drew upon him severe censure. Moreover, he often disconnected the horrors of the old legends with those religious agencies by which they had been originally forced on, prefacing them by motives of a more refined character, which carried no sense of awful compulsion: thus the considerations by which the Euripidean Alkmæôn was reduced to the necessity of killing his mother appeared to Aristotle ridiculous. After the time of this great poet, his successors seem to have followed him in breathing into their characters the spirit of common life, but the names and plot were still borrowed from the stricken mythical families of Tantalus, Kadmus, &c.; and the heroic exaltation of all the individual personages introduced, as contrasted with the purely human character of the Chorus, is still numbered by Aristotle among the essential points of the theory of tragedy.

The tendency then of Athenian tragedy – powerfully manifested in Æschylus, and never wholly lost – was to uphold an unquestioning faith and a reverential estimate of the general mythical world and its personages, but to treat the particular narratives rather as matter for the emotions than as recitals of actual fact. The logographers worked along with them to the first of these two ends, but not to the second. Their grand object was, to cast the mythes into a continuous readable series, and they were in consequence compelled to make selection between inconsistent or contradictory narratives: to reject some narratives as false, and to receive others as true. Their preference was determined more by their sentiments as to what was appropriate, than by any pretended historical test. Pherekydês, Akusilaus and Hellanikus did not seek to banish miraculous or fantastic incidents from the mythical world: they regarded it as peopled with loftier beings, and expected to find in it phænomena not paralleled in their own degenerate days. They reproduced the fables as they found them in the poets, rejecting little except the discrepancies, and producing ultimately what they believed to be not only a continuous but an exact and trustworthy history of the past – wherein they carry indeed their precision to such a length, that Hellanikus gives the year, and even the day of the capture of Troy.

Hekatæus of Milêtus (500 B.C.), anterior to Pherekydês and Hellanikus, is the earliest writer in whom we can detect any disposition to disallow the prerogative and specialty of the mythes, and to soften down their characteristic prodigies, some of which however still find favour in his eyes, as in the case of the speaking ram who carried Phryxus over the Hellespont. He pronounced the Grecian fables to be "many and ridiculous;" whether from their discrepancies or from their intrinsic improbabilities we do not know. We owe to him the first attempt to force them within the limits of historical credibility; as where he transforms the three-headed Cerberus, the dog of Hadês, into a serpent inhabiting a cavern on Cape Tænarus – and Geryôn of Erytheia into a king of Epirus rich in herds of oxen. Hekatæus traced the genealogy of himself and the gens to which he belonged through a line of fifteen progenitors up to an initial god, the clearest proof both of his profound faith in the reality of the mythical world, and of his religious attachment to it as the point of junction between the human and the divine personality.

We have next to consider the historians, especially Herodotus and Thucydidês. Like Hekatæus, Thucydidês belonged to a gens which traced its descent from Ajax, and through Ajax to Æakus and Zeus. Herodotus modestly implies that he himself had no such privilege to boast of. Their curiosity respecting the past had no other materials to work upon except the mythes which they found already cast by the logographers into a continuous series, and presented as an aggregate of antecedent history, chronologically deduced from the times of the gods. In common with the body of the Greeks, both Herodotus and Thucydidês had imbibed that complete and unsuspecting belief in the general reality of mythical antiquity, which was interwoven with the religion and the patriotism, and all the public demonstrations of the Hellenic world. To acquaint themselves with the genuine details of this fore-time, was an inquiry highly interesting to them. But the increased positive tendencies of their age, as well as their own habits of personal investigation, had created in them an *historical sense* in regard to the past as well as to the present. Having acquired a habit of appreciating the intrinsic tests of historical credibility and probability, they found the particular narratives of the poets and logographers, inadmissible as a whole even in the eyes of Hekatæus, still more at variance with their stricter canons of criticism. We thus observe in them the constant struggle, as well as the resulting compromise, between these two opposite tendencies: on one hand a firm belief in the reality of the mythical world, on the other hand an inability to accept the details which their only witnesses, the poets and logographer, told them respecting it.

Each of them however performed the process in his own way. Herodotus is a man of deep and anxious religious feeling: he often recognises the special judgments of the gods as determining historical events: his piety is also partly tinged with that mystical vein which the last two centuries had gradually infused into the religion of the Greeks – for he is apprehensive of giving offence to the gods by reciting publicly what he has heard respecting them: he frequently stops short in his narrative and intimates that there *is* a sacred legend, but that he will not tell it: in other cases, where he feels compelled to speak out, he entreats forgiveness for doing so from the gods and heroes. Sometimes he will not even mention the name of a god, though be generally thinks himself authorised to do so, the names being matter of public notoriety. Such pious reserve, which the open-hearted Herodotus avowedly proclaims as chaining up his tongue, affords a striking contrast with the plain-spoken and unsuspecting tone of the ancient epic, as well as of the popular legends, wherein the gods and their proceedings were the familiar and interesting subjects of common talk as well as of common sympathy, without ceasing to inspire both fear and reverence.

Herodotus expressly distinguishes, in the comparison of Polykratês with Minôs, the human race to which the former belonged, from the divine or heroic race which comprised the latter. He has a firm belief in the authentic personality and parentage of all the names in the mythes, divine, heroic and human, as well as in the trustworthiness of their chronology computed by generations. He counts back 1600 years from his own day to that of Semelê, mother of Dionysus: 900 years to Hêraklês, and 800 years to Penelopê, the Trojan war being a little earlier in date. Indeed even the longest of these periods must have seemed to him comparatively short, seeing that he apparently accepts the prodigious series of years which the Egyptians professed to draw from a recorded chronology – 17,000 years from their god Hêraklês, and 15,000 years from their god Osiris or Dionysus, down to their king Amasis (550 B.C.) So much was his imagination familiarised with these long chronological computations barren of events, that he treats Homer and Hesiod as "men of yesterday," though separated from his own age by an interval which he reckons as four hundred years.

Herodotus had been profoundly impressed with what be saw and heard in Egypt. The wonderful monuments, the evident antiquity, and the peculiar civilisation of that country, acquired such preponderance in his mind over his own native legends, that be is disposed to trace even the oldest religious names or institutions of Greece to Egyptian or Phœnician original, setting aside in favour of this hypothesis the Grecian legends of Dionysus and Pan. The oldest Grecian mythical genealogies are thus made ultimately to lose themselves in Egyptian or Phœnician antiquity, and in the full extent of these genealogies Herodotus firmly believes. It does not seem that any doubt had ever crossed his mind as to the real personality of those who were named or described in the popular mythes: all of them have once had reality, either as men, as heroes, or as gods. The eponyms of cities, dêmes and tribes, are all comprehended in this affirmative category: the supposition of fictitious personages being apparently never entertained. Deukaliôn, Hellên, Dôrus, Iôn, with his four sons, the eponyms of the old Athenian tribes, the autochthonous Titakus and Dekelus, Danaus, Lynkeus, Perseus, Amphitryôn, Alkmêna, and Hêraklês, Talthybius, the heroic progenitor of the privileged heraldic gens at Sparta, the Tyndarids and Helena, Agamemnôn, Menelaus, and Orestês, Nestôr and his son Peisistratus, Asôpus, Thêbê, and Ægina, Inachus and Iô, Æêtês and Mêdea, Melanippus, Adrastus, and Amphiaraüs, as well as Jasôn and the Argô, all these are occupants of the real past time, and predecessors of himself and his contemporaries. In the veins of the Lacedæmonian kings flowed the blood both of Kadmus and of Danaus, their splendid pedigree being traceable to both of these great mythical names: Herodotus carries the lineage up through Hêraklês first to Perseus and Danaê, then through Danaê to Akrisius and the Egyptian Danaus; but he drops the paternal lineage when he comes to Perseus (inasmuch as Perseus is the son of Zeus by Danaê, without any reputed human father, such as Amphitryôn was to Hêraklês), and then follows the higher members of the series through Danaê alone. He also pursues the same regal genealogy, through the mother of Eurysthenês and Proclês, up to Polynikês, Œdipus, Laius, Labdakus, Polydôrus and Kadmus: he assigns various ancient inscriptions which he saw in the temple of the Ismenian Apollo at Thêbes, to the ages of Laius and Œdipus. Moreover, the sieges of Thêbes and Troy, the Argônautic expedition, the invasion of Attica by the Amazons, the protection of the Herakleids, and the defeat and death of Eurystheus, by the Athenians, the death of Mêkisteus and Tydeus before Thêbes by the hands of Melanippus, and the touching calamities of Adrastus and Amphiaraüs connected with the same enterprise, the sailing of Kastôr and Pollux in the Argô, the abductions of Iô, Eurôpe, Mêdea and Helena, the emigration of Kadmus in quest of Eurôpa, and his coming to Bœôtia, as well as the attack of the Greeks upon Troy to recover Helen, all these events seem to him portions of past history, not less unquestionably certain, though more clouded over by distance and misrepresentation, than the battles of Salamis and Mykalê.

Though Herodotus is thus easy of faith in regard both to the persons and to the general facts of Grecian mythes, yet when he comes to discuss particular facts taken separately, we find him applying to them stricter tests of historical credibility, and often disposed to reject as well the miraculous as the extravagant. Thus even with respect to Hêraklês, he censures the levity of the Greeks in ascribing to him absurd and incredible exploits: he tries their assertion by the philosophical standard of nature, or of determinate powers and conditions governing the course of events. "How is it consonant to *nature* (he asks), that Hêraklês, being, as he was, according to the statement of the Greeks, *still a man* (*i.e.* having not yet been received among the gods), should kill many thousand persons? I pray that indulgence may be shown to me both by gods and heroes for saying so much as this." The religions feelings of Herodotus here told him that he was trenching upon the utmost limits of admissible scepticism.

Another striking instance of the disposition of Herodotus to rationalise the miraculous narratives of the current mythes, is to be found in his account of the oracle of Dôdôna and its alleged Egyptian origin. Here, if in any case, a miracle was not only in full keeping, but apparently indispensable to satisfy the exigences of the religious sentiment: anything less than a miracle would have appeared tame and unimpressive to the visitors of so revered a spot, much more to the residents themselves. Accordingly, Herodotus heard, both from the three priestesses and from the Dôdônæans generally, that two black doves had started at the same time from Thêbes in Egypt: one of them went to Libya, where it directed the Libyans to establish the oracle of Zeus Ammon: the other came to the grove of Dôdôna, and perched on one of the venerable oaks, proclaiming with a human voice that an oracle of Zeus must be founded on that very spot. The injunction of the speaking dove was respectfully obeyed.

Such was the tale related and believed at Dôdôna. But Herodotus had also heard, from the priests at Thêbes in Egypt, a different tale, ascribing the origin of all the prophetic establishments, in Greece as well as in Libya, to two sacerdotal women, who had been carried away from Thêbes by some Phœnician merchants and sold, the one in Greece, the other in Libya. The Theban priests boldly assured Herodotus that much pains had been taken to discover what had become of these women so exported, and that the fact of their having been, taken to Greece and Libya had been accordingly verified.

The historian of Halicarnassus cannot for a moment think of admitting the miracle which harmonised so well with the feelings of the priestesses and the Dodonæans. "How (he asks) could a dove speak with human voice?" But the narrative of the priests at Thêbes, though its prodigious improbability hardly requires to be stated, yet involved no positive departure from the laws of nature and possibility, and therefore Herodotus makes no difficulty in accepting it, The curious circumstance is, that he turns the native Dodonæan legend into a figurative representation, or rather a misrepresentation, of the supposed true story told by the Thêban priests. According to his interpretation, the woman who came from Thêbes to Dôdôna was called a dove, and affirmed to utter sounds like a bird, because she was non-Hellenic and spoke a foreign tongue: when she learned to speak the language of the country, it was then said that the dove spoke with a human voice. And the dove was moreover called black, because of the woman's Egyptian colour.

That Herodotus should thus bluntly reject a miracle, recounted to him by the prophetic women themselves as the prime circumstance in the *origines* of this holy place, is a proof of the hold which habits of dealing with historical evidence had acquired over his mind; and the awkwardness of his explanatory mediation between the dove and the woman, marks not less his anxiety, while discarding the legend, to let it softly down into a story quasi-historical and not intrinsically incredible.

We may observe another example of the unconscious tendency of Herodotus to eliminate from the mythes the idea of special aid from the gods, in his remarks upon Melampus. He designates Melampus "as a clever man, who had acquired for himself the art of prophecy;" and had procured.through Kadmus much information about the religious rites and customs of Egypt, many of which he introduced into Greece – especially the name, the sacrifices, and the phallic processions of Dionysus: he adds, "that Melampus himself did not accurately comprehend or bring out the whole doctrine, but wise men who came after mm made the necessary additions." Though the name of Melampus is here maintained, the character described is something in the vein of Pythagoras – totally different from the great seer and leech of the old epic mythes – the founder of the gifted family of the Amythaonids, and the grandfather of Amphiaraüs. Tthat which is most of all at variance with the genuine legendary spirit, is the opinion expressed by Herodotus (and delivered with some emphasis as *his own*), that Melampus "was a clever man, who had acquired for himself prophetic powers." Such a supposition would have appeared inadmissible to Homer or Hesiod, or indeed to Solôn, in the preceding century, in whose view even inferior arts come from the gods, while Zeus or Apollo bestows the power of prophesying. The intimation of such an opinion by Herodotus, himself a thoroughly pious man, marks the sensibly diminished omnipresence of the gods, and the increasing tendency to look for the explanation of phænomena among more visible and determinate agencies.

We may make a similar remark on the dictum of the historian respecting the narrow defile of Tempê, forming the embouchure of the Pêneus and the efflux of all the waters from the Thessalian basin. The Thessalians alleged that this whole basin of Thessaly had once been a lake, but that Poseidôn had split the chain of mountains and opened the efflux; upon which primitive belief, thoroughly conformable to the genius of Homer and Hesiod, Herodotus comments as follows: "The Thessalian statement is reasonable. For whoever thinks that Poseidôn shakes the earth, and that the rifts of an earthquake are the work of that god, will, on seeing the defile in question, say that Poseidôn has caused it. For the rift of the mountains is, as appeared to me (when I saw it), the work of an earthquake." Herodotus admits the reference to Poseidôn, when pointed out to him, but it stands only in the background: what is present to his mind is the phenomenon of the earthquake, not as a special act, but as part of a system of habitual operations.

Herodotus adopts the Egyptian version of the legend of Troy, founded on that capital variation which seems to have originated with Stesichorus, and according to which Helen never left Sparta at all – her *eidôlon* had been taken to Troy in her place. Upon this basis a new story had been framed, midway between Homer and Stesichorus, representing Paris to have really carried off Helen from Sparta, but to have been driven by storms to Egypt, where she remained during the whole siege of Troy, having been detained by Prôteus, the king of the country, until Menelaus came to reclaim her after his triumph. The Egyptian priests, with their usual boldness of assertion, professed to have heard the whole story from Menelaus himself – the Greeks had besieged Troy, in the full persuasion that Helen and the stolen treasures were within the walls, nor would they ever believe the repeated denials of the Trojans as to the fact of her presence. In intimating his preference for the Egyptian narrative, Herodotus betrays at once his perfect and unsuspecting confidence that he is dealing with genuine matter of history, and his entire distrust of the epic poets, even including Homer, upon whose authority that supposed history rested. His reason for rejecting the Homeric version is that it teems with historical improbabilities. If Helen had been really in Troy (he says), Priam and the Trojans would never have been so insane as to retain her to their own utter ruin; but it was the divine judgment which drove them into the miserable alternative of neither being able to surrender Helen, nor to satisfy the Greeks of the real fact that they had never had possession of her – in order that mankind might plainly read, in the utter destruction of Troy, the great punishments with which the gods visit great misdeeds. Homer (Herodotus thinks) had heard this story, but designedly departed from it, because it was not so suitable a subject for epic poetry.

Enough has been said to show how wide is the difference between Herodotus and the logographers with their literal transcript of the ancient legends. Though he agrees with them in admitting the full series of persons and generations, he tries the circumstances narrated by a new standard. Scruples have arisen in his mind respecting violations of the laws of nature: the poets are unworthy of trust, and their narratives must be brought into conformity with historical and ethical conditions, before they can be admitted as truth. To accomplish this conformity, Herodotus is willing to mutilate the old legend in one of its most vital points: he sacrifices the personal presence of Helena in Troy, which ran through every one of the ancient epic poems belonging to the Trojan cycle,

227

and is indeed, under the gods, the great and present moving force throughout.

Thucydidês places himself generally in the same point of view as Herodotus with regard to mythical antiquity, yet with some considerable differences. Though manifesting no belief in present miracles or prodigies, he seems to accept without reserve the pre-existent reality of all the persons mentioned in the mythes, and of the long series of generations extending back through so many supposed centuries: in this category, too, are included the eponymous personages, Hellen, Kekrops, Eumolpus, Pandiôn, Amphilochus the son of Amphiaraüs, and Akarnan. On the other hand, we find no trace of that distinction between a human and an heroic ante-human race, which Herodotus still admitted, nor any respect for Egyptian legends. Thucydidês, regarding the personages of the mythes as men of the same breed and stature with his own contemporaries, not only tests the acts imputed to them by the same limits of credibility, but presumes in them the same political views and feelings as he was accustomed to trace in the proceedings of Peisistratus or Periklês. He treats the Trojan war as a great political enterprise, undertaken by all Greece: brought into combination through the imposing power of Agamemnôn, not (according to the legendary narrative) through the influence of the oath exacted by Tyndareus. Then he explains how the predecessors of Agamemnôn arrived at so vast a dominion – beginning with Pelops, who came over (as he says) from Asia with great wealth among the poor Peloponnesians. and by means of this wealth so aggrandised himself, though a foreigner, as to become the eponym of the peninsula. Next followed his son Atreus, who acquired after the death of Eurystheus the dominion of Mykênae, which had before been possessed by the descendants of Perseus: here the old legendary tale, which described Atreus as having been banished by his father Pelops in consequence of the murder of his elder brother Chrysippus, is invested with a political bearing, as explaining the reason why Atreus retired to Mykênæ. Another legendary tale – the defeat and death of Eurystheus by the fugitive Herakleids in Attica, so celebrated in Attic tragedy as having given occasion to the generous protecting intervention of Athens – is also introduced as furnishing the cause why Atreus succeeded to the deceased Eurystheus; "for Atreus, the maternal uncle of Eurystheus, had been entrusted by the latter with his government during the expedition into Attica, and had effectually courted the people, who were moreover in great fear of being attacked by the Herakleids." Thus the Pelopids acquired the supremacy in Peloponnêsus, and Agamemnôn was enabled to get together his 1200 ships and 100,000 men for the expedition against Troy. Considering that contingents were furnished from every portion of Greece, Thucydidês regards this as a small number, treating the Homeric Catalogue as an authentic muster-roll, perhaps rather exaggerated than otherwise. He then proceeds to tell us why the armament was not larger. Many more men could have been furnished, but there was not sufficient money to purchase provisions for their subsistence: hence they were compelled, after landing and gaining a victory, to fortify their camp, to divide their army, and to send away one portion for the purpose of cultivating the Chersonese, and another portion to sack the adjacent towns. This was the grand reason why the siege lasted so long as ten years. For if it had been possible to keep the whole army together, and to act with an undivided force, Troy would have been taken both earlier and at smaller cost.

Such is the general sketch of the war of Troy, as given by Thucydidês. So different is it from the genuine epical narrative, that we seem hardly to be reading a description of the same event: still less should we imagine that the event was known, to him as well as to us, only through the epic poets themselves. The men, the numbers, and the duration of the siege, do indeed remain the same; but the cast and juncture of events, the determining forces, and the characteristic features, are altogether heterogeneous. But, like Herodotus, and still more than Herodotus, Thucydidês was under the pressure of two conflicting impulses. He shared the general faith in the mythical antiquity, but at the same time he could not believe in any facts which contradicted the laws of historical credibility or probability. He was thus under the necessity of torturing the matter of the old mythes into conformity with the subjective exigencies of his own mind: he left out, altered, recombined, and supplied new connecting principles and supposed purposes, until the story became such as no one could have any positive reason for calling in question: though it lost the impressive mixture of religion, romance, and individual adventure, which constituted its original charm, it acquired a smoothness and plausibility, and a poetical *ensemble,* which the critics were satisfied to accept as historical truth. And historical truth it would doubtless have been, if any independent evidence could have been found to sustain it. Had Thucydidês been able to produce such new testimony, we should have been pleased to satisfy ourselves that the war of Troy, as he recounted it, was the real event; of which the war of Troy, as sung by the epic poets, was a misreported, exaggerated, and ornamented recital. But in this case the poets are the only real witnesses, and the narrative of

Thucydidês is a mere extract and distillation from their incredibilities.

A few other instances may be mentioned to illustrate the views of Thucydidês respecting various mythical incidents. **1.** He treats the residence of the Homeric Phæakians at Korkyra as an undisputed fact, and employs it partly to explain the efficiency of the Korkyrean navy in times preceding the Peloponnesian war. **2.** He notices, with equal confidence, the story of Têreus and Proknê, daughter of Pandiôn, and the murder of the child Itys by Proknê his mother, and Philomêla: and he produces this ancient mythe with especial reference to the alliance between the Athenians and Têrês, king of the Odrysian Thracians, during the time of the Peloponnesian war, intimating that the Odrysian Têrês was neither of the same family nor of the same country as Têreus the husband of Proknê. The conduct of Pandiôn, in giving his daughter Proknê in marriage to Têreus, is in his view dictated by political motives and interests. **3.** He mentions the Strait of Messina as the place through which Odysseus is said to have sailed. **4.** The Cyclôpes and the Læstrygones (he says) were the most ancient reported inhabitants of Sicily, but he cannot tell to what race they belonged, nor whence they came. **5.** Italy derived its name from Italus, king of the Sikels. **6.** Eryx and Egesta in Sicily were founded by fugitive Trojans after the capture of Troy; also Skionê, in the Thracian peninsula of Pallênê, by Greeks from the Achæan town of Pellênê, stopping thither in their return from the siege of Troy: the Amphtiochian Argôs in the Gulf of Ambrakia was in like manner founded by Amphilochus son of Amphiaraüs, in his return from the same enterprise. The remorse and mental derangement of the matricidal Alkmæôn, son of Amphiaraüs, is also mentioned by Thucydidês, us well as the settlement of his son Akarnan in the country called after him Akarnania.

Such are the special alluvions made by this illustrious author in the the course of his history to mythical events. From the tenor of his language we may see that he accounted all that could be known about them to be uncertain and unsatisfactory; but he has it much at heart to show, that even the greatest were inferior in magnitude and importance to the Peloponnesian war. In this. respect his opinion seems to have been at variance with that which was popular among his contemporaries.

To touch a little upon the later historians by whom these mythes were handled, we find that Anaximenês of Lampsacus composed a consecutive history of events, beginning from the Theogony down to the battle of Mantineia. But Ephorus professed to omit all the mythical narratives which are referred to times anterior to the return of the Herakleids, (such restriction would of course have banished the siege of Troy), and even reproved those who introduced mythes into historical writing; adding, that everywhere truth was the object to be aimed at. Yet in practice he seems often to have departed from his own rule. Theopompus, on the other hand, openly proclaimed that he could narrate fables in his history better than Herodotus, or Ktêsias, or Hellanicus. The fragments which remain to us exhibit some proof that this promise was performed as to quantity; though as to his style of narration, the judgment of Dionysius is unfavourable. Xenophôn ennobled his favourite amusement of the chase by numerous examples chosen from the heroic world, tracing their portraits with all the simplicity of an undiminished faith. Kallisthenês, like Ephorus, professed to omit all mythes which referred to a time anterior to the return of the Herakleids; yet we know that he devoted a separate book or portion of his history to the Trojan war. Philistus introduced some mythes in the earlier portions of his Sicilian history; but Timæus was distinguished above all others for the copious and indiscriminate way in which he collected and repeated such legends. Some of these writers employed their ingenuity in transforming the mythical circumstances into plausible matter of history: Ephorus, in particular, converted the serpent Pythô, slain by Apollo, into a tyrannical king.

The author who pushed this transmutation of legend into history to the greatest length, was the Messênian Euêmerus, contemporary of Kassander of Macedôn. He melted down in this way the divine persons and legends, as well as the heroic – representing both gods and heroes as having been mere earthborn men, though superior to the ordinary level in respect of force and capacity, and deified or heroified after death as a recompense for services or striking exploits. In the course of a voyage into the Indian sea, undertaken by command of Kassander, Euêmerus professed to have discovered a fabulous country called Panchaia, in which was a temple of the Triphylian Zeus: he there described a golden column, with an inscription purporting to have been put up by Zeus himself, and detailing his exploits while on earth. Some eminent men, among whom may be numbered Polybius, followed the views of Euêmerus, and the Roman poet Ennius translated his Historia Sacra; but on the whole he never acquired favour, and the unblushing inventions which he put into circulation were of themselves sufficient to disgrace both the author and his opinions. The doctrine that all the gods had once existed as mere men offended the religious pagans, and drew upon Euêmerus the imputation of atheism; but, on the other hand, it came to be warmly espoused by several of the Christian assailants of paganism, by Minucius Felix, Lactantius, and St. Augustin, who found the ground ready prepared for them in their efforts to strip Zeus and the other pagan gods of the attributes of deity. They believed not only in the main theory, but also in the copious details of Euêmerus; and the same man whom Strabo casts aside as almost a proverb for mendacity, was extolled by them as an excellent specimen of careful historical inquiry.

But though the pagan world repudiated that "lowering tone of explanation," which effaced the superhuman personality of Zeus and the great gods of Olympus, the mythical persons and narratives generally came to be surveyed more and more from the point of view of history, and subjected to such alterations as might make them look more like plausible matter of fact. Polybius, Strabo, Diodôrus, and Pausanias, cast the mythes into historical statements – with more or less of transformation, as the case may require, assuming always that there is a basis of truth, which may be discovered by removing poetical exaggerations and allowing for mistakes. Strabo, in particular, lays down that principle broadly and unequivocally in his remarks upon Homer. To give pure fiction, without any foundation of fact, was in his judgment utterly unworthy of so great a genius: and he comments with considerable acrimony. On the geographer Eratosthenês, who maintains the opposite opinion. Again, Polybius tells us that the Homeric Æolus, the dispenser of the winds by appointment from Zeus, was in reality a man eminently skilled in navigation, and exact in predicting the weather; that the Cyclôpes and Læstrygones, were wild and savage real men in Sicily; and that Scylla and Charybdis were a figurative representation of dangers arising from pirates in the Strait of Messina. Strabo speaks of the amazing expeditions of Dionysus and Hêraklês, and of the long wanderings of Jasôn, Menelaus, and Odysseus, in the same category with the extended commercial range of the Phœnician merchant-ships: he explains the report of Thesêus and Peirithous having descended to Hadês, by their dangerous earthly pilgrimages, and the invocation of the Dioskuri as the protectors of the imperilled mariner, by the celebrity which they had acquired as real men and navigators.

Diodôrus gave at considerable length versions of the current fables respecting the most illustrious names in the Grecian mythical world, compiled confusedly out of distinct and incongruous authors. Sometimes the mythe is reproduced in its primitive simplicity, but for the most part it is partially, and sometimes wholly, historicised. Amidst this jumble of dissentient authorities we can trace

XVI. GRECIAN MYTHES, AS SEEN BY THE GREEKS.

little of a systematic view, except the general conviction that there was at the bottom of the mythes a real chronological sequence of persons, and real matter of fact, historical or ultra-historical. Nevertheless, there are some few occasions on which Diodôrus brings us back a step nearer to the point of view of the old logographers. For, in reference to Hêraklês, he protests against the scheme of cutting down the mythes to the level of present reality, and contends that a special standard of ultra-historical credibility ought to be constituted, so as to include the mythe in its native dimensions, and do fitting honour to the grand, beneficent, and superhuman personality of Hêraklês and other heroes or demi-gods. To apply to such persons the common measure of humanity (he says), and to cavil at the glorious picture which grateful man has drawn of them, is at once ungracious and irrational. All nice criticism into the truth of the legendary narratives is out of place: we show our reverence to the god by acquiescing in the incredibilities of his history, and we must be content with the best guesses which we can make, amidst the inextricable confusion and numberless discrepancies which they present. Yet though Diodôrus here exhibits preponderance of the religious sentiment over the purely historical point of view, and thus reminds us of a period earlier than Thucydidês – he in another place inserts a series of stories which seem to be derived from Euêmerus, and in which Uranus, Kronus, and Zeus appear reduced to the character of human kings celebrated for their exploits and benefactions. Many of the authors, whom Diodôrus copies, have so entangled together Grecian, Asiatic, Egyptian, and Libyan fables, that it becomes impossible to ascertain how much of this heterogeneous mass can be considered as at all connected with the genuine Hellenic mind.

Pausanias is far more strictly Hellenic in his view of the Grecian mythes than Diodôrus: his sincere piety makes him inclined to faith generally with regard to the mythical narratives, but subject nevertheless to the frequent necessity of historicising or allegorising them. His belief in the general reality of the mythical history and chronology is complete, in spite of the many discrepancies which he finds in it, and which he is unable to reconcile.

Another author who seems to have conceived clearly, and applied consistently, the semi-historical theory of the Grecian mythes, is Palæphatus, of whose work what appears to be a short abstract has been preserved. In the short preface of this treatise "concerning Incredible Tales," he remarks, that some men, from want of instruction, believe all the current narratives; while others, more searching and cautious, disbelieve them altogether. Each of these extremes he is anxious to avoid. On the one hand, he thinks that no narrative could ever have acquired credence unless it had been founded in truth: on the other, it is impossible for him to accept so much of the existing narratives as conflicts with the analogies of present natural phænomena. If such things ever had been, they would still continue to be – but they never have so occurred; and the extra-analogical features of the stories are to be ascribed to the license of the poets. Palæphatus wishes to adopt a middle course, neither accepting all nor rejecting all; accordingly, he had taken great pains to separate the true from the false in many of the narratives: he had visited the localities wherein they had taken place, and made careful inquiries from old men and others. The results of his researches are presented in a new version of fifty legends, among the most celebrated and the most fabulous, comprising the Centaurs, Pasiphaê, Aktæôn, Kadmus and the Sparti, the Sphinx, Cycnus, Dædalus, the Trojan horse, Æolus, Scylla, Geryôn, Bellerophôn, &c.

It must be confessed that Palæphatus has performed his promise of transforming the "incredibilia" into narratives in themselves plausible and unobjectionable, and that in doing so he always follows some thread of analogy, real or verbal. The Centaurs (he tells us) were a body of young men from the village of Nephelê in Thessaly, who first trained and mounted horses for the purpose of repelling a herd of bulls belonging to Ixiôn king of the Lapithæ, which had run wild and done great damage: they pursued these wild bulls on horseback, and pierced them with their spears, thus acquiring both the name of *Prickers* (κέντορες) and the imputed attribute of joint body with the horse. Aktæôn was an Arcadian, who neglected the cultivation of his land for the pleasures of hunting, and was thus eaten up by the expense of his hounds. The dragon whom Kadmus killed at Thêbes, was in reality Drako, king of Thêbes: and the dragon's teeth which he was said to have sown, and from whence sprung a crop of armed men, were in point of fact elephants' teeth, which Kadmus as a rich Phœnician, had brought over with him: the sons of Drako sold these elephants' teeth and employed the proceeds to levy troops against Kadmus. Dædalus, instead of flying across the sea on wings, had escaped from Krête in a swift sailing-boat under a violent storm: Kottus, Briareus,and Gygês were not persons with one hundred hands, but inhabitants of the village of Hekatoncheiria in Upper Macedonia, who warred with the inhabitants of Mount Olympus against the Titans: Scylla, whom Odysseus so narrowly escaped, was a fast-sailing piratical vessel, as was also Pegasus, the alleged winged horse of

Bellerophôn.

By such ingenious conjectures, Palæphatus eliminates all the incredible circumstances, and leaves to us a string of tales perfectly credible and commonplace, which we should readily believe, provided a very moderate amount of testimony could be produced in their favour. If his treatment not only disenchants the original mythes, but even effaces their generic and essential character, we ought to remember that this is not more than what is done by Thucydidês in his sketch of the Trojan war. Palæphatus handles the mythes consistently, according to the semi-historical theory, and his results exhibit the maximum which that theory can ever present By aid of conjecture, we get out of the impossible, and arrive at matters intrinsically plausible, but totally uncertified; beyond this point we cannot penetrate, without the light of extrinsic evidence, since there is no intrinsic mark to distinguish truth from plausible fiction.

It remains that we should notice the manner in which the ancient mythes were received and dealt with by the philosophers. The earliest expression which we hear, on the part of philosophy, is the severe censure bestowed upon them on ethical grounds by Xenophanês of Kolophôn, and seemingly by some others of his contemporaries. It was apparently in reply to such charges, which did not admit of being directly rebutted, that Theagenês of Rhêgium (about 520 B.C.) first started the idea of a double meaning in the Homeric and Hesiodic narratives, an interior sense, different from that which the words in their obvious meaning bore, yet to a certain extent analogous, and discoverable by sagacious divination. Upon this principle, he allegorised especially the battle of the gods in the Iliad. In the succeeding century, Anaxagoras and Metrodôrus carried out the allegorical explanation more comprehensively and systematically: the former representing the mythical personages as mere mental conceptions, invested with name and gender, and illustrative of ethical precepts, the latter connecting them with physical principles and phænomena. Metrodôrus resolved not only the persons of Zeus, Hêrê, and Athênê, but also those of Agamemnôn, Achillês, and Hectôr, into various elemental combinations and physical agencies, and treated the adventures ascribed to them as natural facts concealed under the veil of allegory. Empedoklês, Prodikus, Antisthenês, Parmenidês, Hêrakleidês of Pontus, and in a later age, Chrysippus, and the Stoic philosophers generally, followed more or less the same principle of treating the popular gods as allegorical personages; while the expositors of Homer (such as Stesimbrotus, Glaukôn, and others, even down to the Alexandrine age), though none of them proceeded to the same extreme length as Metrodôrus, employed allegory amongst other media of explanation for the purpose of solving difficulties, or eluding reproaches against the poet.

In the days of Plato and Xenophôn, this allegorising interpretation was one of the received methods of softening down the obnoxious mythes – though Plato himself treated it as an insufficient defence, seeing that the bulk of youthful hearers could not see through the allegory, but embraced the story literally as it was set forth. Pausanias tells us, that when he first began to write his work, he treated many of the Greek legends as silly and undeserving of serious attention; but as he proceeded, he gradually arrived at the full conviction, that the ancient sages had designedly spoken in enigmatical language, and that there was valuable truth wrapped up in their narratives: it was the duty of a pious man, therefore, to study and interpret, but not to reject, stories current and accredited respecting the gods. And others, arguing from the analogy of the religious mysteries, which could not be divulged without impiety to any except such as had been specially admitted and initiated, maintained that it would be a profanation to reveal directly to the vulgar, the genuine scheme of nature and the divine administration: the ancient poets and philosophers had taken the only proper course, of talking to the many in types and parables, and reserving the naked truth for privileged and qualified intelligences. The allegorical mode of explaining the ancient fables became more and more popular in the third and fourth centuries after the Christian æra, especially among the new Platonic philosophers being both congenial to their orientalised turn of thought, and useful as a shield against the attacks of the Christians.

It was from the same strong necessity, of accommodating the old mythes to a new standard both of belief and of appreciation, that both the historical and the allegorical schemes of transforming them arose: the literal narrative being decomposed for the purpose of arriving at a base either of particular matter of fact, or of general physical or moral truth. Instructed men commonly disposed to historicise only the heroic legends, and to allegorise more or less of the divine legends: the attempt of Euêmerus to historicise the latter was for the most part denounced as irreligious, while that of Metrodôrus to allegorise the former met with no success. In allegorising, moreover, even the divine legends, it was usual to apply the scheme of allegory only to the inferior gods, though some of the great Stoic philosophers carried it farther, and allegorised all the separate personal gods, leaving only an all-pervading cosmic Mind, essential as a coefficient along with Matter, yet not separable from Matter. But many pious pagans seem to have perceived that allegory pushed to this extent was fatal to all living religious faith, inasmuch as it divested the gods of their character of Persons, sympathising with mankind and modifiable in their dispositions according to the conduct and prayers of the believer; and hence they permitted themselves to employ allegorical interpretation only to some of the obnoxious legends connected with the superior gods, leaving the personality of the latter unimpeached.

One novelty, however, introduced seemingly by the philosopher Empedoklês and afterwards expanded by others, deserves notice, inasmuch as it modified considerably the old religious creed by drawing a pointed contrast between gods and dæmons, a distinction hardly at all manifested in Homer, but recognised in the Works and Days of Hesiod. Empedoklês widened the gap between the two, and founded upon it important consequences. The gods were good, immortal, and powerful agents, having volition and intelligence, but without appetite, passion, or infirmity: the dæmons were of a mixed nature between gods and men, ministers and interpreters from the former to the latter, but invested also with an agency and dispositions of their own. Though not immortal they were still long lived, and subject to the passions and propensities of men, so that there were among them beneficent and maleficent dæmons with every shade of intermediate difference. It had been the mistake (according to these philosophers) of the old mythes to ascribe to the gods proceedings really belonging ta the dæmons, who were always the immediate communicants with mortal nature, inspiring prophetic power to the priestesses of the oracles, sending dreams and omens, and perpetually interfering either for good or for evil. The wicked and violent dæmons, having committed many enormities, had thus sometimes incurred punishment from the gods; besides which, their bad dispositions had imposed upon men the necessity of appeasing them by religious ceremonies of a kind acceptable to such beings: hence, the human sacrifices, the violent, cruel, and obscene exhibitions, the wailings and fastings, the tearing and eating of raw flesh, which it had become customary to practise on various consecrated occasions, and especially in the Dionysiac solemnities. Moreover, the discreditable actions imputed to the gods, the terrific combats, the Typhonic and Titanic convulsions, the rapes, abductions, flight, servitude, and concealment, all these were really the doings and sufferings of bad dæmons, placed far below the sovereign agency – equable, undisturbed, and unpolluted – of the immortal gods. The action of such dæmons upon mankind was fitful and intermittent: they sometimes perished or changed their local abode, so that oracles which had once been inspired became after a time forsaken and disfranchised.

This distinction between gods and dæmons appeared to save in a great degree both the truth of the old legends and the dignity of the gods: it obviated the necessity of pronouncing either that the gods were unworthy, or the legends untrue. Yet although devised for the purpose of satisfying a more scrupulous religious sensibility, it was found inconvenient afterwards, when assailants arose against paganism generally. For while it abandoned as indefensible a large portion of what had once been genuine faith, it still retained the same word *dæmons* with an entirely altered signification. The Christian writers in their controversies found ample warrant among the *earlier* pagan authors for treating all the gods as dæmons – and not less ample warrant among the *later* pagans for denouncing the dæmons generally as evil beings.

Such were the different modes in which the ancient mythes were treated, during the literary life of Greece, by the four classes above named – poets, logographers, historians, and philosophers.

Literal acceptance, and unconscious, un-inquiring faith, such as they had obtained from the original auditors to whom they were addressed, they now found only among the multitude – alike retentive of traditional feeling and fearful of criticising the proceedings of the gods. But with instructed men they became rather subjects of respectful and carious analysis – all agreeing that the Word as tendered to them was inadmissible, yet all equally convinced that it contained important meaning, though hidden yet not undiscoverable. A very large proportion of the force of Grecian intellect was engaged in searching after this unknown base, by guesses, in which sometimes the principle of semi-historical interpretation was assumed, sometimes that of allegorical, without any collateral evidence in either case, and without possibility of verification. Out of the one assumption grew a string of allegorised phænomenal truths, out of the other a long series of seeming historical events and chronological persons, both elicited from the transformed mythes and from nothing else.

The utmost which we accomplish by means of the semi-historical theory, even in its most successful applications, is, that after leaving out from the mythical narrative all that is miraculous or high-coloured or extravagant, we arrive at a series of credible incidents – incidents which *may, perhaps,* have really occurred, and against which no intrinsic presumption can be raised. This is exactly the character of a well-written modern novel (as, for example, several among the compositions of Defoe), the whole story of which is such as may well have occurred in real life: it is plausible fiction, and nothing beyond. To raise plausible fiction up to the superior dignity of truth, some positive testimony or positive ground of inference must be shown; even the highest measure of intrinsic probability is not alone sufficient. A man who tells us that, on the day of the battle of Platæa, rain fell on the spot of ground where the city of New York now stands, will neither deserve nor obtain credit, because he can have had no means of positive knowledge; though the statement is not in the slightest degree improbable. On the other hand, statements in themselves very improbable may well deserve belief, provided they be supported by sufficient positive evidence: thus the canal dug by order of Xerxês across the promontory of Mount Athos, and the sailing of the Persian fleet through it, is a fact which I believe, because it is well-attested – notwithstanding its remarkable improbability, which so far misled Juvenal as to induce him to single out the narrative as a glaring example of Grecian mendacity. Again, many critics have observed that the general tale of the Trojan war (apart from the superhuman agencies) is not more improbable than that of the Crusades, which every one admits to be an historical fact. But (even if we grant this position, which is only true to a small extent), it is not sufficient to show an analogy between the two cases in respect to negative presumptions alone; the analogy ought to be shown to hold between them in respect to positive certificate also. The Crusades are a curious phænomenon in history, but we accept them nevertheless, as an unquestionable fact, because the antecedent improbability is surmounted by adequate contemporary testimony. When the like testimony, both in amount and kind, is produced to establish the historical reality of a Trojan war, we shall not hesitate to deal with the two events on the same footing.

Semi historical theory of Greek mythe.

In applying the semi-historical theory to Grecian mythical narrative, it has been often forgotten that a certain strength of testimony, or positive ground of belief, must first be tendered, before we can be called upon to discuss the antecedent probability or improbability of the incidents alleged. The belief of the Greeks themselves, without the smallest aid of special or contemporary witnesses, has been tacitly assumed as sufficient to support the case, provided only sufficient deduction be made from the mythical narratives to remove all antecedent improbabilities. It has been taken for granted that the faith of the people must have rested originally upon some particular historical event, involving the identical persons, things, and places which the original mythes exhibit, or at least the most prominent among them. But when we examine the pyschagogic influences predominant in the society among whom this belief originally grew up, we shall see that their belief is of little or no evidentiary value, and that the growth and diffusion of it may be satisfactorily explained without supposing any special basis of matters of fact. The popular faith, so far as it counts for anything, testifies in favour of the entire and literal mythes, which are now universally rejected as incredible. We have thus the very minimum of positive proof, and the maximum of negative presumption: we may diminish the latter by conjectural omissions and interpolations, but we cannot by any artifice increase the former: the narrative ceases to be incredible, but it still remains uncertified, – a mere common-place possibility. Nor is fiction always, or essentially, extravagant and incredible. It is often not only plausible and coherent but, even more like truth (if a paradoxical phrase may be allowed) than truth itself. Nor can we, in the absence of any extrinsic test, reckon upon any intrinsic mark to discriminate the one from the other.

In the semi-historical theory respecting Grecian mythical narrative, the critic unconsciously transports into the Homeric age those habits of classification and distinction, and that standard of acceptance or rejection, which he finds current in his own. Amongst us, the distinction between historical fact and fiction is highly valued as well as familiarly understood: we have a long history of the past, deduced from a study of contemporary evidences; and we have a body of fictitious literature, stamped with its own mark and interesting in its own way. Speaking generally, no man could now hope to succeed permanently in transferring any striking incident from the latter category into the former, nor could any man deliberately attempt it without incurring well-merited obloquy. But this *historical sense,* now so deeply rooted in the modern mind that we find a difficulty in conceiving any people to be without it, is the fruit of records and inquiries, first applied to the present, and then preserved and studied by subsequent generations; while in a society which has not yet formed the habit of recording its present, the real facts of the past can never be known: the difference between attested matter of fact and plausible fiction – between truth and that which is like truth – can neither be discerned nor sought for. Yet it a precisely upon the supposition that this distinction is present to men's habitual thoughts, that the semi-historical theory of the mythes is grounded.

It is perfectly true, as has often been stated, that the Grecian epic contains what are called traditions respecting the past – the larger portion of it, indeed, consists of nothing else. But what are these traditions? They are the matter of those songs and stories which have acquired hold on the public mind; they are the creations of the poets and storytellers themselves, each of whom finds some pre-existing, and adds others of his own, new and previously untold, under the impulse and authority of the inspiring Muse. Homer doubtless found many songs and stories current with respect to the siege of Troy: he received and transmitted some of these traditions, re-cast and transformed others, and enlarged the whole mass by new creations of his own. To the subsequent poets, such as Arktinus and Leschês, these Homeric creations formed portions of pre-existing tradition, with which they dealt in the same manner; so that the whole mass of traditions constituting the tale of Troy became larger and larger with each successive contributor. To assume a generic difference between the older and the newer strata of tradition – to treat the former as morsels of history, and the latter as appendages of fiction – is an hypothesis gratuitous at the least, not to say inadmissible. For the farther we travel back into the past, the more do we recede from the clear day of positive history, and the deeper do we plunge into the unsteady twilight and gorgeous clouds of fancy and feeling. It was one of the agreeable dreams of the Grecian epic, that the man who travelled far enough northward beyond the Rhipæan mountains, would in time reach the delicious country and genial climate of the virtuous Hyperboreans – the votaries and favourites of Apollo, who dwelt in the extreme north beyond the chilling blasts of Boreas. Now the hope that we may, by carrying our researches up the stream of time, exhaust the limits of fiction, and land ultimately upon some points of solid truth, appears to me no less illusory than this northward journey in quest of the Hyperborean elysium.

The general disposition to adopt the semi-historical theory as to the genesis of Grecian mythes, arises in part from reluctance in critics to impute to the mythopœic ages extreme credulity or fraud; together with the usual presumption, that where much is believed some portion of it must be true. There would be some weight in these grounds of reasoning, if the ages under discussion had been supplied with records and accustomed to critical inquiry. But amongst a people unprovided with the former and strangers to the latter, credulity is naturally at its maximum, as well in the narrator himself as in his hearers: the idea of deliberate fraud is moreover inapplicable, for if the hearers are disposed to accept what is related to them as a revelation from the Muse, the *œstrus* of composition is quite sufficient to impart a similar persuasion to the poet whose mind is penetrated with it. The belief of that day can hardly be said to stand apart by itself as an act of reason. It becomes confounded with vivacious imagination and earnest emotion; and in every case where these mental excitabilities are powerfully acted upon, faith ensues unconsciously and as a matter of course. How active and prominent such tendencies were among the early Greeks, the extraordinary beauty and originality of their epic poetry may teach us.

It is, besides, a presumption far too largely and indiscriminately applied, even in our own advanced age, that where much is believed, something must necessarily be true – that accredited fiction is always traceable to some basis of historical truth. The influence of imagination and feeling is not confined simply to the process of retouching, transforming, or magnifying narratives originally founded on fact; it will often create new narratives of its own, without any such preliminary basis. Where there is any general body of sentiment pervading men living in society, whether it be religious or political – love, admiration, or antipathy – all incidents tending to illustrate that sentiment are eagerly welcomed, rapidly circulated and (as a general rule) easily accredited. If real incidents are not at hand, impressive fictions will be provided to satisfy the demand. The perfect harmony of such fictions with the prevalent feeling stands in the place of certifying testimony, and causes men to hear them not merely with credence, but even with delight: to call them in question and require proof, is a task which cannot be undertaken without incurring obloquy. Of such tendencies in the human mind, abundant evidence is furnished by the innumerable religious legends which have acquired currency in various parts of the world, and of which no country was more fertile than Greece – legends which derived their origin, not from special facts misreported and exaggerated, but from pious feelings pervading the society, and translated into narrative by forward and imaginative minds – legends, in which not merely the incidents, but often even the personages are unreal, yet in which the generating sentiment is conspicuously discernible, providing its own matter as well as its own form. Other sentiments also, as well as the religious, provided they be fervent and widely diffused, will find expression in current narrative, and become portions of the general public belief – every celebrated and notorious character is the source of a thousand fictions exemplifying his peculiarities. If it be true, as I think present observation may show us, that such creative agencies are even now visible and effective, when the materials of genuine history are copious and critically studied – much more are we warranted in concluding that, in ages destitute of records, strangers to historical testimony, and full of belief in divine inspiration both as to the future and as to the past, narratives purely fictitious will acquire ready and un-inquiring credence, provided only they be plausible and in harmony with the preconceptions of the auditors.

The allegorical interpretation of the mythes has been by several learned investigators, especially by Creuzer, connected with the hypothesis of an ancient and highly instructed body of priests, having their origin either in Egypt or in the East, and communicating to the rude and barbarous Greeks religious, physical, and historical knowledge under the veil of symbols. At a time (we are told) when language was yet in its infancy, visible symbols were the most vivid means of acting upon the minds of ignorant hearers: the next step was to pass to symbolical language and expressions – for a plain and literal exposition, even if understood at all, would at least have been listened to with indifference, as not corresponding with any mental demand. In such allegorising way, then, the early priests set forth their doctrines inspecting god, nature, and humanity – a refined monotheism and a theological philosophy – and to this purpose the earliest mythes were turned. Another class of mythes, more popular and more captivating, grew up under the hands of the poets – mythes purely epical, and descriptive of real or supposed past events. The allegorical mythes, being taken up by the poets, insensibly became confounded in the same category with the purely narrative mythes – the matter symbolised was no longer thought of, while the symbolising words came to be construed in their own literal meaning – and the basis of the early allegory, thus lost among the general public, was only preserved as a secret among various religious fraternities, composed of members allied together by initiation in certain mystical ceremonies, and administered by hereditary families of presiding priests. In the Orphic and Bacchic sects, in the Eleusinian and Samothracian mysteries, was thus treasured up the secret doctrine of the old theological and philosophical mythes, which had once constituted the primitive legendary stock of Greece, in the hands of the original priesthood and in ages anterior to Homer. Persons who had gone through the preliminary ceremonies of initiation, were permitted at length to hear, though under strict obligation of secrecy, this ancient religious and cosmogonic doctrine, revealing the destination of men and the certainty of posthumous rewards and punishments – all disengaged from the corruptions of poets, as well as from the symbols and allegories under which they still remained buried in the eyes of the vulgar. The mysteries of Greece were thus traced up to the earliest ages, and represented as the only faithful depository channels of that purer theology and physics which had originally been communicated, though under the unavoidable inconvenience of a symbolical expression, by an enlightened priesthood coming from abroad to the then rude barbarians of the country.

But this theory, though advocated by several learned man, has been shown to be unsupported and erroneous. It implies a mistaken view both of the antiquity and the purport of the mysteries, which cannot be safely carried up even to the age of Hesiod and which, though imposing and venerable as religious ceremonies, included no recondite or esoteric teaching.

Supposed ancient meaning is modern interpretation.

The doctrine, supposed to have been originally symbolised and subsequently overclouded, in the Greek mythes, was in reality first intruded into them by the unconscious fancies of later interpreters. It was one of the various roads which instructed men took to escape from the literal admission of the ancient mythes, and to arrive at some new form of belief, more consonant with their ideas of what the attributes and character of the gods ought to be. It was one of the ways of constituting, by help of the mysteries, a philosophical religion apart from the general public, and of connecting that distinction with the earliest periods of Grecian society. Such a distinction was both avowed and justified among the superior men of the later pagan world. Varro and Scævola distributed theology into three distinct departments, – the mythical or fabulous, the civil, and the physical. The first had its place in the theatre, and was left without any interference to the poets: the second belonged to the city of political community as such, – it comprised the regulation of all the public worship and religious rites, and was consigned altogether to the direction of the magistrate: the third was the privilege of philosophers, but was reserved altogether for private discussion in the schools, apart from the general public. As a member of the city, the philosopher sympathised with the audience in the theatre, and took a devout share in the established ceremonies, nor was he justified in trying what he heard in the one or saw in the other by his own ethical standard. In the private assemblies of instructed or inquisitive men, he enjoyed the fullest liberty of canvassing every received tenet, and of broaching his own theories unreservedly, respecting the existence and nature of the gods. By these discussions, the activity of the philosophical mind was maintained and truth elicited; but it was such truth as the body of the people ought not to hear, lest their faith in their own established religious worship should be overthrown. In thus distinguishing the civil theology from the fabulous, Varro was enabled to cast upon the poets all the blame of the objectionable points in the popular theology, and to avoid the necessity of pronouncing censure on the magistrates, who (he contended) had made as good a compromise with the settled prejudices of the public as the case permitted.

The same conflicting sentiments which led the philosophers to decompose the divine mythes into allegory, impelled the historians to melt down the heroic mythes into something like continuous political history, with a long series of chronology calculated upon the heroic pedigrees. The one process as well as the other was interpretative guesswork, proceeding upon unauthorised assumptions, and without any verifying test or evidence; while it frittered away the characteristic beauty of the mythe into something essentially anti-mythical, it sought to arrive both at history and philosophy by impracticable roads. That the superior men of antiquity should have striven hard to save the dignity of legends which constituted the charm of their literature as well as the substance of the popular religion, we cannot be at all surprised; but it is gratifying to find Plato discussing the subject in a more philosophical spirit. The Platonic Sokratês, being asked whether he believed the current Attic fable respecting the abduction of Oreithyia (daughter of Erechtheus) by Boreas, replies, in substance, – "It would not be strange if I disbelieved it, as the clever men do: I might then show my cleverness by saying that a gust of Boreas blew her down from the rocks above while she was at play, and that, having been killed in this manner, she was reported to have been carried off by Boreas. Such speculations are amusing enough, but they belong to men ingenious and busy-minded overmuch, and not greatly to be envied, if it be only for this reason, *that, after having set right one fable, they are under the necessity of applying the same process to a host of others –* Hippocentaurs, Chimæras, Gorgons, Pegasus, and numberless other monsters and incredibilities. A man, who, disbelieving these stories, shall try to find a probable basis for each of them, will display an ill-placed acuteness and take upon himself an endless burden, for which I at least have no leisure: accordingly I forego such researches, and believe in the current version of tht stories."

These remarks of Plato are valuable, not simply because they point out the uselessness of digging for a supposed basis of truth in the mythes, but because they at the same time suggest the true reason for mistrusting all such tentatives. The mythes form a class apart, abundant as well as peculiar. To remove any individual mythe from its own class into that of history or philosophy, by simple conjecture, and without any collateral evidence, is of no advantage, unless you can perform a similar process on the remainder. If the process be trustworthy, it ought to be applied to all: and *e converso,* if it be not applicable to all, it is not trustworthy as applied to any one specially; always assuming no special evidence to be accessible. To detach any individual mythe from the class to which it belongs, is to present it in an erroneous point of view: we have no choice except to admit them as they stand, by putting ourselves approximatively into the frame of mind of those for whom they were destined and to whom they appeared worthy of credit.

If Plato thus discountenances all attempts to transform the mythes by interpretation into history or philosophy, indirectly recognising the generic difference between them – we find substantially the same view pervading the elaborate precepts in his treatise on the Republic. He there regards the mythes, not as embodying either matter-of-fact or philosophical principle, but as portions of religious and patriotic faith, and instruments of ethical tuition. Instead of allowing the poets to frame them according to the impulses of their own genius, and with a view to immediate popularity, he directs the legislator to provide types of his own for the characters of the gods and heroes, and to suppress all such divine and heroic legends as are not in harmony with these pre-established canons. In the Platonic system, the mythes are not to be matters of history, nor yet of spontaneous or casual fiction, but of prescribed faith: he supposes that the people will believe, as a thing of course, what the poets circulate, and he therefore directs that the latter shall circulate nothing which does not tend to ennoble and improve the feelings. He conceives the mythes as stories composed to illustrate the general sentiments of the poets and the community, respecting the character and attributes of the gods and heroes, or respecting the social relations, and ethical duties as well as motives of mankind; hence the obligation upon the legislator to prescribe beforehand the types of character which shall be illustrated, and to restrain the poets from following out any opposing fancies. "Let us neither believe ourselves the exclaims), nor permit any one to circulate, that Thêseus son of Poseidôn and Peirithous son of Zeus, or any other hero or son of a god, could ever have brought themselves to commit abductions or other enormities each as are now falsely ascribed to them. We must compel the poets to say, either that such persons were not the sons of gods, or that they were not the perpetrators of such misdeeds."

Most of the mythes which the youth hear and repeat (according to Plato) are false, but some of them are true: the great and prominent mythes which appear in Homer and Hesiod are no less fictions than the rest. But fiction constitutes one of the indispensable instruments of mental training as well as truth; only the legislator must take care that the fiction so employed shall be beneficent and not mischievous. As the mischievous fictions (he says) take their rise from wrong preconceptions respecting the character of the gods and heroes, so the way to correct them is to enforce, by authorised compositions, the adoption of a more correct standard.

The comments which Plato has delivered with so much force in his Republic, and the enactments which he deduces from them, are in the main an expansion of that sentiment of condemnation, which he shared with so many other philosophers, towards a large portion of the Homeric and Hesiodic stories. The manner in which he has set forth this opinion, unfolds to us more clearly the real character of the mythical narratives. They are creations of the productive minds in the community, deduced from the supposed attributes of the gods and heroes: so Plato views them, and in such character he proposes to amend them. The legislator would cause to be prepared a better and truer picture of the fore-time, because he would start from truer (that is to say, more creditable) conceptions of the gods and heroes. For Plato rejects the mythes respecting Zeus and Hêrê, or Thesêus and Peirithous, not from any want of evidence, but because they are unworthy of gods and heroes: he proposes to call forth new mythes, which, though he admits them at the outset to be fiction, he knows will soon be received as true, and supply more valuable lessons of conduct.

We may consider, then, that Plato disapproves of the attempt to identify the old mythes either with exaggerated history or with disguised philosophy. He shares in the current faith, without any suspicion or criticism, as to Orpheus, Palamêdês, Dædalus, Amphiôn, Thesêus, Achillês, Cheirôn, and other mythical personages; but what chiefly fills his mind is, the inherited sentiment of deep reverence for these superhuman characters and for the age to which they belonged, – a sentiment sufficiently strong to render him not only an unbeliever in such legends as conflict with it, but also a deliberate creator of new legends for the purpose of expanding and gratifying it. The more we examine this sentiment, both in the mind of Plato as well as in that of the Greeks generally, the more shall we be convinced that it formed essentially and inseparably a portion of Hellenic religious faith. The mythe both presupposes, and springs out of, a settled basis, and a strong expansive force of religious, social, and patriotic feeling, operating upon a past which is little better than a blank as to positive knowledge. It resembles history, in so far as its form is narrative: it resembles philosophy, in so far as it is occasionally illustrative; but in its essence and substance, in the mental tendencies by which it is created as well as in those by which it is judged and upheld, it is a popularised expression of the divine and heroic faith of the people.

Grecian antiquity cannot be at all understood except in connection with Grecian religion. It begins with gods and it ends with historical men, the former being recognised not simply as gods, but as primitive ancestors, and connected with the latter by a long mythical genealogy, partly heroic and partly human. Now the whole value of such genealogies arises from their being taken entire: the god or hero at the top is in point of fact the most important member of the whole; for the length and continuity of the series arises from anxiety on the part of historical men to join themselves by a thread of descent with the being whom they worshipped in their gentile sacrifices. Without the ancestorial god, the whole pedigree would have become not only acephalous, but worthless and uninteresting. The pride of the Herakleids, Asklêpiads, Æakids, Nêleids, Dædalids, &c. was attached to the primitive eponymous hero and to the god from whom they sprung, not to the line of names, generally long and barren, through which the divine or heroic dignity gradually dwindled down into common manhood. Indeed, the length of the genealogy (as I have before remarked) was an evidence of the humility of the historical man, which led him to place himself at a respectful distance from the gods or heroes; for Hekatæus of Milêtus, who ranked himself as the fifteenth descendant of a god, might perhaps have accounted it an overweening impiety in any living man to claim a god for his immediate father.

The whole chronology of Greece, anterior to 776 B.C., consists of calculations founded upon these mythical genealogies, especially upon that of the Spartan kings and their descent from Hêraklês, – thirty years being commonly taken as the equivalent of a generation, or about three generations to a century. This process of computation was altogether illusory, as applying historical and chronological conditions to a case on which they had no bearing.

XVI. GRECIAN MYTHES, AS SEEN BY THE GREEKS.

Though the domain of history was seemingly enlarged, the religious element was tacitly set aside: when the heroes and gods were chronologised, they became insensibly approximated to the limits of humanity, and the process indirectly gave encouragement to the theory of Euêmerus. Personages originally legendary and poetical were erected into definite landmarks for measuring the duration of the fore-time, thus gaining in respect to historical distinctness, but not without loss on the score of religious association. Both Euêmerus and the subsequent Christian writers, who denied the original and inherent divinity of the pagan gods, had a great advantage in carrying their chronological researches strictly and consistently upwards – for all chronology fails as soon as we suppose a race superior to common humanity.

Moreover, it is to be remarked that the pedigree of the Spartan kings, which Apollodôrus and Eratosthenês selected as the basis of their estimate of time, is nowise superior in credibility and trustworthiness to the thousand other gentile and family pedigrees with which Greece abounded: it is rather indeed to be numbered among the most incredible of all, seeing that Hêraklês as a progenitor is placed at the head of perhaps more pedigrees than any other Grecian god or hero. The descent of the Spartan king Leonidas from Hêraklês rests upon no better evidence than that of Aristotle or Hippocratês from Asklêpius, – of Evagoras or Thucydidês from Æakus, – of Sokratês from Dædalus, – of the Spartan heraldic family from Talthybius, – of the prophetic Iamid family in Elis from Iamus, – of the root-gatherers in Pêlion from Cheirôn, – and of Hekatæus and his gens from some god in the sixteenth ascending line of the series. There is little exaggeration in saying, indeed, that no permanent combination of men in Greece, religious, social, or professional, was without a similar pedigree; all arising out of the same exigences of the feelings and imagination, to personify as well as to sanctify the bond of union among the members. Every one of these *gentes* began with a religious and ended with an historical person. At some point or other in the upward series, entities of history were exchanged for entities of religion; but where that point is to be found we are unable to say, nor had the wisest of the ancient Greeks any means of determining. Thus much, however, we know, that the series taken as a whole, though dear and precious to the believing Greek, possesses no value as chronological evidence to the historian.

When Hekatæus visited Thêbes in Egypt, he mentioned to the Egyptian priests, doubtless with a feeling of satisfaction and pride, the imposing pedigree of the gens to which he belonged, – with fifteen ancestors in ascending

249

249

line, and a god as the initial progenitor. But he found himself immeasurably overdone by the priests "who genealogised against him." They showed to him three hundred and forty-one wooden colossal statues, representing the succession of chief priests in the temple in uninterrupted series from father to son, through a space of 11,300 years. Prior to the commencement of this long period (they said), the gods dwelling along with men, had exercised sway in Egypt; but they repudiated altogether the idea of men begotten by gods or of heroes.

Both these counter genealogies, are, in respect to trustworthiness and evidence, on the same footing. Each represents partly the religious faith, partly the retrospective imagination, of the persons from whom it emanated: in each, the lower members of the series (to what extent we cannot tell) are real, the upper members fabulous; but in each also the series derived all its interest and all its imposing effect from being conceived unbroken and entire. Herodotus is much perplexed by the capital discrepancy between the Grecian and Egyptian chronologies, and vainly employs his ingenuity in reconciling them. There is no standard of objective evidence by which either the one or the other of them can be tried: each has its own subjective value, in conjunction with the faith and feelings of Egyptians and Greeks, and each presupposes in the believer certain mental prepossessions which are not to be found beyond its own local limits. Nor is the greater or less extent of duration at all important, when we once pass the limits of evidence and verifiable reality. One century of recorded time, adequately studded with authentic and orderly events, presents a greater mass and a greater difficulty of transition to the imagination than a hundred centuries of barren genealogy. Herodotus, in discussing the age of Homer and Hesiod, treats an anterior point of 400 years as if it were only yesterday: the reign of Henry VI. is separated from us by an equal interval, and the reader will not require to be reminded how long that interval now appears.

The mythical age was peopled with a mingled aggregate of gods, heroes, and men, so confounded together that it was often impossible to distinguish to which class any individual name belonged. In regard to the Thracian god Zalmoxis, the Hellespontic Greeks interpreted his character and attributes according to the scheme of Euemerism. They affirmed that he had been a man, the slave of the philosopher Pythagoras at Samos, and that he had by abilities and artifice established a religious ascendency over the minds of the Thracians, and obtained from them divine honours. Herodotus cannot bring himself to believe this story, but he frankly avows his inability to determine whether Zalmoxis was a god or a man, nor can he extricate himself from a similar embarrassment in respect to Dionysus and Pan. Amidst the confusion of the Homeric fight, the goddess Athênê confers upon Diomêdês the miraculous favour of dispelling the mist from his eyes, so as to enable him to discriminate gods from men; and nothing less than a similar miracle could enable a critical reader of the mythical narratives to draw an ascertained boundary-line between the two. The original hearers of the mythes felt neither surprise nor displeasure from this confusion of the divine with the human individual. They looked at the past with a film of faith over their eyes – neither knowing the value, nor desiring, the attainment, of an unclouded vision. The intimate companionship, and the occasional mistake of identity between gods and men, were in full harmony with their reverential retrospect. We accordingly, see the poet Ovid in his Fasti, when he undertakes the task of unfolding the legendary antiquities of early Rome, reacquiring, by the inspiration of Juno, the power of seeing gods and men in immediate vicinity and conjunct action, such as it existed before the development of the critical and historical sense.

To resume, in brief, what has been laid down in this and the preceding chapters respecting the Grecian mythes:

1. They are a special product of the imagination and feelings, radically distinct both from history and philosophy: they cannot be broken down and decomposed into the one, nor allegorised into the other. There are indeed some particular and even assignable mythes, which raise intrinsic presumption of an allegorising tendency; and there are doubtless some others, though not specially assignable, which contain portions of matter of fact, or names of real persons, embodied in them. But such matter of fact cannot be verified by any intrinsic mark, nor we are entitled to presume its existence in any given case unless some collateral evidence can be produced.

2. We are not warranted in applying to the mythical world the rules either of historical credibility or chronological sequence. Its personages are gods, heroes, and men, in constant juxtaposition and reciprocal sympathy: men, too, of whom we know a large proportion to be fictitious, and of whom we can never ascertain how many may have been real. No series of such personages can serve as materials for chronological calculation.

3. The mythes were originally produced in an age which had no records, no philosophy, no criticism, no canon of belief, and scarcely any tincture either of astronomy or geography – but which, on the other hand, was full of religious faith, distinguished for quick and susceptible imagination, seeing personal agents where we look only for objects and connecting laws: an age, moreover, eager for new narrative, accepting with the unconscious impressibility of children (the question of truth or falsehood being never formally raised) all which ran in harmony with its pre-existing feelings, and penetrable by inspired prophets and poets in the same proportion that it was indifferent to positive evidence. To such hearers did the primitive poet or story-teller address himself: it was the glory of his productive genius to provide suitable narrative expression for the faith and emotions which he shared in common with them, and the rich stock of Grecian mythes attests how admirably he performed his task. As the gods and the heroes formed the conspicuous object of national reverence, so the mythes were partly divine, partly heroic, partly both in one. The adventures of Achillês, Helen, and Diomêdês, of Œdipus and Adrastus, of Meleager and Althæa, of Jasôn and the Argô, were recounted by the same tongues, and accepted with the same unsuspecting confidence, as those of Apollo and Artemis, of Arês and Aphroditê, of Poseidôn and Hêraklês.

4. The time however came, when this plausibility ceased to be complete. The Grecian mind made an important advance, socially, ethically, and intellectually. Philosophy and history were constituted, prose writing and chronological records became familiar: a canon of belief more or less critical came to be tacitly recognised. Moreover, superior men profited more largely by the stimulus, and contracted habits of judging different from the vulgar: the god Elenchus (to use a personification of Menander) the giver and prover of truth, descended into their minds. Into the new intellectual medium, thus altered in its elements, and no longer uniform in its quality, the mythes descended by inheritance; but they were found, to a certain extent, out of harmony even with the feelings of the people, and altogether dissonant with those of instructed men. Yet the most superior Greek was still a Greek, cherishing the common reverential sentiment towards the fore-time of his country. Though he could neither believe nor respect the mythes as they stood, he was under an imperious mental necessity to transform them into a state worthy of his belief and respect. Whilst the literal mythe still continued to float among the poets and the people, critical men interpreted, altered, decomposed, and added, until they found something which satisfied their minds as a supposed real basis. They manufactured some dogmas of supposed original philosophy, and a long series of fancied history and chronology, retaining the mythical names and generations even when they were obliged to discard or recast the mythical events. The interpreted mythe was thus promoted into a reality, while the literal mythe was degraded into a fiction.

The habit of distinguishing the interpreted from the literal mythe has passed from the literary men of antiquity to those of the modern world, who have for the most part construed the divine mythes as allegorised philosophy, and the heroic mythes as exaggerated, adorned, and over-coloured history. The early ages of Greece have thus been peopled with quasi-historical persons and quasi-historical events, all extracted from the mythes after making certain allowances for poetical ornament. We must not treat this extracted product as if it were the original substance: we cannot properly understand it except by viewing it in connection with the literal mythes out of which it was obtained, in their primitive age and appropriate medium, before the superior minds had yet outgrown the common faith in an all-personified Nature, and learned to restrict the divine free-agency by the supposition of invariable physical laws. It is in this point of view that the mythes are important for any one who would correctly appreciate the general tone of Grecian thought and feeling; for they were the universal mental stock of the Hellenic world – common to men and women, rich and poor, instructed and ignorant: they were in every one's memory and in every one's mouth, while science and history were confined to comparatively few. We know from Thucydidês how erroneously and carelessly the Athenian public of his day retained the history of Peisistratus, only one century past; but the adventures of the gods and heroes, the numberless explanatory legends attached to visible objects and periodical ceremonies, were the theme of general talk, and any man unacquainted with there would have found himself partially excluded from the sympathy of his neighbours. The theatrical representations, exhibited to the entire city population, and listened to with enthusiastic interest, both presupposed and perpetuated acquaintance with the great lines of heroic fable. In later times even the pantomimic dancers embraced in their representations the whole field of mythical incident, and their immense success proves at once how popular and how well known such subjects were. The names and attributes of the heroes were incessantly alluded to in the way of illustration, to point out a consoling, admonitory, or repressive moral: the simple mention of any of them sufficed to call up in every one's mind the principal events of his life, and the poet or rhapsode could thus calculate on touching chords not less familiar than susceptible.

A similar effect was produced by the multiplied religious festivals and processions, as well as by the oracles and prophecies which circulated in every city. The annual departure of the Theôric ship from Athens to the sacred island of Dêlos, kept alive, in the minds of Athenians generally, the legend of Thesêus and his adventurous enterprise in Krête; and in like manner most of the other public rites and ceremonies were of a commemorative character, deduced from some mythical person or incident familiarly known to natives, and forming to strangers a portion of the curiosities of the place. During the period of Grecian subjection under the Romans, these curiosities, together with their works of art and their legends, were especially clung so as a set-off against present degradation. The Thêban citizen who found himself restrained from the liberty enjoyed by all other Greeks, of consulting Amphiaraüs as a prophet, though the sanctuary and chapel of the hero stood in his own city – could not be satisfied without a knowledge of the story which explained the origin of such prohibition, and which conducted him back to the originally hostile relations between Amphiaraüs and Thêbes. Nor can we suppose among the citizens of Sikyôn anything less than a perfect and reverential conception of the legend of Thêbes, when we read the account given by Herodotus of the conduct of the despot Kleisthenês in regard to Adrastus and Melanippus. The Trœzenian youths and maidens, who universally, when on the eve of marriage, consecrated an offering of their hair at the Herôon of Hippolytus, maintained a lively recollection of the legend of that unhappy recusant whom Aphroditê had so cruelly punished. Abundant relics preserved in many Grecian cities and temples, served both as mementos and attestations of other legendary events; and the tombs of the heroes counted among the most powerful stimulants of mythical reminiscence. The sceptre of Pelops and Agamemnôn, still preserved in the days of Pausanias at Chæroneia in Bœotia, was the work of the god Hêphæstos. While many other alleged productions of the same divine hand were preserved in different cities of Greece, this is the only one which Pausanias himself believed to be genuine: it had been carried by Elektra, daughter of Agememnôn to Phôkis, and received divine honours from the citizens of Chæroneia. The spears of Mêrionês and Odysseus were treasured up at Engyium in Sicily, that of Achilles at Phasêlis: the sword of Memnôn adorned the temple of Asklêpius at Nicomêdia: and Pausanias, with unsuspecting confidence, adduces the two latter as proofs that the arms of the heroes were made of brass. The hide of the Kalydonian boar was guarded and shown by the Tegeates as a precious possession: the shield of Euphorbus was in like manner suspended in the temple of Branchiæ near Milêtus, as well as in the temple of Hêrê in Argôs. Visible relics of Epeius and Philoktêtês were not wanting, while Strabo raises his voice with indignation against the numerous Palladia which were shown in different cities, each pretending to be the genuine image from Troy. It would be impossible to specify the number of chapels, sanctuaries, solemnities, foundations of one sort or another, said to have been first commenced by heroic or mythical personages, – by Hêraklês, Jasôn, Mêdea, Alkmæôn, Diomêdês, Odysseus, Danaus, and his daughters, &c. Perhaps in some of these cases particular critics might raise objections, but the great bulk of the people entertained a firm and undoubted belief in the current legend.

If we analyse the intellectual acquisitions of a common Grecian townsman, from the rude communities of Arcadia or Phôkis even up to the enlightened Athens, we shall find that, over and above the rules of art or capacities requisite for his daily wants, it consisted chiefly of the various mythes connected with his gens, his city, his religious festivals, and the mysteries in which he might have chosen to initiate himself, as well as with the works of art and the more striking natural objects which he might see around him, – the whole set off and decorated by some knowledge of the epic and dramatic poets. Such was the intellectual and imaginative reach of an ordinary Greek, considered apart from the instructed few: it was an aggregate of religion, of social and patriotic retrospect, and of romantic fancy, blended into one indivisible faith. Thus the subjective value of the mythes, looking at them purely as elements of Grecian thought and feeling, will appear indisputably great, however little there may be of objective reality, either historical or philosophical, discoverable under them.

Nor must we omit the incalculable importance of the mythes as stimulants to the imagination of the Grecian artist in sculpture, in painting, in carving, and in architecture. From the divine and heroic legends and personages were borrowed those paintings, statues, and reliefs, which rendered the temples, porticos, and public buildings, at Athens and elsewhere, objects of surpassing admiration; and such visible reproduction contributed again to fix the types of the gods and heroes familiarly and indelibly on the public mind. The figures delineated on cups and vases, as well as on the walls of private houses, were chiefly drawn from the same source – the mythes being the great storehouse of artistic scenes and composition.

To enlarge on the characteristic excellence of Grecian art would here be out of place: I regard it only in so far as, having originally drawn its materials from the mythes, it reacted upon the mythical faith and imagination – the reaction imparting strength to the former as well as distinctness to the latter. To one who saw constantly before him representations of the battles of the Centaurs or the Amazons, of the exploits performed by Perseus and Bellerophôn, of the incidents composing the Trojan war or the Kalydonian boar-hunt – the process of belief, even in the more fantastic of these conceptions, became easy in proportion as the conception was familiarised. If any person had been slow to believe in the efficacy of the prayers of Æakus, whereby that devout hero once obtained special relief from Zeus, at a moment when Greece was perishing with long-continued sterility, his doubts would probably vanish when, on visiting the Æakeium at Ægina, there were exhibited to him the statues of the very envoys who had come on the behalf of the distressed Greeks to solicit that Æakus would pray for them. A Grecian temple was not simply a place of worship, but the actual dwelling-place of a god, who was believed to be introduced by the solemn dedicatory ceremony, and whom the imagination of the people identified in the most intimate manner with his statue. The presence or removal of the statue was conceived as identical with that of the being represented, – and while the statue was solemnly washed, dressed, and tended with all the respectful solicitude which would have been bestowed upon a real person, miraculous tales were often rife respecting the manifestation of real internal feeling in the wood and the marble. At perilous or critical moments, the statue was affirmed to have sweated, to have wept, to have closed its eyes, or brandished the spear in its hands, in token of sympathy or indignation. Such legends, springing up usually in times of suffering and danger, and finding few men bold enough openly to contradict them, ran in complete harmony with the general mythical faith, and tended to strengthen it in all its various ramifications. The renewed nativity of the god or hero both brought to mind and accredited the pre-existing mythes connected with his name. When Boreas, during the invasion of Greece by Xerxês, and in compliance with the fervent prayers of the Athenians, had sent forth a providential storm, to the irreparable damage of the Persian armada, the sceptical minority (alluded to by Plato), who doubted the mythe of Boreas and Oreithyia, and his close connection thus acquired with Erechtheus, and the Erechtheids generally, must for the time have been reduced to absolute silence.

XVII. GRECIAN MYTHE COMPARED WITH MODERN EUROPE.

I have already remarked that the existence of that popular narrative talk, which the Germans express by the significant word *Sage* or *Volks-Sage,* in a greater or less degree of perfection or development, is a phenomenon common to almost all stages of society and to almost all quarters of the globe. It is the natural effusion of the unlettered, imaginative, and believing man, and its maximum of influence belongs to an early state of the human mind; for the multiplication of recorded facts, the diffusion of positive science, and the formation of a critical standard of belief, tend to discredit its dignity and to repress its easy and abundant flow. It supplies to the poet both materials to recombine and adorn, and a basis as well as a stimulus for further inventions of his own; and this at a time when the poet is religious teacher, historian, and philosopher, all in one, – not, as he becomes at a more advanced period, the mere purveyor of avowed, though interesting, fiction.

Such popular stories, and such historical songs (meaning by historical, simply that which is accepted as history) are found in most quarters of the globe, and especially among the Teutonic and Celtic populations of early Europe. The old Gothic songs were cast into a continuous history by the historian Ablavius; and the poems of the Germans respecting Tuisto the earth-born god, his son Mannus, and his descendants the eponyms of the various German tribes, as they are briefly described by Tacitus, remind us of Hesiod, or Eumêlus, or the Homeric Hymns. Jacob Grimm, in his learned and valuable Deutsche Mythologie, has exhibited copious evidence of the great fundamental analogy, along with many special differences, between the German, Scandinavian, and Grecian mythical world: and the Dissertation of Mr. Price (prefixed to his edition of Warton's History of English Poetry) sustains and illustrates Grimm's view. The same personifying imagination – the same ever-present conception of the will, sympathies, and antipathies of the gods as the producing causes of phenomena, and as distinguished from a course of nature with its invariable sequence – the same relations between gods, heroes, and men, with the like difficulty of discriminating the one from the other in many individual names – a similar wholesale transfer of human attributes to the gods, with the absence of human limits and liabilities – a like belief in Nymphs, Giants, and other beings, neither gods nor men – the same coalescence of the religious with the patriotic feeling and faith – these are positive features common to the early Greeks with the early Germans; and the negative conditions of the two are not less analogous – the absence of prose writing, positive records, and scientific culture. The preliminary basis and encouragements for the mythopœic faculty were thus extremely similar.

But though the prolific forces were the same in kind, the results were very different in degree, and the developing circumstances were more different still.

First, the abundance, the beauty, and the long continuance of early Grecian poetry, in the purely poetical age, is a phenomenon which has no parallel elsewhere.

Secondly, the transition of the Greek mind from its poetical to its comparatively positive state was self-operated, accomplished by its own inherent and expansive force – aided indeed, but by no means either impressed or provoked, from without. From the poetry of Homer, to the history of Thucydidês and the philosophy of Plato and Aristotle, was a prodigious step, but it was the native growth of the Hellenic youth into an Hellenic man: and what is of still greater moment, it was brought about without breaking the thread either of religious or patriotic tradition – without any coercive innovation or violent change in the mental feelings. The legendary world, though the ethical judgments and rational criticisms of superior men had outgrown it, still retained its hold upon their feelings as an object of affectionate and reverential retrospect.

Far different from this was the development of the early Germans. We know little about their early poetry, but we shall run no risk of error in affirming that they had nothing to compare with either Iliad or Odyssey. Whether, if left to themselves, they would have possessed sufficient progressive power to make a step similar to that of the Greeks, is a question which we cannot answer. Their condition, mental as well as political, was violently changed by a foreign action from without. The influence of the Roman empire introduced artificially among them new institutions, new opinions, habits, and luxuries, and, above all, a new religion: the Romanised Germans becoming themselves successively the instruments of this revolution with regard to such of their brethren as still remained heathen. It was a revolution often brought about by penal and coercive means: the old gods Thor and Woden were formally deposed and renounced, their images were crumbled into dust, and the sacred oaks of worship and prophecy hewn down. But even where conversion was the fruit of preaching and persuasion, it did not the less break up all the associations of a German with respect to that mythical world which he called his past, and of which the ancient gods constituted both the charm and the sanctity: he had now only the alternative of treating them either as men or as dæmons. That mixed religious and patriotic retrospect, formed by the coalescence of piety with ancestral feeling, which constituted the appropriate sentiment both of Greeks and of Germans towards their unrecorded antiquity, was among the latter banished by Christianity; and while the root of the old mythes was thus cankered, the commemorative ceremonies and customs with which they were connected, either lost their consecrated character or disappeared altogether. Moreover, new influences of great importance were at the same time brought to bear. The Latin language, together with some tinge of Latin literature – the habit of writing and of recording present events – the idea of a systematic law and pacific adjudication of disputes, – all these formed a part of the general working of Roman civilisation, even after the decline of the Roman empire, upon the Teutonic and Celtic tribes. A class of specially-educated men was formed, upon a Latin basis and upon Christian principles, consisting too almost entirely of priests, who were opposed, as well by motives of rivalry as by religious feeling, to the ancient bards and storytellers of the community: the "lettered men" were constituted apart from "the men of story," and Latin literature contributed along with religion to sink the mythes of untaught heathenism. Charlemagne, indeed, at the same time that he employed aggressive and violent proceedings to introduce Christianity among the Saxons, also took special care to commit to writing and preserve the old heathen songs. There can be little doubt that this step was the suggestion of a large and enlightened understanding peculiar to himself. The disposition general among lettered Christians of that age is more accurately represented by his son Louis le Débonnaire, who, having learned these songs as a boy, came to abhor them when he arrived at mature years, and could never be induced either to repeat or tolerate them.

According to the old heathen faith, the pedigree of the Saxon, Anglian, Danish, Norwegian, and Swedish kings, – probably also those of the German and Scandinavian kings generally, – was traced to Odin, or to some of his immediate companions or heroic sons. I have already observed that the value of these genealogies consisted not so much in their length, as in the reverence attached to the name serving as primitive source. After the worship attached to Odin had been extinguished, the genealogical line was lengthened up to Japhet or Noah, – and Odin, no longer accounted worthy to stand at the top, was degraded into one of the simple human members of it. And we find this alteration of the original mythical genealogies to have taken place even among the Scandinavians, although the introduction of Christianity was in those parts both longer deferred, so as to leave time for a more ample development of the heathen poetical vein – and seems to have created a less decided feeling of antipathy (especially in Iceland) towards the extinct faith. The poems and tales composing the Edda, though first committed to writing after the period of Christianity, do not present the ancient gods in a point of view intentionally odious or degrading.

The transposition above alluded to, of the genealogical root from Odin to Noah, is the more worthy of notice, as it illustrates the genuine character of these genealogies, and shows that they sprung, not from any erroneous historical data, but from the turn of the religious feeling; also that their true value is derived from their being taken entire, as connecting the existing race of men with a divine original. If we could imagine that Grecian paganism had been superseded by Christianity in the year 500 B.C., the great and venerated gentile genealogies of Greece would have undergone the like modification: the Herakleids, Pelopids, Æakids, Asklêpiads, &c. would have been merged in some larger aggregate branching out from the archaeology of the Old Testament. The old heroic legends connected with these ancestral names would either have been forgotten, or so transformed as to suit the new vein of thought: for the altered worship, ceremonies, and customs would have been altogether at variance with them, and the mythical feeling would have ceased to dwell upon those to whom prayers were no longer offered. If the oak of Dôdôna had been cut down, or the Theôric ship had ceased to be sent from Athens to Dêlos, the mythes of Thesêus and of the two black doves would have lost their pertinence, and died away. As it was, the change from Homer to Thucydidês and Aristotle took place internally, gradually, and imperceptibly. Philosophy and history went superinduced in the minds of the superior few, but the feelings of the general public continued unshaken – the sacred objects remained the same both to the eye and to the heart – and the worship of the ancient gods was even adorned by new architects and sculptors who greatly strengthened its imposing effect.

While then in Greece the mythopœic stream continued in the same course, only with abated current and influence, in modern Europe its ancient bed was blocked up, and it was turned into new and divided channels. The old religion – though as an ascendent faith, unanimously and publicly manifested, it became extinct – still continued in detached scraps and fragments, and under various alterations of name and form. The heathen gods and goddesses, deprived as they were of divinity, did not pass out of the recollection and fears of their former worshippers, but were sometimes represented (on principles like those of

XVII. GRECIAN MYTHE COMPARED WITH MODERN EUROPE.

Euêmerus) as having been eminent and glorious men – sometimes degraded into dæmons, magicians, elfs, fairies, and other supernatural agents, of an inferior grade and generally mischievous cast. Christian writers, such as Saxo Grammaticus and Snorro Sturleson, committed to writing the ancient oral songs of the Scandinavian Scalds, and digested the events contained in them into continuous narrative – performing in this respect a task similar to that of the Grecian logographers Pherekydês and Hellanikus, in reference to Hesiod and the Cyclic poets. But while Pherekydês and Hellanikus compiled under the influence of feelings substantially the same as those of the poets on whom they bestowed their care, the Christian logographers felt it their duty to point out the Odin and Thor of the old Scalds as evil dæmons, or cunning enchanters, who had fascinated the minds of men into a false belief in their divinity. In some cases, the heathen recitals and ideas were modified so as to suit Christian feeling. But when preserved without such a change, they exhibited themselves palpably, and were designated by their compilers, as at variance with the religious belief of the people, and as associated either with imposture or with evil spirits.

A new vein of sentiment had arisen in Europe, unsuitable indeed to the old mythes, yet leaving still in force the demand for mythical narrative generally. And this demand was satisfied, speaking generally, by two classes of narratives, – the legends of the Catholic Saints and the Romances of Chivalry, corresponding to two types of character, both perfectly accommodated to the feelings of the time, – the saintly ideal and the chivalrous ideal.

Both these two classes of narrative correspond, in character as well as in general purpose, to the Grecian mythes – being stories accepted as realities, from their full conformity with the predispositions and deep-seated faith of an uncritical audience, and prepared beforehand by their authors, not with any reference to the conditions of historical proof, but for the purpose of calling forth sympathy, emotion, or reverence. The type of the saintly character belongs to Christianity, being the history of Jesus Christ as described in the gospels, and that of the prophets in the Old Testament; whilst the lives of holy men who acquired a religious reputation from the fourth to the fourteenth century of the Christian sera, were invested with attributes, and illustrated with ample details, tending to assimilate them to this revered model. The numerous miracles, the cure of diseases, the expulsion of dæmons, the temptations and sufferings, the teachings and commands, with which the biography of Catholic saints abounds, grew chiefly out of this pious feeling, common to the writer and to his readers. Many of the other incidents, recounted in the same performances, take their rise from misinterpreted allegories, from ceremonies and customs of which it was pleasing to find a consecrated origin, or from the disposition to convert the etymology of a name into matter of history: many have also been suggested by local peculiarities, and by the desire of stimulating or justifying the devotional emotions of pilgrims who visited some consecrated chapel or image. The dove was connected, in the faith of the age, with the Holy Ghost, the serpent with Satan: lions, wolves, stags, unicorns, &c. were the subjects of other emblematic associations; and such modes of belief found expression for themselves in many narratives which brought the saints into conflict or conjoint action with these various animals. Legends of this kind, so indefinitely multiplied and so pre-eminently popular and affecting, in the Middle Ages, are not exaggerations of particular matters of fact, but emanations in detail of some current faith or feeling, which they served to satisfy, and by which they were in turn amply sustained and accredited.

Readers of Pausanias will recognise the great general analogy between the stories recounted to him at the temples which he visited, and these legends of the Middle Ages. Though the type of character which the latter illustrate is indeed materially different, yet the source as well as the circulation, the generating as well as the sustaining forces, were in both cases the same. Such legends were the natural growth of a religious faith, earnest, un-examining, and interwoven with the feelings at a time when the reason does not need to be cheated. The lives of the Saints bring us even back to the simple and ever-operative theology of the Homeric age: so constantly is the hand of God exhibited even in the minutest details, for the succour of a favoured individual, – so completely is the scientific point of view, respecting the phenomena of nature, absorbed into the religious. During the intellectual vigour of Greece and Rome, a sense of the invariable course of nature and of the scientific explanation of phenomena had been created among the superior minds, and through them indirectly among the remaining community; thus limiting to a certain extent the ground open to be occupied by a religious legend. With the decline of the pagan literature and philosophy, before the sixth century of the Christian æra, this scientific conception gradually passed out of sight, and left the mind free to a religious interpretation of nature not less simple and *naïf* than that which had prevailed under the Homeric paganism. The great religious movement of the Reformation, and the gradual formation of critical and philosophical habits in the modern mind, have caused these legends of the Saints, – once the charm and cherished creed of a numerous public, to pass altogether out of credit, without even being regarded, among Protestants at least, as worthy of a formal scrutiny into the evidence, – a proof of the transitory value of public belief, however sincere and fervent, as a certificate of historical truth, if it be blended with religious predispositions.

The same mythopœic vein, and the same susceptibility and facility of belief, which had created both supply and demand for the legends of the Saints, also provided the abundant stock of romantic narrative poetry, in amplification and illustration of the chivalrous ideal. What the legends of Troy, of Thêbes, of the Kalydonian boar, of Œdipus, Thesêus, &c. were to an early Greek, the tales of Arthur, of Charlemagne, of the Niebelungen, were to an Englishman, or Frenchman, or German, of the twelfth or thirteenth century. They were neither recognised fiction nor authenticated history: they were history, as it is felt and welcomed by minds unaccustomed to investigate evidence, and unconscious of the necessity of doing so. That the Chronicle of Turpin, a mere compilation of poetical legends respecting Charlemagne, was accepted as genuine history, and even pronounced to be such by papal authority, is well known; and the authors of the Romances announce themselves, not less than those of the old Grecian epic, as being about to recount real matter of fact. It is certain that Charlemagne is a great historical name, and it is possible, though not certain, that the name of Arthur may be historical also. But the Charlemagne of history, and the Charlemagne of romance, have little except the name in common nor could we ever determine, except by independent evidence (which in this case we happen to possess), whether Charlemagne was a real or a fictitious person. That illustrious name, as well as the more problematical Arthur, is taken up by the romancers, not with a view to celebrate realities previously verified, but for the purpose of setting forth or amplifying an ideal of their own, in such manner as both to rouse the feelings and captivate the faith of their hearers.

To inquire which of the personages of the Carlovingian epic were real and which were fictitious, – to examine whether the expedition ascribed to Charlemagne against Jerusalem had ever taken place or not, – to separate truth from exaggeration in the exploits of the Knights of the Round Table, – these were problems which an audience of that day had neither disposition to undertake nor means to resolve. They accepted the narrative as they heard it, without suspicion or reserve: the incidents related, as well as the connecting links between them, were in full harmony with their feelings, and gratifying as well to their sympathies as to their curiosity: nor was anything farther wanting to induce them to believe it, though the historical basis might be ever so slight or even non-existent.

The romances of chivalry represented, to those who heard them, real deeds of the fore-time – "glories of the foregone men," to use the Hesiodic expression —at the same time that they embodied and filled up the details of an heroic ideal, such as that age could conceive and admire – a fervent piety, combined with strength, bravery, and the love of adventurous aggression, directed sometimes against infidels, sometimes against enchanters or monsters, sometimes in defence of the fair sex. Such characteristics were naturally popular, in a century of feudal struggles and universal insecurity, when the grand subjects of common respect and interest were the Church and the Crusades, and when the latter especially were embraced with an enthusiasm truly astonishing.

The long German poem of the Niebelungen Lied, as well as the Volsunga Saga and a portion of the songs of the Edda, relate to a common fund of mythical, superhuman personages, and of fabulous adventure, identified with the earliest antiquity of the Teutonic and Scandinavian race, and representing their primitive sentiment towards ancestors of divine origin. Sigurd, Brynhilde, Gudrun, and Atle, are mythical characters celebrated as well by the Scandinavian Scalds as by the German epic poets, but with many varieties and separate additions to distinguish the one from the other. The German epic, later and more elaborated, includes various persons not known to the songs in the Edda, in particular the prominent name of Dieterich of Bern – presenting, moreover, the principal characters and circumstances as Christian, while in the Edda there is no trace of anything but heathenism. There is, indeed, in this the old and heathen version, a remarkable analogy with many points of Grecian mythical narrative. As in the ease of the short life of Achillês, and of the miserable Labdakids of Thêbes – so in the family of the Volsungs, though sprung from and protected by the gods – a curse of destiny hangs upon them and brings on their ruin, in spite of pre-eminent personal qualities. The more thoroughly this old Teutonic story has been traced and compared, in its various transformations and accompaniments, the less can any well-established connection be made out for it with authentic historical names or events. We must acquiesce in its personages as distinct in original conception from common humanity, and as belonging to the subjective mythical world of the race by whom they were sung.

Such were the compositions which not only interested the emotions, but also satisfied the un-distinguishing historical curiosity, of the ordinary public in the middle ages. The exploits of many of these romantic heroes resemble in several points those of the Grecian: the adventures of Perseus, Achillês, Odysseus, Atalanta, Bellerophôn, Jasôn, and the Trojan war, or Argônautic expedition generally, would have fitted in perfectly to the Carlovingian or other epics of the period. That of the middle ages, like the Grecian, was eminently expansive in its nature. New stories were successively attached to the names and companions of Charlemagne and Arthur, just as the legend of Troy was enlarged by Arktinus, Leschês, and Stesichorus, – that of Thêbes, by fresh miseries entailed on the fated head of Œdipus, – and that of the Kalydônian boar, by the addition of Atalanta. Altogether, the state of mind of the hearers seems in both cases to have been much the same, – eager for emotion and sympathy, and receiving any narrative attuned to their feelings, not merely with hearty welcome, but also with unsuspecting belief.

Nevertheless, there were distinctions deserving of notice, which render the foregoing proposition more absolutely exact with regard to Greece than with regard to the middle ages. The tales of the epic, and the mythes in their most popular and extended signification, were the only intellectual nourishment with which the Grecian public was supplied, until the sixth century before the Christian æra: there was no prose writing, no history, no philosophy. But such was not exactly the case at the time when the epic of the middle ages appeared. At that time, a portion of society possessed the Latin language, the habit of writing, and some tinge both of history and philosophy: there were a series of chronicles, scanty, indeed, and imperfect, but referring to contemporary events and preventing the real history of the past from passing into oblivion: there were even individual scholars, in the twelfth century, whose acquaintance with Latin literature was sufficiently considerable to enlarge their minds and to improve their judgments. Moreover, the epic of the middle ages, though deeply imbued with religious ideas, was not directly amalgamated with the religion of the people, and did not always find favour with the clergy; while the heroes of the Grecian epic were not only linked in a thousand ways with existing worship, practices, and sacred localities, but Homer and Hesiod pass with Herodotus for the constructors of Grecian theology. We thus see that the ancient epic was both exempt from certain distracting influences by which that of the middle ages was surrounded, and more closely identified with the veins of thought and feeling prevalent in the Grecian public. Yet these counteracting influences did not prevent Pope Calixtus II. from declaring the Chronicle of Turpin to be a genuine history.

Brute the Trojan.

If we take the history of England as it was conceived and written from the twelfth to the seventeenth century by Hardyng, Fabyan, Grafton, Hollinshed, and others, we shall find that it was supposed to begin with Brute the Trojan, and was carried down from thence, for many ages and through a long succession of kings, to the times of Julius Caesar. A similar belief of descent from Troy, arising seemingly from a reverential imitation of the Romans and of their Trojan origin, was cherished in the fancy of other European nations. With regard to the English, the chief circulator of it was Geoffrey of Monmouth, and it passed with little resistance or dispute into the national faith – the kings from Brute downward being enrolled in regular chronological series with their respective dates annexed. In a dispute which took place during the reign of Edward I. (A.D. 1301) between England and Scotland, the descent of the kings of England from Brute the Trojan was solemnly embodied in a document put forth to sustain the rights of the crown of England, as an argument bearing on the case then in discussion; and it passed without attack from the opposing party, – an incident which reminds us of the appeal made by Æschinês, in the contention between the Athenians and Philip of Macedôn, respecting Amphipolis, to the primitive dotal rights of Akamas son of Theseûs – and also of the defence urged by the Athenians to sustain their conquest of Sigeium, against the reclamations of the Mityleneans, wherein the former alleged that they had as much right to the place as any of the other Greeks who had formed part of the victorious armament of Agamemnôn.

The tenacity with which this early series of British kings was defended, is no less remarkable than the facility with which it was admitted. The chroniclers at the beginning of the seventeenth century warmly protested against the intrusive scepticism which would cashier so many venerable sovereigns and efface so many noble deeds. They appealed to the patriotic feelings of their hearers, represented the enormity of thus setting up a presumptuous criticism against the belief of ages, and insisted on the danger of the precedent as regarded history generally. How this controversy stood, at the time and in the view of the illustrious author of Paradise Lost, I shall give in his own words, as they appear in the second page of his History of England. After having briefly touched upon the stories of Samothes son of Japhet, Albion son of Neptune, &c., he proceeds:

XVII. GRECIAN MYTHE COMPARED WITH MODERN EUROPE.

"But now of Brutus and his line, with the whole progeny of kings to the entrance of Julius Caesar, we cannot so easily be discharged: descents of ancestry long continued, law and exploits not plainly seeming to be borrowed or devised, which on the common belief have wrought no small impression: *defended by many, denied utterly by few.* For what though Brutus and the whole Trojan pretence were yielded up, seeing they, who first devised to bring us some noble ancestor, were content at first with Brutus the Consul, till better invention, though not willing to forego the name, taught them to remove it higher into a more fabulous age, and by the same remove lighting on the Trojan tales, in affectation to make the Briton of one original with the Roman, pitched there: *Yet those old and inborn kings, never any to have been real persons, or done in their lives at least some part of what so long hath been remembered, cannot be thought without too strict incredulity.* For these, and those causes above mentioned, that which hath received approbation from so many, I have chosen not to omit. Certain or uncertain, be that upon the credit of those whom I must follow: *so far as keeps aloof from impossible or absurd,* attested by ancient writers from books more ancient, I refuse not, as the due and proper subject of story."

Yet in spite of the general belief of so many centuries – in spite of the concurrent persuasion of historians and poets – in spite of the declaration of Milton, extorted from his feelings rather than from his reason, that this long line of quasi-historical kings and exploits could not be *all* unworthy of belief – in spite of so large a body of authority and precedent, the historians of the nineteenth century begin the history of England with Julius Cæsar. They do not attempt either to settle the date of king Bladud's accession, or to determine what may be the basis of truth in the affecting narrative of Lear. The standard of historical credibility, especially with regard to modem events, has indeed been greatly and sensibly failed within the last hundred years.

In regard to ancient Grecian history, the rules of evidence still continue relaxed. The dictum of Milton, regarding the ante-Cæsarian history of England, still represents pretty exactly the feeling now prevalent respecting the mythical history of Greece: "Yet those old and inborn kings (Agamemnôn, Achillês, Odysseus, Jasôn, Adrastus, Amphiaraüs, Meleager, &c.), never any to have been real persons, or done in their lives at least some part of what so long hath been remembered, cannot be thought without too strict incredulity." Amidst much fiction (we are still told), there must be some truth; but how is such truth to be singled out? Milton does not even attempt to make the severance: he contents himself with "keeping aloof from the impossible and the absurd," and ends in a narrative which has indeed the merit of being sober-coloured, but which he never for a moment thinks of recommending to his readers as true. So in regard to the legends of Greece, – Troy, Thêbes, the Argonauts, the Boar of Kalydôn, Hêraklês, Thesêus, Œdipus, – the conviction still holds in men's minds, that there must be something true at the bottom: and many readers of this work may be displeased, I fear, not to see conjured up before them the Eidôlon of an authentic history, even though the vital spark of evidence be altogether wanting.

I presume to think that our great poet has proceeded upon mistaken views with respect to the old British fables, not less in that which he leaves out than in that which he retains. To omit the miraculous and the fantastic, (it is that which he really meant by "the impossible and the absurd,") is to suck the life-blood out of these once popular narratives, – to divest them at once both of their genuine distinguishing mark, and the charm by which they acted on the feelings of believers. Still less ought we to consent to break up and disenchant in a similar manner the mythes of ancient Greece, – partly because they possess the mythical beauties and characteristics in far higher perfection, partly because they sank deeper into the mind of a Greek, and pervaded both the public and private sentiment of the country to a much greater degree than the British fables in England.

Two courses, and two only, are open; either to pass over the mythes altogether, which is the way in which modern historians treat the old British fables, or else to give an account of them as mythes; to recognise and respect their specific nature, and to abstain from confounding them with ordinary and certifiable history. There are good reasons for pursuing this second method in reference to the Grecian mythes; and when so considered, they constitute an important chapter in the history of the Grecian mind, and indeed in that of the human race generally. The historical faith of the Greeks, as well as that of other people, in reference to early and unrecorded times, is as much subjective and peculiar to themselves as their religious faith: among the Greeks, especially, the two are confounded with an intimacy which nothing less than great violence can disjoin. Gods, heroes, and men – religion and patriotism – matters divine, heroic, and human – were all woven together by the Greeks into one indivisible web, in which the threads of truth and reality, whatever they might originally have been, were neither intended to be, nor were actually, distinguishable. Composed of such; and animated by the electric spark of genius, the mythical antiquities of Greece formed a whole at once trustworthy and captivating to the faith and feelings of the people; but neither trustworthy nor captivating, when we sever it from these subjective conditions, and expose its naked elements to the scrutiny of an objective criticism. Moreover, the separate portions of Grecian mythical fore-time ought to be considered with reference to that aggregate of which they form a part: to detach the divine from the heroic legends, or some one of the heroic legends from the remainder, as if there were an essential and generic difference between them, is to present the whole under an erroneous point of view. The mythes of Troy and Thêbes are no more to be handled objectively, with a view to detect an historical base, than those of Zeus in Krête, of Apollo and Artemis in Delos, of Hermês, or of Promêtheus. To single out the Siege of Troy from the other mythes, as if it were entitled to pre-eminence as an ascertained historical and chronological event, is a proceeding which destroys the true character and coherence of the mythical world: we only transfer the story (as has been remarked in the preceding chapter) from a class with which it is connected by every tie both of common origin and fraternal affinity, to another with which it has no relationship, except such as violent and gratuitous criticism may enforce.

By drawing this marked distinction between the mythical and the historical world, – between matter appropriate only for subjective history, and matter in which objective evidence is attainable, – we shall only carry out to its proper length the just and well-known position long ago laid down by Varro. That learned man recognised three distinguishable periods in the time preceding his own age: "First, the time from the beginning of mankind down to the first deluge: a time wholly unknown. Secondly, the period from the first deluge down to the first Olympiad, which is called *the mythical period,* because many fabulous things are recounted in it. Thirdly, the time from the first Olympiad down to ourselves, which is called *the historical period,* because the things done in it are comprised in true histories."

Taking the commencement of true or objective history at the point indicated by Varro, I still consider the mythical and historical periods to be separated by a wider gap than he would have admitted. To select any one year as an absolute point of commencement, is of course not to be understood literally; but in point of fact, this is of very little importance in reference to the present question, seeing that the great mythical events – the sieges of Thêbes and Troy, the Argônautic expedition, the Kalydônian boar-hunt, the Return of the Herakleids,

&c. – are all placed long anterior to the first Olympiad, by those who have applied chronological boundaries to the mythical narratives. The period immediately preceding the first Olympiad is one exceedingly barren of events: the received chronology recognises four hundred years, and Herodotus admitted five hundred years, from that date back to the Trojan war.

XVIII. LAST DAYS OF LEGENDARY GREECE. - DARKNESS
BEFORE HISTORICAL GREECE.

I. Return of the Herakleids into Peloponnesus.

In one of the preceding chapters, we have traced the descending series of the two most distinguished mythical families in Peloponnêsus, – the Perseids and the Pelopids: we have followed the former down to Hêraklês and his son Hyllus, and the latter down to Orestês son of Agamemnôn, who is left in possession of that ascendancy in the peninsula which had procured for his father the chief command in the Trojan war. The Herakleids, or sons of Hêraklês, on the other hand, are expelled fugitives, dependent upon foreign aid or protection: Hyllus had perished in single combat with Echemus of Tegea, (connected with the Pelopids by marriage with Timandra sister of Klytæmnêstra), and a solemn compact had been made, as the preliminary condition of this duel, that no similar attempt at an invasion of the peninsula should be undertaken by his family for the space of one hundred years. At the end of the stipulated period the attempt was renewed, and with complete success; but its success was owing, not so much to the valour of the invaders as to a powerful body of new allies. The Herakleids re-appear as leaders and companions of the Dorians, – a northerly section of the Greek name, who now first come into importance, – poor, indeed, in mythical renown, since they are never noticed in the Iliad, and only once casually mentioned in the Odyssey, as a fraction among the many-tongued inhabitants of Krête, – but destined to form one of the grand and predominant elements throughout all the career of historical Hellas.

The son of Hyllus – Kleodæus – as well as his grandson Aristomachus, were now dead, and the lineage of Hêraklês was represented by the three sons of the latter, – Têmenus, Kresphontês, and Aristodêmus, and under their conduct the Dorians penetrated into the peninsula. The mythical account traced back this intimate union between the Herakleids and the Dorians to a prior war, in which Hêraklês himself had rendered inestimable aid to the Dorian king Ægimius, when the latter was hard pressed in a contest with the Lapithæ. Hêraklês defeated the Lapithæ, and slew their king Korônus; in return for which Ægimius assigned to his deliverer one third part of his whole territory, and adopted Hyllus as his son. Hêraklês desired that the territory thus made over might be held in reserve until a time should come when his descendants might stand in need of it; and that time did come, after the death of Hyllus, (see Chap. V.) Some of the Herakleids then found shelter at Trikorythus in Attica, but the remainder, turning their steps towards Ægimius, solicited from him the allotment of land which had been promised to their valiant progenitor. Ægimius received them according to his engagement, and assigned to them the stipulated third portion of his territory. From this moment the Herakleids and Dorians became intimately united together into one social communion. Pamphylus and Dymas, sons of Ægimius, accompanied Têmenus and his two brothers in their invasion of Peloponnêsus.

Such is the mythical incident which professes to explain the origin of those three tribes into which all the Dorian communities were usually divided, – the Hyllêis, the Phamphyli, and the Dymanes, – the first of the three including certain particular families, such as that of the kings of Sparta, who bore the special name of Herakleids. Hyllus, Pamphylus, and Dymas are the eponymous heroes of the three Dorian tribes.

Têmenus and his two brothers resolved to attack Peloponnêsus, not by a land-march along the Isthmus, such as that in which Hyllus had been previously slain, but by sea, across the narrow inlet between the promontories of Rhium and Antirrhium, with which the Gulf of Corinth commences. According to one story, indeed, – which, however, does not seem to have been known to Herodotus, – they are said to have selected this line of march by the express direction of the Delphian god, who vouchsafed to expound to them an oracle which had been delivered to Hyllus in the ordinary equivocal phraseology. Both the Ozolian Lokrians, and the Ætolians, inhabitants of the northern coast of the Gulf of Corinth, were favourable to the enterprise, and the former granted to them a port for building their ships, from which memorable circumstance the port ever afterwards bore the name of Naupaktus. Aristodêmus was here struck with lightning and died, leaving twin sons, Eurysthenês and Proklês; but his remaining brothers continued to press the expedition with alacrity.

At this juncture, an Akarnanian prophet named Karnus presented himself in the camp under the inspiration of Apollo, and uttered various predictions: he was, however, so much suspected of treacherous collusion with the Peloponnesians, that Hippotês, great-grandson of Hêraklês through Phylas and Antiochus, slew him. His death drew upon the army the wrath of Apollo,

XVIII. LAST DAYS OF LEGENDARY GREECE. - DARKNESS BEFORE HISTORICAL GREECE.

who destroyed their vessels and punished them with famine. Têmenus, in his distress, again applying to the Delphian god for succour and counsel, was made acquainted with the cause of so much suffering, and was directed to banish Hippotês for ten years, to offer expiatory sacrifice for the death of Karnus, and to seek as the guide of the army a man with three eyes. On coming back to Naupaktus, he met the Ætolian Oxylus, son of Andræmôn, returning to his country, after a temporary exile in Elis, incurred for homicide: Oxylus had lost one eye, but as he was seated on a horse, the man and the horse together made up the three eyes required, and he was adopted as the guide prescribed by the oracle. Conducted by him, they refitted their ships, landed on the opposite coast of Achaia, and marched to attack Tisamenus son of Orestês, then the great potentate of the peninsula. A decisive battle was fought, in which the latter was vanquished and slain, and in which Pamphylus and Dymas also perished. This battle made the Dorians so completely masters of the Peloponnêsus, that they proceeded to distribute the territory among themselves. The fertile land of Elis had been by previous stipulation reserved for Oxylus, as a recompense for his services as conductor; and it was agreed that the three Herakleids, – Têmenus, Kresphontês, and the infant sons of Aristodêmus, – should draw lots for Argôs, Sparta, and Messênê. Argôs fell to Têmenus, Sparta to the sons of Aristodêmus, and Messênê to Kresphontês; the latter having secured for himself this prize, the most fertile territory of the three, by the fraud of putting into the vessel out of which the lots were drawn, a lump of clay instead of a stone, whereby the lots of his brothers were drawn out while his own remained inside. Solemn sacrifices were offered by each upon this partition; but as they proceeded to the ceremony, a miraculous sign was seen upon the altar of each of the brothers, – a toad corresponding to Argôs, a serpent to Sparta, and a fox to Messênê. The prophets, on being consulted, delivered the import of these mysterious indications: the toad, as an animal slow and stationary, was an evidence that the possessor of Argôs would not succeed in enterprises beyond the limits of his own city; the serpent denoted the aggressive and formidable future reserved to Sparta; the fox prognosticated a career of wile and deceit to the Messênian.

Such is the brief account given by Apollodôrus of the Return of the Herakleids, at which point we pass, as if touched by the wand of a magician, from mythical to historical Greece. The story bears on the face of it the stamp, not of history, but of legend – abridged from one or more of the genealogical poets, and presenting such an account as they thought satisfactory, of the first formation of the great Dorian establishments in Peloponnêsus, as well as of the semi-Ætolian Elis. Its incidents are so conceived as to have an explanatory bearing on Dorian institutions, – upon the triple division of tribes, characteristic of the Dorians, – upon the origin of the great festival of the Karneia at Sparta, alleged to be celebrated in expiation of the murder of Karnus, – upon the different temper and character of the Dorian states among themselves, – upon the early alliance of the Dorians with Elis, which contributed to give ascendency and vogue to the Olympic games, – upon the reverential dependence of Dorians towards the Delphian oracle, – and, lastly, upon the etymology of the name Naupaktus. If we possessed the narrative more in detail, we should probably find many more examples of colouring of the legendary past suitable to the circumstances of the historical present.

Above all, this legend makes out in favour of the Dorians and their kings a mythical title to their Peloponnesian establishments; Argôs, Sparta, and Messênê are presented as rightfully belonging, and restored by just retribution, to the children of Hêraklês. It was to them that Zeus had specially given the territory of Sparta; the Dorians came in as their subjects and auxiliaries. Plato gives a very different version of the legend, but we find that he, too, turns the story in such a manner as to embody a claim of right on the part of the conquerors. According to him, the Achæans, who returned from the capture of Troy, found among their fellow-citizens at home – the race which had grown up during their absence – an aversion to re-admit them: after a fruitless endeavour to make good their rights, they were at last expelled, but not without much contest and bloodshed. A leader named Dorieus, collected all these exiles into one body, and from him they received the name of Dorians instead of Achæans; then marching back, under the conduct of the Herakleids into Peloponnêsus, they recovered by force the possessions from which they had been shut out, and constituted the three Dorian establishments under the separate Herakleid brothers, at Argôs, Sparta, and Messênê. These three fraternal dynasties were founded upon a scheme of intimate union and sworn alliance one with the other, for the purpose of resisting any attack which might be made upon them from Asia, either by the remaining Trojans or by their allies. Such is the story as Plato believed it; materially different in the incidents related, yet analogous in

XVIII. LAST DAYS OF LEGENDARY GREECE. - DARKNESS BEFORE HISTORICAL GREECE.

mythical feeling, and embodying alike the idea of a rightful reconquest. Moreover, the two accounts agree in representing both the entire conquest and the triple division of Dorian Peloponnêsus as begun and completed in one and the same enterprise, – so as to constitute one single event, which Plato would probably have called the Return of the Achæans, but which was commonly known as the Return of the Herakleids. Though this is both inadmissible and inconsistent with other statements which approach close to the historical times, yet it bears every mark of being the primitive view originally presented by the genealogical poets. The broad way in which the incidents are grouped together, was at once easy for the imagination to follow, and impressive to the feelings.

The existence of one legendary account must never be understood as excluding the probability of other accounts, current at the same time, but inconsistent with it; and many such there were as to the first establishment of the Peloponnesian Dorians. In the narrative which I have given from Apollodôrus, conceived apparently under the influence of Dorian feelings, Tisamenus is stated to have been slain in the invasion. According to another narrative, which seems to have found favour with the historical Achæans on the north coast of Peloponnêsus, Tisamenus, though expelled by the invaders from his kingdom of Sparta or Argôs, was not slain; he was allowed to retire under agreement, together with a certain portion of his subjects, and he directed his steps towards the coast of Peloponnêsus south of the Corinthian Gulf, then occupied by the Iônians. As there were relations, not only of friendship, but of kindred origin, between Iônians and Achæans, (the eponymous heroes Iôn and Achæus pass for brothers, both sons of Xuthus, (Tisamenus solicited from the Ionians admission for himself and his fellow-fugitives into their territory. The leading Ionians declining this request, under the apprehension that Tisamenus might be chosen as sovereign over the whole, the latter accomplished his object by force. After a vehement struggle, the Ionians were vanquished and put to flight, and Tisamenus thus acquired possession of Helikê, as well as of the northern coast of the peninsula, westward from Sikyôn; which coast continued to be occupied by the Achæans, and received its name from them, throughout all the historical times. The Ionians retired to Attica, many of them taking part in what is called the Ionic emigration to the coast of Asia Minor, which followed shortly after. Pausanias, indeed, tells us that Tisamenus, having gained a

275

decisive victory over the Ionians, fell in the engagement, and did not himself live to occupy the country of which his troops remained masters. This story of the death of Tisamenus seems to arise from a desire, on the part of Pausanias, to blend together into one narrative two discrepant legends; at least the historical Achæans in later times continued to regard Tisamenus himself as having lived and reigned in their territory, and as having left a regal dynasty which lasted down to Ogygês, after whom it was exchanged for a popular government.

The conquest of Têmenus, the eldest of the three Herakleids, originally comprehended only Argôs and its neighbourhood; it was from thence that Trœzen, Epidaurus, Ægina, Sikyôn, and Phlius were successfully occupied by Dorians, the sons and son-in-law of Têmenus – Dêiphontês, Phalkês, and Keisus – being the leaders under whom this was accomplished. At Sparta, the success of the Dorians was furthered by the treason of a man named Philonomus, who received as recompense the neighbouring town and territory of Amyklæ. Messênia is said to have submitted without resistance to the dominion of the Herakleid Kresphontês, who established his residence at Stenyklarus: the Pylian Melanthus, then ruler of the country, and representative of the great mythical lineage of Nêleus and Nestôr, withdrew with his household gods and with, a portion of his subjects to Attica.

The only Dorian establishment in the peninsula not directly connected with the triple partition is Corinth, which is said to have been Dorised somewhat later and under another leader, though still a Herakleid. Hippotês – descendant of Hêraklês in the fourth generation, but not through Hyllus, – had been guilty (as already mentioned) of the murder of Karnus the prophet at the camp of Naupaktus, for which he had been banished and remained in exile for ten years; his son deriving the name of Alêtês from the long wanderings endured by the father. At the head of a body of Dorians, Alêtês attacked Corinth: he pitched his camp on the Solygeian eminence near the city, and harassed the inhabitants with constant warfare until he compelled them to surrender. Even in the time of the Peloponnesian war, the Corinthians professed to identify the hill on which the camp of these assailants had been placed. The great mythical dynasty of the Sisyphids was expelled, and Alêtês became ruler and Œkist of the Dorian city; many of the inhabitants, however, Æolic or Ionic, departed.

The settlement of Oxylus and his Ætolians in Elis is said by some to have been accomplished with very little opposition; the leader professing himself to be descended from Ætolus, who had been in a previous age banished from Elis into Ætôlia, and the two people, Epeians and Ætolians, acknowledging a kindred origin one with the other. At first, indeed, according to Ephorus, the Epeians appeared in arms, determined to repel the intruders, but at length it was agreed on both sides to abide the issue of a single combat. Degmenus, the champion of the Epeians, confided in the long shot of his bow and arrow; but the Ætolian Pyræchmês came provided with his sling, – a weapon then unknown and recently invented by the Ætolians, – the range of which was yet longer than that of the bow of his enemy: he thus killed Degmenus, and secured the victory to Oxylus and his followers. According to one statement, the Epeians were expelled; according to another, they fraternised amicably with the new-comers. Whatever may be the truth as to this matter, it is certain that their name is from this moment lost, and that they never reappear among the historical elements of Greece: we hear from this time forward only of Eleians, said to be of Ætolian descent.

One most important privilege was connected with the possession of the Eleian territory by Oxylus, coupled with his claim on the gratitude of the Dorian kings. The Eleians acquired the administration of the temple at Olympia, which the Achæans are said to have possessed before them; and in consideration of this sacred function, which subsequently ripened into the celebration of the great Olympic games, their territory was solemnly pronounced to be inviolable. Such was the statement of Ephorus: we find, in this case as in so many others, that the return of the Herakleids is made to supply a legendary basis for the historical state of things in Peloponnêsus.

It was the practice of the great Attic tragedians, with rare exceptions, to select the subjects of their composition from the heroic or legendary world, and Euripidês had composed three dramas, now lost, on the adventures of Têmenus with his daughter Hyrnethô and his son-in-law Dêiphontês, – on the family misfortunes of Kresphontês and Meropê, – and on the successful valour of Archelaus the son of Têmenus in Macedonia, where he was alleged to have first begun the dynasty of the Temenid kings. Of these subjects the first and second were eminently tragical, and the third, relating to Archelaus, appears to have been undertaken by Euripidês in compliment to his contemporary sovereign and patron, Archelaus king of Macedonia: we are even told that those exploits which the usual version of the legend ascribed to Têmenus, were reported in the drama of Euripidês to have been performed by Archelaus his son. Of all the heroes, touched upon by the three Attic tragedians, these Dorian Herakleids stand lowest in the descending genealogical series, – one mark amongst others that we are approaching the ground of genuine history.

Though the name Achæans, as denoting a people, is henceforward confined to the North-Peloponnesian territory especially called Achaia, and to the inhabitants of Achæa, Phthiôtis, north of Mount Œta, – and though the great Peloponnesian states always seem to have prided themselves on the title of Dorians, – yet we find the kings of Sparta, ever, in the historical age, taking pains to appropriate to themselves the mythical glories of the Achæans, and to set themselves forth as the representatives of Agamemnôn and Orestês. The Spartan king Kleomenês even went so far as to disavow formally any Dorian parentage; for when the priestess at Athens refused to permit him to sacrifice in the temple of Athênê, on the plea that it was peremptorily closed to all Dorians, he replied: "I am no Dorian, but an Achæan." Not only did the Spartan envoy, before Gelôn of Syracuse, connect the indefeasible title of his country to the supreme command of the Grecian military force, with the ancient name and lofty prerogatives of Agamemnôn, – but, in farther pursuance of the same feeling, the Spartans are said to have carried to Sparta both the bones of Orestês from Tegea, and those of Tisamenus from Helikê, at the injunction of the Delphian oracle. There is also a story that Oxylus in Elis was directed by the same oracle to invite into his country an Achæan, as Œkist conjointly with himself; and that he called in Agorius, the great-grandson of Orestês, from Helikê, with a small number of Achæans who joined him. The Dorians themselves, being singularly poor in native legends, endeavoured, not unnaturally, to decorate themselves with those legendary ornaments which the Achæans possessed in abundance.

As a consequence of the Dorian establishments in Peloponnêsus, several migrations of the pre-existing inhabitants are represented as taking place. 1. The Epeians of Elis are either expelled, or merged in the new-comers under Oxylus, and lose their separate name 2. The Pylians, together with the great heroic family of Nêleus and his son Nestôr, who preside over them, give place to the Dorian establishment of Messênia, and retire to Athens, where their leader, Melanthus, becomes king: a large portion of them take part in the subsequent Ionic emigration. 3. A portion of the Achæans, under Penthilus and other descendants of Orestês, leave Peloponnêsus, and form what is called the Æolic emigration, to Lesbos, the Trôad, and the Gulf of

XVIII. LAST DAYS OF LEGENDARY GREECE. - DARKNESS BEFORE HISTORICAL GREECE.

Adramyttium; the name *Æolians,* unknown to Homer, and seemingly never applied to any separate tribe at all, being introduced to designate a large section of the Hellenic name, partly in Greece Proper, and partly in Asia. **4.** Another portion of Achæans expel the Ionians from Achaia, properly so called, in the north of Peloponnêsus; the Ionians retiring to Attica.

The Homeric poems describe Achæans, Pylians, and Epeians, in Peloponnêsus, but take no notice of Ionians in the northern district of Achaia: on the contrary, the Catalogue in the Iliad distinctly includes this territory under the dominions of Agamemnôn. Though the Catalogue of Homer is not to be regarded as an historical document, fit to be called as evidence for the actual state of Peloponnêsus at any prior time, it certainly seems a better authority than the statements advanced by Herodotus and others respecting the occupation of northern Peloponnêsus by the Ionians, and their expulsion from it by Tisamenus. In so far as the Catalogue is to be trusted, it negatives the idea of Ionians at Helikê, and countenances what seems in itself a more natural – apposition, – that the historical Achæans in the north part of Peloponnêsus are a small undisturbed remnant of the powerful Achæan population once distributed throughout the peninsula, until it was broken up and partially expelled by the Dorians.

The Homeric legends, unquestionably the oldest which we possess, are adapted to a population of Achæans, Danaans, and Argeians, seemingly without any special and recognised names, either aggregate or divisional, other than the name of each separate tribe or kingdom. The post-Homeric legends are adapted to a population classified quite differently, – Hellens, distributed into Dorians, Ionians, and Æolians. If we knew more of the time and circumstances in which these different legends grew up, we should probably be able to explain their discrepancy; but in our present ignorance we can only note the fact.

Whatever difficulty modern criticism may find in regard to the event called "The Return of the Herakleids," no doubt is expressed about it even by the best historians of antiquity. Thucydidês accepts it as a single and literal event, having its assignable date, and carrying at one blow the acquisition of Peloponnêsus. The date of it he fixes as eighty years after the capture of Troy. Whether he was the original determiner of this epoch, or copied it from some previous author, we do not know. It must have been fixed according to some computation of generations, for there were no other means accessible,

– probably by means of the lineage of the Herakleids, which, as belonging to the kings of Sparta, constituted the most public and conspicuous thread of connection between the Grecian real and mythical world, and measured the interval between the Siege of Troy itself and the first recorded Olympiad. Hêraklês himself represents the generation before the siege, and his son Tlepolemus fights in the besieging army. If we suppose the first generation after Hêraklês to commence with the beginning of the siege, the fourth generation after him will coincide with the ninetieth year after the same epoch; and therefore, deducting ten years for the duration of the struggle, it will coincide with the eightieth year after the capture of the city; thirty years being reckoned for a generation. The date assigned by Thucydidês will thus agree with the distance in which Têmenus, Kresphontês, and Aristodêmus, stand removed from Hêraklês. The interval of eighty years, between the capture of Troy and the Return of the Herakleids, appears to have been admitted by Apollodôrus and Eratosthenês, and some other professed chronologists of antiquity; but there were different reckonings which also found more or less of support.

II. Migration of Thessalians and Bœotians.

In the same passage in which Thucydidês speaks of the Return of the Herakleids, he also marks out the date of another event a little antecedent, which is alleged to have powerfully affected the condition of Northern Greece. "Sixty years after the capture of Troy (he tells us) the Bœotians were driven by the Thessalians from Arnê, and migrated into the land then called Kadmêis, but now Bœotia, wherein there had previously dwelt a section of their race, who had contributed the contingent to the Trojan war."

The expulsion here mentioned, of the Bœotians from Arnê "by the Thessalians," has been construed, with probability, to allude to the immigration of the Thessalians, properly so called, from the Thesprôtid in Epirus into Thessaly. That the Thessalians had migrated into Thessaly from the Thesprôtid territory, is stated by Herodotus, though he says nothing about time or circumstances. Antiphus and Pheidippus appear in the Homeric Catalogue as commanders of the Grecian contingent from the islands of Kôs and Karpathus, on the south-east coast of Asia Minor: they are sons of Thessalus, who is himself the son of Hêraklês. A legend ran that these two chiefs, in the dispersion which ensued after the victory, had been driven by storms into the Ionian Gulf, and cast upon the coast of Epirus, where they landed and settled at Ephyrê in the Thesprôtid. It was Thessalus, grandson of Pheidippus, who was reported to have conducted the Thesprotians across the passes of Pindus into Thessaly, to have conquered the fertile central plain of that country, and to have imposed upon it his own name instead of its previous denomination Æolis.

Whatever we may think of this legend as it stands, the state of Thessaly during the historical ages renders it highly probable that the Thessalians, properly so called, were a body of immigrant conquerors. They appear always as a rude, warlike, violent, and uncivilised race, distinct from their neighbours the Achæans, the Magnetes, and the Perrhæbians, and holding all the three in tributary dependence: these three tribes stand to them in a relation analogous to that of the Lacedæmonian Periœki towards Sparta, while the Penestæ, who cultivated their lands, are almost an exact parallel of the Helots. Moreover, the low level of taste and intelligence among the Thessalians, as well as certain points of their costume, assimilates them more to Macedonians or Epirots than to Hellens. Their position in Thessaly is in many respects analogous to that of the Spartan Dorians in Peloponnêsus, and there seems good reason for concluding that the former, as well as the latter, were originally victorious invaders, though we cannot pretend to determine the time at which the invasion took place. The great family of the Aleuads, and probably other Thessalian families besides, were descendants of Hêraklês, like the kings of Sparta.

There are no similar historical grounds, in the case of the alleged migration of the Bœotians from Thessaly to Bœotia, to justify a belief in the main fact of the legend, nor were the different legendary stories in harmony one with the other. While the Homeric Epic recognises the Bœotians in Bœotia, but not in Thessaly, Thucydidês records a statement which he had found of their migration from the latter into the former; but in order to escape the necessity of flatly contradicting Homer, he inserts the parenthesis that there had been previously an outlying fraction of Bœotians in Bœotia at the time of the Trojan war, from whom the troops who served with Agamemnôn were drawn. Nevertheless, the discrepancy with the Iliad, though less strikingly obvious, is not removed, inasmuch as the Catalogue is unusually copious in enumerating the contingents from Thessaly, without once mentioning Bœotians. Homer distinguishes Orchomenus from Bœotia, and he does not specially notice Thêbes in the Catalogue: in other respects his enumeration of the towns coincides pretty well with the ground historically known afterwards under the name of Bœotia.

Pausanias gives us a short sketch of the events which he supposes to have intervened in this section of Greece between the Siege of Troy and the Return of the Herakleids. Peneleôs, the leader of the Bœotians at the siege, having been slain by Eurypylus the son of Telephus, Tisamenus, son of Thersander and grandson of Polynikês, acted as their commander, both during the remainder of the siege and after their return. Autesiôn, his son and successor, became subject to the wrath of the avenging Erinnyes of Laius and Œdipus: the oracle directed him to expatriate, and he joined the Dorians. In his place, Damasichthôn, son of Opheltas and grandson of Peneleôs, became king of the Bœotians: he was succeeded by Ptolemæus, who was himself followed by Xanthus. A war having broken out at that time between the Athenians and Bœotians, Xanthus engaged in single combat with Melanthus son of Andropompus, the champion of Attica, and perished by the cunning of his opponent. After the death of Xanthus, the Bœotians passed from kingship to popular government. As Melanthus was of the lineage of the Neleids, and had migrated from Pylus to Athens in consequence of the successful establishment of the Dorians in Messênia, the duel with Xanthus must have been of course subsequent to the Return of the Herakleids.

Here then we have a summary of alleged Bœotian history between the Siege of Troy and the Return of the Herakleids, in which no mention is made of the immigration of the mass of Bœotians from Thessaly, and seemingly no possibility left of fitting in so great and capital an incident The legends followed by Pausanias are at variance with those adopted by Thucydidês, but they harmonise much better with Homer.

So deservedly high is the authority of Thucydidês, that the migration here distinctly announced by him is commonly set down as an ascertained datum, historically as well as chronologically. But on this occasion it can be shown that he only followed one amongst a variety of discrepant legends, none of which there were any means of verifying.

Pausanias recognised a migration of the Bœotians from Thessaly, in early times anterior to the Trojan war; and the account of Ephorus, as given by Strabo, professed to record a series of changes in the occupants of the country: First, the non-Hellenic Aones and Temmikes, Leleges and Hyantes; next, the Kadmeians, who, after the second siege of Thêbes by the Epigoni, were expelled by the Thracians and Pelasgians, and retired into Thessaly,

XVIII. LAST DAYS OF LEGENDARY GREECE. - DARKNESS BEFORE HISTORICAL GREECE.

where they joined in communion with the inhabitants of Arnê, – the whole aggregate being called Bœotians. After the Trojan war, and about the time of the Æolic emigration, these Bœotians returned from Thessaly and reconquered Bœotia, driving out the Thracians and Pelasgians, – the former retiring to Parnassus, the latter to Attica. It was on this occasion (he says) that the Minyæ of Orchomenus were subdued, and forcibly incorporated with the Bœotians. Ephorus seems to have followed in the main, the same narrative as Thucydidês, about the movement of the Bœotians out of Thessaly; coupling it, however, with several details current as explanatory of proverbs and customs.

The only fact which we make out, independent of these legends, is, that there existed certain homonymies and certain affinities of religious worship, between parts of Bœotia and parts of Thessaly, which appear to indicate a kindred race. A town named Arnê, similar in name to the Thessalian, was enumerated in the Bœotian Catalogue of Homer, and antiquaries identified it sometimes with the historical town Chæroneia, sometimes with Akræphium. Moreover, there was near the Bœotian Korôneia a river named Kuarius, or Koralius, and a venerable temple dedicated to the Itonian Athênê, in the sacred ground of which the Pambœotia, or public council of the Bœotian name, was held; there was also a temple and a river of similar denomination in Thessaly, near to a town called Iton, or Itônus. We may from these circumstances presume a certain ancient kindred between the population of these regions, and such a circumstance is sufficient to explain the generation of legends describing migrations backward and forward, whether true or not in point of fact.

What is most important to remark is, that the stories of Thucydidês and Ephorus bring us out of the mythical into the historical Bœotia. Orchomenus is Bœotised, and we hear no more el the once-powerful Minyæ: there are no more Kadmeians at Thêbes, nor Bœotians in Thessaly. The Minyæ and the Kadmeians disappear in the Ionic emigration, which will be presently adverted to. Historical Bœtia is now constituted, apparently in its federative league, under the presidency of Thêbes, just as we find it in the time of the Persian and Peloponnesian wars.

III. Emigrations from Greece to Asia and the Islands of the Ægean.

1. ÆOLIC. – 2. IONIC – 3. DORIC

LEGENDARY GREECE

To complete the transition of Greece from its mythical to its historical condition, the secession of the races belonging to the former must follow upon the introduction of those belonging to the latter. This is accomplished by means of the Æolic and Ionic migrations.

The presiding chiefs of the Æolic emigration are the representatives of the heroic lineage of the Pelopids: those of the Ionic emigration belong to the Neleids; and even in what is called the Doric emigration to Thêra, the Œkist Thêras is not a Dorian but a Kadmeian, the legitimate descendant of Œdipus and Kadmus.

The Æolic, Ionic, and Doric colonies were planted along the western coast of Asia Minor, from the coasts of the Propontis southward down to Lykia (I shall in a future chapter speak more exactly of their boundaries); the Æolic occupying the northern portion, together with the islands of Lesbos and Tenedos; the Doric occupying the southernmost, together with the neighbouring islands of Rhodes and Kôs; and the Ionic being planted between them, comprehending Chios, Samos, and the Cyclades islands.

Æolic Emigration.

The Æolic emigration was conducted by the Pelopids: the original story seems to have been, that Orestês himself was at the head of the first batch of colonists, and this version of the event is still preserved by Pindar and by Hellanikus. The more current narratives represented the descendants of Orestês as chiefs of the expeditions to Æolis, – his illegitimate son Penthilus, by Erigonê daughter of Ægisthus, together with Echelatus and Gras, the son and grandson of Penthilus, – also Kleuês and Malaus, descendants of Agamemnôn through another lineage. According to the account given by Strabo, Orestês began the emigration, but died on his route in Arcadia; his son Penthilus, taking the guidance of the emigrants, conducted them by the long land-journey through Bœotia and Thessaly to Thrace; from whence Archelaus, son of Penthilus, led them across the Hellespont, and settled at Daskylium on the Propontis. Gras, son of Archelaus, crossed over to Lesbos and possessed himself of the island. Kleuês and Malaus, conducting another body of Achæans, were longer on their journey, and lingered a considerable time near Mount Phrikium, in the territory of Lokris; ultimately, however, they passed over by sea to Asia and took possession of Kymê, south of the Gulf of Adramyttium, the most considerable of all the Æolic cities on the continent. From Lesbos and Kymê, the other less considerable Æolic towns,

XVIII. LAST DAYS OF LEGENDARY GREECE. - DARKNESS BEFORE HISTORICAL GREECE.

spreading over the region of Ida as well as the Trôad, and comprehending the island of Tenedos, are said to have derived their origin.

Though there are many differences in the details, the accounts agree in representing these Æolic settlements as formed by the Achæans expatriated from Lacônia under the guidance of the dispossessed Pelopids. We are told that in their journey through Bœotia they received considerable reinforcements, and Strabo adds that the emigrants started from Aulis, the port from whence Agamemnôn departed in the expedition against Troy. He also informs us that they missed their course and experienced many losses from nautical ignorance, but we do not know to what particular incidents he alludes.

Ionic Emigration.

The Ionic emigration is described as emanating from and directed by the Athenians, and connects itself with the previous legendary history of Athens, which must therefore be here briefly recapitulated.

The great mythical hero Thesêus, of whose military prowess and errant exploits we have spoken in a previous chapter, was still more memorable in the eyes of the Athenians as an internal political reformer. He was supposed to have performed for them the inestimable service of transforming Attica out of many states into one. Each dême, or at least a great many out of the whole number, had before his time enjoyed political independence under its own magistrates and assemblies, acknowledging only a federal union with the rest under the presidency of Athens: by a mixture of conciliation and force, Thesêus succeeded in putting down all these separate governments, and bringing them to unite in one political system, centralised at Athens. He is said to have established a constitutional government, retaining for himself a defined power as king, or president, and distributing the people into three classes: Eupatridæ, a sort of sacerdotal noblesse; Geômori and Demiurgi, husbandmen and artisans. Having brought these important changes into efficient working, he commemorated them for his posterity by introducing solemn and appropriate festivals. In confirmation of the dominion of Athens over the Megarid territory, he is said farther to have erected a pillar at the extremity of the latter towards the Isthmus, marking the boundary between Peloponnêsus and Iônia.

A revolution so extensive was not consummated without creating much discontent; and Menestheus, the rival of Thesêus, – the first specimen, as we are told, of an artful demagogue, – took advantage of this feeling to assail and undermine him. Thesêus had quitted Attica, to accompany and assist his friend Peirithoüs, in his journey down to the under-world, in order to carry off the goddess Persephonê, – or (as those who were critical in legendary story preferred recounting) in a journey to the residence of Aidôneus, king of the Molossians in Epirus, to carry off his daughter. In this enterprise, Peirithoüs perished, while Thesêus was cast into prison, from whence he was only liberated by the intercession of Hêraklês. It was during his temporary absence, that the Tyndarids Castôr and Pollux invaded Attica for the purpose of recovering their sister Helen, whom Thesêus had at a former period taken away from Sparta and deposited at Aphidnæ; and the partisans of Menestheus took advantage both of the absence of Thesêus and of the calamity which his licentiousness had brought upon the country, to ruin his popularity with the people. When he returned, he found them no longer disposed to endure his dominion, or to continue to him the honours which their previous feelings of gratitude had conferred. Having, therefore, placed his sons under the protection of Elephenôr, in Eubœa, he sought an asylum with Lykomêdês, prince of Scyros, from whom, however he received nothing but an insidious welcome and a traitorous death.

Menestheus, succeeding to the honours of the expatriated hero, commanded the Athenian troops at the Siege of Troy. But though he survived the capture, he never returned to Athens, – different stories being related of the place where he and his companions settled. During this interval, the feelings of the Athenians having changed, they restored the sons of Thesêus, who had served at Troy under Elephenôr, and had returned unhurt, to the station and functions of their father. The Theseids Demophoôn, Oxyntas, Apheidas, and Thymœtes had successively filled this post for the space of about sixty years, when the Dorian invaders of Peloponnêsus (as has been before related) compelled Melanthus and the Neleid family to abandon their kingdom of Pylus. The refugees found shelter at Athens, where a fortunate adventure soon raised Melanthus to the throne. A war breaking out between the Athenians and Bœotians, respecting the boundary tract of Œnoê, the Bœotian king Xanthus challenged Thymœtês to single combat: the latter declining to accept it, Melanthus not only stood forward in his place, but practised a cunning stratagem with such success as to kill his adversary. He was forthwith chosen king, Thymœtês being constrained to resign.

XVIII. LAST DAYS OF LEGENDARY GREECE. - DARKNESS BEFORE HISTORICAL GREECE.

Melanthus and his son Kodrus reigned for nearly sixty years, during which time large bodies of fugitives, escaping from the recent invaders throughout Greece, were harboured by the Athenians: so that Attica became populous enough to excite the alarm and jealousy of the Peloponnesian Dorians. A powerful Dorian force, under the command of Alêtês from Corinth and Althæmenês from Argôs, were accordingly despatched to invade the Athenian territory, in which the Delphian oracle promised them success, provided they abstained from injuring the person of Kodrus. Strict orders were given to the Dorian army that Kodrus should be preserved unhurt; but the oracle had become known among the Athenians, and the generous prince determined to bring death upon himself as a means of salvation to his country. Assuming the disguise of a peasant, he intentionally provoked a quarrel with some of the Dorian troops, who slew him without suspecting his real character. No sooner was this event known, than the Dorian leaders, despairing of success, abandoned their enterprise – and evacuated the country. In retiring, however, they retained possession of Megara, where they established permanent settlers, and which became from this moment Dorian, – seemingly at first a dependency of Corinth, though it afterwards acquired its freedom and became an autonomous community. This memorable act of devoted patriotism, analogous to that of the daughters of Erechtheus at Athens, and of Menœkeus at Thêbes, entitled Kodrus to be ranked among the most splendid characters in Grecian legend.

Kodrus is numbered as the last king of Athens: his descendants were styled Archons, but they held that dignity for life, – a practice which prevailed during a long course of years afterwards. Medon and Neileus, his two sons, having quarrelled about the succession, the Delphian oracle decided in favour of the former; upon which the latter, affronted at the preference, resolved upon seeking a new home. There were at this moment many dispossessed sections of Greeks, and an adventitious population accumulated in Attica, who were anxious for settlements beyond sea. The expeditions which now set forth to cross the Ægean, chiefly under the conduct of members of the Kodrid family, composed collectively the memorable Ionic Emigration, of which the Ionians, recently expelled from Peloponnêsus, formed a part, but, as it would seem, only a small part; for we hear of many quite distinct races, some renowned in legend, who withdraw from Greece amidst this assemblage of colonists. The Kadmeians, the Minyæ of

Orchomenus, the Abantes of Eubœa, the Dryopes; the Molossi, the Phokians, the Bœotians, the Arcadian Pelasgians, and even the Dorians of Epidaurus, – are represented as furnishing each a proportion of the crews of these emigrant vessels. Nor were the results unworthy of so mighty a confluence of different races. Not only the Cyclades islands in the Ægean, but the great islands of Samos and Chios, near the Asiatic coast, and ten different cities on the coast of Asia Minor, from Milêtus in the south to Phokæa in the north, were founded, and all adopted the Ionic name. Athens was the metropolis or mother city of all of them: Androklus and Neileus, the Œkists of Ephesus and Milêtus, and probably other Œkists also, started from the Prytaneium at Athens, with those solemnities, religious and political, which usually marked the departure of a swarm of Grecian colonists.

Other mythical families, besides the heroic lineage of Nêleus and Nestôr, as represented by the sons of Kodrus, took a leading part in the expedition. Herodotus mentions Lykian chiefs, descendants from Glaukus son of Hippolochus, and Pansanias tells us of Philôtas descendant of Peneleôs, who went at the head of a body of Thebans: both Glaukus and Peneleôs are commemorated in the Iliad. It is a remarkable fact mentioned by Pausanias (though we do not know on what authority), that the inhabitants of Phokæa, – which was the northernmost city of Ionia on the borders of Æolis, and one of the last founded, – consisting mostly of Phokian colonists under the conduct of the Athenians Philogenês and Dæmon, were not admitted into the Pan-Ionic Amphiktyony until they consented to choose for themselves chiefs of the Kodrid family. Proklês, the chief who conducted the Ionic emigrants from Epidaurus to Samos, was said to be of the lineage of Iôn, son of Xuthus.

Of the twelve Ionic states constituting the Pan-Ionic Amphiktyony – some of them among the greatest cities in Hellas – I shall say no more at present, as I have to treat of them again when I come upon historical ground.

Doric Emigrations.

The Æolic and Ionic emigrations are thus both presented to us as direct consequences of the event called the Return of the Herakleids; and in like manner the formation of the Dorian Hexapolis in the south-western corner of Asia Minor: Kôs, Knidus, Halikarnassus, and Rhodes, with its three separate cities, as well as the Dorian establishments in Krête, Melos, and Thêra, are all traced more or less directly to the same great revolution.

XVIII. LAST DAYS OF LEGENDARY GREECE. - DARKNESS
BEFORE HISTORICAL GREECE.

Thêra, more especially, has its root in the legendary world. Its Œkist was Thêras, a descendant of the heroic lineage of Œdipus and Kadmus, and maternal uncle of the young kings of Sparta, Eurysthenês and Proklês, during whose minority he had exercised the regency. On their coming of age, his functions were at an end; but being unable to endure a private station, he determined to put himself at the head of a body of emigrants. Many came forward to join him, and the expedition was farther reinforced by a body of interlopers, belonging to the Minyæ, of whom the Lacedæmonians were anxious to get rid. These Minyæ had arrived in Lacônia, not long before, from the island of Lêmnos, out of which they had been expelled by the Pelasgian fugitives from Attica. They landed without asking permission, took up their abode and began to "light their fires" on Mount Taygetus. When the Lacedæmonians sent to ask who they were, and wherefore they had come, the Minyæ replied that they were sons of the Argônauts who had landed at Lêmnos, and that, being expelled from their own homes, they thought themselves entitled to solicit an asylum in the territory of their fathers: they asked, withal, to be admitted to share both the lands and the honours of the state. The Lacedæmonians granted the request, chiefly on the ground of a common ancestry, – their own great heroes, the Tyndarids, having been enrolled in the crew of the Argô: the Minyæ were then introduced as citizens into the tribes, received lots of land, and began to intermarry with the pre-existing families. It was not long, however, before they became insolent: they demanded a share in the kingdom (which was the venerated privilege of the Herakleids), and so grossly misconducted themselves in other ways, that the Lacedæmonians resolved to put them to death, and began by casting them into prison. While the Minyæ were thus confined, their wives, Spartans by birth, and many of them daughters of the principal men, solicited permission to go in and see them; leave being granted, they made use of the interview to change clothes with their husbands, who thus escaped and fled again to Mount Taygetus. The greater number of them quitted Laconia, and marched to Triphylia, in the western regions of Peloponnêsus, from whence they expelled the Paroreatæ and the Kaukones, and founded six towns of their own, of which Lepreum was the chief. A certain proportion, however, by permission of the Lacedæmonians, joined Thêras, and departed with him to the island of Kallistê, then possessed by Phœnician inhabitants, who were descended from the kinsmen and companions of Kadmus, and who had been left there by that prince, when he came forth in search of Eurôpa, eight generations preceding. Arriving thus among men of kindred lineage with himself, Thêras met with a fraternal reception, and the island derived from him the name, under which it is historically known, of Thêra.

Such is the foundation-legend of Thêra, believed both by the Lacedæmonians and by the Theræans, and interesting as it brings before us, characteristically as well as vividly, the persons and feelings of the mythical world, – the Argônauts, with the Tyndarids as their children companions and Minyæ as their children. In Lepreum, as in the other towns of Triphylia, the descent from the Minyæ of old seems to have been believed in the historical times, and the mention of the river Minyëius in those regions by Homer tended to confirm it. People were not unanimous as to the legend by which that descent should be made out; while some adopted the story just cited from Herodotus, others imagined that Chlôris, who had come from the Minyeian town of Orchomenus as the wife of Nêleus to Pylus, had brought with her a body of her countrymen.

These Minyæ from Lêmnos and Imbros appear again as portions of another narrative respecting the settlement of the colony of Melôs. It has already been mentioned, that when the Herakleids and the Dorians invaded Lacônia, Philonomus, an Achæan, treacherously betrayed to them the country, for which he received as his recompense the territory of Amyklæ. He is said to have peopled this territory by introducing detachments of Minyæ from Lêmnos and Imbros, who, in the third generation after the return of the Herakleids, became so discontented and mutinous, that the Lacedæmonians resolved to send them out of the country as emigrants, under their chiefs Polis and Delphus. Taking the direction of Krête, they stopped in their way to land a portion of their colonists on the island of Mêlos, which remained throughout the historical times a faithful and attached colony of Lacedæmôn. On arriving in Krête, they are said to have settled at the town of Gortyn. We find, moreover, that other Dorian establishments, either from Lacedæmôn or Argôs, were formed in Krête; and Lyktos in particular, is noticed, not only as a colony of Sparta, but as distinguished for the analogy of its laws and customs. It is even said that Krête, immediately after the Trojan war, had been visited by the wrath of the gods, and depopulated by famine and pestilence; and that, in the third generation afterwards, so great was the influx of emigrants, the entire population of the island was renewed, with the exception of the Eteokrêtes at Polichnæ and Præsus.

There were Dorians in Krête in the time of the Odyssey: Homer mentions

XVIII. LAST DAYS OF LEGENDARY GREECE. - DARKNESS BEFORE HISTORICAL GREECE.

different languages and different races of men, Eteokrêtes, Kydônes, Dorians, Achæans, and Pelasgians, as all co-existing in the island, which he describes to be populous, and to contain ninety cities. A legend given by Andrôn, based seemingly upon the statement of Herodotus, that Dôrus the son of Hellên had settled in Histiæôtis, ascribed the first introduction of the three last races to Tektaphus son of Dôrus, — who had led forth from that country a colony of Dorians, Achæans, and Pelasgians, and had landed in Krête during the reign of the indigenous king Krês. This story of Andrôn so exactly fits on to the Homeric Catalogue of Kretan inhabitants, that we may reasonably presume it to have been designedly arranged with reference to that Catalogue, so as to afford some plausible account, consistently with the received legendary chronology, how there came to be Dorians in Krête before the Trojan war, — the Dorian colonies after the return of the Herakleids being of course long posterior in supposed order of time. To find a leader sufficiently early for his hypothesis, Andrôn ascends to the primitive Eponymus Dôrus, to whose son Tektaphus he ascribes the introduction of a mixed colony of Dorians, Achæans, and Pelasgians into Krête: these are the exact three races enumerated in the Odyssey, and the king Krês, whom Andrôn affirms to have been then reigning in the island, represents the Eteokrêtes and Kydônes in the list of Homer. The story seems to have found favour among native Kretan historians, as it doubtless serves to obviate what would otherwise be a contradiction in the legendary chronology.

Another Dorian emigration from Peloponnêsus to Krête, which extended also to Rhodes and Kôs, is farther said to have been conducted by Althæmenês, who had been one of the chiefs in the expedition against Attica, in which Krodus perished. This prince, a Herakleid, and third in descent from Têmenus, was induced to expatriate by a family quarrel, and conducted a body of Dorian colonists from Argôs first to Krête, where some of them remained; but the greater number accompanied him to Rhodes, in which island, after expelling the Karian possessors, he founded the three cities of Lindus, Ialysus, and Kamairus.

It is proper here to add, that the legend of the Rhodian archæologists respecting their Œkist Althæmenês, who was worshipped in the island with heroic honours, was something totally different from the preceding. Althæmenês was a Kretan, son of the king Katreus, and grandson of Minôs. An oracle predicted to him that he would one day kill his father. Eager to escape so terrible a destiny, he quitted Krête, and conducted a colony to Rhodes, where the famous temple of the Atabyrian Zeus, on the lofty summit of Mount Atabyrum, was ascribed to his foundation, built so as to command a view of Krête. He had been settled on the island for some time, when his father Katreus, anxious again to embrace his only son, followed him from Krête: he landed in Rhodes during the night without being known, and a casual collision took place between his attendants and the islanders. Althæmenês hastened to the shore to assist in repelling the supposed enemies, and in the fray had the misfortune to kill his aged father.

Either the emigrants who accompanied Althæmenês, or some other Dorian colonists afterwards, are reported to have settled at Kôs, Knidus, Karpathus, and Halikarnassus. To the last mentioned city, however, Anthês of Trœzên is assigned as theŒkist: the emigrants who accompanied him were said to have belonged to the Dymanian tribe, one of the three tribes always found in a Doric state; and the city seems to have been characterised as a colony sometimes of Trœzên, sometimes of Argôs.

We thus have the Æolic, the Ionic, and the Doric colonial establishments in Asia, all springing out of the legendary age, and all set forth as consequences, direct or indirect, of what is called the Return of the Herakleids, or the Dorian conquest of Peloponnêsus. According to the received chronology, they are succeeded by a period, supposed to comprise nearly three centuries, which is almost an entire blank, before we reach authentic chronology and the first recorded Olympiad, – and they thus form the concluding events of the mythical world, out of which we now pass into historical Greece, such as it stands at the last-mentioned epoch. It is by these migrations that the parts of the Hellenic aggregate are distributed into the places which they occupy at the dawn of historical daylight, – Dorians, Arcadians, Ætolo-Eleians, and Achæans, sharing Peloponnêsus unequally among them, – Æolians, Ionians, and Dorians, settled both in the islands of the Ægean and the coast of Asia Minor. The Return of the Herakleids, as well as the three emigrations, Æolic, Ionic, and Doric, present the legendary explanation, suitable to the feelings and belief of the people, showing how Greece passed from the heroic races who besieged Troy and Thêbes, piloted the adventurous Argô, and slew the monstrous boar of Kalydôn, to the historical races, differently named and classified, who furnished victors to the Olympic and Pythian games.

A patient and learned French writer, M. Raoul Rochette, – who construes

XVIII. LAST DAYS OF LEGENDARY GREECE. - DARKNESS BEFORE HISTORICAL GREECE.

all the events of the heroic age, generally speaking, as so much real history, only making allowance for the mistakes and exaggerations of poets, – is greatly perplexed by the blank and interruption which this supposed continuous series of history presents, from the Return of the Herakleids down to the beginning of the Olympiads. He cannot explain to himself so long a period of absolute quiescence, after the important incidents and striking adventures of the heroic age; and if there happened nothing worthy of record during this long period, – as he presumes, from the fact that nothing has been transmitted, – he concludes that this must have arisen from the state of suffering and exhaustion in which previous wars and revolution had left the Greeks; a long interval of complete inaction being required to heal such wounds.

Assuming M. Rochette's view of the heroic ages to be correct, and reasoning upon the supposition that the adventures ascribed to the Grecian heroes are matters of historical reality, transmitted by tradition from a period of time four centuries before the recorded Olympiads, and only embellished by describing poets, – the blank which he here dwells upon is, to say the least of it, embarrassing and unaccountable. It is strange that the stream of tradition, if it had once begun to flow, should (like several of the rivers in Greece) be submerged for two or three centuries and then reappear. But when we make what appears to me the proper distinction between legend and history, it will be seen that a period of blank time between the two is perfectly conformable to the conditions under which the former is generated. It is not the immediate past, but a supposed remote past, which forms the suitable atmosphere of mythical narrative, – a past originally quite undetermined in respect to distance from the present, as we see in the Iliad and Odyssey. Even when we come down to the genealogical poets, who affect to give a certain measure of bygone time, and a succession of persons as well as of events, still, the names whom they most delight to honour and upon whose exploits they chiefly expatiate, are those of the ancestral gods and heroes of the tribe and their supposed contemporaries; ancestors separated by a long lineage from the present hearer. The gods and heroes were conceived as removed from him by several generations, and the legendary matter which was grouped around them appeared only the more imposing when exhibited at a respectful distance, beyond the days of father and grandfather, and of all known predecessors. The Odes of Pindar strikingly illustrate this tendency. We thus see how it happened that, between the times assigned to heroic adventure and those of historical record, there existed an intermediate blank, filled with inglorious names; and how, amongst the same society which cared not to remember proceedings of fathers and grandfathers, there circulated much popular and accredited narrative respecting real or supposed ancestors long past and gone. The obscure and barren centuries which immediately precede the first recorded Olympiad, form the natural separation between the legendary return of the Herakleids and and the historical wars of Sparta against Messênê; – between the province of legend, wherein matter of fact (if any there be) is so intimately combined with its accompaniments of fiction, as to be undistinguishable without the aid of extrinsic evidence, – and that of history where some matters of fact can be ascertained, and where a sagacious criticism may be usefully employed in trying to add to their number.

XIX. CHRONOLOGY APPLIED TO LEGEND.

I need not repeat, what has already been sufficiently set forth in the preceding pages, that the mass of Grecian incident anterior to 776 B.C. appears to me not reducible either to history or to chronology, and that any chronological system which may be applied to it must be essentially uncertified and illusory. It was, however, chronologised in ancient times, and has continued to be so in modern; and the various schemes employed for this purpose may be found stated and compared in the first volume (the last published) of Mr. Fynes Clinton's Fasti Hellenici. There were among the Greeks, and there still are among modern scholars, important differences as to the dates of the principal events; Eratosthenês dissented both from Herodotus and from Phanias and Kallimachus, while Larcher and Raoul Rochette (who follow Herodotus), stand opposed to O. Müller and to Mr. Clinton. That the reader may have a general conception of the order in which these legendary events were disposed, I transcribe from the Fasti Hellenici a double chronological table, contained in p. 139, in which the dates are placed in series, from Phorôneus to the Olympiad of Corœbus in B.C. 776, – in the first column according to the system of Eratosthenês, in the second according to that of Kallimachus.

"The following Table (says Mr. Clinton) offers a summary view:

TABLE

Years before fall of Troy		Years Intervening between the different events	B.C. Eratosh.	B.C. Kallimach
(570)	*Phroneus*, p. 19	287	(1753)	(1697)
(283)	*Daneus*, p. 73	33	(1466)	(1410)
	Pelasgus V. p, 13, 88			
(250)	*Deukalion*, p. 42	50	(1433)	(1377)
(200)	*Erechtheus*	50	(1383)	(1327)
	Dardanus, p. 88			
(150)	*Azan, Aphida, Elatus*	20	(1333)	(1277)
130	*Kadmus*, p. 85	30	1313	1257
(100)	*Pelops*	22	(1283)	(1227)
78	Birth of *Heracles*	36	1261	1205
(42)	Argonauts	12	(1225)	(1169)

30	First Theban war, p. 51, h.	4	1213	1157
26	Death of *Heracles*	2	1209	1153
24	Death of *Eurystheus*, p. 106, x	4	1207	1151
20	Death of *Hyllus*	2$^{y.}$ 9$^{m.}$	1203	1147
18	Accession of *Agamemnon*	2	1200	1144
16	Second Theban war, p. 87, l	6	1198	1142
10	Trojan expedition (9$^{y.}$ 1$^{m.}$)	9	1192	1136
Years after the fall of Troy				
	Troy taken	7	1183	1127
8	*Orestes* reigns at Argos in the 8th year	52	1176	1120
60	The *Thessali* occupy Thessaly		1124	1068
	The *Bœoti* return to Bœotia in the 60th, yr.	20		
	Æolic migration under *Penthilus*			
80	Return of the *Heraclidæ* in the 80th year	29	1104	1048
109	*Aletes* reigns at Cornith, p. 130, m	1	1075	1019
110	Migration of *Theras*	21	1074	1018
131	Lesbos occupied 130 years after the æra	8	1053	997
139	Death of *Codrus*	1	1045	989
140	Ionic migrations 60 years after the Return	11	1044	988
151	Cymê founded 150 years after the æra	18	1033	977
169	Smyrna, 168 years after the æra, p. 105, t	131	1015	959

299

169	Olympiad of *Iphitus*	108	884	828
		52		
408	Olympiad of *Corœbus*	. . .	776	776
352				

The dates, distinguished from the rest by braces, are proposed as mere conjectures founded upon the probable length of generations.

of the leading periods from Phorôneus to the Olympiad of Corœbus, and exhibits a double series of dates; the one proceeding from the date of Eratosthenês, the other from a date founded on the reduced calculations of Phanias and Kallimachus, which strike out fifty-six years from the amount of Eratosthenês. Phanias, as we have seen, omitted fifty-five years between the Return and the registered Olympiads; for so we may understand the account: Kallimachus, fifty-six years between the Olympiad of Iphitus and the Olympiad in which Corœbus won.

"The first column of this Table exhibits the *current* year before and after the fall of Troy: in the second column of dates the *complete* intervals are expressed."

Whatever chronology is possible, researches such as those of Mr. Clinton, which have conduced so much to the better understanding of the later times of Greece, deserve respectful attention. But the ablest chronologist can accomplish nothing, unless he is supplied with a certain basis of matters of fact, pure and distinguishable from fiction, and authenticated by witnesses both knowing the truth and willing to declare it. Possessing this preliminary stock, he may reason from it to refute distinct falsehoods and to correct partial mistakes; but if all the original statements submitted to him contain truth (at least wherever there *is* truth) in a sort of chemical combination with fiction, which he has no means of decomposing, – he is in the condition of one who tries to solve a problem without data: he is first obliged to construct his own data, and from them to extract his conclusions. The statements of the epic poets, our only original witnesses in this case, correspond to the description here given. Whether the proportion of truth contained in them be smaller or greater, it is at all events un-assignable, – and the constant and intimate admixture of fiction is both indisputable in itself, and, indeed, essential to the purpose and profession of those from whom the tales proceed. Of such a character are all the deposing witnesses, even where their tales agree; and it is out of a heap of such tales, not agreeing, but discrepant in a thousand ways, and without a morsel of pure authenticated truth, – that the critic is called upon to draw out a methodical series of historical events adorned with chronological dates.

If we could imagine a modern critical scholar transported into Greece at the time of the Persian war, – endued with his present habits of appreciating historical evidence, without sharing in the religious or patriotic feelings of the country, – and invited to prepare, out of the great body of Grecian epic which then existed, a History and Chronology of Greece anterior to 776 B.C., assigning reasons as well for what he admitted as for what he rejected, – I feel persuaded that he would have judged the undertaking to be little better than a process of guesswork. But the modern critic finds that not only Pherekydês and Hellanikus, but also Herodotus and Thucydidês, have either attempted the task or sanctioned the belief that it was practicable, – a matter not at all surprising, when we consider both their narrow experience of historical evidence and the powerful ascendency of religion and patriotism in predisposing them to antiquarian belief, – and he therefore accepts the problem as they have bequeathed it, adding his own efforts to bring it to a satisfactory solution. Nevertheless, he not only follows them with some degree of reserve and uneasiness, but even admits important distinctions quite foreign to their habits of thought. Thucydidês talks of the deeds of Hellên and his sons with as much confidence as we now speak of William the Conqueror: Mr. Clinton recognises Hellên, with his sons Dôrus, Æolus, and Xuthus, as fictitious persons. Herodotus recites the great heroic genealogies down from Kadmus and Danaus, with a belief not less complete in the higher members of the series than in the lower; but Mr. Clinton admits a radical distinction in the evidence of events before and after the first recorded Olympiad, or 776 B.C., – "the first date in Grecian chronology (he remarks, p. 123), which can be fixed upon *authentic evidence*," – the highest point to which Grecian chronology, *reckoning upward,* can be carried. Of this important epoch in Grecian development, – the commencement of authentic chronological life, – Herodotus and Thucydidês had no knowledge or took no account: the later chronologists, from Timæus downwards, noted it, and made it serve as the basis of their chronological comparisons, so far as it went; but neither Eratosthenês nor Apollodôrus seem to have recognised (though Varro and Africanus did recognise) a marked difference in respect of certainty or authenticity between the period before and the period after.

In farther illustration of Mr. Clinton's opinion that the first recorded

XIX. CHRONOLOGY APPLIED TO LEGEND.

Olympiad is the earliest date which can be fixed upon authentic evidence, we have, in p. 138, the following just remarks in reference to the dissentient views of Eratosthenês, Phanias, and Kallimachus, about the date of the Trojan war: "The chronology of Eratosthenês (he says), founded on a careful comparison of circumstances, and approved by those to whom the same stores of information were open, is entitled to our respect. But we must remember that a conjectural date can never rise to the authority of evidence; that what is accepted as a substitute for testimony is not an equivalent: witnesses only can prove a date, and in the want of these, the knowledge of it is plainly beyond our reach. If in the absence of a better light we seek for what is probable, we are not to forget the distinction between conjecture and proof between what is probable and what is certain. The computation, then, of Eratosthenês for the war of Troy is open to inquiry; and if we find it adverse to the opinions of many preceding writers, who fixed a lower date, and adverse to the acknowledged length of generation in the most authentic dynasties, we are allowed to follow other guides, who give us a lower epoch."

Here Mr. Clinton again plainly acknowledges the want of evidence, and the irremediable uncertainty of Grecian chronology before the Olympiads; and the reasonable conclusion from his argument is, not simply, that "the computation of Eratosthenês was open to inquiry," (which few would be found to deny), but that both Eratosthenês and Phanias had delivered positive opinions upon a point on which no sufficient evidence was accessible, and therefore that neither the one nor the other was a guide to be followed. Mr. Clinton does, indeed, speak of authentic dynasties prior to the first recorded Olympiad, but if there be any such, reaching up from that period to a supposed point coeval with or anterior to the war of Troy, – I see no good reason for the marked distinction which he draws between chronology before and chronology after the Olympiad of Korœbus, or for the necessity which he feels of suspending his upward reckoning at the last-mentioned epoch, and beginning a different process, called "a downward reckoning," from the higher epoch (supposed to be somehow ascertained without any upward reckoning) of the first patriarch from whom such authentic dynasty emanates. Herodotus and Thucydidês might well, upon this supposition, ask of Mr. Clinton, why he called upon them to alter their method of proceeding at the year 776 B.C., and why they might not be allowed to pursue their "upward chronological reckoning," without interruption, from Leonidas up to

Danaus, or from Peisistratus up to Hellên and Deukaliôn, without any alteration in the point of view. Authentic dynasties from the Olympiads, up to an epoch above the Trojan war, would enable us to obtain chronological proof for the latter date, instead of being reduced (as Mr. Clinton affirms that we are) to "conjecture" instead of proof.

The whole question, as to the value of the reckoning from the Olympiads up to Phorôtneus, does in truth turn upon this point: Are those genealogies, which profess to cover the space between the two, authentic and trustworthy, or not? Mr. Clinton appears to feel that they are not so, when he admits the essential difference in the character of the evidence and the necessity of altering the method of computation, before and after the first recorded Olympiad; yet, in his Preface, he labours to prove that they possess historical worth and are in the main correctly set forth: moreover, that the fictitious persons, wherever any such are intermingled, may be detected and eliminated. The evidences upon which he relies, are: **1.** Inscriptions; **2.** The early poets.

1. An inscription, being nothing but a piece of writing on marble, carries evidentiary value under the same conditions as a published writing on paper. If the inscriber reports a contemporary fact which he had the means of knowing, and if there be no reason to suspect misrepresentation, we believe his assertion: if, on the other hand, he records facts belonging to a long period before his own time, his authority counts for little, except in so far as we can verify and appreciate his means of knowledge.

In estimating, therefore, the probative force of any inscription, the first and most indispensable point is to assure ourselves of its date. Amongst all the public registers and inscriptions alluded to by Mr. Clinton, there is not one which can be positively referred to a date anterior to 776 B.C. The quoit of Iphitus, – the public registers at Sparta, Corinth, and Elis, – the list of the priestesses of Juno at Argôs, – are all of a date completely uncertified. O. Müller does, indeed, agree with Mr. Clinton (though in my opinion without any sufficient proof) in assigning the quoit of Iphitus to the age ascribed to that prince; and if we even grant thus much, we shall have an inscription as old (adopting Mr. Clinton's determination of the age of Iphitus) as 828 B.C. But when Mr. Clinton quotes O. Müller as admitting the registers of Sparta, Corinth, and Elis, it is right to add that the latter does not profess to guarantee the authenticity of these documents, or the age at which such registers began to be kept. It is not to be doubted that there were registers of the kings of Sparta carrying them up to Hêraklês, and of the kings of Elis from Oxylus to Iphitus; but the question is, at what time did lists begin to be kept continuously? This is a point which we have no means of deciding, nor can we accept Mr. Clinton's unsupported conjecture, when he tells us: "*Perhaps* these were begun to be written as early as B.C. 1048, the probable time of the Dorian conquest." Again, be tells us: "At Argos, a register was preserved of the priestesses of Juno, which *might be* more ancient than the catalogues of the kings of Sparta or Corinth. That register, from which Hellanikus composed his work, contained the priestesses from the earliest times down to the age of Hellanikus himself. But this catalogue *might have* been commenced as early as the Trojan war itself, and even at a still earlier date." (Pp. x. xi.) Again, respecting the inscriptions quoted by Herodotus from the temple of the Ismenian Apollo at Thêbes, in which Amphitryo and Laodamas are named, Mr. Clinton says, "They were ancient in the time of Herodotus, which *may* perhaps carry them back 400 years before his time; and in that case they *might* approach within 300 years of Laodamas and within 400 years of the probable time of Kadmus himself." – "It is granted (he adds, in a note), that these inscriptions were *not genuine,* that is, not of the date to which they were assigned by Herodotus himself. But that they were ancient, cannot be doubted," &c.

The time when Herodotus saw the temple of the Ismenian Apollo at Thêbes can hardly have been earlier than 450 B.C. reckoning upwards from hence to 776 B.C., we have an interval of 326 years: the inscriptions which Herodotus saw may well therefore have been *ancient,* without being earlier than the first recorded Olympiad. Mr. Clinton does, indeed, tell us that *ancient* "may perhaps" be construed as 400 years earlier than Herodotus. But no careful reader can permit himself to convert such bare possibility into a ground of inference, and to make it available, in conjunction with other similar possibilities before enumerated, for the purpose of showing that there really existed inscriptions in Greece of a date anterior to 776 B.C. Unless Mr. Clinton can make out this, he can derive no benefit from inscriptions, in his attempt to substantiate the reality of the mythical persons or of the mythical events.

The truth is, that the Herakleid pedigree of the Spartan kings (as has been observed in a former chapter) is only one out of the numerous divine and heroic genealogies with which the Hellentic world abounded, – a class of documents which become historical evidence only so high in the descending series as the names composing them are authenticated by contemporary, or nearly contemporary, enrolment. At what period this practice of enrolment began, we have no information. Two remarks, however, may be made, in reference to any approximative guess as to the time when actual registration commenced: First, that the number of names in the pedigree, or the length of past time which it professes to embrace, affords no presumption of any superior antiquity in the time of registration. Secondly, that, looking to the acknowledged paucity and rudeness of Grecian writing, even down to the 60th Olympiad (540 B.C.), and to the absence of the habit of writing, as well as the low estimate of its value, which such a state of things argues, the presumption is, that written enrolment of family genealogies, did not commence until a long time after 776 B.C., and the obligation of proof falls upon him who maintains that it commenced earlier. This second remark is farther borne out, when we observe that there is no registered list, except that of the Olympic victors, which goes up even so high as 776 B.C. The next list which O. Müller and Mr. Clinton produce, is that of the Karneonikæ, or victors at the Karneian festival, which reaches only up to 676 B.C.

If Mr. Clinton then makes little out of inscriptions to sustain his view of Grecian history and chronology anterior to the recorded Olympiads, let us examine the inferences which he draws from his other source of evidence, – the early poets. Here it will be found: First, that in order to maintain the credibility of these witnesses, he lays down positions respecting historical evidence both indefensible in themselves, and especially inapplicable to the early times of Greece: Secondly, that his reasoning is at the same time inconsistent, – inasmuch as it includes admissions, which, if properly understood and followed out, exhibit these very witnesses as habitually, indiscriminately, and unconsciously mingling truth and fiction, and therefore little fit to be believed upon their solitary and unsupported testimony.

To take the second point first, he says, Introduction, p. ii. iii. – "The authority even of the genealogies has been called in question by many able and learned persons, who reject Danaus, Kadmus, Hercules, Thesêus, and many others, as fictitious persons. It is evident that any fact would come from the hands of the poets embellished with many fabulous additions; and fictitious genealogies were undoubtedly composed. Because, however, some genealogies were fictitious, we are not justified in concluding that all were fabulous. . . . In estimating, then, the historical value of the genealogies transmitted by the early poets, we may take a middle course; not rejecting them as wholly false, nor yet implicitly receiving all as true. The genealogies *contain many real persons,* but these are *incorporated with many fictitious names.* The fictions, however, will have a basis of truth: the genealogical expression may be false, but the connection which it describes is real. Even to those who reject the whole as fabulous, the exhibition of the early times which is presented in this volume may still be not unacceptable: because it is necessary to the right understanding of antiquity that the opinions of the Greeks concerning their own origin should be set before us, even if these are erroneous opinions, and that their story should be told as they have told it themselves. The names preserved by the ancient genealogies may be considered of three kinds; either they were the name of a race or clan converted into the name of an individual, or they were altogether fictitious, or lastly, they were real historical names. An attempt is made, in the four genealogical tables inserted below, to distinguish these three classes of names. . . . Of those who are left in the third class (*i.e.* the real) all are not entitled to remain there. But I have only placed in the third class those names concerning which there seemed to be little doubt The rest are left to the judgment of the reader."

Pursuant to this principle of division, Mr. Clinton furnishes four genealogical tables, in which the names of persons representing races are printed in capital letters, and those of purely fictitious persons in italics. These tables exhibit a curious sample of the intimate commixture of fiction with that which he calls truth: real son and mythical father, real husband and mythical wife, or *vice versâ.*

Upon Mr. Clinton's tables we may remark:

1. The names singled out as fictitious are distinguished by no common character, nor any mark either assignable or defensible, from those which are left as real. To take an example (p. 40), why is Itônus the first pointed out as a fiction, while Itônus the second, together with Physcus, Cynus, Salmôneus, Ormenus, &c., in the same page, are preserved as real, all of them being eponyms of towns just as much as Itônus?

2. If we are to discard Hellên, Dôrus, Æolus, Iôn, &c., as not being real individual persons, but expressions for personified races, why are we to retain Kadmus, Danaus, Hyllus, and several others, who are just as much eponyms of races and tribes as the four above mentioned? Hyllus, Pamphylus, and Dymas are the eponyms of the three Dorian tribes, just as Hoplês and the other three sons of Iôn were of the four Attic tribes: Kadmus and Danaus stand in the same relation to the Kadmeians and Danaans, as Argus and Achæus to the Argeians and Achæans. Besides, there are many other names really eponymous, which we cannot now recognise to be so, in consequence of our imperfect acquaintance with the subdivisions of the Hellenic population, each of which, speaking generally, had its god or hero, to whom the original of the name was referred. If, then, eponymous names are to be excluded from the category of reality, we shall find that the ranks of the real men will be thinned to a far greater extent than is indicated by Mr. Clinton's tables.

3. Though Mr. Clinton does not carry out consistently either of his disfranchising qualifications among the names and persons of the old mythes, he nevertheless presses them far enough to strike out a sensible proportion of the whole. By conceding thus much to modern scepticism, he has departed from the point of view of Hellanikus and Herodotus, and the ancient historians generally; and it is singular that the names, which he has been the most forward to sacrifice, are exactly those to which they were most attached, and which it would have been most painful to their faith to part with, – I mean the eponymous heroes. Neither Herodotus, nor Hellanikus, nor Eratosthenês, nor any one of the chronological reckoners of antiquity, would have admitted the distinction which Mr. Clinton draws between persons real and persons fictitious in the old mythical world, though they might perhaps occasionally, on special grounds, call in question the existence of some individual characters amongst the mythical ancestry of Greece; but they never dreamed of that general severance into real and fictitious persons, which forms the principle of Mr. Clinton's "middle course." Their chronological computations for Grecian antiquity assumed that the mythical characters, in their full and entire sequence, were all real persons. Setting up the entire list as real, they calculated so many generations to a century, and thus determined the number of centuries which separated themselves from the gods, the heroes, or the indigenous men who formed in their view the historical starting point. As soon as it is admitted that the personages in the mythical world are divisible into two classes, partly real and partly fictitious, the integrity of the series is broken up, and it can be no longer employed as a basis for chronological calculation. In the estimate of the ancient chronologers, three succeeding persons of the same lineage – grandfather, father, and son, – counted for a century; and this may pass in a rough way, so long as you are thoroughly satisfied that they are all real persons; but if in the

XIX. CHRONOLOGY APPLIED TO LEGEND.

succession of persons A, B, C, you strike out B as a fiction, the continuity of data necessary for chronological computation disappears. Now Mr. Clinton is inconsistent with himself in this – that while he abandons the unsuspecting historical faith of the Grecian chronologers, he nevertheless continues his chronological computations upon the data of that ancient faith, – upon the assumed reality of all the persons constituting his ante-historical generations. What becomes, for example, of the Herakleid genealogy of the Spartan kings, when it is admitted that eponymous persons are to be cancelled as fictions; seeing that Hyllus, through whom those kings traced their origin to Hêraklês comes in the most distinct manner under that category, as much so as Hoplês the son of Iôn? It will be found that, when we once cease to believe in the mythical world as an uninterrupted and unalloyed succession of real individuals, it becomes unfit to serve as a basis for chronological computations, and that Mr. Clinton, when he mutilated the data of the ancient chronologists, ought at the same time to have abandoned their problems as insoluble. Genealogies of real persons, such as Herodotus and Eratosthenês believed in, afford a tolerable basis for calculations of time, within certain limits of error: "genealogies containing many real persons, but incorporated with many fictitious names," (to use the language just cited from Mr. Clinton), are essentially unavailable for such a purpose.

It is right here to add, that I agree in Mr. Clinton's view of these eponymous persons: I admit, with him, that "the genealogical expression may often be false, when the connection which it describes is real." Thus, for example, the adoption of Hyllus by Ægimius, the father of Pamphylus and Dymas, to the privileges of a son and to a third fraction of his territories, may reasonably be construed as a mythical expression of the fraternal union of the three Dorian tribes, Hyllêis, Pamphyli, and Dymanes: so about the relationship of Iôn and Achæus, of Dôrus and Æolus. But if we put this construction on the name of Hyllus, or Iôn, or Achæus, we cannot at the same time employ either of these persons as units in chronological reckoning: nor is it consistent to recognise them in the lump as members of a distinct class, and yet to enlist them as real individuals in measuring the duration of past time.

4. Mr. Clinton, while professing a wish to tell the story of the Greeks as they have told it themselves, seems unconscious how capitally his point of view differs from theirs. The distinction which he draws between real and fictitious persons would have appeared unreasonable, not to say offensive, to

305

Herodotus or Eratosthenês. It is undoubtedly right that the early history (if so it is to be called) of the Greeks should be told as they have told it themselves, and with that view I have endeavoured in the previous narrative, as far as I could, to present the primitive legends in their original colour and character, – pointing out at the same time the manner in which they were transformed and distilled into history by passing through the retort of later annalists. It is the legend, as thus transformed, which Mr. Clinton seems to understand as the story told by the Greeks themselves, – which cannot be admitted to be true, unless the meaning of the expression be specially explained. In his general distinction, however, between the real and fictitious persons of the mythical world, he departs essentially from the point of view even of the later Greeks. If he had consistently followed out that distinction in his particular criticisms, he would have found the ground slipping under his feet in his upward march even to Troy, – not to mention the series of eighteen generations farther up, to Phorôneus; but he does *not* consistently follow it out, and therefore, in practice, he deviates little from the footsteps of the ancients.

Enough has been said to show that the witnesses upon whom Mr. Clinton relies, blend truth and fiction habitually, indiscriminately, and unconsciously, even upon his own admission. Let us now consider the positions which he lays down respecting historical evidence. He says (Introduct. pp. vi. vii.):

"We may acknowledge as real persons all those whom there is no reason for rejecting. The presumption is in favour of the early tradition, if no argument can be brought to overthrow it. The persons may be considered real, when the description of them is consonant with the state of the country at that time: when no national prejudice or vanity could be concerned in inventing them: when the tradition is consistent and general: when rival or hostile tribes concur in the leading facts: when the acts ascribed to the person (divested of their poetical ornament) enter into the political system of the age, or form the basis of other transactions which fall within known historical times. Kadmus and Danaus appear to be real persons: for it is conformable to the state of mankind, and perfectly credible, that Phœnician and Egyptian adventurers, in the ages to which these persons are ascribed, should have found their way to the coasts of Greece; and the Greeks (as already observed) had no motive from any national vanity to feign these settlements. Hercules was a real person. His acts were recorded by those who were not friendly to the Dorians; by Achæans and Æolians, and Ionians, who had no vanity to gratify in celebrating the hero of a hostile and rival people. His descendants in many branches remained in many states down to the historical times. His son Tlepolemus, and his grandson and great-grandson Cleodæus and Aristomachus, are acknowledged (*i.e.* by O. Müller) to be real persons; and there is no reason that can be assigned for receiving these, which, will not be equally valid for establishing the reality both of Hercules and Hyllus. Above all, Hercules is authenticated by the testimonies both of the Iliad and Odyssey."

These positions appear to me inconsistent with any sound views of the conditions of historical testimony. According to what is here laid down, we are bound to accept as real all the persons mentioned by Homer, Arktinus, Leschês, the Hesiodic poets, Eumêlus, Asius, &c., unless we can adduce some positive ground in each particular case to prove the contrary. If this position be a true one, the greater part of the history of England, from Brute the Trojan down to Julius Caesar, ought at once to be admitted as valid and worthy of credence. What Mr. Clinton here calls the *early tradition,* is in point of fact, the narrative of these early poets. The word *tradition* is an equivocal word, and begs the whole question; for while in its obvious and literal meaning it implies only something handed down, whether truth or fiction, – it is tacitly understood to imply a tale descriptive of some real matter of fact, taking its rise at the time when that fact happened, and originally accurate, but corrupted by subsequent oral transmission. Understanding, therefore, by Mr. Clinton's words *early tradition,* the tales of the old poets, we shall find his position totally inadmissible, – that we are bound to admit the persons or statements of Homer and Hesiod as real unless where we can produce reasons to the contrary. To allow this, would be to put them upon a par with good contemporary witnesses; for no greater privilege can be claimed in favour even of Thucydidês, than the title of his testimony to be believed unless where it can be contradicted on special grounds. The presumption in favour of an asserting witness is either strong or weak, or positively nothing, according to the compound ratio of his means of knowledge, his moral and intellectual habits, and his motive to speak the truth. Thus, for instance, when Hesiod tells us that his father quitted the Æolic Kymê, and came to Askra in Bœotia, we may fully believe him; but when he describes to us the battles between the Olympic gods and the Titans, or between Hêraklês and Kyknus, – or when Homer depicts the efforts of Hectôr, aided by Apollo, for the defence of Troy, and the struggles of

307

Achilles and Odysseus, with the assistance of Hêrê and Poseidon, for the destruction of that city, events professedly long past and gone, – we cannot presume either of them to be in any way worthy of belief. It cannot be shown that they possessed any means of knowledge, while it is certain that they could have no motive to consider historical truth: their object was to satisfy an uncritical appetite for narrative, and to interest the emotions of their hearers. Mr. Clinton says, that "the persons may be considered real when the description of them is consistent with the state of the country at that time." But he has forgotten, first, that we know nothing of the state of the country except what these very poets tell us; next, that fictitious persons may be just as consonant to the state of the country as real persons. While, therefore, on the one hand, we have no independent evidence either to affirm or to deny that Achilles or Agamemnôn are consistent with the state of Greece or Asia Minor, at a certain supposed date 1183 B.C., so, on the other hand, even assuming such consistency to be made out, this of itself would not prove them to be real persons.

Mr. Clinton's reasoning altogether overlooks the existence of *plausible fiction,* – fictitious stories which harmonise perfectly well with the general course of facts, and which are distinguished from matters of fact not by any internal character, but by the circumstance that matter of fact has some competent and well-informed witness to authenticate it, either directly or through legitimate inference. Fiction may be, and often is, extravagant and incredible; but it may also be plausible and specious, and in that case there is nothing but the want of an attesting certificate to distinguish it from truth. Now all the tests, which Mr. Clinton proposes as guarantees of the reality of the Homeric persons, will be just as well satisfied by plausible fiction as by actual matter of fact: the plausibility of the fiction consists in its satisfying those and other similar conditions. In most cases, the tales of the poets *did* fall in with the existing current of feelings in their audience: "prejudice and vanity" are not the only feelings, but doubtless prejudice and vanity were often appealed to, and it was from such harmony of sentiment that they acquired their hold on men's belief. Without any doubt, the Iliad appealed most powerfully to the reverence for ancestral gods and heroes among the Asiatic colonists who first heard it: the temptation of putting forth an interesting tale is quite a sufficient stimulus to the invention of the poet, and the plausibility of the tale a sufficient passport to the belief of the hearers. Mr. Clinton talks of "consistent and general tradition." But that the tale of a poet, when once told with effect and beauty, acquired general belief, – is no proof that it was founded on fact; otherwise, what are we to say to the divine legends, and to the large portion of the Homeric narrative which Mr. Clinton himself sets aside as untrue, under the designation of "poetical ornament?" When a mythical incident is recorded as "forming the basis" of some known historical fact or institution, – as, for instance, the successful stratagem by which Melanthus killed Xanthus, in the battle on the boundary, as recounted in my last chapter, – we may adopt one of two views; we may either treat the incident as real, and as having actually given occasion to what is described as its effect, – or we may treat the incident as a legend imagined in order to assign some plausible origin of the reality, – "Aut ex re nomen, aut ex vocabulo fabula." In cases where the legendary incident is referred to a time long anterior to any records, – as it commonly is, – the second mode of proceeding appears to me far more consonant to reason and probability than the first. It is to be recollected that all the persons and facts, here defended as matter of real history, by Mr. Clinton, are referred to an age long preceding the first beginning of records.

I have already remarked that Mr. Clinton shrinks from his own rule in treating Kadmus and Danaus as real persons, since they are as much eponyms of tribes or races as Dôrus and Hellen. If he can admit Hêraklês to be a real man, I cannot see upon what reason he can consistently disallow any one of the mythical personages, for there is not one whose exploits are more strikingly at variance with the standard of historical probability. Mr. Clinton reasons upon the supposition that "Hercules was a *Dorian* hero;" but he was Achæan and Kadmeian as well as Dorian, though the legends respecting him are different in all the three characters. Whether his son Tlepolemus and his grandson Kleodæus belong to the category of historical men, I will not take upon me to say, though O. Müller (in my opinion without any warranty) appears to admit it; but Hyllus certainly is not a real man, if the canon of Mr. Clinton himself respecting the eponyms is to be trusted. "The descendants of Hercules (observes Mr. Clinton) remained in many states down to the historical times." So did those of Zeus and Apollo, and of that god whom the historian Hekatæus recognised as his progenitor in the sixteenth generation; the titular kings of Ephesus, in the historical times, as well as Peisistratus, the despot of Athens, traced their origin up to Æolus and Hellên, yet Mr. Clinton does not hesitate to reject Æolus and Hellên as fictitious persons. I dispute the propriety of quoting the Iliad and Odyssey (as

Mr. Clinton does) in evidence of the historic personality of Herculês. For, even with regard to the ordinary men who figure in those poems, we have no means of discriminating the real from the fictitious; while the Homeric Hêraklês is unquestionably more than an ordinary man, – he is the favourite son of Zeus, from his birth predestined to a life of labour and servitude, as preparation for a glorious immortality. Without doubt, the poet himself believed in the reality of Hercules, but it was a reality clothed with superhuman attributes.

Mr. Clinton observes (Intro. p. ii.), that "because some genealogies were fictitious, we are not justified in concluding that all were fabulous." It is no way necessary that we should maintain so extensive a position: it is sufficient that all are fabulous so far as concerns gods and heroes, – *some* fabulous throughout, – and none ascertainably true, for the period anterior to the recorded Olympiads. How much, or what particular portions, may be true, no one can pronounce. The gods and heroes are, from our point of view, essentially fictitious; but from the Grecian point of view they were the most real (if the expression may be permitted, *i. e.* clung to with the strongest faith) of all the members of the series. They not only formed parts of the genealogy as originally conceived, but were in themselves the grand reason why it was conceived, – as a golden chain to connect the living man with a divine ancestor. The, genealogy, therefore, taken as a whole, (and its value consists in its being-taken as a whole), was from the beginning a fiction; but the names of the father and grandfather of the living man, in whose day it first came forth, were doubtless those of real men. Wherever, therefore, we can verify the date of a genealogy, as applied to some living person, we may reasonably presume the two lowest members of it to be also those of real persons; but this has no application to the time anterior to the Olympiads, – still less to the pretended times of the Trojan war, the Kalydônian boar-hunt, or the deluge of Deukalion. To reason (as Mr. Clinton does, Introd. p. vi.), – "Because Aristomachus was a real man, therefore his father Cleodæus, his grandfather Hyllus, and so farther upwards, &c., must have been real men," – is an inadmissible conclusion. The historian Hekatæus was a real man, and doubtless his father Hegesander, also, – but it would be unsafe to march up his genealogical ladder fifteen steps, to the presence of the ancestral god of whom he boasted: the upper steps of the ladder will be found broken and unreal. Not to mention that the inference, from real son to real father, is inconsistent with the admissions in Mr. Clinton's own genealogical tables; for he there inserts the names of several mythical fathers as having begotten real historical sons.

The general authority of Mr. Clinton's book, and the sincere respect which I entertain for his elucidations of the later chronology, have imposed upon me the duty of assigning those grounds on which I dissent from his conclusions prior to the first recorded Olympiad. The reader who desires to see the numerous and contradictory guesses (they deserve no better name) of the Greeks themselves in the attempt to chronologise their mythical narratives, will find them in the copious notes annexed to the first half of his first volume. As I consider all such researches not merely as fruitless, in regard to any trustworthy result, but as serving to divert attention from the genuine form and really illustrative character of Grecian legend, I have not thought it right to go over the same ground in the present work. Differing as I do, however, from Mr. Clinton's views on this subject, I concur with him in deprecating the application of etymology (Intr. pp. xi. xii.) as a general scheme of explanation, to the characters and events of Greek legend. Amongst the many causes which operated as suggestives and stimulants to Greek fancy in the creation of these interesting tales, doubtless Etymology has had its share; but it cannot be applied (as Hermann, above all others, has sought to apply it) for the purpose of imparting supposed sense and system to the general body of mythical narrative. I have already remarked on this topic in a former chapter.

It would be curious to ascertain at what time, or by whom, the earliest continuous genealogies, connecting existing persons with the supposed antecedent age of legend, were formed and preserved. Neither Homer nor Hesiod mentioned any verifiable *present* persons or circumstances: had they done so, the age of one or other of them could have been determined upon good evidence, which we may fairly presume to have been impossible, from the endless controversies upon this topic among ancient writers. In the Hesiodic Works and Days, the heroes of Troy and Thêbes are even presented as an extinct race, radically different from the poet's own contemporaries, who are a new race, far too depraved to be conceived as sprung from the loins of the heroes; so that we can hardly suppose Hesiod (though his father was a native of the Æolic Kymê) to have admitted the pedigree of the Æolic chiefs, as reputed descendants of Agamemnôn. Certain it is, that the earliest poets did not attempt to measure or bridge over the supposed interval, between their own age and the war of Troy, by any definite series of fathers and sons: whether Eumêlus or Asius made any such attempt, we cannot tell, but the earliest continuous backward genealogies which we find mentioned are those of Pherekydês, Hellanikus, and Herodotus. It is well known that Herodotus, in his manner of computing the upward genealogy of the Spartan kings, assigns the date of the Trojan war to a period 800 years earlier than himself, equivalent about to B.C. 1270-1250; while the subsequent Alexandrine chronologists, Eratosthenês and Apollodôrus, place that event in 1184 and 1183 B.C.; and the Parian marble refers it to an intermediate date, different from either, – 1209 B.C. Ephorus, Phanias, Timæus, Kleitarchus, and Duris, had each his own conjectural date; but the computations of the Alexandrine chronologists was the most generally followed by those who succeeded them, and seems to have passed to modern times as the received date of this great legendary event, – though some distinguished inquirers have adopted the epoch of Herodotus, which Larcher has attempted to vindicate in an elaborate but feeble dissertation. It is unnecessary to state that, in my view, the inquiry has no other value except to illustrate the ideas which guided the Greek mind, and to exhibit its progress from the days of Homer to those of Herodotus. For it argues a considerable mental progress when men begin to methodise the past, even though they do so on fictitious principles, being as yet unprovided with those records which alone could put them on a better course. The Homeric man was satisfied with feeling, imagining, and believing particular incidents of a supposed past, without any attempt to graduate the line of connection between them and himself: to introduce fictitious hypotheses and media of connection is the business of a succeeding age, when the stimulus of rational curiosity is first felt, without any authentic materials to supply it. We have, then, the form of history operating upon the matter of legend, – the transition-state between legend and history; less interesting, indeed, than either separately, yet necessary as a step between the two.

XX. SOCIETY & MANNERS IN GRECIAN LEGEND.

Though the particular persons and events, chronicled in the legendary poems of Greece, are not to be regarded as belonging to the province of real history, those poems are, nevertheless, full of instruction as pictures of life and manners; and the very same circumstances, which divest their composers of all credibility as historians, render them so much the more valuable as unconscious expositors of their own contemporary society. While professedly describing an uncertified past, their combinations are involuntarily borrowed from the surrounding present. For among communities, such as those of the primitive Greeks, without books, without means of extended travel, without acquaintance with foreign languages and habits, the imagination, even of highly gifted men, was naturally enslaved by the circumstances around them to a far greater degree than in the later days of Solôn or Herodotus; insomuch that the characters which they conceived and the scenes which they described would for that reason bear a stronger generic resemblance to the realities of their own time and locality. Nor was the poetry of that age addressed to lettered and critical authors, watchful to detect plagiarism, sated with simple imagery, and requiring something of novelty or peculiarity in every fresh production. To captivate their emotions, it was sufficient to depict, with genius and fervour, the more obvious manifestations of human adventure or suffering, and to idealise that type of society, both private and public, with which the hearers around were familiar. Even in describing the gods, where a great degree of latitude and deviation might have been expected, we see that Homer introduces into Olympus the passions, the caprices, the love of power and patronage, the alternation of dignity and weakness, which animated the bosom of an ordinary Grecian chief; and this tendency, to reproduce in substance the social relations to which he had been accustomed, would operate still more powerfully when he had to describe simply human characters, – the chief and his people, the warrior and his comrades, the husband, wife, father, and son, – or the imperfect rudiments of judicial and administrative proceeding. That his narrative on all these points, even with fictitious characters and events, presents a close approximation to general reality, there can be no reason to doubt. The necessity under which he lay of drawing from a store, then happily un-exhausted, of personal experience and observation, is one of the causes of that freshness and vivacity of description for which he stands unrivalled, and which constituted the imperishable charm of the Iliad and Odyssey from the beginning to the end of Grecian literature.

While, therefore, we renounce the idea of chronologising or historicising the events of Grecian legend, we may turn them to profit as valuable memorials of that state of society, feeling, and intelligence, which must be to us the starting-point of the history of the people. Of course, the legendary age, like all those which succeeded it, had its antecedent causes and determining conditions; but of these we know nothing, and we are compelled to assume it as a primary fact, for the purpose of following out its subsequent changes. To conceive absolute beginning or origin (as Niebuhr has justly remarked) is beyond the reach of our faculties: we can neither apprehend nor verify anything beyond progress, or development, or decay – change from one set of circumstances to another, operated by some definite combination of physical or moral laws. In the case of the Greeks, the legendary age, as the earliest in any way known to us, must be taken as the initial state from which this series of changes commences. We must depict its prominent characteristics as well as we can, and show, – partly how it serves to prepare, partly how it forms a contrast to set off, – the subsequent ages of Solôn, of Periklês, and of Demosthenês.

1. The political condition, which Grecian legend everywhere presents to us, is in its principal features strikingly different from that which had become universally prevalent among the Greeks in the time of the Peloponnesian war. Historical oligarchy, as well as democracy, agreed in requiring a certain established system of government, comprising the three elements of specialised functions, temporary functionaries, and ultimate responsibility (under some forms or other) to the mass of qualified citizens, – either a Senate or an Ecclesia, or both. There were, of course, many and capital distinctions between one government and another, in respect to the qualification of the citizen, the attributes and efficiency of the general assembly, the admissibility to power, &c.; and men might often be dissatisfied with the way in which these questions were determined in their own city. But in the mind of every man, some determining rule or system – something like what in modern times is called a *constitution* – was indispensable to any government entitled to be called legitimate, or capable of creating in the mind of a Greek a feeling of moral obligation to obey it. The functionaries who exercised authority under it might be more or less competent or popular; but his personal feelings towards them were commonly lost in his attachment or aversion to the general system. If any energetic man could by audacity or craft break down the constitution, and render himself permanent ruler according to his own will and pleasure, – even though he might govern well, he could never inspire the people with any sentiment of duty towards him. His sceptre was illegitimate from the beginning, and even the taking of his life, far from being interdicted by that moral feeling which condemned the shedding of blood in other cases, was considered meritorious. Nor could he be mentioned in the language except by a name (τύραννος, *despot*) which branded him as an object of mingled fear and dislike.

The king.

If we carry our eyes back from historical to legendary Greece, we find a picture the reverse of what has been here sketched. We discern a government in which there is little or no scheme or system, – still less any idea of responsibility to the governed, – but in which the mainspring of obedience on the part of the people consists in their personal feeling and reverence towards the chief. We remark, first and foremost, the king: next, a limited number of subordinate kings or chiefs; afterwards, the mass of armed freemen, husbandmen, artisans, freebooters, &c.; lowest of all, the free labourers for hire, and the bought slaves. The king is not distinguished by any broad or impassable boundary from the other chiefs, to each of whom the title *Basileus* is applicable as well as to himself: his supremacy has been inherited from his ancestors, and passes by descent, as a general rule, to his eldest son, having been conferred upon the family as a privilege by the favour of Zeus. In war, he is the leader, foremost in personal prowess, and directing all military movements; in peace, he is the general protector of the injured and oppressed; he farther offers up those public prayers and sacrifices which are intended to obtain for the whole people the favour of the gods. An ample domain is assigned to him as an appurtenance of his lofty position, while the produce of his fields and his cattle is consecrated in part to an abundant, though rude hospitality. Moreover, he receives frequent presents, to avert his enmity, to conciliate his favour, or to buy off his exactions; and when plunder is taken from the enemy, a large previous share, comprising probably the most alluring female captive, is reserved for him, apart from the general distribution.

Such is the position of the king, in the heroic times of Greece, – the only person (if we except the heralds and priests, each both special and subordinate), who is then presented to us as clothed with any individual authority, – the person by whom all the executive functions, then few in number, which the society requires, are either performed or directed. His personal ascendency – derived from divine countenance, bestowed both upon himself individually and upon his race, and probably from accredited divine descent – is the salient feature in the picture. The people hearken to his voice, embrace his propositions, and obey his orders: not merely resistance, but even criticism upon his acts, is generally exhibited in an odious point of view, and is, indeed, never heard of except from some one or more of the subordinate princes. To keep alive and justify such feelings in the public mind, however, the king must himself possess various accomplishments, bodily and mental, and that too in a superior degree. He must be brave in the field, wise in the council, and eloquent in the agora; he must be endued with bodily strength and activity above other men, and must be an adept, not only in the use of his arms, but also in those athletic exercises which the crowd delight to witness. Even the more homely varieties of manual acquirements are an addition to his character, – such as the craft of the carpenter or shipwright, the straight furrowing of the ploughman, or the indefatigable persistence of the mower without repose or refreshment throughout the longest day. The conditions of voluntary obedience, during the Grecian heroic times, are family descent with personal force and superiority mental as well as bodily, in the chief, coupled with the favour of the gods: an old chief, such as Pêleus and Laërtes, cannot retail his position. On the other hand, where these elements of force are present, a good deal of violence, caprice, and rapacity is tolerated: the ethical judgment is not exact in scrutinising the conduct of individuals so pre-eminently endowed. As in the case of the gods, the general epithets of *good, just,* &c., are applied to them as euphemisms arising from submission and fear, being not only not suggested, but often pointedly belied, by their particular acts. These words signify the man of birth, wealth, influence, and daring, whose arm is strong to destroy or to protect, whatever may be the turn of his moral sentiments; while the opposite epithet, *bad,* designates the poor, lowly, and weak; from whose dispositions, be they ever so virtuous, society has little either to hope or to fear.

Aristotle, in his general theory of government, lays down the position, that the earliest sources of obedience and authority among mankind are personal, exhibiting themselves most perfectly in the type of paternal supremacy; and that therefore the kingly government, as most conformable to this stage of social sentiment, became probably the first established everywhere. In fact it still continued in his time to be generally prevalent among the non-Hellenic nations, immediately around; though the Phœnician cities and Carthage, the most civilised of all non-Hellenic states, were republics. Nevertheless, so completely were the feelings about kingship reversed among his contemporary Greeks, that he finds it difficult to enter into the voluntary obedience paid by his ancestors to their early heroic chiefs. He cannot explain to his own satisfaction how any one man should have been so much superior to the companions around him as to maintain such immense personal ascendency: he suspects that in such small communities great merit was very rare, so that the chief had few competitors. Such remarks illustrate strongly the revolution which the Greek mind had undergone daring the preceding centuries, in regard to the internal grounds of political submission. The connecting link, between the Homeric and the republican schemes of government, is to be found in two adjuncts of the Homeric royalty, which are now to be mentioned, – the Boulê, or council of chiefs, and the agora, or general assembly of freemen.

The Boulê and the Agora.

These two meetings, more or less frequently convoked, and interwoven with the earliest habits of the primitive Grecian communities, are exhibited in the monuments of the legendary age as opportunities for advising the king, and media for promulgating his intentions to the people, rather than as restraints upon his authority. Unquestionably, they must have conduced in practice to the latter result as well as to the former; but this is not the light in which the Homeric poems describe them. The chiefs, kings, princes, or Gerontes – for the same word in Greek designates both an old man and a man of conspicuous rank and position – compose the council, in which, according to the representations in the Iliad, the resolutions of Agamemnôn on the one side, and of Hectôr on the other, appear uniformly to prevail. The harshness and even contempt with which Hectôr treats respectful opposition from his ancient companion Polydamas, – the desponding tone and conscious inferiority of the latter, and the unanimous assent which the former obtains, even when quite in the wrong – all this is clearly set forth in the poem; while in the Grecian camp we see Nestôr tendering his advice in the most submissive and delicate manner to Agamemnôn, to be adopted or rejected, as "the king of men" might determine. The council is a purely consultative body, assembled, not with any power of peremptorily arresting mischievous resolves of the king, but solely for his information and guidance. He himself is the presiding (Boulephorus, or) member of council; the rest, collectively as well as individually, are his subordinates.

We proceed from the Council to the Agora. According to what seems the received custom, the king, after having talked over his intentions with the former, proceeds to announce them to the people. The heralds make the crowd sit down in order, and enforce silence: any one of the chiefs or councillors – but as if seems, no one else – is allowed to address them: the king first promulgates his intentions, which are then open to be commented upon by others. In the Homeric agora, no division of affirmative or negative voices ever takes place, nor is any formal resolution ever adopted. The nullity of positive function strikes us even more in the Agora than in the Council. It is an assembly for talk, communication and discussion to a certain extent, by the chiefs, in presence of the people as listeners and sympathisers, – often for eloquence, and sometimes for quarrel, – but here its ostensible purposes end.

The Agora in Ithaka, in the second book of the Odyssey, is convened by the youthful Telemachus, at the instigation of Athênê, not for the purpose of submitting any proposition, but in order to give formal and public notice to the suitors to desist from their iniquitous intrusion and pillage of his substance, and to absolve himself farther, before gods and men, from all obligations towards them, if they refuse to comply. For the slaughter of the suitors, in all the security of the festive hall and banquet (which forms the catastrophe of the Odyssey), was a proceeding involving much that was shocking to Grecian feeling, and therefore required to be preceded by such ample formalities, as would leave both the delinquents themselves without the shadow of excuse, and their surviving relatives without any claim to the customary satisfaction. For this special purpose, Telemachus directs the heralds to summon an agora; but what seems most of all surprising is, that none had ever been summoned or held since the departure of Odysseus himself, – an interval of twenty years. "No agora or session has taken place amongst us (says the grey-headed Ægyptius, who opens the proceedings) since Odysseus went on shipboard: and now, who is he that has called us together? What man, young or old, has felt such a strong necessity? Has he received intelligence from our absent warriors, or has he other public news to communicate? He is our good friend for doing this: whatever his projects may be, I pray Zeus to grant him success." Telemachus, answering the appeal forthwith, proceeds to tell the assembled Ithakans that he has no public news to communicate, but that he has convoked them upon his own private necessities. Next, he sets forth, pathetically, the wickedness of the suitors, calls upon them personally to desist, and upon the people to restrain them, and concludes by solemnly warning them, that, being henceforward free from all obligation towards them, he will invoke the avenging aid of Zeus, so "that they may be slain in the interior of his own house, without bringing upon him any subsequent penalty."

We are not of course to construe the Homeric description as anything more than an *idéal,* approximating to actual reality. But, allowing all that can be required for such a limitation, it exhibits the Agora more as a special medium of publicity and intercommunication, from the king to the body of the people, than as including any idea of responsibility on the part of the former or restraining force on the part of the latter, however such consequences may indirectly grow out of it. The primitive Grecian government is essentially monarchical, reposing on personal feeling and divine right: the memorable dictum in the Iliad is borne out by all that we hear of the actual practice; "The ruler of many is not a good thing: let us have one ruler only, – one king, – him to whom Zeus has given the sceptre and the tutelary sanctions."

The second book of the Iliad, full as it is of beauty and vivacity, not only confirms our idea of the passive, recipient, and listening character of the Agora, but even presents a repulsive picture of the degradation of the mass of the people before the chiefs. Agamemnôn convokes the Agora for the purpose of immediately arming the Grecian host, under a full impression that the gods have at last determined forthwith to crown his arms with complete victory. Such impression has been created by a special visit of Oneirus (the Dream-god), sent by Zeus during his sleep, – being, indeed, an intentional fraud on the part of Zeus, though Agamemnôn does not suspect its deceitful character. At this precise moment, when he may be conceived to be more than usually anxious to get his army into the field and snatch the prize, an unaccountable fancy seizes him, that, instead of inviting the troops to do what he really wishes, and encouraging their spirits for this one last effort, he will adopt a course directly contrary: he will try their courage by professing to believe that the siege had become desperate, and that there was no choice except to go on shipboard and flee. Announcing to Nestôr and Odysseus, in preliminary council, his intention to hold this strange language, he at the same time tells them that he relies upon them to oppose it and counter-work its effect upon the multitude. The agora is presently assembled, and the king of men pours forth a speech full of dismay and despair, concluding by a distinct exhortation to all present to go aboard and return home at once. Immediately the whole army, chiefs as well as people, break up and proceed to execute his orders: every one rushes off to get his ship afloat, except Odysseus, who looks on in mournful silence and astonishment. The army would have been quickly on its voyage home, had not the goddesses Hêrê and Athênê stimulated Odysseus to an instantaneous interference. He hastens among the dispersing crowd and diverts them from their purpose of retreat: to the chiefs he addresses flattering words, trying to shame them by gentle expostulation; but the people he visits with harsh reprimand and blows from his sceptre, thus driving them back to their seats in the agora.

Amidst the dissatisfied crowd thus unwillingly brought back, the voice of Thersitês is heard the longest and the loudest, – a man ugly, deformed, and unwarlike, but fluent in speech, and especially severe and unsparing in his censure of the chiefs, Agamemnôn, Achillês, and Odysseus. Upon this occasion, he addresses to the people a speech denouncing Agamemnôn for selfish and greedy exaction generally, but particularly for his recent ill-treatment of Achillês, – and he endeavours, moreover, to induce them to persist in their scheme of departure. In reply, Odysseus not only rebukes Thersitês sharply for his impudence in abusing the commander-in-chief, but threatens that, if ever such behaviour is repeated, he will strip him naked, and thrash him out of the assembly with disgraceful blows; as an earnest of which, he administers to him at once a smart stroke with the studded sceptre, imprinting its painful mark in a bloody weal across his back. Thersitês, terrified and subdued, sits down weeping; while the surrounding crowd deride him, and express the warmest approbation of Odysseus for having thus by force put the reviler to silence.

Both Odysseus and Nestôr then address the agora, sympathising with Agamemnôn for the shame which the retreat of the Greeks is about to inflict upon him, and urging emphatically upon every one present the obligation of persevering until the siege shall be successfully consummated. Neither of them animadverts at all upon Agamemnôn, either for his conduct towards Achillês, or for his childish freak of trying the temper of the army.

There cannot be a clearer indication than this description – so graphic in the original poem – of the true character of the Homeric agora. The multitude who compose it are listening and acquiescent, not often hesitating, and never refractory to the chief. The fate which awaits a presumptuous critic, even where his virulent reproaches are substantially well-founded, is plainly set forth in the treatment of Thersitês; while the unpopularity of such a character is attested even more by the excessive pains which Homer takes to heap upon him repulsive personal deformities, than by the chastisement of Odysseus; – he is lame, bald, crook-backed, of misshapen head, and squinting vision.

But we cease to wonder at the submissive character of the agora, when we read the proceedings of Odysseus towards the people themselves; – his fine words and flattery addressed to the chiefs, and his contemptuous reproof and manual violence towards the common men, at a moment when both were doing exactly the same thing, – fulfilling the express bidding of Agamemnôn, upon whom Odysseus does not offer a single comment. This scene, which excited a sentiment of strong displeasure among the democrats of historical Athens, affords a proof that the feeling of personal dignity, of which philosophic observers in Greece – Herodotus, Xenophôn, Hippocratês, and Aristotle – boasted, as distinguishing the free Greek citizen from the slavish Asiatic, was yet undeveloped in the time of Homer. The ancient epic is commonly so filled with the personal adventures of the chiefs, and the people are so constantly depicted as simple appendages attached to them, that we rarely obtain a glimpse of the treatment of the one apart from the other, such as this memorable Homeric agora affords.

There remains one other point of view in which we are to regard the Agora of primitive Greece, – as the scene in which justice was administered. The king is spoken of as constituted by Zeus the great judge of society: he has received from Zeus the sceptre, and along with it the powers of command and sanction: the people obey these commands and enforce these sanctions, under him, enriching him at the same time with lucrative presents and payments. Sometimes the king separately, sometimes the kings or chiefs or Gerontes in the plural number, are named as deciding disputes and awarding satisfaction to complainants; always, however, in public, in the midst of the assembled agora. In one of the compartments of the shield of Achillês, the details of a judicial scene are described, While the agora is full of an eager and excited crowd, two men are disputing about the fine of satisfaction for the death of a murdered man, – one averring, the other denying, that the fine had already been paid, and both demanding an inquest. The Gerontes are ranged on stone seats, in the holy circle, with two talents of gold lying before them, to be awarded to such of the litigants as shall make out his case to their satisfaction. The heralds with their sceptres, repressing the warm sympathies of the crowd in favour of one or other of the parties, secure an alternate hearing to both. This interesting picture completely harmonises with the brief allusion of Hesiod to the judicial trial – doubtless a real trial – between himself and his brother Persês. The two brothers disputed about their paternal inheritance, and the cause was carried to be tried by the chiefs in agora; but Persês bribed them, and obtained an unjust verdict for the whole. So at least Hesiod affirms, in the bitterness of his heart; earnestly exhorting his brother not to waste a precious time, required for necessary labours, in the unprofitable occupation of witnessing and abetting litigants in the agora, – for which (he adds) no man has proper leisure, unless his subsistence for the year beforehand be safely treasured up in his garners. He repeats, more than once, his complaints of the crooked and corrupt judgments of which the Kings were habitually guilty; dwelling upon abuse of justice as the crying evil of his day, and predicting as well as invoking the vengeance of Zeus to repress it. Homer ascribes the tremendous violence of the autumnal storms to the wrath of Zeus against those judges who disgrace the agora with their wicked verdicts.

Though it is certain that, in every state of society, the feelings of men when assembled in multitude will command a certain measure of attention, yet we thus find the agora, in judicial matters still more than in political, serving merely the purpose of publicity. It is the king who is the grand personal mover of Grecian heroic society. He is on earth, the equivalent of Zeus in the agora of the gods: the supreme god of Olympus is in the habit of carrying on his government with frequent publicity, of hearing some dissentient opinions, and of allowing himself occasionally to be wheedled by Aphroditê, or worried into compliance by Hêrê; but his determination is at last conclusive, subject only to the overruling interference of the Mœræ, or Fates. Both the society of gods, and the various societies of men, are, according to the conceptions of Grecian legend, carried on by the personal rule of a legitimate sovereign, who does not derive his title from the special appointment of his subjects, though he governs with their full consent. In fact, Grecian legend presents to us hardly anything else, except these great individual personalities. The race, or nation, is as it were absorbed into the prince: eponymous persons, especially, are not merely princes, but fathers and representative unities, each the equivalent of that greater or less aggregate to which he gives name.

Though, in the primitive Grecian government, the king is the legitimate as well as the real sovereign, he is always conceived as acting through the council and agora. Both the one and the other are established and essential media through which his ascendency is brought to bear upon the society: the absence of such assemblies is the test and mark of savage men, as in the ease of the Cyclôpes. Accordingly, he must possess qualities fit to act with effect upon these two assemblies: wise reason for the council, unctuous eloquence for the agora. Such is the *idéal* of the heroic government: a king, not merely full of valour and resource as a soldier, but also sufficiently superior to those around him to insure both the deliberate concurrence of the chiefs, and the hearty adhesion of the masses. That this picture is not, in all individual cases, realised, is unquestionable; but the endowments so often predicated of good kings show it to have been the type present to the mind of the describer. Xenophôn, in his Cyropædia, depicts Cyrus as an improved edition of the Homeric Agamemnôn, – "a good king and a powerful soldier," thus idealising the perfection of personal government.

It is important to point out these fundamental conceptions of government, discernible even before the dawn of Grecian history, and identified with the social life of the people. It shows us that the Greeks, in their subsequent revolutions, and in the political experiments which their countless autonomous communities presented, worked upon pre-existing materials, – developing and exalting elements which had been at first subordinate, and suppressing, or remodelling on a totally new principle, that which had been originally predominant. When we approach historical Greece, we find that (with the exception of Sparta) the primitive hereditary, un-responsible monarch, uniting in himself all the functions of government, has ceased to reign, – while the feeling of legitimacy, which originally induced his people to obey him willingly, has been exchanged for one of aversion towards the character and title generally. The multifarious functions which he once exercised, have been parcelled out among temporary nominees. On the other hand, the Council, or Senate, and the Agora, originally simple media through which the king acted, are elevated into standing and independent sources of authority, controlling and holding in responsibility the various special officers to whom executive duties of one kind or another are confided. The general principle here indicated is common both to the oligarchies and the democracies which grew up in historical Greece: much as these two governments differed from each other, and many as were the varieties even between one oligarchy or democracy and another, they all stood in equal contrast with the principle of the heroic government. Even in Sparta, where the hereditary kingship lasted, it was preserved with lustre and influence exceedingly diminished, and such timely diminution of its power seems to have been one of the essential conditions of its preservation. Though the Spartan kings had the hereditary command of the military forces, yet, even in all foreign expeditions, they habitually acted in obedience to orders from home; while in affairs of the interior, the superior power of the ephors sensibly overshadowed them. So that, unless possessed of more than ordinary force of character, they seem to have exercised their chief influence as presiding members of the senate.

Public speaking.

There is yet another point of view in which it behoves us to take notice of the council and the agora as integral portions of the legendary government of the Grecian communities. We are thus enabled to trace the employment of public speaking, as the standing engine of government and the proximate cause of obedience, to the social infancy of the nation. The power of speech in the direction of public affairs becomes more and more obvious, developed, and irresistible, as we advance towards the culminating period of Grecian history, the century preceding the battle of Chæroneia. That its development was greatest among the most enlightened sections of the Grecian name, and smallest among the more obtuse and stationary, is matter of notorious fact; nor is it less true, that the prevalence of this habit was one of the chief causes of the intellectual eminence of the nation generally. At a time when all the countries around were plunged comparatively in mental torpor, there was no motive sufficiently present and powerful to multiply so wonderfully the productive minds of Greece, except such as arose from the rewards of public speaking. The susceptibility of the multitude to this sort of guidance, their habit of requiring and enjoying the stimulus which it supplied, and the open discussion, combining regular forms with free opposition, of practical matters, political as well as judicial, – are the creative causes which formed such conspicuous adepts in the art of persuasion. Nor was it only professed orators who were thus produced; didactic aptitude was formed in the background, and the speculative tendencies were supplied with interesting phenomena for observation and combination, at a time when the truths of physical science were almost inaccessible. If the primary effect was to quicken the powers of expression, the secondary, but not less certain result, was to develop the habits of scientific thought. Not only the oratory of Demosthenês and Periklês, and the colloquial magic of Sokratês, but also the philosophical speculations of Plato, and the systematic politics, rhetoric, and logic of Aristotle, are traceable to the same general tendencies in the minds of the Grecian people; and we find the germ of these expansive forces in the senate and agora of their legendary government. The poets, first epic and then lyric, were the precursors of the orators, in their power of moving the feelings of an assembled crowd; whilst the Homeric poems – the general training-book of educated Greeks – constituted a treasury of direct and animated expression, full of concrete forms, and rare in the use of abstractions, and thence better suited to the workings of oratory. The subsequent critics had no difficulty in selecting from the Iliad and Odyssey, samples of eloquence in all its phases and varieties.

On the whole, then, the society depicted in the old Greek poems is loose and unsettled, presenting very little of legal restraint, and still less of legal protection, – but concentrating such political power as does exist in the hands of a legitimate hereditary king, whose ascendency over the other chiefs is more or less complete according to his personal force and character. Whether that ascendency be greater or less, however, the mass of the people is in either case politically passive and of little account, Though the Grecian freeman of the heroic age is above the degraded level of the Gallic *plebs,* as described by Cæsar, he is far from rivalling the fierce independence and sense of dignity, combined with individual force, which characterise the Germanic tribes before their establishment in the Roman empire. Still less does his condition, or the society in which he moves, correspond to those pleasing dreams of spontaneous rectitude and innocence, in which Tacitus and Seneca indulge with regard to primitive man.

2. The state of moral and social feeling, prevalent in legendary Greece, exhibits a scene in harmony with the rudimentary political fabrics just described. Throughout the long stream of legendary narrative on which the Greeks looked back as their past history, the larger social motives hardly ever come into play: either individual valour and cruelty, or the personal attachments and quarrels of relatives and war-companions, or the feuds of private enemies, are ever before us. There is no sense of obligation then existing, between man and man as such, – and very little between each man and the entire community of which he is a member; such sentiments are neither operative in the real world, nor present to the imaginations of the poets. Personal feelings, either towards the gods, the king, or some near and known individual, fill the whole of a man's bosom: out of them arise all the motives to beneficence, and all the internal restraints upon violence, antipathy, or rapacity; and special communion, as well as special solemnities, are essential to their existence. The ceremony of an oath, so imposing, so paramount, and so in dispensable in those days, illustrates strikingly this principle. Even in the case of the stranger suppliant, – in which an apparently spontaneous sympathy manifests itself, – the succour and kindness shown to him arise mainly from his having gone through the consecrated formalities of supplication, such as that of sitting down in the ashes by the sacred hearth, thus obtaining a sort of privilege of sanctuary. That ceremony exalts him into something more than a mere suffering man, – it places him in express fellowship with the master of the house, under the tutelary sanctions of Zeus Hiketêsios. There is great difference between one form of supplication and another; the suppliant, however, in any form, becomes more or less the object of a particular sympathy.

The sense of obligation towards the gods manifests itself separately in habitual acts of worship, sacrifice, and libations, or by votive presents, such as that of the hair of Achillês, which he has pledged to the river-god Spercheius, and such as the constant dedicated offerings which men who stand in urgent need of the divine aid first promise and afterwards fulfil. But the feeling towards the gods also appears, and that not less frequently, as mingling itself with and enforcing obligations towards some particular human person. The tie which binds a man to his father, his kinsman, his guest, or any special promise respecting which he has taken the engagement of an oath, is conceived in conjunction with the idea of Zeus, as witness and guarantee; and the intimacy of the association is attested by some surname or special appellation of the god. Such personal feelings composed all the moral influences of which a Greek of that day was susceptible, – a state of mind which we can best appreciate by contrasting it with that of the subsequent citizen of historical Athens. In the view of the latter, the great impersonal authority, called "The Laws," stood out separately, both as guide and sanction, distinct from religious duty or private sympathies; but of this discriminated conception of positive law and positive morality, the germ only can be detected in the Homeric poems. The appropriate Greek word for human laws never occurs. Amidst a very wavering phraseology, we can detect a gradual transition from the primitive idea of a personal goddess Themis, attached to Zeus, first to his sentences or orders called Themistes, and next by a still farther remove to various established customs, which those sentences were believed to sanctify, – the authority of religion and that of custom coalescing into one indivisible obligation.

The family relations, as we might expect, are set forth in our pictures of the legendary world as the grand sources of lasting union and devoted attachment. The paternal authority is highly reverenced: the son who lives to years of maturity, repays by affection to his parents the charge of his maintenance in infancy, which the language notes by a special word; whilst on the other hand, the Erinnys, whose avenging hand is put in motion by the curse of a father or mother, is an object of deep dread.

Marriage & respect paid to a wife.

In regard to marriage, we find the wife occupying a station of great dignity and influence, though it was the practice for the husband to purchase her by valuable presents to her parents, – a practice extensively prevalent among early communities, and treated by Aristotle as an evidence of barbarism. She even seems to live less secluded and to enjoy a wider sphere of action than was allotted to her in historical Greece. Concubines are frequent with the chiefs, and occasionally the jealousy of the wife breaks out in reckless excess against her husband, as may be seen in the tragical history of Phœnix. The continence of Laërtês, from fear of displeasing his wife Antikleia, is especially noticed. A large portion of the romantic interest which Grecian legend inspires is derived from the women: Penelopê, Andromachê, Helen, Klytæmnêstra, Eriphylê, Iokasta, Hekabê, &c., all stand in the foreground of the picture, either from their virtues their beauty, their crimes, or their sufferings.

Not only brothers, but also cousins, and the more distant blood-relations and clansmen, appear connected together by a strong feeling of attachment, sharing among them universally the obligation of mutual self-defence and revenge, in the event of injury to any individual of the race. The legitimate brothers divide between them by lot the paternal inheritance, – a bastard brother receiving only a small share: he is, however, commonly very well treated, though the murder of Phôkus, by Telamôn and Pêleus, constitutes a flagrant exception. The furtive pregnancy of young women, often by a god, is one of the most frequently recurring incidents in the legendary narratives; and the severity with which such a fact, when discovered, is visited by the father, is generally extreme. As an extension of the family connection, we read of larger unions, called the phratry and the tribe, which are respectfully, but not frequently, mentioned.

The generous readiness with which hospitality is afforded to the stranger who asks for it, the facility with which he is allowed to contract the peculiar connection of guest with his host, and the permanence with which that connection, when created by partaking of the same food and exchanging presents, is maintained even through a long period of separation, and even transmitted from father to son – these are among the most captivating features of the heroic society. The Homeric chief welcomes the stranger who comes to ask shelter in his house, first gives him refreshment, and then inquires his name and the purpose of his voyage. Though not inclined to invite strangers to his house, he cannot repel them when they spontaneously enter it craving a lodging. The suppliant is also commonly a stranger, but a stranger under peculiar circumstances; who proclaims his own calamitous and abject condition, and seeks to place himself in a relation to the chief whom he solicits, something like that in which men stand to the gods. Onerous as such special tie may become to him, the chief cannot decline it, if solicited in the proper form: the ceremony of supplication has a binding effect, and the Erinnys punish the hardhearted person who disallows it. A conquered enemy may sometimes throw himself at the feet of his conqueror, and solicit mercy, but he cannot by doing so acquire the character and claims of a suppliant properly so called: the conqueror has free discretion either to kill him, or to spare him and accept a ransom.

There are in the legendary narratives abundant examples of individuals who transgress in particular acts even the holiest of these personal ties, but the savage Cyclops is the only person described as professedly indifferent to them, and careless of that sanction of the gods which in Grecian belief accompanied them all. In fact, the tragical horror which pervades the lineage of Athamas or Kadmus, and which attaches to many of the acts of Hêraklês, of Pêleus and Telamôn, of Jasôn and Mêdea, of Atreus and Thyestês, &c., is founded upon a deep feeling and sympathy with those special obligations, which conspicuous individuals, under the temporary stimulus of the maddening Atê, are driven to violate. In such conflict of sentiments, between the obligation generally reverenced and the exceptional deviation in an individual otherwise admired, consists the pathos of the story.

These feelings – of mutual devotion between kinsmen and companions in arms – of generous hospitality to the stranger, and of helping protection to the suppliant, – constitute the bright spots in a dark age. We find them very generally prevalent amongst communities essentially rude and barbarous, – amongst the ancient Germans as described by Tacitus, the Druses in Lebanon, the Arabian tribes in the desert, and even the North American Indians.

They are the instinctive manifestations of human sociality, standing at first alone, and for that reason appearing to possess a greater tutelary force than really belongs to them, – beneficent, indeed, in a high degree, with reference to their own appropriate period, but serving as a very imperfect compensation for the impotence of the magistrate, and for the absence of any all-pervading sympathy or sense of obligation between man and man. We best appreciate their importance when we compare the Homeric society with that of barbarians like the Thracians, who tattooed their bodies, as the mark of a generous lineage, – sold their children for export as slaves, – considered robbery, not merely as one admissible occupation among others, but as the only honourable mode of life; agriculture being held contemptible, – and above all, delighted in the shedding of blood as a luxury. Such were the Thracians in the days of Herodotus and Thucydidês; and the Homeric society forms a mean term between that which these two historians yet saw in Thrace, and that which they witnessed among their own civilised countrymen.

When, however, among the Homeric men we pass beyond the influence of the private ties above enumerated, we find scarcely any other moralising forces in operation. The acts and adventures commemorated imply a community wherein neither the protection nor the restraints of law are practically felt, and where in ferocity, rapine, and the aggressive propensities generally, seem restrained by no internal counterbalancing scruples. Homicide, especially, is of frequent occurrence, sometimes by open violence, sometimes by fraud. Expatriation for homicide is among the most constantly recurring acts of the Homeric poems; and savage brutalities are often ascribed, even to admired heroes, with apparent indifference. Achilles sacrifices twelve Trojan prisoners on the tomb of Patroklus, while his son Neoptolemus not only slaughters the aged Priam, but also seizes by the leg the child Astyanax (son of the slain Hectôr) and hurls him from one of the lofty towers of Troy. Moreover, the celebrity of Autolykus, the maternal grandfather of Odysseus, in the career of wholesale robbery and perjury, and the wealth which it enabled him to acquire, are described with the same unaffected admiration as the wisdom of Nestôr or the strength of Ajax. Achillês, Menelaus, Odysseus, pillage in person, wherever they can find an opportunity, employing both force and stratagem to surmount resistance. The vocation of a pirate is recognised and honourable, so that a host, when he asks his guest what is the purpose of his voyage enumerates enrichment by indiscriminate maritime plunder as among those projects which may naturally enter into his contemplation. Abduction of cattle, and expeditions for unprovoked ravage as well as for retaliation, between neighbouring tribes, appear ordinary phenomena; and the established inviolability of heralds seems the only evidence of any settled feeling of obligation between one community and another. While the house and property of Odysseus, during his long absence, enjoys no public protection, those unprincipled chiefs, who consume his substance, find sympathy rather than disapprobation among the people of Ithaka. As a general rule, he who cannot protect himself finds no protection from society: his own kinsmen and immediate companions are the only parties to whom he can look with confidence for support. In this respect, the representation given by Hesiod makes the picture even worse. In his emphatic denunciation of the fifth age, that poet deplores not only the absence of all social justice and sense of obligation among his contemporaries, but also the relaxation of the ties of family and hospitality. There are marks of querulous exaggeration in the poem of the Works and Days; yet the author professes to describe the real state of things around him, and the features of his picture, soften them as we may, will still appear dark and calamitous. It is, however to be remarked, that he contemplates a state of peace, – thus forming a contrast with the Homeric poems. His copious catalogue of social evils scarcely mentions liability to plunder by a foreign enemy, nor does he compute the chances of predatory aggression as a source of profit.

There are two special veins of estimable sentiment, on which it may be interesting to contrast heroic and historical Greece, and which exhibit the latter as an improvement on the former, not less in the affections than in the intellect.

The law of Athens was peculiarly watchful and provident with respect both to the persons and the property of orphan minors; but the description given in the Iliad of the utter and hopeless destitution of the orphan boy, despoiled of his paternal inheritance, and abandoned by all the friends of his father, whom he urgently supplicates, and who all harshly cast him off, is one of the most pathetic morsels in the whole poem. In reference again to the treatment of the dead body of an enemy we find all the Greek chiefs who come near (not to mention the conduct of Achilles himself) piercing with their spears the corpse of the slain Hectôr, while some of them even pass disgusting taunts upon it. We may add, from the lost epics, the mutilation of the dead bodies of Paris and Deiphobus by the hand of Menelaus. At the time of the Persian invasion, it was regarded as unworthy of a right-minded Greek to maltreat in any way the dead body of an enemy, even where such a deed might seem to be justified on the plea of retaliation. After the battle of Platæa, a proposition was made to the Spartan king Pausanias, to retaliate upon the dead body of Mardonius the indignities which Xerxês had heaped upon that of Leonidas at Thermopylæ. He indignantly spurned the suggestion, not without a severe rebuke, or rather a half-suppressed menace, towards the proposer; and the feeling of Herodotus himself goes heartily along with him.

The different manner of dealing with homicide presents a third test, perhaps more striking yet, of the change in Grecian feelings and manners during the three centuries preceding the Persian invasion. That which the murderer in the Homeric times had to dread, was, not public prosecution and punishment, but the personal vengeance of the kinsmen and friends of the deceased, who were stimulated by the keenest impulses of honour and obligation to avenge the deed, and were considered by the public as specially privileged to do so. To escape from this danger, he is obliged to flee the country, unless he can prevail upon the incensed kinsmen to accept of a valuable payment (we must not speak of coined money, in the days of Homer) as satisfaction for their slain comrade. They may, if they please, decline the offer, and persist in their right of revenge; but if they accept, they are bound to leave the offender unmolested, and he accordingly remains at home without farther consequences. The chiefs in agora do not seem to interfere, except to insure payment of the stipulated sum.

Here we recognise once more the characteristic attribute of the Grecian heroic age, – the omnipotence of private force, tempered and guided by family sympathies, and the practical nullity of that collective sovereign afterwards called *The City,* – who in historical Greece becomes the central and paramount source of obligation, but who appears yet only in the background, as a germ of promise for the future. The manner in which, in the case of homicide, that germ was developed into a powerful reality, presents an interesting field of comparison with other nations.

For the practice, here designated, of leaving the party guilty of homicide to compromise by valuable payment with the relatives of the deceased, and also of allowing to the latter a free choice whether they would accept such compromise or enforce their right of personal revenge, – has been remarked in many rude communities, but is particularly memorable among the early German tribes. Among the many separate Teutonic establishments which rose upon the ruins of the Western empire of Rome, the right as well as duty of private revenge, for personal injury or insult offered to any member of a family, – and the endeavour to avert its effects by means of a pecuniary composition levied upon the offender, chiefly as satisfaction to the party injured, but partly also as perquisite to the king, – was adopted as the basis of their legislation. This fundamental idea was worked out in elaborate detail as to the valuation of the injury inflicted, wherein one main circumstance was the rank, condition, and power of the sufferer. The object of the legislator was to preserve the society from standing feuds, but at the same time to accord such full satisfaction as would induce the injured person to waive his acknowledged right of personal revenge, – the full luxury of which, as it presented itself to the mind of an Homeric Greek, may be read in more than one passage of the Iliad. The German codes begin by trying to bring about the acceptance of a fixed pecuniary composition as a constant voluntary custom, and proceed ultimately to enforce it as a peremptory necessity: the idea of society is at first altogether subordinate, and its influence passes only by slow degrees from amicable arbitration into imperative control.

The Homeric society, in regard to this capital point in human progression, is on a level with that of the German tribes at described by Tacitus. But the subsequent course of Grecian legislation takes a direction completely different from that of the German codes: the primitive and acknowledged right of private revenge (unless where bought off by pecuniary payment), instead of being developed into practical working, is superseded by more comprehensive views of a public wrong requiring public intervention, or by religious fears respecting the posthumous wrath of the murdered person. In historical Athens, this right of private revenge was discountenanced and put out of sight, even so early as the Drakonian legislation, and at last restricted to a few extreme and special cases; while the murderer came to be considered, first as having offended against the gods, next as having deeply injured the society, and thus at once as requiring absolution and deserving punishment. On the first of these two grounds, he is interdicted from the agora and from all holy places, as well as from public functions, even while yet untried and simply a suspected person; for if this were not done, the wrath of the gods would manifest itself in bad crops and other national calamities. On the second ground, he is tried before the council of Areiopagus, and if found guilty, is condemned to death, or perhaps to disfranchisement and banishment, The idea of a propitiatory payment to the relatives of the deceased has ceased altogether to be admitted: it is the protection of society which dictates, and the force of society which inflicts, a measure of punishment calculated to deter for the future.

Slaves and Thetês.

3. The society of legendary Greece includes, besides the chiefs, the general mass of freemen (λαοί), among whom stand out by special names certain professional men, such as the carpenter, the smith, the leather-dresser, the leech, the prophet, the bard, and the fisherman. We have no means of appreciating their condition. Though lots of arable land were assigned in special property to individuals, with boundaries both carefully marked and jealously watched, yet the larger proportion of surface was devoted to pasture. Cattle formed both the chief item in the substance of a wealthy man, the chief means of making payments, and the common ground of quarrels, – bread and meat, in large quantities, being the constant food of every one. The estates of the owners were tilled, and their cattle tended, mostly by bought slaves, but to a certain degree also by poor freemen called Thêtes, working for hire and for stated periods. The principal slaves, who were entrusted with the care of large herds of oxen, swine, or goats, were of necessity men worthy of confidence, their duties placing them away from their master's immediate eye. They had other slaves subordinate to them, and appear to have been well-treated: the deep and unshaken attachment of Eumtæus the swineherd and Philœtius the neat-herd to the family and affairs of the absent Odysseus, is among the most interesting points in the ancient epic. Slavery was a calamity, which in that period of insecurity might befall any one: the chief who conducted a freebooting expedition, if he succeeded, brought back with him a numerous troop of slaves, as many as he could seize, – if he failed, became very likely a slave himself. Such that the slave was often by birth of equal dignity with his master: Eumæus was himself the son of a chief, conveyed away when a child by his nurse, and sold by Phœnician kidnappers to Laërtês. A slave of this character, if he conducted himself well, might often expect to be enfranchised by his master and placed in an independent holding.

On the whole, the slavery of legendary Greece does not present itself as existing under a peculiarly harsh form, especially if we consider that all the classes of society were then very much upon a level in point of taste, sentiment, and instruction. In the absence of legal security or an effective social sanction, it is probable that the condition of a slave under an average master, may have been as good as that of the free Thête. The class of slaves whose lot appears to have been the most pitiable were the females, – more numerous than the males, and performing the principal work in the interior of the house. Not only do they seem to have been more harshly treated than the males, but they were charged with the hardest and most exhausting labour which the establishment of a Greek chief required: they brought in water from the spring, and turned by hand the house-mills, which ground the large quantity of flour consumed in his family. This oppressive task was performed generally by female slaves, in historical as well as legendary Greece. Spinning and weaving was the constant occupation of women, whether free or slave, of every rank and station: all the garments worn both by men and women were fashioned at home, and Helen as well as Penelopê is expert and assiduous at the occupation. The daughters of Keleos at Eleusis go to the well with their basins for water, and Nausikaa, daughter of Alkinous, joins her female slaves in the business of washing her garments in the river. If we are obliged to point out the fierceness and insecurity of an early society, we may at the same time note with pleasure its characteristic simplicity of manners: Rebecca, Rachel, and the daughters of Jethro, in the early Mosaic narrative, as well as the wife of the native Macedonian chief (with whom the Temenid Perdiccas, ancestor of Philip and Alexander, first took service on retiring from Argos), baking her own cakes on the hearth, exhibit a parallel in this respect to the Homeric pictures.

We obtain no particulars respecting either the common freemen generally, or the particular class of them called Thêtes. These latter, engaged for special jobs, or at the harvest and other busy seasons of field labour, seem to have given their labour in exchange for board and clothing: they are mentioned in the same line with the slaves, and were (as has been just observed) probably on the whole little better off. The condition of a poor freeman in those days, without a lot of land of his own, going about from one temporary job to another, and having no powerful family and no social authority to look up to for protection, must have been sufficiently miserable. When Eumæus indulged his expectation of being manumitted by his masters, he thought at the same time that they would give him a wife, a house, and a lot of land near to themselves; without which collateral advantages, simple manumission might perhaps have been no improvement in his condition. To be Thête in the service of a very poor farmer is selected by Achilles as the maximum of human hardship: such a person could not give to his Thête the same ample food, and good shoes and clothing, as the wealthy chief Eurymachus, while he would exact more severe labour. It was probably among such smaller occupants, who could not advance the price necessary to purchase slaves, and were glad to save the cost of keep when they did not need service, that the Thêtes found employment: though we may conclude that the brave and strong amongst these poor freemen found it preferable to accompany some freebooting chief and to live by the plunder acquired. The exact Hesiod advises his farmer, whose work is chiefly performed by slaves, to employ and maintain the Thête. during summer-time, but to dismiss him as soon as the harvest is completely got in, and then to take into his house for the winter a woman "without any child;" who would of course be more useful than the Thête for the indoor occupations of that season.

In a state of society such as that which we have been describing, Grecian commerce was necessarily trifling and restricted. The Homeric poems mark either total ignorance or great vagueness of apprehension respecting all that lies beyond the coasts of Greece and Asia Minor, and the islands between or adjoining them. Libya and Egypt are supposed so distant as to be known only by name and hearsay: indeed, when the city of Kyrene was founded, a century and a half after the first Olympiad, it was difficult to find anywhere a Greek navigator who had ever visited the coast of Libya, or was fit to serve as guide to the colonists. The mention of the Sikels in the Odyssey, leads us to conclude that Korkyra, Italy, and Sicily were not wholly unknown to the poet: among seafaring Greeks, the knowledge of the latter implied the knowledge of the two former, – since the habitual track, even of a well-equipped Athenian trireme during the Peloponnesian war, from Peloponnêsus to Sicily, was by Korkyra and the Gulf of Tarentum. The Phokæans, long afterwards, were the first Greeks who explored either the Adriatic or Tyrrhenian sea. Of the Euxine sea no knowledge is manifested in Homer, who, as a general rule, presents to us the names of distant regions only in connection with romantic or monstrous accompaniments. The Kretans, and still more the Taphians (who are supposed to have occupied the western islands off the coast of Akarnania), are mentioned as skilful mariners, and the Taphian Mentês professes to be conveying iron to Temesa to be there exchanged for copper; but both Taphians and Kretans are more corsairs than traders. The strong sense of the dangers of the sea, expressed by the poet Hesiod, and the imperfect structure of the early Grecian ship, attested by Thucydidês (who points out the more recent date of that improved ship-building which prevailed in his time), concur to demonstrate the then narrow range of nautical enterprise.

Such was the state of the Greeks, as traders, at a time when Babylon combined a crowded and industrious population with extensive commerce, and when the Phœnician merchant-ships visited in one direction the southern coast of Arabia, perhaps even the island of Ceylon, – in another direction, the British islands.

The Phœnician, the kinsman of the ancient Jew, exhibits the type of character belonging to the latter, – with greater enterprise and ingenuity, and less of religious exclusiveness, yet still different from, and even antipathetic to, the character of the Greeks. In the Homeric poems, he appears somewhat like the Jew of the Middle Ages, a crafty trader, turning to profit the violence and rapacity of others, – bringing them ornaments, decorations, the finest and brightest products of the loom, gold, silver, electrum, ivory, tin, &c., in exchange for which he received landed produce, skins, wool, and slaves, the only commodities which even a wealthy Greek chief of those early times had to offer, – prepared at the same time for dishonest gain, in any manner which chance might throw in his way. He is, however, really a trader, not undertaking expeditions with the deliberate purpose of surprise and plunder, and standing distinguished in this respect from the Tyrrhenian, Kretan, or Taphian pirate. Tin, ivory, and electrum, all of which are acknowledged in the Homeric poems, were the fruit of Phœnician trade with the West as well as with the East.

Thucydidês tells us that the Phœnicians and Karians, in very early periods, occupied many of the islands of the Ægean, and we know, from the striking remnant of their mining works which Herodotus himself saw in Thasus, off the coast of Thrace, that they had once extracted gold from the mountains of that island, – at a period indeed very far back, since their occupation must have been abandoned prior to the settlement of the poet Archilochus. Yet few of the islands in the Ægean were rich in such valuable products, nor was it in the usual course of Phœnician proceeding to occupy islands, except where there was an adjoining mainland with which trade could be carried on. The traffic of these active mariners required no permanent settlement, but as occasional visitors they were convenient, in enabling a Greek chief to turn his captives to account, – to get rid of slaves or friendless Thêtes who were troublesome, – and to supply himself with the metals, precious as well as useful. The halls of Alkinous and Menelaus glitter with gold, copper, and electrum; while large stocks of yet unemployed metal – gold, copper, and iron – are stored up in the treasure-chamber of Odysseus and other chiefs. Coined money is unknown to the Homeric age, – the trade carried on being one of barter. In reference also to the metals, it deserves to be remarked that the Homeric descriptions universally suppose copper, and not iron, to be employed for arms, both offensive and defensive. By what process the copper was tempered and hardened, so as to serve the purposes of the warrior, we do not know; but the use of iron for these objects belongs to a later age, though the Works and Days of Hesiod suppose this change to have been already introduced.

Weapons & mode of fighting.

The mode of fighting among the Homeric heroes is not less different from the historical times, than the material of which their arms were composed. The Hoplites, or heavy-armed infantry of historical Greece, maintained a close order and well-dressed line, charging the enemy with their spears protended at even distance, and coming thus to close conflict without breaking their rank: there were special troops, bowmen, slingers, &c., armed with missiles, but the hoplite had no weapon to employ in this manner. The heroes of the Iliad and Odyssey, on the contrary, habitually employ the spear as a missile, which they launch with tremendous force: each of them is mounted in his war-chariot, drawn by two horses, and calculated to contain the warrior and his charioteer; in which latter capacity a friend or comrade will sometimes consent to serve. Advancing in his chariot at full speed, in front of his own soldiers, he hurls his spear against the enemy: sometimes, indeed, he will fight on foot, and hand to hand, but the chariot is usually near to receive him if he chooses, or to insure his retreat. The mass of the Greeks and Trojans, coming forward to the charge, without any regular step or evenly-maintained line, make their attack in the same way by hurling their spears. Each chief wears habitually a long sword and a short dagger, besides his two spears to be launched forward, – the spear being also used, if occasion serves, as a weapon for thrust. Every man is protected by shield, helmet, breastplate, and greaves; but the armour of the chiefs is greatly superior to that of the common men, while they themselves are both stronger and more expert in the use of their weapons. There are a few bowmen, as rare exceptions, but the general equipment and proceeding is as here described.

Such loose array, immortalised as it is in the Iliad, is familiar to every one; and the contrast which it presents, with those inflexible ranks, and that irresistible simultaneous charge which bore down the Persian throng at Platæa and Kunaxa, is such as to illustrate forcibly the general difference between heroic and historical Greece. While in the former, a few splendid figures stand forward, in prominent relief, the remainder being a mere unorganised and ineffective mass, – in the latter, these units have been combined into a system, in which every man, officer and soldier, has his assigned place and duty, and the victory, when gained, is the joint work of all. Pre-eminent individual prowess is indeed materially abridged, if not wholly excluded, – no man can do more than maintain his station in the line; but on the other hand, the grand purposes, aggressive or defensive, for which alone arms are taken up, become more assured and easy, and long-sighted combinations of the general are rendered for the first time practicable, when he has a disciplined body of men to obey him. In tracing the picture of civil society, we have to remark a similar transition – we pass from Hêraklês, Thesêus, Jasôn, Achillês, to Solôn, Pythagoras, and Periklês – from "the shepherd of his people," (to use the phrase in which Homer depicts the good side of the heroic king), to the legislator who introduces, and the statesman who maintains, a preconcerted system by which willing citizens consent to bind themselves. If commanding individual talent is not always to be found, the whole community is so trained as to be able to maintain its course under inferior leaders; the rights as well as the duties of each citizen being predetermined in the social order, according to principles more or less wisely laid down. The contrast is similar, and the transition equally remarkable, in the civil as in the military picture. In fact, the military organisation of the Grecian republics is an element of the greatest importance in respect to the conspicuous part which they have played in human affairs, – their superiority over other contemporary nations in this respect being hardly less striking than it is in many others, as we shall have occasion to see in a subsequent stage of this history.

Even at the most advanced point of their tactics, the Greeks could effect little against a walled city, whilst the heroic weapons and array were still less available for such an undertaking as a siege. Fortifications are a feature of the age deserving considerable notice. There was a time, we are told, in which the primitive Greek towns or villages derived a precarious security, not from their walls, but merely from sites lofty and difficult of access. They were not built immediately upon the shore, or close upon any convenient landing-place, but at some distance inland, on a rock or elevation which could not be approached without notice or scaled without difficulty. It was thought sufficient at that time to guard against piratical or marauding surprise: but as the state of society became assured, – as the chance of sudden assault comparatively diminished and industry increased, – these uninviting abodes were exchanged for more convenient sites on the plain or declivity beneath; or a portion of the latter was enclosed within larger boundaries and joined on to the original foundation, which thus became the Acropolis of the new town. Thêbes, Athens, Argôs, &c., belonged to the latter class of cities; but there were in many parts of Greece deserted sites on hilltops, still retaining, even in historical times, the traces of former habitation, and some of them still bearing the name of the old towns. Among the mountainous parts of Krête, in Ægina and Rhodes, in portions of Mount Ida and Parnassus, similar remnants might be perceived.

Probably, in such primitive hill villages, a continuous circle of wall would hardly be required as an additional means of defence, and would often be rendered very difficult by the rugged nature of the ground. Thucydidês represents the earliest Greeks – those whom he conceives anterior to the Trojan war – as living; thus universally in unfortified villages, chiefly on account of their poverty, rudeness, and thorough carelessness for the morrow. Oppressed, and held apart from each other by perpetual fear, they had not yet contracted the sentiment of fixed abodes – they were unwilling even to plant fruit-trees because of the uncertainty of gathering the produce, – and were always ready to dislodge, because there was nothing to gain by staying, and a bare subsistence might be had anywhere. He compares them to the mountaineers of Ætolia and of the Ozolian Lokris in his own time, who dwelt in their unfortified hill villages with little or no intercommunication, always armed and fighting, and subsisting on the produce of their cattle and their woods, – clothed in undressed hides, and eating raw meat. The picture given by Thucydidês, of these very early and unrecorded times, can only be taken as conjectural, – the conjectures, indeed, of a statesman and a philosopher, – generalised too, in part, from the many particular instances of contention and expulsion of chiefs which he found in the old legendary poems. The Homeric poems, however, present to us a different picture. They recognise walled towns, fixed abodes, strong local attachments, hereditary individual property in land, vineyards planted and carefully cultivated, established temples of the gods, and splendid palaces of the chiefs. The description of Thucydidês belongs to a lower form of society, and bears more analogy to that which the poet himself conceives as antiquated and barbarous, – to the savage Cyclôpes, who dwell on the tops of mountains, in hollow caves, without the plough, without vine or fruit culture, without arts or instruments, – or to the primitive settlement of Dardanus son of Zeus, on the higher ground of Ida, while it was reserved for his descendants and successors to found the holy Ilium on the plain. Ilium or Troy represents the perfection of Homeric society. It is a consecrated spot, containing temples of the gods as well as the palace of Priam, and surrounded by walls which are the fabric of the gods; while the antecedent form of ruder society, which the poet briefly glances at, is the parallel of that which the theory of Thucydidês ascribes to his own early semi-barbarous ancestors.

Walled towns serve thus as one of the evidences, that a large part of the population of Greece had, even in the Homeric times, reached a level higher than that of the Ætolians and Lokrians of the days of Thucydidês. The remains of Mykênæ and Tiryns demonstrate the massy and Cyclopian style of architecture employed in those early days: but we may remark that, while modern observers seem inclined to treat the remains of the former as very imposing, and significant of a great princely family, Thucydidês, on the contrary, speaks of it as a small place, and labours to elude the inference, which might be deduced from its insignificant size, in disproof of the grandeur of Agamemnôn. Such fortifications supplied a means of defence incomparably superior to those of attack. Indeed, even in historical Greece, and after the invention of battering engines, no city could be taken except by surprise or blockade, or by ruining the country around, and thus depriving the inhabitants of their means of subsistence. In the two great sieges of the legendary time, Troy and Thêbes, the former is captured by the stratagem of the wooden horse, while the latter is evacuated by its citizens, under the warning of the gods, after their defeat in the field.

This decided superiority of the means of defence over those of attack, in rude ages, has been one of the grand promotive causes both of the growth of civic life and of the general march of human improvement. It has enabled the progressive portions of mankind not only to maintain their acquisitions against the predatory instincts of the ruder and poorer, and to surmount the difficulties of incipient organisation. – but ultimately, when their organisation has been matured, both to acquire predominance, and to uphold it until their own disciplined habits have in part passed to their enemies. The important truth here stated is illustrated not less by the history of ancient Greece, than by that of modern Europe during the Middle Ages. The Homeric chief, combining superior rank with superior force, and ready to rob at every convenient opportunity, greatly resembles the feudal baron of the Middle Ages, but circumstances absorb him more easily into a city life, and convert the independent potentate into the member of a governing aristocracy. Traffic by sea continued to be beset with danger from, pirates, long after it had become tolerably assured by land: the "wet ways" have always been the last resort of lawlessness and violence, and the Ægean, in particular, has in all times suffered more than other waters under this calamity.

Aggressions of the sort here described were of course most numerous in those earliest times when the Ægean was not yet an Hellenic sea, and when many of the Cyclades were occupied, not by Greeks, but by Karians, – perhaps by Phœnicians: the number of Karian sepulchres discovered in the sacred island of Delus seems to attest such occupation as an historical fact. According to the legendary account, espoused both by Herodotus and by Thucydidês, it was the Kretan Minôs who subdued these islands and established his sons as rulers in them; either expelling the Karians, or reducing them to servitude and tribute. Thucydidês presumes that he must of course have put down piracy, in order to enable his tribute to be remitted in safety, like the Athenians during the time of their hegemony. Upon the legendary thalassocraty of Minôs, I have already remarked in another place: it is sufficient here to repeat, that, in the Homeric poems (long subsequent to Minôs in the current chronology), we find piracy both frequent and held in honourable estimation, as Thucydidês himself emphatically tells us, – remarking, moreover, that the vessels of those early days were only half decked, built and equipped after the piratical fashion, in a manner upon which the nautical men of his time looked back with disdain. Improved and enlarged shipbuilding, and the trireme, or ship with three banks of oars, common for warlike purposes during the Persian invasion, began only with the growing skill, activity, and importance of the Corinthians, three quarters of a century after the first Olympiad. Corinth, even in the Homeric poems, is distinguished by the epithet of wealthy, which it acquired principally from its remarkable situation on the Isthmus, and from its two harbours of Lechæum and Kenchreæ, the one on the Corinthian, the other on the Sardônic gulf. It thus supplied a convenient connection between Epirus and Italy on the one side, and the Ægean sea on the other, without imposing upon the unskilful and timid navigator of those days the necessity of circumnavigating Peloponnêsus.

The extension of Grecian traffic and shipping is manifested by a comparison of the Homeric with the Hesiodic poems; in respect to knowledge of places and countries, – the latter being probably referable to dates between B.C. 740 and B.C. 640. In Homer, acquaintance is shown (the accuracy of such acquaintance, however, being exaggerated by Strabo and other friendly critics) with continental Greece and its neighbouring islands, with Krête and the principal islands of the Ægean, and with Thrace, the Trôad, the Hellespont, and Asia Minor between Paphlagonia northward and Lykia southward. The Sikels are mentioned in the Odyssey, and Sikania in the last book of that poem, but nothing is said to evince a knowledge of Italy or the realities of the western world. Libya, Egypt, and Phœnike, are known by name and by vague hearsay, but the Nile is only mentioned as "the river Egypt:" while the Euxine sea is not mentioned at all. In the Hesiodic poems, on the other hand, the Nile, the Ister, the Phasis, and the Eridanus, are all specified by name; Mount Ætna, and the island of Ortygia near to Syracuse, the Tyrrhenians and Ligurians in the west, and the Scythians in the north, were also noticed. Indeed, within forty years after the first Olympiad, the cities of Korkyra and Syracuse were founded from Corinth, – the first of a numerous and powerful series of colonies, destined to impart a new character both to the south of Italy and to Sicily.

In reference to the astronomy and physics of the Homeric Greek, it has already been remarked that he connected together the sensible phenomena which form the subject matter of these sciences by threads of religious and personifying fancy, to which the real analogies among them were made subordinate; and that these analogies did not begin to be studied by themselves, apart from the religious element by which they had been at first overlaid, until the age of Thales, – coinciding as that period did with the increased opportunities for visiting Egypt and the interior of Asia. The Greeks obtained access in both of these countries to an enlarged stock of astronomical observations, to the use of the gnomon, or sun-dial, and to a more exact determination of the length of the solar year, than that which served as the basis of their various lunar periods. It is pretended that Thales was the first who predicted an eclipse of the sun, – not, indeed; accurately, but with large limits of error as to the time of its occurrence, – and that he also possessed so profound an acquaintance with meteorological phenomena and probabilities, as to be able to foretell an abundant crop of olives for the coming year, and to realise a large sum of money by an olive speculation. From Thales downward we trace a succession of astronomical and physical theories, more or less successful, into which I do not intend here to enter: it is sufficient at present to contrast the father of the Ionic philosophy with the times preceding him, and to mark the first commencement of scientific prediction among the Greeks, however imperfect at the outset, as distinguished from the inspired dicta of prophets or oracles, and from those special signs of the purposes of the gods, which formed the habitual reliance of the Homeric man. We shall see these two modes of anticipating the future, – one based upon the philosophical, the other upon the religious appreciation of nature, – running simultaneously on throughout Grecian history, and sharing between them in unequal portions the empire of the Greek mind; the former acquiring both greater predominance and wider application among the intellectual men, and partially restricting, but never abolishing, the spontaneous employment of the latter among the vulgar.

Neither coined money, nor the art of writing, nor painting, nor sculpture, nor imaginative architecture, belong to the Homeric and Hesiodic times. Such rudiments of arts, destined ultimately to acquire so great a development in Greece, as may have existed in these early days, served only as a sort of nucleus to the fancy of the poet, to shape out for himself the fabulous creations ascribed to Hephæstus or Dædalus. No statues of the gods, not even of wood, are mentioned in the Homeric poems. All the many varieties, in Grecian music, poetry, and dancing, – the former chiefly borrowed from Lydia and Phrygia, – date from a period considerably later than the first Olympiad: Terpander, the earliest musician whose date is assigned, and the inventor of the harp with seven strings instead of that with four strings, does not come until the 26th Olympiad, or 676 B.C.: the poet Archilochus is nearly of the same date. The iambic and elegiac metres – the first deviations from the primitive epic strain and subject – do not reach up to the year 700 B.C.

It is this epic poetry which forms at once both the undoubted prerogative and the solitary jewel of the earliest era of Greece. Of the many epic poems which existed in Greece during the eight century before the Christian æra, none have been preserved except the Iliad and Odyssey: the Æthiopis of Arktinus, the Ilias Minor of Leschês, the Cyprian Verses, the Capture of Œchalia, the Returns of the Heroes from Troy, the Thêbaïs and the Epigoni, – several of them passing in antiquity under the name of Homer, – have all been lost. But the two which remain are quite sufficient to demonstrate in the primitive Greeks, a mental organisation unparalleled in any other people, and powers of invention and expression which prepared, as well as foreboded, the future eminence of the nation in all the various departments to which thought and language can be applied. Great as the power of thought afterwards became among the Greeks, their power of expression was still greater: in the former, other nations have built upon their foundations and surpassed them, – in the latter, they still remained unrivalled. It is not too much to say that this flexible, emphatic, and transparent character of the language as an instrument of communication, – its perfect aptitude for narrative and discussion, as well as for stirring all the veins of human emotion without ever forfeiting that character of simplicity which adapts it to all men and all times, – may be traced mainly to the existence and the wide-spread influence of the Iliad and Odyssey. To us, these compositions are interesting as beautiful poems, depicting life and manners, and unfolding certain types of character with the utmost vivacity and artlessness: to their original hearer, they possessed all these sources of attraction, together with others more powerful still, to which we are now strangers. Upon him, they bore with the full weight and solemnity of history and religion combined, while the charm of the poetry was only secondary and instrumental. The poet was then the teacher and preacher of the community, not simply the amuser of their leisure hours: they looked to him for revelations of the unknown past and for expositions of the attributes and dispensations of the gods, just as they consulted the prophet for his privileged insight into the future. The ancient epic comprised many different poets and poetical compositions, which fulfilled this purpose with more or less completeness; but it is the exclusive prerogative of the Iliad and Odyssey, that, after the minds of men had ceased to be in full harmony with their original design, they yet retained their empire by the mere force of secondary excellences; while the remaining epics – though serving as food for the curious, and as storehouses for logographers, tragedians, and artists – never seem to have acquired very wide popularity even among intellectual Greeks.

I shall, in the succeeding chapter, give some account of the epic cycle, of its relation to the Homeric poems, and of the general evidences respecting the latter, both as to antiquity and authorship.

XXI. GRECIAN EPIC. – HOMERIC POEMS.

At the head of the once abundant epical compositions of Greece, most of them unfortunately lost, stand the Iliad and Odyssey, with the immortal name of Homer attached to each of them, embracing separate portions of the comprehensive legend of Troy. They form the type of what may be called the heroic epic of the Greeks, as distinguished from the genealogical, in which latter species some of the Hesiodic poems – the Catalogue of Women, the Eoiai, and the Naupaktia – stood conspicuous. Poems of the Homeric character (if so it may be called, though the expression is very indefinite), – being confined to one of the great events, or great personages of Grecian legendary antiquity, and comprising a limited number of characters, all contemporaneous, made some approach, more or less successful, to a certain poetical unity; while the Hesiodic poems, tamer in their spirit, and unconfined both as to time and as to persons, strung together distinct events without any obvious view to concentration of interest, – without legitimate beginning or end. Between these two extremes there were many gradations: biographical poems, such as the Herakleia, or Theseïs, recounting all the principal exploits performed by one single hero, present a character intermediate between the two, but bordering more closely on the Hesiodic. Even the hymns to the gods, which pass under the name of Homer, are epical fragments, narrating particular exploits or adventures of the god commemorated.

Both the didactic and the mystico-religious poetry of Greece began in Hexameter verse, – the characteristic and consecrated measure of the epic; but they belong to a different species, and burst out from a different vein in the Grecian mind. It seems to have been the more common belief among the historical Greeks, that such mystic effusions were more ancient than their narrative poems, and that Orpheus, Musæus, Linus, Olên, Pamphus, and even Hesiod, &c. &c., the reputed composers of the former, were of earlier date than Homer. But there is no evidence to sustain this opinion, and the presumptions are all against it. Those compositions, which in the sixth century before the Christian æra passed under the name of Orpheus and Musæus, seem to have been unquestionably post-Homeric, nor can we even admit the modified conclusion of Hermann, Ulrici, and others, that the mystic poetry as a genus (putting aside the particular compositions falsely ascribed to Orpheus and others) preceded in order of time the narrative.

XXI. GRECIAN EPIC. – HOMERIC POEMS.

Besides the Iliad and Odyssey, we make out the titles of about thirty lost epic poems, sometimes with a brief hint of their contents.

Concerning the legend of Troy there were five: the Cyprian Verses, the Æthiopis, and the Capture of Troy, both ascribed to Arktinus; the Lesser Iliad, ascribed to Leschês; the Returns (of the Heroes from Troy), to which the name of Hagias of Trœzên is attached; and the Telegonia, by Eugammôn, a continuation of the Odyssey. Two poems, – the Thebaïs and the Epigoni (perhaps two parts of one and the same poem) were devoted to the legend of Thêbes, – the two sieges of that city by the Argeians. Another poem, called Œdipodia, had for its subject the tragical destiny of Œdipus and his family; and perhaps that which is cited as Eurôpia, or verses on Eurôpa, may have comprehended the tale of her brother Kadmus, the mythical founder of Thêbes.

The exploits of Hêraklês were celebrated in two compositions, each called Hêrakleia, by Kinæthôn and Pisander, – probably also in many others, of which the memory has not been preserved. The capture of Œchalia, by Hêraklês, formed the subject of a separate epic. Two other poems, the Ægimius and the Minyas, are supposed to have been founded on other achievements of this hero, – the effective aid which he lent to the Dorian king Ægimius against the Lapithæ, his descent to the under-world for the purpose of rescuing the imprisoned Thesêus, and his conquest of the city of the Minyæ, the powerful Orchomenus.

Other epic poems – the Phorônis, the Danaïs, the Alkmæônis, the Atthis, the Amazonia – we know only by name, and can just guess obscurely at their contents so far as the name indicates. The Titanomachia, the Gigantomachia, and the Corinthiaca, three compositions all ascribed to Eumêlus, afford by means of their titles an idea somewhat clearer of the matter which they comprised. The Theogony ascribed to Hesiod still exists, though partially corrupt and mutilated: but there seem to have been other poems, now lost, of the like import and title.

Of the poems composed in the Hesiodic style, diffusive and full of genealogical detail, the principal were, the Catalogue of Women and the Great Eoiai; the latter of which, indeed, seems to have been a continuation of the former. A large number of the celebrated women of heroic Greece were commemorated in these poems, one after the other, without any other than an arbitrary bond of connection. The Marriage of Kêyx, – the Melampodia, – and a string of fables called Astronomia, are farther ascribed to Hesiod: and the poem above mentioned, called Ægimius, is also sometimes connected with his name, sometimes with that of Kerkops. The Naupaktian Verses (so called, probably, from the birthplace of their author), and the genealogies of Kinæthôn and Asius, were compositions of the same rambling character, as far as we can judge from the scanty fragments remaining. The Orchomenian epic poet Chersias, of whom two lines only are preserved to us by Pausanias, may reasonably be referred to the same category.

Epic poets & the epic cycle.

The oldest of the epic poets, to whom any date, carrying with it the semblance of authority, is assigned, is Arktinus of Milêtus, who is placed by Eusebius in the first Olympiad, and by Suidas in the ninth. Eugammôn, the author of the Telegonia, and the latest of the catalogue, is placed in the fifty-third Olympiad, B.C. 566. Between these two we find Asius and Leschês, about the thirtieth Olympiad, – a time when the vein of the ancient epic was drying up, and when other forms of poetry – elegiac, iambic, lyric, and choric – had either already arisen, or were on the point of arising, to compete with it.

It has already been stated in a former chapter, that in the early commencements of prose-writing, Hekatæus, Pherekydês, and other logographers, made it their business to extract from the ancient fables something like a continuous narrative, chronologically arranged. It was upon a principle somewhat analogous that the Alexandrine literati, about the second century before the Christian æra, arranged the multitude of old epic poets into a series founded on the supposed order of time in the events narrated, – beginning with the intermarriage of Uranus and Gæa, and the Theogony, – and concluding with the death of Odysseus by the hands of his son Telegonus. This collection passed by the name of the Epic Cycle, and the poets, whose compositions were embodied in it, were termed Cyclic poets. Doubtless, the epical treasures of the Alexandrine library were larger than had ever before been brought together and submitted to men both of learning and leisure: so that multiplication of such compositions in the same museum rendered it advisable to establish some fixed order of perusal, and to copy them in one corrected and uniform edition. It pleased the critics to determine precedence, neither by antiquity nor by excellence of the compositions themselves, but by the supposed sequence of narrative, so that the whole taken together constituted a readable aggregate of epical antiquity.

XXI. GRECIAN EPIC. – HOMERIC POEMS.

Much obscurity exists, and many different opinions have been expressed, respecting this Epic Cycle: I view it, not as an exclusive canon, but simply as an all-comprehensive classification, with a new edition founded thereupon. It would include all the epic poems in the library older than the Telegonia, and apt for continuous narrative; it would exclude only two classes, – first, the recent epic poets, such as Panyasis and Antimachus; next, the genealogical and desultory poems, such as the Catalogue of Women, the Eoiai, and others, which could not be made to fit in to any chronological sequence of events. Both the Iliad and the Odyssey were comprised in the Cycle, so that the denomination of cyclic poet did not originally or designedly carry with it any association of contempt. But as the great and capital poems were chiefly spoken of by themselves, or by the title of their own separate authors, so the general name of *poets of the Cycle* came gradually to be applied only to the worst, and thus to imply vulgarity or common-place; the more so, as many of the inferior compositions included in the collection seem to have been anonymous, and their authors in consequence describable only under some such common designation as that of the cyclic poets. It is in this manner that we are to explain the disparaging sentiment connected by Horace and others with the idea of a cyclic writer, though no such sentiment was implied in the original meaning of the Epic Cycle.

The poems of the Cycle were thus mentioned in contrast and antithesis with Homer, though originally the Iliad and Odyssey had both been included among them; and this alteration of the meaning of the word has given birth to a mistake as to the primary purpose of the classification, as if it had been designed especially to part off the inferior epic productions from Homer. While some critics are disposed to distinguish the cyclic poets too pointedly from Homer, I conceive that Welcker goes too much into the other extreme, and identifies the Cycle too closely with that poet. He construes it as a classification deliberately framed to comprise all the various productions of the Homeric epic, with its unity of action and comparative paucity, both of persons and adventures, – as opposed to the Hesiodic epic, crowded with separate persons and pedigrees, and destitute of central action as well as of closing catastrophe. This opinion does, indeed, coincide to a great degree with the fact, inasmuch as few of the Hesiodic epics appear to have been included in the Cycle: to say that *none* were included, would be too much, for we cannot venture to set aside either the Theogony or the Ægimius; but we may account for their absence perfectly well without supposing any design to exclude them, for it is obvious that their rambling character (like that of the Metamorphoses of Ovid) forbade the possibility of interweaving them in any continuous series. Continuity in the series of narrated events, coupled with a certain degree of antiquity in the poems, being the principle on which the arrangement called the Epic Cycle was based, the Hesiodic poems generally were excluded, not from any preconceived intention, but because they could not be brought into harmony with such orderly reading.

What were the particular poems which it comprised, we cannot now determine with exactness. Welcker arranges them as follows: Titanomachia, Danaïs, Amazonia (or Atthis), Œdipodia, Thebaïs (or Expedition of Amphiaraüs), Epigoni (or Alkmæônis), Minyas (or Phokaïs), Capture of Œchalia, Cyprian Verses, Iliad, Æthiopis, Lesser Iliad, Iliupersis or the Taking of Troy, Returns of the Heroes, Odyssey, and Telegonia, Wuellner, Lange, and Mr. Fynes Clinton enlarge the list of cyclic poems still farther. But all such reconstructions of the Cycle are conjectural and destitute of authority: the only poems which we can affirm on positive grounds to have been comprehended in it, are, first, the series respecting the heroes of Troy, from the Cypria to the Telegonia, of which Proclus has preserved the arguments, and which includes the Iliad and Odyssey, – next, the old Thebaïs, which is expressly termed cyclic, in order to distinguish it from the poem of the same name composed by Antimachus. In regard to other particular compositions, we have no evidence to guide us, either for admission or exclusion, except our general views as to the scheme upon which the Cycle was framed. If my idea of that scheme be correct, the Alexandrine critics arranged therein *all* their old epical treasures, down to the Telegonia, – the good as well as the bad; gold, silver, and iron, – provided only they could be pieced in with the narrative series. But I cannot venture to include, as Mr. Clinton does, the Eurôpia, the Phorônis, and other poems of which we know only the names, because it is uncertain whether their contents were such as to fulfil their primary condition: nor can I concur with him in thinking that, where there were two or more poems of the same title and subject, one of them must necessarily have been adopted into the Cycle to the exclusion of the others. There may have been two Theogonies, or two Herakleias, both comprehended in the Cycle; the purpose being (as I before remarked), not to sift the better from the worse, but to determine some fixed order, convenient for reading and reference, amidst a multiplicity of scattered compositions, as the basis of a new, entire, and corrected edition.

XXI. GRECIAN EPIC. – HOMERIC POEMS.

Whatever may have been the principle on which the cyclic poems were originally strung together, they are all now lost, except those two unrivalled diamonds, whose brightness, dimming all the rest, has alone sufficed to confer imperishable glory even upon the earliest phase of Grecian life. It has been the natural privilege of the Iliad and Odyssey, from the rise of Grecian philology down to the present day, to provoke an intense curiosity, which, even in the historical and literary days of Greece, there were no assured facts to satisfy. These compositions are the monuments of an age essentially religious and poetical, but essentially also unphilosophical, unreflecting, and un-recording: the nature of the case forbids our having any authentic transmitted knowledge respecting such a period; and the lesson must be learned, hard and painful though it be, that no imaginable reach of critical acumen will of itself enable us to discriminate fancy from reality, in the absence of a tolerable stock of evidence. After the numberless comments and acrimonious controversies to which the Homeric poems have given rise, it can hardly be said that any of the points originally doubtful have obtained a solution such as to command universal acquiescence. To glance at all these controversies, however briefly, would far transcend the limits of the present work; but the most abridged Grecian history would be incomplete without some inquiry respecting *the Poet* (so the Greek critics in their veneration denominated Homer), and the productions which pass now, or have heretofore passed, under his name.

Who was Homer?

Who or what was Homer? What date is to be assigned to him? What were his compositions?

A person, putting these questions to Greeks of different towns and ages, would have obtained answers widely discrepant and contradictory. Since the invaluable labours of Aristarchus and the other Alexandrine critics on the text of the Iliad and Odyssey, it has, indeed, been customary to regard those two (putting aside the Hymns, and a few other minor poems) as being the only genuine Homeric compositions; and the literary men called Chorizontes, or the Separators, at the head of whom were Xenôn and Hellanikas, endeavoured still farther to reduce the number by disconnecting the Iliad and Odyssey, and pointing out that both could not be the work of the same author. Throughout the whole course of Grecian antiquity, the Iliad and the Odyssey, and the Hymns, have been received as Homeric.; but if we go back to the time of Herodotus, or still earlier, we find that several other epics also were ascribed to Homer, – and there were not wanting critics, earlier than the Alexandrine age, who regarded the whole Epic Cycle, together with the satirical poem called Margitês, the Batrachomyomachia, and other smaller pieces, as Homeric works. The cyclic Thebaïs and the Epigoni (whether they be two separate poems, or the latter a second part of the former) were in early days currently ascribed to Homer: the same was the case with the Cyprian Verses: some even attributed to him several other poems, the Capture of Œchalia, the Lesser Iliad, the Phokaïs, and the Amazonia. The title of the poem called Thebaïs to be styled Homeric, depends upon evidence more ancient than any which can be produced to authenticate the Iliad and Odyssey: for Kallinus, the ancient elegiac poet (B.C. 640), mentioned Homer as the author of it, – and his opinion was shared by many other competent judges. From the remarkable description given by Herodotus, of the expulsion of the rhapsodes from Sikyôn, by the despot Kleisthenês, in the time of Solôn (about B.C. 580), we may form a probable judgment that the Thebaïs and the Epigoni were then rhapsodised at Sikyôn as Homeric productions. It is clear from the language of Herodotus, that in his time the general opinion ascribed to Homer both the Cyprian Verses and the Epigoni. though he himself dissents. In spite of such dissent, however, that historian must have conceived the names of Homer and Hesiod to be nearly co-extensive with the whole of the ancient epic; otherwise, he would hardly have delivered his memorable judgment, that they two were the framers of Grecian Theogony.

The many different cities which laid claim to the birth of Homer (seven is rather below the truth, and Smyrna and Chios are the most prominent among them), is well known, and most of them had legends to tell respecting his romantic parentage, his alleged blindness, and his life as an itinerant bard, acquainted with poverty and sorrow. The discrepancies of statement respecting the date of his reputed existence are no less worthy of remark; for out of the eight different epochs assigned to him, the oldest differs from the most recent by a period of 460 years.

Thus conflicting would have been the answers returned in different portions of the Grecian world to any questions respecting the person of Homer. But there were a poetical gens (fraternity or guild) in the Ionic island of Chios, who, if the question had been put to them, would have answered in another manner. To them, Homer was not a mere antecedent man, of kindred nature with themselves, but a divine or semi-divine eponymous and progenitor, whom they worshipped in their gentile sacrifices, and in whose ascendent name and glory the individuality of every member of the gens was merged. The compositions of each separate Homêrid, or the combined efforts of many of them in conjunction, were the works of Homer: the name of the individual bard perishes and his authorship is forgotten, but the common gentile father lives and grows in renown, from generation to generation, by the genius of his self-renewing sons.

Such was the conception entertained of Homer by the poetical gens called Homêridæ, or Homêrids; and in the general obscurity of the whole case, I lean towards it as the most plausible conception. Homer is not only the reputed author of the various compositions emanating from the gentile members, but also the recipient of the many different legends and of the divine genealogy, which it pleases their imagination to confer upon him. Such manufacture of fictitious personality, and such perfect incorporation of the entities of religion and fancy with the real world, is a process familiar, and even habitual, in the retrospective vision of the Greeks.

It is to be remarked, that the poetical gens here brought to view, the Homêrids, are of indisputable authenticity. Their existence and their considerations were maintained down to the historical times in the island of Chios. If the Homêrids were still conspicuous, even in the days of Akusilaus, Pindar, Hellanikus, and Plato, when their productive invention had ceased, and when they had become only guardians and distributors, in common with others, of the treasures bequeathed by their predecessors, – far more exalted must their position have been three centuries before, while they were still the inspired creators of epic novelty, and when the absence of writing assured to them the undisputed monopoly of their own compositions.

Homer, then, is no individual man, but the divine or heroic father (the ideas of worship and ancestry coalescing, as they constantly did in the Grecian mind) of the gentile Homêrids, and he is the author of the Thebaïs, the Epigoni, the Cyprian Verses, the Procems, or Hymns, and other poems, in the same sense in which he is the author of the Iliad and Odyssey, – assuming that these various compositions emanate, as perhaps they may, from different individuals numbered among the Homêrids. But this disallowance of the historical personality of Homer is quite distinct from the question, with which it has been often confounded, whether the Iliad and Odyssey are originally entire poems, and whether by one author or otherwise. To us, the name of Homer means these two poems, and little else: we desire to know as much as can be learned respecting their date, their original composition, their preservation, and their mode of communication to the public. All these questions are more or less complicated one with the other.

Dates of the Iliad and Odyssey.

Concerning the date of the poems, we have no other information except the various affirmations respecting the age of Homer, which differ among themselves (as I have before observed) by an interval of 460 years, and which for the most part determine the date of Homer by reference to some other event, itself fabulous and unauthenticated, – such as the Trojan war, the Return of the Hêrakleids, or the Ionic migration. Kratês placed Homer earlier than the Return of the Hêrakleids, and less than eighty years after the Trojan war: Eratosthenês put him one hundred years after the Trojan war: Aristotle, Aristarchus, and Castôr made his birth contemporary with the Ionic migration, while Apollodôrus brings him down to 100 years after that event, or 240 years after the taking of Troy. Thucydidês assigns to him a date much subsequent to the Trojan war. On the other hand, Theopompus and Euphoriôn refer his age to the far more recent period of the Lydian king, Gygês, (Ol. 18-23, B.C. 708-688), and put him 500 years after the Trojan epoch. What were the grounds of these various conjectures, we do not know; though in the statements of Kratês and Eratosthenês, we may pretty well divine. The oldest dictum preserved to us respecting the date of Homer, – meaning thereby the date of the Iliad and Odyssey, – appears to me at the same time the most credible, and the most consistent with the general history of the ancient epic Herodotus places Homer four hundred years before himself; taking his departure, not from any fabulous event, but from a point of real and authentic time. Four centuries anterior to Herodotus would be a period commencing with 800 B.C. so that the composition of the Homeric poems would thus fall in a space between 850 and 800 B.C. We may gather from the language of Herodotus that this was his own judgment, opposed to a current opinion, which assigned the poet to an earlier epoch.

To place the Iliad and Odyssey at some periods between 850 B.C. and 776 B.C., appears to me more probable than any other date, anterior or posterior, – more probable than the latter, because we are justified in believing these two poems to be older than Arktinus, who comes shortly after the first Olympiad; – more probable than the former, because, the farther we push the poems back, the more do we enhance the wonder of their preservation, already sufficiently great, down from such an age and society to the historical times.

The mode in which these poems, and indeed all poems, epic as well as lyric, down to the age (probably) of Peisistratus, were circulated and brought to bear upon the public, deserves particular attention. They were not read by individuals alone and apart, but sung or recited at festivals or to assembled companies. This seems to be one of the few undisputed facts with regard to the great poet: for even those who maintain that the Iliad and Odyssey were preserved by means of writing, seldom contend that they were read.

In appreciating the effect of the poems, we must always take account of this great difference between early Greece and our own times, – between the congregation mustered at a solemn festival, stimulated by community of sympathy, listening to a measured and musical recital from the lips of trained bards or rhapsodes, whose matter was supposed to have been inspired by the Muse, – and the solitary reader, with a manuscript before him; such manuscript being, down to a very late period in Greek literature, indifferently written, without division into parts, and without marks of punctuation. As in the case of dramatic performances, in all ages, so in that of the early Grecian epic, – a very large proportion of its impressive effect was derived from the talent of the reciter and the force of the general accompaniments, and would have disappeared altogether in solitary reading. Originally, the bard sung his own epical narrative, commencing with a procemium or hymn to one of the gods; his profession was separate and special, like that of the carpenter, the leech, or the prophet: his manner and enunciation must have required particular training no less than his imaginative faculty. His character presents itself in the Odyssey as one highly esteemed; and in the Iliad, even Achilles does not disdain to touch the lyre with his own hands, and to sing heroic deeds. Not only did the Iliad and Odyssey, and the poems embodied in the Epic Cycle, produce all their impression and gain all their renown by this process of oral delivery, but even the lyric and choric poets who succeeded them were known and felt in the same way by the general public, even after the full establishment of habits of reading among lettered men. While in the case of the epic, the recitation or singing had been extremely simple, and the measure comparatively little diversified, with no other accompaniment than that of the four-stringed harp, – all the variations superinduced upon the original hexameter, beginning with the pentameter and iambus, and proceeding step by step to the complicated strophês of Pindar and the tragic writers, still left the general effect of the poetry greatly dependent upon voice and accompaniments, and pointedly distinguished from mere solitary reading of the words. In the dramatic poetry, the last in order of time, the declamation and gesture of the speaking actor alternated with the song and dance of the Chorus, and with the instruments of musicians, the whole being set off by imposing visible decorations. Now both dramatic effect and song are familiar in modern times, so that every man knows the difference between reading the words and hearing them under the appropriate circumstances; but poetry, as such, is, and has now long been, so exclusively enjoyed by reading, that it requires an especial memento to bring us back to the time when the Iliad and Odyssey were addressed only to the ear and feelings of a promiscuous and sympathising multitude. Readers there were none, at least until the century preceding Solôn and Peisistratus: from that time forward, they gradually increased both in number and influence; though doubtless small, even in the most literary period of Greece, as compared with modern European society. So far as the production of beautiful epic poetry was concerned, however, the select body of instructed readers, furnished a less potent stimulus than the unlettered and listening crowd of the earlier periods. The poems of Chœrilus and Antimachus, towards the close of the Peloponnesian war, though admired by erudite men, never acquired popularity; and the emperor Hadrian failed in his attempt to bring the latter poet into fashion at the expense of Homer.

It will be seen by what has been here stated, that that class of men, who formed the medium of communication between the verse and the ear, were of the highest importance in the ancient world, and especially in the earlier periods of its career, – the bards and rhapsodes for the epic, the singers for the lyric, the actors and singers jointly with the dancers for the chorus and drama. The lyric and dramatic poets taught with their own lips the delivery of their compositions, and so prominently did this business of teaching present itself to the view of the public, that the name Didaskalia, by which the dramatic exhibition was commonly designated, derived from thence its origin.

Among the number of rhapsodes who frequented the festivals at a time when Grecian cities were multiplied and easy of access, for the recitation of the ancient epic, there must have been of course great differences of excellence; but that the more considerable individuals of the class were elaborately trained and highly accomplished in the exercise of their profession, we may assume as certain. It happens that Sokratês, with his two pupils Plato and Xenophôn, speak contemptuously of their merits; and many persons have been disposed, somewhat too readily, to admit this sentence of condemnation as conclusive, without taking account of the point of view from which it was delivered. These philosophers considered Homer and other poets with a view to instruction, ethical doctrine, and virtuous practice. They analysed the characters whom the poet described, sifted the value of the lessons conveyed, and often struggled to discover a hidden meaning, where they disapproved that which was apparent. When they found a man like the rhapsode, who professed to impress the Homeric narrative upon an audience, and yet either never meddled at all, or meddled unsuccessfully, with the business of exposition, they treated him with contempt; indeed, Sokratês depreciates the poets themselves, much upon the same principle, as dealing with matters of which they could render no rational account. It was also the habit of Plato and Xenophôn to disparage generally professional exertion of talent for the purpose of gaining a livelihood, contrasting it often in an indelicate manner with the gratuitous teaching and ostentatious poverty of their master. But we are not warranted in judging the rhapsodes by such a standard. Though they were not philosophers or moralists, it was their province – and it had been so, long before the philosophical point of view was opened – to bring their poet home to the bosoms and emotions of an assembled crowd, and to penetrate themselves with his meaning so far as was suitable for that purpose, adapting to it the appropriate graces of action and intonation. In this their genuine task they were valuable members of the Grecian community, and seem to have possessed all the qualities necessary for success.

These rhapsodes, the successors of the primitive Aœdi, or Bards, seem to have been distinguished from them by the discontinuance of all musical accompaniment. Originally, the bard sung, enlivening the song with occasional touches of the simple four-stringed harp: his successor, the rhapsode, recited, holding in his hand nothing but a branch of laurel and depending for effect upon voice and manner, – a species of musical and rhythmical declamation, which gradually increased in vehement emphasis and gesticulation until it approached to that of the dramatic actor. At what time this change look place, or whether the two different modes of enunciating the ancient epic may for a certain period have gone on simultaneously, we have no means ef determining. Hesiod receives from the Muse a branch of laurel, as a token of his ordination into their service, which marks him for a rhapsode; while the ancient bard with his harp is still recognised in the Homeric Hymn to the Delian Apollo, as efficient and popular at the Panionic festivals in the island of Delos. Perhaps the improvements made in the harp, to which three strings, in addition to the original four, were attached by Terpander (B.C. 660), and the growing complication of instrumental music generally, may have contributed to discredit the primitive accompaniment, and thus to promote the practice of recital: the story, that Terpander himself composed music, not only for hexameter poems of his own, but also for those of Homer, seems to indicate that the music which preceded him was ceasing to find favour. By whatever steps the change from the bard to the rhapsode took place, certain it is that before the time of Solôn, the latter was the recognised and exclusive organ of the old Epic; sometimes in short fragments before private companies, by single rhapsodes, – sometimes several rhapsodes in continuous succession at a public festival.

When were the Homeric poems written?

Respecting the mode in which the Homeric poems were preserved, during the two centuries (or as some think, longer interval) between their original composition and the period shortly preceding Solôn, – and respecting their original composition and subsequent changes, – there are wide differences of opinion among able critics. Were they preserved with or without being written? Was the Iliad originally composed as one poem, and the Odyssey in like manner, or is each of them an aggregation of parts originally self-existent and unconnected? Was the authorship of each poem single-headed or many-headed?

Either tacitly or explicitly, these questions have been generally coupled together and discussed with reference to each other, by inquiries into the Homeric poems; though Mr. Payne Knight's Prolegomena have the merit of keeping them distinct. Half a century ago, the acute and valuable Prolegomena of F. A. Wolf, turning to account the Venetian Scholia which had then been recently published, first opened philosophical discussion as to the history of the Homeric text. A considerable part of that dissertation (though by no means the whole) is employed in vindicating the position, previously announced by Bentley, among others, that the separate constituent portions of the Iliad and Odyssey had not been cemented together into any compact body and unchangeable order until the days of Peisistratus, in the sixth century before Christ. As a step towards that conclusion, Wolf maintained that no written copies of either poem could be shown to have existed during the earlier times to which their composition is referred, – and that without writing, neither the perfect symmetry of so complicated a work could have been originally conceived by any poet, nor, if realised by him, transmitted with assurance to posterity. The absence of easy and convenient writing, such as must he indispensably supposed for long manuscripts, among the early Greeks, was thus one of the points in Wolf's case against the primitive integrity of the Iliad and Odyssey. By Nitzsch and other leading opponents of Wolf, the connection of the one with the other seems to have been accepted as he originally put it; and it has been considered incumbent on those, who defended the ancient aggregate character of the Iliad and Odyssey, to maintain that they were written poems from the beginning.

To me it appears that the architectonic functions ascribed by Wolf to Peisistratus and his associates, in reference to the Homeric poems, are nowise admissible. But much would undoubtedly be gained towards that view of the question, if it could be shown that, in order to controvert it, we were driven to the necessity of admitting long written poems in the ninth century before the Christian era. Few things, in my opinion, can be more improbable; and Mr. Payne Knight, opposed as he is to the Wolfian hypothesis, admits this no less than Wolf himself. The traces of writing in Greece, even in the seventh century before the Christian era, are exceedingly trifling. We have no remaining inscription earlier than the 40th Olympiad, and the early inscriptions are rude and unskilfully executed: nor can we even assure ourselves whether Archilochus, Simonidês of Amorgus, Kallinus, Tyrtæus, Xanthus, and the other early elegiac and lyric poets, committed their compositions to writing, or at what time the practice of doing so became familiar. The first positive ground, which authorises us to presume the existence of a manuscript of Homer, is in the famous ordinance of Solôn with regard to the rhapsodes at the Panathenæa; but for what length of time, previously, manuscripts had existed, we are unable to say.

Those who maintain the Homeric poems to have been written from the beginning, rest their case, not upon positive proofs, – nor yet upon the existing habits of society with regard to poetry, for they admit generally that the Iliad and Odyssey were not read, but recited and heard, – but upon the supposed necessity that there must have been manuscripts, to insure the preservation of the poems, – the unassisted memory of reciters being neither sufficient nor trustworthy. Here we only escape a smaller difficulty by running into a greater; for the existence of trained bards, gifted with extraordinary memory, is far less astonishing than that of long manuscripts in an age essentially non-reading and non-writing, and when even suitable instruments and materials for the process are not obvious. Moreover, there is a strong positive reason for believing that the bard was under no necessity for refreshing his memory by consulting a manuscript. For if such had been the fact, blindness would have been a disqualification for the profession, which we know that it was not; as well from the example of Demodokus in the Odyssey, as from that of the blind bard of Chios, in the hymn to the Delian Apollo, whom Thucydidês, as well as the general tenor of Grecian legend, identifies with Homer himself. The author of that Hymn, be he who he may, could never have described a blind man as attaining the utmost perfection in his art, if he had been conscious that the memory of the bard was only maintained by constant reference to the manuscript in his chest.

Nor will it be found, after all, that the effort of memory required, either from bards or rhapsodes, even for the longest of these old Epic poems, – though doubtless great, was at all superhuman. Taking the case with reference to the entire Iliad and Odyssey, we know that there were educated gentlemen at Athens who could repeat both poems by heart; but in the professional recitations, we are not to imagine that the same person did go through the whole: the recitation was essentially a joint undertaking, and the rhapsodes who visited a festival would naturally understand among themselves which part of the poem should devolve upon each particular individual. Under such circumstances, and with such means of preparation beforehand, the quantity of verse which a rhapsode could deliver would be measured, not so much by the exhaustion of his memory, as by the physical sufficiency of his voice, having reference to the sonorous, emphatic, and rhythmical pronunciation required from him.

But what guarantee have we for the exact transmission of the text tor a space of two centuries by simply oral means? It may be replied, that oral transmission would hand down the text as exactly as in point of fact it was handed down. The great lines of each poem, – the order of parts, – the vein of Homeric feeling, and the general style of locution, and, for the most part, the true words, – would be maintained: for the professional training of the rhapsode, over and above the precision of his actual memory, would tend to Homerise his mind (if the expression may be permitted), and to restrain him within this magic circle. On the other hand, in respect to the details of the text, we should expect that there would be wide differences and numerous inaccuracies; and so there really were, as the records contained in the Scholia, together with the passages cited in ancient authors, but not found in our Homeric text, abundantly testify.

Moreover, the state of the Iliad and Odyssey, in respect to the letter called the Digamma, affords a proof that they were recited for a considerable period before they were committed to writing, insomuch that the oral pronunciation underwent during the interval a sensible change. At the time when these poems were composed, the Digamma was an effective consonant, and figured as such in the structure of the verse: at the time when they were committed to writing, it had ceased to be pronounced, and therefore never found a place in any of the manuscripts, – insomuch that the Alexandrine critics, though they knew of its existence in the much later poems of Alkæus and Sapphô, never recognised it in Homer. The hiatus, and the various perplexities of metre, occasioned by the loss of the Digamma, were corrected by different grammatical stratagems. The whole history of this lost letter is very curious, and is rendered intelligible only by the supposition that the Iliad and Odyssey belonged for a wide space of time to the memory, the voice, and the ear, exclusively.

At what period these poems, or, indeed, any other Greek poems, first began to be written, must be matter of conjecture, though there is ground for assurance that it was before the time of Solôn. If, in the absence of evidence, we may venture upon naming any more determinate period, the question at once suggests itself, what were the purposes which, in that stage of society, a manuscript at its first commencement must have been intended to answer? For whom was a written Iliad necessary? Not for the rhapsodes; for with them it was not only planted in the memory, but also interwoven with the feelings, and conceived in conjunction with all those flexions and intonations of voice, pauses, and other oral artifices, which were required for emphatic delivery, and which the naked manuscript could never reproduce. Not for the general public, – *they* were accustomed to receive it with its rhapsodic delivery, and with its accompaniments of a solemn and crowded festival. The only persons for whom the written Iliad would be suitable, would be a select few; studious and curious men, – a class of readers, capable of analysing the complicated emotions which they had experienced as hearers in the crowd, and who would, on perusing the written words, realise in their imaginations a sensible portion of the impression communicated by the reciter.

Incredible as the statement may seem in an age like the present, there is in all early societies, and there was in early Greece, a time when no such reading class existed. If we could discover at what time such a class first began to be formed, we should be able to make a guess at the time when the old Epic poems were first committed to writing. Now the period which may with the greatest probability be fixed upon as having first witnessed the formation even of the narrowest reading class in Greece, is the middle of the seventh century before the Christian era (B.C. 660 to B.C. 630), – the age of Terpander, Kallinus, Archilochus, Simonidês of Amorgus, &c. I ground this supposition on the change then operated in the character and tendencies of Grecian poetry and music, – the elegiac and iambic measures having been introduced as rivals to the primitive hexameter, and poetical compositions having been transferred from the epical past to the affairs of present and real life. Such a change was important at a time when poetry was the only known mode of publication (to use a modern phrase not altogether suitable, yet the nearest approaching to the sense). It argued a new way of looking at the old epical treasures of the people, as well as a thirst for new poetical effect; and the men who stood forward in it may well be considered as desirous to study, and competent to criticise, from their own individual point of view, the written words of the Homeric rhapsodes, just as we are told that Kallinus both noticed and eulogised the Thebaïs as the production of Homer. There seems, therefore, ground for conjecturing, that (for the use of this newly-formed and important, but very narrow class) manuscripts of the Homeric poems and other old epics – the Thebaïs and the Cypria as well as the Iliad and the Odyssey – began to be compiled towards the middle of the seventh century B.C.; and the opening of Egypt to Grecian commerce, which took place about the same period, would furnish increased facilities for obtaining the requisite papyrus to write upon. A reading class, when once formed, would doubtless slowly increase, and the number of manuscripts along with it; so that before the time of Solôn, fifty years afterwards, both readers and manuscripts, though still comparatively few, might have attained a certain recognised authority, and formed a tribunal of reference, against the carelessness of individual rhapsodes.

We may, I think, consider the Iliad and Odyssey to have been preserved without the aid of writing, for a period near upon two centuries. But is it true, as Wolf imagined, and as other able critics have imagined, also, that the separate portions of which these two poems are composed were originally distinct epical ballads, each constituting a separate whole and intended for separate recitation? Is it true, that they had not only no common author, but originally, neither common purpose nor fixed order, and that their first permanent arrangement and integration was delayed for three centuries, and accomplished at last only by the taste of Peisistratus conjoined with various lettered friends?

This hypothesis – to which the genius of Wolf first gave celebrity, but which has been since enforced more in detail by others, especially by William Müller and Lachmann – appears to me not only unsupported by any sufficient testimony, but also opposed to other testimony as well as to a strong force of internal probability. The authorities quoted by Wolf are Josephus, Cicero, and Pausanias; Josephus mentions nothing about Peisistratus, but merely states (what we may accept as the probable fact) that the Homeric poems were originally unwritten, and preserved only in songs or recitations, from which they were at a subsequent period put into writing: hence many of the discrepancies in the text. On the other hand, Cicero and Pausanias go farther, and affirm that Peisistratus both collected, and arranged in the existing order, the rhapsodies of the Iliad and Odyssey, (implied as poems originally entire, and subsequently broken into pieces), which he found partly confused and partly isolated from each other, – each part being then remembered only in its own portion of the Grecian world. Respecting Hipparchus the son of Peisistratus, too, we are told in the Pseudo-Platonic dialogue which bears his name, that he was the first to introduce into Attica, the poetry of Homer, and that he prescribed to the rhapsodes to recite the parts of the Panathenaic festival in regular sequence.

Wolf and William Müller occasionally speak as if they admitted something like an Iliad and Odyssey as established aggregates prior to Peisistratus; but for the most part they represent him or his associates as having been the first to put together Homeric poems which were before distinct and self-existent compositions. Lachmann, the recent expositor of the same theory, ascribes to Peisistratus still more unequivocally this original integration of parts in reference to the Iliad, – distributing the first twenty-two books of the poem into sixteen separate songs, and treating it as ridiculous to imagine that the fusion of these songs, into an order such as we now read, belongs to any date earlier than Peisistratus.

Upon this theory we may remark, first, that it stands opposed to the testimony existing respecting the regulations of Solôn; who, before the time of Peisistratus, had enforced a fixed order of recitation on the rhapsodes of the Iliad at the Panathenaic festival; not only directing that they should go through the rhapsodies *seriatim,* and without omission or corruption, but also establishing a prompter or censorial authority to insure obedience, – which implies the existence (at the same time that it proclaims the occasional infringement) of an orderly aggregate, as well as of manuscripts professedly complete. Next, the theory ascribes to Peisistratus a character not only materially different from what is indicated by Cicero and Pausanias, – who represent him, not as having put together atoms originally distinct, but as the renovator of an ancient order subsequently lost, – but also in itself unintelligible, and inconsistent with Grecian habit and feeling. That Peisistratus should take pains to repress the license, or make up for the unfaithful memory, of individual rhapsodes, and to ennoble the Panathenaic festival by the most correct recital of a great and venerable poem, according to the standard received among the best judges in Greece, – this is a task both suitable to his position, and requiring nothing more than an improved recension, together with exact adherence to it on the part of the rhapsodes. But what motive had he to string together several poems, previously known only as separate, into one new whole? What feeling could he gratify by introducing the extensive changes and transpositions surmised by Lachmann, for the purpose of binding together sixteen songs, which the rhapsodes are assumed to have been accustomed to recite, and the people to hear, each by itself apart? Peisistratus was not a poet, seeking to interest the public mind by new creations and combinations, but a ruler, desirous to impart solemnity to a great religious festival in his native city. Now such a purpose would be answered by selecting, amidst the divergences of rhapsodes in different parts of Greece, that order of text which intelligent men could approve as a return to the pure and pristine Iliad; but it would be defeated if he attempted large innovations of his own, and brought out for the first time a new Iliad by blending together, altering, and transposing, many old and well-known songs. A novelty so bold would have been more likely to offend than to please both the critics and the multitude. If it were even enforced by authority, at Athens, no probable reason can be given why all the other towns, and all the rhapsodes throughout Greece, should abnegate their previous habits in favour of it, since Athens at that time enjoyed no political ascendency such as she acquired during the following century. On the whole, it will appear that the character and position of Peisistratus himself go far to negative the function which Wolf and Lachmann put upon him. His interference presupposes a certain foreknown and ancient aggregate, the main lineaments of which were familiar to the Grecian public, although many of the rhapsodes in their practice may have deviated from it both by omission and interpolation. In correcting the Athenian recitations conformably with such understood general type, he might hope both to procure respect for Athens, and to constitute a fashion for the rest of Greece. This step of "collecting the torn body of sacred Homer," is something genetically different from the composition of a new Iliad out of pre-existing songs; the former is as easy, suitable, and promising, as the latter is violent and gratuitous.

To sustain the inference, that Peisistratus was the first architect of the Iliad and Odyssey, it ought at least to be shown that no other long and continuous poems existed during the earlier centuries. But the contrary of this is known to be the fact. The Æthiopis of Arktinus, which contained 9100 verses, dates from a period more than two centuries earlier than Peisistratus: several other of the lost cyclic epics, some among them of considerable length, appear during the century succeeding Arktinus; and it is important to notice, that three or four at least of these poems passed currently under the name of Homer. There is no greater intrinsic difficulty in supposing long epics to have begun with the Iliad and Odyssey than with the Æthiopis: the ascendency of the name of Homer and the subordinate position of Arktinus, in the history of early Grecian poetry, tend to prove the former in preference to the latter.

Moreover, we find particular portions of the Iliad which expressly pronounce themselves, by their own internal evidence, as belonging to a large whole, and not as separate integers. We can hardly conceive the Catalogue in the second book, except as a fractional composition, and with reference to a series of approaching exploits; for, taken apart by itself, such a barren enumeration of names could have stimulated neither the fancy of the poet, nor the attention of the listeners. But the Homeric Catalogue had acquired a sort of canonical authority even in the time of Solôn, insomuch that he interpolated a line into it, or was accused of doing so, for the purpose of gaining a disputed point against the Megarians, who, on their side, set forth another version. No such established reverence could have been felt for this document, unless there had existed for a long time prior to Peisistratus, the habit of regarding and listening to the Iliad as a continuous poem. When the philosopher Xenophanês, contemporary with Peisistratus, noticed Homer as the universal teacher, and denounced him as an unworthy describer of the gods, he must have connected this great mental sway, not with a number of unconnected rhapsodies, but with an aggregate Iliad and Odyssey; probably with other poems, also, ascribed to the same author, such as the Cypria, Epigoni, and Thebaïs.

We find, it is true, references in various authors to portions of the Iliad, each by its own separate name, such as the Teichomachy, the Aristeia (pre-eminent exploits) of Diomedês, or Agamemnôn, the Doloneia, or Night-expedition (of Dolôn as well as of Odysseus and Diomedês), &c., and hence, it has been concluded, that these portions originally existed as separate poems, before they were cemented together into an Iliad. But such references prove nothing to the point; for until the Iliad was divided by Aristarchus and his colleagues into a given number of books, or rhapsodies, designated by the series of letters in the alphabet, there was no method of calling attention to any particular portion of the poem except by special indication of its subject-matter. Authors subsequent to Peisistratus, such as Herodotus and Plato, who unquestionably conceived the Iliad as a whole, cite the separate fractions of it by designations of this sort.

The Wolf hypothesis.

The foregoing remarks on the Wolfian hypothesis respecting the text of the Iliad, tend to separate two points which are by no means necessarily connected, though that hypothesis, as set forth by Wolf himself, by W. Müller, and by Lachmann, presents the two in conjunction. First, was the Iliad originally projected and composed by one author, and as one poem, or were the different parts composed separately and by unconnected authors, and subsequently strung together into an aggregate? Secondly, assuming that the internal evidences of the poem negative the former supposition, and drive us upon the latter, was the construction of the whole poem deferred, and did the parts exist only in their separate state, until a period so late as the reign of Peisistratus? It is obvious that these two questions are essentially separate, and that a man may believe the Iliad to have been put together out of pre-existing songs, without recognising the age of Peisistratus as the period of its first compilation. Now, whatever may be the steps through which the poem passed to its ultimate integrity, there is sufficient reason for believing that they had been accomplished long before that period: the friends of Peisistratus found an Iliad already existing and already ancient in their time, even granting that the poem had not been originally born in a state of unity. Moreover, the Alexandrine critics, whose remarks are preserved in the Scholia, do not even notice the Peisistratic recension among the many manuscripts which they had before them; and Mr. Payne Knight justly infers from their silence that either they did not possess it, or it was in their eyes of no great authority; which could never have been the case if it had been the prime originator of Homeric unity.

The line of argument, by which the advocates of Wolf's hypothesis negative the primitive unity of the poem, consists in exposing gaps, incongruities, contradictions, &c., between the separate parts. Now, if in spite of all these incoherences, standing mementos of an antecedent state of separation, the component poems were made to coalesce so intimately as to appear as if they had been one from the beginning, we can better understand the complete success of the proceeding and the universal prevalence of the illusion, by supposing such coalescence to have taken place at a very early period, during the productive days of epical genius, and before the growth of reading and criticism. The longer the aggregation of the separate poems was deferred, the harder it would be to obliterate in men's minds the previous state of separation, and to make them accept the new aggregate as an original unity. The bards or rhapsodes might have found comparatively little difficulty in thus piecing together distinct songs, during the ninth or eighth century before Christ; but if we suppose the process to be deferred until the latter half of the sixth century, – if we imagine that Solôn, with all his contemporaries and predecessors, knew nothing about any aggregate Iliad, but was accustomed to read and hear only those sixteen distinct epical pieces into which Lachmann would dissect the Iliad, each of the sixteen bearing a separate name of its own, – no compilation then for the first time made by the friends of Peisistratus could have effaced the established habit, and planted itself in the general convictions of Greece as the primitive Homeric production. Had the sixteen pieces remained disunited and individualised down to the time of Peisistratus, they would in all probability have continued so ever afterwards; nor could the extensive changes and transpositions which (according to Lachmann's theory) were required to melt them down into our present Iliad, have obtained at that late period universal acceptance.

Assuming it to be true that such changes and transpositions did really take place, they must at least be referred to a period greatly earlier than Peisistratus or Solôn.

The whole tenor of the poems themselves confirms what is here remarked. There is nothing either in the Iliad or Odyssey which savours of *modernism,* applying that term to the age of Peisistratus; nothing which brings to our view the alterations, brought about by two centuries, in the Greek language, the coined money, the habits of writing and reading, the despotisms and republican governments, the close military array, the improved construction of ships, the Amphiktyonic convocations, the mutual frequentation of religious festivals, the Oriental and Egyptian veins of religion, &c., familiar to the latter epoch. These alterations Onomakritus and the other literary friends of Peisistratus, could hardly have failed to notice even without design, had they then for the first time undertaken the task of piecing together many self-existent epics into one large aggregate. Everything in the two great Homeric poems, both in substance and in language, belongs to an age two or three centuries earlier than Peisistratus. Indeed, even the interrelations (or these passages which on the best grounds are pronounced to be such) betray no trace of the sixth century before Christ, and may well have been heard by Archilochus and Kallinus, – in some cases even by Arktinus and Hesiod, – as genuine Homeric matter. As far as the evidences on the case, as well internal as external, enable us to judge, we seem warranted in believing that the Iliad and Odyssey were recited substantially as they now stand, (always allowing for partial divergences of text, and interpolations), in 776 B.C., our first trustworthy mark of Grecian time. And this ancient date, – let it be added, – as it is the best-authenticated fact, so it is also the most important attribute of the Homeric poems, considered in reference to Grecian history. For they thus afford us an insight into the ante-historical character of the Greeks, – enabling us to trace the subsequent forward march of the nation, and to seize instructive contrasts between their former and their later condition.

Rejecting, therefore, the idea of compilation by Peisistratus, and referring the present state of the Iliad and Odyssey to a period more than two centuries earlier, the question still remains, by what process, or through whose agency, they reached that state? Is each poem the work of one author, or of several? If the latter, do all the parts belong to the same age? What ground is there for believing, that any or all of these parts existed before, as separate poems, and have been accommodated to the place in which they now appear, by more or less systematic alteration?

The acute and valuable Prolegomena of Wolf, half a century ago, powerfully turned the attention of scholars to the necessity of considering the Iliad and Odyssey with reference to the age and society in which they arose, and to the material differences in this respect between Homer and more recent epic poets. Since that time, an elaborate study has been bestowed upon the early manifestations of poetry (Sagen-poesie) among other nations; and the German critics especially, among whom this description of literature has been most cultivated, have selected it as the only appropriate analogy for the Homeric poems. Such poetry, consisting for the most part of short, artless effusions, with little of deliberate or far-sighted combination, has been assumed by many critics as a fit standard to apply for measuring the capacities of the Homeric age: an age exclusively of speakers, singers, and hearers, not of readers or writers. In place of the unbounded admiration which was felt for Homer, not merely as a poet of detail, but as constructor of a long epic, at the time when Wolf wrote his Prolegomena, the tone of criticism passed to the opposite extreme, and attention was fixed entirely upon the defects in the arrangement of the Iliad and Odyssey. Whatever was to be found in them of symmetry or pervading system, was pronounced to be decidedly post-Homeric Under such preconceived anticipations, Homer seems to have been generally studied in Germany, during the generation succeeding Wolf, the negative portion of whose theory was usually admitted, though as to the positive substitute, – what explanation was to be given of the history and present constitution of the Homeric poems, – there was by no means the like agreement. During the last ten years, however, a contrary tendency has manifested itself; the Wolfian theory has been re-examined and shaken by Nitzsch, who, as well as O. Müller, Welcker, and other scholars, have revived the idea of original Homeric unity, under certain modifications. The change in Gothe's opinion, coincident with this new direction, is recorded in one of his latest works. On the other hand, the original opinion of Wolf has also been reproduced within the last five years, and fortified with several new observations on the text, of the Iliad, by Lachmann.

The point is thus still under controversy among able scholars, and is probably destined to remain so. For, in truth, our means of knowledge are so limited, that no man can produce arguments sufficiently cogent to contend against opposing preconceptions; and it creates a painful sentiment of diffidence when we read the expressions of equal and absolute persuasion with which the two opposite conclusions have both been advanced. We have nothing to teach us the history of these poems except the poems themselves. Not only do we possess no collateral information respecting them or their authors, but we have no one to describe to us the people or the age in which they originated: our knowledge respecting contemporary Homeric society, is collected exclusively from the Homeric compositions themselves. We are ignorant whether any other, or what other, poems preceded them, or divided with them the public favour; nor have we anything better than conjecture to determine either the circumstances under which they were brought before the hearers, or the conditions which a bard of that day was required to satisfy. On all these points, moreover, the age of Thucydidês and Plato seems to have been no better informed than we are, except in so far as they could profit by the analogies of the cyclic and other epic poems, which would doubtless in many cases have afforded valuable aid.

Nevertheless, no classical scholar can be easy without *some* opinion respecting the authorship of these immortal poems. And the more defective the evidence we possess, the more essential is it that all that evidence should be marshalled in the clearest order, and its bearing upon the points in controversy distinctly understood beforehand. Both these conditions seem to have been often neglected, throughout the long-continued Homeric discussion.

To illustrate the first point: Since two poems are comprehended in the problem to be solved, the natural process would be, first, to study the easier of the two, and then to apply the conclusions thence deduced as a means of explaining the other. Now, the Odyssey, looking at its aggregate character, is incomparably more easy to comprehend than the Iliad. Yet most Homeric critics apply the microscope at once, and in the first instance, to the Iliad.

To illustrate the second point: What evidence is sufficient to negative the supposition that the Iliad or the Odyssey is a poem originally and intentionally one? Not simply particular gaps and contradictions, though they be even gross and numerous; but the preponderance of these proofs of mere unprepared coalescence over the other proofs of designed adaptation scattered throughout the whole poem. For the poet (or the co-operating poets, if more than one) may have intended to compose an harmonious whole, but may have realised their intention incompletely, and left partial faults; or, perhaps, the contradictory lines may have crept in through a corrupt text. A survey of the whole poem is necessary to determine the question; and this necessity, too, has not always been attended to.

If it had happened that the Odyssey had been preserved to us alone, without the Iliad, I think the dispute respecting Homeric unity would never have been raised. For the former is, in my judgment, pervaded almost from beginning to end by marks of designed adaptation; and the special faults which Wolf, W Müller, and B. Thiersch, have singled out for the purpose of disproving such unity of intention, are so few, and of so little importance, that they would have been universally regarded as mere instances of haste or unskillfulness on the part of the poet, had they not been seconded by the far more powerful battery opened against the Iliad. These critics, having laid down their general presumptions against the antiquity of the long epopee, illustrate their principles by exposing the many flaws and fissures in the Iliad, and then think it sufficient if they can show a few similar defects in the Odyssey, – as if the breaking up of Homeric unity in the former naturally entailed a similar necessity with regard to the latter; and their method of proceeding, contrary to the rule above laid down, puts the more difficult problem in the foreground, as a means of solution for the easier. We can hardly wonder, however, that they have applied their observations in the first instance to the Iliad, because it is in every man's esteem the more marked, striking, and impressive poem of the two, – and the character of Homer is more intimately identified with it than with the Odyssey. This may serve as an explanation of the course pursued; but be the case as it may in respect to comparative poetical merit, it is not the less true, that, as an aggregate, the Odyssey is more simple and easily understood, and therefore, ought to come first in the order of analysis.

Now, looking at the Odyssey by itself, the proofs of an unity of design seem unequivocal and everywhere to be found. A premeditated structure, and a concentration of interest upon one prime hero, under well-defined circumstances, may be traced from the first book to the twenty-third. Odysseus is always either directly or indirectly kept before the reader, as a warrior returning from the fulness of glory at Troy, exposed to manifold and protracted calamities during his return home, on which his whole soul is so bent that he refuses even the immortality offered by Calypsô; – a victim, moreover, even after his return, to mingled injury and insult from the suitors, who have long been plundering his property, and dishonouring his house; but at length obtaining, by valour and cunning united, a signal revenge, which restores him to all that he had lost. All the persons and all the events in the poem are subsidiary to this main plot; and the divine agency, necessary to satisfy the feeling of the Homeric man, is put forth by Poseidôn and Athênê, in both cases from dispositions directly bearing upon Odysseus. To appreciate the unity of the Odyssey, we have only to read the objections taken against that of the Iliad, – especially in regard to the long withdrawal of Achillês, not only from the scene, but from the memory, – together with the independent prominence of Ajax, Diomedês, and other heroes. How far we are entitled from hence to infer the want of premeditated unity in the Iliad, will be presently considered; but it is certain that the constitution of the Odyssey, in this respect, everywhere demonstrates the presence of such unity. Whatever may be the interest attached to Penelopê, Telemachus, or Eumæus, we never disconnect them from their association with Odysseus. The present is not the place for collecting the many marks of artistical structure dispersed throughout this poem; but it may be worth while to remark, that the final catastrophe realised in the twenty-second book, – the slaughter of the suitors in the very house which they were profaning, – is distinctly and prominently marked out in the first and second books, promised by Teiresias in the eleventh, by Athênê in the thirteenth, and by Helen in the fifteenth, and gradually matured by a series of suitable preliminaries, throughout the eight looks preceding its occurrence. Indeed, what is principally evident, and what has been often noticed, in the Odyssey, is, the equable flow both of the narrative and the events; the absence of that rise and fall of interest which is sufficiently conspicuous in the Iliad.

To set against these evidences of unity, there ought, at least, to be some strong cases produced of occasional incoherence or contradiction. But it is remarkable how little of such counter-evidence is to be found, although the arguments of Wolf, W. Müller, and B. Thiersch stand so much in need of it. They have discovered only one instance of undeniable inconsistency in the parts, – the number of days occupied by the absence of Telemachus at Pylus and Sparta. That young prince, though represented as in great haste to depart, and refusing pressing invitations to prolong his stay, must, nevertheless, be supposed to have continued for thirty days the guest of Menelaus, in order to bring his proceedings into chronological harmony with those of Odysseus, and to explain the first meeting of father and son in the swine-fold of Eumæus. Here is undoubtedly an inaccuracy, (so Nitzsch treats it, and I think justly) on the part of the poet, who did not anticipate, and did not experience in ancient times, so strict a scrutiny; an inaccuracy certainly not at all wonderful; the matter of real wonder is, that it stands almost alone, and that there are no others in the poem.

Now, this is one of the main points on which W. Müller and B. Thiersch rest their theory, – explaining the chronological confusion by supposing that the journey of Telemachus to Pylos and Sparta, constituted the subject of an epic originally separate (comprising the first four books and a portion of the fifteenth), and incorporated at second-hand with the remaining poem. They conceive this view to be farther confirmed by the double assembly of the gods, (at the beginning of the first book as well as of the fifth), which they treat as an awkward repetition, such as could not have formed part of the primary scheme of any epic poet. But here they only escape a small difficulty by running into another and a greater. For it is impossible to comprehend how the first four books and part of the fifteenth can ever have constituted a distinct epic; since the adventures of Telemachus have no satisfactory termination, except at the point of confluence with those of his father, when the unexpected meeting and recognition takes place under the roof of Eumæus, – nor can any epic poem ever have described that meeting and recognition without giving some account how Odysseus came thither. Moreover, the first two books of the Odyssey distinctly lay the ground, and carry expectation forward, to the final catastrophe of the poem, – treating Telemachus as a subordinate person, and his expedition as merely provisional towards an ulterior result. Nor can I agree with W. Müller, that the real Odyssey might well be supposed to begin with the fifth book. On the contrary, the exhibition of the suitors and the Ithakesian agora, presented to us in the second book, is absolutely essential to the full comprehension of the books subsequent to the thirteenth. The suitors are far too important personages in the poem to allow of their being first introduced in so informal a manner as we read in the sixteenth book: indeed, the passing allusions of Athênê (xiii 310, 375) and Eumæus (xiv. 41, 81) to the suitors, presuppose cognisance of them on the part of the hearer.

Lastly, the twofold discussion of the gods, at the beginning of the first and fifth books, and the double interference of Athênê, far from being a needless repetition, may be shown to suit perfectly both the genuine epical conditions and the unity of the poem. For although the final consummation, and the organisation of measures against the suitors, was to be accomplished by Odysseus and Telemachus jointly, yet the march and adventures of the two, until the moment of their meeting in the dwelling of Eumæus, were essentially distinct. According to the religious ideas of the old epic, the presiding direction of Athênê was necessary for the safety and success of both of them. Her first interference arouses and inspires the son, her second produces the liberation of the father, – constituting a point of union and common origination for two lines of adventures, in both of which she takes earnest interest, but which are necessarily for a time kept apart in order to coincide at the proper moment.

It will thus appear that the twice-repeated agora of the gods in the Odyssey, bringing home, as it does to one and the same divine agent, that double start which is essential to the scheme of the poem, consists better with the supposition of premeditated unity than with that of distinct self-existent parts. Assuredly, the manner in which Telemachus and Odysseus, both by different roads, are brought into meeting and conjunction at the dwelling of Eumæus, is something not only contrived, but very skilfully contrived. It is needless to advert to the highly interesting character of Eumæus, rendered available as a rallying-point, though in different ways, both to the father and the son, over and above the sympathy which he himself inspires.

If the Odyssey be not an original unity, of what self-existent parts can we imagine it to have consisted? To this question it is difficult to imagine a satisfactory reply: for the supposition that Telemachus and his adventures may once have formed the subject of a separate epos, apart from Odysseus, appears inconsistent with the whole character of that youth as it stands in the poem, and with the events in which he is made to take part. We could better imagine the distribution of the adventures of Odysseus himself into two parts, – one containing his wanderings and return, the other handling his ill-treatment by the suitors, and his final triumph. But though either of these two subjects might have been adequate to furnish out a separate poem, it is nevertheless certain that, as they are presented in the Odyssey, the former cannot be divorced from the latter. The simple return of Odysseus, as it now stands in the poem, could satisfy no one as a final close, so long as the suitors remain in possession of his house, and forbid his reunion with his wife. Any poem which treated his wanderings and return separately, must have represented his reunion with Penelopê and restoration to his house, as following naturally upon his arrival in Ithaka, – thus taking little or no notice of the suitors. But this would be a capital mutilation of the actual epical narrative, which considers the suitors at home as an essential portion of the destiny of the much-suffering hero, not less than his shipwrecks and trials at sea. His return (separately taken) is foredoomed, according to the curse of Polyphemus, executed by Poseidôn, to be long deferred, miserable, solitary, and ending with destruction in his house to greet him; and the ground is thus laid, in the very recital of his wanderings, for a new series of events which are to happen to him after his arrival in Ithaka. There is no tenable halting-place between the departure of Odysseus from Troy, and the final restoration to his house and his wife. The distance between these two events may, indeed, be widened, by accumulating new distresses and impediments, but any separate portion of it cannot be otherwise treated than as a fraction of the whole. The beginning and the end are here the data in respect to epical genesis, though the intermediate events admit of being conceived as variables, more or less numerous: so that the conception of the whole may be said without impropriety both to precede and to govern that of the constituent parts.

The general result of a study of the Odyssey may be set down as follows: **1.** The poem, as it now stands, exhibits unequivocally adaptation of parts and continuity of structure, whether by one or by several consentient hands: it may, perhaps be a secondary formation, out of a pre-existing Odyssey of smaller dimensions; but, if so, the parts of the smaller whole must have been so far recast as to make them suitable members of the larger, and are noway recognisable by us. **2.** The subject-matter of the poem not only does not favour, but goes far to exclude, the possibility of the Wolfian hypothesis. Its events cannot be so arranged as to have composed several antecedent substantive epics, afterwards put together into the present aggregate. Its authors cannot have been mere compilers of pre-existing materials, such as Peisistratus and his friends: they must have been poets, competent to work such matter as they found, into a new and enlarged design of their own. Nor can the age in which this long poem, of so many thousand lines, was turned out as a continuous aggregate, be separated from the ancient, productive, inspired age of Grecian epic.

Arriving at such conclusions from the internal evidence of the Odyssey, we can apply them by analogy to the Iliad. We learn something respecting the character and capacities of that early age which has left no other mementos except these two poems. Long continuous epics (it is observed by those who support the views of Wolf), with an artistical structure, are inconsistent with the capacities of a rude and non-writing age. Such epics (we may reply) are *not inconsistent* with the early age of the Greeks, and the Odyssey is a proof of it; for in that poem the integration of the whole, and the composition of the parts, must have been simultaneous. The analogy of the Odyssey enables us to rebut that preconception under which many ingenious critics sit down to the study of the Iliad, and which induces them to explain all the incoherences of the latter by breaking it up into smaller unities, as if short epics were the only manifestation of poetical power which the age admitted. There ought to be no reluctance in admitting a presiding scheme and premeditated unity of parts, in so far as the parts themselves point to such a conclusion.

That the Iliad is not so essentially one piece as the Odyssey, every man agrees. It includes a much greater multiplicity of events, and what is yet more important, a greater multiplicity of prominent personages: the very indefinite title which it bears, as contrasted with the speciality of the name, *Odyssey,* marks the difference at once. The parts stand out more conspicuously from the whole, and admit more readily of being felt and appreciated in detached recitation. We may also add, that it is of more unequal execution than the Odyssey, – often rising to a far higher pitch of grandeur, but also, occasionally, tamer: the story does not move on continuously; incidents occur without plausible motive, nor can we shut our eyes to evidences of incoherence and contradiction.

To a certain extent, the Iliad is open to all these remarks, though Wolf and William Müller, and above all Lachmann, exaggerate the case in degree. From hence has been deduced the hypothesis which treats the parts in their original state as separate integers, independent of and unconnected with, each other, and forced into unity only by the afterthought of a subsequent age; or sometimes, not even themselves as integers, but as aggregates grouped together out of fragments still smaller, – short epics formed by the coalescence of still shorter songs. Now there is some plausibility in these reasonings, so long as the discrepancies are looked upon as the whole of the case. But in point of fact they are not the whole of the case; for it is not less true, that there are large portions of the Iliad which present positive and undeniable evidences of coherence as antecedent and consequent, though we are occasionally perplexed by inconsistencies of detail. To deal with these latter, is a portion of the duties of the critic. He is not to treat the Iliad as if inconsistency prevailed everywhere throughout its parts; for coherence of parts – symmetrical antecedence and consequence – is discernible throughout the larger half of the poem.

Now the Wolfian theory explains the gaps and contradictions throughout the narrative, but it explains nothing else. If (as Lachmann thinks) the Iliad originally consisted of sixteen songs, or little substantive epics, (Lachmann's sixteen songs cover the space only as far as the 22nd book, or the death of Hectôr, and two more songs would have to be admitted for the 23d and 24th books), – not only composed by different authors, but by each without any view to conjunction with the rest, – we have then no right to expect any intrinsic continuity between them; and all that continuity which we now find must be of extraneous origin. Where are we to look for the origin? Lachmann follows Wolf, in ascribing the whole constructive process to Peisistratus and his associates, at a period when the creative epical faculty is admitted to have died out. Upon this supposition, Peisistratus (or his associates) must have done much more than omit, transpose, and interpolate, here and there; he must have gone far to rewrite the whole poem. A great poet might have recast pre-existing separate songs into one comprehensive whole, but no mere arrangers or compilers would be competent to do so; and we are thus left without any means of accounting for that degree of continuity and consistence which runs through so large a portion of the Iliad, though not through the whole. The idea that the poem, as we read it, grew out of atoms not originally designed for the places which they now occupy, involves us in new and inextricable difficulties, when we seek to elucidate either the mode of coalescence or the degree of existing unity.

Admitting then premeditated adaptation of parts to a certain extent as essential to the Iliad, we may yet inquire, whether it was produced all at once, or gradually enlarged, – whether by one author, or by several; and, if the parts be of different age, which is the primitive kernel, and which are the additions.

Theory of Welcker, Lange & Nitzsch.

Welcker, Lange, and Nitzsch treat the Homeric poems as representing a second step in advance, in the progress of popular poetry. First, comes the age of short narrative songs; next, when these have become numerous, there arise constructive minds, who recast and blend together many of them into a larger aggregate, conceived upon some scheme of their own. The age of the epos is followed by that of the epopee, – short, spontaneous effusions preparing the way, and furnishing materials, for the architectonic genius of the poet. It is farther presumed by the above-mentioned authors, that the pre-Homeric epic included a great abundance of such smaller songs, – a fact which admits of no proof, but which seems countenanced by some passages in Homer, and is in itself no way improbable. The transition from such songs, assuming them to be ever so numerous, to a combined and continuous poem, forms an epoch in the intellectual history of the nation, implying mental qualities of a higher order than those upon which the songs themselves depend. Nor is it to be imagined that the materials pass unaltered from their first state of isolation into their second state of combination. They must of necessity be recast, and undergo an adapting process, in which the genius of the organising poet consists; nor can we hope, by simply knowing them as they exist in the second stage, ever to divine how they stood in the first. Such, in my judgment, is the right conception of the Homeric epoch. – an organising poetical mind, still preserving that freshness of observation and vivacity of details which constitutes the charm of the ballad.

Iliad originally an Achillêis.

Nothing is gained by studying the Iliad as a congeries of fragments once independent of each other: no portion of the poem can be shown to have ever been so, and the supposition introduces difficulties greater than those which it removes. But it is not necessary to affirm that the whole poem as we now read it, belonged to the original and preconceived plan. In this respect, the Iliad produces, upon my mind, an impression totally different from the Odyssey. In the latter poem, the characters and incidents are fewer, and the whole plot appears of one projection, from the beginning down to the death of the suitors: none of the parts look as if they had been composed separately, and inserted by way of addition into a pre-existing smaller poem. The Iliad, on the contrary, presents the appearance of a house built upon a plan comparatively narrow, and subsequently enlarged by successive additions. The first book, together with the eighth, and the books from the eleventh to the twenty second, inclusive, seem to form the primary organisation of the poem, then properly an Achillêis: the twenty-third and twenty-fourth books are, perhaps, additions at the tail of this primitive poem, which still leave it nothing more than an enlarged Achillêis. Whereas the books from the second to the seventh, inclusive, together with the tenth, are of a wider and more comprehensive character, and convert the poem from an Achillêis into an Iliad. The primitive frontispiece, inscribed with the anger of Achilles, and its direct consequences, yet remains, after it has ceased to be coextensive with the poem. The parts added, however, are not necessarily inferior in merit to the original poem: so far is this from being the case, that amongst them are comprehended some of the noblest efforts of the Grecian epic. Nor are they more recent in date than the original; strictly speaking, they must be a little more recent, but they belong to the same generation and state of society as the primitive Achillêis. These qualifications are necessary to keep apart different questions, which, in discussions of Homeric criticism, are but too often confounded.

If we take those portions of the poem which I imagine to have constituted the original Achillêis, it will be found that the sequence of events contained in them is more rapid, more unbroken, and more intimately knit together in the way of cause and effect, than in the other books. Heyne and Lachmann, indeed, with other objecting critics, complains of the action in them as being too much crowded and hurried, since one day lasts from the beginning of the eleventh book to the middle of the eighteenth, without any sensible halt in the march throughout so large a portion of the journey. Lachmann, likewise, admits that those separate songs, into which he imagines that the whole Iliad may be dissected, cannot be severed with the same sharpness, in the books subsequent to the eleventh, as in those before it. There is only one real halting-place from the eleventh book to the twenty-second, – the death of Patroclus; and this can never be conceived as the end of a separate poem; though it is a capital step in the development of the Achillêis, and brings about that entire revolution in the temper of Achilles which was essential for the purpose of the poet. It would be a mistake to imagine that there ever could have existed a separate poem called Patrocleia, though a part of the Iliad was designated by that name. For Patroclus has no substantive position: he is the attached friend and second of Achilles, but nothing else, – standing to the latter in a relation of dependence resembling that of Telemachus to Odysseus. The way in which Patroclus is dealt with in the Iliad, is, (in my judgment), the most dexterous and artistical contrivance in the poem, – that which approaches nearest to the neat tissue of the Odyssey.

The great and capital misfortune which prostrates the strength of the Greeks, and renders them incapable of defending themselves without Achillês, is the disablement, by wounds, of Agamemnôn, Diomêdês, and Odysseus; so that the defence of the wall and of the ships is left only to heroes of the second magnitude (Ajax alone excepted), such as Idomeneus, Leonteus, Polypœtês, Merionês, Menelaus, &c. Now, it is remarkable that all these three first-rate chiefs are in full force at the beginning of the eleventh book: all three are wounded in the battle which that book describes, and at the commencement of which Agamemnôn is full of spirits and courage.

Nothing can be more striking than the manner in which Homer concentrates our attention in the first book upon Achilles as the hero, his quarrel with Agamemnôn, and the calamities to the Greeks which are held out as about to ensue from it, through the intercession of Thetis with Zeus. The incidents dwelt upon from the beginning of the second book down to the combat between Hectôr and Ajax in the seventh, animated and interesting as they are, do nothing to realise this promise. They are a splendid picture of the Trojan war generally, and eminently suitable to that larger title under which the poem has been immortalised, – but the consequences of the anger of Achilles do not appear until the eighth book. The tenth book, or Doloneia, is also a portion of the Iliad, but not of the Achillêis: while the ninth book appears to me a subsequent addition, nowise harmonising with that main stream of the Achillêis which flows from the eleventh book to the twenty-second. The eighth book ought to be read in immediate connection with the eleventh, in order to see the structure of what seems the primitive Achillêis; for there are several passages in the eleventh and the following books, which prove that the poet who composed them could not have had present to his mind the main event of the ninth book, – the outpouring of profound humiliation by the Greeks, and from Agamemnôn, especially, before Achilles, coupled with formal offers to restore Brisêis, and pay the amplest compensation for past wrong. The words of Achilles (not less than those of Patroclus and Nestôr) in the eleventh and in the following books, plainly imply that the humiliation of the Greeks before him, for which he thirsts, is as yet future and contingent; that no plenary apology has yet been tendered, nor any offer made of restoring Brisêis; while both Nestôr and Patroclus, with all their wish to induce him to take arms, never take notice of the offered atonement and restitution, but view him as one whose ground for quarrel stands still the same as it did at the beginning. Moreover, if we look at the first book, – the opening of the Achillêis, – we shall see that this prostration of Agamemnôn and the chief Grecian heroes before Achilles, would really be the termination of the whole poem; for Achilles asks nothing more from Thetis, nor Thetis anything more from Zeus, than that Agamemnôn and the Greeks may be brought to know the wrong they have done to their capital warrior, and humbled in the dust in expiation of it. We may add, that the abject terror in which Agamemnôn appears in the ninth book, when he sends the supplicatory message to Achilles, as it is not adequately accounted for by the degree of calamity which the Greeks have experienced in the preceding (eighth) book, so it is inconsistent with the gallantry and high spirit with which he shines at the beginning of the eleventh. The situation of the Greeks only becomes desperate when the three great chiefs, Agamemnôn, Odysseus, and Diomêdês, are disabled by wounds; this is the irreparable calamity which works upon Patroclus, and through him upon Achilles. The ninth book, as it now stands, seems to me an addition, by a different hand, to the original Achillêis, framed so as both to forestall and to spoil the nineteenth book, which is the real reconciliation of the two inimical heroes: I will venture to add, that it carries the pride and egotism of Achilles beyond even the largest exigences of insulted honour, and is shocking to that sentiment of Nemesis which was so deeply seated in the Grecian mind. We forgive any excess of fury against the Trojans and Hectôr, after the death of Patroclus; but that he should remain unmoved by restitution, by abject supplications, and by the richest atoning presents, tendered from the Greeks, indicates an implacability such as neither the first book, nor the books between the eleventh and seventeenth, convey.

It is with the Grecian agora, in the beginning of the second book, that the Iliad (as distinguished from the Achillêis) commences, – continued through the Catalogue, the muster of the two armies, the single combat between Menelaus and Paris, the renewed promiscuous battle caused by the arrow of Pandarus, the (Epipôlêsis, or) personal circuit of Agamemnôn round the army, the Aristeia, or brilliant exploits of Diomêdês, the visit of Hectôr to Troy for the purposes of sacrifice, his interview with Andromachê, and his combat with Ajax, – down to the seventh book. All these are beautiful poetry, presenting to us the general Trojan war, and its conspicuous individuals under different points of view, but leaving no room in the reader's mind for the thought of Achilles. Now, the difficulty for an enlarging poet was, to pass from the Achillêis in the first book, to the Iliad in the second, and it will accordingly be found that here is an awkwardness in the structure of the poem, which counsel on the poet's behalf (ancient or modern) do not satisfactorily explain.

In the first book, Zeus has promised Thetis, that he will punish the Greeks for the wrong done to Achilles: in the beginning of the second book, he deliberates how he shall fulfil the promise, and sends down for that purpose "mischievous Oneirus" (the Dream-god) to visit Agamemnôn in his sleep, to assure him that the gods have now with one accord consented to put Troy into his hands, and to exhort him forthwith to the assembling of his army for the attack. The ancient commentators were here perplexed by the circumstance that Zeus puts a falsehood into the mouth of Oneirus. But there seems no more difficulty in explaining this, than in the narrative of the book of I Kings (chap. xxii. 20), where Jehovah is mentioned to have put a lying spirit into the mouth of Ahab's prophets, – the real awkwardness is, that Oneirus and his falsehood produce no effect. For in the first place, Agamemnôn takes a step very different from that which his dream recommends, – and in the next place, when the Grecian army is at length armed and goes forth to battle, it does not experience defeat, (which would be the case if the exhortation of Oneirus really proved mischievous), but carries on a successful day's battle, chiefly through the heroism of Diomêdês. Instead of arming the Greeks forthwith, Agamemnôn convokes first a council of chiefs, and next an agora of the host. Though himself in a temper of mind highly elate with the deceitful assurances of Oneirus, he deliberately assumes the language of despair in addressing the troops, having previously prepared Nestôr and Odysseus for his doing so, – merely in order to try the courage of the men, and with formal instructions, given to these two other chiefs, that they are to speak in opposition to him. Now this intervention of Zeus and Oneirus, eminently unsatisfactory when coupled with the incidents which now follow it, and making Zeus appear, but only appear, to realise his promise of honouring Achilles as well as of hurting the Greeks, – forms exactly the point of junction between the Achillêis and the Iliad. The freak which Agamemnôn plays off upon the temper of his army, though in itself childish, serves a sufficient purpose, not only because it provides a special matter of interest to be submitted to the Greeks, but also because it calls forth the splendid description, so teeming with vivacious detail, of the sudden breaking up of the assembly after Agamemnôn's harangue, and of the decisive interference of Odysseus to bring the men back, as well as to put down Thersitês. This picture of the Greeks in agora, bringing out the two chief speaking and counselling heroes, was so important a part of the general Trojan war, that the poet has permitted himself to introduce it by assuming an inexplicable folly on the part of Agamemnôn; just as he has ushered in another fine scene in the third book, – the Teichoskopy, or conversation, between Priam and Helen on the walls of Troy, – by admitting the supposition that the old king, in the tenth year of the war, did not know the persons of Agamemnôn and the other Grecian chiefs. This may serve as an explanation of the delusion practised by Agamemnôn towards his assembled host; but it does not at all explain the tame and empty intervention of Oneirus.

If the initial incident of the second book, whereby we pass out of the Achilles into the Iliad, is awkward so also the final incident of the seventh book, immediately before we come back into the Achillêis, is not less unsatisfactory, – I mean, the construction of the wall and ditch round the Greek camp. As the poem now stands, no plausible reason is assigned why this should be done. Nestôr proposes it without any constraining necessity: for the Greeks are in a career of victory, and the Trojans are making offers of compromise which imply conscious weakness, – while Diomêdês is so confident of the approaching ruin of Troy that he dissuades his comrades from receiving even Helen herself, if the surrender should be tendered. "Many Greeks have been slain," it is true, as Nestôr observes; but an equal or greater number of Trojans have been slain, and all the Grecian heroes are yet in full force: the absence of Achilles is not even adverted to.

Now this account of the building of the fortification seems to be an afterthought, arising out of the enlargement of the poem beyond its original scheme. The original Achillêis, passing at once from the first to the eighth, and from thence to the eleventh book, might well assume the fortification, – and talk of it as a thing existing, without adducing any special reason why it was erected. The hearer would naturally comprehend and follow the existence of a ditch and wall round the ships, as a matter of course, provided there was nothing in the previous narrative to make him believe that the Greeks had originally been without these bulwarks. Since the Achillêis, immediately after the promise of Zeus to Thetis, at the close of the first book, went on to describe the fulfilment of that promise and the ensuing disasters of the Greeks, there was nothing to surprise any one in hearing that their camp was fortified. The case was altered when the first and the eighth books were parted asunder, in order to make room for descriptions of temporary success and glory on the part of the besieging army. The brilliant scenes sketched in the books, from the second to the seventh, mention no fortification, and even imply its non-existence; yet, since notice of it occurs amidst the first description of Grecian disasters in the eighth book, the hearer, who had the earlier books present to his memory, might be surprised to find a fortification mentioned immediately afterwards, unless the

383

construction of it were specially announced to have intervened. It will at once appear, that there was some difficulty in finding a good reason why the Greeks should begin to fortify at this juncture, and that the poet who discovered the gap might not be enabled to fill it up with success. As the Greeks have got on, up to this moment, without the wall, and as we have heard nothing but tales of their success, why should they now think farther laborious precautions for security necessary? We will not ask, why the Trojans should stand quietly by and permit a wall to be built, since the truce was concluded expressly for burying the dead.

The tenth book, (or Doloneia) was considered by some of the ancient scholiasts, and has been confidently set forth by the modern Wolfian critics, as originally a separate poem, inserted by Peisistratus into the Iliad. How it can ever have been a separate poem, I do not understand. It is framed with great specialty for the antecedent circumstances under which it occurs, and would suit for no other place; though capable of being separately recited, inasmuch as it has a definite beginning and end, like the story of Nisus and Euryalus in the Æneid. But while distinctly presupposing and resting upon the incidents in the eighth book, and in line 88 of the ninth, (probably, the appointment of sentinels on the part of the Greeks, as well of the Trojans, formed the close of the battle described in the eighth book), it has not the slightest bearing upon the events of the eleventh or the following books: it goes to make up the general picture of the Trojan war, but lies quite apart from the Achillêis. This is one mark of a portion subsequently inserted, – that, though fitted on to the parts which precede, it has no influence on those which follow.

If the proceedings of the combatants on the plain of Troy, between the first and the eighth book, have no reference either to Achilles, or to an Achillêis, we find Zeus in Olympus still more completely putting that hero out of the question, at the beginning of the fourth book. He is in this last-mentioned passage the Zeus of the Iliad, not of the Achillêis. Forgetful of his promise to Thetis, in the first book, he discusses nothing but the question of continuance or termination of the war, and manifests anxiety only for the salvation of Troy, in opposition to the miso-Trojan goddesses, who prevent him from giving effect to the victory of Menelaus over Paris, and the stipulated restitution of Hellen, – in which case, of course, the wrong offered to Achilles would remain un-expiated. An attentive comparison will render it evident that the poet who composed the discussion among the gods, at the beginning of the fourth book, has not been careful to put himself in harmony either with the Zeus of the first book, or with the Zeus of the eighth.

So soon as we enter upon the eleventh book, the march of the poem becomes quite different. We are then in a series of events, each paving the way for that which follows, and all conducing to the result promised in the first book, – the reappearance of Achilles, as the only means of saving the Greeks from ruin, – preceded by ample atonement, and followed by the maximum both of glory and revenge. The intermediate career of Patroclus introduces new elements, which, however, are admirably woven into the scheme of the poem, as disclosed in the first book, I shall not deny that there are perplexities in the detail of events, as described in the battles at the Grecian wall, and before the ships, from the eleventh to the sixteenth books, but they appear only cases of partial confusion, such as may be reasonably ascribed to imperfections of text: the main sequence remains coherent and intelligible. We find no considerable events which could be left out without breaking the thread, nor any incongruity between one considerable event and another. There is nothing between the eleventh and twenty-second books, which is at all comparable to the incongruity between the Zeus of the fourth book and the Zeus of the first and eighth. It may, perhaps, be true, that the shield of Achilles is a superadded amplification of that which was originally announced in general terms, – because the poet, from the eleventh to the twenty-second books, has observed such good economy of his materials, that he is hardly likely to have introduced one particular description of such disproportionate length, and having so little connection with the series of events. Yet I see no reason for believing that it is an addition materially later than the rest of the poem.

Hypothesis of an enlarged Achillêis.

It must be confessed, that the supposition here advanced, in reference to the structure of the Iliad, is not altogether free from difficulties, because the parts constituting the original Achillêis have been more or less altered or interpolated, to suit the additions made to it, particularly in the eighth book. But it presents fewer difficulties than any other supposition, and it is the only means, so far as I know, of explaining the difference between one part of the Iliad and another; both the continuity of structure, and the conformity to the opening promise, which are manifest when we read the books in the order i. viii. xi. to xxii, as contrasted with the absence of these two qualities in books

ii. to vii., ix. and x. An entire organisation, preconceived from the beginning, would not be likely to produce any such disparity, nor is any such visible in the Odyssey; still less would the result be explained by supposing integers originally separate, and brought together without any designed organisation. It is between these three suppositions that our choice has to be made. A scheme, and a large scheme too, must unquestionably be admitted as the basis of any sufficient hypothesis. The Achillêis would have been a long poem, half the length of the present Iliad, and probably not less compact in its structure than the Odyssey. Moreover, being parted off only by an imaginary line from the boundless range of the Trojan war, it would admit of enlargement more easily, and with greater relish to hearers, than the adventures of one single hero; while the expansion would naturally take place by adding new Grecian victory, – since the original poem arrived at the exaltation of Achilles only through a painful series of Grecian disasters. That the poem under these circumstances should have received additions, is no very violent hypothesis: in fact, when we recollect that the integrity both of the Achillêis and of the Odyssey was neither guarded by printing nor writing, we shall perhaps think it less wonderful that the former was enlarged, than that the latter was not. Any relaxation of the laws of epical unity is a small price to pay for that splendid poetry, of which we find so much between the first and the eighth books of our Iliad.

The question respecting unity of authorship is different, and more difficult to determine, than that respecting consistency of parts, and sequence in the narrative. A poem conceived on a comparatively narrow scale may be enlarged afterwards by its original author, with greater or less coherence and success: the Faust of Goethe affords an example even in our own generation. On the ether hand, a systematic poem may well have been conceived and executed by prearranged concert between several poets; among whom probably one will be the governing mind, though the rest may be effective, and perhaps equally effective, in respect to execution of the parts. The age of the early Grecian epic was favourable to such fraternisation of poets, of which the Gens called Homerids probably exhibited many specimens. In the recital or singing of a long unwritten poem, many bards must have conspired together, and in the earliest times the composer and the singer were one and the same person. Now the individuals comprised in the Homeric Gens, though doubtless very different among themselves in respect of mental capacity, were yet homogeneous in respect of training, means of observation and instruction, social experience, religious feelings and theories, &c., to a degree much greater than individuals in modern times. Fallible as our inferences are on this point, where we have only internal evidence to guide us, without any contemporary points of comparison, or any species of collateral information respecting the age, the society, the poets, the hearers, or the language, – we must nevertheless, in the present case, take coherence of structure, together with consistency in the tone of thought, feeling, language, customs, &c., as presumptions of one author; and the contrary as presumptions of severalty; allowing, as well as we can, for that inequality of excellence which the same author may at different times present.

Now, the case made out against single-headed authorship of the Odyssey, appears to me very weak; and those who dispute it, are guided more by their *à priori* rejection of ancient epical unity, than by any positive evidence which the poem itself affords. It is otherwise with regard to the Iliad. Whatever presumptions a disjointed structure, several apparent inconsistencies of parts, and large excrescence of actual matter beyond the opening promise, can sanction, – may reasonably be indulged against the supposition that this poem all proceeds from a single author. There is a difference of opinion on the subject among the best critics, which is, probably, not destined to be adjusted, since so much depends partly upon critical feeling, partly upon the general reasonings, in respect to ancient epical unity, with which a man sits down to the study. For the champions of unity, such as Mr. Payne Knight, are very ready to strike out numerous and often considerable passages as interpolations, thus meeting the objections raised against unity of authorship, on the ground of special inconsistencies. Hermann and Boeckh, though not going the length of Lachmann in maintaining the original theory of Wolf, agree with the latter in recognising diversity of authors in the poem, to an extent overpassing the limit of what can fairly be called interpolation. Payne Knight and Nitzsch are equally persuaded of the contrary. Here, then, is a decided contradiction among critics, all of whom have minutely studied the poems since the Wolfian question was raised. It is such critics alone who can be said to constitute authority; for the cursory reader, who dwells upon the parts simply long enough to relish their poetical beauty, is struck only by that general sameness of colouring which Wolf himself admits to pervade the poem.

Having already intimated that, in my judgment, no theory of the structure of the poem is admissible which does not admit an original and preconcerted

Achillêis, – a stream which begins at the first book and ends with the death of Hectôr, in the twenty-second, although the higher parts of it now remain only in the condition of two detached lakes, the first book and the eighth, – I reason upon the same basis with respect to the authorship. Assuming continuity of structure as a presumptive proof, the whole of this Achillêis must be treated as composed by one author. Wolf, indeed, affirmed, that he never read the poem continuously through without being painfully impressed with the inferiority and altered style of the last six books, – and Lachmann carries this feeling farther back, so as to commence with the seventeenth book. If I could enter fully into this sentiment, I should then be compelled, not to deny the existence of a preconceived scheme, but to imagine that the books from the eighteenth to the twenty-second, though forming part of that scheme, or Achillêis, had yet been executed by another and an inferior poet. It is to be remarked, first, that inferiority of poetical merit, to a certain extent, is quite reconcilable with unity of authorship; and, secondly, that the very circumstances upon which Wolf's unfavourable judgment is built, seem to arise out of increased difficulty in the poet's task, when he came to the crowning cantos of his designed Achillêis. For that which chiefly distinguishes these books, is the direct, incessant, and manual intervention of the gods and goddesses, formerly permitted by Zeus, – and the repetition of vast and fantastic conceptions to which such superhuman agency gives occasion; not omitting the battle of Achilles against Skamander and Simois, and the burning up of these rivers by Hephæstus. Now, looking at this vein of ideas with the eyes of a modern reader, or even with those of a Grecian critic of the literary ages, it is certain that the effect is unpleasing: the gods, sublime elements of poetry when kept in due proportion, are here somewhat vulgarised. Though the poet here has not succeeded, and probably success was impossible, in the task which he has prescribed to himself, – yet the mere fact of his undertaking it, and the manifest distinction between his employment of divine agency in these latter cantos as compared with the preceding, seems explicable only on the supposition that they *are* the latter cantos, and come in designed sequence, as the continuance of a previous plan. The poet wishes to surround the coming forth of Achilles with the maximum of glorious and terrific circumstance; no Trojan enemy can for a moment hold out against him; the gods must descend to the plain of Troy and fight in person, while Zeus, who at the beginning of the eighth book, had forbidden them to take part, expressly encourages them to do so at the beginning of the twentieth. If, then, the nineteenth book (which contains the reconciliation between Achilles and Agamemnôn, a subject naturally somewhat tame) and the three following books (where we have before us only the gods, Achilles, and the Trojans, without hope or courage) are inferior in execution and interest to the seven preceding books (which describe the long-disputed and often doubtful death-struggle between the Greeks and Trojans without Achilles), as Wolf and other critics affirm, – we may explain the difference without supposing a new poet as composer; for the conditions of the poem had become essentially more difficult, and the subject more unpromising. The necessity of keeping Achilles above the level, even of heroic prowess, restricted the poet's means of acting upon the sympathy of his hearers.

The last two books of the Iliad may have formed part of the original Achillêis. But the probability rather is, that they are additions; for the death of Hectôr satisfies the exigencies of a coherent scheme, and we are not entitled to extend the oldest poem beyond the limit which such necessity prescribes. It has been argued on one side by Nitzsch and O. Müller, that the mind could not leave off with satisfaction at the moment in which Achilles sates his revenge, and while the bodies of Patroclus and Hectôr are lying unburied, – also, that the more merciful temper which he exhibits in the twenty-fourth book, must always have been an indispensable sequel, in order to create proper sympathy with his triumph. Other critics, on the contrary, have taken special grounds of exception against the last book, and have endeavoured to set it aside as different from the other books both in tone and language. To a certain extent, the peculiarities of the last book appear to me undeniable, though it is plainly a designed continuance, and not a substantive poem. Some weight also is due to the remark about the twenty-third book, that Odysseus and Diomêdês, who have been wounded and disabled during the fight, now reappear in perfect force, and contend in the games: here is no case of miraculous healing, and the inconsistency is more likely to have been admitted by a separate enlarging poet, than by the schemer of the Achillêis.

The splendid books from the second to v. 322 of the seventh, are equal, in most parts, to any portion of the Achillêis, and are pointedly distinguished from the latter by the broad view which they exhibit of the general Trojan war, with all its principal personages, localities, and causes, – yet without advancing the result promised in the first book, or, indeed, any final purpose whatever. Even the desperate wound inflicted by Tlepolemus on Sarpedon, is forgotten, when the latter hero is called forth in the subsequent Achillêis. The arguments of Lachmann, who dissects these six books into three or four separate songs, carry no conviction to my mind; and I see no reason why we should not consider all of them to be by the same author, bound together by the common purpose of giving a great collective picture which may properly be termed an Iliad. The tenth book, or Doloneia, though adapted specially to the place in which it stands, agrees with the books between the first and eighth in belonging only to the general picture of the war, without helping forward the march of the Achillêis; yet it seems conceived in a lower vein, in so far as we can trust our modern ethical sentiment. One is unwilling to believe that the author of the fifth book, (or Aristeia of Diomêdês) would condescend to employ the hero whom he there so brightly glorifies, – the victor even over Arês himself, – in slaughtering newly-arrived Thracian sleepers, without any large purpose or necessity. The ninth book, of which I have already spoken at length, belongs to a different vein of conception, and seems to me more likely to have emanated from a separate composer.

While intimating these views respecting the authorship of the Iliad, as being in my judgment the most probable, I must repeat that, though the study of the poem carries to my mind a sufficient conviction respecting its structure, the question between unity and plurality of authors is essentially less determinable. The poem consists of a part original, and other parts superadded; yet it is certainly not impossible that the author of the former may himself have composed the latter; and such would be my belief if I regarded plurality of composers as an inadmissible idea. On this supposition, we must conclude that the poet, while anxious for the addition of new, and for the most part, highly interesting matter, has not thought fit to recast the parts and events in such manner as to impart to the whole a pervading thread of *consensus* and organisation, such as we see in the Odyssey.

That the Odyssey is of later date than the Iliad, and by a different author, seems to be now the opinion of most critics, especially of Payne Knight and Nitzsch; though O. Müller leans to a contrary conclusion, at the same time adding that he thinks the arguments either way not very decisive. There are considerable differences of statement in the two poems in regard to some of the gods: Iris is messenger of the gods in the Iliad, and Hermês in the Odyssey: Æolus, the dispenser of the winds in the Odyssey, is not noticed in the twenty-third book of the Iliad, but, on the contrary, Iris invites the winds, as independent gods, to come and kindle the funeral pile of Patroclus; and, unless we are to expunge the song of Demodokus in the eighth book of the

Odyssey, as spurious, Aphroditê there appears as the wife of Hêphæstus, – a relationship not known to the Iliad. There are also some other points of difference enumerated by Mr. Knight and others, which tend to justify the presumption that the author of the Odyssey is not identical either with the author of the Achillêis or his enlargers, which G. Hermann considers to be a point unquestionable. Indeed, the difficulty of supposing a long coherent poem to have been conceived, composed, and retained, without any aid of writing, appears to many critics even now, insurmountable, though the evidences on the other side, are, in my view, sufficient to outweigh any negative presumption thus suggested. It is improbable that the same person should have powers of memorial combination sufficient for composing two such poems, nor is there any proof to force upon us such a supposition.

Presuming a difference of authorship between the two poems, I feel less convinced about the supposed juniority of the Odyssey. The discrepancies in manners and language in the one and the other, are so little important, that two different persons, in the same age and society, might well be imagined to exhibit as great or even greater. It is to be recollected that the subjects of the two are heterogeneous, so as to conduct the poet, even were he the same man, into totally different veins of imagination and illustration. The pictures of the Odyssey seem to delineate the same heroic life as the Iliad, though looked at from a distinct point of view: and the circumstances surrounding the residence of Odysseus, in Ithaka are just such as we may suppose him to have left in order to attack Troy. If the scenes presented to us are for the most part pacific, as contrasted with the incessant fighting of the Iliad, this is not to be ascribed to any greater sociality or civilisation in the real hearers of the Odyssey, but to the circumstances of the hero whom the poet undertakes to adorn: nor can we doubt that the poems of Arktinus and Leschês, of a later date than the Odyssey, would have given us as much combat and bloodshed as the Iliad. I am not struck by those proofs of improved civilisation which some critics affirm the Odyssey to present: Mr. Knight, who is of this opinion, nevertheless admits that the mutilation of Melanthius, and the hanging up of the female slaves by Odysseus, in that poem, indicate greater barbarity than any incidents in the fights before Troy. The more skilful and compact structure of the Odyssey, has been often considered as a proof of its juniority in age; and in the case of two poems by the same author, we might plausibly contend that practice would bring with it improvement in the combining acuity. In reference to the poems before us, we must recollect, first, that in all probability the Iliad (with which the comparison is taken) is not a primitive but an enlarged poem, and that the primitive Achillêis might well have been quite as coherent as the Odyssey; secondly, that between different authors, superiority in structure is not a proof of subsequent composition, inasmuch as, on that hypothesis, we should be compelled to admit that the later poem of Arktinus would be an improvement upon the Odyssey; thirdly, that, even if it were so, we could only infer that the author of the Odyssey had *heard* the Achillêis or the Iliad; we could not infer that he lived one or two generations afterwards.

On the whole, the balance of probabilities seems in favour of distinct authorship for the two poems, but the same age, – and that age a very early one, anterior to the first Olympiad. They may thus be used as evidences, and contemporary evidences, for the phenomena of primitive Greek civilisation; while they also show that the power of constructing long premeditated epics, without the aid of writing, is to be taken as a characteristic of the earliest known Greek mind. This was the point controverted by Wolf, which a full review of the case (in my judgment) decides against him: it is, moreover, a valuable result for the historian of the Greeks, inasmuch as it marks out to him the ground from which he is to start in appreciating their ulterior progress.

Whatever there may be of truth in the different conjectures of critics respecting the authorship and structure of these unrivalled poems, we are not to imagine that it is the perfection of their epical symmetry which has given them their indissoluble hold upon the human mind, as well modern as ancient. There is some tendency in critics, from Aristotle downwards, to invert the order of attributes in respect to the Homeric poems, so as to dwell most on recondite excellences which escape the unaided reader, and which are even to a great degree disputable. It is given to few minds (as Goethe has remarked) to appreciate fully the mechanism of a long poem, and many feel the beauty of the separate parts, who have no sentiment for the aggregate perfection of the whole.

Nor were the Homeric poems originally addressed to minds of the rarer stamp. They are intended for those feelings which the critic has in common with the unlettered mass, not for that enlarged range of vision and peculiar standard which he has acquired to himself. They are of all poems the most absolutely and unreservedly popular: had they been otherwise, they could not have lived so long in the mouth of the rhapsodes, and the ear and memory of the people; and it was *then* that their influence was first acquired, never afterwards to be shaken. Their beauties belong to the parts taken separately, which revealed themselves spontaneously to the listening crowd at the festival, – far more than to the whole poem taken together, which could hardly be appreciated unless the parts were dwelt upon and suffered to expand in the mind. The most unlettered hearer of those times could readily seize, while the most instructed reader can still recognise, the characteristic excellence of Homeric narrative, – its straightforward, unconscious, unstudied simplicity, – its concrete forms of speech and happy alternation of action with dialogue, – its vivid pictures of living agents, always clearly and sharply individualised, whether in the commanding proportions of Achilles and Odysseus, in the graceful presence of Helen and Penelopê, or in the more humble contrast of Eumæus and Melanthius; and always, moreover, animated by the frankness with which his heroes give utterance to all their transient emotions and even all their infirmities, – its constant reference to those coarser veins of feeling and palpable motives which belong to all men in common, – its fulness of graphic details, freshly drawn from the visible and audible world, and though often homely, never tame, nor trenching upon that limit of satiety to which the Greek mind was so keenly alive, – lastly, its perpetual junction of gods and men in the same picture, and familiar appeal to ever-present divine agency, in harmony with the interpretation of nature at that time universal.

It is undoubtedly easier to feel than to describe the impressive influence of Homeric narrative; but the time and circumstances under which that influence was first, and most powerfully felt, preclude the possibility of explaining it by comprehensive and elaborate comparisons, such as are implied in Aristotle's remarks upon the structure of the poems. The critic who seeks the explanation in the right place will not depart widely from the point of view of those rude auditors to whom the poems were originally addressed, or from the susceptibilities and capacities common to the human bosom in every stage of progressive culture. Though the refinements and delicacies of the poems, as well as their general structure, are a subject of highly interesting criticism, yet it is not to these that Homer owes his widespread and imperishable popularity. Still less is it true, as the well-known observations of Horace would lead us to believe, that Homer is a teacher of ethical wisdom akin and superior to Chrysippus or Crantor. No didactic purpose is to be found in the Iliad and Odyssey; a philosopher may doubtless extract, from the incidents and strongly marked characters which it contains, much illustrative matter for his exhortations, but the ethical doctrine which he applies must emanate from his own reflection. The Homeric hero manifests virtues or infirmities, fierceness or compassion, with the same straightforward and simple-minded vivacity, unconscious of any ideal standard by which his conduct is to be tried; nor can we trace in the poet any ulterior function beyond that of the inspired organ of the Muse, and the nameless, but eloquent, herald of lost adventures out of the darkness of the past.

SOPHRON EDITOR
CATALOGUE 2016

Caesar's Commentaries: The Complete Gallic War. Revised. 8vo., xxiv.507 pp.; Introduction, Latin text of all eight Books, Notes, Companion, Grammar, Exercises, Vocabularies, 17 Maps, illus., all based on Francis W. Kelsey. ISBN 978-0-9850811 1 9 . . . . $19.95

Virgil's Aeneid Complete, Books I-XII. With Introduction, Latin text and Notes by W. D. Williams. 8vo., xxviii. 739 pp., 2 maps. Glossary, Index. ISBN 978-0-9850811 6 4 . . . . $27.95

***Praxis Grammatica.* A New Edition.** John Harmer. 12 mo., xviii,116 pp.; Introduction by Mark Riley. ISBN 978-0-9850811 2 6 . . . . $3.95

The *Other* Trojan War. Dictys & Dares. 12 mo., xxii.397 pp.; Latin/English Parallel Texts; Frazer's Introduction & Notes, Index. ISBN 978-0-9850811 5 7 . . . . $14.95

The Stoic's Bible: *a Florilegium for the Good Life.* Giles Laurén. 8vo., xxx,657 pp., 2 illus., Introduction, Bibliography. ISBN 978-0-9850811-0-2 . . . . $24.95

Why Don't We Learn from History? B. H. Liddell Hart. 12 mo., 126 pp. ISBN 978-0-9850811 3 3 . . . . $4.95

Quintilian. Institutionis Oratoriae. Liber Decimus. Text, Notes & Introductory Essays by W. Peterson. Foreword by James J. Murphy. 8vo., cvi,291 pp., Harleian MS facsimile, Indexes. ISBN 978-0-9850811-8-8 . . . . $19.95

Schools of Hellas. Kenneth Freeman. 12 mo., xxi.279 pp., illus., Indexes. ISBN 978-0-9850811-9-5 . . . . $14.95

Cornelius Nepos Vitae. 12 mo., xviii.314 pp., 3 maps. notes, exercises, & vocabulary by John Rolf. ISBN 978-0-9850811-7-1 . . . . $14.95

Greek Reader. Mark Riley. Based on the selection of Wilamowitz-Moellendorff, with additions, notes and a vocabulary. 12 mo., ix,328 pp., maps & illus. ISBN 978-0-9897836-0-6 . . . . $12.95

Quintilian: *A Roman Educator and his Quest for the Perfect Orator.* Revised Edition. George A. Kennedy. 12 mo., 188 pp. Index. ISBN 978-0-9897836-1-3 . . . . $9.95

Diodorus Siculus. I *The Library of History* in Forty Books. Vol. I. (books I-XIV). 8vo., xxvii, 590 pp., illus. ISBN 978-0-9897836-2-0 . . . . $19.95

Diodorus Siculus. II *The Library of History* in Forty Books. Vol. II. (books XV-XL). 8vo., xiv.493 pp., illus. ISBN 978-0-9897836-3-7 . . . . $19.95

Foulquié. Paul. *La Dialectique.* in-8. 160 pp. ISBN 978-1-4954688-3-4 . . . . $6.95

Horace. *The Complete Horace.* 8vo., xli,620 pp., 2 illus., introduction & notes after Bennett & Rolfe. ISBN 978-0-9897836-4-4 . . . . $19.95

Grote's Legendary Greece. The Pre-history. Being Chapters I-XXI of *A History of Greece*, 4th. Ed. Complete, *without* footnotes, frontis. port. lvi.450 pp edited by Giles Laurén. ISBN 978-0-9897836-6-8 . . . . $17.50

Available from SOPHRON EDITOR (CreateSpace and Amazon worldwide)

In Preparation: **Jebb's Isokrates.** edited by Edward Schiappa, David Timmerman.

George Grote. *A History of Greece.*

Greeks and Romans on the State, Law and Justice: A Source Book.

Giles Laurén, 4020 Grande Vista #114, St. Augustine, FL 32084 enasophron@gmail.com 904 429-9533

Made in the USA
Charleston, SC
08 January 2016